A Methodology for
Client/Server
and
Web Application Development

ISBN 0-13-598426-2

90000

9 780135 984260

Selected Titles from the
YOURDON PRESS COMPUTING SERIES
Ed Yourdon, *Advisor*

ANDREWS AND LEVENTHAL Fusion: Integrating IE, CASE, and JAD
ANDREWS AND STALICK Business Reengineering: The Survival Guide
AUGUST Joint Application Design
BODDIE The Information Asset: Rational DP Funding and Other Radical Notions
BOULDIN Agents of Change: Managing the Introduction of Automated Tools
BRILL Building Controls into Structured Systems
COAD AND NICOLA Object-Oriented Programming
COAD AND YOURDON Object-Oriented Analysis, 2/E
COAD AND YOURDON Object-Oriented Design
COAD AND MAYFIELD Java Design: Building Better Apps and Applets
COAD WITH NORTH AND MAYFIELD Object Models: Strategies, Patterns, and Applications, 2/E
CONNELL AND SHAFER Object-Oriented Rapid Prototyping
CONNELL AND SHAFER Structured Rapid Prototyping
CONSTANTINE Constantine on Peopleware
CONSTANTINE AND YOURDON Structured Design
DEGRACE AND STAHL Wicked Problems, Righteous Solutions
DeMARCO Controlling Software Projects
DeMARCO Structured Analysis and System Specification
EMBLEY, KURTZ, AND WOODFIELD Object-Oriented Systems Analysis
FOURNIER A Methodology for Client/Server and Web Application Development
GARMUS AND HERRON Measuring the Software Process: A Practical Guide to Functional Measurements
GLASS Software Conflict: Essays on the Art and Science of Software Engineering
GROCHOW Information Overload: Creating Value with the New Information Systems Technology
HAYES AND ULRICH The Year 2000 Software Crisis: The Continuing Challenge
JONES Assessment and Control of Software Risks
KING Project Management Made Simple
McMENAMIN AND PALMER Essential System Design
MOSLEY The Handbook of MIS Application Software Testing
PAGE-JONES Practical Guide to Structured Systems Design, 2/E
PUTMAN AND MYERS Measures for Excellence: Reliable Software on Time within Budget
RUBLE Practical Analysis and Design for Client/Server and GUI Systems
SHLAER AND MELLOR Object Lifecycles: Modeling the World in States
SHLAER AND MELLOR Object-Oriented Systems Analysis: Modeling the World in Data
STARR How to Build Shlaer-Mellor Object Models
THOMSETT Third Wave Project Management
ULRICH AND HAYES The Year 2000 Software Crisis: Challenge of the Century
YOURDON Death March: The Complete Software Developer's Guide to Surviving "Mission Impossible" Projects
YOURDON Decline and Fall of the American Programmer
YOURDON Rise and Resurrection of the American Programmer
YOURDON Managing the Structured Techniques, 4/E
YOURDON Managing the System Life-Cycle, 2/E
YOURDON Modern Structured Analysis
YOURDON Object-Oriented Systems Design
YOURDON Techniques of Program Structure and Design
YOURDON AND ARGILA Case Studies in Object-Oriented Analysis and Design
YOURDON, WHITEHEAD, THOMANN, OPPEL, AND NEVERMANN Mainstream Objects: An Analysis and Design Approach for Business
YOURDON INC. YOURDON Systems Method: Model-Driven Systems Development

A Methodology for
Client/Server
and
Web Application Development

Roger Fournier

YOURDON PRESS
Prentice Hall Building
Upper Saddle River, NJ 07458
www.phptr.com

Library of Congress Cataloging-in-Publication Data

Fournier, Roger, 1952–
    A methodology for client/server and web application development /
    Roger Fournier.
        p.   cm. -- (Yourdon Press computing series)
        Includes bibliographical references and index.
        ISBN 0-13-598426-2 (pbk. : alk. paper)
        1. Client/server computing.   2. Web sites--Design.   I. Title.
    II. Series.
    QA76.9.C55F68   1998
    004'.36--dc21   98-20471
                                                 CIP

Editorial/production supervision: *Patti Guerrieri*
Cover design director: *Jerry Votta*
Cover designer: *Anthony Gemmellaro*
Manufacturing manager: *Alexis R. Heydt*
Marketing manager: *Dan Rush*
Acquisitions editor: *Stephen Solomon*
Editorial assistant: *Bart Blanken*

Published by Prentice Hall PTR
Prentice-Hall, Inc.
A Simon & Schuster Company
Upper Saddle River, NJ 07458

Prentice Hall books are widely used by corporations and government agencies
for training, marketing, and resale.

The publisher offers discounts on this book when ordered in bulk quantities.
For more information, contact: Corporate Sales Department, Phone: 800-382-3419;
Fax: 201-236-7141; E-mail: corpsales@prenhall.com; or write: Prentice Hall PTR,
Corp. Sales Dept., One Lake Street, Upper Saddle River, NJ 07458.

Printed in the United States of America
10 9 8 7 6 5 4 3 2

ISBN   0-13-598426-2

Prentice-Hall International (UK) Limited, *London*
Prentice-Hall of Australia Pty. Limited, *Sydney*
Prentice-Hall Canada Inc., *Toronto*
Prentice-Hall Hispanoamericana, S.A., *Mexico*
Prentice-Hall of India Private Limited, *New Delhi*
Prentice-Hall of Japan, Inc., *Tokyo*
Simon & Schuster Asia Pte. Ltd., *Singapore*
Editora Prentice-Hall do Brasil, Ltda., *Rio de Janeiro*

Contents

4 Design   193

5 Construction   321

9 Client-Server and Web Technology Architecture and Support Services   445

10 Joint Facilitated Sessions   553

11   Web Database Application Development   575

12   Key Graphical User Interface Concepts   611

Preface

WHY THIS BOOK?

This book proposes a comprehensive methodology that guides you through the successful development of large-scale and complex client-server or Web database applications. Doing so, it also explains how to circumvent critical issues and potential dangers that might adversely affect the development of large software systems.

Moreover, this book offers several powerful techniques that can be used by your IT organization to accelerate the construction of large and complex business applications, such as iterative/incremental system development, prototyping, timeboxing, and joint facilitated sessions with users.

Similarly, the book strongly recommends the use of component-based application development architectures to maximize reusability and hence reduce the cycle time associated with the system development process.

WHAT MAKES THIS BOOK UNIQUE?

This book addresses the various sets of technical activities that must be conducted to effectively develop a sound client-server or Web database system. However, rather than concentrating on the "how to," this publication primarily focuses on the "what to do."

The book contains numerous guidelines, suggested best practices, hints, and checklists that are based on practical experience and that can be advantageously used by practitioners to successfully develop quality-oriented client-server and Web-based software systems.

This book also emphasizes the importance of enterprises investing efforts in developing and implementing a robust yet flexible enterprise technology infrastructure. An efficient enterprise technology infrastructure is mandatory to effectively support the accelerated development of large software systems. The current enterprise technology infrastructures must be re-engineered or extended to appropriately account for the introduction of new development tools, technologies, and techniques. The new enterprise technology infrastructures must be built on industry-wide standards to accommodate the emergence of new and improved technologies, as time goes by.

WHAT DOESN'T THIS BOOK CONTAIN?

This book does not address the set of project management processes that must be conducted to effectively plan, organize, manage, track, and control the development process of large software systems. It addresses solely the technical activities that are involved in developing large software systems. However, a companion publication will likely be developed in the near future, to address the most critical project management best practices and therefore complement the technical information provided in this current book.

This book is not your typical *"one-minute"* methodology cookbook to client-server and Web database application development. Its content is at the right level of detail for large software development undertakings. In fact, the book is primarily intended for "real-world" software practitioners who must work in the "trenches," often with newer technologies, and yet are hard pressed by their customers to deliver workable system solutions in a compressed timeframe.

As such, this book does not promise you silver bullets. It does not attempt to fool you into thinking that large-scale software development efforts are easy and can be achieved overnight, only with the help of the latest RAD tool available on the market, and without the support of a solid information technology infrastructure. Those involved in developing large and complex software systems know better than this the perils of any particular software development process.

WHO SHOULD READ THIS BOOK?

This book should be read by IT executives, managers, project leaders, developers, specific information technology specialists, software testers, and operations staff around the world who are involved in developing large and complex client-server or Web database applications.

The book is also intended for modern IT organizations who are currently in the process of renewing themselves while planning the introduction of new client-server and Web technologies in their enterprise. These organizations will then be interested in reading the chapter titled *Client-Server and Web Technology Architecture and Support*

Services. This chapter provides the readers with a holistic view of the major issues involved in planning, designing, and implementing the new type of enterprise technology infrastructure that is required to successfully nurture the development, deployment, and support of large client-server or Web database applications.

Finally, the book can be used as a textbook for college or university courses on the development of large client-server and Web database systems.

BOOK ROADMAP

Looking at Figure P-1, the book consists of an introduction chapter, which is then followed by three broad logical sections, identified as sections A, B, and C.

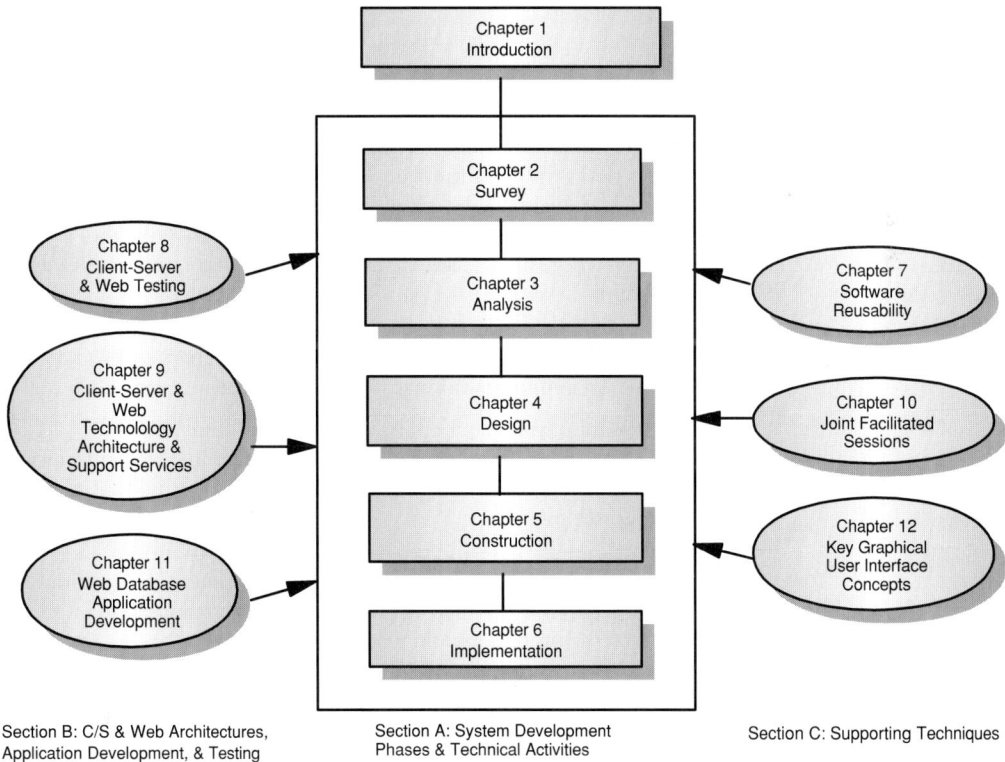

Figure P–1 Book roadmap.

Following is a brief description of the introduction chapter and the three major sections A, B, and C.

INTRODUCTION

The introduction chapter provides an overview of the book and discusses how it is organized. It presents the fundamental concepts that are critical to support the proposed client-server and Web database application development methodology. The process-driven system development methodology that is provided in this book is suited for a variety of business projects of different sizes and complexities. However, it is particularly well-adapted for large and complex client-server or Web database applications.

SECTION A

Section A contains the five core chapters that describe in detail the particular system development phases and set of technical activities that should be performed to successfully build a quality client-server or Web database application.

Table P-1 provides a brief description of these five chapters.

Table P–1 Section A

CHAPTER	DESCRIPTION
Chapter 2: Survey Phase	The preliminary business needs that point toward a client-server/Web application system solution are identified and documented during this stage. A sketch of the initial scope and boundaries of the proposed system are outlined jointly with the customers. Similarly, the development team assesses the major project assumptions, risks, and constraints.
	The survey phase technical activities can be conducted either through a series of joint facilitated sessions, with the active participation of the users, or in a more traditional system development approach.
Chapter 3: Analysis Phase	A blueprint of the major application data and functional requirements is quickly captured with the direct involvement of the customers. A series of joint facilitated sessions can be used specifically for this purpose.
	The preliminary data and process application distribution requirements are also documented at this stage, along with additional system requirements, such as the security, performance, and hardware/software/networking application needs.
	If necessary, the system is partitioned into smaller chunks, where core functions can be implemented more rapidly by the development team, either in sequence or in parallel. Moreover, a first stab at defining the system data conversion, training, and testing strategies is done with the users during this phase.

Table P–1 Section A (cont.)

	Finally, a live system prototype is quickly constructed to demonstrate the graphical user interface and some of the core functionality elements of the proposed client-server or Web database application. Reusable GUI classes or application system templates are used to speed up the delivery of the initial application graphical interface. This fully interactive prototype is used to firm up the initial set of critical user requirements that center on the application graphical interface.
Chapter 4: Design Phase	During this phase, the design of the client-server or Web-based system solution is gradually refined and augmented with all the necessary automated solution details. The application reusable GUI classes and system templates may be created or extended, where applicable.
	The sets of reusable functions that can be effectively reutilized across the application are developed first, prior to developing the application custom functions.
	The detailed design of the database(s) that is(are) required to support the system information needs is finalized, including stored procedures and triggers.
	The data and process distribution design solutions are revisited and expanded with more detailed information. Similarly, the system training, data conversion, and testing strategies are refined and augmented with more detailed information. Based on the design specifications, high-level test cases are defined by the developers toward the end of the design phase.
Chapter 5: Construction Phase	The detailed functional components of the client-server or Web application are coded, unit tested, and then gradually integrated into a complete and robust application system.
	In parallel to the coding and testing activities, the development team gradually sets up the initial user training and data conversion system environments.
Chapter 6: Implementation Phase	During this phase, user training is completed. Final user acceptance tests are performed by selected groups of user representatives.
	Finally, the new client-server or Web system is transferred into a production environment, along with its converted data. The maintenance environment is closely monitored, and the client-server system evolution plan is activated.
	During a short period of time, the application is closely monitored and fine-tuned to achieve optimal performance.
	A post-mortem study is launched to identify what went wrong and what went well during the project. The outcome of the post-mortem study is used to revise and confirm the best internal software development practices.

SECTION B

Section B logically consists of Chapters 8, 9, and 11. The technical information provided in each of these chapters directly supports and/or reinforces the system development methodology proposed in Section A.

Table P-2 provides a brief description of these three chapters.

Table P–2 Section B

CHAPTER	DESCRIPTION
Chapter 8: Client-Server and Web Testing	The development of large and complex client-server or Web database applications emphasizes the necessity for a flexible yet effective testing process, specifically adapted to these newer technology paradigms. This chapter proposes a software-test life cycle that promotes the development of quality-oriented client-server and Web database systems.
	Some of the new components that need to be tested in a client-server and/or Web environment include Graphical User Interfaces (GUI), servers, networks, and a variety of middleware technologies.
	Besides the more traditional types of testing scenarios, I discuss in this chapter new categories of test cases that are specifically intended to verify client-server and Web database systems. These include a variety of test cases such as client configuration testing, server or client-workstation load testing, database server testing, and Web browser application interface testing.
	I also discuss the relevance to implement or not automated testing tools in a client-server or Web development environment in this chapter.
Chapter 9: Client-Server and Web Technology Architecture & Support Services	This chapter presents a holistic view of the major technology infrastructure components that must be put in place to successfully enable and support the rapid development and deployment of large client-server or Web database applications across and sometimes beyond the enterprise.
	I also discuss in this chapter the most critical enterprise systems management activities and support services that must be implemented to efficiently manage and support the distributed client-server and Web technology infrastructures.
	I also include a brief overview of the most desirable characteristics that an integrated software development tool suite must possess to construct effective Web database applications.

Table P–2 Section B (cont.)

Chapter 11: Web Database Application Development	Building on all the material that I cover in the previous chapters, this chapter discusses some of the major application development activities that are involved in successfully planning, analyzing, designing, constructing, and deploying mission-critical Web database applications, in the context of Internet, intranet, or extranet environments.
	This chapter also provides numerous guidelines for designing sound Web graphical user interfaces.

SECTION C

Section C consists of Chapters 7, 10, and 12. Both Chapters 7 and 10 present some specific concepts and techniques that can be used to help accelerate the system development process proposed in this book, such as joint facilitated sessions and software reusability. Chapter 12 covers some fundamental graphical user interface design concepts.

Table P-3 provides a brief description of these three chapters.

Table P–3 Section C

CHAPTER	DESCRIPTION
Chapter 7: Software Re- usability	This chapter discusses the merits and challenges of implementing a software development process that encourages the construction of reusable software components.
	It also provides some basic guidelines to help construct software reusable components across the enterprise.
	Finally, I discuss briefly the major characteristics of three popular distributed software component architectures, namely: DCOM/ ActiveX, CORBA, and JavaBeans for Enterprise.
Chapter 10: Joint Facilitated Sessions	This chapter describes the set of guidelines that are recommended throughout this book to plan, prepare, and successfully conduct effective joint facilitated sessions.
	The joint facilitated session process is frequently used during the analysis and design phases of large projects to dynamically capture, with the active participation of the users, the major external requirements of the system.
	You can also use joint facilitated sessions advantageously during the design, construction, and implementation phases.

Table P–3 Section C (cont.)

Chapter 12: Key Graphical User Interface Concepts	This chapter discusses various topics that relate to the design of sound client-server/Web graphical user interfaces.
	The first part covers the different types of windows an application system can use and their anatomy.
	The second part covers the different types of users that an application might need to support and some essential graphical user interface usability criteria.
	Finally, the third part describes in detail the different types of graphical objects that can be used to design a client-server graphical window, along with several hints to help determine when using them is appropriate or not.

DISCLAIMER

Despite the great attention provided by the author to ensure up-to-date and accurate technical information, this publication could contain technical inaccuracies or typographical errors. All Web site addresses provided in this publication were carefully verified for completeness and accuracy purposes. However, due to the dynamic nature of the Web, no one can guarantee that these Web site addresses will remain unchanged over time.

The views and opinions expressed in this publication are solely those of the author and do not represent the views of anyone else. The names of the vendors and/or products mentioned in this publication should not be interpreted as a recommendation from the author. All references of vendor products and/or services in this book are done as a means of providing background information to discussions that relate to the use of different tools and technologies, and are for illustrative purposes only. Any reference to vendor-related products and/or services made in this publication should not be viewed or construed as either positive or negative comment on those products and/or services, neither should the inclusion of a product or vendor, or the omission of a product or vendor on the part of the author.

TRADEMARK ACKNOWLEDGMENT

The following list recognizes the commercial and intellectual property of the trademark holders whose products and/or services are mentioned in this book. All other products, services, or company names mentioned herein are claimed as trademarks and trade names by their respective companies. Any omission from this list is inadvertent:

The browser-based screen-prints presented in this publication were made using Netscape Communicator, with the permission of Netscape Communications Corporation. Netscape Communicator is a trademark of Netscape Communications Corporation. Netscape Communications Corporation has not authorized, sponsored, or endorsed, or approved this publication and is not responsible for its content. Netscape and the Netscape Communications Corporate Logos are trademarks and trade names of Netscape Communications Corporations. All other product names and/or logos are trademarks of their respective owners.

The clip-art illustrations used in this publication are extracted from: Masterclips, which is a trademark of IMSI Inc. and Corel Gallery, which is a trademark of Corel Corporation.

ActiveX is a trademark of Microsoft Corporation.

CORBA is a trademark of Object Management Group.

DB2 is a trademark of IBM Corporation.

DCOM is a trademark of Microsoft Corporation.

Encina is a trademark of IBM Corporation.

IPX/SPX is a trademark of Novell Corporation.

Java and JavaBeans are trademarks of Sun Microsystems.

JavaScript is a trademark of Netscape Communications Corporation.

Lotus Notes and Domino are trademarks of IBM Corporation.

NetWare is a trademark of Novell Corporation.

ODBC and OLE are trademarks of Microsoft Corporation.

Oracle7/Oracle8 are trademarks of Oracle Corporation.

UNIX is a registered trademark licensed exclusively through X/Open Company.

Windows is a trademark of Microsoft Corporation.

Acknowledgments

I would like to acknowledge the contributions of several individuals who offered help and support during the creation and production of this book.

- Thanks to Paul Becker for his overall encouragement and support during the initial inception of the book, especially when this one was barely just a vague idea in the mind of the author.
- Thanks to Rex Hogan and Gerry Pasternak for providing a myriad of insightful comments and suggestions for improving the format and content of several sections of this book, especially while it was still an unstructured manuscript.
- Thanks to Ed Yourdon for kindly suggesting, during a brief encounter at a social gathering in Montreal, to add some material in the book on Web technology.
- Thanks to the cast of professionals at Prentice Hall who directly or indirectly contributed to the production of this book, especially Stephen Solomon (acquisition editor), Bart Blanken (editorial assistant), Diane Spina, Bernard Goodwin, Patti Guerrieri, Christa Carroll, Penny Baker, Carolyn Gauntt, and Anthony Gemmellaro.
- Thanks to two young and very promising Java software developers, Tho Le and Christian Tarlet, for their assistance in providing the author with some Web-related database application screen pictures, even if those graphics unfortunately did not make their way into the final publication.
- Special thanks and sincere apologies to my two wonderful and extremely patient kids, Karen and Alex, who have coped with a workaholic daddy for merely a year and a half. Alex and Karen, let's go out and play baseball and soccer. Please, show me how to roller skate so you can have good laughs on me!
- Thanks to my "younger" brother Réjean, who simply wanted to have his name appear in a book. There, it is done!
- Finally, many thanks to you, the reader. I sincerely hope that this book will be useful to you. Please read the Afterword if you would like to send me your comments on the content of this book.

1

Introduction

1.1 THE NEED FOR A ROBUST YET FAST AND FLEXIBLE SOFTWARE ENGINEERING METHODOLOGY

The primary motivation behind this book has been the numerous software practitioners and managers around the world who strongly believe that a disciplined yet flexible approach to software engineering can lead to the timely delivery of quality software systems at a reasonable cost.

Time over time, no matter which new technology knocks at the door of the Information Technology organizations all around the world, the construction of business applications performed without a sound strategy to harness the software development process challenges often leads to distressing, costly, and unrewarding experience.

By using wisely the system development processes prescribed in this book, several organizations can improve the quality, productivity, and economics of their internal software development life cycle process. The best part is that these organizations can meet all these objectives while delivering applications on a faster time scale than what many of them can currently achieve at the present time.

Be careful, though! This book does not provide you any silver bullet. Similarly, it does not pretend to sell you a secret recipe that will instantaneously solve all the problems that plague the software development industry.

To succeed with a rapid application development process, the software factory shop must gradually change their traditional development framework and mindset. This change takes time, resources, and unconditional management dedication and commitment, over an extended period of time.[1]

---

1. This transition does not mean that the software development organization suddenly needs to abandon the best development practices that they have accumulated over the years on how to build quality software.

1

However, the benefits can be significant for organizations that must compete in the global market economy, since getting quality software applications through the door as rapidly as possible should not be seen anymore as a competitive advantage but rather a competitive necessity. I assume that your organization really wants not only to survive but also to dominate its market.

The software engineering methodology advocated in this book integrates a set of modern yet well proven software-engineering practices that are successfully used in several organizations around the world to accelerate the development of large and complex client-server and Web database systems. Depending on the type of project at hand, these accelerators might include a variety of techniques such as:

- Evolutionary development life cycle
- Joint facilitated sessions
- Prototyping
- Timeboxing
- Partitioning large projects into smaller, more manageable sub-projects that can each be implemented within a six- to eighteen-month time frame.[2]
- High-performance development teams

Rather than concentrating on the detailed "how to," this comprehensive guide on software engineering primarily addresses the "what to do." It also recognizes the fact that a methodology should reflect an organization's corporate culture and should be augmented by the diversified experiences and various technical backgrounds of the personnel in place. While the software engineering process must impose discipline to ensure a successful project completion, likewise it must nurture creativity, innovation, and adaptation. A software engineering process that remains static over time and is never challenged by developers is indeed a dying process.

Consequently, this technical guide to software engineering advocates that software practitioners make their own choices as to which particular technical activities should be selected to develop their system, based not only on those prescribed in the book but also on their own cumulative knowledge and experience in the field. I highly recommend adapting the proposed software methodology to fit the specific needs of a project rather than trying to blindly squeeze the project into fitting the methodology.

In fact, the organization's own best software development practices should be gradually captured and integrated with those prescribed in this book to provide a repeatable, predictable software development process that can be applied to the construction

---

2. An evolutionary development life cycle allows the gradual delivery to the customers of application segments of the complete business system solution. This approach delivers earlier benefits to users. Each application segment is a fully functional product or service. The application segments can be developed in parallel and/or in series.

of well-engineered software systems. From there on, the process-driven knowledge base should be continually improved, based upon the organization's project experiences and emerging industry best practices. Organizations should institutionalize the continuous process improvement philosophy across the entire software development organization so it can be pursued on a regular basis and truly become second nature to all developers.

The prescribed methodology reflects a strong focus on technical deliverables. I do not exaggerate when I say that a concise description of the technical deliverables is just as important as the detailed description of the activities that are executed for producing them. In fact, the sole purpose of the technical activities is to achieve some results, to create deliverables that add value to the software development process, not to perform activities for the sake of doing so. Maybe the term "application development" should be replaced by the term "application delivery" to underline the importance of concentrating our efforts on delivering a system solution in a timely manner.

Finally, the set of management processes and best practices that are required to plan, estimate, organize, staff, control, and monitor a large software development project are not covered in this book.[3] Similarly, I do not address project financial returns on investments.

1.2 PRESENTATION FORMAT OF THE TECHNICAL ACTIVITIES

All the technical activities that cover the system development life cycle discussed in this book share a common presentation format, as shown in Figure 1-1.

Activity number:
Activity name:
Purpose:
Input(s):
Output(s):
Activity description:

Figure 1–1 Methodology activity template.

---

3. At the time of writing, the development of a companion book will likely be underway, to address what are currently considered best software project management practices. This new book will complement the technical activities described in this present book.

Each technical activity is characterized by:

1. A unique activity identification number that has the following structure: XX-YY, where XX is a two-letter acronym that identifies the specific development phase during which the activity is conducted and YY is a one or two-digit number uniquely assigned to each distinct activity. Table 1-1 lists each two-letter acronym that corresponds to a specific system development life cycle phase.

Table 1–1 An Acronym For Each System Development Life Cycle Phase

Mnemonic	System Development Life Cycle Phase
SU	Survey
AN	Analysis
DE	Design
CO	Construction
IM	Implementation

For example, the identification number SU-3 indicates that this activity is performed during the survey phase and is uniquely identified within that phase by the number 3.

2. A descriptive name of the activity.
3. A brief statement describing the purpose of the activity.
4. A list identifying the prerequisite technical deliverables that are normally required as input to execute the activity.
5. A list identifying the technical deliverables that are produced as a result of performing the activity.
6. A brief description of the detailed steps or tasks involved in performing the activity itself.

At the end of each activity, some practical tips and guidelines are provided to help the software developers perform successfully the detailed steps in each activity. In several instances, some potential pitfalls or alternative ways of performing the activity are also cited.

In each particular introduction section for Chapters 2 through 6, I provide a basic activity network diagram to illustrate the relationships that exist among the technical activities. To enhance the clarity of the diagrams, I do not show the input deliverables that are necessary to perform each individual activity and the output deliverables produced by the activity.

Finally, the execution of the technical activities can be done in an iterative and incremental fashion. Even though some of the activities seem to be set out in a natural order, they do not necessarily need to be performed in sequence. Sometimes, certain activities can proceed in parallel while others can even overlap on each other. Depending on the situation at hand, certain activities may be started before preceding activities are fully completed. A few activities might also be mandatory predecessors to other activities and must be fully completed prior to initiating the subsequent activities. Finally, some activities can be regrouped together and performed following a spiral development process.

1.3 MODELING A BUSINESS SYSTEM

The construction of a model of a relatively large or highly complex business system is a sound approach to attempt to manage its size and complexity. Breaking the system down into its major functional components is useful, from the most general down to the most detailed level.

The resulting architectural blueprint identifies the desirable functional characteristics that the system should possess to meet the users' needs. The model then becomes a very useful tool not only to understand the major business drivers of the area under study but also to validate and confirm the developer's understanding of the users' requirements.

For a very large and mission-critical system, business modeling is a relatively inexpensive process, if we consider that the modeling is done long before the new system reaches a fully functional stage and is entirely constructed. The principle behind software modeling is based on a simple observation: Modifying the critical functional requirements of a large system when they are still being modeled on a drawing board and subsequently prototyped is far easier, and cheaper, than when the system itself is in production.

When the business application model is created at least, two major perspectives are captured, as shown in Figure 1-2.

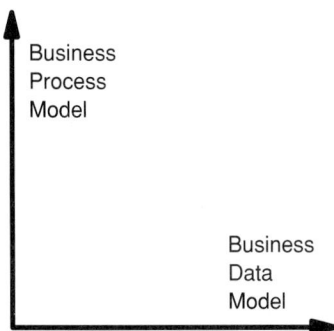

Figure 1–2 Generic, process-based software development life cycle.

The business process model describes the critical business functions of the system and the major interactions that exist among them. The emphasis during business process modeling is to understand the business and its functional requirements. This model is process-oriented because the focus is on modeling the business context and functions of the system.

The business data model describes the system data entities and their relationships. Using entity-relationship diagrams, it captures the inherent properties of data and the underlying business policies and rules that characterize the relationships between the data entities. This model is data-oriented because the emphasis is put primarily on modeling the structure of the data itself.

Note that even though these two models emphasize a specific dimension of the same system, they also complement each other very well. They have in reality strong interdependencies, and they should be developed in a way that ensures consistency among them.

To use an analogy, the business process and data models are like the two parallel tracks of a railway. One model helps to better understand and validate the other.

On one hand, the functions of the system are analyzed along with the data that are required to perform them. However, the emphasis is not on the data structures themselves but rather on the system functions and the graphical user interface that will be required to execute them.

On the other hand, the emphasis with data modeling is mostly put on identifying the data entities that are manipulated by the system and the relationships that exist among them. This effort cannot be done without addressing a portion of the functional aspects of the system, since data on their own have very little intrinsic value. In reality, the business policies that are associated with the data entities often dictate the types of relationships that exist among them.

1.4 FORMAL AND INFORMAL REVIEWS

The software engineering methodology proposed in this book strongly advocates the consistent use of both formal and informal reviews throughout the entire software development process. The development of the most critical technical deliverables should be concluded with a formal review of its contents. You can do this using a specialized review technique called *structured walkthrough*.

On the other end, the methodology also encourages conducting small, informal reviews among the members of the development team and with the users or other software engineering support groups, wherever necessary. The time spent in formal and informal reviews is a very good long-term investment into software quality, if it is done with discipline.

1.5 A QUICK OVERVIEW OF THE MOST CRITICAL SOFTWARE DEVELOPMENT PROCESSES

The software development life cycle can be viewed from a purely process-based stand-point. Figure 1-3 shows ten critical software development processes that must be performed to successfully deliver a high-quality, well engineered application system, regardless of its size and how you might decide to regroup these processes into a set of discrete development phases.[4] These ten generic software development processes must take place whether you build a small client-server application, a large web database application, an electronic commerce application or even a sophisticated data warehouse solution. Each is a generic enough process that it can be tailored to develop a large variety of software applications.

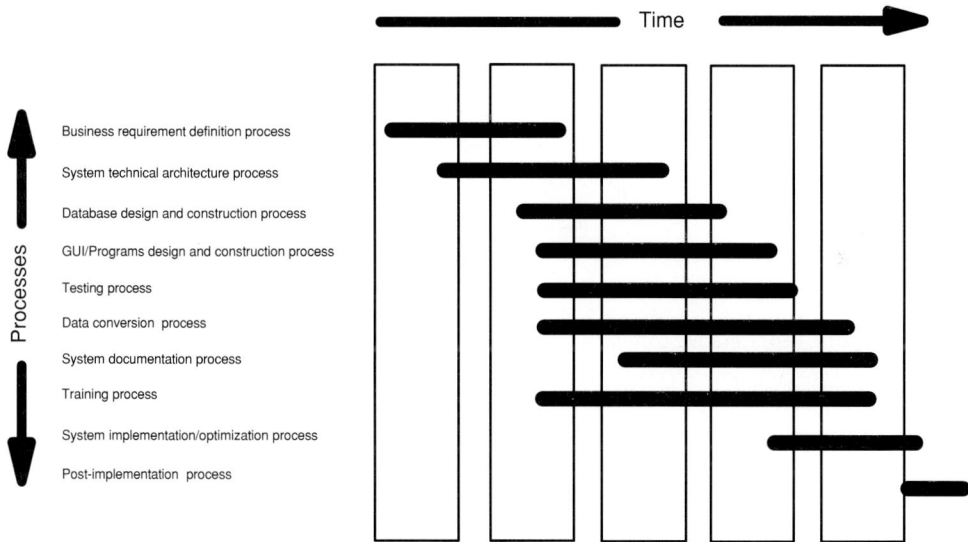

Figure 1–3 Generic, process-based software development life cycle.

For large-scale and complex projects, each major development process shown in Figure 1-3 can even represent a software engineering practice on its own, which then can require specialized skills in order to perform each process successfully.

---

4. This model presupposes that if necessary, the business re-engineering and strategic system planning processes already have been completed, prior to launching the development of a specific business application system.

Similarly, Figure 1-4 reinforces the concept that the software development process can often be performed incrementally through a series of iterations, through which the creation of deliverables is gradually performed over a given time period, either in a specific development phase or across several development phases. Similarly, major software development processes can sometimes overlap each other or often can be intertwined with one another.

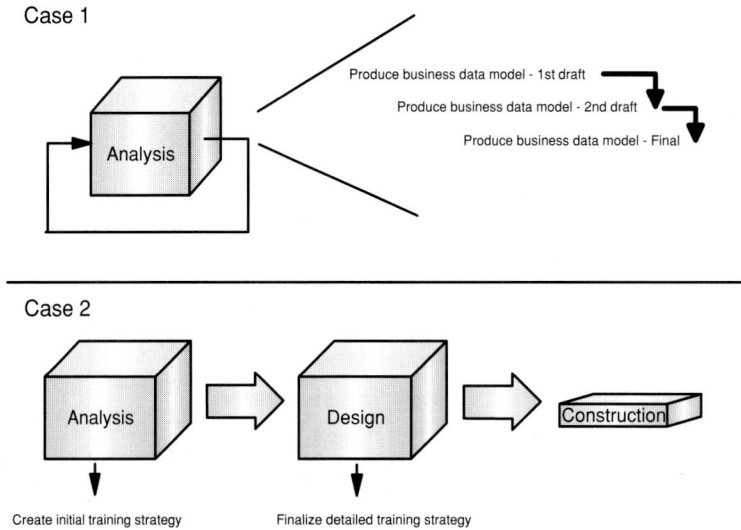

Figure 1–4 Iterative software development processes.

Finally, Table 1-2 provides a brief description of the major software development processes that appear in Figure 1-3.

Table 1–2 The Most Critical Software Development Processes

Process	Description
Business requirements definition process	This process entails the definition of the business requirements for the application. Business problems and opportunity analysis are investigated in this development process. A business data and process model is usually constructed to capture the data and functional needs of the application. Other application requirements are detailed during this process, such as the operational, security, control, and performance requirements.

Table 1-2 The Most Critical Software Development Processes (cont.)

System technical architecture process	This process entails developing an initial technical architecture for the system. If the system will operate on a computing platform that is totally new in the enterprise, then some additional work might be required to ensure that the new architecture will fit with the existing technical architecture. The major components of the technical architecture include items such as the system capacity plan, the hardware/software/networking equipment and facilities, and the distribution architecture. It also covers the type of technology that will be used to secure and control the system, as well as supporting the database backup and recovery process. It might also cover all the middleware technology required to integrate all the heterogeneous computing platforms on or with which the system must operate or communicate. Finally, the technical architecture also explicitly covers the development tools and computing platform that will be used to construct the system.
Database design and construction process	This process entails the design and construction of the physical databases that are required to support the data needs of the system. It starts with the transformation of the business data model into a set of logical database structures. Then the logical database structures are gradually refined to satisfy the data access and performance needs of the application. Finally, the logical database structures are transformed into physical database structures, taking into consideration the data distribution and the detailed system capacity plan requirements.
GUI/Programs design and construction process	This process entails the design and construction of all the programs that are required to automate the application processes. It starts with defining the graphical user interface for the application and building a quick prototype to demonstrate the graphical user interface in a real-life mode. Then it basically consists of designing and constructing all the batch and online programs that are required to support the application system.
Testing process	The testing process entails verifying that the new system does meet the stated functional specifications and satisfy the operations, security, and control requirements. The testing process starts as early as possible during the system development life cycle. The four major testing processes include unit testing the application programs, testing their integration into a complete system, testing the functionality and level of operability/performance of the system, and finally the testing and acceptance of the system by the users themselves.

Table 1–2 The Most Critical Software Development Processes (cont.)

Data conversion process	This process entails the conversion of existing data from the legacy system to the new system. Populating the new system files and databases with completely new data from scratch might also be necessary. The process starts by defining the data conversion requirements for the new application. Then an initial strategy is developed to satisfy these requirements. Subsequently, a detailed plan is produced, describing all the conversion activities that must be performed, along with a proposed timetable. A conversion environment is set up to design, create, and test all required conversion programs. Then the conversion process itself is executed.
System documentation process	The system documentation process entails the creation of all the user and system manuals that are required to use and support the system. These high-quality manuals can be produced in either a paper or electronic format, or both.
Training process	The training process entails training the users on how to use the application in an effective manner. It also entails training the various systems personnel on how to operate and support the new system in its production environment. The process starts by determining the training requirements for the application. Then a training strategy is developed to satisfy these requirements. Specific training materials are created, and the training process is finally executed.
System implementation and optimization process	The system implementation and optimization process entails the migration of the new system into a production environment and fine-tunes it where necessary. The system implementation requirements are first defined. Then an installation strategy is developed to satisfy the system implementation requirements.
Post-implementation process	The post-implementation process entails all the activities that are necessary to support and evolve the system through its useful lifetime. I do not cover the post-implementation process in this book.

1.6 TAILORING THE METHODOLOGY TO YOUR UNIQUE PROJECT DEVELOPMENT NEEDS

No single methodology in the world can adequately satisfy all the different types of business application development projects that can be conducted in an organization. In other words, the "one size fits all" development approach simply does not exist. Those of you who are looking for a silver bullet to solve all your system development problems should stop reading this book.

However, the methodology that I propose in this book can be custom-tailored to accommodate the distinct needs of any particular business-oriented project, whether large or small. It represents a broad road map to software development, which can be adapted by the practitioners to best satisfy the particular needs of their projects.

When properly orchestrated, organizing a software project into a set of distinct development phases constitutes a sound strategy to harness the critical software development processes that appear in Figure 1-3.

The development team needs to carefully examine at least two critical factors when adapting the methodology to satisfy the specific needs of their project: the size and complexity of the proposed system.

The size of a system can be measured primarily by the set of common criteria that are described in Table 1-3.

Table 1–3 Common Factors Influencing The Size Of A System

• Functional scope	• Number and types of users
• Number of interfaces with other systems	• Number of data entities and attributes

The size of a system can be expressed in different metric terms such as lines of code, function points, number of person-months required to develop the system, or development costs.

Evaluating the level of complexity of a system can sometimes be a more tricky process than evaluating its size. Nonetheless, the overall complexity of a system can be measured by different criteria such as those that are listed in Table 1-4.

Table 1–4 Factors Influencing The Complexity Of A System

• Complexity of the business processes that need to be automated • Complexity of the business rules that must be enforced by the system • Volume of transactions to process per unit of time • Geographical locations of the users	• Complexity of the relationships that exist between the various data entities that the system uses • Type and level of maturity of the technology that is required to run the system

As a rule of thumb, when the size and complexity of a system increases, then the number of development phases that should be included into the project development plan should also augment accordingly. The partitioning of a large system development effort into a set of discrete development phases allows the application development team to:

• Better track the progress made during each discretionary development phase

• Assess whether the project is still on-track when major milestones are reached

• Evaluate the level of effort involved in completing the remainder of the project

Figure 1-5 shows three distinct phasing models that are being proposed in this book to assist developers in choosing a specific development method that might more closely fit their particular project requirements.

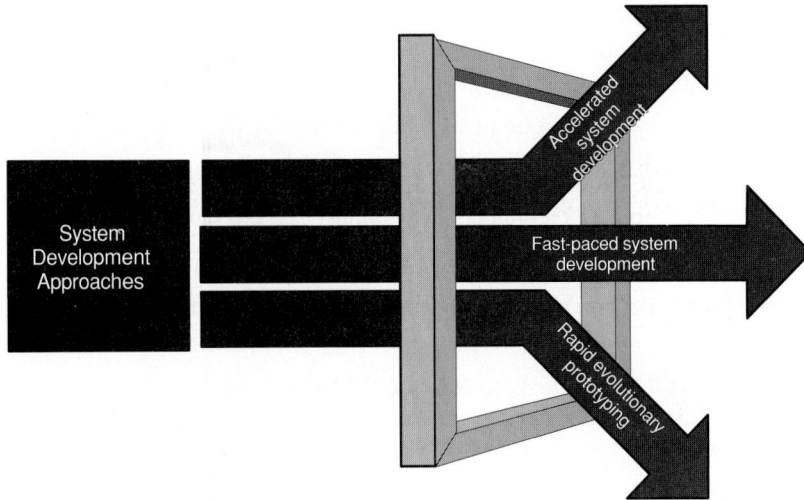

Figure 1–5 Accelerated system development approach, fast-paced development approach, and rapid evolutionary prototyping approach.

Figure 1-6 illustrates the relationship that exists between the size and complexity of a system and how these two factors might affect the selection of one of the three development approaches that are proposed in this book.

Any experienced software developer will recognize that besides the size and complexity of a system, other factors will likely influence the type of development approach that can be used to build a system. Following is a brief discussion of at least three additional factors that can also directly influence the selection of a particular development approach over another one. These factors are:

- The development time allocated to the project
- The importance of the system for the organization's survival in a global market
- The type of technology base that will be used to develop and run the system

The total development time that is required to complete the project is an important factor that must be considered when selecting one of the three particular application development models that are being proposed in this section. Figure 1-7 illustrates the

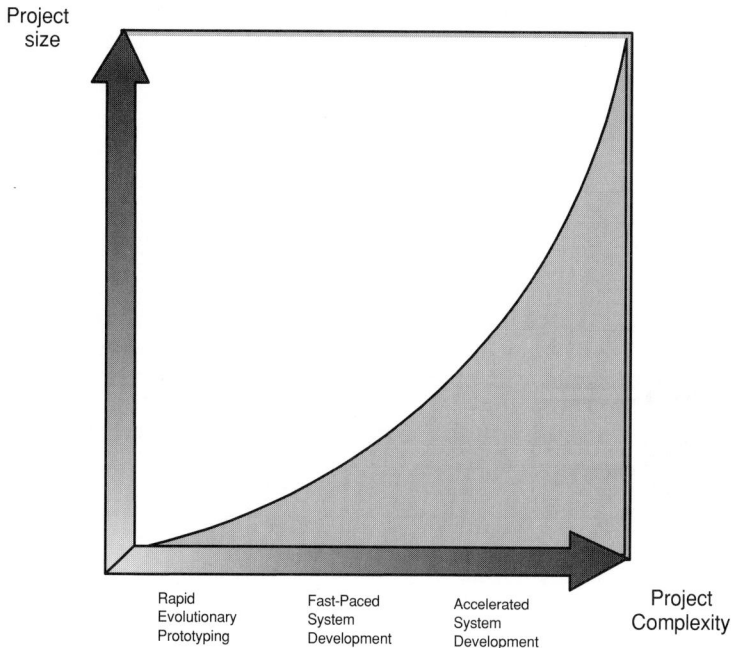

Figure 1–6 System development approaches in relation with system size and complexity.

relationship that exists between the total system development time and each of the three system development approaches.

The level of criticality of a system can also be a determining factor that will likely influence the selection of one of the proposed three systems development approaches. If the system is mission-critical and turns out to be essential for the survival of the enterprise, then a more secure and phased development approach will likely be used to develop the system, along with the insertion of more control points during the project to minimize the risk of failure.

The type of technology that will be used to build and run the system and its level of maturity will also affect the system development approach. For instance, even if the system is relatively small, the chosen development approach might require some additional verification steps if it uses new or very complex technologies with which the developers are not familiar. A well known fact is that in several client-server or Web development projects, several different technologies can be used to develop a system. However, bringing together different technologies introduces an opportunity for failure, which needs to be minimized and managed appropriately.

The following sections provide a brief description of each of the three application development approaches that appear in Figure 1-5.

Proposed
Development
Approach

Rapid
Evolutionary
Prototyping

Fast-Paced
System
Development

Accelerated
System
Development

Months

1   2   3   4   5   6   7   8   9   10 11 12 13 14 15 16 17 18

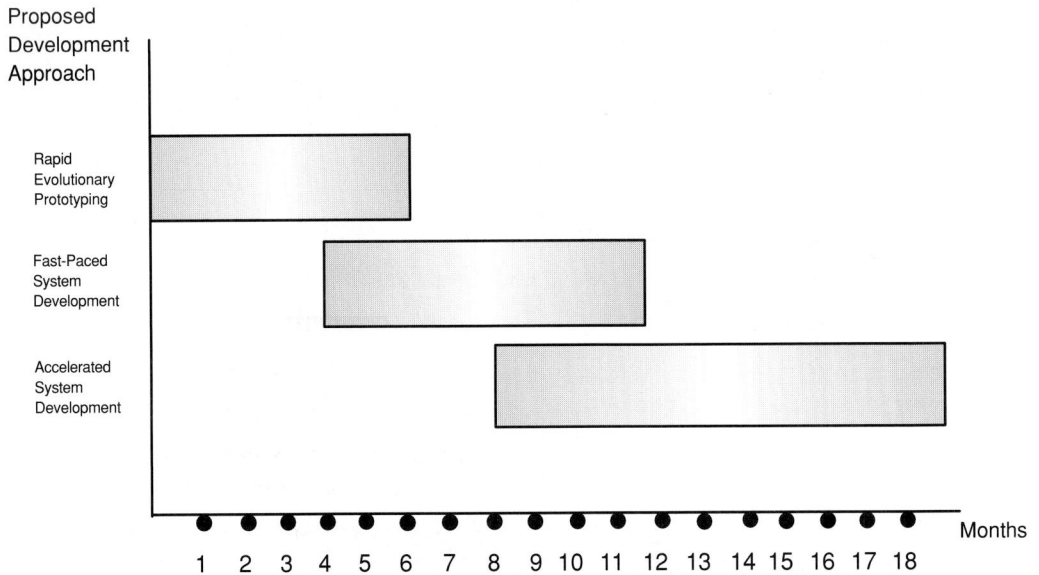

Figure 1–7 System development approaches in relation with estimated development time.

1.7   ACCELERATED SYSTEM DEVELOPMENT APPROACH FOR LARGE PROJECTS

I highly recommend the accelerated system development approach for very large and complex projects.

As shown in Figure 1-8, the accelerated development approach is organized into five major development phases. This approach maximizes the overall productivity of the large number of developers who usually get involved in sizeable software projects.

The system technical deliverables are progressively refined in a step-by-step manner throughout the software development process, with increasing details being added in each particular development phase. As shown in Figure 1-8, technical activities that lead to the delivery of a critical product are not arbitrarily confined to a single development phase. Also, the structuring of technical activities into discrete development phases is not totally rigid. For instance, some design activities can start prior to the completion of the analysis phase. Nevertheless, such a development phasing approach minimizes the risks of divergence from the original users' requirements and of costly retrofits of the deliverables at later stages of the development cycle.

The accelerated system development approach is in fact the only development method that is fully documented in detail in this book. The fast-paced and rapid evolutionary development approaches are not documented, simply because they turn out

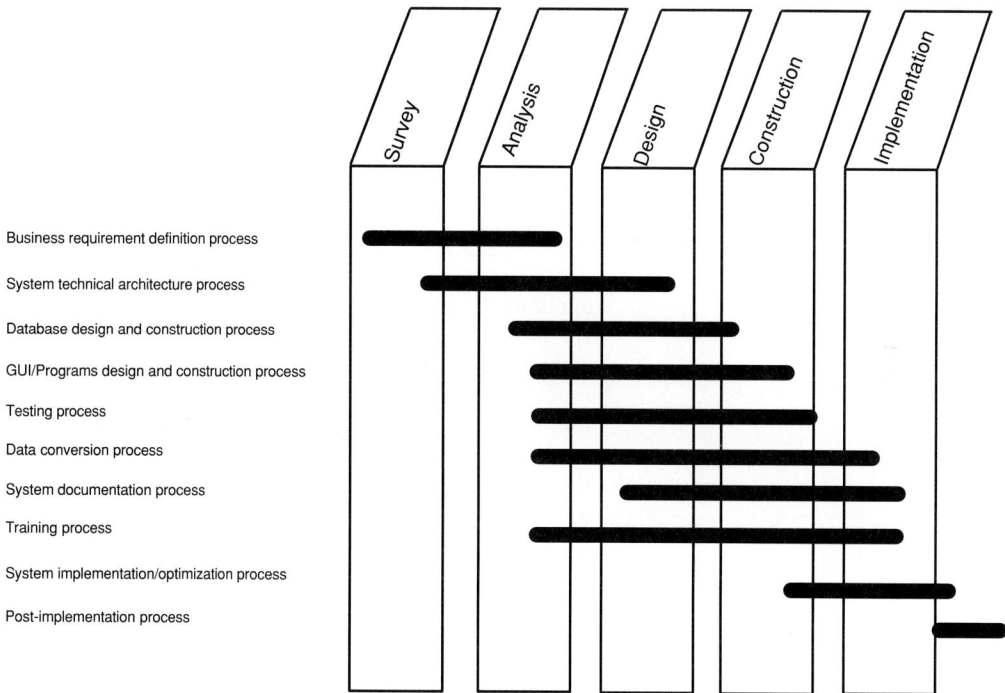

Figure 1–8 Accelerated system development approach.

to somehow be a condensed or expurgated version of the accelerated system development approach for large projects.

Table 1-5 provides a brief description of the purpose and major objectives of each of the five distinct development phases that support the accelerated system development approach.

Table 1–5 Accelerated System Development Approach

Phase	Description
Survey	The purpose of the survey phase is to define the user's business needs, business objectives, project scope, and project constraints and risks.
Analysis	The purpose of the analysis phase is to define the detailed requirements for the business application. A business data and process model is created to capture the functional and data requirements of the application. The technical architecture requirements that are required to operate and

Table 1–5 Accelerated System Development Approach (cont.)

	support the application are also captured at this stage, such as the system security, control, performance, and hardware/software/networking requirements. A high-level testing, training, and data conversion strategy is elaborated during this phase. A working prototype of the system graphical user interface is also constructed during this phase and reviewed with the users.
Design	The purpose of the design phase is to transform the business application requirements into a set of detailed system specifications, which must be kept in line with the technical architecture required to run the system. The business data model is transformed into a logical database design. The business process model is transformed into a detailed and complete set of system transactions that are carefully designed with their appropriate graphical user interface. The testing, training, and data conversion strategies are refined, and detailed plans are produced outlining the activities that must be performed to satisfy the identified testing, training, and data conversion requirements.
Construction	The purpose of the construction phase is to code and test all required application programs to verify that they work as per the stated system specifications. The test and production databases are also created. Depending on the number of programs that need to be developed, the system programs can be developed all at the same time or through an incremental series of fast builds.
Implementation	The purpose of the implementation phase is to migrate the system into a production environment and convert the legacy data into the new system files and databases. The users who will utilize the system and the Information Systems personnel who will operate the system are trained. The old system is phased out.

The accelerated system development approach for large projects that I propose in this book highly recommends the use of several specialized techniques to help compress and speed up the entire development process, such as those indicated in Table 1-6.

Table 1–6 Accelerator Techniques For Large Projects

• Joint facilitated sessions   • Prototyping   • Timeboxing   • Iterative development

Table 1–6 Accelerator Techniques For Large Projects (cont.)

• Partitioning of large projects into smaller, more manageable sub-projects that can be implemented within a six- to eighteen-month time frame
• Use of a component-based, reusable application development architecture

All these accelerators are integrated into the five development phases, where appropriate.

1.8 THE FAST-PACED SYSTEM DEVELOPMENT APPROACH FOR MEDIUM-SIZED PROJECTS

The fast-paced systems development approach is recommended for medium-sized projects. It requires less formalism than for large projects. It is also characterized by a more limited number of major milestones and intermediate system deliverables. This development approach consists of three major development phases, as indicated in Figure 1-9.

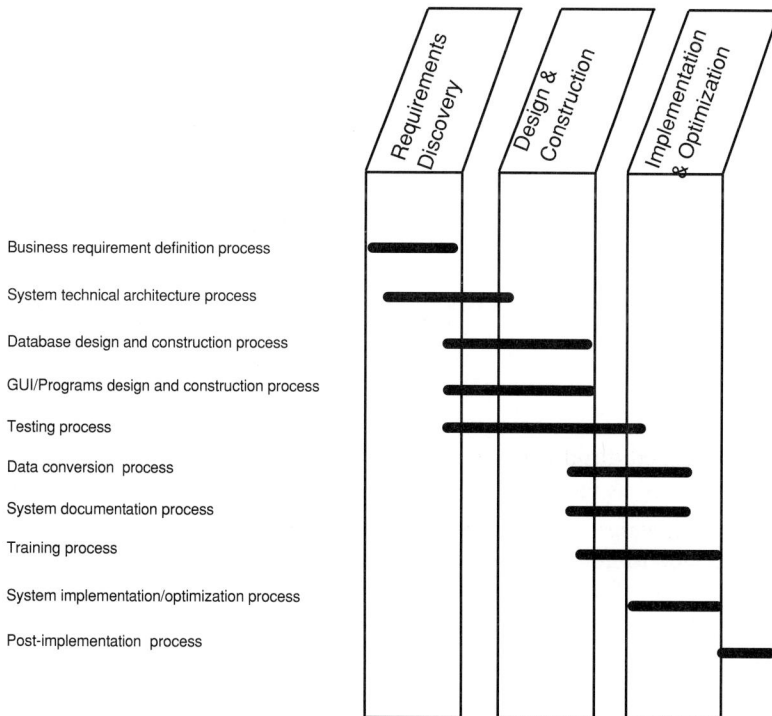

Figure 1–9 Fast-paced system development approach.

Table 1-7 provides a brief description of the purpose and major objectives of each of the three distinct development phases that are supported in the fast-paced systems development approach.

Table 1–7 Fast-paced System Development Approach

Phase	Description
Requirements	The purpose of the requirements investigation phase is to quickly define the system's scope and requirements to a level of detail that will be sufficient to develop the business application in a shortened time frame. During this phase, the development team also determines what is the best strategy for testing the system during the next phase, training the users and systems personnel, and performing the data conversion process.
Design and construction	The purpose of the design and construction phase is to quickly develop and test the system solution that will satisfy the application requirements that were documented during the requirements investigation phase.
Implementation and optimization	The purpose of the implementation and optimization phase is to transfer the new system into its production environment, convert the legacy data, and train the users and systems personnel on how to use and operate the application. Once the system has been migrated, fine-tuning it may be necessary so that it smoothly runs in its production environment.

1.9 RAPID EVOLUTIONARY PROTOTYPING APPROACH FOR SMALL PROJECTS

I particularly recommend the rapid evolutionary prototyping approach for small-sized projects. This more fluid development approach primarily consists of two major development phases, as indicated in Figure 1-10.

Table 1-8 provides a brief description of the purpose and major objectives of the two distinct development phases that are supported in the rapid evolutionary prototyping approach.

The rapid evolutionary prototyping approach slightly diverges from the two previous application development methods. Both the accelerated and rapid system development approaches capture the critical user requirements and system specifications with a modeling approach that focuses initially on *what* the system should do as opposed to the *how to*. Even though a working prototype of the graphical user interface

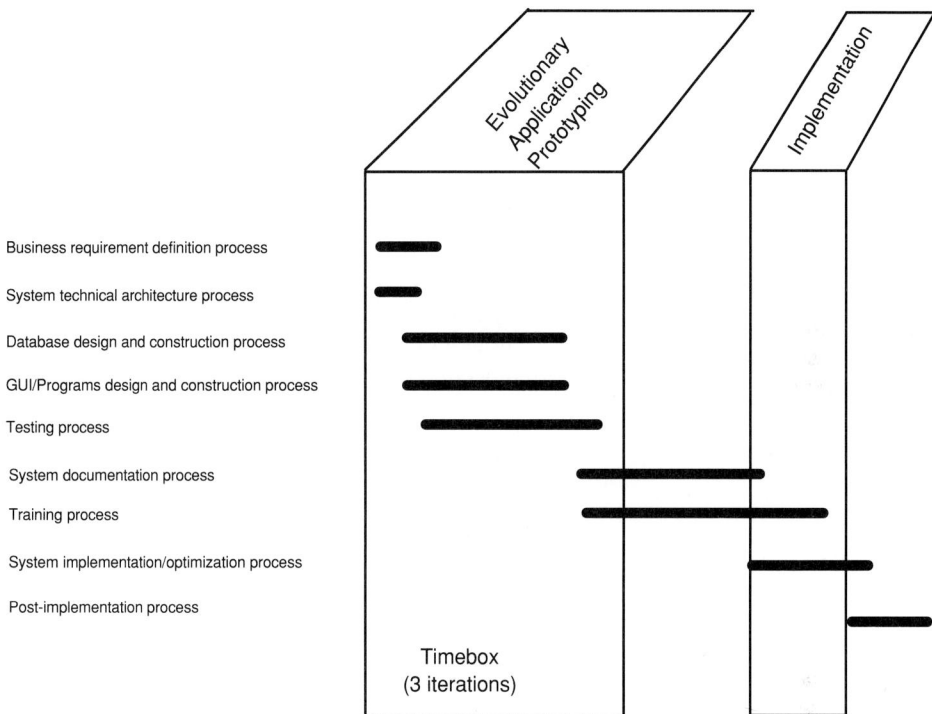

Figure 1–10 Rapid evolutionary prototyping approach.

might very well be created, more emphasis is given to written artifacts with the accelerated and rapid development techniques.

At the opposite end, the rapid evolutionary prototyping approach utilizes the evolving system prototype itself as a means to directly demonstrate to the users how the system solution they are building in an incremental approach will satisfy their needs. In other words, the prototype is used to determine the system requirements as the system is gradually being built over time. With this approach, a more limited set of intermediate documents are produced. Besides the most critical software artifacts that must be developed such as the data model, the overall software documentation is kept minimal and the developers use self-documenting source code techniques, for instance.

The rapid evolutionary prototyping approach is very attractive for the users since they can visually see, in a very tangible manner, what their system looks like as its actual construction is taking place. However, this approach must be properly managed to avoid certain pitfalls, such as developing a system that can turn out to be unstable and hard to maintain as it evolves over time, once it is transferred into a production environment.

Table 1–8 Rapid Evolutionary Prototyping Approach

Phase	Description
Evolutionary Application Prototyping	The purpose of the evolutionary application prototype approach is to directly construct the system solution with an evolutionary prototyping method.
	The prototype gradually evolves into a fully functional system through a pre-determined number of development iterations.
	Each iteration of the evolutionary prototype is executed inside a rigid timebox to control the possibility of creeping functionality and to ensure the system is delivered as per the time frame agreed with the users.
Implementation	The purpose of the implementation phase is to transfer the new system into its production environment and quickly train the users and systems personnel on how to use and operate the application.

Lastly, the rapid evolutionary prototyping approach might require some additional development steps if the system that is being constructed is replacing an existing system, such as the usual activities that are associated with the data conversion process, for instance.

1.10 FINAL NOTES ON THE METHODOLOGY CUSTOMIZATION PROCESS

In all fairness, I can admit that the technical activities that are prescribed in the methodology proposed in this book do not always bear the same weight for each project. Some technical activities can be far more extensive than others, depending on the type of project at hand.

For example, if the application system will run on a computing platform that is already well established in the organization, then defining the technology architecture that will be used to run and support the system becomes a straightforward process. On the other end, if the project introduces brand-new technologies into the organization, then implementing and testing this technology on its own may be imperative, prior to starting to lay down the application architecture. A small prototype can be implemented to verify the technology architecture components as a whole, in order to minimize the potential risks of failure.

Hence, you must not use an autocratic approach whereby all the technical activities need to be performed blindly regardless of the value or non-added value they might bring to the development process of a particular system.

Also, I need to point out that tailoring the methodology might not only imply eliminating, modifying, or combining the technical development activities that are proposed in this book. It might also entail the addition of new technical activities that might be necessary to satisfy the specific needs of a particular project. Adapting the baseline methodology to the needs of a specific system is not a static process, and new technical activities can certainly be added to the development process to tune the methodology to address specific situations.

The development team might also be facing several constraints, such as limited time and limited staff resources with less than optimal technical skills to develop the system or some severe budgetary restrictions. In such situations, I strongly recommend downsizing the number of functions to be embedded in the new system or building special contingencies in the project development plan, rather than attempting to cut corners in the development process.

2

Survey

2.1 INTRODUCTION

The primary objective of the survey phase is to define the core business objectives for the new system and obtain a realistic project scope, especially if the system is fairly large and complex.

Table 2-1 describes the detailed objectives of the survey phase.

Table 2–1 Survey Phase Objectives

- To examine the current problems to be eliminated from the business environment under study and also the business opportunities that can be better exploited
- To derive from the users' business needs a clear set of business objectives for the new application system
- To define the initial scope of the system and set delimiters around the functional areas that will be covered by the project at hand
- To identify the high-level set of business functions that the new system is to support
- To identify project constraints, risks and assumptions

Table 2-2 summarizes the major technical activities that are conducted during the survey phase, along with a list of the anticipated technical deliverables.

Figure 2-1 pictorially presents, at a high-level, the relationships that exist among the individual technical activities of the survey phase.

The survey phase technical activities can be performed using an iterative approach, gradually refining the activity deliverables in incremental steps. On the other hand, certain types of activities might not easily lend themselves to an iterative development approach.

Table 2–2 Survey Phase

ACTIVITY	DELIVERABLE(S)
1. Analyze current situation	1. Current problems, opportunities, users' needs
2. Define system mission and project business objectives	2. System mission & project business objectives
3. Create system context diagram	3. System context diagram
4. Create data context diagram	4. Data context diagram
5. Identify project constraints, risks, and assumptions	5. Project constraints, risks, and assumptions
6. Determine initial project scope	6. Initial project scope

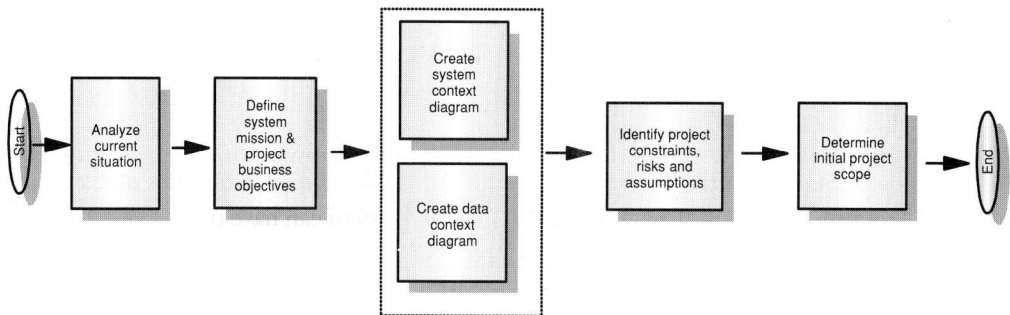

Figure 2–1 Survey phase technical activities diagram.

At the completion of each survey phase major activity, a formal walkthrough should be scheduled to review the deliverables that are produced by the activity.

Finally, the development team has two alternatives to develop the survey phase technical deliverables: the traditional survey phase approach as described in the following sections or the joint facilitated session approach, as described at the end of this chapter.

2.2 INITIATE THE SURVEY PHASE

Depending on the level of maturity the organization has achieved in planning its corporate systems requirements, the survey phase can be initiated in two different ways:

1. **Starting with a strategic system plan.** This plan outlines the portfolio of corporate systems that must be developed to support the global business goals of the enterprise. The plan is based on a corporate-wide business strategy, and the

strategic information systems are implemented according to a predetermined sequence over a given period of time.

2. ***Upon receipt of a request for service from a user representative.*** Typically, the business problems and opportunities are identified at the operational level. This situation leads users to issue a request to the MIS organization to develop a system. However, this system may or may not be in line with the strategic directions set in the enterprise corporate systems plan.

In the first context, justification for the project should be easily accomplished, as the implementation of the system has already been planned at a corporate level. Thus, it will likely support the strategic, long-range business goals and objectives of the organization. Furthermore, the total effort required to conduct the survey phase tasks should normally take far less time than with a traditional survey phase. The reason is that the high-level technical deliverables that were developed during the enterprise-wide strategic planning effort can be used to finalize quickly some of the survey phase technical deliverables, such as the system and data context diagrams, the system mission, and so forth.

In the second context, the project proposal must be elaborated with enough detail to indicate clearly that the proposed system not only will satisfy the immediate business needs of a particular business area but also does in fact support the overall strategic business objectives of the organization. Additionally, members of the development team must carefully examine the potential impact the system can have on its direct users and also on the organization at large. Although this need for corporate alignment is true for all systems, it is especially important for large projects, as the investment for developing a large and complex system is proportionally far greater than for a smaller system.

Activity number:	SU-1
Activity name:	Analyze current situation
Purpose:	To identify the users' business needs
Inputs:	User request for service Current system documentation
Outputs:	SU-T1 Current problems/opportunities/users' needs
Activity description:	• Based on a brief investigation of the service request for a new system, identify all the business areas and related systems that will likely be affected by the proposed project request. • For each prospective business area involved, identify the names of the key user representatives to contact during the initial project assessment activities. Confirm their participation in the survey phase activities and get an agreement on their anticipated roles, responsibilities, and availability.

- Conduct preliminary interviews and meetings with the individuals who represent each affected business area.
- Describe the problems that are currently being experienced in each business area and also the new business opportunities that can be exploited by the construction of a new system.
- If some problems or opportunities appear to be in conflict with one another, document the related issues and submit them to the user's management for guidance and resolution.
- Assign a priority to each critical problem/opportunity that was identified during the preliminary fact-gathering processes.
- Walk through the identified problems/opportunities/users' needs to ensure they truly reflect the current situation and that all major affected business areas have been covered during this preliminary assessment study.

2.3   ANALYZE THE CURRENT SITUATION

The primary objective of this activity is to meet with the prime business areas that will likely be affected by the proposed project and derive the core business needs that must be satisfied by the new system.

Obviously, the users would not request a new system if the current environment was considered adequate in the first place. Therefore, even during the preliminary information gathering sessions, you must document not only the existing problems but also the specific users' views that can lead to the discovery of business opportunities.

Sometimes situations might arise in which the business problems at hand cannot be resolved by the implementation of a computerized system. Typically, these problems are the results of organizational deficiencies in the working place that can be resolved by restructuring the operations of the business department(s) involved or re-engineering some of the most critical business processes.

Problem definition is not always a straightforward process. Invariably, it necessitates a thorough understanding of the current situation, which should carefully be examined in its proper context. Figure 2-2 presents some of the fact-gathering techniques that the analysts can use to better comprehend the current situation.

Regardless of the data-gathering technique used, Table 2-3 lists the most common types of information that should be gathered from each affected business area, while assessing the current situation. However, this list is far from exhaustive. Consequently, the analysts should not limit themselves to this list.

The following section is not intended to be exhaustive in terms of describing the fact-gathering techniques shown in Figure 2-2. Rather, the aim here is to highlight some important points the analysts should consider when using any of these fact-finding techniques.

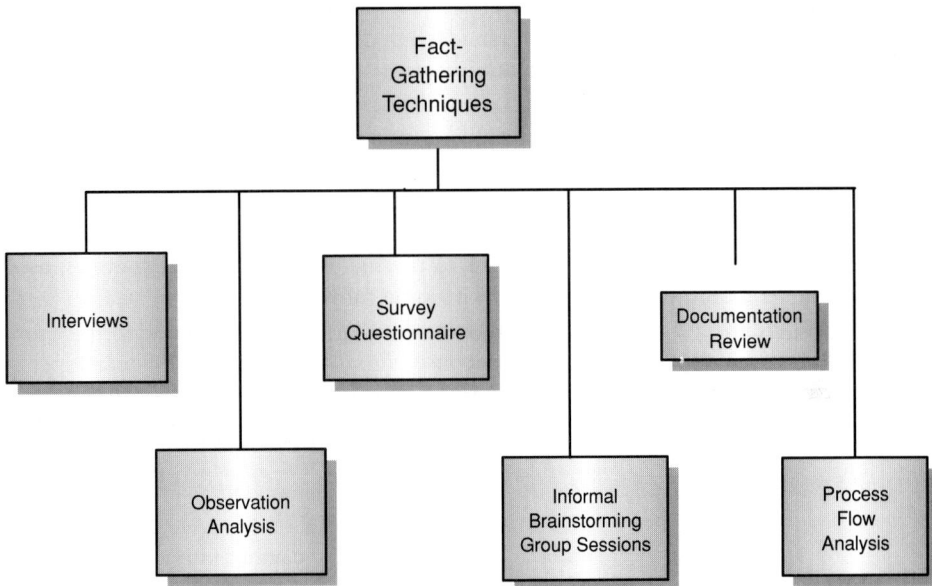

Figure 2–2 Fact-gathering techniques.

Table 2–3 Major Type Of Information To Be Gathered

- Business goals and objectives
- Problems and opportunities
- High-level business processes
- Assumptions
- Critical success factors
- High-level information needs
- External agents and major business events to which the business area must react

2.3.1 INTERVIEWS

Depending on the number of affected departments, the users' business needs can be uncovered through a series of interviews. The first step in the interviewing process consists of identifying the most relevant users, who should then be interviewed by the analyst. One simple way of doing so is to obtain from the users an organizational chart of all the business units that will likely participate in the project. Verifying that such charts are accurate and up-to-date is imperative. The key individuals who should be interviewed in each particular user area are then identified, usually by following the established line of authority, starting from the head of the department downward.

The analyst should obtain the assistance of the department managers to identify both the various people who should be interviewed and how to obtain their cooperation. The interviews can then be scheduled in advance. Sometimes, right at the outset, knowing which individuals will provide the most critical and valuable information about the current situation is hard. For this reason, the analysts might, during the fact-gathering process, add new persons to the list of candidate interviewees, as their potential contributions to the project become more apparent.

Before meeting with a user representative, the analysts should carefully prepare the interview. Although this book's purpose is not to discuss in any detail specific interviewing techniques, the basic guidelines provided in Table 2-4 should be useful.

Table 2–4 Basic Interview Guidelines

Before	• Identify the objectives of the interview
	• Schedule the interview ahead of time. Avoid just dropping in without an appointment. Unplanned interviews can turn out to be quite disruptive for the users.
	• Identify the current position and responsibilities of the interviewees before the meeting.
	• Set up the interview at a time that is convenient for the user. Wherever possible, choose a quiet area, which eliminates potential disruptions.
	• Gather as much pertinent information as you can on the functions that are performed in the interviewee's area, including the appropriate business forms and report samples.
	• Since the major objective of the interview is to gather information, and since the interviewee values his or her time, an appropriate measure might be to prepare an outline of the interview and give an advance copy to the interviewees so they can prepare themselves in advance, if required.
During	• Present yourself, inform the interviewee of the purpose of the interview, and explain the objectives you hope to achieve with this interview.
	• If you take notes, explain what you are doing and why you are doing so. Various tools other than the traditional pencil and paper outfit can be used to record the discussion, such as a tape recorder or even a video camera. However, the analyst should keep in mind that these devices can make the user reluctant or unwilling to discuss openly issues he or she feels are politically oriented.
	• As a rule of thumb, do not take more than half an hour to a full hour for conducting the interview. If necessary, schedule several interviews with the same person to cover completely the related subject of interest.

Table 2–4 Basic Interview Guidelines (cont.)

	• If you plan to do so, ask for permission to talk to the interviewee's staff later on. • Explain that all the information gathered during the interview will be submitted for his or her approval before being officially published. • Toward the end of the interview, summarize the major points that were discussed to confirm your understanding of what has been said. • Terminate the interview on a positive note, thanking the interviewee for her or his contribution.
After	• Document all relevant points that were gathered during the interview. • Send the documentation to the interviewee for final approval. • If further clarification is needed, contact the interviewee to set up another meeting. • Issue the outcome of the interview to the appropriate users and managers.

While conducting interviews, the analyst should be careful about the following three particular situations:

1. The user concentrates on the symptoms of the problems rather than on the real causes of the problems.

2. The user expresses his or her needs in terms of predetermined computer solutions without understanding the real nature of the problems. In many instances, the user may not be familiar with the facilities that a computerized system can or cannot provide to ease the current situation. Therefore, the user can make false assumptions about computerized solutions, such as thinking that an automated system will magically solve all existing problems, no matter what they are.

3. During the course of an interview, the analyst suddenly realizes that some disparities might exist between the official version of how the existing system manual and automated procedures should operate and what really happens at the operational level. If so, the analyst should use tact and diplomacy when reporting these discrepancies to management. Personnel at the operational level may be reluctant to admit that the business operations do not always conform to the working patterns officially endorsed by upper management.

When any of the above-mentioned situations are encountered, the analyst should acknowledge these inconsistencies while still trying to discover the real causes of the problems. For this reason, the analyst should be highly skilled in the techniques of interviewing. Different users will have different viewpoints that will likely influence their own perceptions of the current situation.

2.3.2 SURVEY QUESTIONNAIRE

Survey

The survey questionnaire is a technique that is frequently used to gather different types of information. This particular fact-gathering tool is very convenient when a large number of users must be canvassed, as is often the case in very large organizations, where several user groups can be dispersed in many locations throughout the country or around the world. In these situations, having an analyst interview all the people at all the sites would be impractical. This is where a survey questionnaire becomes a valuable technique to solicit and gather information from a large and geographically dispersed user population. Later on, once all the information gathered with the questionnaire is analyzed, specific follow-up interviews can be organized with selective users whose potential contributions to the project has become more apparent.

The use of a survey questionnaire has some potential drawbacks. One serious disadvantage is that communication with users is seriously restricted; no real face-to-face exchange of information takes place. For this reason, the decision to use a survey questionnaire should be carefully weighed against its shortcomings. Typically, the preparation of a well-written questionnaire requires a considerable amount of time. Furthermore, the questions must be structured in a way that will be user-friendly and meaningful to the people who fill them out. Ideally, they must be formulated without anticipating the way the users will respond.

A variety of formats can be used to construct the questionnaire, such as multiple-choice, checklist, and fill-in-the-blank questions, for example. In all cases, the questionnaire should be developed in a manner that minimizes the time needed to fill it out. Allowing the respondent to make a choice by checking off or circling the answer might be advantageous. This will also facilitate the compilation of the results. The target audience for a survey can be customers, partners, suppliers, and internal business process owners.

Table 2-5 outlines some of the basic steps to follow when using survey questionnaires.

Table 2–5 Survey Questionnaire Guidelines

Prepare the questionnaire	• Identify the type of information you want to gather, such as problems experienced or opportunities to exploit.
	• Once your requirements are defined, choose an appropriate format for the questionnaire. Construct the questions in a simple, clear, and concise manner.
	• If you include questions that require a narrative answer, make sure you provide sufficient space for the reply.
	• The questions addressing a specific topic should be grouped together and identified under a main heading.
	• Ideally, the questionnaire should be accompanied by a cover letter written by a senior executive to emphasize the importance of this survey for the organization.

Table 2–5 Survey Questionnaire Guidelines (cont.)

Identify respondents	• Adding the name, job title, and address of each respondent can help to personalize the questionnaire. • A log, which identifies all the people who will receive the questionnaire, must be developed. It will be used to monitor the status of the questionnaires that have been distributed.
Distribute the questionnaire	• Distribute the questionnaire, along with detailed instructions on how to fill it out. Clearly indicate a time limit for returning the questionnaire.
Analyze respondents' answers	• Analyze and consolidate the information provided in the returned questionnaires. • Document the major findings. • Send a copy of the major findings to each respondent as a courtesy for having taken the time to participate in the survey.

2.3.3 DOCUMENT REVIEW

Document review is one of the most popular ways to gather information about the current situation. Internal procedure manuals, existing system documentation, forms and documents that are used to perform departmental business tasks, and reports produced by the current system – all are important sources of information that describe the user environment. (A worthwhile point about document review is that it can be performed before, during, and after other fact-gathering techniques).

Quite often, the multiplicity of documents flowing through the environment justifies the need to start building an inventory of what currently exists, in terms of forms, reports, and other, similar documents. This list often becomes a useful reference point for planning and organising interviews and observations.

2.3.4 OBSERVATION ANALYSIS

Observation analysis is a very effective fact-gathering technique. It can be used for several purposes, such as processing and confirming the results of an interview, identifying the documents that should be collected for further analysis, clarifying what is being done in the current environment and how it is done, and similar tasks. The technique is relatively simple. For a given period of time, the analyst observes users on-site as they perform their daily activities. Although the analyst can observe without directly intervening in the process, most of the time he or she will interact with the persons being observed. The analyst frequently will ask questions in order to understand how an operation is done. To the limit possible, the analyst should perform a user's activities in order to gain a better understanding of how users operate in their own environment.

Observation analysis presupposes that proper management approval has been secured with the users in the first place. You also need to explain to the people who will be observed what you will do and why. This precautionary measure will help to prevent situations in which those under observation feel they are under some form of police surveillance. Table 2-6 describes the basic activities that should be performed before, during, and after an observation study.

Table 2–6 Observation Study Guidelines

Before	• Identify the user areas and business processes to be observed. • Obtain the proper management approval to carry out the observations. • Obtain the names and titles of the key people who will be involved in the observation study. • Explain the purpose of the study.
During	• Familiarize yourself with the workplace being observed. • Note the current organizational groupings. • Observe the current manual and automated facilities in use. • Collect samples of the documents and written procedures that are used for each specific process being observed. • Amass statistical information on job duties: frequency of occurrence, volume estimates, time duration for each person being observed, and the like. • While interacting with the users, always try to remain objective and do not comment on their mode of operation in a non-constructive way. • Observe not only the normal business operations but also how the exceptions are handled. • Once the observations are completed, thank the people for their support.
After	• Document the findings resulting from the observations made. • Consolidate the results. • Review the consolidated results with the individual observed and/or their managers.

In particular instances, observation analysis has some potential drawbacks. For one, the overall process can be quite time-consuming. In other cases, analysts might also be misled in their observations. Nonetheless, this technique is widely accepted by many people in the data processing field and can often be used to complement the findings obtained with the use of other fact-gathering techniques.

2.3.5 PROCESS FLOW ANALYSIS

Sometimes, user problems have nothing to do with the software system in place. More often than not, these non-system-related problems can be directly connected to the way the business processes themselves are performed in the user's environment. Typically, the symptoms leading to workflow problems of this nature are associated with complaints about unnecessary interactions, time lost by inability to proceed, too many errors occurring in the workplace, and quite often, an impression that a lot of work is duplicated among various departments for no apparent reason.

Ordinarily, this situation happens when the user's work is partitioned into several processes that are performed by so many business departments that nobody can figure out the big picture. Process flow analysis can then be used to analyze the current situation. In the context of this book, process flow analysis can be used primarily to pictorially represent the relationships among various activities that must be performed within a sub-process.

Process flow analysis is a problem identification technique that has its roots in industrial engineering. It has been successfully used for several decades in various engineering disciplines to study the general flow of processes that cross several functional areas, such as from the engineering departments down to the shop floor areas, for instance.

The technique uses a simple graphical language that depicts the flow of processes that are performed by different departments. The detailed processes are often shown on a flowchart that is displayed on a wall.

Before I describe the symbols that can be used to construct a process flowchart, I want to define the terminology that is used in process flowcharting. A *process* is a series of business operations that are conducted in a department and produce some outputs. *Analysis* means studying a process to divide it into simpler elements and see whether they can be enhanced.

Figure 2-8 illustrates the nine basic symbols that are needed to draw a process flowchart.

Table 2-7 provides a brief description of each symbol.

Figure 2-9 schematically illustrates a typical process flowchart, once it is completed.

The various user departments involved in the process workflow are usually identified on the left-hand side of the diagram and are separated by horizontal lines. Quite often, the people who participate in the study use a special process flow analysis toolkit that includes all the materials required to easily create a giant flowchart diagram on a wall.

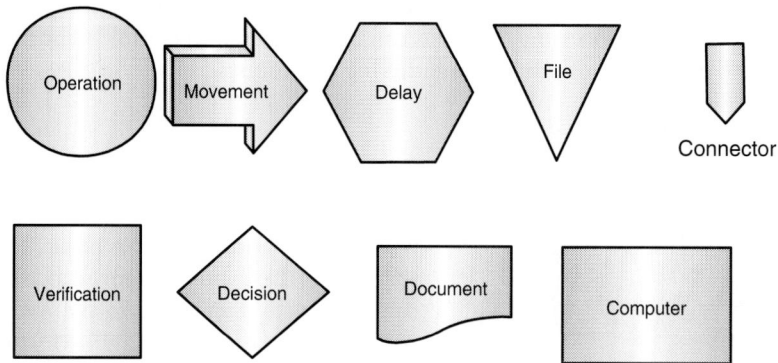

Figure 2–8 Process flowchart symbols.

Table 2–7 Process Flowchart Symbol Description

Operation	A large circle represents a particular operation that is manually performed within a specific process. As a result of this operation, something is created or modified. Examples: Fill out a request for purchase, reproduce a document, prepare a report.
Movement	An arrow is used to represent the physical movement of an item. Examples: Walk to a filing cabinet, walk to a storage area, deliver a report to a user.
Delay	An octagon is used to identify a temporary delay in the work process. Examples: Wait for an authorisation, wait for a reply, delay the publication of a report until month's end.
File	A triangle is used to represent the act of storing a document. Examples: Dispose of a document, file or classify a document, record information on microfiche.
Verification	A square is used when an appraisal task is performed. It represents the task of verifying something. Examples: Verify for completeness, authorize document, verify for conformance to requirements.
Decision	A diamond-shaped form means a decision must be made. Subsequently, the process workflow is divided into at least two paths. Examples: Reach a yes/no conclusion, reach a conditional settlement.
Document	A document symbol denotes an output that is produced when executing an operation or an input. Examples: A sales report, a customer invoice.
Computer	A rectangle represents a software system or an automated process. Examples: Program computes sales history, program validates a customer credit line.

Table 2–7 Process Flowchart Symbol Description (cont.)

Connector	A page connector is used to join different components of the process workflow. The page connector is used whenever the addition of workflows would clutter the diagram.

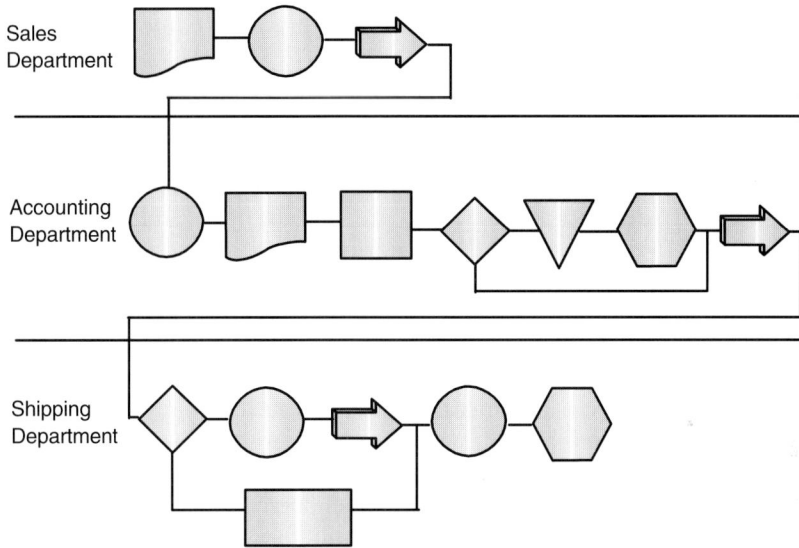

Figure 2–9 Process flowchart sample.

The participants can then visualize all at once the complete process under study. Once completed, the participants carefully examine the process flowchart. Each particular operation is scrutinized to determine whether it adds value and is really required in the overall process. If yes, how can it be improved? Can the overall business cycle time be reduced? Which process or sub-process needs to be scrutinized to improve the quality of the process outcome? What are the major process deterrents?

The flow of operations and documents is traced throughout the different departments that are involved in the work process. In this technique, the sequence of operations performed by the users across several organizational units can sometimes be simplified and improved. Delays or bottlenecks can be eliminated or reduced by re-sequencing some operations. In some instances, the results of a process flow analysis study can clearly indicate some disparities between the official organizational structure and the actual structure that indeed might exist at a lower operational level.

This technique has always sounded very attractive to users of all professions because it is relatively simple to use and quite easy to understand. However, selecting the right people to attend a process flow analysis workshop is very important. The study team should be composed of at least one representative from each department who has its "share" of the process being analyzed. He or she should always be the one individual who is the most knowledgeable about the process being described.

If the development team realizes that the core business processes under study require significant re-engineering work, then completely removing them from the scope of the project might be preferable until they are properly addressed by a thorough business process re-engineering effort. Launching a large-scale business process re-engineering effort requires time, resources, and the full support of the corporate executives.

2.3.6 INFORMAL BRAINSTORMING GROUP SESSION

A particular approach that is often useful to gather information quickly on the current situation is dynamic group sessions. For example, the identification of several problems or opportunities can be performed via the use of the brainstorming technique.

The most knowledgeable user representatives who are involved in the project simply attend a group discussion led by a mediator. The users can nominate this person themselves, if necessary. During the session, all work-related problems and opportunities that might exist in the environment are first identified and thereafter reviewed by the group participants.

The principle behind the brainstorming concept is not new; several heads are better than one. Furthermore, one person's identification of a problem or opportunity might trigger further suggestions from the other attendees.

Some user representatives may have difficulty formulating their problems in a way that naturally leads to an analytical statement of the current situation. When this is the case, the brainstorming technique can turn out to be very useful, because the other user participants and the mediator can provide assistance to those having difficulty in formulating a concise and logical statement of the problem or opportunity at hand. In other words, the collective knowledge and experience of the team participants is used to identify the problems and possibly generate creative solutions to resolve them permanently. I now discuss the basic steps that are involved in conducting a brainstorming session. Although the brainstorming technique can be used to generate a lot of creative and innovative ideas, the process itself is conducted in a structured manner, following a well-defined set of ground rules.

Select Participants

The participants should be carefully selected. They should be invited because of the direct contributions they can provide during the session. The presence of knowledgeable people from different functional groups will ensure a good representation level. If the group turns out to be a mixture of high-ranking and lower-ranking personnel, everyone must understand that during the session, they all operate at the same level. The group should be completely uninhibited to truly operate at a creative level.

A BRIEF NOTE ON THE ORIGINS OF BRAINSTORMING

> Brainstorming is based on a fundamental principle: The human brain carries its thinking activities in two basic modes of operation, analytical and logical. The right side of the brain operates using the mechanisms that are typically associated with creativity, intuition, inventiveness, and sensitivity. The left side of the brain has a tendency to operate in an analytical, rational mode. When we think with the left side of our brain, we examine things in a logical, intellectual, deductive, and systematic manner.
>
> Researchers realized through various experiments that when most human beings think, they normally use either side of their brain, but not both at the same time. If people want to be creative, then they should try to momentarily put to sleep the left side of their brain. If people want to be analytical, they should use the left side of their brain and turn off the right side. If the person does not make a conscious effort to control one side of the brain versus the other, the creative and analytical sides will then struggle with each other.

Explain The Technique And The Rules To Follow

The session leader explains the basic concepts behind brainstorming and the rules that must be followed during the session. The session leader should be an impartial individual.

Produce A Quantity Of Ideas

The first step is simple. The participants generate as many ideas as they can on the topic being brainstormed, such as:

- the identification of problems in the work environment
- the symptoms and causes of a problem
- new opportunities that are waiting to be exploited
- different suggestions to solve a problem

Ideally, only one topic at a time should be selected for a brainstorming session.

The participants are invited, one at a time, to come up with a single idea as their turn arises. If someone has trouble offering an idea, that person simply passes his/her turn and waits for the next round. Thus, everyone is invited to contribute one at a time and in a clockwise manner.

The group session leader controls the session to ensure everyone's participation and that the rules are followed. Participation is very important, but above all, the most critical rule to keep in mind is to forbid any form of criticism whatsoever. People must put aside their analytical skills. The ideas submitted should not be evaluated at all at this early stage. Consequently, the overall process must be fast-paced to increase the number of proposed ideas. This pace will ensure that people do not "switch" their minds to the analytical mode of thinking. It is like a windmill that turns rapidly to generate as many ideas as possible, as quickly as possible.

Write Down The Ideas

The session leader records the ideas on a whiteboard or flipchart as soon as they are mentioned. They should be visible to the entire audience. In several instances, an idea already suggested by a participant will likely encourage the other participants to come up with several variations centered on the same theme. In a brainstorming session, such an approach is perfectly admissible. Once again, no judgment is made about the propositions. No good or bad ideas result, only ideas that are candidly submitted by the participants. The first part of the brainstorming session should be pleasant and people uninhibited. They should let their imaginations flow freely.

Analyze The Ideas

Before starting to analyze the proposed ideas, the group should pause for a few minutes. Once the analysis review has started, the people "activate" the analytical side of their brain. The ideas are reviewed one at a time, and those considered valuable by the group are retained for further analysis.

Table 2-8 resumes the basic set of ground rules that must be observed while conducting a typical brainstorming session.

Table 2–8 Brainstorming Session Ground Rules

- Only one individual may speak at a time
- Participants remain silent unless their input is solicited from the facilitator
- In creative mode, there are no stupid ideas
- No one criticizes someone elses suggestions
- Everyone must participate in proposing ideas
- All the ideas are recorded by the facilitator on a flowchart or whiteboard in clear sight of all attendees
- The number of attendees generally varies between 3 and 15 individuals

2.3.7 PRIORITIZING THE PROBLEMS/OPPORTUNITIES

Some of the most common types of problems that might be experienced or opportunities that might trigger the need for a new computer system are listed in Table 2-9. The problems and/or opportunities described by the users should be prioritized by order of importance. This ranking is necessary to differentiate between those issues that are very important and those that, although nice to address, are not essential for the project at hand. One possible way of categorising the problems or opportunities is indicated in Table 2-10.

Furthermore, the problems and opportunities should be easily traceable back to the departments that originally identified them.

A wide range and variety of problems/opportunities can exist in the current business environment. Not only do you need to rank them by order of importance, but also consider them in terms of the ranking categories that are listed in Table 2-11.

Table 2–9 Most Common Problems/Opportunities

- A new or revised corporate policy that must be enforced
- Contractual obligations that must be satisfied
- Mandatory government regulations or laws that must be implemented
- Major technology breakthroughs that need to be exploited to gain or sustain a competitive advantage
- Increased company revenues or costs avoidance
- Enhancements to existing core business services or processes
- The support of new services or business processes
- Reduction of various business operating costs
- Gaining or retaining a competitive market edge
- New system interfaces must be added
- Shrinking time-to-market situations
- Reduction in business process cycle time
- Quality improvements in products or services
- Existing system deficiencies, such as
  - Obsolete technology
  - Excessive maintenance costs
  - System throughput limitations
  - System information reliability/integrity/accuracy problems
  - System's lack of flexibility to support new business processes or sub-processes

Table 2–10 Business Problems/Opportunities Prioritisation

Essential	Requirements without which the user could not properly operate in the business environment.
Adaptable	Requirements that, if need be, can be partly modified to allow alternative modes of operation.
Nice to have	Requirements that the users are willing to document but that can be excluded from the system list of requirements, if they prove to be too costly to satisfy.

Table 2–11 Ranking Problems/Opportunities By Categories

Category 1	Problems/opportunities over which the involved business departments have full control, as well as full authority to solve them permanently.
Category 2	Problems/opportunities for which the involved business units have no direct control. Despite this restriction, though, they can still exercise some influence on the decision-making process that could lead to a permanent solution to resolve the current problems.
Category 3	Problems/opportunities over which the involved business areas have no direct control whatsoever. Furthermore, they have no influence at all on the solutions that could permanently solve the problems.

2.3.8 DOCUMENTATION OF FACT-GATHERING FINDINGS

You should write all the documentation resulting from the project fact-gathering tasks using the user's terminology. All business terms should be clearly comprehensible, and avoid the use of acronyms wherever possible. You can include a glossary of terms at the end of the survey phase document, if necessary. Furthermore, file all the intermediary documents that have led to a consolidated statement of user needs and make them available on request.

2.3.9 USER PARTICIPATION

You must obtain active participation from the users during the survey phase. This is, without the shadow of a doubt, a very critical success factor. For instance, the business needs and objectives of the project cannot be properly developed without the users' firm commitment to actively participate in their formulation. Ensuring user participation is the only way to assure that the requested system will be precisely aligned with the business goals of the affected departments and of the entire enterprise.

Hence, users must actively participate in the survey phase activities and articulate their own business needs. In fact, this statement remains true for all the deliverables that are produced during the survey phase, from the initial definition of users' needs up to the last set of activities for this phase.

This emphasis on user involvement should be seen as conducive to the success of the project. The system that will be developed will be as effective in supporting the users' functional areas as the users will be in participating in the development of the system's requirements, especially during the crucial stages of the analysis process. Graph A in Figure 2-10 illustrates user involvement in a traditional project. Graph B shows the desired level of user participation required to ensure the successful development of a modern computer system.

In summary, the most successful projects are often those that are placed under the formal responsibility of the users. Although software professionals will develop the system, the ultimate responsibility of the project lies in the hands of knowledgeable and capable user representatives who are officially held accountable for the new system.

2.3.10 USER TRAINING

You need to familiarize the user representatives with the fact-gathering techniques that will be used during the survey phase for very large projects. This familiarization approach will help bridge the communication gap that might exist between the user representatives and the developers.

Some courses are designed specifically to help remove the cloud of mystery surrounding the development of a software system. In general, these courses describe the system development process in simple terms that are easy to understand from a user point of view. During these seminars, the specialized (and often esoteric) software concepts and vocabulary used by software developers are also explained, along with a brief description of the various graphical tools and techniques that are applied during the data and process modeling tasks.

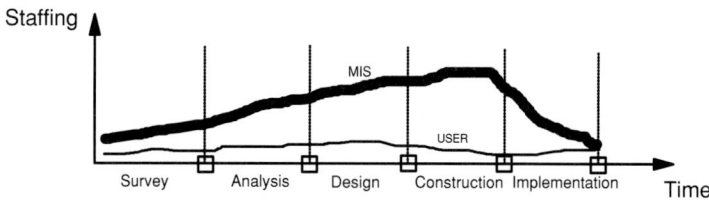

Graph A

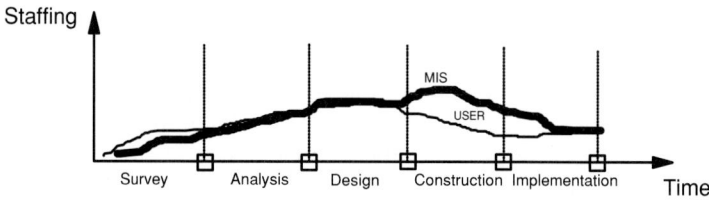

Graph B

Figure 2–10 User involvement in project development.

A brief system development overview course that is tailored specifically for user representatives is a small price to pay for attempting to deliver high-quality system requirements that aim at truly satisfying the users' needs.

Activity number:	SU-2
Activity name:	Define system mission and project business objectives
Purpose:	To identify the system mission and state the major business objectives of the project
Inputs:	Request for service SU-T1 Current problems/opportunities/users' needs
Outputs:	SU-T2 System mission and project business objectives
Activity description:	• Define the mission of the proposed system. • Document the business objectives that must be achieved with the implementation of this system. • Prioritize the business objectives by order of importance and degree of emergency. • For each listed business objective, identify the specific business areas associated with it. • Walk through the system mission and project business objectives to ensure that they are complete and that the objectives are expressed as much as possible in quantifiable terms.

2.4 DEFINE SYSTEM MISSION AND PROJECT BUSINESS OBJECTIVES

2.4.1 SYSTEM MISSION

The primary role of the system mission is to clarify the true "raison d'être" of the system. Whereas the system development life cycle methodology is used to develop the system right the first time, the system mission addresses an essential question: Are we building the right system?

This response may sound like a trivial exercise, but arriving at a consensus as to the exact reason for a system's existence is not always easy. An important step is to develop a clear understanding of the role that the system will play in light of the corporate environment it will support. This will help to avoid potential directional drifts later on during the next development phases of the project.

Once the mission is clearly defined and agreed to by all involved parties, the team can then produce a development strategy that aims at accomplishing that mission. The system mission statement should be formulated in the context of the entire enterprise by answering the fundamental questions listed in Table 2-12.

Table 2–12 System Mission Formulation Questionnaire

• Why should this system exist?
• Which business needs and processes does it support?
• Where does this system fit in the overall corporate picture?

2.4.2 PROJECT BUSINESS OBJECTIVES

Given the formulation of the current situation and of the system mission, the business objectives of the project must also be defined in conjunction with the users. The business objectives serve as the basic framework for elaborating the justification of the system solution. As mentioned, the system must be directed toward helping the organization fulfil its mission and meet its corporate business goals.

The definition of the project business objectives is produced in relation to the problems and/or opportunities that were identified during the analysis of the current situation. A business objective is aimed at either resolving a business problem or capitalizing on exploiting an opportunity. Consequently, you should have at least as many business objectives as the number of major problems/opportunities that were identified earlier during the assessment of the current situation.

Consequently, business objectives are not created equal. Objectives do not carry the same weight and some can be more important than others. A business objective should be assigned a priority that is more or less equivalent to the one assigned to the related problem or opportunity. Table 2-13 illustrates the close relationship between the problems/opportunities and the proposed business objectives.

Table 2–13 Business Objectives To Problems/Opportunities Association Matrix

Business objective	Corresponding problem or opportunity addressed
• Objective 1 • Objective 2 • Objective 3	• Business problem 1 • Business opportunity 1 • Business problem 2

Business objectives can be stated in either qualitative or quantitative terms. However, to be truly meaningful, a business objective should be clearly stated in a quantifiable and measurable format whenever possible. Typically, objectives are formulated as short-term targets that can be achieved within a 6- to 18-month time frame.

Table 2-14 provides a basic set of guidelines that can be used to formulate business objectives.

Table 2–14 Business Objectives Definition Guidelines

Conciseness	A business objective must be clear and concise, no more than one to three sentences. The objective statement should be directed toward achieving an end result, not the intermediate steps that are required to accomplish this result. In other words, a business objective should not try to identify the work to be done but, rather, the desirable end result. Objectives are targets for achievement.
Measurability	A business objective must be measurable, to ensure that we can ascertain whether or not the objective has been fulfilled once the system has been put into production. Measurable terms that use dollar values, percentages, or time factors must be employed wherever possible, as in these examples: • To reduce the control inventory costs by 20 percent within the first two years of operation. • To reduce the control inventory costs by $500,000 within one year. • To increase our ability to handle customer requests on the status of their orders from 50 to 75 percent, within the next year of operation. • To reduce the elapsed time that exists between receiving a customer order and validating the customer's credit status by 15 percent.
Attainability	A business objective must be attainable in light of the current organizational context. In some instances, you may not be able to satisfy a business objective by the means of a new business system simply because there are still some technological or operational constraints in the environment that cannot be resolved by the project at hand. Furthermore, the business objective should be attainable within a reasonable time frame. Thus, a realistic target date must be determined.

Project business objectives should not be confused with system objectives. Business objectives are primarily used to define the productivity/quality gains that must be achieved once the proposed system is implemented. In most instances, they are directed toward the definition of business goals, such as the reduction of operating costs; the increase in efficiency, quality, and responsiveness; the reinforcement of the enterprise's competitive position in the marketplace; or being in a position to provide better services or facilities.

Well-stated and verifiable business objectives will help the organization to better determine the added value that the system will provide to the users' business community at large. Too often, once the system has been implemented, the actual return on investment is not validated against the original figures that were advanced at the beginning of the project. This verification can be done only if the original business objectives of the project are properly formulated, along with a statement of the strategy that will be used to verify them later on.

Be sure to understand that defining objectives, whether business- or system-oriented, is in fact a highly iterative process. Definitions will be modified or refined throughout the entire business requirement definition process. Table 2-15 shows some fairly common measurement indicators that can be used to formulate quantitative business objectives.

Activity name:	Create system context diagram
Purpose:	To situate the system within the overall business environment
Inputs:	Existing system documentation SU-T1 Current problems/opportunities/users' needs SU-T2 System mission and project business objectives
Activity number:	SU-3
Outputs:	SU-T3 System context diagram
Activity description	• Situate the proposed system within the existing business environment and in context with the enterprise at large. • Document all the graphical elements that are depicted in the system context diagram with supportive narrative descriptions. • Verify that the proposed system is not redundant with other systems that might already be in place somewhere else in the enterprise or currently in development. • Identify the high-level business processes that should be included in the proposed system scope, as well as those that should be excluded • Walk through the system context diagram to ensure that all the external agents to the proposed system are properly identified and that each major information flow depicted on the diagram is well described.

Table 2–15 List Of Common Measurement Indicators

- Diminution of operating costs
- Throughput capacity (increase or decrease)
- Level of quality
- Degree of responsiveness
- Accuracy level
- Volume capacity
- Reduction in overall business cycle time
- Degree of customer satisfaction or delight
- Degree of conformance to requirements
- Percentage productivity increase
- Business process cycle time reduction
- Period of time
- Reduction of process overall turnaround time
- Reduction of inventories
- Production costs decrease

2.5 CREATE SYSTEM CONTEXT DIAGRAM

2.5.1 SYSTEM CONTEXT DIAGRAM

The prime purpose of the system context diagram is to situate the system in the enterprise's business environment. It is a very useful tool that will help the development team later on to clarify and formalize the initial scope of the project. All the business areas that have a stake in the proposed system should, by looking at this diagram, have a better grasp of what could or should be the external boundaries of the system and the major external agents that interact with the system from the outside.

I need to mention that, at this early stage, the scope of the project is not yet entirely crystallized. The boundaries may still expand or shrink, at least until the end of the analysis phase. At that time, more detailed information will be available to the development team, allowing a better understanding of what should and should not be included in the scope of the project.

Construction of the system context diagram should start when the analyst is familiar enough with the business area under study, at least at a high level. The input or output information flows shown on the diagram can include several items such as reports, information sent to or received from other systems, and other similar types of documents. The external agents represent the various external suppliers, vendors, individual customers, or organizations that are external to the system and that are interfacing with it. Either these external entities initiate events that the business area under study must respond to in a pre-planned manner, or they receive results from the business processes that are performed within the business area.

Typically, the system context diagram can be developed iteratively, in the following manner:

- Depict the boundary of the proposed system by placing a single process in a rectangle positioned at the center of the diagram. Label it with the a good descriptive name of the system, which represents the domain of study.

- Review the list of external agents that communicate with the system or receive some output from it. The external agents that supply source data to the system (i.e. stimulus) should be identified preferably on the left side of the diagram. The external agents that receive data from the system (i.e. response) should be represented preferably on the right side of the diagram. Identify each external agent with its appropriate name.

- For each external agent shown on the diagram, depict all the information flows that are entering into the proposed system and all the information flows that are leaving it. Identify each specific information flow.

2.5.2 INTERNAL BUSINESS PROCESSES

Once the external agents that interact with the system have been properly identified and the nature of their interactions have been documented at a high level, the next step is to identify the high-level set of major business processes that are performed within the system, in response to external events.

For each high-level business process, the following information should be provided:

- The name of the business process.
- A brief narrative description of the business process.
- The name of the business unit responsible for the business process. If the business process is performed across different business units, list all the stakeholders.

At this stage, the analysts should not be overly concerned about how these high-level business processes are actually performed but, rather, should concentrate their efforts on identifying them as completely as possible. The purpose of this exercise is to tentatively identify and isolate the major business processes that will fall within the boundaries of the proposed system. These high-level business processes will then be studied in greater detail during the analysis phase. At that time, other business processes might be added and others modified or even removed, depending on the final scope of the project.

If a corporate strategic system plan does exist, then the major components of the system context diagram should be mapped against the appropriate high-level business process components of the corporate business process model. Any discrepancy should be documented, and a notification to update either the corporate or application business process model should be initiated at this stage.

Activity number:	SU-4
Activity name:	Create data context diagram
Purpose:	To identify the major data entities used by the system and the relationships that exist among them
Inputs:	Existing system documentation SU-T1 Current problems/opportunities/users' needs SU-T2 System mission and project business objectives SU-T3 System context diagram
Outputs:	SU-T4 Data context diagram
Activity description:	• Construct a high-level data context diagram using the entity-relationship technique. • Document all the major entities that are depicted in the data context diagram with their supporting narrative descriptions. • Walk through the data context diagram to ensure that all the major data entities used by the system are shown and well documented.

2.6 CREATE DATA CONTEXT DIAGRAM

The data context diagram is to the business data model what the system context diagram is to the business process model. It illustrates, at a high level, the critical data entities that are handled by the system under study, with the most critical relationships that exist among them.

Like the system context diagram, it is a very high-level diagram, and because of this, the detailed data attributes of the entities are not shown at this early stage. The initial data context diagram will be expanded and refined during the analysis phase. At that time, more details will be added, including all the data attributes that are associated with an entity or a relationship and the detailed corresponding business rules.

Typically, the high-level data context diagram can be developed in the following manner:

• Identify the major data entities that are of interest to the business area(s) under study.

• Depict the data entities that are manipulated by the system. Label each entity with a unique name.

• Identify the major relationships that exist among the data entities. Label each relationship with a unique name that well describes the relationship. If necessary, document the high-level critical business policies that dictate the nature of the associations established between the entities.

- Identify and surround with dotted lines the data entities and relationships that in some way are related to the proposed system but that are considered outside the immediate boundary of the system's domain of information.

The relationships that exist among the data entities that are directly manipulated and those that are indirectly manipulated by the system can also be shown on the data context diagram.

However, the entities that are clearly outside the boundaries of the proposed system are surrounded with dotted lines. A multitude of connections can be established among a given group of data entities. In fact, the larger the number of data entities, the larger the number of possible connections among them. In practice, what is important is not to identify all the possible relationships that can be established arbitrarily, but rather to identify only those that are of direct interest to the business area being modeled. If a conceptual data model for the enterprise already exists, the data entities shown on the local application model should be mapped against those identified in the corporate data model.

Do realize that even though I discuss the task of constructing the data context diagram after the task of constructing the system context diagram, both diagrams can be constructed in parallel? In some situations, the data context diagram can be constructed even before the system context diagram.

Activity number:	SU-5
Activity name:	Identify project constraints, risks, and assumptions
Purpose:	To define the project constraints, risks, and assumptions that can affect the initial search for tentative solutions
Inputs:	SU-T1 Current problems/opportunities/users' needs SU-T2 System mission and project business objectives SU-T3 System context diagram SU-T4 Data context diagram
Outputs:	SU-T5 Project constraints, risks, and assumptions
Activity description:	• Identify the potential business or technical constraints that might affect the scope and objectives of the project. • Identify the potential business or technical risks that might affect the scope and objectives of the project. • Identify the potential business or technical assumptions that might affect the scope and objectives of the project.

- Identify the stated project business objectives that may somehow conflict with the identified constraints, risks, or assumptions. Evaluate the degree of conflict, document the related issues, and present them to management for resolution.
- Walk through the project constraints, risks, and assumptions to ensure that their potential impact on this project is clearly understood and well described.

2.7 IDENTIFY PROJECT CONSTRAINTS, RISKS AND ASSUMPTIONS

The business and technically-oriented constraints, risks, and assumptions pertain to those conditions that are usually considered outside the direct influence or control of the project team members. At the same time, however, they might have a direct impact on the scope of the project, its schedule, and the proposed implementation solution alternatives. Their potential impact on the project must be well understood by the development team and management. They must be fully described and carefully highlighted so that they will be taken into consideration by all involved parties when the project moves on to the next development phases. You also need to describe, in a risk-mitigation plan, how the project team intends to minimize the technical major risks that potentially might be associated with the creation of the new system.

Table 2-16 lists some of the most common constraints or risks that might affect the viability of a project.

Table 2–16 List Of Common Project Constraints Or Risks

• Corporate practices and directives	• Government regulations
• Business risks (new business processes never supported before)	• Hardware/software/networking considerations
• Budget limitations	• Personnel considerations
• Union regulations	• Technology limitations
• Schedule considerations	• New technology never used before in the enterprise
• Political considerations	
• Legal considerations	• Operational limitations
• Environmental considerations	• organizational policies

The following discussion provides some typical examples of project constraints and risks that the development team should highlight explicitly, where applicable.

2.7.1 BUSINESS CONSTRAINTS

The fact that the new system must be developed using the database management system already in place is a good example of a possible technical constraint on the software side. Another example might be the necessity to use the Java Integrated Development Environment (IDE) toolkit already in place to develop the application code. A third case in point could be the physical limitations of the hardware equipment being used currently.

2.7.2 BUSINESS RISK

The decision to develop a decentralized system to support an organization that in the past was highly centralized might involve a certain element of business risk. A strong resistance to the decentralisation process can occur. Therefore, this situation can result in a destabilisation period that can turn out to be quite harmful to the enterprise, in the long run.

2.7.3 TECHNICAL RISK

Technical risks must be appraised and prioritized early in the software development process of a large system. For instance, if brand-new technologies are introduced to develop and implement new mission-critical systems, then the developers and their management must make a careful assessment of the situation. Is the project technically feasible, based on the organization's current technology infrastructure? Does the current infrastructure need to be beefed up? Does the organisation have the capacity to undertake the project, in terms of costs, development time, skills, and resources? Is the project technically within reach, based on a brief assessment of these factors?

What steps can be taken to mitigate the technology risks? Can you hire contractors who already have gained a proven expertise in this technology, to help reduce the risk of failure for this project? If the technology is so new that finding anyone out there who has some practical experience on it is difficult, then can the potential risks of failure be contained with a proof of concept? Could you launch a small pilot project to experiment with that new technology, prior to implementing it at large?

Activity number:	SU-6
Activity name:	Determine initial project scope
Purpose:	To delineate the domain of the study that will be associated with the project
Inputs:	SU-T1 Current problems/opportunities/users' needs SU-T2 System mission and project business objectives SU-T3 System context diagram SU-T4 Data context diagram SU-T5 Project constraints/risks/assumptions
Outputs:	SU-T6 Initial project scope
Activity description:	• Identify the high-level business processes and data entities that fall within the boundaries of the proposed system scope.

- Identify the set of external agents that fall within the scope of this project.
- Walk through the project scope to ensure that it truly reflects the major business processes to be supported by the new system, as well as the data entities that fall under its jurisdiction.

2.8 DETERMINE INITIAL PROJECT SCOPE

Several projects have failed in the past because the development team did not succeed in obtaining a clear agreement from the users and the information system management as to the scope of the project. In reality, one of the biggest challenges of the survey phase is to define the scope of the system properly. Special attention should be given to include only those areas involved in the business environment of the proposed system. But, if in doubt, you might want to include the business area in question within the project scope. During the analysis phase, a more detailed examination of the situation will determine whether this particular area should remain.

In theory, the ideal process-based system does not necessarily have organisational boundaries. On the other hand, a project is the logical process by which the boundaries of the system are arbitrarily restricted to a manageable size in order to ensure the system's successful implementation. This is one reason why a first draft of the system context diagram should be completed before the project constraints, risks, and assumptions are identified by the development team. Doing so will decrease the risk that the development team might prematurely exclude some business areas from the study that indeed should be investigated thoroughly.

At such an early stage, determining how much of the existing user environment should be included within the scope of the project is not always easy. Experienced analysts are quite aware that a given problem that was originally identified in one business area of the organisation might turn out to have its root cause in some other area. If so, such a situation should be highlighted to management, and a decision should be made by management to include the business area in question, if necessary.

2.9 CONDUCTING JOINT FACILITATED SESSION(S) FOR THE SURVEY PHASE

Organizing and conducting a single or even a brief series of short but intensive workshops using the joint facilitated session process can drastically shorten the time cycle that is typically required to produce the survey phase technical deliverables. Moreover, the users directly participate in the definition of the system's high-level requirements and its initial scope, using structured dynamic group discussions. This direct involvement, which allows the users to publicly voice and share their ideas and concerns, can only strengthen the users' buy-in into the new system that is being developed for them.

The survey phase joint facilitated session process usually lasts from one to five days, depending on the size and complexity of the system.

The next section describes in more detail how to use the joint facilitated session process to more rapidly create the survey phase technical deliverables. You can consult the additional information provided in Chapter 10 for a more detailed description of the joint facilitated session process in general.

2.9.1 STEP 1: PLAN THE SURVEY PHASE JOINT FACILITATED SESSION(S)

The first step consists of planning the joint facilitated session for the survey phase. The facilitator must obtain a high-level understanding of the project in general and the scope of the proposed facilitated session, with the project leader and project sponsor. Sometimes she might also have to interview additional key individuals within the organization.

The most common points that are reviewed during this preparatory step are highlighted in Table 2-17.

Table 2–17 Survey Phase Joint Facilitated Session Preparatory Tasks

• Gain some background on the project in general
• Understand the purpose and scope of the survey phase effort
• Determine the high-level management and business objectives to be achieved
• Identify the potential issues, constraints, or assumptions that can affect the survey phase workshop
• Identify the participants and their respective organizations
• Decide the number of sessions required and their timetables
• Decide the location where the session(s) will be held
• Determine the expected deliverables and their formats

If necessary, the joint session facilitator might decide to gather various business documents to acquaint himself/herself with the business organization. The facilitator might also decide to interview some key, knowledgeable users and their management. The information gathered at this stage will help to prepare the visual aids that will be used during the survey phase workshop. These documents can include reports, filled-in forms, online transactions, and other similar material that can be used to quickly identify the high-level business processes supported by the current system.

Through this acquaintance process, the facilitator or project sponsor/leader must also ensure that the user participants in each affected business area can attend the series of sessions that are being planned and provide a strong commitment to its success.

Since the user requirements are gathered at a high level during the survey phase, the facilitator typically plays the role of both session facilitator as well as process and data modeler. This extra role assumes that this individual already has some practical experience in both process and data modeling.

Usually a scribe will be assigned with the responsibility of documenting all the technical deliverables as they are created during the survey phase joint facilitated session. Last but not least, the business users themselves must attend the sessions as full-time participants. These people are the subject-matter experts that will provide all the business knowledge and tactical perspective required for creating the set of technical deliverables that will be the outcome of the survey phase. The best business people must attend the session to achieve quality results.

2.9.2 STEP 2: PREPARE THE SURVEY PHASE JOINT FACILITATED SESSION(S)

Specific arrangements are made for the session room, equipment, and supplies.

The facilitator develops the workshop approach and also prepares the visual aids for the workshop. The visual aids might include different items such as:

- The Survey phase joint facilitated session agenda
- A brief explanation of the basic concepts associated with the joint facilitated session process
- The purpose, scope, and objectives of the survey phase joint facilitated session
- Constraints and assumptions
- Expected survey phase technical deliverables
- Proposed joint facilitated session rules and guidelines

The joint facilitated session facilitator can also assist the project sponsor to prepare a kick-off memo to invite the session participants. Once completed, this memo is distributed immediately to all workshop participants. The memo must describe the purpose of the survey phase workshop and its importance for the project. The sponsor must also request a strong commitment, from all participants, to ensure the success of the session.

The following letter provides a sample of a generic memo that can be used to invite participants to a survey phase joint facilitated session. This memo can be modified easily to schedule other types of joint facilitated sessions.

Date: YYYYMMDD

TO   :   \<List of Joint Facilitated Session Attendees\>
FROM   :   \<Executive Sponsor\>
SUBJECT   :   \<Project Name\> - Joint Facilitated Session(s) – Survey phase
DATE   :   \<Facilitated Session Start and End Dates\>
LOCATION   :   \<Facilitated Session Start Time and Place\>

You have been chosen to actively participate in a joint facilitated session for the \<business application or project name\>. The purpose of this workshop is to \<workshop purpose\>. The group session(s) will be led by \<facilitator's name\>, who is an accomplished joint facilitated session leader.

Similar joint facilitated sessions were successfully conducted \<in several organizations like ours\> or \<in other departments within our company\>. No secret recipe exists, though. A successful workshop always depends on the ability and willingness of each participant to positively contribute to the overall process. In this regard, I know your personal contribution will be important because of the business knowledge and on-the-job experience you will bring along with you during the facilitated session.

I, for one, fully support this workshop and sincerely hope you will too. By working together as a pro-active team, we can make this joint facilitated session a great success. This is very important to us all. I look forward to seeing you on \<Joint Facilitated Session Start Date\>.

If, in the meantime, you have any questions on this important subject, please do not hesitate to contact \<project manager's name\> or myself.

Sincerely,

\<Executive Sponsor\>

A typical list of joint facilitated session ground rules and guidelines is provided in Chapter 10, titled "Joint Facilitated Sessions." The joint facilitated session ground rules are used to establish a formal contract between all participants and the facilitator about how the session will be conducted. For a survey phase workshop, sticking to the proposed agenda as much as possible is important.

Likewise, you will need to explain to the participants that the purpose of the survey phase joint facilitated session is to work on finding the high-level business requirements and initial project scope. It also entails the identification of the high-level, core business processes and events to which the business must react, not a discussion of technical solutions. Thus, including this additional rule to the proposed list of rules of the land might be wise, if it is not already covered.

Table 2-18 shows a typical agenda for a survey phase joint facilitated session. Please note that the sequence in which the items are shown does not necessarily indicate the order in which they need to be covered. An experienced session facilitator will feel his/her way as the session progresses and may alter its mainstream course.

Table 2–18 Survey Phase Joint Facilitated Session Agenda

- Introduce participants to the joint facilitated session process
- Analyze the current situation and identify high-level business requirements
- Identify user areas involved
- Formulate the system mission
- Determine the project business objectives/anticipated benefits
- Develop the system and data context diagrams
  - Situate the proposed system within its business environment and identify the external agents that communicate with it or receive some output from it
  - Identify the high-level business processes that are performed in the involved business area(s) and the data entities that are used
  - Create a preliminary list of major events to which the business area(s) must react
- Define the initial project scope
  - Determine the functional areas in scope
  - Determine the functional areas out of scope
- Identify the project constraints, risks, and assumptions

2.9.3 STEP 3: CONDUCT THE SURVEY PHASE JOINT FACILITATED SESSION(S)

As I stated earlier, the order in which the survey phase activities are executed during the workshop is not necessarily linear. The exact steps will vary, depending on the discovery of new facts that relate to the survey phase deliverables, which are progressively created with the participants. The set of generic activities that follow can be tailored to satisfy the needs of specific survey phase joint facilitated session objectives. Adopting a flexible approach in joint facilitated sessions is paramount to achieve success.

- Kick off the joint facilitated session
  - Welcome the participants
  - Ask each participant to introduce himself or herself
  - Allow the project sponsor to provide the appropriate opening remarks
  - Review the proposed survey phase workshop agenda
  - Describe the joint facilitation process
  - Describe the process and data modeling techniques that will be used to construct the system and data context diagrams
  - Present the workshop objectives and proposed timetable
  - Review and discuss with the participants the proposed workshop rules of the land

- Guide the participants through the tasks of creating the following set of technical deliverables:
  - Current situation assessment
  - System mission and project business objectives
  - System context diagram
  - High-level business processes that are performed within the boundaries of the system
  - Data context diagram
  - Project constraints, risks, and assumptions
  - Initial project scope

Table 2-19 provides a sample of some of the leading questions that the facilitator should address with all the participants during a typical survey phase workshop. The questions are formulated in relation with some of the technical deliverables highlighted above.

Table 2–19 Survey Phase Joint Facilitated Session Questionnaire

Current situation	• What are the five major process-oriented problems that the business area is currently facing? • Are some important business opportunities not yet fully exploited?
Business objectives	• What are the business objectives of this project? • Why are we building this software system? • Can this system provide strategic advantages to the enterprise? • Do we anticipate major upcoming changes in the enterprise's way of doing business? • How can the system allow us to become more efficient, more effective, and more competitive?
Expected Benefits	• What major benefits can be derived from this application? • Can we quantify these benefits? • Are there some intangible benefits?
Constraints, risks, and assumptions	• Can some business risk, constraint, or assumption be associated with this system or project? • Can some technical risks, constraints, or assumptions be associated with this system or project? • Do any time constraints exist (i.e., the system needs to be completed in a six-month timeframe)? • Do any financial constraints exist? • Does any specific staffing limitation exist (i.e., no contractors are allowed)?

Table 2–19 Survey Phase Joint Facilitated Session Questionnaire (cont.)

	• Do some specific hardware/software/networking limitations exist? • Do some technical risks exist due to the use of some new technologies (i.e., use of a new object-oriented database management system)? • Do some legal or governmental obligations need to be fulfilled?
External events	• What types of external events does the business area under study need to react to (i.e., reception of a customer order, a customer inquiry, etc.)? • For each event, what type of information is transmitted from the external agents to the system? • What type of information is sent to external agents by the system?
Internal events	• What types of time-dependent events are triggered inside the boundaries of the proposed system (i.e., a monthly financial report must be sent to all customers)?
High-level processes	• What are the high-level processes that are performed by the business area? • What are the critical success factors associated with each high-level process?
Information requirements	• What type of information is used in each high-level business process?

- Conclude and wrap up the joint facilitated session
  - Review all outstanding issues with participants and ensure that each of them is assigned to someone and a target completion date has been identified for its resolution
  - Seek participants' feedback on the work achieved during the session

2.9.4 STEP 4: PRODUCE AND ISSUE THE SURVEY PHASE JOINT FACILITATED SESSION(S) FINAL DOCUMENT

- Gather all the relevant information that was documented during the session
- Analyze, edit, and consolidate all session information into a final document
- Issue final document and, if necessary, schedule a final review with the session participants
- Discuss the session main outcome with the executive champion and project manager

3

Analysis

3.1 INTRODUCTION

The prime goal of the analysis phase is to express concisely the detailed requirements for the new application system. To achieve this goal, the analysis phase uses a combination of both top-down and bottom-up analysis techniques to describe and document the set of critical business processes, data, and system operational requirements for the new application system.

For large projects, the prime analysis methods that are used to describe the users' functional and data requirements are the business process and data modeling techniques. Basically, the business data and process models can be created by means of two different information-gathering approaches.

The first approach is based on conducting special interactive workshops, called joint facilitated sessions, with the active participation of a focused group of users, for short periods of time.

The second approach is focused on conducting a series of individual interviews with the users who are responsible for executing the business processes and who are therefore very knowledgeable about the business.

Sometimes, a mixture of the two approaches can be used to quickly formulate the detailed requirements for the new application system.

Either way, the business process and data modeling deliverables are developed in a highly iterative fashion. The construction of the business process model gradually progresses from an initial description of the high-level business processes that are performed by the business area under study to a more detailed description of the lower-level, more elementary business processes. The same iterative approach is also used to construct the business data model, through a series of successive and gradually more detailed refinement analysis steps.

Table 3-1 describes a set of objectives for the analysis phase.

Table 3–1 Analysis Phase Objectives

- Rapidly develop a quality business process and data model that is complete and that accurately reflects the business requirements for the new application system
- Define the detailed operational requirements for the new application system
- Determine a technical architecture of hardware, software, and networking components and their configuration requirements on which the new application system will run
- Define, at a high level, the preliminary data conversion, training, and testing system strategies

Table 3-2 summarizes the major technical activities that are conducted during the analysis phase, along with a list of the anticipated technical deliverables.

Table 3–2 Analysis Phase

ACTIVITY	DELIVERABLE(S)
1. Create the business process model	1. Business process model
2. Create the business data model	2. Business data model
3. Partition the business application into system transactions	3. System transactions
4. Conduct graphical user interface joint facilitated session	4. System graphical user interface
5. Construct graphical user interface prototype	5. System graphical user interface prototype
6. Define initial system distribution strategy	6. Initial system distribution strategy
7. Define the system interface requirements	7. System interface requirements
8. Define the system security and control requirements	8. System security and control requirements
9. Define the system operational requirements	9. System operational requirements
10. Develop initial capacity plan	10. Initial capacity plan
11. Develop initial data conversion strategy	11. Initial data conversion strategy
12. Develop initial backup/recovery strategy	12. Initial backup/recovery strategy
13. Develop initial testing strategy	13. Initial testing strategy
14. Develop initial training strategy	14. Initial training strategy
15. Define the hardware/software/networking requirements	15. Hardware/software/networking requirements

Figure 3-1 pictorially presents, at a high level, the relationships that exist among the individual activities of the analysis phase.

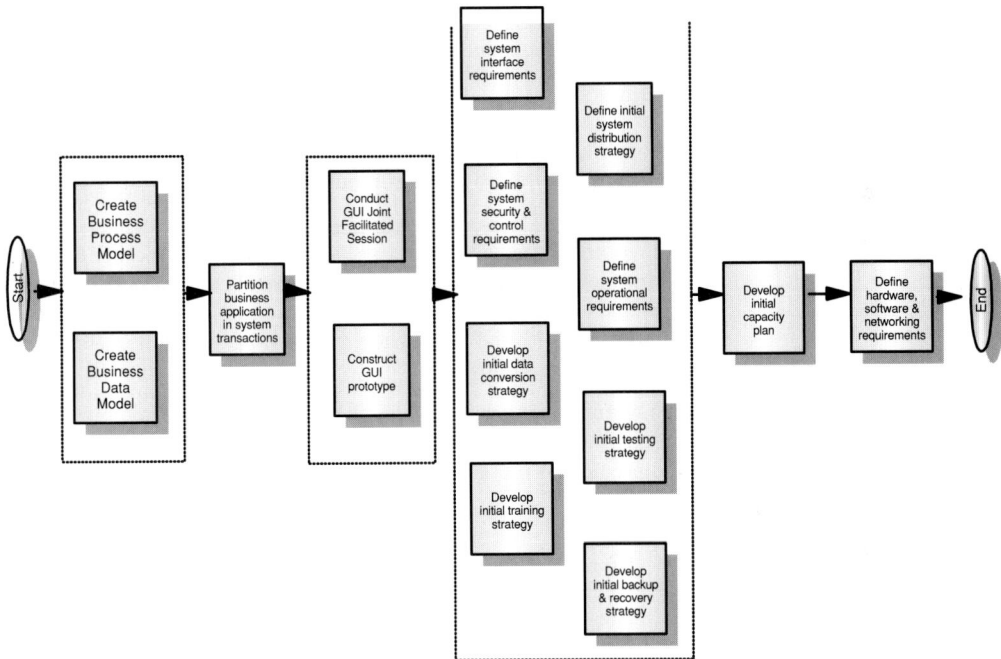

Figure 3–1 Analysis phase activities.

Although the linear sequence in which the analysis phase activities are shown in Figure 3-1 might suggest that one specific activity must be completed prior to beginning the next one, in fact they can be performed in parallel or in different sequences.

Furthermore, several of these activities can be performed with an iterative approach, gradually refining the activity deliverables in incremental steps. On the other hand, certain types of activities might not easily lend themselves to an iterative development approach.

At the completion of each major analysis phase activity, a formal walkthrough should be scheduled to review the final outcome of each activity, which is comprised of a set of specific system deliverables. Finally, Table 3-3 provides a brief list of some of the most important characteristics that relate to good requirement specifications.

Table 3–3 Requirements Specifications Characteristics

Explicit	Each requirement should be stated in a way that leaves no room for ambiguity as to how it can be interpreted by different people.
Concise	Each requirement should be documented in a manner that is concise and precise, with a terminology that can be understood by the users.
Complete	Each requirement should be complete and not be in conflict with other requirement(s).
Traceable	Each requirement should be uniquely identified and traceable back to its originator and/or the group responsible for it. If the requirement evolves over time, all changes should be identified through a version number.
Priority	All requirements do not carry the same weight of criticality through the eyes of the users. Contrary to what several developers might think, they are not all created equals. Hence, you should discuss their relative importance with the users. Each requirement should be classified as high, medium, or low.
Inter-dependency	If a requirement has inter-dependency with other requirement(s), then this relationship should be explicitly documented. For instance, requirement A must be fulfilled prior to satisfying requirement B.

Activity number:	AN-1
Activity name:	Create the business process model
Purpose:	Develop a business process model to depict the business processes that will be supported by the application system
Inputs:	SU-T1 Current problems/opportunities/users' needs
	SU-T2 System mission and project business objectives
	SU-T3 System context diagram
	SU-T6 Initial project scope
	Current system documentation
Outputs:	AN-T1 Business process model
Activity description:	• Review the system context diagram that was constructed during the survey phase.
	• Gradually decompose into sub-processes, through successive iterations, the major business processes that are identified in the system context diagram.

- Repeat the process decomposition procedure until the lower-level business processes are identified in the top-down process hierarchy.
- Describe the business processes, documenting their major functional characteristics.
- Using the event analysis technique, identify the lowest-level business processes (a.k.a. elementary business processes) that provide value to the end users.
- Describe the elementary business processes, documenting their major characteristics. If necessary, depict, with the use of a diagram, the input and output data streams that enter and leave each elementary process. Document the business procedural logic that must be performed by each elementary business process.
- Walk through the business process model deliverable.

3.2   CREATE THE BUSINESS PROCESS MODEL

This section discusses the detailed steps involved in creating the business process model. It also provides useful tips on how to execute that process, along with descriptions of some basic terminology.

Figure 3-2 illustrates the hierarchical nature of the business process model.

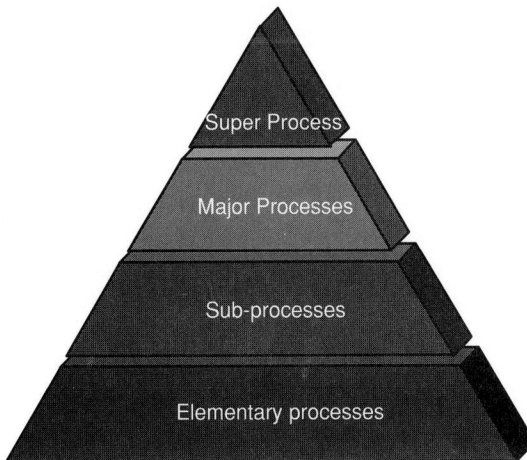

Figure 3–2 Business process model hierarchy.

At the top of the pyramid is a parent super process, which is comprised of a set of major subordinate processes. In turn, these major processes are themselves composed of middle-level or intermediate processes, which finally can be decomposed into a set of lower-level processes.

Tables 3-4 and 3-5 provide a definition for the terms "business process" and "elementary business process."

Table 3–4 Business Process Definition

A business process is composed of a set of generic activities that transform some input(s) into some output(s). The final outcome of a business process is a product or service that provides added value to a customer. High level business processes transcend organizational boundaries.

Table 3–5 Elementary Business Process Definition

An elementary business process is defined as the smallest set of basic activities that must be performed by a business unit in response to the activation of a discrete business event, such as a customer who places an order. An elementary business process cannot be further decomposed into other sub-processes.

3.2.1   USING AN ITERATIVE APPROACH TO CONSTRUCT THE BUSINESS PROCESS MODEL

If the scope of the business area under study is fairly large, then the business process model is developed with an iterative development approach. Depending on the number and magnitude of high-level business processes involved in the process analysis effort, you might need to divide the process modeling activities between multiple teams. Each specific team should be assigned a set of closely related processes. Furthermore, each team should coordinate their sub-model with the other teams to ensure a smooth integration of all sub-models later on.

The high-level business processes that are shown in the initial system context diagram are gradually decomposed into sub-processes, through a succession of controlled iterations. Each consecutive iteration incrementally provides more detailed information about the functional components that are shown in the business process model.

As a rule of thumb, the construction of the business process model is usually performed in three major iterations. The following sub-sections provide a brief description of each of the three steps.

STEP 1: Decompose the high-level business processes into sub-processes
During a first iteration, the high-level business processes that are performed by the business area are quickly decomposed into a hierarchical set of intermediate and lower-level business process layers.

The outcome of this activity is then verified and validated with the end users for completeness and accuracy. The resulting functional hierarchy must somehow reflect the logical grouping of top, middle, and bottom layers of business processes into a cohesive set, along with their interdependencies. However, at this stage, you do not have to spend a substantial amount of time trying to improve the overall structure of this hierarchical classification of business processes. What is really important is the identification of the elementary business processes that are performed at the bottom layer of the business process hierarchy.

The pictorial, hierarchical view of the business processes is primarily used as a registry that helps to identify all the elementary business processes that are performed within the business application. It can also be used as a checklist to verify the completeness of the business process model. If the business area already has a hierarchical representation model that depicts the set of business processes that are performed in it, then this document can be used as a starting point to identify an initial draft of all the business events to which the business must respond.

STEP 2: Identify all major business events
During the second iteration, all the major business events that drive the business area are identified with the active participation of the users. This step is done by carefully analyzing in more detail the processes that are shown in the hierarchical business process model. The identification of the business events will also help to verify the completeness of the business process model and especially its bottom layer, which depicts the elementary business processes that are performed by the business. Some critical business events may not have elementary business processes shown on the business process model. In such a case, these elementary business processes were simply not discovered through the pure functional decomposition of business processes into subordinate lower-level processes.

STEP 3: Describe and document the elementary business processes
During the third iteration, the elementary business processes are described and documented along with the detailed business-oriented procedural tasks that are used to perform them. The complete business process model with all its deliverables is then verified with the user for completeness, accuracy, and consistency.

Figure 3-3 shows a holistic view of a business process model hierarchy.

3.2.2   DISCOVERING BUSINESS PROCESSES

Business processes and their sub-processes can be discovered using a variety of different approaches, such as those indicated in Table 3-6.

DECOMPOSING BUSINESS PROCESSES
In a real-life business environment, common practice includes dealing with business processes that cover a large business scope. For instance, the high-level business process *"order fulfillment"* that is performed in a manufacturing organization that specializes in producing sophisticated gas turbine engines for airplanes can indeed be rather complex and quite large in scope.

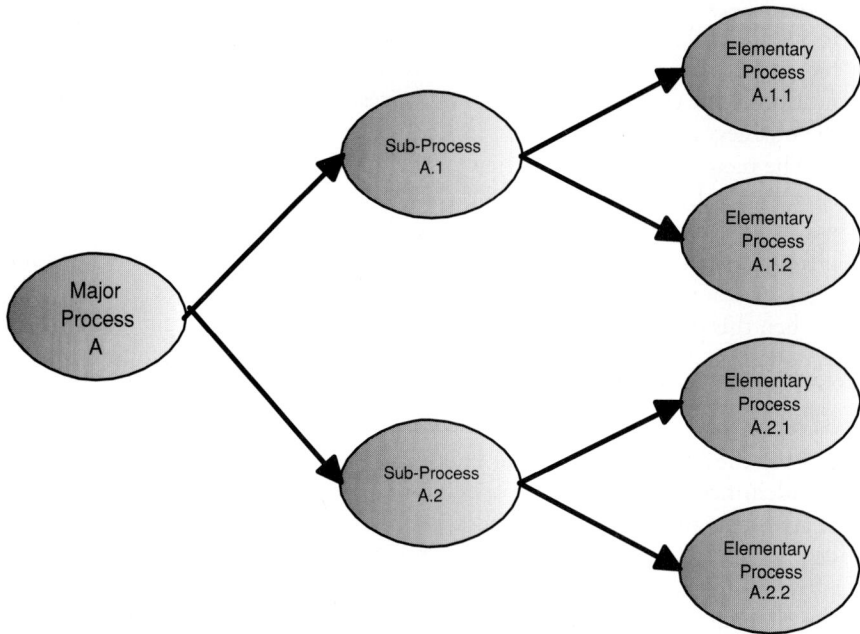

Figure 3–3 Holistic view of a business process model hierarchy.

Table 3–6 Various Ways To Discover Business Processes

• Invite the users to describe their job functions, within the context of the business domain under study
• Identify the business processes that create, delete, or update important business entities
• Identify the business processes that are activated by external or internal business events
• Identify the core business processes that are used to plan, procure, utilize, dispose, and control the use of various business resources
• Identify the business processes that are required to produce core products and services
• Observe the users while they perform their business tasks in their business environment

However, the *"order fulfillment"* super business process can be broken down into distinct high-level processes that can then be dealt with more easily by the development team. One of these high-level processes could be *"parts procurement,"* for example. In turn, *"parts procurement"* could be divided into two distinct sub-processes, such as *"procure raw material"* and *"procure finished parts."* Each distinct sub-process is in reality a complete process on its own, but breaking them into smaller chunks makes them easier to analyze and manage.

The developers can use a variety of techniques to decompose high-level processes into sub-processes as indicated in Table 3-7.

Table 3–7 Three Useful Techniques To Help Decompose Business Processes

- Business process resource life cycle
- Business process specialization
- Business process partitioning along the time dimension

The following sub-sections briefly describe the three decomposition techniques indicated in Table 3-7.

Business Process Resource Life Cycle (BPRLC)

The business process resource life cycle method can be used to break down high-level processes into subordinate sub-processes by studying the core business resources that are managed by the business. In a typical enterprise, some of the most common types of raw resources that are managed by the business include subjects such as those indicated in Table 3-8.

Table 3–8 List Of Common Business Raw Resources

- Suppliers, customers, employees, partners
- Physical equipment and objects
- Financial entities
- Products and services

When using the business process resource life cycle technique, the high-level business processes that are shown at the top level of a functional hierarchy model are decomposed by breaking them into sub-processes that match a model of discrete life cycle stages that appear in Figure 3-4.

Figure 3–4 Resource discrete life cycle stages.

Using the resource life cycles model shown in Figure 3-4, the development team can analyze a high-level process and decompose it into subordinate processes by asking themselves basic questions such as what are the planning sub-processes, the acquisition sub-processes, and so forth. For instance, if the business resource is parts, then some potential sub-processes can be forecast parts, procure parts, procure raw material, procure finished parts, scratch parts, etc.

Business Process Specialization

Certain categories of business processes can achieve the same final outcome by per-forming similar but yet slightly different set of activities. A case in point is the *"process order"* business process. Depending on the way in which the order is received from the customer, a different set of activities might be performed by the employee who must take the order. For instance, if the order is taken directly via the telephone, then the *"take customer order"* process can be fulfilled by a set of activities slightly different from those if the order is processed via the reception of a customer letter or fax. Two addi-tional alternate paths would be receiving an order via either electronic data inter-change (EDI) or the Web. Yet at the end, the final outcome is identical. That is, a customer order has been processed and it will be fulfilled shortly thereafter.

Figure 3-5 illustrates how the "take customer sales order" process can be subdivided into a series of specialized sub-processes that produce the same final outcome.

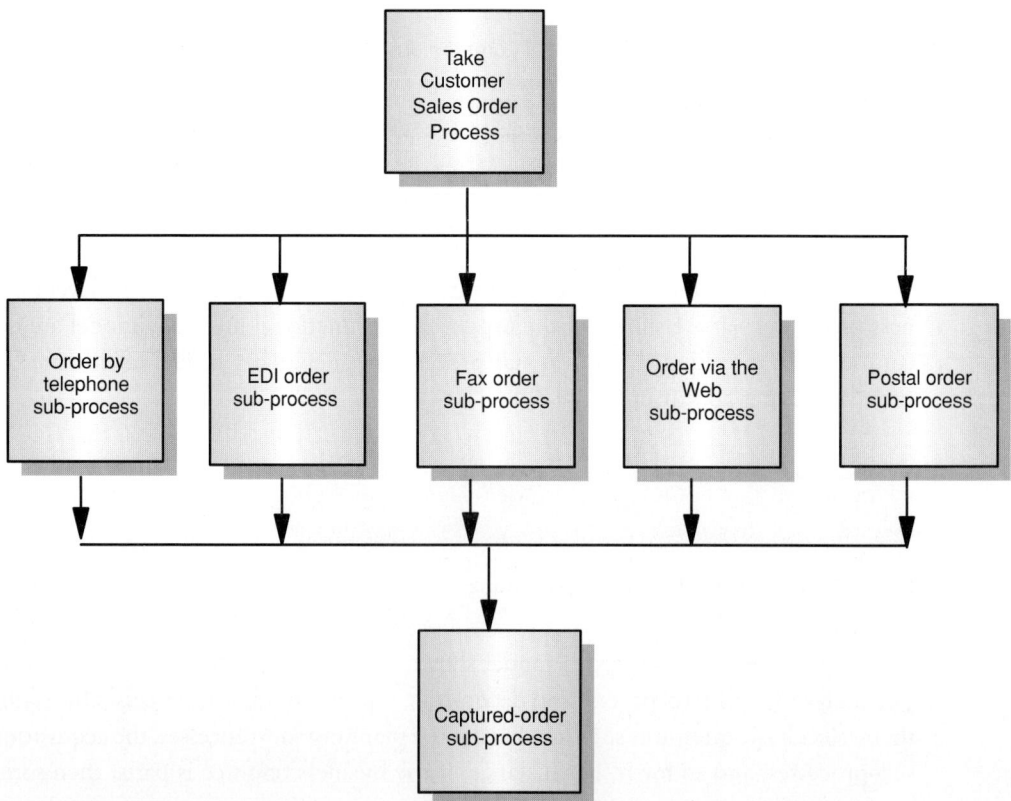

Figure 3–5 Decomposing a process via specialization.

As you have just seen, the set of discrete activities that must be accomplished to carry on some business processes can be somewhat different, even though the final output is identical. In such cases, partitioning these business processes into a set of distinct sub-processes that carry on a different set of tasks might be useful. Each resulting sub-process can be seen as a distinct child of the same parent business process.

Table 3-9 provides additional hints that might help developers to discover and decompose business processes that can be fulfilled by a series of slightly distinct, specialized activity paths.

Table 3–9 Specialization Of Business Processes

• The business process generates almost identical products or services, but some variations exist in the set of activities that produce or deliver them
• The business process is triggered by similar events that use slightly different means to provide input data
• The execution of the process is characterized by several exception cases rather than a more standardized set of generic activities

Business Process Partitioning Along A Time-dependent Dimension

Sometimes, large and complex business processes can be partitioned into discrete sub-processes that are organized along a time-dependent axis. First, the discrete activities that are included in the business process are identified with the users. Then the specific activities that can be carried out either in sequential or parallel modes of operation are logically regrouped into sub-processes, aligned around a time axis. However, all the distinct sub-processes must be carried out together as a homogenous set to adequately fulfill the original parent's business process.

DESCRIBING BUSINESS PROCESSES

Table 3-10 indicates the major characteristics that are used to document a business process.

Table 3–10 Business Process Description

Purpose	A brief textual description of the purpose of the business process
Description	A brief textual description of the business process itself, in relation with the products or services that are generated by it
Frequency	The number of times the business process is initiated per unit of time. If significant peak periods exist during the day, they should be documented also.
Priority	An indication of the importance of the business process for the organization. The values can be high, medium, or low.
Information needs	A list of the major input/output information that is used to carry on the business process

NAMING BUSINESS PROCESSES

The next two sections provide suggestions to name high-level or low-level business processes.

High-level Business Processes

Uniquely identifying and naming each business process is important. The high-level processes that reside at the top of the process hierarchy model should be identified with a descriptive noun that usually contains one or two words such as: *marketing, engineering, inventory control, procurement*, etc. Remember that higher-level business processes are ongoing in the enterprise.

Also note that business processes should not reflect a specific organizational structure but rather a purely generic, logical view of a business process. Quite often, a high-level process can transcend several departments across the enterprise.

Low-level Business Processes

A beginning and end state often characterize the lower-level business processes that exist in the enterprise. As a rule of thumb, a good practice is to construct the name of the lower-level business processes with an active verb followed by an object such as: *ship goods, hire applicant, forecast parts demand, define reorder quantity.*

3.2.3   UNDERSTANDING BUSINESS EVENTS

Business processes can activate other business processes. Similarly, business processes can also be activated by what are called business events. One example of a business event that activates a business process is the *"take customer order"* elementary business process, which can be triggered by the business event called *"customer places order."*

Table 3-11 provides a definition of a business event.

Table 3–11 Business Event Definition

A business event is a happening that activates a business process. The business process responds to the business event in a pre-determined manner. An event can be internal or external to an organization.

External agents that are located outside the boundaries of the business area under study frequently initiate the external business events. An example is a customer who calls a company sales representative to place an order for certain parts. The external business event is often characterized by a flow of data that goes into the business process it triggers. For example, the *"customer makes payment"* event is associated with an incoming flow of data, which in this case could be a check or a payment with a credit card, for example.

Business events can also be temporal. Temporal business events are triggered by the passage of time. They are characterized by a frequency of execution but no agents are behind them and they do not generate an incoming flow of data into a process. Table 3-12 provides some examples of temporal business events.

Table 3–12 Examples Of Temporal Events

- Create the month end financial statements
- Weekly status reports are due!
- Checks are produced every two weeks on Thursday at 3:00 p.m. sharp!

For each of the temporal events mentioned in Table 3-12, the system must automatically respond in a pre-determined manner to appropriately address this event.

IDENTIFYING BUSINESS EVENTS

The business processes that are shown in the business process model hierarchy are used to facilitate the search and identification of business events that are critical for the enterprise. For a small system, the business events can be discovered through a series of interviews with the users. For a medium to large business application system, an alternate method is suggested, as I describe in the text that follows.

A brainstorming session is conducted with key users. During this joint facilitated session, specific subsections of the business process model are canvassed, one at a time, to uncover the candidate business events that are relevant to the business. Each stimulus from the external world to which the application system must react in a pre-planned manner is identified with the users. The external and internal events are listed during a first pass. During a second pass, the temporal events are then listed. Usually, date-triggered processes automatically generate the temporal events to which the system must react in a pre-planned manner.

As a complementary approach to discover business events, the system context diagram can also be examined to help identify all the external agents that exchange information with the system. As you have seen previously, external agents are often responsible for initiating business events to which the system must respond in a pre-determined manner.

All the external events that have been discovered are then scrutinized carefully with the active involvement of the users to identify whether they carry some incoming flow of data along with them.

Another method that can be used to identify business events consists of analyzing the data entities that are documented in the business data model. Several categories of business events often provoke a state of change within the business entities shown on the model. The state of change causes modifications to certain attributes of a particular entity, or the deletion or creation of an entity.

NAMING BUSINESS EVENTS

Each discrete business event should have a meaningful name.

For each temporal business event, a brief sentence is used to convey its prime intent, such as: *"time to prepare monthly status report," "time to produce invoices," "payment overdue recall," "seminar confirmation attendance due."* I usually recommend starting a temporal business event sentence with the expression "time to" or to terminate the sentence with the word "due."

Each external business event should be named with a sentence that identifies the originator of the business event and what is done to initiate the event, for example: *"customer places order," "customer inquires on order status," "customer cancels insurance policy."*

DESCRIBING BUSINESS EVENTS

Tables 3-13 and 3-14 indicate the major characteristics that are used to describe external, internal, or temporal business events.

Table 3–13 External/internal Business Event Description

Description	A brief textual description of the external business event. The originator of the business event should be identified, along with a short description of the purpose of the business event and the incoming data flow(s) that are associated with it.
Frequency	The number of times the business event is initiated per unit of time. If the business event is characterized by significant peak periods, then these should be clearly documented.
Data Flow	Identification of the high-level incoming data flow that usually notifies the business area of the occurrence of an event.

Table 3–14 Temporal Business Event Description

Description	A brief textual description of the temporal business event, including a short description of the business context that causes the event to be initiated.
Frequency	The number of times the temporal business event occurs per unit of time. If significant peak periods exist, they should be clearly documented.

3.2.4   IDENTIFYING ELEMENTARY BUSINESS PROCESSES

As you have seen earlier in this chapter, an elementary business process is defined as the smallest set of procedural steps that must be performed by a business unit in response to the activation of a discrete business event.

Elementary business processes are usually discovered by carefully examining all the business events that have been identified so far in a shopping list. For each distinct business event, at least one elementary business process should be assigned to it. The elementary business process stands for the operation that the application system should take in response to the business event.

Table 3-15 provides some basic guidelines to validate the elementary business processes and the upper-level process to which they belong.

Table 3–15 Elementary Business Process Characteristics

- The scope of an elementary business process should include all the logical tasks that are required to adequately answer a business event, which was initiated either by an external agent or internally by a business unit.
- An elementary business process should contain a set of business tasks that each share a very high level of cohesion.
- An elementary business process should respond to a business event in a manner that is logical and meaningful from a user's standpoint. It describes the functionality that the users desire from the application system, in direct response to a certain event.
- An elementary business process has a clear beginning and end.
- An elementary business process has some input data and output data. Given some input data, it produces some output result.
- Each elementary business process should be independent of other elementary business processes. If two elementary processes are not totally independent of one another, then perhaps they should be merged into a single elementary business process.
- Quite often, an elementary business process changes the state of a data entity or it queries some information that is stored about an entity.
- The actions performed inside an elementary business process do not have time dependencies or constraints. Once the elementary process is activated, it can only progress to its final conclusion, with no time dependency interruptions.
- When the activities that are performed inside an elementary business process are completed, the elementary business process remains idle until another business event is initiated and activates it again.

NAMING ELEMENTARY BUSINESS PROCESSES

An elementary business process name consists of an active verb followed by a few words. The name should be a short, concise sentence. For example: *"take customer order," "provide customer with order status," "cancel customer insurance policy," "open customer's bank account,"* and *"modify customer information details."*

DESCRIBING ELEMENTARY BUSINESS PROCESSES

Each elementary business process should be concisely described and documented as indicated in Table 3-16.

DESCRIBING ELEMENTARY BUSINESS PROCESS PROCEDURAL LOGIC

You should further describe each elementary business process with a narrative specification that documents the tasks that must be done to produce the outcome of the pro-

Table 3–16 Elementary Process Description

Description	A brief textual description of the elementary business process that delineates its purpose and scope. The description should be written in a business language that the users can understand naturally without effort.
Frequency	The number of times the elementary business process is performed per unit of time, as a number per day, week, month, or year. If significant peak periods exist during the day, they should be clearly documented also.
Data flow	Identification of the incoming data flow(s) that supply data to the elementary business process and the output result(s).
Response time	The identification of the response time that is requested by the users of the elementary business process. This is the time taken from the point at which the elementary business process is initiated, to the point at which it is terminated.
Expected growth	The rate at which the frequency is expected to increase over a given period of time. The rate is usually expressed as an absolute number or a percentage.

cess. Remember that the procedural logic should describe what the system should do, not all the technical details on how to achieve it. The description of the procedural logic should also avoid the use of business or technical jargon. Users should easily understand it, preferably with a terminology to which they can easily relate.

Several methods can be used to document the procedural logic of an elementary process. The methods can vary from very informal to formal approaches. The decision to use a formal or informal documentation method will vary from one organization to another, depending on their corporate culture. However, if the internal procedural logic of an elementary process is highly complex, then using a formal, structured method to describe it might be useful. Table 3-17 provides a brief list of some of the most common methods that can be used by developers to describe medium to complex procedural logic or algorithms that pertain to the execution of an elementary business process.

Special procedural logic that might be required to handle unusual case scenarios, exception handling, or error handling should be documented, preferably after the procedural logic required to handle the normal cases has been described. This approach will allow the developers to concentrate their initial efforts on documenting the procedural logic required to handle the normal transactional paths, as opposed to devoting too much time to document what should be done to handle the few exceptional paths with which the users must deal.

Table 3–17 Methods To Document Elementary Business Process Procedural Logic

Standard narrative text	The procedural logic of the elementary process is simply documented with some standard text narrative.
Structured English	Structured English uses a subset of the English language that has been specifically adapted to describe logical program statements that can be easily translated into a computer language, later on.
Action diagrams	An action diagram uses several logical constructs borrowed from the basic tenets of structured programming such as sequence, iteration, selection, condition, subroutine, and data access to express high-level to detailed procedural logic, in a structured manner.
Decision table	A decision table is a graphic tool that is used to provide a tabular representation of the conditions versus the actions that must be taken to perform a task, based on a unique set of existing conditions.
Decision tree	A decision tree utilizes a tree structure to alternatively show the set of conditions and actions that are required to solve a logic specification.

3.2.5   UNDERSTANDING JOINT FACILITATED SESSIONS FOR PROCESS MODELING

Small to medium business process modeling efforts can be achieved by interviewing some key users and by analyzing supportive material that has been gathered within the business area under study.

In fact, even a large business process modeling effort can be performed with traditional data-gathering and analysis techniques that are also complemented with user serial interviews. With such a method, the business process model is gradually constructed out of the information that is extracted from key user interviews and analysis of various business documents. This approach can certainly lead to a quality business process model that reflects the critical business processes that make up the business. However, a long period of time may pass before the analysts complete and validate the business process model, depending on the availability of the key users that need to be interviewed.

On the other hand, conducting a series of short but intensive business process modeling workshops using the joint facilitated session process can drastically shorten the time cycle required to produce a complete business process model. Moreover, the users directly participate in the construction of the process model, in a real-time fashion. This direct involvement will strengthen their buy-in into the system that is being developed for them. Such a strong buy-in is rarely achieved via serial interviews.

At the opposite end, a joint facilitated session process will usually generate a stronger consensus among the users when the final deliverable is ultimately completed.

Likewise, as a group, the users gradually develop and share a common understanding of the key business events that drive their business area and the responses that the business makes for each of those events, in the form of elementary business processes.

The next section describes how to use the joint facilitated session process to construct a business model. You can consult the additional information provided in Chapter 10 for a more detailed description of the joint facilitated session process in general.

STEP 1: Plan the business process modeling joint facilitated session
The first step consists of planning the joint facilitated session for process modeling. The facilitator must review the scope of the proposed facilitated session with the project leader and project sponsor. The detailed points that are reviewed during the meeting include:

- Background on the project in general
- The purpose and scope of the process modeling effort
- Management and business objectives to be achieved
- Potential issues, constraints, or assumptions that can affect the process modeling workshop
- Identification of the participants and their respective organizations
- The number of sessions required and their timetables
- The location where the sessions will be held
- Expected deliverables
- The types of process modeling technique that will be used to develop and document the business processes that will be uncovered during the facilitated sessions

If necessary, the facilitator might decide to gather various business documents to acquaint himself/herself with the business organization. The facilitator might also decide to interview some key, knowledgeable users and their management. The information gathered at this stage will help to prepare visual aids for the process modeling workshop. These documents can include reports, filled-in forms, online transactions, and other material that can be used to quickly identify the major processes of the system.

Through this process, the facilitator or project sponsor/leader must also ensure that the user participants in each affected business unit can attend the series of sessions that are being planned and provide a strong commitment to its success.

Be sure to select a facilitator who has a good knowledge of the process modeling technique that will be used to construct the business process model. For a small- to medium-sized process model, the facilitator can play the role of both facilitator and process modeler, assuming this individual has already some practical experience in process modeling.

However, for a large process model that involves the participation of several cross-functional user areas, having one facilitator and one process modeler might be preferable. The role of the process modeler is to assist the facilitator in leading the group through the process of creating the process model and verifying it along the way. Asking leading questions to the participants does this. The answers to these questions will dictate how the decomposition of the high-level business processes into lower-level processes should be done. The role of the facilitator then is to keep the workshop on track and ensure that everyone participates. For this approach to work, though, a very good complicity must exist between the facilitator and the process modeler.

A scribe will document the definitions of the processes and business events that make up the business process model, as it is progressively constructed through a series of iterations. Last but not least, the business users themselves must attend the sessions as full-time participants. These people are the subject-matter experts who will provide all the business knowledge required for creating the process model. The best business people must attend the session to achieve quality results.

STEP 2: Prepare the process modeling joint facilitated session
The arrangements are made for the session room, equipment, and supplies.

The facilitator develops the workshop approach and also prepares the visual aids for the workshop. The visual aids might include different items such as:

- The process modeling session agenda
- A brief explanation of the basic concepts associated with process modeling
- Purpose, scope, and objectives of the process modeling session
- Constraints and assumptions
- Expected process modeling deliverables
- Proposed session rules and guidelines

The joint facilitated session facilitator can also assist the project sponsor to prepare a kick-off memo to invite the session participants. Once completed, this memo is distributed immediately to all workshop participants. The memo must describe the purpose of the process modeling workshop and its importance for the project. The sponsor must also request a strong commitment, from all participants, to ensure the success of the session.

The following letter provides a sample generic memo that can be used to invite participants to a joint facilitated session. This memo can be modified easily to schedule other types of joint facilitated sessions.

I provide a typical list of joint facilitated session rules and guidelines in Chapter 10. The joint facilitated session rules are used to establish a formal contract between all participants and the facilitator, describing how all participants must behave during the session. For a process modeling workshop, be sure to stick to the proposed agenda. Likewise, an important step is to explain to the participants that the purpose of the process modeling session is to work on finding the business process requirements and events, not to discuss technical solutions. Thus, you might include this additional rule to the proposed list of rules of the land, if it is not already there.

STEP 3: Conduct the process modeling joint facilitated session

Note that the order in which the process modeling activities are executed during the workshop is not necessarily linear. The exact steps will vary, depending on the type of process model being developed and the discovery of new facts that relate to the processes that are modeled with the participants. The set of generic activities that follow can be tailored to the needs of specific modeling session objectives. Adopting a flexible approach in a joint facilitated session is paramount to its success.

- Kick off the joint facilitated session
  - Welcome the participants
  - Ask participants to introduce themselves
  - Allow the project sponsor to provide the appropriate opening remarks
  - Review the proposed process modeling workshop agenda
  - Describe the joint facilitation process
  - Describe the process modeling technique that will be used to construct the business process model
  - Present the workshop objectives
  - Review and discuss with the participants the proposed workshop rules of the land
- Investigate the business process requirements and progressively construct the business process model

Some session facilitators might prefer to work out this activity in a purely traditional top-down fashion, whereas others might prefer to do it by adopting a bottom-up approach. With the bottom-up approach, the business events are usually identified first, and then the business processes that respond to them are uncovered. In reality, both methods can achieve some good results, and the experienced facilitator will often use either technique at different points in time during the joint facilitated session.

- Analyze the scope of the process modeling workshop
  - Review the system context diagram that was created during the project survey phase
  - Identify the high-level business processes that are performed within the boundary of the system context diagram and the associated major external contributors
- Progressively decompose the high-level business processes into lower-level business processes, using the functional decomposition technique. This step is done by breaking down the high-level processes into a hierarchy of sub-processes in which the successively lower layers of the hierarchical structure provide

gradually more detailed information as to what the business is required to do in response to business events.

- – Identify and provide a summary description of the mid-level processes that are performed under the umbrella of a high-level parent process
- – Identify and provide a summary description of the elementary level processes that are performed under the umbrella of a mid-level process. An elementary process cannot be further decomposed into other sub-processes.
- – Review and validate with the users the business process hierarchy and verify its level of accuracy and completeness

- • Identify and describe all the business events to which the business must respond

Business events can be external (i.e., they are initiated outside the business area), temporal (i.e., they are initiated at a given point in time), or internal (i.e., they are initiated inside the business area). Each specific business event should be uniquely identified and named. The event should be described in business terms, not in technical terms. The facilitator might also want to capture some additional information on each particular event, such as its frequency and how soon the business must respond to it.

- – For each identified business event, identify the business process that is performed in response to it. Then identify the process's inputs and outputs data streams.
- – For each business elementary process, identify and document the detailed business tasks that make it up, along with the sequence and conditions that govern their execution
- – Review and validate with the users the list of business events and all the elementary business processes. Verify their level of completeness and accuracy.

- • Conclude and wrap up the joint facilitated session
- – Review all outstanding issues with participants and ensure that each of them is assigned to someone and a target completion date has been identified for its resolution
- – Seek participants' feedback on the work achieved during the session

STEP 4: Produce and issue the process modeling final document

- • Gather all the relevant information that was documented during the session
- • Analyze, edit, and consolidate all session information into a final document
- • Issue final document and, if necessary, schedule a final review with the session participants
- • Review the outcome of the session with the executive sponsor and project manager

3.2.6   IDENTIFYING BUSINESS PROCESS RE-ENGINEERING ISSUES

I assume that the processes that are performed by the business area under study have already been streamlined or re-engineered prior to being used as the foundation for developing the new application system.

Nonetheless, Table 3-18 provides a list of symptoms that might help the development team members to uncover inefficient business processes. If the inefficiencies discovered in the business processes can be corrected relatively easily without too much effort, then the development team should fix them.

Table 3–18 Symptoms Pointing Out Inefficient Processes

• Too many handoffs inside a department • Too many approval layers • Significant time delays between processes • Too many rigid procedures • Too many rejects generated at the outcome of a process • Processes that are still executed even though they do not add value to the products or services provided by the organization • Overall turnaround time too long	• Too many review cycles • Too many handoffs across multiple departments • Duplication of work across multiple departments • Work that is too dispersed and fragmented • Not enough standard work methods, causing inconsistent work methods • Too much paper-oriented work methods

On the other hand, the work involved in correcting these inefficiencies may require a significant amount of time and resources or necessitate some drastic changes in current business practices. Such a situation usually becomes evident when the business process is overly complex, or when the users themselves are uncertain about how to resolve the numerous business problems that are identified with the process. If so, then all the analysis work that is currently done on the delinquent business processes should be halted until management assigns a special team of users to properly address all critical issues related to these processes.

Activity number:	AN-2
Activity name:	Create the business data model
Purpose:	Develop a conceptual data model depicting the relationships that exist between the business entities required by the application system
Inputs:	SU-T1 Current problems/opportunities SU-T2 System mission and project business objectives

	SU-T3 Data context diagram SU-T6 Initial project scope Current system documentation
Outputs:	AN-T2 Business data model
Activity description:	Using the entity-relationship data modeling technique, perform the following tasks:

Step 1: Develop a first cut of the entity-relationship diagram

- Identify the business entities for which information needs to be maintained by the application system. In the case of a large application system, group the business entities into logical domains or subject areas
- Identify the business relationships that exist between the entities, based on the set of business rules that regulate how the business is conducted
- Describe and document the entities and relationships that are shown on the diagram
- Determine whether the entities can be broken down into supertype/subtype roles
- For each relationship that connects two entities, determine its cardinality, identifying how many instances of each of the two entities must be accounted for in the model

Step 2: Refine the entity-relationship diagram by adding the entities' attributes

- For each entity or relationship shown on the entity-relationship diagram, identify all the attributes that characterize them
- Describe each specific attribute, including their respective domains
- Identify the attribute(s) that uniquely identify an occurrence of an entity

Step 3: Normalize the entity-relationship diagram

- Normalize into at least a third-normal form the data shown on the entity-relationship diagram
  - For each entity:
    - Remove the repeating data groups
    - Remove attributes that do not depend on the whole key
    - Remove attributes that do not depend directly and entirely on the whole key
  - For each relationship:
    - Resolve the relationships that contain data
- Walk through the logical data model deliverable

3.3   CREATE THE BUSINESS DATA MODEL

This section discusses the detailed steps involved in creating the business data model. It also provides useful tips on how to execute that process, along with descriptions of some basic terminology.

3.3.1   INTRODUCTION

In this activity, the business data model is created with the active participation of the customers. The business data model is used to document the structure of all the data that the business area utilizes or creates. The business data model components are graphically depicted with the entity-relationship technique. This data modeling method is used to describe all the information needs of the users in terms of data entities, attributes, relationships, business rules, domains, unique identifiers, and alternative identifiers.

The business data model should truly reflect the business environment because it primarily consists of the various business objects that are used by the organization. It also describes the conditions under which the business objects interact with one another, according to the precise business rules that govern them. The business data model will provide the basis for the design of the system's logical databases during the design phase.

The business data model is constructed in parallel with the business process model. In some instances, it can also be constructed before the business process model, such as when a preliminary prototype of the system needs to be built quickly. In fact, both models are necessary in order to fully convey the desired functional and data characteristics of the business application required by the users.

Table 3-19 describes the major components of an entity-relationship diagram.

Table 3–19 Entity-relationship Diagram Components

Entity	An entity is any object or thing that is of interest to the organization and for which some data must be stored.
Attribute	An attribute is a descriptive element, which is used to characterize an entity or a relationship. Attributes are the fields that describe an entity.
Relationship	A relationship describes the way entities interact with each other, along with the business conditions under which they associate with one another.
Cardinality	The cardinality describes the number of entity instances that can exist at each end of a relationship. Typically, the cardinality is expressed as a qualifier, such as one-to-one, one-to-many, or many-to-many relationships.

Table 3–19 Entity-relationship Diagram Components (cont.)

Entity supertype/ subtype	An entity can be divided into two or more subtype entities. Each subtype entity has attributes of its own, which are unique. An entity that has subtypes is called a supertype entity.
Entity instance	An entity instance is a single occurrence of an entity.
Synonyms	Synonyms are aliases or other names of an entity or one of its attributes.
Unique identifier	A unique identifier is the combination of attributes and relationships that uniquely identify each instance of the entities.

The following sections describe how to create the business data model with the entity-relationship method. It also suggests some considerations on how to avoid potential pitfalls.

3.3.2   IDENTIFYING ENTITIES

Entities can be discovered by examining a large variety of business documents such as: reports, business process description documents, company procedures, business plans, existing systems user interfaces, forms, and file/database layouts. Entities can also be identified by conducting various interviews with the customers or by organizing a data modeling joint facilitated session.

Table 3-20 lists some of the most common entities that business organizations normally deal with while conducting their business.

Table 3–20 Most Common Business Entities

Customers	Employees
Vendors/suppliers/partners	Products/services
Parts	Locations/places/sites/plants
Physical assets	Financial assets

Looking at Table 3-20 above, entities can be loosely grouped into five generic categories, as indicated in Table 3-21.

NAMING ENTITIES

Be sure to assign unique, meaningful names to the entities shown on the model. The names should reflect as closely as possible the terminology that the users utilize when

Table 3–21 Entity Categories

People	Employees, suppliers, vendors, customers
Place	Important locations that are relevant to the organization, such as headquarters, field offices, customer locations, plants
Things	Various physical items that are important to the organization, such as products, machines, parts, desks, tools, books
Logical concepts	These entities usually include conceptual objects such as the various services that are provided by the organization, either to internal or external customers. For instance, legal services, financial services, manufacturing services, consulting services. They can also be logical abstractions such as plans, strategies, business objectives.
Events	These are time-sequenced entities, such as recurring events (i.e., weekly, monthly meetings, weekly status report creation). They can also be internal/external stimuli to which the application must respond in a pre-planned manner.

they accomplish their business activities. The following conventions can be used to name an entity:

- Always use singular names.

- Each entity name must be unique.

- The entity name must clearly convey what the entity represents. If necessary, provide a qualifier to make the name more meaningful.

DESCRIBING ENTITIES

All entities in the business data model must be described clearly with explicit terms. Coming up with a meaningful description is more difficult than it might initially seem at first glance. Although an entity should not be described only with concrete examples, it might be useful sometimes to complement the textual description of an entity by providing a set of representative examples.

Also, be very sure to understand that the entity-relationship model is often constructed in multiple iterations, meaning that the developers should not insist on completing the detailed description of all the elements that are used to describe an entity in a complete and thorough manner all at once. The description of the entities should be refined gradually as the data model is progressively developed with the users through a series of iterations.

Each entity should be described with an outline similar to the one provided in Table 3-22.

Table 3–22 Entity Characteristics

PROPERTIES	DESCRIPTION
Entity name	Name that uniquely identifies an entity
Alias(es)	Used to describe other terms that might be utilized within the organization to identify the same entity
Definition	Description, in meaningful terms, of the role and purpose of the entity in the context of the organization
Existence constraints	Specifies whether an entity depends on other entities for its existence or identification
Business rules	A business rule is a business policy, which defines one or more assertions that represent constraints, which regulate the behavior of the entity. Often, the business rules will dictate the specific business conditions under which an entity is created, deleted, or modified.
Volumetrics	Describes the number of occurrences of the entity, covering the lower-, upper-, and mid-range boundary values
Attributes	List of all the attributes that are used to characterize and describe the entity
Example(s)	This optional section lists concrete examples of the entity

3.3.3 IDENTIFYING RELATIONSHIPS

Relationships can be discovered in different ways, such as:

- Conducting interviews with the users
- Conducting a joint facilitated session
- Examining various business or system documents
- Conducting event analysis

NAMING RELATIONSHIPS

In an entity-relationship model, each relationship appears as a line that connects two entities, with a verb phrase that is normally written along the line. The verb phrase should contain a meaningful verb in the present tense. Figure 3-6 shows a one-to-many relationship between ORDER and ORDER ITEM, using the IDEF1X data modeling technique.

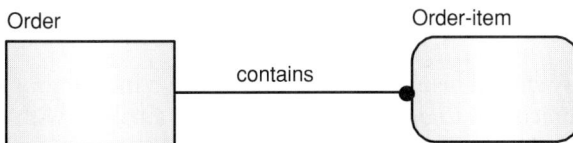

Figure 3–6 A one-to-many relationship.

DESCRIBING RELATIONSHIPS

Relationships between entities can convey a great deal of information. To a large extent, the relationship that might exist between two entities is established in accordance with the current business policies and work practices of the organization.

The description of each relationship that is shown on the entity-relationship diagram is important since the identification of relationships is one of the key vehicles by which the enterprise business rules are captured and documented. The discussions about relationships with the users often uncover important business policies and rules that will govern the behavior of the logical data structure and its data objects.

Each relationship should be described with an outline similar to the one provided in Table 3-23.

Table 3–23 Relationship Characteristics

PROPERTIES	DESCRIPTION
Relationship name	Name that uniquely identifies a relationship
Description	Definition of the relationship in meaningful terms, describing its role and purpose
Cardinality classification	Statements that describe how many instances of the parent entity are connected to how many instances of the child entity, such as one-to-one, one-to-many, or many-to-many
Existence constraints	Specifies whether a relationship depends on other components shown on the entity-relationship diagram for its existence and identification
Business rules	A business rule is a business policy, which defines one or more assertions that represent constraints, which regulate the behavior of the relationship. Often, the business rules will dictate the business conditions under which a relationship is created, modified, or deleted.

3.3.4   IDENTIFYING ATTRIBUTES

The attributes of an entity can be discovered in different ways, such as:

- Conducting interviews with the users
- Conducting a joint facilitated session
- Examining various business or system documents

NAMING ATTRIBUTES

Each attribute of an entity should be uniquely identified with a meaningful name. As a rule of thumb, a good practice is to precede the name of the attribute with the name of the entity. The attribute names should always be singular.

DESCRIBING ATTRIBUTES

Each attribute that characterizes an entity should be described with an outline similar to the one provided in Table 3-24.

Table 3–24 Attribute Main Characteristics

PROPERTIES	DESCRIPTION
Attribute name	Name that uniquely identifies an attribute
Alias	Used to describe other names that might be utilized within the organization to identify the same attribute
Definition	Description, in meaningful terms, of the role and purpose of the attribute, in its proper business context
Existence constraints	Specifies whether an attribute depends on other data for its existence and identification
Business rules	A business rule is a business policy, which defines one or more assertions that represent constraints, which regulate the behavior of the attribute. Often, the business rules will dictate the business conditions under which an attribute is created, deleted, or modified.
Domain	A domain is a set of specific values or value ranges an attribute is permitted to take.
Format	Characterizes the attribute with the values of numeric, text, date, time, or money. Sometimes it can be other forms, such as sound or video multimedia elements.
Length	Characterizes the attribute with the maximum number of characters or digits the value can take
Default value	Initial value an attribute can take when it is instantiated for the first time
Derivation algorithm	Describes the algorithm by which a derivable attribute is computed from the values of other attributes

Describing in further detail the more specialized categories of attributes, such as base, group, or derived, is beyond the scope of this book. However, I do want to provide some additional definitions for attributes, which pertain also to the relational data model, as described in Table 3-25.

DERIVABLE ATTRIBUTES

A derivable attribute is an attribute whose value can be calculated based on the values of other attributes, such as totals, for instance. Normally, you leave derivable attributes

Table 3–25 Additional Attribute Characteristics

ATTRIBUTE TYPE	DEFINITION
Primary key	A primary key is an attribute or combination of attributes that are used to uniquely identify an occurrence of an entity. In other words, a primary key is a unique identifier.
Access key	An access key is an attribute or a set of attributes that will be used often to access an entity, but not via the primary key. However, an attempt to access the entity via an access key may not necessarily result in retrieving only one instance of an entity. Several access keys can exist for an entity. For example, the entity "Customer" can be accessed via the following candidate access keys: Customer Code, Customer Name, Customer Telephone Number, or Customer Address.
Foreign key	A foreign key is an attribute or set of attributes of an entity that is used as a primary key in another entity.

out of the business data model and add them back in during the database design stage, if they are required.

However, experienced developers should know when breaking the rules makes sense. If developers feel, through discussions with the users, that including derived attributes in the model is useful, then they should be added. However, they need to be identified as such in the data model. Similarly, you also need to describe the procedural algorithms that are used to derive these composite attributes.

SPECIFYING THE DOMAINS

A domain of an attribute is the set of permissible values or value ranges that an attribute can take. You need to clearly describe the set of allowed values the attribute can take, while specifying the various characteristics of an attribute. Later on, when the physical data model will be created, the attributes shown in the physical data structure will be able to take only the permissible values that originate from their domains.

Sometimes, the domain of an attribute consists of a series of codes. In such a case, a good practice is always to not only identify the permissible values that the attribute can have, but also provide the definitions of the codes themselves. For example, the attribute 'employee-status' can have the following set of codes as permissible values: A, I. Also documenting the meaning of these codes would make sense, such as: A = active, I = inactive.

SYNONYMS AND HOMONYMS

During the building of the business data model, attribution of data elements to the various data entities of the system may expose new categories of problems, such as those associated with the detection of synonyms and homonyms. Synonyms occur when two different names are used to identify the same entity or the same attribute. Example: Customer-invoice and customer-bill are synonyms if both have the same definition in the context of a given system (e.g., a list of the goods sold to the customer along with a description of the corresponding charges and terms). Homonyms occur when the same name is used to identify two entities or attributes that, in reality, have different meanings in different contexts. Example: An "assembly" in one department is used to identify a specific part of an engine, whereas another department uses the word "assembly" to identify the complete engine itself, with all its constituent parts.

When inconsistencies of this nature are detected in the data model, you should clarify them with the users as soon as possible. Ideally, a consensus should be reached among the users as to which terminology should prevail. In practice, though, this task may prove to be quite difficult, especially if a strong data administration function has not yet been established in the user organization itself. Such a situation might prevail when the myriad business documents that are being processed in several user areas utilize slightly different terminology. Changing all the existing documentation or creating new forms to reflect a consistent terminology across the entire organization might not be too practical, especially for those areas that fall outside the scope of the present system. As a compromise, though, discrepancies of this nature should at least be recorded in the corporate data dictionary and aliases could be created to reflect the current situation.

Eventually, the synonyms and homonyms should then be gradually phased out with the eventual replacement of the systems already in place.

3.3.5 IDENTIFYING AND SPECIFYING THE BUSINESS RULES

Business rules are the policies by which the enterprise runs the business. In several instances, the proper implementation of the most important business rules will help differentiate an organization from its competition. Certain rules might change frequently in response to changing business conditions, government and industry regulations, or new innovative competitive schemes. Other types of business rules are fairly stable and change rarely.

Quite often, though, business rules designate some specific constraints on the data used within the enterprise. Although business rules can be either formally or informally documented, they nevertheless rule the way the enterprise conducts its business operations. For this reason, capturing and accurately describing all the business rules that are important to the organization's core operations is crucial.

The business rules can be found in many places while developing the entity-relationship data model, such as in:

- Entities
- Relationships
- Attributes
- Domains

They can also simply hide in the heads of the organization's most valued workers. Then the job of the data modeler is to uncover these by asking the right questions of knowledgeable business users.

Table 3-26 provides a list of some of the most common types of business rules that should be considered while constructing the entity-relationship data model with the users.

Table 3–26 Business Rules Identification

Attributes	• Business rules stating that certain values are mandatory for attributes of an entity • Business rules stating the conditions under which a value of an attribute is modified or accessed • Business rules stating the conditions under which the value of an attribute is dependent on the value(s) of other attributes
Relationships	• Business rules stating the conditions under which a relationship is created between two entities • Business rules stating the conditions under which a relationship is dependent on the existence of other relationship(s)

Entities	• Business rules stating the conditions under which an entity is created, updated, or deleted
	• Business rules stating the conditions under which an entity is deleted, such as:
	  – Are related entities deleted, too?
	  – The entity cannot be deleted if other entities relate to it
	  – When the entity is deleted, the relationships in which the entity participates are deleted also?
	• Business rules stating the conditions under which an entity is classified into sub-entities (i.e., subtypes)

Triggering operations	• Business rules that carry the notion that specific actions should be automatically triggered when insert, update, or delete operations are performed on an entity or attribute and when certain conditions are encountered

Most of the time, business rules should be application-independent. They can be simply documented with the following basic construct:

If <existence of certain condition(s)> then <operation> statements.

Note that at this stage, the business discussions surrounding the business rules are still done at a logical level. They should be kept strictly at a business level.

3.3.6 DISTINGUISHING ENTITY SUPERTYPE/SUBTYPE

During the course of creating the entity-relationship data model, sometimes categorizing entities as supertype and subtype is useful. An entity can be subdivided into two or more subtype entities. Each subtype entity has attributes of its own, which are unique. An entity that has subtypes is called a supertype entity. The supertype/subtype construct is based on the notions of generalization and specialization. Generalization is based on the principle that objects are subtypes of more global objects. At the opposite end, the notion of specialization implies that objects come in various types that are different from each other.

The inclusion of the supertype/subtype construct in the data model has several advantages. For instance, it can help to identify specific information structures and simplify them. Similarly, if the business situation requires it, supertype/subtype constructs can improve the communication process with the users during analysis. Finally, it can help to uncover important business rules about entities and their relationships that otherwise could be ignored. Figure 3-7 shows a classic example where a supertype/subtype construct is utilized in a business data model for a banking environment, using the IDEF1X data modeling technique.

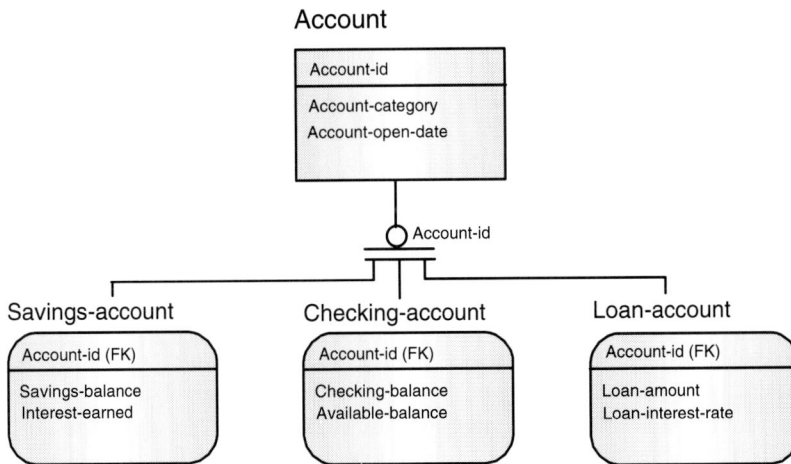

Figure 3–7 Supertype/subtype construct.

Table 3-27 documents a set of basic rules that govern the use of a generic supertype/subtype construct in an entity-relationship diagram.

3.3.7 UNDERSTANDING THE DATA NORMALIZATION PROCESS

This section reviews the normalization process without going into a deep discussion of the subject. It presents the fundamental principles behind the normalization tech-

Table 3–27 Entity Supertype/Subtype Association Guidelines

- A subtype entity should normally have more than one distinctive attribute to justify its creation
- A supertype entity should normally have more than one subtype associated with it
- A subtype entity can have separate relationships with other entities
- Subtypes entities should normally contain attributes that are distinct from one another or used differently, depending on the business context
- The attributes that are common to all the subtypes should be located in the supertype entity
- Subtypes should normally be mutually exclusive

nique and shows some basic examples. For a rigorous treatment of the normalization theory, I provide several references on this topic at the end of this book.

To start the discussion on normalization, I want to define in non-mathematical terms what is involved in normalization. Normalization is a formal technique that is used to develop a highly structured data model. Through three basic normalization steps the data shown in an entity-relationship diagram are gradually structured in a way such that:

- Data redundancy is progressively controlled and eliminated
- The data is structured for future ease of maintenance and modification considerations. This structuring is done by reducing create, update, and delete anomalies of data.
- After normalization, the resulting data structure is more stable. However, it can still be viewed as a logical data model that is independent of the hardware and software that will be used to implement the physical database.

A BRIEF NOTE ON THE SEMANTICS OF THE NORMALIZATION PROCESS

The normalization of the business data model can be seen by some hard-liner data analysts as a purely technical process that will pave the way to the design of a flexible database.

However, from a business perspective, the normalization of the logical data model is done primarily to ensure that the proper business rules are correctly reflected in the model. For this reason, the focus should still remain on the user environment and its related business standards, rules, and policies, instead of design-related intricacies.

If business rules are found to be incorrect, they should then be revisited with the users and appropriately corrected. In reality, many of the business rules that were discovered while constructing the entity-relationship model are verified via the application of the normalization process.

Normal forms are the steps that are commonly used to normalize data. Following is a description of the three normalization steps that are performed to create a data model that is said to be in a third normal form.

In fact, five normalization forms have been identified so far but I limit the discussion to the first three normalization steps. As a rule of thumb, a data model in its third normal form has already achieved a satisfactory level of data redundancy elimination and more often than not will already be in fourth and fifth normal form.

FIRST NORMAL FORM

All the attributes of an entity must have exactly one single occurrence in each instance. In other words, all attributes of an entity must not be repeated. Figure 3-8 shows an entity called EMPLOYEE with some attributes, using the IDEF1X notation.

Employee

Employee-id
Employee-name Employee--address Employee-skills

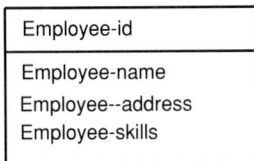

Figure 3–8 Entity shown with the IDEF1X data modeling notation.

Since the attribute employee-skills shown in Figure 3-8 is not single valued, because an employee can have many skills, this entity is violating the first normal form rule. The repeating attribute employee-skills is the offender. To fix this problem, the entity EMPLOYEE must be transformed into the structure shown in Figure 3-9, using the IDEF1X notation.

In fact, an additional entity called SKILL has been created and a one-to-many relationship has been produced between the entity EMPLOYEE and the newly created entity SKILL.

SECOND NORMAL FORM

Every non-key attribute of an entity must be fully dependent upon the entity's entire key. Figure 3-10 shows two entities called Employee and Department, along with their respective set of attributes. (Figure 3-10 and subsequent figures use a notation different from IDEF1X.)

The attribute Dept-location in the entity Employee is not dependent upon the entire key Employee-id. In fact, the attribute Dept-location is dependent upon the key Department-id, which belongs to the entity DEPARTMENT. Thus the entity EMPLOYEE is violating the second normal form rule. The attribute Dept-location is the offender in this case. To fix this problem, the attribute Dept-location must be transferred to the entity DEPARTMENT as shown in Figure 3-11.

Employee

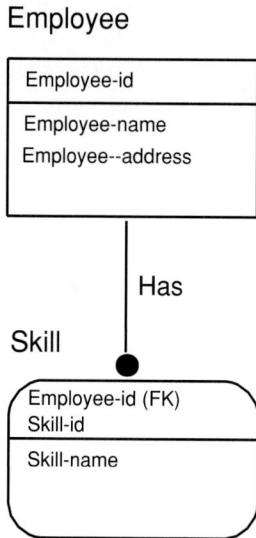

Figure 3–9 Entity in first normal form.

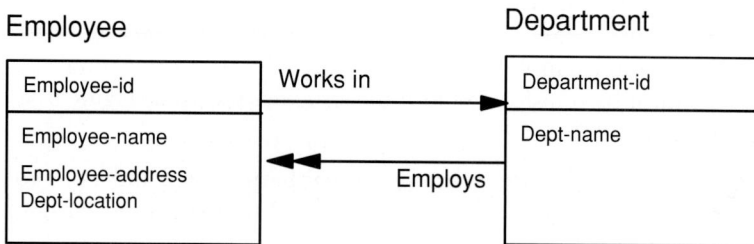

Figure 3–10 Employee/department entity-relationship.

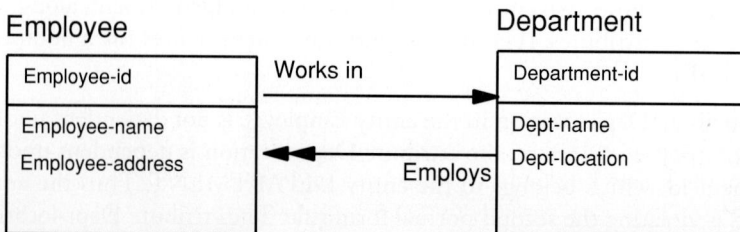

Figure 3–11 Employee/department entity-relationship in second normal form.

THIRD NORMAL FORM

An entity is in third normal form if (a) it is already in second normal form and (b) every non-key attribute of this entity must not be dependent upon another non-key attribute. Figure 3-12 shows the entity ORDER with its attributes.

Order

Order-id
Order-date
Order-description
Customer-id
Customer-name

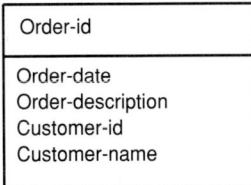

Figure 3–12 Order entity.

Since the attribute Customer-name is dependent upon the Customer-id attribute, the entity ORDER is violating the third normal form rule. To fix this problem, a new entity called CUSTOMER is created, and the attribute customer-name is transferred to that entity, as shown in Figure 3-13.

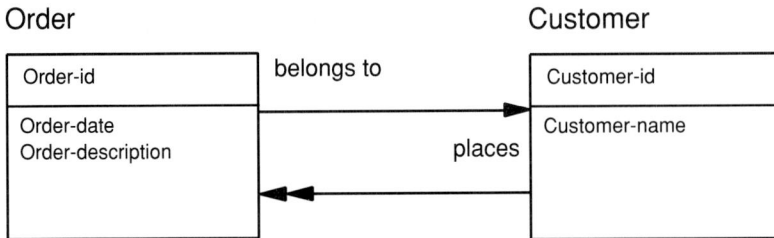

Order   Customer

Order-id	belongs to		Customer-id
Order-date		places	Customer-name
Order-description			

Figure 3–13 Customer/order entity-relationship in third normal form.

3.3.8   VARIOUS DATA MODELING NOTATIONS AND TOOLS

Several entity-relationship data modeling notations are used in industry. Table 3-28 lists six of the most popular ones. Data analysts frequently utilize these six data modeling notations. These notations are used to graphically depict the entities and their relationships, along with their associated attributes. Several of these notations are supported by various CASE data modeling tools.

Table 3–28 Different Entity-relationship Data Modeling Notations

- Chen
- Merise
- NIAM (Nijssen's Information Analysis Methodology)
- IDEF1X
- Information Engineering (IE) Data Modeling Technique
- Unified Modeling Language (UML)

In Europe, Merise is very popular. In North America, data modelers frequently use IDEF1X, Chen, and IE. Some of the criteria to consider while selecting a notation versus another one might be:

- Does an automated tool support this data modeling technique?
- Can I follow courses or seminars to learn how to use this data modeling technique?
- Can I buy books that describe how to use this data modeling technique?

Following are the addresses of vendor Web sites that offer automated logical data modeling and database diagramming tools.

http://www.logicworks.com	(Erwin/ERX)
http://www.oracle.com	(Oracle Database Designer)
http://www.sybase.com	(PowerDesigner)
http://www.popkin.com	(SA/Data Architect)
http://www.visible.com	(Visual Analyst Workbench)
http://www.infomodelers.com	(InfoModeler)
http://www.rational.com	(Rational Rose)

Several of the data modeling tools identified in the above-mentioned list support the creation of logical data models that are independent of the various types of physical database models they can generate. The logical data model contains generic data types. When the physical database model is generated from the logical data model, the generic data types are automatically converted into actual data field types that specific commercial DBMS software can handle.

Some of these data modeling tool vendors also support some of the most popular object-oriented modeling conventions such as Object Role Modeling (ORM), Coad-Yourdon, and Booch.

3.3.9   DATA MODELING BEST PRACTICES

Finally, Table 3-29 provides a brief list of best practices for data modeling.

Table 3–29 Data Modeling Best Practices

• Select the data entities that are of interest to the application system
• Identify the critical relationships that associate different entities
• Assign the proper attributes to the proper entities
• Identify the set of business rules that reflect the enterprise's way of doing business
• Document with accuracy the entities, attributes, and relationships
• Identify the proper prime key attributes of each entity to ensure that all attributes depend on the whole key and nothing else
• Assign simple but meaningful names to the entities, relationships, and attributes

3.3.10 JOINT FACILITATED SESSIONS FOR DATA MODELING

Small to medium data modeling efforts (5 to 30 entities) can be achieved by interviewing some key users and by analyzing supportive material that has been gathered within the business area under study.

In fact, even a large data modeling effort (30 to 100+ entities) can be completed with simple information-gathering techniques such as collecting and analyzing a variety of business documents that are then complemented with user serial interviews. With such methods, the data model is gradually constructed by consolidating the information that is extracted from user interviews and analysis of various business documents.

This approach can certainly lead to a quality data model that reflects the important business rules, which govern the use of data within an organization. However, quite a while may pass before the data analyst completes and validates for this purpose the data model, depending on the availability of the key users that need to be interviewed.

On the other hand, conducting short data modeling workshops using the joint facilitated session process can drastically shorten the time cycle required to produce a complete data model. Moreover, the users directly participate in the construction of the data model. This participation will strengthen their buy-in into the system that is being developed for them.

Such a strong buy-in is rarely achieved via serial interviews, whereas a joint facilitated session process will usually generate a stronger consensus among the users when the final deliverable is completed. Likewise, the users gradually develop together a better understanding of the business rules and policies that regulate the usage of corporate data in their business environment.

The next section describes how to use the joint facilitated session process to construct a data model. The reader can consult the information provided in Chapter 10 for a more detailed description of the joint facilitated session process in general.

STEP 1: Plan the data modeling joint facilitated session

The first step consists of planning the joint facilitated session for data modeling. The facilitator must review the scope of the proposed facilitated session with the project leader and project sponsor. The detailed points that are reviewed during the meeting include:

- Background on the project in general
- The purpose and scope of the data modeling effort
- Management and business objectives to be achieved
- Potential issues, constraints, or assumptions that can affect the data modeling workshop
- The participants and their respective organizations
- The number of sessions required and the timetable
- The location where the sessions will be held
- Expected deliverables and a basic description of their contents
- The type of data modeling technique that will be used during the facilitated sessions to construct the business data model

If necessary, the facilitator might decide to gather various business documents to acquaint himself/herself with the business organization. The facilitator might also decide to interview some key users. The information gathered at this stage will help to prepare visual aids for the data modeling workshop. These documents can include reports, filled-in forms, online transactions, and other material that can be used to quickly identify the major data entities of the system.

Through this process, the facilitator or project sponsor/leader must also ensure that the user participants in each affected business unit will be able to attend the series of sessions that are being planned and provide a strong commitment to its success.

Be sure to select a facilitator who has at least a high-level knowledge of the data modeling technique that will be used to construct the business data model. For a small to a medium data model, the facilitator can play the role of both facilitator and data modeler, assuming this individual has already some practical experience in data modeling.

However, for a large data model that involves the participation of several users from different business units, having one facilitator and one data modeler might be preferable. The role of the data modeler is to assist the facilitator in leading the group through the process of creating the data model and verifying it along the way. This is done by asking various questions to the participants that bring out the most important business rules, which will dictate the type of relationships that are established between the entities. The role of the facilitator then is to keep the workshop on track. For this approach to work, though, a very good complicity must exist between the facilitator and the data modeler.

A scribe will document the definitions of the entities, attributes, relationships, and business rules that make up the business data model, as it is progressively constructed. Last but not least, the business users themselves must attend the sessions as full-time participants. These people are the subject-matter experts who will provide all the business knowledge required for creating the data model. The most knowledgeable and experienced business people must attend the session to achieve quality results.

STEP 2: Prepare the data modeling joint facilitated session

The arrangements are made for the session room, equipment, and supplies.

The facilitator develops the workshop approach and also prepares the visual aids for the workshop. The visual aids might include different items such as:

- The data modeling session agenda

- A brief explanation of the basic concepts associated with data modeling

- Purpose, scope, and objectives of the data modeling session

- Constraints and assumptions

- Expected data modeling deliverables

- Proposed session rules and guidelines

The joint facilitated session facilitator can also assist the project sponsor to prepare a kick-off memo to invite the session participants. Once completed, this memo is distributed immediately to all workshop participants. The memo must describe the purpose of the data modeling workshop and its importance for the project.

The sponsor must also request a strong commitment, from all participants, to ensure the success of the session. The following letter provides a sample generic memo that can be used to invite participants to a joint facilitated session. This memo can be modified easily to schedule other types of joint facilitated sessions.

Date: YYYYMMDD

TO: \<List of Joint Facilitated Session Attendees\>
FROM: \<Executive Sponsor\>
SUBJECT: \<Project Name\> - Joint Facilitated Session(s) – Data modeling
DATE: \<Facilitated Session Start and End Dates\>
LOCATION: \<Facilitated Session Start Time and Place\>

You have been chosen to actively participate in a joint facilitated session for the \<business application or project name\>. The purpose of this workshop is to \<workshop purpose\>. The group session(s) will be led by \<facilitator's name\>, who is an accomplished joint facilitated session leader.

Similar joint facilitated sessions were successfully conducted <in several organizations like ours> or <in other departments within our company>. No secret recipe exists, though. A successful workshop always depends on the ability and willingness of each participant to positively contribute to the overall process. In this regard, I know your personal contribution will be important because of the business knowledge and on-the-job experience you will bring along with you during the facilitated session.

I, for one, fully support this workshop and sincerely hope you will, too. By working together as a pro-active team, we can make this joint facilitated session a great success. This is very important to us all. I look forward to seeing you on <Joint Facilitated Session Start Date>.

If, in the meantime, you have any questions on this important subject, please do not hesitate to contact <project manager's name> or myself.

Sincerely,

<Executive Sponsor>

A typical list of joint facilitated session rules and guidelines is provided in Chapter 10. The joint facilitated session rules establish a formal contract between all participants and the facilitator. For a data modeling workshop, be sure to stick to the proposed agenda. Likewise, you will need to explain to the participants that the purpose of the data modeling session is to work on finding data requirements and business rules, not to discuss solutions. Thus, you might want to include this additional rule to the proposed list of rules of the land.

STEP 3: Conduct the data modeling joint facilitated session
The order in which the data modeling activities are executed during the workshop is not necessarily linear. The exact steps will vary, depending on the type of data model being developed and the discovery of new facts that relate to the data being modeled with the participants. The set of generic activities that follow can be tailored to the needs of a specific joint facilitated data modeling session. Adopting a flexible approach in joint facilitated sessions is paramount to its success.

- Kick off the joint facilitated session
  - Welcome the participants
  - Ask each participant to introduce himself/herself
  - Allow the project sponsor to provide the appropriate opening remarks
  - Review the proposed data modeling workshop agenda
  - Describe the joint facilitation process
  - Describe the data modeling technique that will be used to construct the data model

  – Present the workshop objectives
  – Review and discuss with the participants the proposed rules of the land
- Investigate the data requirements and progressively construct the data model
  – Analyze the scope of the data modeling workshop
    – Review the system context diagram that was created during the project survey phase
    – Identify the high-level business processes that are performed within the boundary of the system context diagram and the associated major external contributors
  – Identify the data objects that are used within the stated business domain, such as entities, attributes, and relationships

> *At this early stage, the data modeler normally does not make attempts at diagramming the relationships between the entities. Rather, the different data objects are simply listed with meaningful business-oriented names on a suitable medium such as a whiteboard or an overhead transparency that is clearly visible to all session attendees.*

  – Classify the data objects

> *The data modeler asks pertinent questions of the participants that are used to appropriately classify the objects as entities, attributes, or relationships.*

  – Depict the data entities and their attributes

> *The data modeler depicts on a diagram all the entities and attributes that were identified in the previous step. The attributes of an entity are appropriately regrouped under this entity. The names of the entities and the attributes might change, depending on the questions that are asked by the data modeler and the feedback provided by the participants. Each attribute should be identified as a single- or multiple-occurrence attribute type. Similarly, each attribute must have a clear and explicit meaning.*

  – Depict the relationships between entities

> *The relationships that exist between the entities are depicted on the entity-relationship model. Here the cardinality that exists between the entities is also discussed and documented on the data model. During this activity, the business rules are stated either with the entity-relationship graphic language or written down under the form of a specification.*

–   Determine the key of each entity

Each entity is assigned a unique key. That unique identifier can be a single attribute or it can be composed of a group of attributes. I suggest identifying at the same time potential alternate keys and also any inversion entries (a.k.a. secondary indexes).

–   Document all the data objects

Although some preliminary definitions of entities, attributes, and relationships might have been documented during earlier data modeling activities, here a formal description of each data object shown on the entity-relationship diagram is documented, with the active participation of the users. This also includes the business rules that were discovered during the workshop.

–   Normalize the data model

The data model is now normalized into a third normal form. The normalization process ensures that the model supports the appropriate business rules. An experienced data modeler might decide to normalize the data model throughout the entire data modeling session, as the need for it arises during any of the previous steps. This approach requires strong data analysis skills, though. The data modeler must then normalize the model with the users in a manner in which the process almost becomes transparent to them. Asking all relevant normalization questions in a business-like manner that the users can easily understand will help the data modeler achieve this goal.

If the business data model is quite complex, then the normalization process can be done later on, as an additional step that falls outside the scope of the workshop.

•   Wrap up the joint facilitated session
    –   Review all outstanding issues with participants and ensure that each issue is assigned to someone and a target completion date has been identified for its resolution
    –   Seek participants' feedback on the work achieved during the session

STEP 4: Produce and issue the data modeling final document

•   Gather all the relevant information that was documented during the session
•   Analyze, edit, and consolidate all session information into a final document

- Issue a final document and, if necessary, schedule a last review with the session participants
- Review the session final outcome with the executive project sponsor and project manager

Activity number:	AN-3
Activity name:	Partition the business application into system transactions
Purpose:	Allocate the business elementary processes to a set of computerized system transactions
Inputs:	AN-T1 Business process model AN-T2 Business data model
Outputs:	AN-T3 System transactions

Activity description:	• Consolidate the business process and data models and verify the level of consistency between them
	• Review the major components of the business process and data models
	• Identify the application process and data components that will be automated versus those that will be manual. For each automated component, identify the recommended automation method, such as:
	  – Online
	  – Batch
	  – Ad Hoc
	  – Automated interfaces with other systems (batch or online)
	• For each automated process component, review the set of elementary business processes that are within its boundary and structure them into a set of cohesive system transactions, based on how the elementary business processes should be carried out and the type of technology chosen to implement the system.
	• Describe the system transactions, documenting their major functional characteristics.
	• Walk through the system transactions deliverable

3.4 PARTITION THE BUSINESS APPLICATION INTO SYSTEM TRANSACTIONS

In this activity, the business data and process models are verified for consistency and stability. Then the major application process and data model components are divided into either manual or automated components. The focus of the development team now gradually shifts from a logical perspective to a more physical perspective. The elementary business processes that are identified in the business process model are gradually transformed into different sets of system business transactions.

Each elementary business process is carefully examined to determine the degree of automation that is required for each internal task and to define whether it will be done manually with some computer assistance or completely automatically by the new application system.

3.4.1   CONSOLIDATING THE BUSINESS PROCESS AND DATA MODELS

Whether the business data and process models are constructed in sequence or in parallel, ensure that both models use consistent naming conventions for common components. These are important to eliminate inconsistencies, especially when several development teams create different sections of the process and data models. The consolidation process should not be a last-minute effort. Rather, it should be an ongoing activity that starts at the very beginning of the analysis phase.

Another important step is to verify the level of stability of the business process and data models. In today's ever-changing business world, no one thinks that the user business environment will remain static over the years. Therefore, the new application system should be constructed in such a way as to allow future expansion while ensuring minimal disruptions in the business environments it supports.

The users and developers should meet to brainstorm and together determine the likelihood of introducing new requirements in the near future that would significantly affect the data and functional architectures of the new business application. The objective is to anticipate certain types of changes, such as those presented in Table 3-30.

Table 3–30 Potential Business Changes Affecting Business Process & Data Models Stability

- Does the organization anticipate moving into a new line of business?
- Will new business processes be required in the next twelve months? In the next three years?
- Can an attribute of an entity become an entity by itself in the near future?
- Can new attributes be added to an entity in the near future?
- Can new entities be introduced in the near future?
- Can new relationships be established between entities to support new business rules?
- Can some fundamental business rules or policies be modified in the years to come, based on anticipated business changes?

To conclude, anticipating foreseeable changes in the business environment might prevent costly system changes in the future, if they are properly reflected in the architecture of the new application system.

3.4.2   MANUAL VERSUS AUTOMATED PROCESSES

Whenever possible, the elementary business processes should be implemented as a set of automated system transactions. However, specific situations may arise in which the use of manual processes is preferable, as indicated in Table 3-31.

Table 3–31   Suggested Hints To Identify Manual Processes

- The decision-making process involves several steps that are never exactly the same and that require some human judgment that cannot be fully implemented with a computer solution. Several exception rules that often change must be applied.
- The implementation of a computerized solution cannot be cost-justified because of the complexity of the process and its associated business rules. The implementation of a manual solution is more economical.
- The process can be implemented more effectively and efficiently with a manual method.

As a rule of thumb, the business processes that are characterized by well organized, well defined series of tasks that are repetitive by nature are often good candidates for automation. Business processes that tend to be unstructured, hard-to-define with a series of well defined tasks that are not repetitive in nature, and can frequently change, are good candidates for manual handling. For example, a manual process that would be hard to automate would be the one whereby a model is selected for the cover page of a fashion magazine.

3.4.3   IDENTIFYING THE SYSTEM TRANSACTIONS

The users will utilize a series of system transactions to interact with the system. A system transaction normally starts when a user or another system decides to use the application to perform a pre-determined business activity. Once the system transaction is started, it usually involves a dialogue between the user that initiated the transaction and the automated system.

In some instances, the customers themselves will initiate the system transaction and interact directly with the system. An example is when a customer withdraws money using an automated teller machine.

For the set of online transactions, creating a live prototype of the user interface frequently complements the process of describing and confirming the more detailed transaction requirements. The prototype shows how the user will interact with the system, based on its capabilities. Section 3.6 discusses the prototyping process in more detail.

Table 3-32 provides a definition of a system transaction.

The identification of business system transactions is an iterative process that requires experience and creativity. Although no formal rules exist for assembling the elementary business processes into a set of cohesive system transactions that will satisfy the user needs, some general guidelines are provided in Table 3-33.

Table 3–32 System Transaction Definition

A system transaction is a complete set of basic computer operations that are required to adequately respond to one or several business events. A system transaction completes one or more computer operations (or "units of works") that are meaningful to the business. A user or a customer who interacts with the system in a specific manner normally activates a system transaction.

Table 3–33 Business System Transaction Characteristics

- Each automated interface with another system can be the subject of a system transaction, either batch or online. In such a case, the system under study either gives information to another system or receives information from another system.
- Each set of basic operations contained in a system transaction must be highly cohesive. All the various operations that are performed under the umbrella of a system transaction must work together toward a common, shared objective.
- All system transactions should be independent of each other for completion. The operations of a given system transaction should not overlap with the operations of another system transaction.
- A system transaction is normally composed of operations that access a limited number of data entities.
- A system transaction is not limited in scope to a single elementary business process. Each system transaction can satisfy one or more elementary business processes.
- Each system transaction has a clear starting and ending point.

Figure 3-14 provides some examples of how various elementary business processes can be implemented into different types of system transactions.

3.4.4 DESCRIBING THE SYSTEM TRANSACTIONS

Each business transaction should be documented with a brief narrative text. The description should include the following elements: automation method, frequency, specific system performance and security requirements, data entities accessed. Since the elementary business processes were already defined and documented, usually you do not need to further detail the internal processing logic of the system transactions. The graphical user interfaces that will be required to support the set of online transactions of a large and complex system will be further described with the active participation of the users through joint facilitated sessions and prototyping.

3.4.5 DEFINING GLOBAL SYSTEM ARCHITECTURE CHARACTERISTICS

As the automated system transactions are defined with the users, they can be regrouped into different logical subsystems, based on their level of functional affinities.

Legend:
P=Process
SP=Sub-process
EP=Elementary process
O=Online
M=Manual

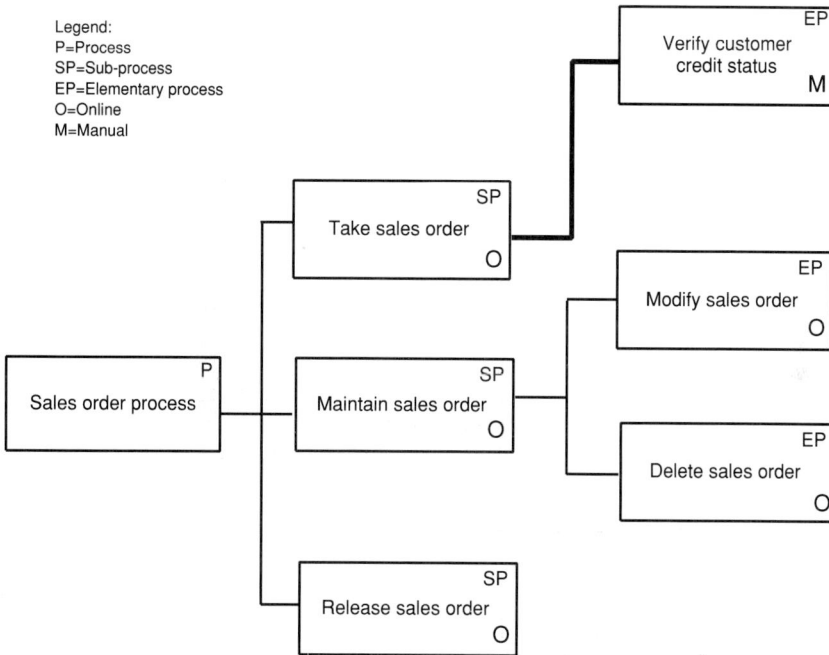

Figure 3–14 Elementary business processes translated in system transactions.

Similarly, the type of client-server configuration that will be used to implement the new application and its set of logical subsystems can be defined at this stage. Will the new application system be implemented in a 2-tier, 3-tier, or N-tier client-server or Web architecture? What type(s) of computing platform(s) will be retained to implement the new application system? What are the different types of technologies that can best enable specific business processes? Which sets of system transactions will be implemented with each proposed enabling technology?

The application target technology components should be selected as much as possible within the context of the standard technology architecture that is currently supported across the enterprise. Some of the factors that might influence the selection of specific technology components for the application at hand are listed in Table 3-34.

3.4.6 FINALIZING THE SYSTEM DEVELOPMENT STRATEGY

Basically, two fundamental approaches exist for developing and implementing an application system. One approach consists of constructing and implementing the entire system all at once. With the second approach, the system is developed and implemented one application segment at a time. Each application segment is identified as a release. For large systems, the best plan is to use the second approach, which often is identified as evolutionary software development.

Table 3–34 Technology Selection Factors

Interoperability principles	• What type and level of interoperability is required between the hardware components of a single, uniform enterprise-computing platform? Across different platforms • What type and level of interoperability is required between the software components across the different computing platforms supported by the enterprise? • What type and level of interoperability is required between the networking components across the different computing platforms supported by the enterprise? • What type and level of interoperability is required between various enterprise business applications?
Vendor selection principles	• What standard technical criteria are used by the enterprise to select a technology vendor? Should all the technology components be selected with a unique vendor or a set of preferred vendors?
Computing platforms principles	• Is a single, homogenous distributed computing platform standard supported across the enterprise? • If a set of heterogeneous distributed computing platforms are supported, what are they? • What type(s) of operating system(s) are supported? • What type(s) of network(s) are supported? • Are 2-tier, 3-tier, or N-tier distributed architectures supported?
Database selection principles	• What type(s) of database software are supported within the enterprise? What types of database middleware?
Security principles	• What are the security technologies that are currently supported by the standard enterprise technology infrastructure?
Distributed component model principles	• What type(s) of distributed component model(s) are supported for application development?
Reliability principles	• If the application is mission-critical for the enterprise, what are the risks involved in selecting a promising but unproven new technology? • Is the technology reliable?

Table 3-35 lists some of the advantages that are associated with developing a large system incrementally with an evolutionary development approach.

On the other hand, the evolutionary software development concept might add some overhead to the development process. This possibility is particularly true in situations where some additional efforts might be required from the development teams to ensure that the different releases of the system remain consistent and synchronized

Table 3–35 Incremental Application Development Benefits

- Reduce the complexity inherent in managing the development of a large and complex system
- Minimize the risks of developing a huge, monolithic system, only to find out later that it does not meet the users' true requirements
- Easier to gain customer confidence and direct participation
- Provide the users with the business processes they most urgently need, long before the whole system actually gets implemented
- Facilitate the division of labor and optimize the utilization of available development resources
- Accommodate evolving business needs

with one another. Table 3-36 lists some of the factors that should be considered to organize the system transactions into a set of distinct application releases.

Table 3–36 Evolutionary Application Partitioning Factors

- The affinities that exist between the various business processes/system transactions and data entities of the system (i.e., various system transactions all using the same data). The business processes that are naturally highly cohesive should be regrouped together.
- The dependencies that exist among certain business processes/system transactions. Each release should have minimal interactions with other releases.
- The necessity for the users to implement as soon as possible particular business processes/system transactions
- The clear distinction between manual versus automated processes
- The availability of developers to construct the entire system all at once
- The types of different distributed computing platforms that might be used to run the various business processes/system transactions
- The development of each release with the participation of a small number of developers and users
- The distribution of business processes/system transactions and data across several geographically dispersed locations
- The size and complexity of the business processes/system transactions and data
- The physical partitioning of the business processes/system transactions into batch and online transactions
- The benefits that will be achieved by implementing earlier some specific business processes/system transactions
- The identification of potential re-usable business processes/system transactions candidates

A final criterion that should be taken into consideration is the timing factor. As a yardstick, each software release should not take more than 6 to 18 months to develop, test, and implement. A six-month timeframe is preferable, whenever feasible.

The next step consists of deciding when and how each development release should be implemented with an evolutionary approach. Figure 3-15 shows the relationship between each release concept and the various development phases of the system development life cycle of large systems.

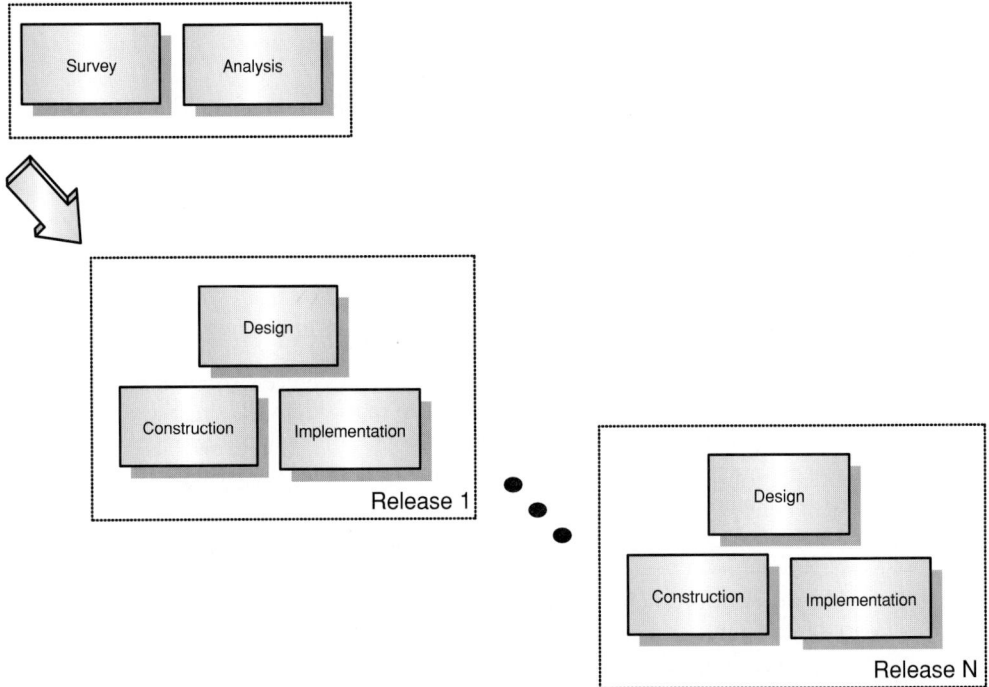

Figure 3–15 Breaking a large system into several development releases.

The system is segmented or partitioned into several releases. Subsequently, the different releases of the system can be developed either in parallel, if sufficient developers are available, or in sequence, with or without some overlapping. Nevertheless, from there on, each particular release is gradually implemented through the execution of the next three development phases: design, construction, and implementation. Similarly, and depending on its size, a release can be developed through a quick series of major versions and interim versions, as illustrated in Figure 3-16. The time to deliver a specific version could range from a few weeks to a few months, depending on the size and complexity of the software release.

Finally, a high-performance team with complementary skills develops each software release. As a rule of thumb, each high-performance team should be composed of a relatively small number of core developers, such as two to seven individuals. The intense

Release 1

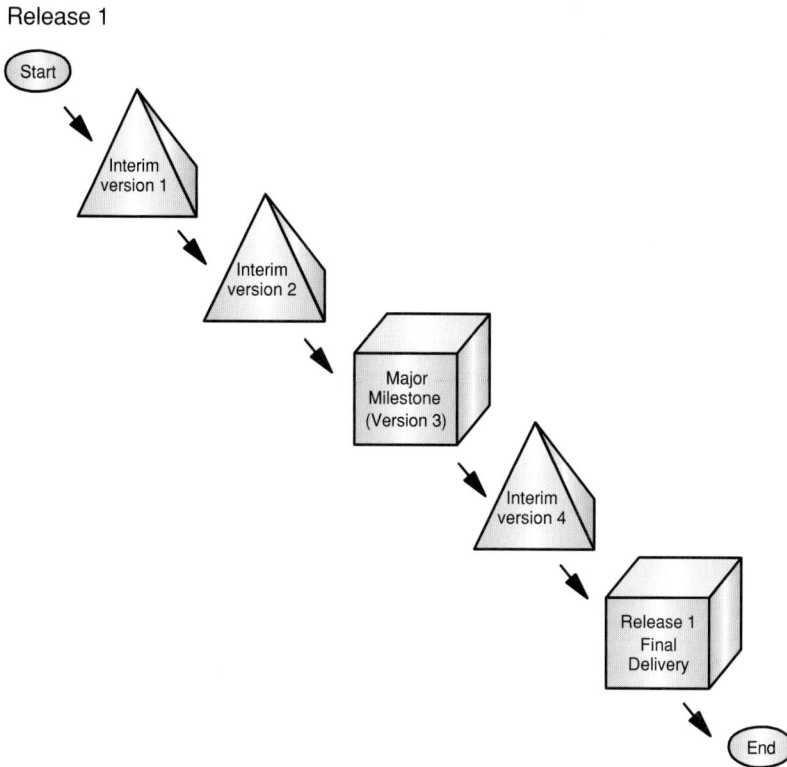

Figure 3–16 Incremental versions within a development release.

interactions that occur among the team members during the development of a release make fostering effective teamwork with larger groups difficult. Likewise, the development team requires a well balanced combination of skills, including technical skills, decision-making skills, business area knowledge skills, problem-solving skills, and good interpersonal skills. High-performance teams must be composed of developers and users who can build trust with each other and are able to work together under intense pressure. True teams have developers who subordinate their personal views and desires to those of the team.

This evolutionary development strategy assumes that the developers are reasonably confident that the architecture of the system (i.e., data and processes) is well defined and stabilized at this stage. Therefore, the dependencies and interfaces that might exist between each release are reasonably well described and well understood by all involved parties.

The implementation of the various releases can be done in different ways when several user sites are affected by the system. Some of the possible implementation scenarios are described in Table 3-37.

Table 3–37 Different Implementation Scenarios

- A particular release is implemented at each user site simultaneously.
- A particular release is installed only at one site initially. Once the major problems are ironed out, the release is then implemented at the other user sites.
- All the releases of the system are first developed and implemented at a unique user site. Then the whole system is implemented at each other user site.

If the development-by-release concept is retained for the system at hand, you might need to develop some additional interfaces for the system. This task might be required to allow the implementation of a release of the new system while supporting at the same time the operations of some portions of the legacy system. For example, you might need to develop some temporary conversion programs that reformat some of the new transactions processed by the new system release into a format compatible with the old system.

The interfaces with the other systems should also be very carefully considered while the system development-by-release strategy is being constructed. For instance, should all the interfaces be established at once or at different points in time? Lastly, while developing the release strategy, pay particular attention to the hardware/software/networking requirements for each particular release. For example, you might need to acquire some hardware equipment ahead of time to support a specific release of the system. In fact, the development team should cross-reference all existing system requirements against each specific release to ensure that they will be properly addressed.

Activity number:	AN-4
Activity name:	Conduct graphical user interface joint facilitated session
Purpose:	To develop a first draft of the application system graphical user interface (GUI)
Inputs:	AN-T1 Business process model AN-T2 Business data model AN-T3 System transactions
Outputs:	AN-T4 System graphical user interface
Activity description:	• Plan the GUI joint facilitated session – Meet with the project sponsor and project leader to discuss the purpose, scope, and objectives of the graphical user interface joint facilitated session

- Determine the technology platform that will be used to deploy the application
- Identify the user participants
- Determine the number of required joint facilitated sessions, their duration, and the location where they will be held
- Schedule the joint facilitated session(s)
- Notify the participants

- Prepare the GUI joint facilitated session
  - Gather and analyze existing material in preparation for the workshop, such as the information contained in the business data and process models, the elementary business processes and the business events that activate them, and the preliminary set of system transactions
  - Determine whether different categories of users will utilize the same graphical user interface, such as at a beginner, intermediate, or advanced level
  - If necessary, observe or interview each category of users to find out how they do their jobs
  - Prepare some presentation material for the workshop, such as visual aids
  - If possible, develop some basic user interface layouts of the proposed GUI, in accordance with the organization's own set of GUI design guidelines, application templates, or generic application GUI classes
  - Develop a proposed joint facilitated session agenda
  - Prior to the first day of the workshop, ensure that the room where the workshop will be conducted has the appropriate seating arrangements, office supplies, and audio-visual equipment and facilities

- Conduct the joint facilitated session
  - If necessary, familiarize the participants with the basic set of design standards and guidelines that must be adhered to across the enterprise while drafting the graphical user interface
  - Present the generic application GUI template(s) that will be used to draft the major application windows
  - Review each system transaction that the system must support, including the entities and attributes that are manipulated to successfully complete each transaction Regroup related transactions that have strong functional and data affinities.

- For each group of system transactions, perform the following tasks, with the active participation of the users:
  - Identify the information that needs to be displayed in a single window or series of dependent windows
  - Place the data elements in the window(s)
  - Regroup the data elements that have strong affinities
  - Identify and position the major window controls elements
  - Identify the major functional menu items
- Create a high-level diagram that depicts the basic navigation capabilities between the different application windows
  - If necessary, repeat the same graphical design process for all the application report and form layouts required to support the application
  - Wrap up the session and conclude the workshop
- Produce and issue the elementary GUI application deliverable

3.5 CONDUCT GRAPHICAL USER INTERFACE JOINT FACILITATED SESSION

This section covers the detailed steps involved in organizing and conducting a joint facilitated session to create the system graphical user interface.

3.5.1 INTRODUCTION

A joint facilitated workshop that focuses on the graphical user interface of a system can take a few hours for a very simple application. On the other end, a workshop that can easily last several days might be required to design a sound graphical user interface for a large-scale application system.

Also, keep in mind that for small or medium-sized systems, you might consider combining the preliminary design of the graphical user interface with the construction of a fully functional prototype.

The initial design of the application graphical user interface is a very creative process. Nonetheless, to be truly successful, this creative process needs to be harnessed to some extent, if the organization wants to achieve a consistent look and feel for the corporate applications that are used across the enterprise. To this end, the joint facilitated session facilitator must be aware of the essential set of GUI design standards that the organization wants to enforce across the enterprise. If no standards exist in the organization, then the facilitator should propose some basic guidelines.

Moreover, the facilitator must have the technical skills and training necessary to successfully lead the users through the intricacies of developing graphical user interfaces that are based on sound and proven graphical design layout practices. If she does not, then the facilitator should work in close cooperation with someone who has practical experience in designing highly usable and efficient graphical user interfaces, with a proven tracked record.

During the entire graphical user interface design process, the attention of the facilitator must constantly focus on the users and how they want the system to help them to do their work. By all accounts, designing GUIs is a user-centered process.

Another major keyword when designing a graphical user interface is *iteration*. Do not expect perfection from the first round of design layouts. First concentrate the initial design efforts on the information content of each window as opposed to the cosmetic aspects. Discussions on the use of colors, fonts, accelerators, windows size/placement, and toolbars should not be allowed at this early stage of the GUI design process. Do not worry; the final look and feel of the windows will be refined later on, during prototyping. Even though the GUI design process begins with some analysis work, it should quickly move into an interactive design session with the workshop participants. Users provide some immediate feedback and then another iteration cycle starts. As a rule of thumb, Figure 3-17 shows a breakdown of the percentage of time that should be spent on various GUI-related design tasks.

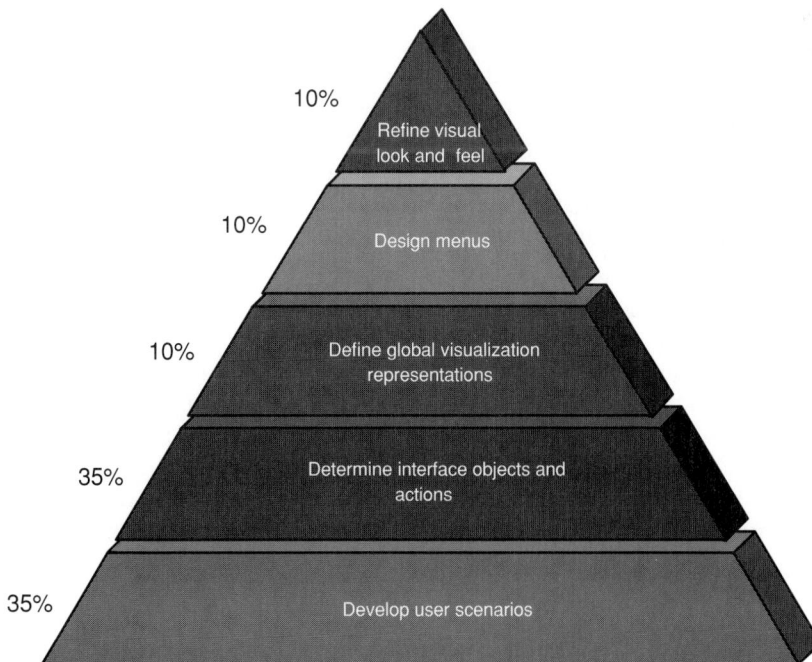

Figure 3–17 Breakdown of GUI design tasks in percentages.

3.5.2   GATHERING THE INITIAL REQUIREMENTS FOR THE GUI JOINT FACILITATED SESSION

The first step in the GUI design process consists of gathering the basic set of user requirements that will help to facilitate the process of designing the initial layouts of the GUI screens. This step can be successfully done in different ways, such as those indicated in Table 3-38.

Table 3–38 List Of Preparatory Tasks For Conducting A GUI Joint Facilitated Session

- Review the process and data business models and their supporting documents
- Interview the different categories of users who will utilize the application graphical interface
- Perform some direct observation of how the users currently perform their tasks
- Perform the actual user tasks themselves for a short period of time

You need to concentrate your initial efforts on the high-level graphical layout requirements as your first attempt. As the GUI design process unfolds, the detailed GUI requirements will surface quickly enough.

3.5.3   UNDERSTANDING WHO THE USERS ARE

You cannot develop for the users the best possible graphical interface that will truly give them what they really need, without understanding first who they are and what they do. This means doing some preliminary field research as to what are the users' current capabilities and skills are, as well as developing a basic understanding of what the main tasks are that they routinely perform on a daily basis. Table 3-39 shows some of the basic questions that should be answered about the types of users who will interact with the system graphical interface.[1]

3.5.4   TOOLS OF THE TRADE FOR GUI DESIGN

Different categories of tools can be used during the GUI joint facilitated session. For example, rapid application development (RAD) tools can be advantageously used to design the GUI interface interactively with the users. Properly used, these tools can facilitate and enforce some standardized interface design. They can be a good approach as long as the individual who uses the RAD tool is mastering perfectly well all the features provided by that tool to visually construct a graphical user interface. Also, using a generic GUI application template as a starting point for constructing the major graphical user interface elements helps tremendously.

---

1.   Chapter 12 provides more information on graphical user interfaces concepts and user profiles.

Table 3–39 Elementary User Profile

- What are the different categories of users who will utilize the system?
- What are their skills?
- What is their level of experience?
- What type of work do they do?
- What are their job responsibilities?
- What are the major tasks they perform routinely? Occasionally?
- What type of information and common business objects do they use while performing their tasks?
- What are the objectives they are trying to achieve while performing their tasks?
- What are the business problems they are trying to solve?
- What kind of technology are they using or is familiar to them?
- What are the physical characteristics of the work environment in which they will use the interface?
- What language(s) do the users use at work?

However, some facilitators prefer to kick off the interface design process with hand-drawn paper versions of the interface. In such a case, they use standard flip charts, whiteboards, transparencies, or storyboards to quickly draw preliminary sketches of the major groups of data elements that should be displayed on the GUI layout. Once the basic groups of data elements are disposed roughly on a transparency sheet, for example, a more fancy visual layout is then created with the use of a powerful RAD tool.

Figure 3-18 illustrates a very basic sketch of an individual screen layout that was quickly created on a transparency and that can subsequently be transposed on a real window screen with the use of a RAD client-server tool. From there, the graphical screen layout can be gradually refined through some iterative prototyping sessions with the users.

3.5.5 OBJECT-ORIENTED USER INTERFACES VERSUS GRAPHICAL USER INTERFACES

As the industry gradually transitions from standard application GUI interfaces toward more object-oriented user interfaces, additional tools can be used to help the GUI designers to deal more easily with various objects that are displayed on the screen. Table 3-40 provides a list of some of the major characteristics that are associated with an object-oriented graphical user interface.

Figure 3-19 illustrates how objects are manipulated when they gradually evolve from a graphical-oriented interface to a more object-oriented interface.

In an object-oriented interface, a drag-and-drop operation is usually performed when the user selects an object on the interface and then manipulates it to achieve some results. One of the best examples to illustrate this point is a user who selects a document and drags it to a printer icon. Then the system automatically prints the doc-

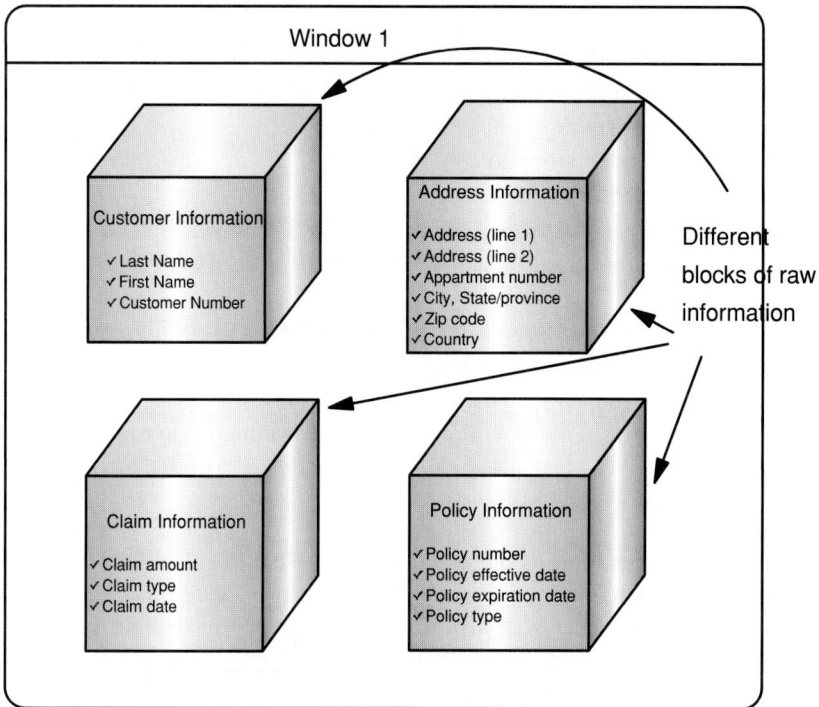

Figure 3–18 Basic sketch of a screen layout.

Table 3–40 Object-oriented User Interface Characteristics

• The interface is composed of a collection of cooperating objects instead of the regular applications and data files that are shown in a traditional GUI • Users work with objects instead of applications • Objects are represented by real-world metaphors and models • The interface is more data-centric than application-centric

ument. A similar process could be repeated with another real-life metaphor such as an icon that shows a picture of a fax machine. As soon as the user drags a document to this fax icon, the system brings up the fax module along with the document that needs to be faxed. One example of a simple tool that can be used to help design interfaces that are more object-oriented is the object manipulation matrix shown in Figure 3-20.

The various objects that are used in the interface are displayed on both the left and top sides of the matrix. Then the objects shown on the left side of the matrix are carefully analyzed, one at a time, to see whether they can be dragged and dropped into any of the objects that are shown in the top portion of the matrix.

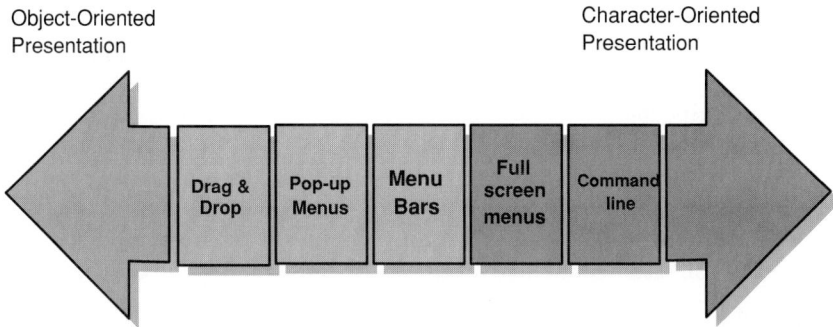

Figure 3–19 Object-oriented versus character-oriented presentations.

	Destination Object				
	Printer Icon	...	...	Fax Icon	...
Source Object					
Customer list	X			X	
Customer					

Figure 3–20 Object manipulation matrix.

The use of object-oriented interfaces is far more intuitive and easier to use than traditional graphical user interfaces, since the users rely on metaphors that simulate the real world, such as desktop, printers, faxes, spreadsheets, mailbox, and in-baskets objects, to perform their business-oriented tasks.

3.5.6 DEVELOPING USER SCENARIOS

If a large number of different groups of users will use the same graphical user interface, then a useful approach might be to develop a series of user scenarios to identify the work patterns of each group and use this information to develop a more flexible graphical user interface. Table 3-41 provides a definition of a user scenario.

User scenarios can be developed for each critical online system transaction. The following text provides an example where the same user performs two different user scenarios.

Table 3–41 User Scenario

> A user scenario is a sequence of basic operations that a user must perform to initiate and successfully complete a system transaction. Each specific operation within a user scenario starts with a specific user action that will trigger a response from the computer system. User scenarios are real-life cases that describe how the users work in their environment.

First, I start with a short profile of a purely fictitious company. The organization is a world leader manufacturer of jet turbine engines. The after-sale "Parts Support" division has 100 sales representatives who perform the following two functions:

- provide various types of information to customers who inquire about various engine parts
- process customer orders for engine parts

You decide, as the person who is responsible for assisting the users in developing the graphical user interface, to interview one of the users. You quickly come up with the following observations as you interview Amelia, one of the most knowledgeable salespeople in the Parts Support organization:

- Amelia uses different objects as she provides information on the engines' parts to her current and potential customers and also as she processes the different customers' orders for various engine parts, such as:
  - Parts inventory list, customer list, parts description catalog, order forms
  - Telephone, fax machine, office calculator, brochures

Amelia eventually uses all the business objects described above when she performs her business activities. However, she does not always use them all at once every time she deals with a customer. Whether or not she uses these objects is based on the tasks and situation at hand, as determined by her customers' requests and her own way of organizing her methods of work.

Now you're ready to start with the two user scenarios:

User Scenario 1:

A potential customer contacts Amelia to get information on an engine compressor. Amelia performs the following tasks:

- She verifies the parts catalog object
- She verifies the prices by consulting the price list object
- She provides the required information to the potential customer
- She offers to send to the customer the latest brochure on the company's latest family of engine compressors

User Scenario 2:

An existing customer contacts Amelia to order an engine part. Amelia performs the following tasks:

- She verifies the inventory list object

- She verifies the price list object

- She verifies the customer's credit line status

- She takes the customer order

Then:

- She verifies the closest warehouse location that has the requested engine part in stock

- She allocates that part to the customer

- She sends to the customer a confirmation letter for the order

As you have just seen, despite the similarities in both scenarios, Amelia did perform her tasks in a slightly different sequence of events. However, she was in control of the situation all the time, manipulating the different business objects she needs to perform her work in a manner she feels comfortable with and that optimizes her personal work methods.

The different users scenarios you have just seen should be taken into consideration by the system designers to provide Amelia with a graphical user interface that is flexible and efficiently supports the way she does her job under different working situations.

3.5.7 GUI DESIGN AND THE 80/20 RULE

When designing the graphical user interface interactively with the users, the joint session facilitator may want to observe the 80/20 Pareto's rule, as described in Table 3-42.

Table 3–42 Pareto's Rule Applied To Joint Facilitated Gui Design Session

Eighty percent of the user population will use twenty percent of the features implemented in the graphical user interface.

In simple terms, this rule means that the facilitator should spend a considerable amount of time during the joint session to design, with the active participation of the users, the most important features that will be used by eighty percent of them. Conversely, less time should be allocated during the facilitated session to attempt to design the intricate features that will be used by only twenty percent of them.

The facilitator should identify and prioritize with the users those important features that will be used regularly by the vast majority of them. The less frequently used features could be designed off-line and then reviewed with a selective group of users to get constructive feedback on their usability.

Activity number:	AN-5
Activity name:	Construct graphical user interface prototype
Purpose:	Develop a high-level prototype of the graphical user interface for the system
Inputs:	AN-T1 Business process model AN-T2 Business data model AN-T3 System transactions AN-T4 System graphical user interface
Outputs:	AN-T5 System graphical user interface prototype

Activity description:	• Plan the prototyping process
	  – Determine the initial application prototyping scope, objectives, and deliverables
	  – Determine any particular constraints and assumptions
	  – Determine the different categories of users groups that will actively participate in the prototyping sessions
	  – Discuss with some key users the number of iterations that will be performed during the prototyping process
	  – For each level of iteration agreed to, clearly identify the set of deliverables that will be prototyped, along with a brief description of the expected level of detail upon which each major deliverable will be demonstrated
	  – Outline, in a high-level plan, the major milestones that reflect the number of prototyping iterations that was agreed with the users and the rigid prototyping timeboxes allocated to each of them
	• Prepare the prototyping process and development environment
	  – Review the set of deliverables that are inputs to the prototyping exercise, including:
	    – Business process model
	      – High-level and intermediate-level business processes
	      – Elementary business processes
	      – External events, internal events, temporal events, and their associated triggers
	      – System transactions
	      – User scenarios
	      – Preliminary layouts of the graphical user interface screens
	    – Business data model
	      – Data entities
	      – Data relationships
	      – Data attributes
	      – Business rules
	• Set up the proper prototyping development environment
	  – Determine whether the prototype will be performed locally on a workstation or whether the prototype will access the database server via the network

- Install and test the proper tools in the development environment, if not already done, including:
  - RAD or Web development tools
  - Pre-established GUI application templates and classes
  - Database server with the preliminary application test data required to exercise the prototype
  - The software middleware required to access the database server, such as Open Data Base Connectivity (ODBC) drivers or native database Application Programming Iinterfaces (APIs). If the prototype will access data that resides on the mainframe from either a client-server or Web-based platform, then another class of middleware will be required, commonly named database gateways
  - Ensure the client workstation is properly set up with the proper hardware/ software/networking configuration
- Construct the application windows prototype
- Review all the source material that has been gathered so far for the required application
- Identify the major windows required to support the system transactions
- Using a set of pre-established application windows templates or classes, quickly create an initial layout of the major data windows that are required to support the application
  - Elementary data window screen layouts
    - Identify the different data groups and elements that must be displayed on each specific window and place them on the window based on their affinities
    - Identify the data controls that must be displayed on the window and place them on the window
  - Elementary navigational window controls
    - Determine how the users will navigate from one window to another, based on business dependencies and different user scenarios
    - Develop the elementary procedural logic required to navigate among the different windows that are related to one another
  - Elementary menu controls
    - Determine the various application functions that require menu item(s)
    - Create the menus classes and menu items
  - Test and verify the prototype
- Conduct an active prototyping session with the users
  - Prepare for the prototype review with the users
  - Demonstrate the prototype to the users
  - Discuss user feedback
  - Document requested changes and enhancements
- Repeat the prototyping cycle for the agreed number of prototype iterations
- Produce and issue the final application prototype document

3.6 CONSTRUCT THE GRAPHICAL USER INTERFACE PROTOTYPE

This section discusses the GUI prototyping process and its detailed steps. It also provides useful guidelines to help manage and control the prototyping process.

3.6.1 PROTOTYPING OBJECTIVES

With this activity, the complete graphical user interface, or some selective component, is prototyped with the active participation of the users.

The construction of the application prototype considerably minimizes the risk of delivering to the users a system that does not meet their needs. This dynamic visual modeling process is achieved by providing the users with visual feedback on how they can interact with the system. The prototype allows the users to verify firsthand the major components of the graphical interface, including the functionality provided in each system window and the overall level of navigability among all windows. The prototyping approach is far better than providing the users with a set of paper specifications in an abstract form that they do not always understand completely. In fact, the formulation of accurate and stable requirements cannot be completed until the users gain some practical experience with the proposed system's interface.

3.6.2 PROTOTYPING BENEFITS AND CHALLENGES

Table 3-43 lists some of the most common benefits and challenges that the developers might face with the use of prototyping.

Table 3–43 Prototyping Advantages Versus Potential Pitfalls

ADVANTAGES	ISSUES
• Increase user participation • Increase user ownership and commitment • Improve communication between the developers and the users • Reduce risk of not satisfying user needs • Provide the users with hands-on experience with a real-life graphical user interface • Help clarify and validate visual requirements reasonably early in the development cycle • Increase the level of usability of the graphical user interface	• Users want to make the prototype the production system immediately • Users keep requesting added functionality that was not in the original project scope • The completed application system is hard to maintain because the prototyping approach was done in an ad hoc manner • Users minimize the amount of time required to actively participate in the prototyping exercise and provide constructive feedback

Well planned and executed prototyping projects provide far more benefits than issues, especially when the developers properly manage the users' expectations and develop a professional relationship with the users. The developers should adopt a structured yet flexible approach to prototyping. In today's age of highly visual application development tools, producing a live prototype of the user interface as early as possible is paramount.

3.6.3   PROTOTYPING DEFINITION

Table 3-44 provides a definition of prototyping.

Table 3–44 Prototyping Definition

Prototyping consists of the construction, in context, of a working model of a system, in a short period of time. This model is generally quickly developed, but can be either thrown away once the system requirements are well understood or gradually expanded to evolve eventually into a full-blown operational system.

Simply stated, the prototype is nothing more than a live model of a system that emphasizes the graphical user interfaces. This model is built for experimentation purposes, for gaining valuable information on the users' needs, and for obtaining a positive confirmation of the initial system requirements.

A generic view of the prototyping process appears in Figure 3-21.

3.6.4   HOW TO CONTROL THE PROTOTYPING PROCESS

The prototyping process is highly intensive in terms of resource utilization. It is done usually in a series of short time intervals. To avoid creeping functionality problems, the number of iterations that will be used to construct the prototype must be well understood in advance by all user participants. Table 3-45 suggests some of the best practices that can be used to better control the prototyping process, using a timeboxing technique.

With the timeboxing development technique, the timetable that the users agree on to deliver a given product at the end of a particular prototyping iteration is critical and cannot be altered. If necessary, scoping or staffing adjustments must be made instead of changing the original product delivery timetable.

3.6.5   DIFFERENT TYPES OF PROTOTYPES FOR DIFFERENT PURPOSES

Several types of prototypes exist. Four of the most common ones are briefly described in Table 3-46.

As you should have guessed by now, functional or evolutionary prototyping is the technique that I primarily describe in this book. This technique is very powerful for fleshing out any missing application requirements and solidify the existing ones.

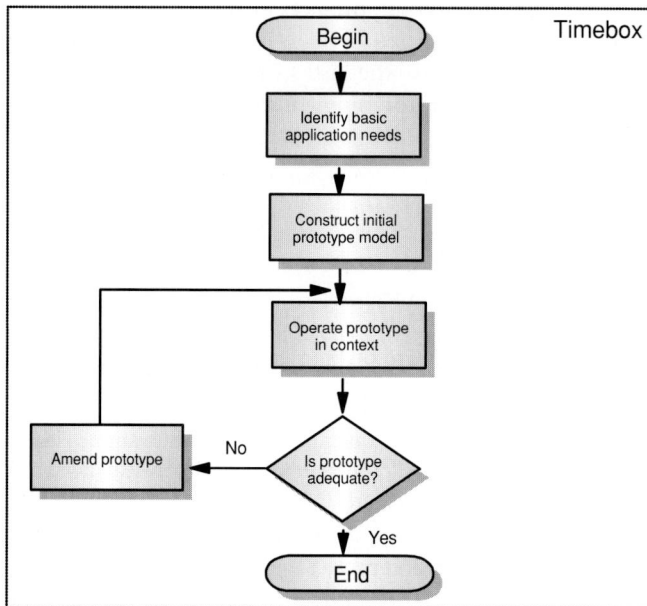

Figure 3–21 Generic view of the prototyping process.

Table 3–45 How To Control The Prototyping Process

- Elaborate a high-level timetable to construct the prototype and adhere to it. Get an agreement with the users on:
  - The overall duration of the entire prototyping exercise
  - The number of iterations allowed
  - The elapsed time between each distinct iteration
  - The system functions that will be prototyped within each specific iteration
  - The types of deliverables that will be produced and level of details they will contain
- Develop a contractual agreement with the users on:
  - How user feedback will be provided
  - How much time the users are willing to provide during the entire prototyping exercise
  - How the requests for added functionality that fall outside the scope of the prototyping exercise will be handled
  - How the user enhancements will be prioritized
- Make sure you keep a backup of the prototyping results that are produced with each iteration

However, feasibility prototyping can be used to technically evaluate and test different technology architectures and configurations. On the other hand, the throwaway

Table 3–46 Different Types Of Prototypes

PROTOTYPING TYPE	DESCRIPTION
Functional	With functional or evolutionary prototyping, a working model of the application windows, frames, menus, reports, and forms is created with the active participation of the users. Typically, the working model is constructed in three iterations. The prototype can gradually evolve into a fully functional system, since the system data is usually retrieved from the database server.
Feasibility	With feasibility or technology prototyping, a live model is created to verify a client-server or Web architecture configuration. Some of the most common components that are tested usually include: • Performance and scalability of both clients and servers • Components compatibility and connectivity • Different configuration schemes • Cost justification of the different solutions This type of prototyping is usually less visual than functional or evolutionary prototyping.
Throwaway	With throwaway prototyping, the final results of the prototype are discarded, and the application system is developed with a different tool from the one that was used to build the prototype.
External prototype	With external prototyping, the graphical user interface is constructed with the users. The emphasis, though, is primarily on the basic layouts of the windows and the navigation between them. The detailed functional aspects of the system are not prototyped, and the system might not access real data that is stored in the backend databases.

prototyping technique can sometimes be useful particularly in situations where the RAD tool that will be utilized to code the application is not yet selected. Finally, an external prototype can be developed with a RAD tool or with a simple pen-and-paper approach, if the system is not too complex.

3.6.6 TECHNOLOGY CONSIDERATIONS

The application can be prototyped on a single workstation where the graphical user interface, application logic, and database server all reside in the same physical location. On the other hand, a large application can be prototyped in a milieu that more closely mirrors the future production environment.

In such a case, the user interface and some of the application logic will reside on the client workstation while the database will be located on a separate server machine. This type of prototype usually leads to a more precise approximation of the type of performance that the users should expect once the full-blown system is transferred in a real-life production environment. Core stored procedures and remote procedures can also be more realistically prototyped in this type of pseudo-production environment. This approach can be especially useful in situations where the future production system will contain several database stored procedures and remote procedures.

If the application prototype will use data to demonstrate more functionality than just a physical layout of the windows, then a preliminary database must be quickly constructed to support the prototyping effort. Once the preliminary database structure is constructed, it is then quickly populated with some meaningful test data with which the users are familiar. You need to use real-life data so the interface prototype looks real to the users.

Activity number:	AN-6
Activity name:	Define initial system distribution strategy
Purpose:	Define the data and process distribution strategy that will be adopted to support the application data and process requirements
Inputs:	AN-T1 Business process model AN-T2 Business data model AN-T3 System transactions AN-T5 System graphical user interface prototype
Outputs:	AN-T6 Initial system distribution strategy

Activity description:	• Review the business data and process models
	• Construct the following data and process association matrices:
	  – System transactions/location matrix
	  – Data entity/location matrix
	  – Data entity/volume matrix
	• Analyze the application requirements to distribute the data and system transactions at different geographical locations
	• Document where the data and system transactions will be distributed and the business rationale for these decisions
	• Verify that the current hardware/software/networking technology architecture can support the application needs for distribution, based on estimated data and transaction processing volumes
	• Walk through the data and system transactions distribution strategy deliverables

3.7 DEFINE THE INITIAL SYSTEM DISTRIBUTION STRATEGY

This section discusses the major steps involved in creating an initial system distribution strategy. It also provides tips on how to execute that process.

3.7.1 INTRODUCTION

In a distributed application environment, the system transactions and their supportive data might be used in different geographical locations. The decision to distribute the system transactions and associated data across different physical sites is usually formulated based on a variety of business and technical factors such as those indicated in Table 3-47.

Table 3–47 Factors Influencing Data And Process Distribution Decisions

- The different geographical locations where the business transactions must be performed and which type of data needs to be shared across the enterprise or remain local
- The organizational structure of the enterprise, which can range from a very centralized to a very decentralized organizational scheme
- The necessity to optimize the overall application system resources and maximize data access performance
- The business need to minimize the impact of a system failure at a single site, as opposed to a more lenient multi-site, distributed software architecture
- The necessity to work around some potential hardware limitations, such as limited capacity data storage devices

Ultimately, the technology complexities that might be involved in setting up and maintaining a complex distributed data and process application environment should always be carefully weighted against the anticipated benefits. To better illustrate this point, Table 3-48 summarizes some of the benefits and potential disadvantages that might be associated with an application environment that supports distributed data.

However, keep in mind that application data allocation design solutions will most likely influence the process allocation design solutions. The reverse statement is also true: process allocation design solutions will influence the application data allocation design solutions.

3.7.2 DISTRIBUTED DATA AND PROCESS ANALYSIS

This section discusses the basic analytical steps that should be performed by the development team to help determine the requirements for distributing the application system transactions and data against different geographical sites, along with a brief description of the tools that support this process.

Table 3–48 Data Distribution

ADVANTAGES	DISADVANTAGES
• More business autonomy for the users at local sites • Better control of local data • Distributed system that is less vulnerable to failure than a unique central site • Reduced network communication overhead and improved system performance because the data is processed locally	• More complex backup and recovery processes because the data is dispersed in different locations and must be synchronized • More difficulty physically securing the distributed database environment, which is spread in different geographical locations • More difficulty maintaining data consistency, integrity, and accuracy

The system distribution analysis process is highly iterative in nature. Hence, the initial system distribution strategy is developed during the analysis phase but will be revisited and refined during the design phase.

STEP 1: Develop data and process distribution matrices
The first step in assessing the potential distribution requirements of the application consists of developing different types of matrices that are used to map the data and system transactions against the different locations where they might be used. Once these data and system transaction usage matrices are constructed, they are then used to analyze the distribution requirements and characteristics of the application at hand.

At least three basic types of usage matrices can be constructed to analyze the potential application data and system transaction distribution ramifications, as listed in Table 3-49.

Table 3–49 Three Different Types Of Data And System Transaction Usage Matrices

• System transaction versus location association matrix • Data entity versus location association matrix • Data entity/volume association matrix

Following is a brief description of each type of usage matrix that appears in Table 3-49, along with some basic guidelines on how to create each of them.

System Transaction/Location Matrix
The system transaction/location matrix is used to map the application system transactions against the different geographical sites where they might be executed. The system transactions are shown along the vertical axis of the matrix. The geographical location(s) where these system transactions are performed is(are) then mapped along the horizontal axis of the matrix.

Inside each relevant cells of the matrix, an estimate of the number of transactions performed per unit of time is indicated for each system transaction, against the appropriate geographical locations. If critical, peak volumes can also be indicated in the matrix cells. Figure 3-22 shows a sample of a system transaction/location matrix.

System Transactions \ Geographical Locations	Site 1	Site 2	...	...	Site n
System Transaction 1	1,000/Day	1,000/Day			
System Transaction 2	1,000/Hour				
...					
System Transaction n					

Figure 3–22 System transaction/location usage matrix.

If necessary, the different categories of users that execute the system transactions at each specific geographical location can also be shown in the matrix, as indicated in Figure 3-23.

System Transactions \ Geographical Locations	Site 1			Site 2	...	...	Site n
	Dept A	Dept B	Dept C				
System Transaction 1							
System Transaction 2		50/D					
...							
System Transaction n							

Figure 3–23 System transaction/location usage matrix with different user categories.

Another variation might consist in showing, besides the frequency estimates, the growth percentage per unit of time, such as per year for instance. Such a matrix is shown in Figure 3-24.

Geographical Locations / System Transactions	Site 1 F	Site 1 G	Site 2 F	Site 2 G	...	...	Site n F	Site n G
System Transaction 1								
System Transaction 2	5000/D	45%						
...								
System Transaction n								

F=Frequency G=Growth % per year

Figure 3–24 System transaction/location usage matrix with frequency/growth estimates per site.

Data Entity/Location Matrix

The data entity/location matrix is used to map the major entities that are processed by the application against the different geographical locations where they are used. The entities appear along the vertical axis of the matrix. The locations where these entities are used are indicated along the top horizontal axis of the matrix.

Inside each relevant cell of the matrix, four different one-letter codes can be shown. Each one-letter code is used to indicate a different type of operation that can be performed against a particular entity, at a given location. The different code values that indicate the type of transaction operations that can be executed are:

C= Create
R= Read
U= Update
D= Delete

Figure 3-25 shows a sample of a data entity-to-location association matrix.

More specifically, the data entity-to-location association matrix is used to identify the locations where a particular data entity can be created, read, deleted, or updated.

The data entity-to-location association matrix, as well as the two other matrices discussed in this section, are just different tools that can help the developers to better assess the potential ways in which they can distribute the application data and system transactions.

Entity \ Geographical Location	Site 1	Site 2	...	...	Site n
Entity 1	CU	R			R
Entity 2	CU	R			U
...					
Entity n	CU	U			D

C=Create
R=Read
U=Update
D=Delete

Figure 3–25 Entity/location usage matrix.

The content of these association matrices gradually evolves as the business application requirements for distribution progressively unfold during the analysis phase. The matrices will also be revisited during the design phase. Similarly, the development team can adapt and modify the format and look and feel of these usage matrices to better suit their specific needs. The developers can also construct new types of matrices to analyze different types of associations between different system objects.

Data Entity/Volume Matrix

The data entity/volume matrix maps the major entities that are processed within the application against the different locations where they are used, along with some volume estimates. The entities appear along the left axis of the matrix. The locations where these entities are used are indicated along the top horizontal axis of the matrix.

Inside each relevant cell of the matrix, an estimate of the number of entity occurrences is indicated for each specific location, along with their projected growth estimates over a given period of time.

This type of matrix can be used to assess, very early on, the database server-sizing requirements of the application, based on the projected volumes of data that need to be stored in each specific geographical location.

Figure 3-26 shows a sample of a data entity-to-volume association matrix.

STEP 2: Analyze in detail the data and process allocation

Once all the different data and system transactions allocation matrices are completed, the information that is mapped in these matrices is then carefully analyzed to decide

Entity \ Geographical Location	Site 1 V	Site 1 G	Site 2 V	Site 2 G	...	...	Site N V	Site N G
Entity 1	40	20	66	35			73	40
Entity 2	15	5	30	10			15	40
...								
Entity n								

V=Volume in 1000s
G=Growth % per year

Figure 3–26 Data entity-to-volume association matrix.

what data and system transactions should be distributed and at which geographical location.

This investigation process evolves as additional functional, performance, or technology constraint factors might gradually surface throughout the analysis phase. At this stage, the preliminary data and system transactions distribution allocation strategy should be done independently of the type of technology that will be used to support the system. It is a logical view of the distributed data and process alternatives.

Table 3-50 provides a set of fundamental questions that can be used by the developers to help determine what might be the basic application requirements for distributed data (i.e., will the data be stored at a central location, replicated at certain sites, or fragmented across different sites?).

Table 3-51 provides some basic guidelines that can assist the developers when the time comes to decide how the allocation of data should be performed, from a geographical standpoint.

As an additional rule of thumb, the application data can be distributed when several sites must use it and when at least one of the following conditions is satisfied:

- The data is used locally at a specific site and does not need to be shared with other sites
- The data is not updated frequently
- The stringent response time requirements that were stated for the application dictate the need to allocate the data as close as possible to the different sites where the data will be accessed

Table 3–50 Data Distribution Strategy Questionnaire

- What type of data is used by the application?
- Who utilizes the data and where? At which sites? Is some data used locally at a given site and unique to that site? Does data need to be shared across several sites?
- Who owns the data? Who controls the data?
- Who is allowed to read the data?
- Who is allowed to update the data?
- Who is allowed to create the data?
- How is the data accessed and when?
- What are the volumes of data involved in the distribution process?
- If a master data set and duplicate copies of that master data set are required:
  - Where will the master data set file reside?
  - Where will the copies of the master data set file reside?
  - How will updates to the master data be propagated to the other copies of that master data set?

Table 3–51 Data Distribution Guidelines

- Always try to maintain the data near the site where it is utilized the most frequently
- If the data is read and updated at a unique site (i.e., location-specific), then allocate the data to that specific site.
- If the data is read by several sites but updated only at a single site, then allocate the master file to the site where the transaction updates occur. The sites that only read the data might be provided with replicated copies of the master file, if deemed necessary.
- If the data is updated at several sites but you cannot fragment* it in a rational manner, then allocate the data to a central site.
- If the data is updated at several sites but can be fragmented* in a rational manner, then fragment the data and allocate each distinct data fragment to the appropriate site(s).
  - * **Fragmentation**: Segmentation of a database into separate physical tables that can be implemented at different physical sites

You also need to determine the frequency at which the data copies should be refreshed from the master data set, based on the application business needs.

STEP 3: Assess data and process distribution technology

Once the logical view of the data and system transaction distribution strategy is completed, its technical feasibility must then be verified against the hardware/software/networking technology architecture that will be required to support it.

Some of the basic technology architecture questions that must be assessed in light of the new distributed application are shown in Table 3-52.

Table 3–52 Distributed Technology Assessment

Hardware	• Can the current servers accommodate the projected application data storage requirements? • Can the current servers support the application processing needs in terms of the expected number of CPU and I/O cycles? • Can the current hardware equipment support the data processing loads that will be generated by the new application?
Software	• Can the current DBMS and operating system architecture support the distributed requirements of the application? • Does a need exist to access legacy data from the mainframe? If so, will the current client-server database gateway provide access to these mainframe database and files? Do you have other alternatives to accessing the mainframe data from the client-server platform?
Networking	• Will the current network infrastructure be able to accommodate the additional volumes of data traffic that will be generated by the new application at the central site, at the remote sites, and between the central and remote sites? • Can the network support the volume of traffic generated by the application users when they will access the master data from different locations? • Will the network be able to effectively support the projected volumes of data traffic, including the expected peaks? • Can the transaction response times needed by the application be satisfied without the need to replicate data?

3.7.3   CONCLUSION

To conclude, the data and process distribution strategy of a very large and complex client-server system might benefit from the construction of a live prototype, via a small pilot project, to verify its technical feasibility and assess potential issues.

During the design phase, the different techniques that are available to distribute the data will be investigated in more detail, along with their unique challenges, such as different types of data replication techniques that can be used to disseminate the data at different locations, the need for synchronizing the data, the backup/recovery issues that a distributed database environment raises, and so forth.

Finally, I provide a discussion on the optimal placement of the application processing logic in the context of a client-server 2-tier or 3-tier architecture in Chapter 9, Section 9.2.3, entitled "Placement of business processes and data". As you will see in Section 9.2.3, the client-server technology enables different application-processing components to be distributed on the client workstations, application servers, or database servers.

Activity number:	AN-7
Activity name:	Define the system interface requirements
Purpose:	To document the high-level interfaces required between the new system and existing systems
Inputs:	AN-T1 Business process model AN-T2 Business data model AN-T3 System transactions SU-T3 System context diagram
Outputs:	AN-T7 System interface requirements
Activity description:	• Review the system context diagram deliverable along with information contained in the business data and process models • Identify all the major data streams that flow into and out of the new system • Document the system data interface requirements for each of the existing systems that requires an interface with the new system • Walk through the system interface requirement deliverables

3.8 DEFINE THE SYSTEM INTERFACE REQUIREMENTS

In this activity, the interfaces that must be set up between the new system and other existing systems are identified and documented to a level of detail where all the functional and data interfaces requirements are well understood. The major characteristics of each required interface should be documented as per the information indicated in Table 3-53.

Activity number:	AN-8
Activity name:	Define the system security and control requirements
Purpose:	To identify and document the security and control requirements of the system
Inputs:	AN-T1 Business process model AN-T2 Business data model AN-T3 System transactions AN-T5 System graphical user interface prototype AN-T6 Initial system distribution strategy AN-T7 System interface requirements

Outputs:	AN-T8 System security and control requirements

Activity description:	• Identify the application system security and control requirements, covering the following items:
	 – Security
	     – Physical
	     – Operating system
	     – Application
	     – Network
	     – Database
	 – Integrity
	 – Audibility
	 – Disaster Recovery
	 • Document the system security and control requirements. Describe, where applicable, the extent to which each of the security and control requirements should be applied across the entire application or only to some distinct components.
	 • Walk through the system security and control requirements deliverable

Table 3–53 System Interface Requirements Documentation

- Name of the interface
- Brief description of the interface and how it should operate
  - Purpose
  - Type (i.e., input or output)
  - Frequency
  - Interface method (online, batch, at specific time intervals, on-demand)
  - Criticality
    - High (i.e., If a problem occurs, it must be resolved immediately)
    - Medium (i.e., If a problem occurs, the new system can still be used without loss of integrity. The problem should be fixed within the next working day.)
    - Low (i.e., If a problem occurs, the new system can still run without any loss of integrity. The problem should be fixed within the next two or three working days.)
- Geographical location of the system interface
- Identification of the type of database or flat files involved, along with volume estimates
- Identification of the information that needs to be exchanged between the current system and the new system
  - Identification of each logical group of data elements that are involved in the interface.
- Description of any dependencies with other systems or data interfaces
- Specific considerations, if any (i.e., technical assumptions, etc.)

3.9 DEFINE THE SYSTEM SECURITY AND CONTROL REQUIREMENTS

This section discusses a variety of security and control requirements that require careful planning when developing a large and complex business system.

3.9.1 INTRODUCTION

The security and control requirements of the system are identified with the users. These include the security, audibility, integrity, and disaster recovery requirements. If the organization has already established different corporate standards on the control, audit, security, and disaster recovery subjects, then this set of standard policies and guidelines should be investigated with the users to ensure that the new client-server or web database system complies with them. The identification of the system security and control requirements should apply to both the manual and automated processes of the system.

3.9.2 SECURITY

This sub-section describes the detailed steps involved in identifying and documenting the system security requirements. It also describes some basic concepts and terminology related to security in an Internet environment.

DETERMINING THE APPLICATION SECURITY NEEDS

The security requirements of the application should be carefully analyzed with the users. Today's corporate enterprises have complex and diversified networks that connect to several sites over large geographical boundaries. The security techniques and procedures must also be adapted to quickly evolving technologies such as complex Internet/intranet/extranet environments.

However, technology by itself cannot overcome a lack of adequate corporate security policies and practices. In parallel to the implementation of technologies that can help to secure corporate information, the organization must implement proper corporate security policies, services, and procedures.

The following section provides a set of basic procedural steps and guidelines that will help the development team to define the critical security requirements of the system.

STEP 1: Identify and classify the application data types
The first step consists of identifying the major categories of data that the application will have to manipulate and assess their respective level of sensitivity.

Some of the most basic questions that the developers and the users must ask themselves to determine whether a need exists to protect the information that the application will manipulate are listed in Table 3-54.

Table 3–54 Basic Questions To Determine Security Needs

- What type of information must be manipulated by the application?
- Are specific segments of information highly sensitive?
- Would the absence of security controls increase the likelihood of losing money, losing a competitive edge, or the disclosure of valuable information to the competition?
- Does the company have legal or contractual obligations that must be fulfilled to protect access to specific information such as financial data?
- Does the company have legal or contractual obligations that must be fulfilled to protect access to private information about individuals or organizations?
- What would be the consequences for the company to have proprietary information about products, suppliers, customers, or partners exposed to the view of outsiders? What about unsolicited access attempts by insiders?
- Where will the information be located? Centrally on a single database or Web server, or physically distributed across different locations?
- Do you have a need to secure information that is in transit (i.e., transmitted from one physical location to another via a private network or the Internet, for example)?

In an attempt to overcome potential information security exposures, several organizations have developed their own security guidelines in which the company's data are classified into different categories of information, each having a specific level of sensitivity directly proportional to its importance.

The different levels of sensitivity are often defined by different classifications such as: non-confidential, confidential, restricted, secret, or top-secret. Thus, the information that is vital to the proper functioning of the organization can be treated by the corporate business applications in accordance with the established information security classification levels.

STEP 2: Identify the different categories of users

Once the application data has been identified and classified in terms of security levels, the second step consists of identifying the different categories of internal or external users who will need access to the information and the types of security threats to which the system can be exposed. Why do different categories of users need to access this information and also what type of system access will they need (i.e., read, update, create, delete) to perform their business functions? You also need to ask yourself which category of people you need to protect the information from, those from inside or those from outside the organization?

STEP 3: Identify the required application security controls

The third step consists of determining the specific types of security controls that need to be implemented to restrict access to the application information, based on the identified security requirements and associated security threats. Finally, the value of the information assets and the cost of protecting them are assessed with the users. A realistic analysis of the situation helps to balance the security risks versus the cost factors involved with the implementation and enforcement of tighter security controls.

Figure 3-27 shows different types of potential security threats, and Figure 3-28 shows some of the problems these security threats might cause to an organization.

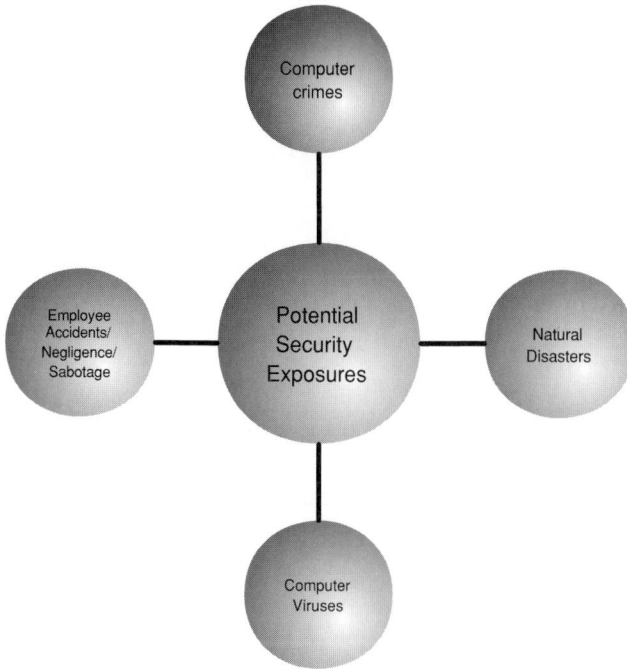

Figure 3–27 Potential security threats.

Finally, Figure 3-29 shows some of the different types of preventive measures that can be used to minimize different security risks.

UNDERSTANDING DIFFERENT TYPES OF SECURITY CONTROLS

Typically, the security controls are categorized as either physical or procedural. They generally cover five different dimensions of the system, as indicated in Figure 3-30.

The following sections briefly discuss each of the five security layers that you see in Figure 3-30.

Physical Security

This layer is the most basic layer of security. The protection of critical computer equipment is normally handled with various physical techniques, such as controlling physical access to sensitive computer areas, installing computer equipment in remote locations, and having emergency auxiliary power units to circumvent potential power

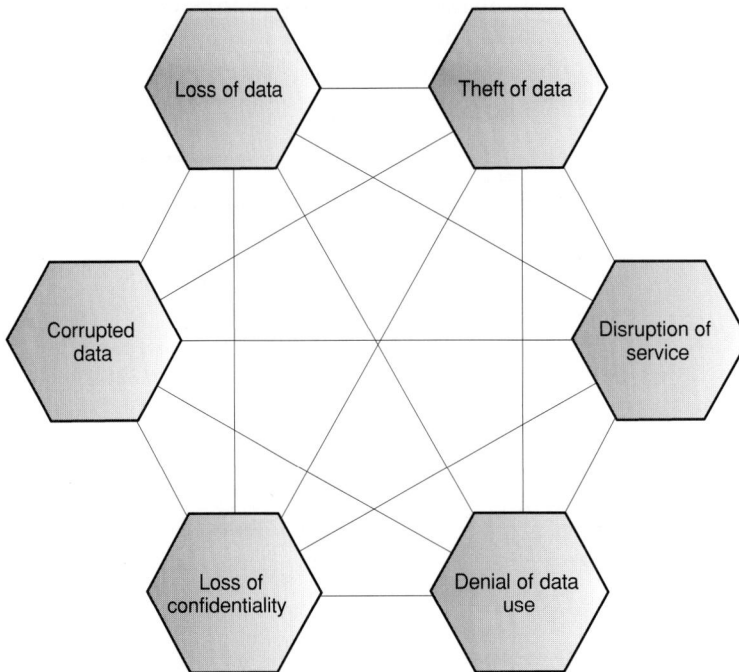

Figure 3–28 Impact of security breaches on organizations.

failures. The physical access to these secured areas is enforced with the use of human and/or electronic control mechanisms. Some of the essential hardware components that are usually secured in restricted areas include:

- Application or Web servers
- Database servers
- Networking equipment, such as routers, bridges, gateways, switches
- Physical data backup units

Besides controlling the physical accesses to critical hardware components, you also need to protect these hardware components against hazards. Hazards relate to unexpected events, such as fire, sabotage, riot, vandalism, and power failures, for instance.

Protecting your mission-critical systems against hazards is important. In one specific instance, a large organization installed its most sophisticated computer equipment in the basement of a building. The security measures that were put in place to control the physical accesses to this remote location were nothing else but impressive. State-of-the-art technology was used and nothing was neglected in terms of security features. They had security guards, magnetic cards to open doors, closed circuit TV monitors—the works. Unfortunately, a very simple point was overlooked by everyone—it was

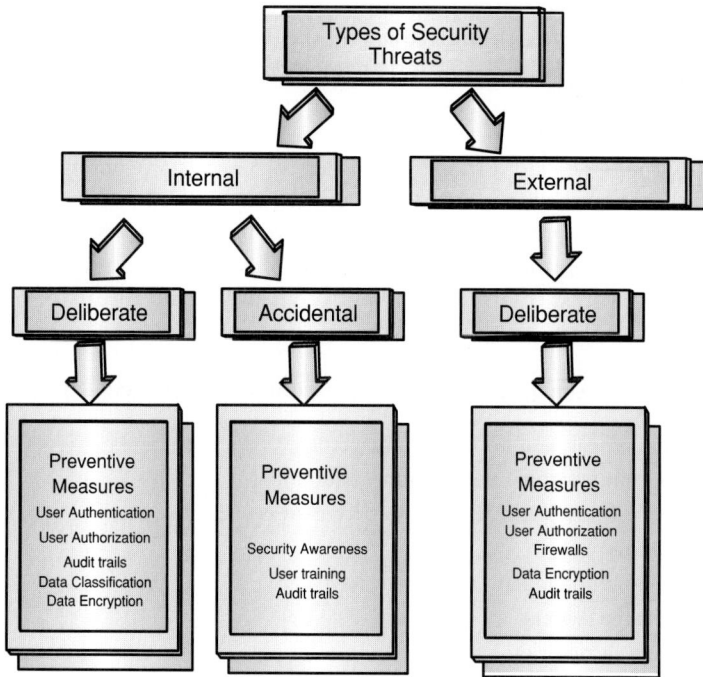

Figure 3–29 Different types of security threats and corresponding preventive measures.

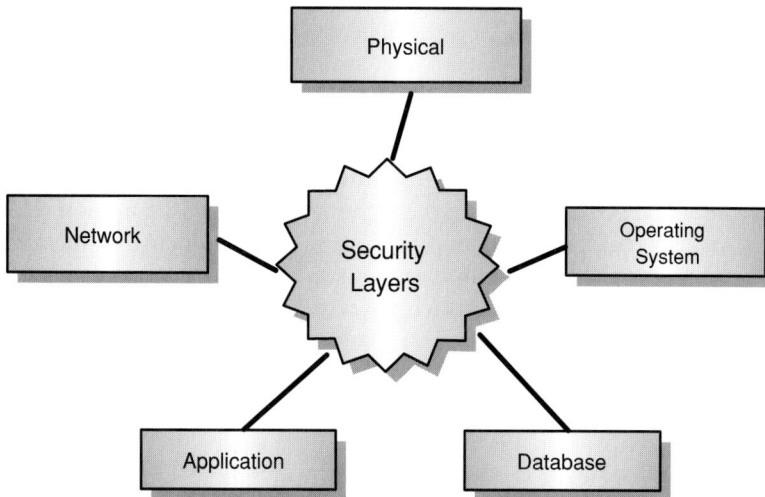

Figure 3–30 Different security layers

probably much too obvious—the possibility of water damage. What had to happen did happen! One day, a severe thunderstorm hit the region and in a matter of one hour, the entire basement was flooded, seriously damaging the computer equipment.

Physical security requirements can vary significantly from one organization to another. Be sure to verify thoroughly the geographical sites and buildings where critical computer equipment will be installed, in order to detect such potential hazards as flood, fire, riots, or power supply shutdowns. If the risks are high, then special security measures should be taken to minimize and circumvent these threats.

Some of the most common security or hazard prevention techniques that can be used to prevent or at least minimize different physical security threats or hazards are listed in Table 3-55.

Table 3–55 Techniques To Circumvent Physical Hazards Or Security Threats

- Use of smoke, fire, gas, and flood alarm detectors
- Installation of uninterrupted power supply equipment
- Enforce control of physical accesses to restricted areas via:
  - Security guards
  - Security locks with regular or magnetic keys
  - Magnetic badge readers
  - Voice pattern recognition facilities
  - Fingerprint or eye iris/retina readers
- Electronic surveillance facilities
  - Digital cameras
  - Videos
- Sign-in/sign-out mechanisms to control physical access to restricted computer areas
- Store sensitive documents in fireproof filing cabinets that can be locked
- Security guards

Operating System

Certain core security functions can be performed at the level of the operating system, either at the client workstation or at the server level. The most common security measure that is performed at the operating system level is when the operating system prompts the users to identify themselves with an appropriate user id and password to access the computer platform on which the system is running. Sometimes the operating system works closely with specialized, additional layers of security access control software.

Database

The database management system software can provide various levels of data access controls. The data that is stored in the databases should be well safeguarded from and only accessed through the utilization of proper database user ids and passwords. Users should be provided with only the minimum set of database access privileges they require to perform the business functions for which they are responsible.

Network

At the network level, the security control measures encompass different dispositions that control and/or limit the access to the network and all its related components, such as packet filtering, virus detection and cleansing, encryption, and password authentication. These security measures are implemented to ensure that the integrity of the data during transmissions will be preserved and that the proper identification of users will be enforced. Ensure that the information that transits through the network is secured from being viewed, altered, or removed by unauthorized people or equipment.

Application

At the application level, the use of certain transactions can be restricted to only those users who need to perform these transactions. Depending on the categories of users, certain functions are hidden from the application's main menu selection.

SECURITY CONTROLS FOR HARD-COPY DATA

Special considerations should also be given to controlling unauthorized access to classified information that is generated by the system in a hard-copy format, such as program dumps, forms, or reports that are printed on paper and stored in filing cabinets.

Special equipment might be required to dispose of such sensitive documents in a secured manner, such as paper shredders, for example. Such equipment should be acquired not only for the production environment but also for the test environment sites, if they are situated at different locations.

SECURITY CONTROLS AT THE WORKSTATION LEVEL

Special attention might be required to enforce some additional security measures at the workstation level. The use of a screen saver software facility that gets activated automatically when the system has not been used for a certain period of time can enforce some additional security control at the desktop level. The re-activation of the application requires the users to re-enter a password to get access to it.

SECURITY CONTROLS FOR MOBILE COMPUTERS

As the computer technology advances, more and more organizations are equipping their personnel who are frequently on the road with powerful PC laptops. Laptops are used by various categories of mobile employees to sometimes perform critical business tasks. Thus, the proper use of PC laptops can significantly increase the productivity of employees.

Similarly, portable laptops can considerably increase security breach risks. The theft of laptops that contain highly competitive information can be very harmful to an organization. In several instances, the replacement cost of the stolen PC laptop is negligible when compared to the loss of strategic corporate information or the potential disclosure of very sensitive corporate data to the competition.

Besides training the mobile task force on how to avoid possible theft situations, several security control mechanisms can be implemented to minimize the risk of exposing valuable corporate information to unauthorized access, such as:

- Implementing a boot protection mechanism on each laptop

- Enforcing a robust password and user id utility

- Encrypting any sensitive data that is stored on the laptop's hard drive or floppy disks

- Using a robust authentication process to allow mobile users to communicate with the central host, from a remote location

To conclude, protecting information that resides in the host computers from hackers who could have stolen the passwords and logons that might have been stored on laptops might also be very important. After all, several organizations allow their mobile task force personnel to directly enter field-related data into their central host computers from remote locations or inversely retrieve data from it.

SECURITY CONTROLS FOR INTERNET/INTRANETS

Internet and intranet environments are a major security concern for several organizations.

Table 3-56 describes in basic terms some of the most common types of attacks that can occur in Internet or intranet environments. However, this table is far from exhaustive. New types of attacks surface almost every week. I assume that you have some knowledge of basic networking and Internet terminology such as "packet" and "Internet Protocol" address.

Table 3–56 Different Categories Of Web Attacks

TYPE OF WEB ATTACK	DESCRIPTION
Spoofing	A spoofing attack occurs when intruders send packets with false source Internet Protocol addresses. This category of attack takes advantage of the applications that use authentication-based Internet Protocol addresses. This type of attack may lead to unauthorized access to an intranet from the outside, by pretending to be someone else.
Snooping	A snooping attack occurs when outside hackers try to break into a site.

Table 3–56 Different Categories Of Web Attacks (cont.)

Sniffing	A sniffing attack occurs when hackers use a program called a sniffer to intercept packets as they go in and out of a site, traveling over the network. Doing so, sensitive information such as passwords and user ids can be grabbed by hackers.
Saturating	A saturating attack occurs when a very large number of messages are sent to a Web site with the intent of creating a disastrous bottleneck situation and overload the Web server.
Shuffling	A shuffling attack occurs when your site receives bad code that will mess it up.

As you can see, the Internet/Intranet environments can present several threats to the security and integrity of your system. Thus, the security requirements for a mission-critical Internet/intranet application might encompass several of the issues that are indicated in Table 3-57.

Table 3–57 Internet/intranet Security Issues

Privacy/confidentiality	How to ensure that data is disclosed only to authorized parties
Integrity	How to ensure that the original data remains complete and has not been altered when it is transmitted through the network (i.e., nothing added or deleted)
Authentication	How to guarantee that both parties that are involved in a business transaction are indeed who they claim they are
Access control	How to allow legitimate users to access only the data they are authorized to see, once they have been authenticated; how to prevent unauthorized users from accessing data they must not see or services they are not allowed to use
Non-repudiation	How to prevent denial of transaction submissions, from either the sending or receiving ends of the communication process; non-repudiation services usually cover the following items: confirmation of the delivery of services, confirmation of the origin of services, and confirmation of the submission of services

As indicated in Table 3-57, authentication is the process of identifying the users and making sure that they are who they claim to be. Furthermore, the authentication process must also ensure that the users are truly accessing the proper servers or services. For example, if Darlene accesses a certain Web site, what mechanism can ensure her that this Web site is really operated by the site's legitimate owner? Access control mechanisms regulate what users can do once they identify themselves. Authentication and access control techniques are paramount to enforce security in an Internet/intranet environment.

At least three common authentication techniques exist, as indicated in Table 3-58. These authentication techniques can be used to validate users or computers that want to communicate with each other.

Table 3–58 Generic User Authentication Mechanisms

Authentication with something the user knows	This authentication mechanism uses the traditional user identification and password technique. If the user id and passwords entered by the user match those stored in a central user profile security file, then the user has access to the system.
Authentication with something the user has in his/her possession	This authentication technique uses some type of token that the user owns, such as a magnetic card or a smart card that contains a computer chip, which are used to authenticate him/her.
Authentication with the use of physical characteristics	This authentication mechanism uses biometrics techniques to authenticate the users, such as fingerprints, retinal scans, and voice recognition.

Figures 3-31 through 3-34 illustrate with pictures the basic concepts of integrity, non-repudiation, confidentiality, and authentication.

As you can see, many challenges occur in building a secure Internet/intranet mission-critical application. Two of the most widely accepted security technologies that

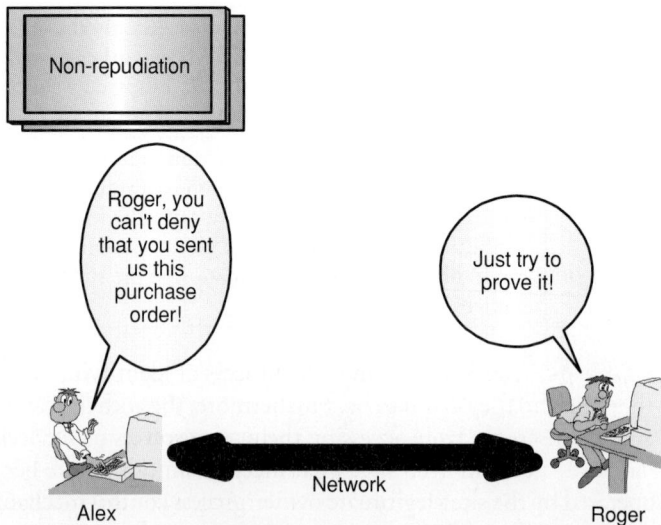

Figure 3–31 Non-repudiation concept.

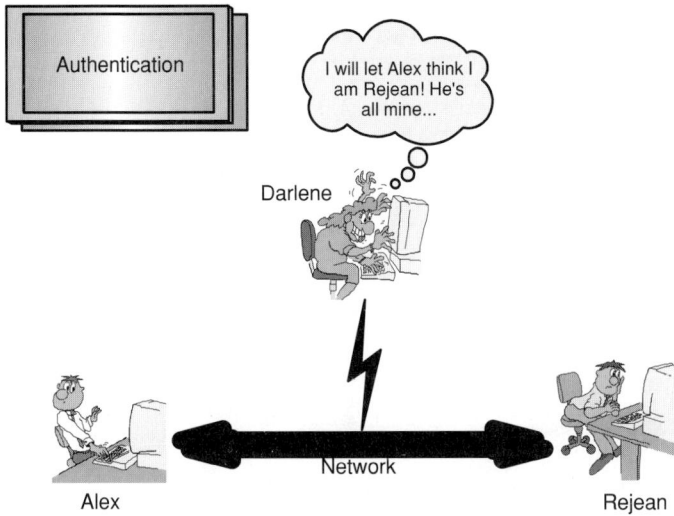

Figure 3–32 Authentication concept.

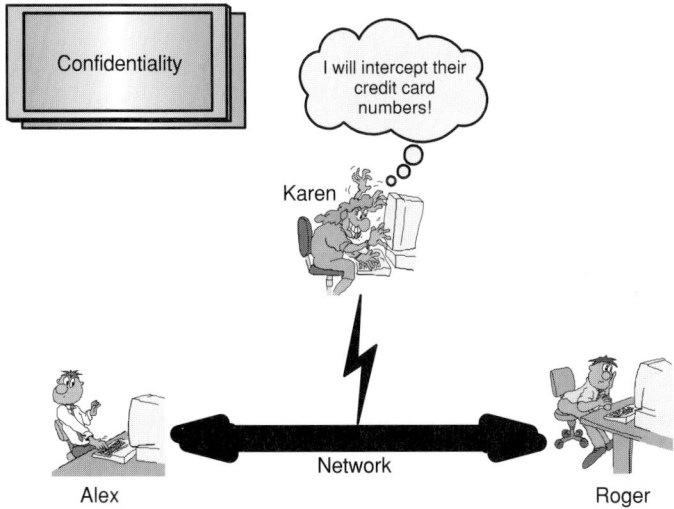

Figure 3–33 Confidentiality concept.

can provide a solution to security issues such as authentication and access control are encryption and digital signature, as indicated in Table 3-59.

Describing in detail the various encryption and digital signature mechanisms that can be enforced in an Internet/intranet environment goes well beyond the scope of this book. If you desire more information on these subjects, you can search the Web,

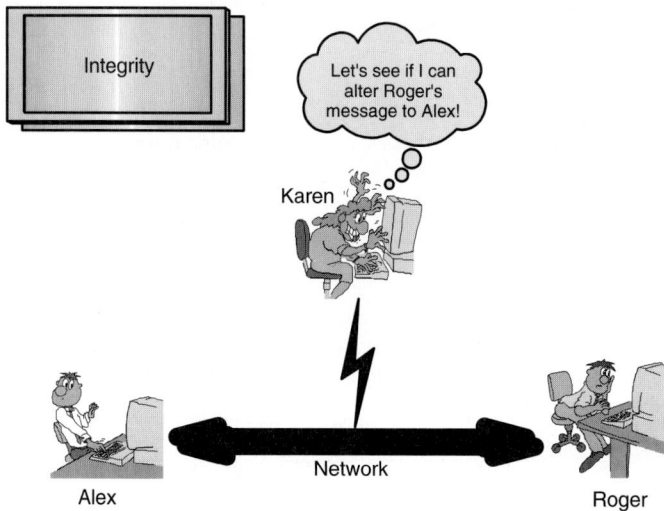

Figure 3–34 Integrity concept.

Table 3–59 Security Issues And Potential Solutions

SECURITY ISSUE	PROPOSED SOLUTION
Access Control	Encryption/Password
Privacy	Encryption
Integrity	Digital Signature
Non-Repudiation	Digital Signature
Authentication	Digital Signature

narrowing down your investigation on the following major cryptographic technologies industry-standard protocols:

• SET – Secure Electronic Transactions
• S/MIME – Secure Multipart Internet Mail Encoding
• SSL – Secure Socket Layer

Nonetheless, Table 3-60 provides a brief description of the major terms that are frequently used by the cryptography industry.

Figure 3-35 depicts the generic process of encrypting and decrypting a document with the use of a key.

Finally, two additional techniques that are complementary to cryptography are often utilized to secure the Internet/intranet environments: digital certificates and firewalls.

Table 3–60 Some Cryptography Buzzwords

CRYPTOGRAPHY TERM	DESCRIPTION
Encryption	The transformation of data into some unreadable form with the use of software or hardware devices. Two common types of encryption techniques exist: symmetric key and asymmetric key.
Decryption	The transformation of encrypted data back into a readable format.
Digital signature	A technique of signing an electronic document with a piece of data that cannot be forged. Digital signatures are the electronic equivalent of the traditional paper signatures.
Signature validation	A technique to verify that a digital signature is valid.

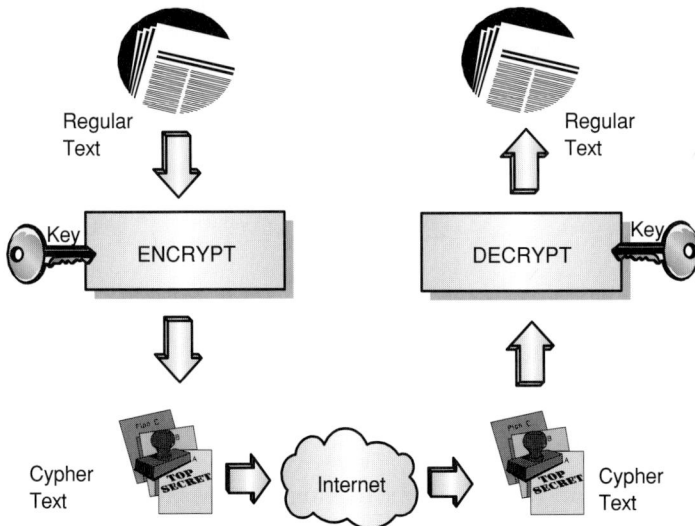

Figure 3–35 Encryption/Decryption mechanism.

A digital certificate identifies you to someone else who requires proof of your identity. This is the same concept as when you enter a high-security site and must show the security guard at the entrance door your badge id with your picture on it. Certificates use a sophisticated electronic form of identification to establish your identity with someone. They are the digital equivalent of an employee's badge id or any other mechanisms established to identify you to the authorities, such as a passport or a birth certificate, for instance. Digital certificates (a.k.a. public-key certificates) are regulated by an ITU standard called X.509.

Firewalls are a necessity for companies that open their networks to Internet traffic. A firewall consists of a set of hardware and/or software components that control all incoming and outgoing transactions. With a firewall, you can determine who is allowed to pass through your security fence and access your corporate network and under what rules. In other words, the prime purpose of a firewall is to protect an enterprise's internal corporate network/intranet surroundings from unauthorized intruders.

The firewall, as shown in Figure 3-36, is placed between internal LANs/WANs and public networks such as the Internet. It identifies applications, Internet protocol addresses, and other properties of the incoming and outgoing data flows and verifies this information against pre-established access rules. I cover firewalls in more detail in Chapter 9.

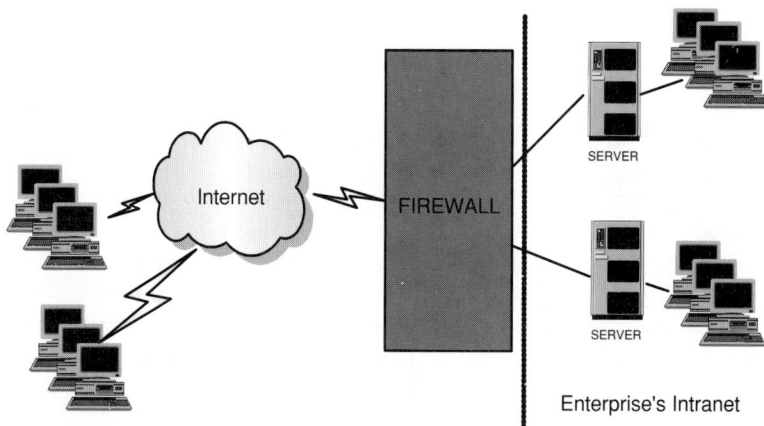

Figure 3–36 Firewall.

3.9.3   INTEGRITY AND AUDIT REQUIREMENTS

This section discusses integrity and audit requirements. It suggests some basic techniques to increase the integrity of a system. It also presents some generic system audit controls.

INTEGRITY REQUIREMENTS

Most data integrity requirements are primarily associated with the validity and correctness of the information that is fed or manipulated by the system. Consequently, the integrity requirements usually put a special emphasis on the characteristics of the system that are required to detect and handle events that can lead to the processing of incorrect or invalid data.

The ability for a system to automatically detect and enforce the correction of data errors will greatly enhance its level of integrity. The processes that are primarily designed to feed the new system with some raw input data should be carefully assessed in light of the integrity mechanism that should be enforced to help maintain the data at an optimal level of accuracy and correctness.

Some of the most common processes that usually require the implementation of specific data integrity procedural routines include data entry functions, data interface functions with other systems, and data transmission functions that are accomplished through either private or public networks.

The internal processes that are used by the new system to generate output data should also be investigated to ensure that specific data integrity routines are used to control the integrity and accuracy of the output data. For the automated batch system interfaces, the integrity process is frequently implemented through the use of various file reconciliation control schemes.

Several techniques can be used to improve the level of accuracy of the data entry process, such as those indicated in Table 3-61.

Table 3–61 Suggested Techniques To Improve The Level Of Accuracy Of The Data Entry Processes

- Reduce the number of keystrokes required to input data into the system
  - Optimize the data entry screens for speed and accuracy. Sequence and dispose the data entry fields that must be captured into logical blocks of data that have strong affinities.
  - Automatically re-display, from screen to screen, frequently used data, so the user does not have to re-key previously entered information from one screen to another.
  - Provide facilities such as list boxes, drop-down list boxes, radio buttons, and checkboxes to allow the customer to make choices and to select data values from existing tables.
  - Use automated data entry technologies such as bar codes.
- Use extensive data editing and validation algorithms for the data entry processes

The integrity of the databases can be enhanced if their data content is always updated via legitimate application programs or special utilities that are provided with the database management system (DBMS) product. The database tables should be updated from a single entry point and always under the control of the DBMS software. Moreover, the integrity of all the data that are stored in the databases should be regularly verified by running special database integrity utilities that thoroughly check all database files to detect potentially corrupted database indexes, bad physical pointers, or referential integrity mismatches.

The level of accuracy provided by the network facilities should be evaluated when frequent transmission of large volumes of data occurs between the physical sites supported by the new system. What types of error-detection mechanisms are used by the network protocol? Do any specific routines automatically detect and correct transmission data errors?

AUDIT REQUIREMENTS

The audit requirements of the system are defined with the users. Because more often than not the developers have a limited experience as to what could be the system auditing requirements, the company's internal auditors should be directly involved in this process, at least on a consulting basis. Auditing is important for financial systems. Table 3-62 indicates some of the most common types of system auditing controls.

Table 3–62 List Of Auditing System Controls

- An audit trail of all the online transactions that update sensitive data stored in the system databases. The software utility used for tracking the execution of transactions should be able to identify the originator of the transaction and the input data used, along with the resulting changes.
- A log of all the transactions rejected by the system, as well as the reasons for their rejection and possibly the identification of the originator of the transaction.
- Verification procedures in the form of manual checklists that can be used to control the accuracy and completeness of the manual operations of the system.
- A mechanism to verify that the data produced by the system are properly distributed to the users and other external system interfaces.
- A procedure to ensure that the various system transactions files are properly balanced and reconciled at the end of the day.
- Procedures to ensure that industry standard accounting practices are properly observed.
- Procedures to ensure that aging data are properly archived to meet the legal obligations associated with the preservation of historical information.

3.9.4   DISASTER RECOVERY REQUIREMENTS

For a mission-critical client-server or Web database system, a sound disaster recovery strategy should be developed with the users. The disaster recovery plan should address both the manual and automated functions of the system. Table 3-63 lists some of the major elements that the proposed disaster recovery strategy should cover.

Table 3–63 Questions To Help Identify The Disaster Recovery Requirements Of The Application

---

- What elements of the system documentation and user operating manuals must be secured in case of a major disaster? Where will this information be stored?
- Which files, databases, and application libraries must be backed up and secured in case of a major disaster recovery event?
- Which applications must be restored first and in what order? What are the priorities?
- Who controls the operations environment in case of a major disaster?
- Who is involved in the recovery plan on the system side? On the user side?
- What are the roles and responsibilities of the users? Of the system operations personnel?
- How quickly can a new site and new hardware/software/networking environment be used?

Finally, the development team should discuss with the users the maximum system outage they can tolerate before their daily business operations start to be seriously affected by the outage.

In the event of a major system failure, the development team and the users should consider some fallback procedures, especially if the application is considered critical to the survival of the organization. For instance, do alternative ways exist for the users to continue to carry out their business activities while the system is down?

Activity number:	AN-9
Activity name:	Define the system operational requirements
Purpose:	To identify the set of operational requirements that the system must satisfy
Inputs:	AN-T1 Business process model AN-T2 Business data model AN-T3 System transactions AN-T5 System graphical user interface prototype AN-T6 Initial system distribution strategy AN-T7 System interface requirements
Outputs:	AN-T9 System operational requirements

Activity description:	• Identify and document the set of critical system transactions for which specific performance level requirements must be met
	• Identify other types of operational service levels requirements
	• Identify and document the following miscellaneous system operational requirements:
	  – System accessibility
	  – System availability
	  – System reliability
	  – Batch reporting requirements
	  – End-user ad hoc query and report requirements
	  – Miscellaneous batch job utility requirements
	  – System printing requirements
	  – Environmental site requirements
	• Walk through the system operational requirements deliverable

3.10 DEFINE THE SYSTEM OPERATIONAL REQUIREMENTS

This section discusses a variety of performance-related requirements, regrouped under the generic term 'operational requirements'. The operational requirements also cover other types of requirements such as overall system availability and reliability.

3.10.1 INTRODUCTION

The system operational requirements can significantly affect the design of a large and complex client-server or web system and the technology architecture required to support it. During the analysis phase, the operational requirements must be stated in a format that can be easily understood by all involved parties, especially the users.

Ideally, the operational requirements must be defined at a level of detail that will facilitate their measurements, once the system is fully operational. The active participation of the users is very important. They must clearly communicate their expectations to the developers.

In some instances, the developers must carefully manage the expectations of their customers. Although they might be perfectly valid from a business standpoint, sometimes users' expectations simply cannot be satisfied with the current state of technology. Similarly, the costs to implement highly sophisticated technology solutions might turn out to be prohibitive for the project at hand.

3.10.2 SYSTEM RESPONSE TIME REQUIREMENTS

The system online transactions can be classified into different categories, based on their expected response time, such as:

- All online transactions in class 1 must have a response time between 1 and 3 seconds
- All online transactions in class 2 must have a response time between 4 and 6 seconds
- All online transactions in class 3 must have a response time between 7 and 10 seconds

The response time of each specific online transaction should be justifiable by the users based on the type of work achieved with the transaction and its level of criticality. For instance, a perfectly justifiable expectation might be for the users to request a 1- to 3-second response time for a transaction that involves an interactive session at the workstation while at the same time the users must interact directly with a customer over a telephone.

The definition of response time requirements normally applies to pre-planned transactions. If the users utilize a query facility for ad hoc inquiries, defining in a precise manner what the response time will be in such a situation might be more difficult.

Thus, the users might need to be educated as to the type of queries they can formulate with these powerful query tools and the adverse effect that some of these queries can have on the overall performance of the system.

3.10.3 OPERATIONAL SERVICE LEVELS REQUIREMENTS

In this task, the requirements for service levels that are required to support the system, besides response time, usually include the following topics:

- System availability, accessibility, and reliability
- The level of technical support provided in case of system failures, level of help desk support provided for answering general-purpose questions from the users or for problem resolution
- Hours of availability for various help desk support services

The service levels requirements identified at this stage will eventually be transposed into formal service level contractual agreements between the user and MIS organizations when the system will be implemented in a production environment.

3.10.4 SYSTEM ACCESSIBILITY REQUIREMENTS

The accessibility requirements apply to the total number of users the system must support at a given point in time. For instance:

- How many users will need direct access to the system in a concurrent mode?
- How many users will access the system in total?
- What will be the ratio of users per workstations?
- Will mobile users require to connect to the system from remote locations?

This type of requirements will directly affect several other deliverables, such as the proposed network configuration, the number of workstations that need to be connected to the network, and so forth. Growth projections should also be estimated, covering the increase of the total number of users over the next two to three years, for instance. This type of information will become handy to plan the system expansion as the number of users potentially increases drastically in the near future.

3.10.5 SYSTEM AVAILABILITY AND RELIABILITY REQUIREMENTS

Table 3-64 resumes some of the most common questions that must be discussed with the users to identify the system availability and reliability requirements. Mission-critical applications might require a detailed system fail-over strategy.

Table 3–64 System Availability And Reliability Requirements

- What is the maximum period of time during which the system must remain fully operational?
    - Only during the traditional 9 am to 5 pm business hours?
    - 24 hours a day, 365 days a year?
- How reliable must the system be? Can the users tolerate small system outages?
- Does a need exist to duplicate or mirror some of the hardware/software/networking components to increase the overall level of reliability of the system?
- In case of a hardware failure, can the most critical system online transactions remain active by rerouting the server traffic to other servers? What about the network traffic?
- Can the application client-server or Web technology support dynamic load balancing?
- Does a need exist to define a fail-over scenario for critical system components?

3.10.6 SYSTEM THROUGHPUT REQUIREMENTS

Table 3-65 resumes some of the most common questions that must be discussed with the users in order to identify the system throughput capacity requirements.

Table 3–65 System Throughput Requirements

- What is the average number of transactions that the system must satisfy per unit of time for:
    - The online transactions?
    - The batch transactions?
    - The manual transactions?
- What is the expected number of transactions annual growth?
- What are the peak loads? At which frequency?
- Can the system handle the peak loads without suffering serious degradation?

For high-volume, mission-critical applications, ideally the computer should be able to process, on average, two days of normal processing work in a single day. This additional reserve capacity could turn out to be extremely useful when two or three days of additional work processing must be recovered following a major system downtime situation.

The throughput requirements of the system manual procedures should also be assessed as accurately as possible. These figures will eventually be used to better quantify the number of personnel required to perform these tasks manually.

3.10.7 BATCH REPORTS/USER QUERIES TURNAROUND REQUIREMENTS

The expected turnaround time requirements for the various types of regular batch reports that the system must produce on a periodic basis (i.e., daily, weekly, monthly, and yearly) should be discussed with the users.

Cases might arise in which the users would like to produce their own online or batch reports and queries. User-friendly reporting and querying tools can provide a solution to these legitimate requirements. Some of the fundamental questions that should be asked of the users to help uncover these requirements are listed in Table 3-66.

Table 3–66 Batch Reports And Queries Turnaround Requirements

- Can the expected number and frequency of requests for ad hoc queries or reports be assessed?
- Should the users make use of query tools simply to read the data that is stored in the operational databases or also to update the data?
- Should the users be allowed to directly access the operational production databases, or should the requested data be periodically downloaded or replicated to other files structures that are more suitable to provide a faster response time to various types of ad hoc queries and report requests (i.e. data warehouses or data marts)?

3.10.8 MISCELLANEOUS BATCH JOB REQUIREMENTS

Any requirements that might relate to the submission of large batch job streams other than those required to produce specific reports should also be discussed with the users and the system operations staff. The daily or overnight window time that can be made available for running these jobs on either mainframes or application servers might be limited.

Some of the batch jobs that might fall into this category can include various software utilities such as:

- database backup/recovery jobs
- database reorganization jobs
- miscellaneous housekeeping jobs
- data archiving jobs

3.10.9 SYSTEM PRINTING REQUIREMENTS

Although it should be the exception rather than the rule, some client-server or even Web-based applications might still have a requirement to print a large volume of data. If this is the case for the project at hand, then the total number of print lines that must be processed by the system per unit of time should be estimated by the development team. These figures should cover the total printing requirements of the central site, as well as the printing needs of each local site. The volumetric data related to printing will be used to help determine the types of printers that should be acquired to support the application.

3.10.10 SYSTEM ENVIRONMENTAL SITE REQUIREMENTS

The main objective for this activity is to determine whether any critical site requirements must be satisfied to accommodate the new client-server or Web application. For each affected site, whether centralized or remote, the following information should be documented:

- A list and brief description of all the major geographical locations where the application must be supported

- A list and brief description of any new or additional computer equipment that will be required to run the new application at the different sites

- A brief description of any major physical site alterations or construction requirements

If necessary, create a preliminary sketch describing where the new or additional computers and peripheral equipment will be installed along with a list of the necessary site alterations.

Activity number:	AN-10
Activity name:	Develop the initial capacity plan
Purpose:	To identify the initial requirements for current and future disk storage capacity and the overall technology infrastructure in place
Inputs:	AN-T1 Business process model AN-T2 Business data model AN-T3 System transactions AN-T6 Initial system distribution strategy AN-T7 System interface requirements AN-T8 System security and control requirements AN-T9 System operational requirements
Outputs:	AN-10 Initial capacity plan
Activity description:	• Review the business process and data models, along with other technical deliverables such as the operational and system interface requirements • Identify what level of technology resources are required to support the system overall disk, memory, processing, and networking requirements • Walk through the initial capacity plan deliverable

3.11 DEVELOP THE INITIAL CAPACITY PLAN

This activity is primarily executed for new, especially large-scale and complex systems that might affect significantly the technology infrastructure that is currently in place.

The prime objective of the capacity planning activity is to estimate the capacity of the current hardware enterprise architecture to be able to run the new system to the required performance level.

The major deliverable for this task is a document, which provides an order-of-magnitude estimate for the total system usage of several critical technology resources such as:

- Overall disk space utilization
- Overall CPU processing utilization
- Overall central memory utilization
- Overall transmission of data through the corporate networks

The type of volumetric data that must be collected to develop the capacity plan can vary from one application system to another one. Depending on the size of the project and the complexity of the algorithms that might be used to calculate the capacity requirements, a capacity planner specialist might be required to produce the final outcome of this activity.

The capacity plan is produced in the following manner:

- The developers (or a capacity planner) create a set of matrices, which contain different volumetric data that describe how the new system will be used. The main source of information that is used to create these matrices is the business process and data models, system interface requirements, system operational requirements, and database sizing estimates deliverables.
- The volumetric information that is contained in the matrices is then converted with the use of special algorithms into specific hardware requirements.

3.11.1 ONLINE USAGE

Tables 3-67, 3-68, and 3-69 show different matrices that are used to specify the estimated total online usage of the system.

- Table 3-67 indicates how the users are geographically distributed in different locations.
- Table 3-68 provides an overview of the different critical transactions that are executed in the system.
- Table 3-69 shows the frequency of execution of each transaction in the system, for each specific location, for a given time window period.

Table 3–67 Geographical Distribution Of Users

Location	Total number of concurrent users at peak time	Average number of concurrent users	Total number of users
Brasilia	130	50	200
Montreal	40	30	75
Paris	20	10	30
New York	250	200	300

Table 3–68 System Transactions Overview

Transaction name	Response time required	Database activity level
Create new customer	3 sec	1 insert
…		

Table 3–69 Transaction Usage Frequency

Transaction name	Window start time	Window stop time	Estimated number of transactions/time
Create new customer	8:30	18:00	25/day
…			

3.11.2 BATCH USAGE

Table 3-70 shows volumetric data on total system batch usage

Table 3–70 System Batch Usage

Batch job	Frequency	Average job execution time	Database activity level
Paycheck print run	Every Monday	6 hours	1000 employee records in read/write mode
Human Resource Database backup	Every night	3 hours	Full database export (1 GIG)
Accounts Payable download	Bi-weekly	2 hours	Access, in read mode only, 15,000 records

3.11.3 INITIAL DISK SPACE SIZING

Table 3-71 shows volumetric data that is extracted from information contained in the business data model. The volumetric information shown in this matrix can be used as the foundation to estimate the initial sizing of the application databases.

Table 3–71 Entity Sizing Estimates

Entity name	Estimated size	Initial number of occurrences	Estimated annual growth	Years of online active life
Customer	300 bytes	18,000	25%	10
Customer invoice	1500 bytes	100,000	10%	5

3.11.4 EXTRA CAPACITY LOAD(S)

Table 3-72 is used to document supplementary loads such as those caused by various types of overhead conditions.

Table 3–72 Additional Requirements To Increase Capacity Load

EXTRA CAPACITY LOAD(S)	DESCRIPTION
• Disk mirroring	• +15% on CPU sizing, +60% on disk capacity
• Database indexes overhead	• + 20% of current database size estimates

3.11.5 NETWORK REQUIREMENTS

Table 3-73 shows the high-level network requirements for the new application system.

Table 3–73 Site Network Requirements

From site	To site	Network type	Protocol	Line speed
...				
...				

3.11.6 TOTAL COMPUTER/NETWORK SIZING

Table 3-74 shows a summary of the total computer machine and local area network (LAN) resource requirements for each specific location. These final resource capacity estimates are derived from all the volumetric information that was contained in the set of system resource matrices that were shown above.

Table 3–74 Total Computer/Network Resource Estimates

Location	Disk space requirements	Memory requirements	CPU requirements	LAN band-width requirements
Tokyo	10 Gbytes	200 MBytes	15 MIPS	30 KBytes
...				

Activity number:	AN-11
Activity name:	Develop the initial data conversion strategy
Purpose:	To define, at a high level, the initial system data conversion requirements and strategy
Inputs:	AN-T1 Business process model AN-T2 Business data model AN-T3 System transactions AN-T6 Initial system distribution strategy AN-T8 System security and control requirements Existing system documentation
Outputs:	AN-T11 Initial data conversion strategy

Activity description:	• Define the scope of the data conversion process, covering:
	  – Legacy databases and files
	  – Automated
	  – Manual
	  – Existing system interfaces
	  – Creation of new data files
	• Verify the level of quality, accuracy, and integrity of the legacy data
	• Identify the major data conversion functional requirements
	• Identify the existing or special software tools and facilities or hardware and networking equipment that will be required to support the data conversion process
	• Derive the optimal data conversion strategy that is required to perform the overall data conversion effort
	• Walk through the data conversion deliverables

3.12 DEVELOP THE INITIAL DATA CONVERSION STRATEGY

This section discusses the detailed steps involved in creating the system data conversion requirements. It also provides useful tips as how to execute that process.

3.12.1 INTRODUCTION

Once the business data and process models are completed, the development team is then able to define the initial data conversion strategy that will be used to convert the data from the legacy system to the new system. The magnitude of the data conversion effort is directly related to the following factors:

- The complexity of the existing and new system data architectures
- The total number of files and volumes of data involved in the data conversion process
- The current level of quality, accuracy, and integrity of the legacy data

For some relatively small client-server or Web systems, the conversion effort will be relatively straightforward. For large-scale systems, it might warrant the creation of a dedicated subproject. The prime objective of this special subproject is to support the complete conversion process, including all necessary data cleansing activities.

3.12.2 DEFINING THE DATA CONVERSION REQUIREMENTS

STEP 1: Analyze the scope of the conversion effort

The first step toward developing the data conversion requirements consists of analyzing the scope of the conversion effort. Essentially, this is done by identifying the following elements:

- The existing application files/databases that need to be converted to the new system
- The set of new files/databases that must be created from scratch
- The estimated amounts of manual data that must be converted to accommodate the new application
- The major business units that should be involved in the conversion process

STEP 2: Identify the potential constraints

During the second step, the potential constraints that might be imposed on the conversion process are identified with the users, such as:

- The expected data conversion target completion dates
- The special handling of highly sensitive data (i.e., special security measures required to handle confidential data)
- The dependencies with other systems and the necessity to construct automated interfaces with them
- The necessity to let the users of the current system utilize the legacy data by synchronizing some of the old and new files/databases until the final system cut-over
- The different business cycle periods (i.e., month ends, quarter ends, and year-end processing) that might impact the timing of the conversion efforts

STEP 3: Verify the integrity and quality of the legacy data

The third step examines the level of quality of the data that is currently stored in the legacy files/databases. If, for whatever reason, the present data are severely corrupted, you might need to come up with an action plan to clean up the existing files/databases and improve their integrity before undertaking the final conversion effort itself. Sometimes, this clean-up process might entail extensive efforts from the users, especially when a large number of discrepancies or integrity issues are detected in the current files or databases.

STEP 4: Identify the required conversion tools and facilities

The fourth step defines the type of software facilities and computer equipment that will be required to support the conversion process. The ultimate responsibility for ensuring the success of the conversion process lies in the hands of the users, who are accountable for the integrity of the data they use. However, the developers will play an important role in supporting the conversion process. They must provide the appropriate software tools (i.e., conversion programs, data validation programs, file comparison facilities, data capturing software) that will be necessary to convert the existing files and databases efficiently. They will also create the various utilities that will be used to produce the various reports that might be needed by the users to verify the final data conversion results.

If legacy data must be transferred from the mainframe environment to a client-server platform, the use of a database gateway might be required by the conversion team.

In some instances, special or additional hardware equipment might be necessary to perform the data conversion activities. For instance, additional workstations might be required for a given period of time to accommodate a massive data entry effort aimed at capturing all the data needed by the new system as rapidly as possible.

3.12.3 ELABORATION OF THE DATA CONVERSION STRATEGY

The data conversion strategy is elaborated based on all the information that has been gathered during the previous steps. The conversion strategy will be largely influenced by the system development and deployment approaches that were retained for the application at hand. If the application will be gradually implemented in a series of releases, then the dependencies that exist among these various releases and the sequences in which they will be developed and deployed will affect the manner in which the conversion process will be performed. In some cases, the creation of temporary bridges between the old and new files/databases will be required until all system releases are finally implemented.

Table 3-75 lists some of the major elements that should be covered in the initial data conversion strategy of a large and complex system.

Table 3–75 Data Conversion Strategy Components

- Overview of the data conversion strategy
- The major objectives of the data conversion process
- Assumptions made
- Potential issues and constraints
- Data conversion scope:
  - Identification of the major files/databases that must be converted
  - Identification of the new files/databases that must be created
  - Identification of the system interfaces
- The type of data conversion that will be performed for each file/database:
  - Automated to automated
  - Manual to automated
  - Automated to manual
  - Manual to manual
- The particular sequences in which the files/databases must be converted and the inter-dependencies that might exist among the different files and databases
- The hardware/software/networking equipment and facilities that are required to support the conversion effort along with an estimate of the volume of data that must be converted per file/database
- The type of reports required by the users to verify the results of the conversion process or to analyze the quality of the legacy data and ultimately clean it up
- The set of fallback procedures that must be put in place in order to recover from an unsuccessful data conversion process
- An estimate of the number of staff required to support the overall conversion effort
- An identification of the special skills that might be required to perform the conversion process
- The identification of the major roles and responsibilities that will be assigned to each user and system group involved in the conversion process
- Timing of the overall conversion effort

If multiple geographic locations are involved in the data conversion process, you will also need to determine the sequence and timing in which each particular site will be converted.

Activity number:	AN-12
Activity name:	Develop the initial backup/recovery strategy
Purpose:	To define, at a high level, the strategy that should be taken to back up and recover the system databases in case of a failure
Inputs:	AN-T1 Business process model AN-T2 Business data model AN-T3 System transactions AN-T6 Initial system distribution strategy AN-T7 System interface requirements AN-T10 Initial capacity plan
Outputs:	AN-T12 Initial backup/recovery strategy
Activity description:	• Identify and document, at a high level, the initial system backup and recovery requirements. • Identify, at a high level, the generic set of techniques that should be used to ensure that the system can be recovered in case of a failure • Identify with the users whether some special paper-based fallback approaches are necessary in case of a system outage • Walk through the backup/recovery requirements

3.13 DEVELOP THE INITIAL BACKUP/RECOVERY STRATEGY

In this activity, an initial high-level strategy is formulated with the users to ensure that the system can be recovered from a failure.

The prime objective of the strategy should be to warrant that the data availability and integrity requirements of the system are satisfied, even when the recovery of data becomes necessary in the event of a system failure. Also, ensuring that the interfaces with other systems can remain in a consistent state when the recovery process is executed is important.

Although the backup/recovery strategy will likely be straightforward if it is based on the organization's existing corporate strategy for backup and recovery, some problematic issues can still occur, especially if some very large databases that contain critical data are involved in the recovery process.

In the case of very large-scale, mission-critical systems, the backup/recovery strategy should cover the list of elements indicated in Table 3-76.

Table 3–76 High-level Backup/Recovery Requirements

- Backups of large databases
- Backups of large flat files
- Backups of interface files, report output files, transaction files
- Off-site backups
- Off-line backups
- Automatic recovery of batch jobs
- Backup scheduling and windows time constraints
- Backup resource requirements
- Special hardware and software requirements

Furthermore, the backup/recovery strategy should include a brief description of the various types of recovery inputs that will be involved during a recovery situation (i.e., a snapshot or full backup along with log inputs that archive changes since the last time a backup was taken). The time that might be required to take full backups and the frequency of these backups should be balanced with the time required to do forward recovery.

Finally, the development team should discuss with the end users the maximum time period they can tolerate a downtime situation caused by either a total system failure or a critical component of a system. Sometimes, a total system failure might require an extended period of time to fully recover the entire system, such as a couple of hours, for example. To cover such problematic situations, you might want to discuss with the users whether some special paper-based fallback approaches are necessary. The maximum recovery time permitted by end users should be documented in a service level agreement.

Activity number:	AN-13
Activity name:	Develop the initial testing strategy
Purpose:	To identify, at a high level, the major application testing requirements, along with the proposed strategy to satisfy them
Inputs:	AN-T1 Business process model AN-T2 Business data model AN-T3 System transactions AN-T5 System graphical user interface prototype AN-T6 Initial system distribution strategy AN-T7 System interface requirements AN-T8 System security and control requirements AN-T9 System operational requirements AN-T11 Initial data conversion strategy AN-T12 Initial backup/recovery strategy

Outputs:	AN-T13 Initial testing strategy

Activity description:	• Determine the high-level scope of the testing process, covering the following elements:
	   – The application automated processes that will be tested, such as:
	    – The online processes
	    – The batch processes
	    – The major application interfaces to other systems
	    – The client-server or Web technology infrastructure environments
	• Determine the broad set of objectives for the overall testing process, covering each specific major testing cycle; also identify the different locations where the testing process will be executed
	• Identify the set of hardware/software/networking components that will be required to support the testing effort and determine the set of application development libraries and databases needed
	• Determine the security and control access requirements associated with each specific test environment
	• Determine the approach that will be used to test the graphical user interface for the application
	• Determine the testing deliverables that should be produced during the overall testing effort
	• Identify the different departments and number of resources that will be involved in the testing effort, along with a brief description of the assigned roles and responsibilities
	• Walk through the testing strategy deliverable

3.14 DEVELOP THE INITIAL TESTING STRATEGY

This section discusses the detailed steps involved in creating a preliminary testing strategy. It also provides some basic tips and guidelines on how to execute the testing process.

3.14.1 INTRODUCTION

The elaboration of the testing strategy provides a high-level statement as to what should be the major objectives of the testing process and the strategy that is proposed to achieve them.

A sound testing strategy is critical for large and complex client-server or Web database applications. The testing process for these sophisticated systems is not always as well structured and executed as it should be to fully warrant the delivery of a stable, quality-oriented application. Thus the need exists to carefully plan the complete testing effort along with the different techniques that will be selected to test and verify the critical components of the system.

Systematic testing will reduce the risk of delivering a system that might contain severe defects. As indicated in several sections of this book, be sure to start testing certain elements of the application as early as possible during the development cycle, like when the graphical user interface prototype is constructed, for instance.

Due to the highly heterogeneous nature of the various technology components that must be assembled together to create web and client-server development and production infrastructures, you might want to carefully test the most complex components of that technology prior to conducting the functional tests themselves. The multiple vendor configurations and versions of hardware, software, and networking components should be verified to see how well they integrate with one another. This verification is especially important for the various points of interfaces where these components connect with one another to exchange system objects.

3.14.2 ELABORATE THE INITIAL TESTING STRATEGY

This section describes the major sections that should be included in the initial testing strategy document.

TESTING SCOPE AND OBJECTIVES

The first step toward elaborating the testing strategy consists of defining the high-level scope and objectives for the overall testing effort and then for each specific testing stage indicated in Table 3-77.

Table 3–77 Four Major Testing Stages

• Unit testing*
• Integration testing*
• System testing*
• User Acceptance testing*
*For more details on each specific testing stage, please consult Chapter 8, about client-server and Web testing.

The scope of the testing effort is based on several deliverables that were produced earlier during the analysis phase, including all the system requirements that are reflected in the business process and data models, the system performance requirements, and other similar requirements. The set of elementary business processes that will be automated and therefore should be tested by the development team should be clearly identified along with the list of other systems that must somehow interface with the new application. You might also want to point out in this section any particular application components that will not be formally verified during the testing effort, if any.

Then the development team documents the major objectives for the testing effort. Table 3-78 provides a list of some of the most common objectives for the testing process in general.

Table 3–78 General Testing Objectives

• Defect detection and elimination
• Verification that the system meets the user functional requirements:
  – Graphical user interface
  – Batch processes
  – Batch and online interfaces
  – Error and exception handling
  – Database accesses
• Compliance with the enterprise standards for:
  – Naming conventions
  – Structured coding practices
  – Graphical user interface standard look and feel
  – Program internal documentation
  – Components re-usability
• Virus protection
• System usability
	• System portability
	• System scalability
	• System performance
	  – Response time
	  – Throughput levels
	• System availability
	• System ease of maintenance
	• System flexibility
	• System security, control, and audibility mechanisms
	• System backup and recovery mechanisms
	• System operability
	• Hardware/software/networking interoperability
	• System multimedia capabilities
	• Stored and remote procedures
	• Middleware testing

TESTING THE CRITICAL SYSTEM INTERFACES

Some of the critical system interface testing characteristics that should be investigated with the users are highlighted in Table 3-79.

Table 3–79 Major Characteristics Of The Critical System Interfaces

• The nature of the interface (internal to the enterprise or external to the enterprise) • The interface frequency (real-time, near real-time, daily, weekly, monthly, quarterly, annually, on request) • The different platforms and technologies involved (mainframe, client-server, and/or internet/intranet) • The volume of information exchanged • The various types of data involved (text, images, sounds, graphics, videos, 3-D) • The mechanisms that should be used to activate the interfacing process

High-level testing requirements should be outlined for each critical system interface. Figure 3-37 provides a simple view of an interface between two systems.

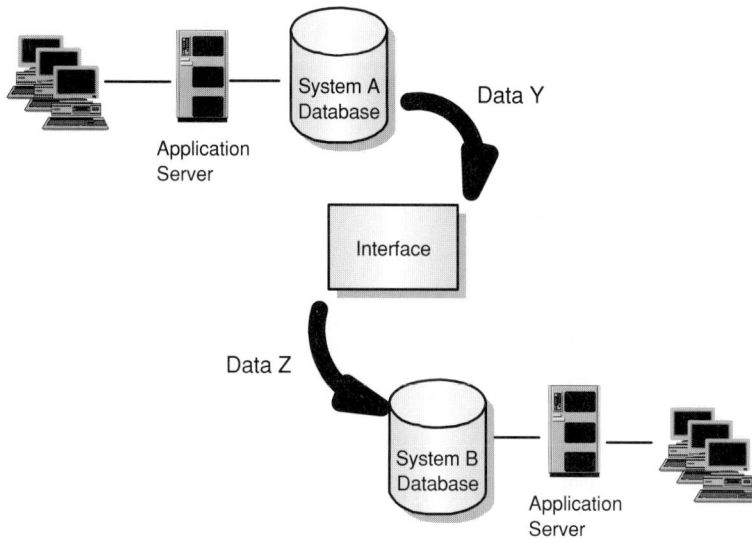

Figure 3–37 Holistic view of a system interface.

TESTING SITES
The major physical sites where the various testing processes will be executed are investigated with the users. The critical elements to review are:

- What are the automated processes that will be tested at each distinct site?
- Will the tests involve client (front-end) and/or server testing (back-end)? Does a need exist to set up some special test configurations?
- What type of test data will be required in order to exercise the tests at each site?
- What are the physical characteristics of these sites?

SECURITY AND CONTROL TESTING REQUIREMENTS
This step consists of determining whether any special security and control requirements need to be enforced to restrict accesses to sensitive data during the execution of the testing process. If so, what are the different types of security requirements (physical, software-oriented, or both) and what are the strategies to verify them?

TESTING TECHNIQUES
The different testing techniques that will be used to verify the system are identified by the development team, along with the level of formality that will be applied in exercising them. Some of the different testing techniques that might be considered include:

- Testing techniques that utilize user scenarios to formulate GUI-oriented test cases
- Formal code reviews via structured walkthroughs

- Informal peer reviews of the program code
- Desktop code inspection
- Automated GUI testing
- Manual GUI testing
- Informal GUI testing
- Usability testing with the users
- Regression testing

The appropriateness of using these various techniques to test the system must be weighed against the level of risk that the enterprise is willing to accept for the application and the amount of time and resources that will be devoted to the testing effort.

In a real-life environment, since the pressure to deliver the system significantly increases as time goes by, the testing process always seem to be constrained by a limited amount of time to test and verify the system's functionality. Thus, a good practice is to prioritize by order of importance the crucial system elements that must be tested first and to what extent. You also want to start testing various system components as early and as often as possible during the project.

If you desire more information on additional testing techniques, you can consult Chapter 8, about client-server and Web testing and entirely dedicated to the testing process.

TESTING ENVIRONMENT AND TOOLS

Assessing whether the existing enterprise technology infrastructure will be able to support the client-server or web testing process is important. If not, additional work might be necessary to select, acquire, install, and test the required additional hardware, software, and networking equipment and facilities.

Furthermore, the development team must assess whether special automated client-server or Web testing tools will be necessary to verify the system. Automated GUI testing tools can help to test the graphical user interfaces of large client-server or Web systems, especially in the context of regression testing. They can also be quite useful to simply complement the manual testing activities that are performed by the testing team.

If new testing tools are acquired, be sure to evaluate whether a need exists to train the testing team members on how to use these sophisticated tools in the most effective manner possible. If training is required and necessitates an extended period of time, then this event should be factored into the overall application development plan. Table 3-80 lists some of the most common types of testing tools.

The development team should also estimate the amount of DASD space that will be necessary to house all the test data, application and database libraries. If the amount of space required turns out to be significant, then you might need to acquire additional disk devices.

Table 3–80 Different Categories Of Testing Tools

• Test data generator tools	• GUI screen capture and playback tools
• Test library configuration tools	• Database and file comparison tools
• Regression testing tools	• Test coverage tools
• Test data management tools	• Test case creation and management tools
• Test data creation tools	• Test database extraction tools
• Defect tracking tools	• Debugging tools
• Server and network load processing tools	• Client load processing tools

Finally, the team should investigate whether a need exists to use a software configuration tool to manage and control the source code of all the programs and objects that will be stored in the different application development and test libraries and their executables.

TEST CASES DEVELOPMENT STRATEGY

The techniques that will be used to create a representative set of test cases should be documented as an integral component of the testing strategy. Likewise, the specific roles and responsibilities of the different groups who will be involved in creating the different categories of test cases and scenarios should also be documented in the testing strategy document.

TEST DATA CREATION/ACQUISITION STRATEGY

For a large and complex system, determining how the test data will be created or acquired might be very important to exercise the system automated processes. Similarly, the development team must factor in the time needed to create or acquire the system test data.

MANAGEMENT TESTING PROCEDURES

The various sets of procedures that will govern the execution, defect tracking, and progress monitoring of all the activities associated with the testing process should be highlighted at this stage. The extent and level of formality at which diverse procedures and control mechanisms will need to be put in place in order to manage the multiple testing activities and its environment should be directly proportional to the magnitude and complexity of the testing effort itself.

Table 3-81 lists some of the most common sets of procedures that can be implemented to manage and control the testing process and its supporting environment.

MAJOR TESTING ROLES AND RESPONSIBILITIES

Lastly, the responsibilities associated with the various user and system groups that will be involved in the testing process should be documented in the testing strategy document.

Table 3–81 Management Testing Procedures

- Change management procedures
- Library management and control procedures
- Problem management procedures
- Defect tracking and resolution procedures
- Progress monitoring procedures

Some experts advocate that individuals who did not participate in the direct development of the system should perform the testing activities, past the unit testing cycle. This approach could be the ideal situation, but the particular context in which each organization operates will ultimately determine the best testing approach, based on the tools, techniques, resources, and time available to the project. Table 3-82 lists some of the questions that should be answered while performing this task.

Table 3–82 General Testing Roles And Responsibilities

- Who will create the test cases and anticipated test results?
- Who will create the test data?
- Who will verify the test results?
- What are the dependencies with other internal or external systems?
- Who will provide the test data for the system interfaces?
- Who will determine the test completion criteria?
- Who will determine the general system acceptance test criteria?
- Who will actually test the system?
- Who will be responsible to report, track and manage the resolution of defects?

PILOT TESTING

If the same system will be implemented in different geographical sites, the users might want to consider conducting a pilot test at one specific location to ensure that the system works properly in an environment as close as possible to a production environment. Once this is done, the system can then be installed at the other locations in either a pre-determined sequence or in parallel, all at once.

PARALLEL TESTING

Typically, parallel testing might be considered when the business inputs and outputs generated by the new system do not differ much from those of the old system. For instance, parallel testing can be a valuable aid if the system is converted almost "as is" from one computer platform to another. The results of the test runs of the new system are compared against the known results of the legacy system while the two operate in parallel with the same input data streams for a certain period of time. For some very critical financial systems, parallel testing can be mandatory.

Activity number:	AN-14
Activity name:	Develop the initial training strategy
Purpose:	To identify the major user training requirements along with the proposed strategy to satisfy them
Inputs:	AN-T1 Business process model AN-T2 Business data model AN-T5 System graphical user interface prototype
Outputs:	AN-T14 Initial training strategy

Activity description:	• Define the scope of the overall training effort
	• Define the major training objectives
	• Identify the broad categories of personnel who will be affected by the implementation of the new system
	  – For each category of personnel, identify the following:
	    – The number of individuals who must be trained
	    – The geographic location of the different groups of personnel who must be trained
	    – The high-level training needs of each group based on current experience level and skill base
	• Develop a preliminary training strategy to address the following points:
	  – An overview to the different training techniques and approaches that will be used along with an identification of what type of training medium/material will be required
	  – How the training material will be developed or what the alternatives are to developing an in-house training program
	  – What the roles and responsibilities of each group involved in planning, developing, and conducting training should be
	  – The number of resources that will be required to support the overall training strategy
	  – Any special hardware/software/networking equipment and facilities that will be required to develop the training material and perform the training effort itself
	  – The high-level training milestones along with the dependencies that might exist between them
	• Walk through the system training strategy deliverable

3.15 DEVELOP THE INITIAL TRAINING STRATEGY

This section discusses the major steps involved in developing the initial system training strategy.

3.15.1 INTRODUCTION

Effective training is a critical success factor to ensure that users will utilize the new system in the most productive manner possible. While it is essential to develop a system that truly meet the users' needs, you must also ensure that the users are properly trained on how to use their new system in an optimal manner. Because of this, a sound and realistic training strategy is required to successfully manage the transition between the old and new system environments.

3.15.2 IDENTIFYING MAJOR CHANGES

Obviously, when the organizational structure that is currently in place does not change drastically or when the new business processes that are introduced with the new system are relatively simple, the transition to the new order of things will likely be relatively straightforward.

Alternately, a large and complex system that will be used by numerous categories of people and that will introduce intensive organizational changes will probably require some special attention because of the massive training effort that must be involved in educating individuals at all levels of the organization.

At this early stage, you might have difficulty assessing completely and precisely the detailed impact that the new system will have on the users and their current business practices. Nonetheless, it is very important to evaluate, at least at a high level, the major types of changes that are likely going to occur in the organizations that will be affected by the new system. It is also important to assess how these changes will affect the different user groups. Table 3-83 lists some of the typical types of changes that can take place when a new system is implemented in an organization.

Table 3–83 Different Types Of Changes

- Business process changes
  - Introduction of new business processes
  - Introduction of new business policies
  - Introduction of new control procedures
  - Enhancement of existing business processes
- Organizational changes
  - Creation of new clerical functions
  - Creation of new managerial functions
- Technological changes
  - Introduction of new application technologies such as client-server or Internet/intranet systems
  - Introduction of new computer equipment such as sophisticated graphical workstations

A brief examination of the nature of these changes can sometimes quickly pinpoint specific areas where some kind of basic training will be required before implementing the system in its production environment. For instance, the creation of new business processes might require that the current task force acquire new skills. For some users, the graphical interfaces that are introduced with client-server or Web database applications might represent a drastic departure from the more traditional character-based applications. Furthermore, the introduction of new sophisticated hardware equipment and facilities such as bar code readers, laser printers, scanners, and optical character readers can become a traumatizing experience for certain personnel if the training is not properly planned and delivered in a timely manner.

The next step consists of identifying the different categories of personnel who might be affected by the changes introduced with the implementation of the new system. The same application can service a variety of personnel, such as executives, middle level managers, supervisors, office clerks, professionals, and staff on the shop floor. Indeed, each category of personnel might have different educational and cultural backgrounds and skill sets that will likely influence the type of training that is best suited for them, as well as the type of new skills that must be acquired by personnel in general.

Besides the users themselves, the particular training needs of the various groups of people in Information Systems, who will be called upon to operate and support the application in the production environment, should not be neglected in the training plan.

Finally, a high-level strategy is developed in an attempt to address all the training needs that have been identified so far. At this point in time, a sufficient approach is to highlight the general goals and objectives associated with the training process, the magnitude of the planned training effort, the type of training methods recommended, and the additional or specialized hardware/software/networking facilities that might be required to support the entire training effort. During the design phase, the training strategy will be refined at a more detailed level.

Activity number:	AN-15
Activity name:	Define the hardware/software/networking requirements
Purpose:	To identify the major hardware, software, and networking requirements of the new system
Inputs:	AN-T1 Business process model AN-T2 Business data model AN-T3 System transactions AN-T5 System graphical user interface prototype AN-T6 Initial system distribution strategy AN-T7 System interface requirements AN-T8 System security and control requirements

	AN-T9 System operational requirements
	AN-T10 Initial capacity plan
	AN-T11 Initial data conversion strategy
	AN-T12 Initial backup/recovery strategy
	AN-T13 Initial testing strategy
	AN-T14 Initial training strategy
Outputs:	AN-T15 Hardware/software/networking requirements
Activity description:	• Review the detailed process and data requirements that are described in the business process and data models. Also review the additional set of requirements that are outlined in the data conversion, training, and testing strategy deliverables. If produced, also review the volumetric data contained in the initial capacity plan for the system.
	• Identify the new classes of hardware components that will be required to support the new client-server or Web system.
	• Identify the new classes of software components that will be required to support the new client-server or Web system.
	• Identify the new classes of network components that will be required to support the new client-server or Web system.
	• Identify the geographic locations where the new system will be used. Describe, in general terms, how the processes and data will be processed and/or distributed at each location. Describe the additional data communication facilities that will be required to support the computerized operations of the proposed system.
	• Consolidate the hardware/software/networking requirements. Determine and document the major characteristics of each critical hardware/software/networking component, along with a description of the supported protocols.
	• Verify that the new hardware/software/networking components and protocols that are required to support the application have a high level of interoperability among themselves and with the current components that comprise the enterprise technology infrastructure.
	• Develop an acquisition and installation strategy.
	• Walk through the hardware/software/networking requirement deliverable.

3.16 DEFINE THE HARDWARE/SOFTWARE/NETWORKING REQUIREMENTS

This section describes the critical steps involved in developing the initial hardware, software and networking system requirements.

3.16.1 INTRODUCTION

Identifying the hardware/software/networking requirements might not be a big task if the proposed application system can be implemented with the technology infrastructure that is already in place. If, on the contrary, the new system will require some new types of hardware/software/networking technologies, then you must define and document these requirements. Sometimes, this task can be difficult, especially when the information that has been gathered so far by the development team about the general system requirements might still be incomplete, in certain areas. Nevertheless, you need to understand the magnitude of these requirements and the impact they can have on the current enterprise technology architecture.

The following sections discuss some important elements that might adversely affect the existing enterprise technology architecture if they are not addressed carefully during the early stages of the system development life cycle.

3.16.2 TOTAL SYSTEM RESOURCE LOAD ESTIMATES

Be sure to analyze the system volumetric information that so far has been gathered on performance-related elements, such as:

- Total estimated number of online transactions per unit of time, including peak periods
- Total estimated number of batch transactions per unit of time
- Total estimated volume of active data to be supported by the system

If the proposed system will replace an existing system, then some of these statistics can be obtained directly from the users or from the system operations people who support the present application. Projections might have to be made for the set of entirely new business processes that will be introduced with the proposed system.

If you determine that the existing computerized environment can absorb the anticipated system resource load estimates, then you might not need to continue this evaluation task. On the other hand, the existing enterprise technology infrastructure may not be able to absorb the additional workload that will be incurred with the implementation of the new system. In such a case, the development team should immediately contact the different technology groups inside the Information Systems organization who are responsible for supporting the technology infrastructure and inform them about the current situation. This early notification should be done as early as possible during the system development life cycle of large systems.

3.16.3 INTEROPERABILITY ISSUES

If the organization has already prescribed a basic set of standards or guidelines that provide guidance to the developers when evaluating and selecting various hardware/

software/networking components, then the risk of acquiring inadequate or incompatible equipment or facilities will be reduced.

When defining the detailed hardware/software/networking requirements, the development team should always view these apparently three distinct entities as one, because they often are very strongly interdependent with one another. In fact, one of the most critical aspects of the decision-making process regarding the selection and acquisition of technology components is the often dreadful interoperability factor. For example, decisions concerning the acquisition of a specific line of hardware servers from a given manufacturer might dictate by default the selection of some very specific operating software components. This constraint might be necessary to maintain an acceptable level of reliability and efficiency for the application at hand.

Even if the same vendor provides a software component that can run on several platforms, this component might not necessarily offer the same level of functionality or efficiency when it runs on different types of platforms. Quite often, the software components are highly optimized for a given platform but only at the detriment of other platforms.

Lastly, you might want to verify that the new software components that are required to support the proposed system are compatible with the existing enterprise technology infrastructure and supported protocols.

3.16.4 HARDWARE COMPONENTS

As indicated in Figure 3-38, the major hardware components for a client-server or Web database system include the client workstations, the server machines, and the network.

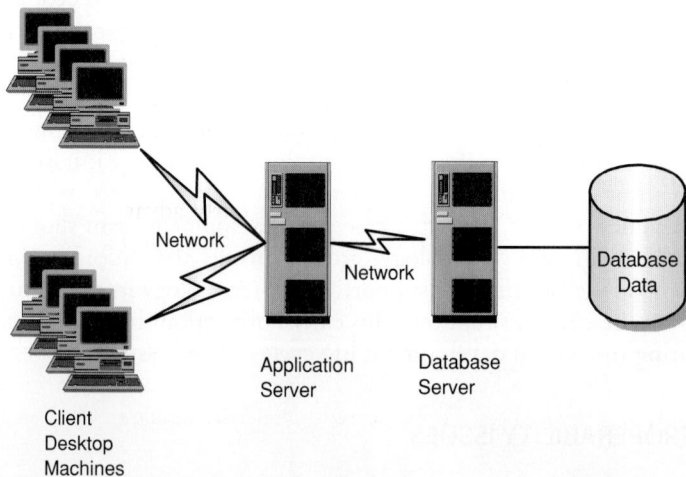

Figure 3–38 Client-server or web application hardware components.

Following is a brief description of the requirements that are usually associated with each of these specific hardware components.

CLIENT MACHINE REQUIREMENTS

The type of client machine and its configuration requirements must be defined and confirmed by the development team. These primarily include the processor, memory, and storage configurations that are required for the client machines. The client machine must be able to support the type of load processing that will be needed to locally process some components of the application software itself and the supporting operating system.

Similarly, the type and number of client machines that must be acquired by categories of users must also be defined with the users. You might want to discuss with the users whether special configurations requirements exist for the client machine and its complementary devices. For example:

- Should the users be provided with a keyboard that supports multiple languages?

- Should the keyboard be adapted for allowing the quick use of specialized functions?

- Should certain machines be equipped with special data capture devices such as bar code readers?

Likewise, the type of workstations needed might be greatly influenced by the locations where they will be installed, such as in an office environment or on the shop floor of a manufacturer. For example, if the working conditions in the manufacturing plants are extreme (heat, cold, dust, vibrations, and corrosive atmosphere), selecting terminals that can withstand such extreme environmental conditions will be very important. Similarly, will thin-client machines be used, as opposed to fat-client machines?

Another important factor to consider is the different categories of personnel who will be equipped with the workstations. For instance, will the workstations be used by people who constantly perform some specialized functions, or will they be used intermittently by different people who must perform various general-purpose business processes?

The use of special-purpose workstations can be fairly advantageous when maximum speed and high accuracy are required, since they can significantly minimize the need for keying data and therefore making potential errors.

On the other hand, multipurpose terminals can increase the flexibility of the users, especially when the users must frequently adjust their working methods or are called upon to perform various non-specialized functions.

Table 3-84 lists some of the most common physical characteristics that should be defined for the client machines.

If a certain class of users will need PC laptops with a dockable workstation, then spell out the physical characteristics of this type of equipment now.

Table 3–84 Client Machine And Complementaty Devices Physical Characteristics

• Type of workstation (PC-based, UNIX-based, PC-Network, etc.) • Workstation internal architectural characteristics (motherboard type, microprocessor family, speed capability, bus architecture, RAM memory speed/size/expandability) • Monitors (screen size, levels of resolution supported, number of colors supported) • Input devices (keyboard, mouse, pen, bar code reader, scanner, OCR, complementary hand-held computer devices) • Output devices (printer, plotter) • Modem (speed, internal/external)	• Type of graphical card for video display (number of colors supported by level of resolution, graphical memory size, 2D/3D graphic acceleration capabilities) • Type of network interface card • Permanent DASD storage (hard disk capacity, read/write speeds) • Type of removable storage media (floppy disk, optical drive, CD-ROM) • Voice recognition • Tape backup unit • Multimedia add-ons (sound card, speakers, video capture card, digital camera, videoconference card)

PRINTER REQUIREMENTS

The speed, types, volumes of data that must be printed per unit of time, and desired print quality will determine the types of printer servers and printers that are required at different user locations. Likewise, the total number of printers that are required to support the system must be determined, based on the number of users to service and the estimated application print loads per user or central locations.

Table 3-85 provides a list of basic questions that can be used by the development team to help them determine the types of printers that are required to support the system.

Table 3–85 Printer Requirements Questionnaire

• For the departmental printers, will black-and-white laser printers suffice or will color laser printers be necessary?   • What about inkjet or impact printers?   • What quality of printing is required for text? For graphics?   • How many pages per minute should the printers support?   • What sizes of paper should the printer support besides the traditional 8 by 11?   • Does anyone have special printing requirements such as the ability to print bar code labels?   • Does anyone need a printer that can support special stationary items such as pre-printed forms or special fonts?

PHYSICAL SERVER REQUIREMENTS

Assuming that the processor, memory, and storage requirements for the application and database servers are known, then the type and number of server machines that must be acquired to support the system must be defined by the development team.

The system growth estimates that cover the next 2 to 4 years' time horizon should also be factored in. Be sure to choose servers that can scale up when the volume of transactions that are processed by the application increases over time. Some of the questions that might be asked to uncover the database (and also application logic-related server) requirements are:

- What type of system processes needs to be supported?
- What type of data needs to be supported?
- What volumes of data or CPU processing power does the server need to hold?
- What will be the server access frequency per unit of time?
- What is the performance of the server?
- What will be the memory size of the application modules?

The types of platform and software operating environments that were chosen to run the application will largely influence the selection of the physical servers. If existing servers are already in place, then they might need to be upgraded and scaled up to satisfy the extra workload that the new application will generate.

Table 3-86 provides a list of some of the most common server characteristics that should be evaluated prior to making a final decision.

Table 3–86 Physical Server Characteristics

• Type of server station (PC-based, UNIX-based, etc.) • Server station internal architectural characteristics (motherboard type, microprocessor family, speed capability, bus architecture, RAM memory speed/size/expandability, number of multiprocessors) • Number of expansion slots	• Type of network interface card • Permanent DASD storage (hard disk capacity, read/write speeds, fault-tolerant characteristic such as redundant arrays of inexpensive disks—RAID—levels, expandability) • Type of removable storage media (floppy disk, optical drive, CD-ROM) • Tape backup unit

Depending on the type of application technology architecture that was chosen to implement the application at hand, the physical server machines can house various software components such as the procedural code used to run the system business logic and the database management system.

NETWORK REQUIREMENTS

The projected volumes of traffic on the network will determine the category of network required to support the application. The total number of client workstations and servers will determine the number of network connections that are required to connect the workstations and the servers to the network itself. Similarly, determine the adequate combination of network hardware and software components that are needed to keep the network traffic flow circulating at an acceptable speed and rate.

Table 3-87 lists some of the most common types of network components that might be required to support the application.

Table 3–87 Network Hardware Components

• Network interface cards (NIC)	• Modems
• Bridges	• Gateways
• B-routers	• Routers
• Hubs	• Network middleware

Network interface cards (NICs) are installed in each client workstation and server station. They are used to manage the flow of data that circulates between the client workstations and the servers. The major characteristics of the NICs that should be determined by the development team are the connection type, bandwidth, and transmission speed supported by the card.

Bridges, routers, hubs, and gateways are utilized to link several networks with varying degrees of transparencies. Table 3-88 provides a brief description of these network devices.

Table 3–88 Different Types Of Network Devices

NETWORK COMPONENT	DESCRIPTION
Bridge	A bridge is a network component that connects two similar LANs, using the same communication protocol.
Router	A router is a network component that connects different types of networks that work with different network communication protocols.
B-router	A B-router is a network device that combines the bridge and router functionality to transparently bridge protocols and performs network-layer routing.
Gateway	A gateway is a hardware/software device that can connect two dissimilar systems.
Hub	A hub is a wiring concentrator that brings together various network connections from several nodes.

The network specialists will determine the optimal network configuration architecture and how to achieve the required level of communication connectivity between the various network components. The network design decisions are primarily based on the application network traffic patterns (i.e., type of information transmitted, such as plain text or graphics, the volume of data transmitted between the different network nodes, and timing).

Nevertheless, be sure to attempt to reduce the complexity of the network architecture by limiting as much as possible the number of different network vendors and protocols used.

At this stage, you should draw a preliminary sketch that illustrates the different geographic locations where the computer processors and their peripheral equipment will be installed. At the same time, answer several questions, such as:

- Can the current site premises satisfy the hardware requirements in terms of floor space, temperature, humidity, and electrical power?

- What changes should be made at the various locations to accommodate the new hardware components?

- What impact will these additions have on the current environment? Do some new construction requirements exist? Do you need to pass network cables between the walls of the buildings?

Also, indicate on the chart the basic requirements for connecting the various pieces of hardware equipment across the different sites. But before doing so, the network analysis steps that are indicated in Table 3-89 should be successfully completed.

COMMUNICATION PROTOCOL REQUIREMENTS

Communication protocols provide program-to-program communications over the local-area networks (LANs) and the wide-area networks (WANs). Examples of LANs include ethernet, token-ring, and fiber distributed data interface (FDDI). Examples of WANs include packet switching and integrated services digital networks (ISDN).

The Transmission Control Protocol/Internet Protocol (TCP/IP) is the de facto client-server networking standard today. If the application needs to communicate to the mainframe environment, then a connection between the TCP/IP protocol and the mainframe protocol, such as the SNA/LU 6.2 protocol, might also be required.

Other types of protocols might be required to support the application, such as:

- File Transfer Protocol (FTP): Used to transfer files over a TCP/IP network

- Simple Mail Transfer Protocol (SMTP): Used to transfer electronic mail over a TCP/IP network

Following is Table 3-90, a sample that can be used to describe the various categories of networks that would be required to support a hypothetical system.

Following is Table 3-91, another sample that can be used to describe, at a high level, the various types of major hardware components that would be required to support a hypothetical system at specific locations.

Table 3–89 Network Analysis Tasks

- Identify the exact locations where the hardware components will be installed. Will the users have their own workstation or will some workstations be located in a common area? Although the vast majority of users will interface with the system at their desks, specific situations might arise in which mobile users will also require access to the system when they are on the road, such as salespeople and field representatives. These people will need PC laptops and a way to be able to securely communicate with the system from remote locations. If this is the case for the application at hand, then the network requirements should reflect the mobile users needs in an accurate manner.
- Determine the network availability requirements. For example, estimate the average number of hours per day and days per week during which each combination of communication connections must remain in operation.
- Determine the type of traffic pattern for each specific network facility, such as: continuous, on-request, intermittent, periodic.
- Determine the types and volume of data that will flow through the network pipes at peak periods, the speed requirements associated with each major category of data transmission, and the maximum number of concurrent users that can be connected at different peak hours. Will the application data transmitted through the network be text, graphic or multimedia?
- Determine the network security requirements. Should data be encrypted?
- Identify the level of degradation that might be tolerated, if any, during a certain period of time in case of overload. Define the network backup requirements in case of failure?
- Analyze the evolving needs of the application covering the foreseeable future while you evaluate different communication network alternatives (i.e., public data networks, public switched networks, meshed networks, local area networks, metropolitan area networks, wide-area networks, the Internet).
- Define the type of protocols will be used to connect the various network links.
- Determine whether legacy data must be accessed by the application from the client-server platform, via the means of a gateway.

Table 3–90 Basic Network Structure

Network id	Purpose	Protocol	Controlling system element	Connections to other network(s)
Network A	New York LAN	TCP/IP	LAN controller PC	Network C
Network B	Singapore LAN	TCP/IP	LAN controller PC	Network C
Network C	Headquarter Sidney WAN/LAN	TCP/IP	Prime server	

Table 3–91 List Of Major Hardware Components

Location	Component type	Number of components	Connections to other network(s)
Atlanta	Server A	1	Network C (WAN)
	PC workstation	25	LAN A
	Laser printer	2	LAN A
Brazilia	Server B	1	Network C (WAN)
	PC workstation	50	LAN B

SOFTWARE REQUIREMENTS

The application software development tools requirements are determined based on the specific needs of the application development team and the selected development and target technology environments. Some of the basic questions that should be answered to uncover these requirements are indicated in Table 3-92.

Table 3–92 Software Requirements Questionnaire

- On what type of computer platform will the application development tools operate? What protocols are supported?
- With what type of software and network operating systems will the application development tools run?
- What are the current release levels of all the different development tool components that must inter-operate together?
- What type of database server will be used with the application? Will native application program interfaces (APIs) be used to connect directly to the database servers or will ODBC-compliant drivers be used?
- What are the software configurations of the current user workstations?
- How well will the different software development tools integrate with each other? With the existing development tools?

Some of the different types of software tools that might be required to support the development process are indicated in Table 3-93.

Also, be very sure to determine the type of operating software and network operating systems that will be used on either the client workstations or servers.

Another important category of software to investigate is middleware. The prime purpose of middleware software is to maintain the integrity of the data and the processes across different networks, computer platforms and protocols. The middleware

Table 3–93 Different Categories Of Software Tools

- Database servers
- Rapid application development tools for client-server or Web applications
- Application testing and debugging tools
- PC-related products that must interface with the custom application such as word processor and spreadsheet tools
- Database query and reporting tools
- CASE tools
- Project management tools
- Project library and software configuration management tools
- Data warehouse tools
- Automated GUI testing tools
- Server load capacity evaluation tools
- Database, message-oriented, object request broker middleware tools

software usually sits somewhere between the network operating system and application layers.

Different categories of middleware are available. One of the most popular categories is the database gateway. Database gateways can tie application access requests from one database type to another. They can also connect clients and server stations that operate on dissimilar networks and platforms. Database gateways are often the preferred solution to large client-server and Web applications that need to access legacy data that reside on the mainframe.

Figure 3-39 shows, at a high level, the generic tasks that are usually performed by database gateways.

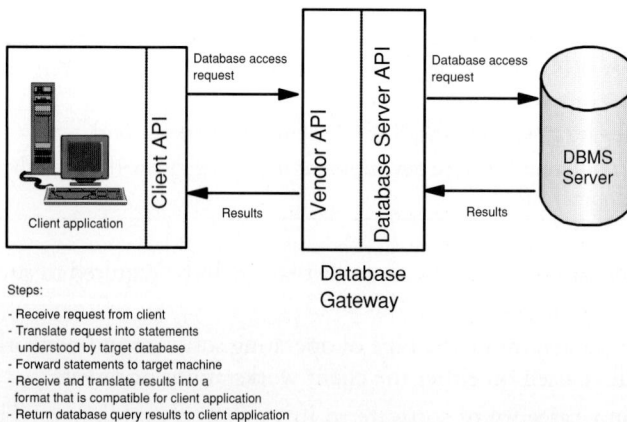

Figure 3–39 Database gateway generic tasks.

All the data conversion and translation tasks that are performed by the database gateway are done in a manner that is completely transparent to the programmer.

I provide more detailed information on database gateways and middleware in Chapter 9.

Finally, the development team must select the type of database management system that will be used to best support the application data requirements. Some of the most basic questions that must be answered to select the appropriate database management system are indicated in Table 3-94.

Table 3–94 Database Server Characteristics

- What type of database system is required: relational, universal server (i.e., able to store multimedia data), object-oriented, multi-dimensional?
- On what type of server platform and software operating system will the database software run?
- What are the major characteristics for which the database software must provide support, such as:
  - Provide support to different types of database gateways
  - Triggers
  - Stored procedures
  - Two-phase commits
  - Referential integrity compliance
  - Database security/audibility features
  - Database backup/recovery features
  - Database replication features
  - Database distributed features, if data is to be distributed
  - Scalability features
  - Performance capabilities
- What are the different categories of communication protocols that must be supported?

3.16.5 THE HARDWARE/SOFTWARE/NETWORKING ACQUISITION AND INSTALLATION STRATEGY

Once all the detailed hardware/software/networking requirements have been identified, a plan of action to acquire and install these commodities must be developed and documented. This plan should address the items that are indicated in Table 3-95.

Depending on the criticality of the system with regard to the well-being of the organization, I recommend in some instances considering additional alternatives for replacing critical hardware items, in case unexpected problems suddenly surface.

For instance, a safe, preventive approach might be necessary to cover unforeseen situations when the much-needed equipment cannot be delivered by the vendor as per the agreed delivery dates or when the equipment clearly does not work as anticipated.

Table 3–95 Hardware/software/networking Acquisition And Installation Strategy Components

- Identification of all critical hardware, software, and networking components that must be acquired and the locations where they should be installed
- Identification of the inter-dependencies that might exist among the related hardware, software, and networking components
- Identification of the sequence in which they must be acquired, installed, and tested for overall functionality and interoperability
- The roles and responsibilities of each group involved in acquiring, installing, and verifying the basic functionality provided by theses commodities
- The expected delivery dates and installation dates of each critical system component

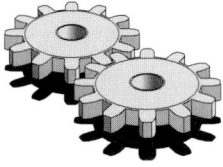

4

Design

4.1 INTRODUCTION

The primary objective of the design phase is to create a design that satisfies the system functional requirements. The graphical user interface prototype that was developed earlier during the analysis phase is gradually refined and extended with all the details required to satisfy the full spectrum of application business functions.

The construction of this preliminary application prototype provided several advantages to the users. Among other things, it allowed them to better visualize the application user interface and its major components. The users had first-hand interactions with the main application windows and their GUI controls. They explored the navigational capabilities provided by the interface and thus had the opportunity to comment on the interface's overall usability and effectiveness.

The creation of this live prototype also provided a solid foundation to identify the detailed functional requirements of the application.

I have no doubt that, through the users' eyes, the graphical user interface is certainly the most important component of the system. After all, through this interface, they will interact with the system to perform their business functions. However, for the developers, the user interface just represents the tip of the iceberg. In fact, the design and integration of several additional internal system components is required to eventually deliver a robust, fully functional system. Figure 4-1 illustrates this point.

For large and complex client-server and Web database applications, the design issues that are associated with the performance, reliability, robustness, scalability, security, and maintainability characteristics of the system are of paramount importance.

The detailed design of the physical database and the application functional components should be engineered in a way that offers as much flexibility and adaptability as possible. This process must take into consideration the existing enterprise technical architecture. It must also take into account the physical constraints that might be imposed by the technology that was selected to implement the system.

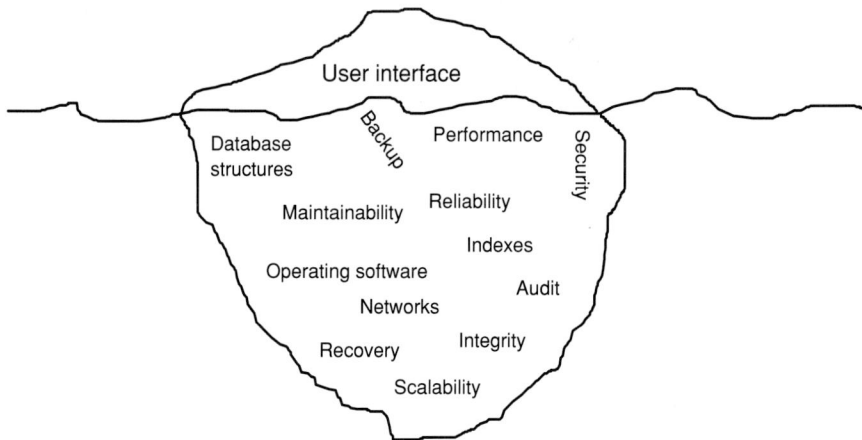

Figure 4–1 System external and internal components

You should properly document any deviation from the original application requirements that might be needed to accommodate specific operational criteria. Discuss thoroughly the alternatives, along with their respective trade-offs, with the users.

During the design phase, the initial system data conversion and testing strategies that were elaborated during the analysis phase are refined with more detailed information. Similarly, detailed test cases are designed to support the different testing stages that will be executed during the construction phase.

Table 4-1 summarizes the major technical activities that are conducted during the design phase, along with a list of the anticipated technical deliverables.

Table 4–1 Design Phase

ACTIVITY	DELIVERABLE(S)
1.Determine GUI design standards and guidelines	1.GUI design standards and guidelines
2.Create logical database design	2.Logical database structures
3.Create physical database design	3.Physical database structures
4.Design database security and audit schemes	4.Database security and audit schemes design
5.Design shared, reusable software components	5.Shared, reusable software components design
6.Design detailed custom application software components	6.Detailed custom application software components design
7.Design system interfaces	7.System interfaces

Table 4–1 Design Phase (cont.)

8.Design data conversion programs	8.Data conversion programs design
9.Design ad hoc report and query environment	9.Ad hoc report and query environment design
10.Create preliminary system documentation	10.Preliminary system documentation
11.Finalize detailed system training strategy	11.Detailed system training strategy
12.Finalize detailed testing strategy	12.Detailed testing strategy
13.Finalize detailed data conversion strategy	13.Detailed data conversion strategy
14.Finalize detailed capacity plan	14.Detailed capacity plan

Figure 4-2 pictorially presents, at a high level, the relationships that exist among the individual activities of the design phase.

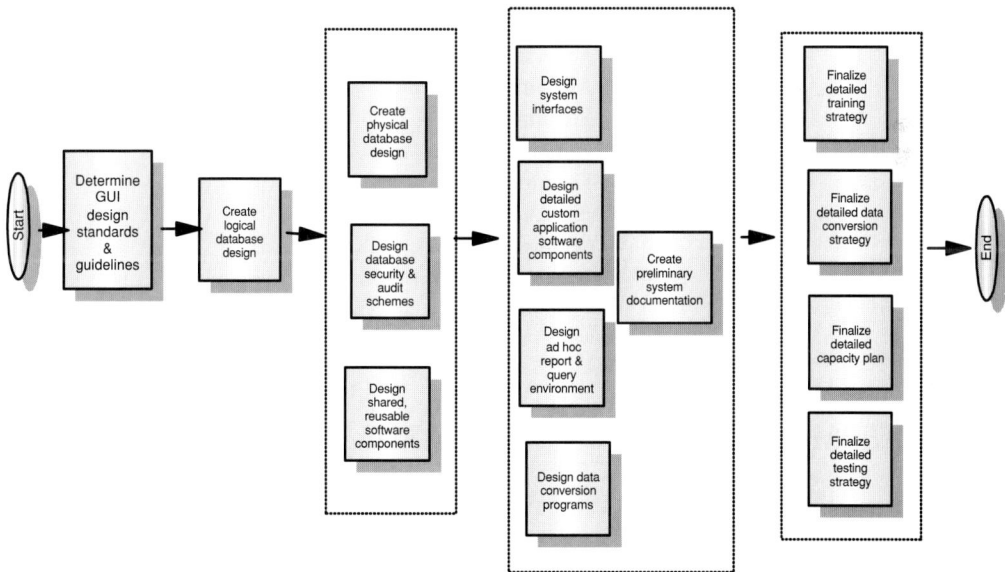

Figure 4–2 Design phase technical activities.

Although the linear sequence in which some of the design activities that are shown in Figure 4-2 might suggest that one specific activity must be completed prior to start the next one, in reality they can be performed in parallel or in different sequences.

Furthermore, several of these activities can be performed by following an iterative approach, gradually refining the deliverables in incremental steps. On the other hand, certain types of activities might not easily lend themselves to an iterative development approach.

At the completion of each major design activity, a formal walkthrough should be scheduled to review the final deliverables.

Activity number:	DE-1
Activity name:	Determine GUI design standards and guidelines
Purpose:	To describe the set of GUI standards and conventions that will be used to design the application
Inputs:	Existing system development standards and guidelines
Outputs:	DE-T1 GUI Design standards and guidelines

Activity description:	• Describe the minimum set of standards that apply to the design of the application graphical interface, covering:
	  – Report layouts and templates
	  – Window layouts and templates
	  – Form layouts and templates
	  – Multimedia interfaces (sound, video, etc.)
	  – Pen interfaces
	  – E-mail interfaces
	  – Fax interfaces
	  – Bar code interfaces
	  – Web interfaces
	• Walk through the minimum set of graphical user interface design standards that should be adhered to by the development team members

4.2 DETERMINE GUI DESIGN STANDARDS AND GUIDELINES

This section discusses basic conventions and guidelines that relate to the design of graphical components such as application windows and menus.

4.2.1 OVERVIEW

The minimum yet essential set of user interface standards, guidelines, or conventions that should be used to design the various application screen layouts must be thoroughly discussed with all development team members.

This review process is a very crucial step toward ensuring the design of a quality system. This statement is especially true when many design teams are called upon to simultaneously develop different sections of a large and complex client-server or Web application. Failure to clearly spell out the most critical graphical user interface conventions might result in reduced application consistency, usability, and maintainability.

If a minimum level of user interface design consistency is achieved across all corporate applications, then the users will be relieved of the painful task of trying to adapt to a myriad of different graphical user interfaces. Moreover, the development team will likely increase the overall efficiency of the users by reducing the likelihood of them making costly errors. Application design consistency should also decrease their level of frustration while they interact with these applications.

Lastly, the learning curve that they must go through while they familiarize themselves with different applications should be minimized significantly since a common graphical user interface will be shared across applications and sustain a predictable behavior. The users should become far more effective and efficient when they use applications that share common "look and feel" characteristics.

Sections 4.2.2 and 4.2.3 discuss some of the different types of graphical user interface standards and conventions that apply to the design and construction of a large-scale client-server application. It also includes advice and commentary on each major set of proposed standards. The two major standards that are covered include:

- Windows conventions

- Menu conventions

Some of these conventions are also relevant to Web database applications. However, you might want to consult Chapter 11 for more specific information on Web application development standards.

I also provide specific guidelines on user interface style definition, screen navigation behavior and on product usability concepts in Chapter 12.

The types of hardware and software tools that are used to develop the system will likely influence the GUI design guidelines. Above all, the design standards and guidelines should remain at a very pragmatic level so developers really use them.

4.2.2   WINDOWS CONVENTIONS

The graphical user interface (GUI) conventions that will be used to design the application windows should at least cover the items that are listed in Table 4-2.

Several good ideas for designing effective, professional-looking user interfaces can be emulated by carefully studying the most popular commercial client-server and Web applications that exist on the market today. In some instances, if the users of the future application are already familiar with a particular product that they use regularly, then

Table 4–2 Windows Components That Require Design Conventions

- Placement and format of command buttons
- Placement and format of status elements such as date, time, page number
- Placement and format of messages (i.e., warning, informative messages)
- Placement and format of menu items
- Placement and format of tool bars, scroll bars, control palettes
- Placement, format, and data representation of input fields (i.e., text and numbers), headers, and labels
- Use of color and fonts for window objects and window backgrounds
- Window screen resolution levels
- Placement and format of multimedia elements such as sounds and video clips
- Placement and format of error messages
- Placement and format of pop-up windows

resorting to developing a similar user interface makes sense in order to take full advantage of that familiarity.

> *Discussing in detail how to design very effective user interfaces is beyond the scope of this book. However, the references that are provided at the end of this book point to references that can be consulted to learn the difficult art of designing highly effective graphical user interfaces. Searching for GUI guidelines that are posted on the world wide web can also be a very effective way of finding some valuable information on this subject.*

Table 4-3 lists some practical conventions that are utilized for the effective design of user-friendly windows.

Table 4–3 General Windows Conventions And Guidelines

SUBJECT	DESIGN GUIDELINE
Number of control buttons	The number of control buttons that are displayed on a window should be limited to avoid confusing the user. Use multiple windows as an alternative to overcrowd a single window with too many controls. The tab folder metaphor can be used to display several tabbed pages that in turn display additional controls.
Controls availability	When controls are not available to users, they should be disabled (i.e., dimmed out).
Controls spacing	Normally, controls should not be clustered physically one against another. White spaces should be inserted between them.

Table 4–3 General Windows Conventions And Guidelines (cont.)

Controls borders	3-D lowered borders are often used to make control buttons stand out as opposed to static text, which usually does not display any form of border delineation.
Keyboard support	At a bare minimum, the user should be able to activate every window control feature not only with the mouse but also directly from the keyboard.
Fonts	As a rule of thumb, a unique font should be consistently used for the same set of application windows. Ideally, this font should be a standard font that is already installed on the user workstation. If required, the same font may be used in a limited number of different font sizes.
Colors	Color should be used with parsimony, such as when some portions of the window must stand out. Careful attention should be given to selecting non-offensive colors that, as much as possible, will not adversely affect the user's default settings.
Amodal window usage	Use non-modal (non-response) windows wherever possible to provide the user with as much control latitude as possible over the presentation interface.
Modal window usage	Use modal (response) windows only when the user must be forced to respond to the information that is displayed in the window.

To a large extent, windows standardization in an application can be achieved through the use of inheritance. With inheritance, a basic set of standard windows can be defined once at the ancestor level and subsequently extended or overridden by an application at a descendant level. Chapter 7 provides more in-depth information on the object-oriented concept of inheritance.

4.2.3 MENU CONVENTIONS

Table 4-4 lists simple conventions that are commonly used for the effective design of standard menus in a client-server application. The use of a common "look and feel" menu across multiple applications will allow the users to utilize different applications that offer the same predictable behavior.

To a large extent, menu standardization in an application can be achieved through the use of inheritance. With inheritance, a standard menu can be defined once at the ancestor level and subsequently extended or overridden by an application at a descendant level.

Table 4–4 General Windows Menu Conventions And Guidelines

SUBJECT	DESIGN GUIDELINE
Number of menu elements	The number of elements that are displayed on a menu should be limited to avoid confusing the user with too many options.
Depth of menu elements	When using a cascading menu, no more than one or two lower levels should be utilized in order to avoid user confusion.
Menu elements availability	When specific elements of the menu are not available to users, they should be disabled (i.e., dimmed out).
Menu elements wording	Each element shown on a menu should carry a descriptive name that clearly indicates its purpose. A menu element should not be composed with more than two simple words, preferably a single word only. Standard names or verbs should be used whenever possible, such as File, Edit, Window, Help.
Menu elements placement	The menu elements in an application should always be positioned at the same location on the menu bar, preferably using the most common standard window conventions (i.e., File, Edit, Window, Help, etc.).
Help menu element	Each menu bar should always contain a help menu element that displays the help information that is specific to the current application.
Keyboard support	Shortcut keys should be used to alternately select a menu item. Accelerator keys should be used to allow quick access to a specific menu element.

Activity number:	DE-2
Activity name:	Create logical database design
Purpose:	To transform the business data model into logical database structure(s)
Inputs:	AN-T1 Business process model AN-T2 Business data model AN-T6 Initial system distribution strategy AN-T10 Initial capacity plan
Outputs:	DE-T2 Logical database structures

Activity description:
- Review the entity-relationship data model that was created earlier during the analysis phase and the initial data distribution and capacity plan deliverables.
- Verify that the business data model and all its related deliverables are complete.
- If you have not already done so, normalize and transform the business data model into first-cut logical database structures:
  - Map each entity to a corresponding table
  - Map each attribute of an entity to a column
  - Assign each table a primary key identifier
- Based on the information contained in the different data access matrices that were developed during the analysis phase, identify the critical primary and/or secondary access path patterns.
  - Verify that the logical database structures can satisfy the data access requirements for both online and batch system transactions.
  - If you determine that some critical system transaction will not be able to meet its stated service-level objectives, either modify the logical database structures to accommodate the required access paths or modify the system transaction itself.
- Determine the initial data views required by the application, based on the access patterns that were identified in the data access matrices.
- Review and refine the business data integrity rules that were documented with the business data model. Decide where and how the application data and referential integrity requirements will be enforced: either in the databases or in the application programs.
- If necessary, denormalize or amend the logical database structures to satisfy specific data access requirements or physical design constraints.
- Walk through the logical database structures.

ADDITIONAL GUI DESIGN GUIDELINES

GUI physical design limitation. While the developers establish the design conventions that should be applied to the layout of the graphical user interfaces, keep in mind that the display capabilities of different types of user workstations might impose some constraints on the available design options. For example, if some users have display monitors that have lower-level resolution capabilities than other users, then you might need to use the lowest level of resolution as a common denominator to design the application windows.

Although less prevalent today, a few users out there may have monochrome monitors. In such a case, the design of the windows should not emphasize the use of colors to highlight special elements of the user interface.

Another constraining design factor might be the display size of the monitors that will be utilized by the users. Will the users utilize workstations that all have the same display size or will they use several types of workstations that have different monitor display sizes?

Multi-platform design limitations. If the application that is being developed will run on different platforms such as UNIX, Microsoft Windows, or Apple Macintosh, then the user interface conventions might slightly differ from one platform to another. Nonetheless, the user interface should be designed, as much as possible, with the lowest common denominator graphical elements that are supported by all target platforms.

International design considerations. If the application is intended to be used by an international audience or in a multilingual setting, then the conventions for the design of the user interface will need to take into account the various cultures and languages of the different countries where it will be used. Cultural differences might be reflected in the choices made while designing the user interfaces.

Help system. The standards that apply to the help system should include guidelines on context sensitivity, different levels of help provided (application level, screen level, field level), and format and general placement of help information.

4.3 CREATE THE LOGICAL DATABASE DESIGN

This section discusses the detailed steps required to transform the application data model into a sound logical database design. It also provides suggestions and tips on how to best perform this process.

4.3.1 INTRODUCTION

In this activity, the business data model is transformed into a first-cut logical database design that can satisfy the data access requirements of the application.

Once this transformation process is done, the logical database design structures are then gradually refined to satisfy the specific operational requirements of the application that relate to performance, security, and data distribution considerations.

Finally, the initial logical database structures might require specific enhancements to accommodate any physical limitations or constraints that might be imposed by the selected database management software and target technology architecture.

4.3.2 TRANSLATING THE BUSINESS DATA MODEL INTO A FIRST-CUT LOGICAL DATABASE DESIGN

Prior to converting the business data model into a set of logical database structures, verify that the data model encompasses all the data needs for the application at hand.

Similarly, all the unique identifiers for each entity should be clearly identified on the business data model.

Once this verification step is done, then you can derive a first-cut logical database structure from the entity-relationship diagram. The major tasks that are involved in this mapping process are listed in Table 4-5.

Table 4–5 Logical Database Design Tasks

Entities with no subtypes	• For each entity documented in the entity-relationship data model, create a single table that contains one column for each specific attribute of the entity • For each relationship that is characterized by a one-to-one association, either add the primary key of one of the data entities as a foreign key column in the other entity's table or implement both entities in one table • For each relationship that is characterized by a one-to-many association, add a foreign key column in the table implementing the entity at the "many" side of the relationship • For each relationship that is characterized by a many-to-many association, create an intersection table whose primary key is a concatenation of the respective primary keys of the two entities involved in the many-to-many relationship
Entities with subtypes	• For complex entities that contain several subtypes, design a table structure using various options, such as: – Create a unique table that implements together the entity supertype and all the subtypes – Create separate tables for the entity supertype and each entity subtype – Create separate tables for each entity subtype but not the supertype

The particular characteristics of each column in a table are directly derived from those that were documented with the attributes for each specific entity, such as length, domain, datatype, and so forth.

Finally, each unique identifier of an entity is usually transformed directly into a primary key identifier for the corresponding table. However, in some specific instances, you may want to implement an artificial unique key. For example, if you can't be certain that the primary key will ever need to be modified, then add an artificial unique key. Another situation might be when the primary key is a composite of several attributes and the entity itself is referenced by several other entities. In such a context, you might want to implement an artificial unique key to save on disk space and possibly eliminate the need to concatenate foreign keys and related concatenated indexes.

4.3.3   DETERMINING THE INITIAL DATA VIEWS

A data view allows the database designer to create a different representation of the data that is stored in the database tables. Views can be used for different purposes, such as to restrict accesses to a predetermined set of rows and/or columns in a table or to facilitate the work of the programmers by allowing them to select data from several tables without forcing them to do a join.

The initial requirements for data views can be determined by carefully examining the data access requirements of the application that are documented in the data access matrices that were developed earlier, during the analysis phase. I discuss data views in more detail in Section 4.4.9, "Creation of database views."

4.3.4   AUGMENTING THE INITIAL LOGICAL DATABASE STRUCTURES WITH ADDITIONAL DATABASE OBJECTS

The logical database structures can be refined by introducing supplementary database objects that might be required to accommodate specific design requirements, such as different application reference code tables or artificial keys, for example. You might also need to create additional tables or columns for data journalizing needs, such as the addition of date and time data as well as user ids. Another example might be the addition of various flags to indicate that the records in a table have been processed in some manner. Lastly, you might consider adding special fields that contain summarized data.

4.3.5   DENORMALIZATION

As I stated earlier, in Chapter 3, the normalization of the business data model helps to eliminate the major difficulties that are associated with updating redundant information and helps to improve the integrity of the data that is stored in the databases.

On the other end, the normalization process can generate a very large number of individual tables for a large database, some of which might need to be joined together to satisfy specific cross-table queries, hence producing a non-negligible amount of overhead in terms of CPU cycles.

Besides simplicity and maintainability, good database design is often measured by its ability to provide good performance. Consequently, some very specific situations might warrant the need to denormalize some of the logical database structures to build a major application that is more responsive, such as the potential cases indicated in Table 4-6.

In all instances, be sure to document the database structural changes that are caused by a denormalization process.

Table 4–6 Denormalization Considerations

Derived data	Derived data entails storing in the database specific data that can be produced from other data, such as the derived field total_invoice_amount, for instance.
Duplicated data	Sometimes you might need to duplicate some specific data from one table to another, to improve performance, for example.
Summary data	Sometimes, you might need to store various types of summary or historical data in the database to ensure a faster response time on certain queries. A typical example would be queries that very frequently access detailed data to calculate a sum. In such a context, I might recommend storing computed values immediately when the data is created at a higher level in the database.

4.3.6   REFINING AND ANALYZING THE CRITICAL DATA ACCESS PATTERNS

The data access matrices that were created during the analysis phase should be revisited and refined with up-to-date volumetric information. The detailed data access paths of the most critical online transactions should be carefully analyzed to ensure that the logical database structures can accommodate them. In the case of a critical batch program, its overall job turnaround time might become critical, especially when the run time of the batch program is constrained by a limited time window.

A critical factor often used to identify the most efficient data access design solutions is estimating the number of rows to be retrieved as a result of each call. From there, the number of I/Os required to access those rows is estimated. Then the associated estimates for CPU time are often compared to identify the best design alternative. Simply plotting the estimated number of I/Os for each data access in a spreadsheet can be a good approach. Another option is to use analytical modeling software tools provided by database or third party vendors. In some cases, a relatively simple prototype may be required to issue SQL calls against real physical databases that contain realistic but artificial data, in order to assess and evaluate the best design alternatives. For very large databases, full-scale prototypes may be essential to obtain realistic estimates of program execution times.

Several alternative designs might be available to improve the response time of the most critical system transactions. In some instances, the logical database structures might need to be modified to accommodate some specific system transactions and associated data access patterns. Sometimes the system transactions and associated data accesses themselves might need to be redesigned to meet the stated response time objectives.

The database designer, with the application developers and even the users if necessary, should also revise the cardinality figures that were documented between the relations shown in the entity-relationship diagram.

The overall data volume estimates should be refined by taking into consideration the enterprise data archival policies that apply to the information contained in the logical database structures. How many years will production data be accessible online, and under which conditions will they be archived? Furthermore, the volume estimates should not only include average occurrences for each specific entity but also the estimated minimum and maximum number of occurrences for an entity. The revised data sizing estimates are used to verify the hardware disk space requirements that were forecasted during the analysis phase. [1]

In some cases, you might also want to verify how often the maximum number of entity occurrences can be encountered while processing the application data. Obtaining this information might be imperative, in order to handle unforeseen situations in large databases. For example, the database structure might be able to support the processing of an average number of entity occurrences but can fail to adequately support the processing of a few occasional but very large numbers of entity occurrences stored in a given table.

4.3.7   DATA INTEGRITY RULES

Each data access operation that creates or deletes a table row should be carefully examined to determine the conditions under which related foreign keys are updated. Also, the data integrity requirements shown in Table 4-7 should be investigated carefully.

Table 4–7 Data Integrity Requirements

• If certain data elements absolutely need to be duplicated in other table(s), what should be the rules to maintain integrity and consistency between them?
• Should derivable data be stored in tables?
• Should derivable data be computed only when it is required?
• Do specific data elements exist for which their presence is conditional to other data elements?
• Do specific data elements exist for which their value is dependent on the value of other data elements?

Enforcing referential integrity can sometimes be very costly. For this reason, you might want to carefully investigate application-enforced versus database-enforced referential integrity pros and cons, especially when some related tables are stored at different physical locations on the network.

---

1. Some of the logical and physical data modeling tools listed in Section 4.4.10 support the calculation of the size of the database tables, indexes and other related objects, according to initial state or estimated growth.

Activity number:	DE-3
Activity name:	Create the physical database design
Purpose:	To transform the logical database structure(s) into physical database structure(s)
Inputs:	DE-T2 Logical data structures AN-T6 Initial system distribution strategy AN-T10 Initial capacity plan
Outputs:	DE-T3 Physical database design

Activity description:	• Transform the logical database structures into physical databases by accomplishing the following tasks:
	DATABASE
	• Analyze the database physical storage requirements based on the volumetric information provided in the capacity plan and the logical database structure(s) deliverables
	  – Review the number of row estimates for each table shown in the logical database structures
	  – Review the predicted database growth estimates that have been projected for a given period of time, such as for the next three years
	  – Determine the total amount of disk space that is required to satisfy the complete database storage requirements, including the database administration disk space overhead
	  – If necessary, refine the initial estimates for the number of physical disk storage devices that are required to store the application data in the production environment
	• Allocate sufficient raw disk space to satisfy the total storage requirements of the complete database
	• Define and create the physical database storage structure
	  – Assign a unique database name
	  – Define and create the database "system" and "data" tablespaces that are required to accommodate the functional groupings of tables, indexes, and rollback segments
	DATABASE TABLES
	• Define and create the table(s) for the database. For each table:
	  – Assign a unique name to the table
	  – Define all the table columns, using the data definition language (DDL) constructs that are supported by the selected relational DBMS. For each specific column in the table, identify the following attributes:

- Column name
- Column data type (i.e., character, varchar, integer, numeric, date, etc.)
- Column data type width and number of decimals supported, where applicable
- If the column data type can contain an empty value (i.e., Nulls)
- Define the column (or set of columns) that constitute the table primary key
- Define the foreign key columns that point to the primary keys of other tables
- Define the type of referential integrity rules that must be enforced for deletes (or updates) of the primary key, such as:
- Restrict referential integrity rule—all associated dependent rows cannot be deleted when the primary key is deleted
- Cascade referential integrity rule—all associated dependent rows are deleted when the primary key is deleted
- Set Null referential integrity rule—all data in the associated dependent rows are set to null when the primary key is deleted
- Identify the column(s) in the table that need to be indexed via other means than the primary or foreign keys. For each indexed field requirement, define:
  - The index name
  - Whether or not the index must be sequenced in ascending or descending order
  - Whether or not the index should be unique or duplicated

DATABASE TABLE VIEWS

- Define and create the physical database views that are required to allow the users to access only specific rows and columns within each selected table or across multiple tables

DATABASE STRUCTURE DIAGRAM

- Create the physical database structure diagram, showing all pertinent database tables and the relationships that exist among them. For each database table, depict all the data fields it contains.
- Walk through the physical database deliverable

4.4 CREATE THE PHYSICAL DATABASE DESIGN

This section describes the detailed steps involved in creating the physical database design. It also provides tips and guidelines on how to perform this highly iterative process.

4.4.1 OVERVIEW

The logical database structures are transformed into a set of physical database structures.[2] Then each physical database structure is progressively refined and optimized to satisfy the complete data access and service-level performance requirements that were identified for the application.

If a preliminary version of the physical database structures was already constructed during the analysis phase in order to support the creation of a live application prototype, then the physical database structures are simply refined to satisfy the additional database requirements that have been identified since then.

4.4.2 DATABASE DESIGN FACTORS

Several application requirements can affect the important design decisions that must be weighed by the database administrator to derive an optimal database structure. Some of the most common design factors, which will likely influence the construction and fine-tuning of the physical database, are listed in Table 4-8.

The various database SQL constructs that are illustrated throughout the next sections apply primarily to the design of an Oracle database. I also assume that you have a basic knowledge of the SQL language.

The data definition language (DDL) command parameters that are shown in the SQL examples will not be discussed in detail, since they truly are beyond the scope of this book. However, most of the examples are generic in nature. They should be relevant to any type of modern relational database server software.

4.4.3 CREATION OF THE DATABASE AND ITS TABLESPACES

Most relational databases are usually partitioned into several logical storage units. In Oracle, these logical storage units are called tablespaces. For example, Figure 4-3 shows

---

2. This transformation can be done with the use of a physical database modeling tool such as Logic Works' ERwin for instance. The database designer can create a physical model of the database, specify the database technology to be used, and generate database data definition language (DDL) statements for the respective database technology selected to implement the physical database. More information is provided in Section 4.4.10 on a variety of automated data modeling tools.

Table 4–8 Physical Database Design Factors

- The volume of live data that must be stored in the database
- The volume of online and batch database transactions that must be processed per unit of time
- The various audit, security, and integrity requirements that must be enforced by the database
- The database backup and recovery requirements, which must be completed in the time windows available
- The database files archival requirements
- The database availability requirements
- The number and different groupings of data objects, data attributes, and relationships that must be supported by the physical database structure and their complexity
- The number of business rules that must be enforced by the database and their complexity
- The proposed application data access sequences
- Efficient database loading

the relationships that exist between an Oracle database, its tablespaces, and its physical data files.

The SYSTEM tablespace contains the data dictionary. It also contains the names and addresses of all the other tablespaces, tables, indexes, and clusters that are associated with the database. The DATA tablespaces contain the actual data tables, indexes, and clusters. A tablespace has a fixed size that can be expanded by the database administrator when it gets full.

Physical Database

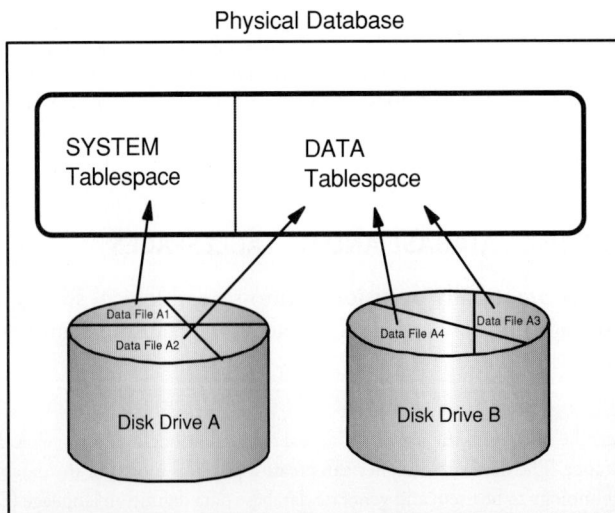

Figure 4–3 Physical database and tablespaces.

One of the first design tasks that the database administrator must perform is to simply define and uniquely name the database and then set up the required database tablespaces.

The database name is created using the 'CREATE DATABASE' DDL command, as shown here. For simplification purposes, this example uses defaults for all the different types of arguments that can be appended at the end of the CREATE command statement.

CREATE DATABASE Database_1

The CREATE TABLESPACE DDL command is used to assign one or more files to a data tablespace, as shown in the following example:

```
CREATE TABLESPACE tabspace_1
DATAFILE 'disk1' SIZE 25M
DEFAULT STORAGE (INITIAL 10K NEXT 40K
                MINEXTENTS 1 MAXEXTENTS 100
                PCTINCREASE 15);
```

The amount of work involved in estimating the sizing of the tablespaces and in the functional grouping of the database tables, indexes, and rollback segments to a given tablespace will vary from one database to another.

Sufficient free space should also be allocated for each tablespace based on the percentage growth of the data they store.

In all cases, the size of the tablespaces should be validated against the database backup and recovery plan. Although this statement might sound subjective, a tablespace is too large if the amount of time needed to recover it is unacceptable (i.e., it does not fit within the backup and recovery window that has been defined as acceptable for recovery).

4.4.4   CREATION OF THE DATABASE TABLES

For the vast majority of relational database management systems, the table is the most fundamental unit of data storage. The database tables house all the data that can be directly accessed by the users. A database table is defined with a unique table name and contains a certain number of columns. The following characteristics must be assigned to each specific column, in an appropriate fashion:

- column name
- datatype (varchar, date, number, etc.)
- data column size or width
- whether the column value is mandatory (i.e., NULL or NOT NULL value)
- whether restrictions are imposed on the permissible values or range of values that are allowed for the column (i.e., CHECK constraints)

Given that the tablespaces have been created for the databases, the various application database tables are now affiliated with their corresponding tablespace. The DDL command 'CREATE TABLE' is used for this purpose, as illustrated in the following example, where an 'Employee' table is created:

```
CREATE TABLE Employee (
Emp_numbernumber,
Emp_namevarchar (30),
Emp_hired_datedate,
Emp_addressvarchar (150))
TABLESPACE tabspace_1;
```

An important factor that must be taken into consideration by the database designer is the association of tables to tablespaces. Following are some basic rules of thumb that might help to optimize the general performance of the database:

- Store index and data components in tablespaces on different disks

- Segregate tables with a high insert/delete rate from more stable tables in size

- Place tables with high access rates in tablespaces on different disk drives

4.4.5   CREATION OF THE PRIMARY KEY

The database primary key is the column or set of columns that uniquely identifies the rows (or records) in the table. The referential integrity constraint PRIMARY KEY is used normally to prohibit duplicate key values in a table. Only one primary key is allowed per table. The following example illustrates how a primary key is defined for the Employee table:

```
CREATE TABLE Employee (
Emp_numbernumber   CONSTRAINT pk_employee PRIMARY KEY,
Emp_namevarchar (30),
Emp_hired_datedate,
Emp_addressvarchar (150))
TABLESPACE tabspace_1;
```

The *pk_employee* constraint assigns the *Emp_number* column as the primary key for the '*Employee*' table. This assignment ensures that no two employees in the '*Employee*' table have the same employee number.

4.4.6   CREATION OF THE FOREIGN KEY(S)

A foreign key is a column or combination of columns that contain some primary key value(s) from another database table. A foreign key constraint, also referred to as a referential integrity constraint, indicates that the values of the foreign key must match the actual values of the primary key in another table. The next example illustrates how to define a foreign key constraint in the '*Employee*' table:

```
CREATE TABLE Employee (
Emp_numbernumber  CONSTRAINT pk_employee PRIMARY KEY,
Emp_namevarchar (30),
Emp_hired_date date,
Emp_addressvarchar (150),
Emp_dept_noNUMBER (4),
CONSTRAINT  fk_dept_no
      FOREIGN KEY (Dept_no)
      REFERENCES  Dept(Dept_no))
TABLESPACE  tabspace_1;
```

The referential integrity constraint *fk_dept_no* enforces the business rule stating that any employee in the *Employee* table must work in a department defined in the department table identified as *'Dept.'*

4.4.7 CREATION OF THE TABLE INDEXES

An index is an object that holds an entry for each value that occurs in an indexed column of a table. Database indexes can improve significantly the performance of database searches against specific table columns. They provide fast and direct access to table rows when the rows are searched in index column sequence, using DML commands such as SELECT, UPDATE, and DELETE.

The data access specifications that were documented in the data access matrices should be scrutinized carefully to identify queries that are performed on data fields that are not primary keys—for example, selecting a customer based on its name and address because the customer number is not known.

Indexes can be created on one or multiple table columns. However, they cannot be created on a view. They are automatically generated and maintained by the database management system. Consequently, indexes are completely transparent to users and applications. The next example illustrates the creation of a database index against the *Emp_name* column in the *Employee* table:

```
CREATE INDEX idx_emp_name ON Employee (Emp_name);
```

Table 4-9 provides some tips on database indexes.

To conclude, the database administrator should carefully weigh the advantages and disadvantages of using database indexes. Generally speaking, database indexes should be built only for non-key table columns that are searched regularly or when storage and processing overhead is not an issue.

Table 4–9 Observations On Database Indexes

- For a large database, first creating the table and inserting all the required rows in it and then creating the database index is generally faster. If the index is created prior to the insertion of the rows, most relational databases will update the index each time a row is inserted into the table. This situation can cause some performance problems when several database tables are populated with a significant number of records.
- The use of database indexes will gradually become more and more attractive as the size of the database tables increases significantly. For instance, the average time needed to locate a particular employee name within a huge table will be dramatically reduced via searching through a database index. On the other hand, small tables that contain 10 to 30 rows might not need to be indexed
- Indexes can take up a significant amount of space for very large indexed database tables. Hence, you need to index only specific non-primary key target columns that are frequently accessed by several database queries.
- Applications with frequent and massive INSERT, DELETE, and UPDATE operations can be slowed down by the abuse of indexes, due to the fact that the execution of each of these database operations against the indexed columns in a table will force the database management system to maintain both the index pointers and the data itself.
- If a query accesses more than 25 to 35 percent of all rows in a table, then performing a full table scan might sometimes be faster than using indexes. In such a case, further investigation might be required to determine which approach provides the best results.
- As a rule of thumb, the database indexes should be physically stored separate from the data in order to optimize database performance

4.4.8 CREATION OF DATABASE CLUSTERS

Clusters provide an alternative method of physically storing table data. A cluster can contain one or multiple tables that together share one or more columns. Clusters, like indexes, are transparent to the users and application developers. The data that is stored in a cluster are accessed in the same manner as the data stored in a non-clustered table.

The judicious use of clusters can favorably increase system performance, especially in situations where the clustered tables are frequently queried in joins. This improvement is due to the fact that the rows that are common to the joined tables are retrieved with a minimum amount of Input-Output (I/O) operations.

On the other hand, the use of clusters is likely to decrease the performance of full table searches. Hence, the potential advantages and disadvantages associated with the use of clusters must be carefully weighed in light of the type of operations that must be performed on the data tables.

4.4.9 CREATION OF DATABASE VIEWS

A view is a customized, logical representation of some of the data that is contained in one or more database tables. Unlike a table, a database view does not actually store physical data. Rather, the view derives its data from the multiple tables that support it. The definition of a database view is permanent, whereas the data content supported by a view is always re-created at execution time.

In many aspects, views can be manipulated very similarly to permanent tables, such as:

- access authorizations can be granted to a view just like for a permanent table
- queries (i.e., SELECT) can be performed on views
- operations such as UPDATE, DELETE, and INSERT commands can be performed on a view (with some restrictions)
- views can be created based on other views

Views also have some limitations when compared to permanent tables, such as:

- indexes cannot be created on views
- integrity constraints and keys cannot be assigned to views
- views are re-created each time they are invoked by an application, since they are derived from permanent tables and do not retain copies of that information
- operations such as UPDATE, DELETE, and INSERT commands can be performed on a view but with some restrictions

Figure 4-4 illustrates the concept of a database view.

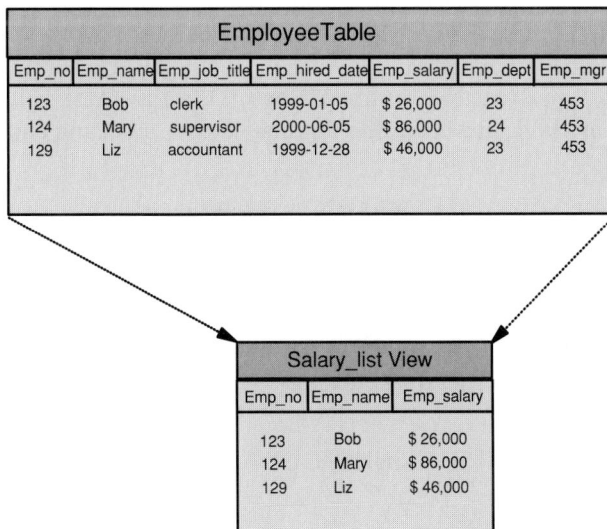

Figure 4–4 Database view.

Although Figure 4-4 shows a view that is created from a single table, a view can be created to unify data that comes from several tables. Views are used often to precisely tailor the accesses to the data in the database. The construction of database views might serve several purposes, such as those listed in Table 4-10.

Table 4–10 Various Utilizations Of Database Views

- To provide improved security by not allowing access to database information that is not relevant to specified users
- To improve usability by hiding data complexity and presenting to users and developers data in a form that is simpler to comprehend and manipulate
- To allow users and developers to retrieve data stored in multiple tables, without needing to perform a join operation
- To present data in different perspectives from the permanent table
- To improve consistency by centralizing in the database the definition of common queries that perform extensive calculations with the data that is stored in the tables. By saving the query as a view, the calculations can be executed automatically every time the view is invoked

4.4.10 AUTOMATED DATABASE DESIGN TOOLS

Several automated tools exist on the market to facilitate the creation and enhancement of multiple types of logical and physical database models. These automated data modeling tools often support a large variety of commercial relational database management systems by generating the appropriate data definition language (DDL) statements. They can also manage various database objects such as stored procedures, views, and triggers.

Furthermore, several of these tools can also reverse engineer several types of physical relational databases directly from their data definition language (DDL) or from the database files that use the Open Database Connectivity (ODBC) protocol. Following are the addresses of vendor's Web sites that offer automated data modeling and database design tools.

http://www.logicworks.com(Erwin/ERX)
http://www.oracle.com(Oracle Database Designer)
http://www.sybase.com(PowerDesigner)
http://www.popkin.com(SA/Data Architect)
http://www.visible.com(Visual Analyst Workbench)
http://www.infomodelers.com(InfoModeler)

4.4.11 DISTRIBUTED DATABASE TECHNOLOGY AND DESIGN CONSIDERATIONS

This section describes some high-level concepts that relate to distributed databases, including:

- Different database distribution techniques
- Database replication mechanisms
- Synchronous or asynchronous replication mechanisms
- Database replication timing mechanisms
- Database replication conflict resolution mechanisms
- Full or partial data refresh mechanisms

It also discusses some basic guidelines that you should consider when designing distributed physical databases. Finally, I present different case scenarios where the database replication technology can be advantageously used.

DIFFERENT DATABASE DISTRIBUTION TECHNIQUES
Table 4-11 describes three different techniques that can be used to distribute data across different locations.

Table 4–11 Various Database Distribution Techniques

Segmentation	Database segmentation is the physical partitioning of a database into a set of separate physical database tables, which then can be stored at different sites. The database tables are not duplicated but only implemented at different sites.
Extraction	For many years, custom database extraction programs have been created by developers to read the data that is stored in databases and create copies of that data either in a flat file format or other formats, for further processing.
Database replication	Database replication allows the automatic generation of several copies of either full or partial database tables. The data replication process is usually performed with built-in database management system (DBMS) utilities. Most relational DBMS vendors also offer sophisticated database replication technologies that support various database objects such as triggers, stored procedures, views, and indexes.

Out of the three techniques that I describe in Table 4-11, the database replication technique is becoming increasingly popular and is supported by all the large relational database management system vendors. The following section briefly discusses the database replication concept.

DATABASE REPLICATION
Database replication is a technique that is frequently used to distribute data from a master database to additional copies that typically are stored at different local sites.

Table 4-12 shows some of the most common benefits that are associated with the database replication technology.

Table 4–12 Database Replication Benefits

- Multiple copies of data can be downloaded to branch offices, where users can access the data locally in a more efficient manner
- Multiple copies of data can help load-balance the traffic on heavily used networks across different locations
- Multiple copies of data can be used for disaster recovery situations
- Database replication can be used for downloading data from the operational, transactional systems to data warehouses or data marts

Fundamentally, two basic types of database replication exist: synchronous and asynchronous replication.

SYNCHRONOUS REPLICATION

Synchronous replication is often used in high-end distributed client-server applications where data consistency, availability, and concurrency are of the utmost importance, such as for a sophisticated airline reservation systems, for example. Also known as "real-time" replication, synchronous replication ensures that the application data is always up-to-date and in-sync at all locations that house a database copy.

Synchronous replication relies on a special two-stage hand-shaking technology protocol called two-phase commit. Figure 4-5 shows a two-phase commit example.

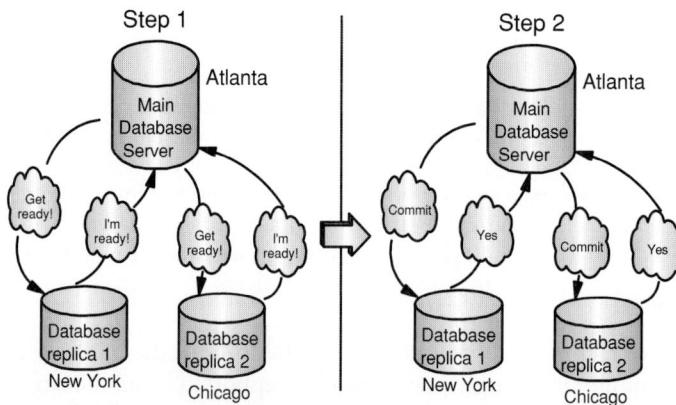

Figure 4–5 Two-phase commit example.

In the first step, all the database servers that need to be updated simultaneously proceed with a synchronized locking of data (i.e., "get ready" and "I'm ready" confirmation tasks). In the second step, all the slave database servers process the update request and do a commit as soon as the master database server instructs them to proceed. The rule is simple: either all the databases must be updated at once or none of them are updated. A failure at any particular node in the distributed network will force a roll-back of the update transaction at all nodes.

ASYNCHRONOUS REPLICATION

With asynchronous replication, the different database copies are allowed to become slightly out of sync with each other, usually for what the business area might consider to be an acceptable period of lag time. Over time, though, all the different database copies eventually converge to the same data values at all the local sites where the database replicas reside.

Asynchronous database replication is not recommended when the business application absolutely needs to know whether a database update has been successfully completed at all the different sites before it can resume its operations.

DIFFERENT PROPAGATION TIMING MECHANISMS

With the asynchronous propagation mechanism, the database updates are stored in a deferred transaction queue. At an appropriate time, the changes are subsequently transmitted to each remote location that must receive the data. The selected RDBMS should have a mechanism that ensures that the database transactions are not eliminated from the deferred transaction queue until they were successfully replicated to each particular remote site. With such an approach, no transactions are ever lost, even in situations in which the network is temporarily down.

The database administrator controls the time at which the data will be transferred to the other database remote locations. For business applications that require almost a continuous data replication scheme, the database administrator can choose a time interval that will propagate the data very close to a real-time mode, usually within a few seconds.

For business applications that do not require a near real-time mode of operation, the database administrator can schedule the replication events at different time intervals, such as every minute, hour, day, or even week, depending on the specific needs of the application.

If the application needs allow it, launching the propagation of data during the night might be convenient, at a time when the network is not overloaded and when the communication costs are usually at their lowest possible rates.

The data replication process can also be triggered by an event-based scheme, such as data value changes, for example, instead of a regular time interval scheme.

Finally, another option is to kick off the replication of data on demand. The on-demand (a.k.a. administrator-initiated) replication scheme might be particularly attractive for applications that support multiple small remote locations that regularly connect to a central database to refresh their database copies. The same approach could also be used for mobile users who are equipped with laptops.

CONFLICT RESOLUTION

In a database distributed environment where all the updates need to be simultaneously applied to the same data across all database copies, update conflicts can sometimes occur. Most distributed RDBMSs offer several options to detect and help resolve these potential conflicts.

Conflict resolution routines are important in a distributed database environment to ensure data convergence. Table 4-13 enumerates some of the standard pre-defined conflict resolution routines that are typically used by most commercially available distributed RDBMSs. The database administrator should opt as much as possible for conflict detection and resolution methods that minimize the need for manual interventions, either from the database administrators or the users themselves.

Table 4–13 Simultaneous Update Conflict Detection And Resolution Routines

• Site priority	• Priority group
• Latest timestamp	• Overwrite
• Earliest timestamp	• Discard

Also, the database administrators should be able to set up their own conflict resolution routines, in situations where they need to address complex application-related business rules.

FULL DATA REFRESH VERSUS PARTIAL DATA REFRESH

Basically, you have two options to replicate data, namely: full or partial refreshes.

A full refresh is performed when the entire content of the database is transferred from the master database to a local copy. Full database refreshes can be suitable for small database applications. However, full database refreshes might not be suitable for large databases, since the network might not be able to support the high volume of data that must be transferred between the different sites.

A partial refresh is performed when only the rows that were updated in the master database are replicated over to the local database copies.

Some of the factors that will influence the selection of a full data refresh approach versus a partial refresh approach appear in Table 4-14.

Table 4–14 Factors Influencing The Distributed Database Refresh Strategy

• The size of the database tables that must be replicated
• The volume of data that is modified and its frequency
• The network bandwidth capacity
• The frequency of the replication process
• The need to maintain associated tables all in sync, timewise, to maintain business integrity

DISTRIBUTED DATABASE CONSIDERATIONS

The Initial Distribution Strategy deliverable that was created earlier during the analysis phase is used as a starting point for designing a distributed database, along with the Logical Database Design and Capacity Plan technical deliverables.

The physical placement of data at different locations can cause several design-related challenges that must be satisfactorily addressed prior to moving forward with the implementation of this strategy.

Table 4-15 lists some of the major points that should be considered by the database administrator and the application development team during the final design stage of a distributed database.

Ideally, the database tables should be stored as closely as possible to where the data is created or where the data is used the most often. If the same data is heavily used at more than one location, then a database replication scheme can be used to create additional local database copies.

AN OVERVIEW OF DIFFERENT TYPES OF DATABASE REPLICATION APPLICATIONS

This section presents a variety of case scenarios in which the database replication technology can be advantageously used to satisfy the business needs for data distribution that were identified earlier during the analysis phase.

Case 1: Central headquarters to branch offices read-only database replication

As shown in Figure 4-6, in this scenario, the data contained in a main database is downloaded from the central headquarters office to multiple branch offices. The data replication process is performed at regular intervals. The users at the branch offices can access the local database replicas only in a read-only mode.

Case 2: Branch offices to central headquarters database replication

As shown in Figure 4-7, in this scenario, the database data is replicated from each branch office back to the central headquarters. The replication process is performed at regular intervals. The data that is uploaded by each branch office to the headquarters office is consolidated in a central database. The consolidated data is then analyzed and processed by the central office for different financial trend and statistical analysis purposes.

Case 3: Database replication to transfer operational data to a data warehouse environment

As shown in Figure 4-8, in this scenario, the data that are stored in the production operational databases are periodically replicated in the data warehouse databases. The databases in the data warehouse environment hold summarized information such as daily, weekly, monthly, or yearly summarized or historical data.

Table 4–15 Distributed Database Design Considerations

- What are the types and amount of data that need to be moved across the network to other sites?
- Will only the database changes be propagated or the entire database tables?
- Will the data move one way or in a bi-directional manner?
- What are the peak loads?
- Who owns the data?
- Where are the user groups located that will access the data?
- How many database servers need to be updated?
- What are the system transactions that create the data? Update the data? Where will they be used?
- What volume of transactions is performed at each different site per unit of time and against which database tables?
- What type of replication mechanism will be used? Synchronous or asynchronous?
  - If asynchronous database replication is used, how up-to-date do the remote sites' database copies need to be?
  - Might multiple time zone constraints affect the scheduling of database updates between the various local sites? What are the data usage patterns by time zones?
  - Can the users work with data that is slightly out-of-date?
  - Can the enterprise network bandwidth sustain the required data transfer rates?
- What mechanism is available to detect the unavailability of the network or the server at a remote site?
- If the network is down between different sites, how will the replicated data be stored for later transmission when the communication facilities are restored?
- In the case of a communication or server failure, how will the initiating application acknowledge and appropriately respond to these failure events?
- What type of processing will be allowed at the local sites when the network is not available?
- How will the database backup and recovery strategy be affected by the distributed data strategy when:
  - The data resides in different geographical sites?
  - The data is stored on different computer platforms?
  - Will the database replication process be performed between databases from different vendors (i.e., cross-platform replication)?
- Will the database replication process involve complex data types such as image, sound, or video data?

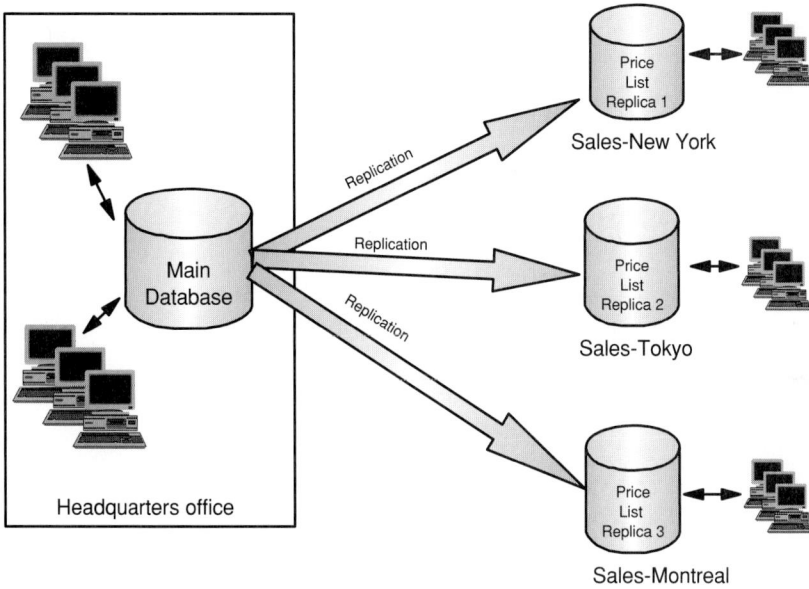

Figure 4–6 Information distribution.

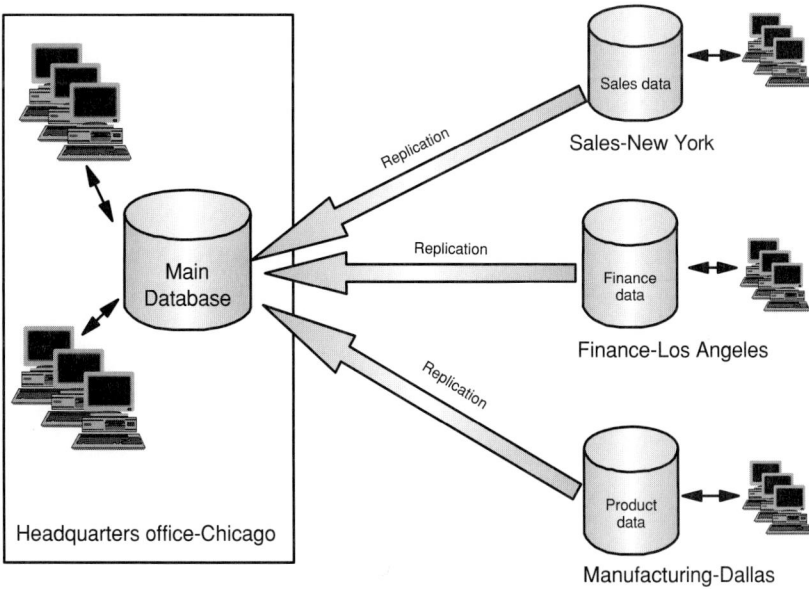

Figure 4–7 Information consolidation.

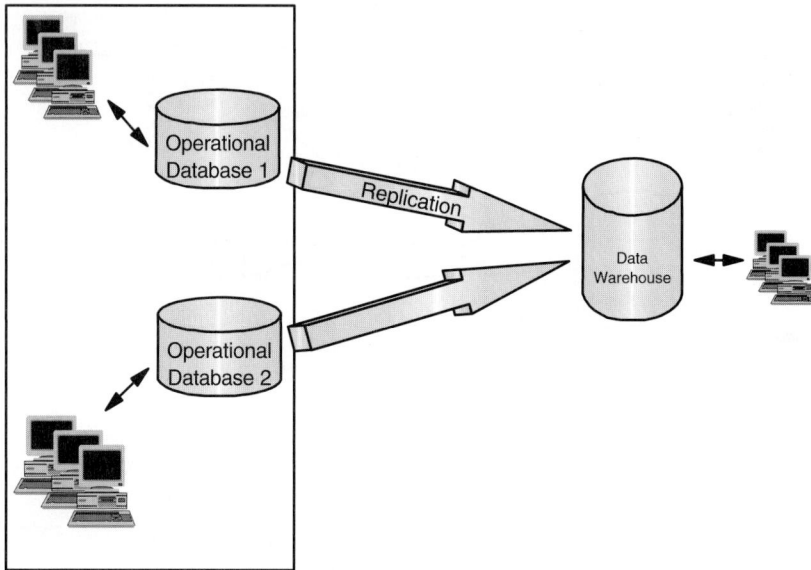

Figure 4–8 Information offloading.

Case 4: Database replication to support mobile users

As shown in Figure 4-9, in this scenario, the mobile users can download data from the corporate databases with the use of a database replication scheme. Later on, the mobile users connect to the central corporate databases and upload the modified data that was stored in their local database replicas back to the corporate databases.

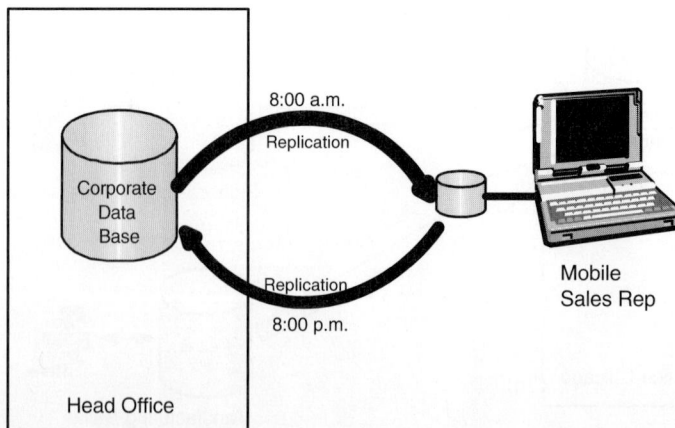

Figure 4–9 Database replication for mobile users.

You can think of several database replication scenarios for mobile users, depending on the users' needs. The one example provided here illustrates a potential use of database replication.

Case 5: Database replication for disaster recovery

As shown in Figure 4-10, in this scenario, complete copies of the corporate databases are periodically replicated to a distinct, secure site, at pre-defined intervals. In the event that a major disaster occurs at the central site, the database replicas can then be used to restore the corporate databases with the data that was previously copied the last time the replication process was done prior to the disaster.

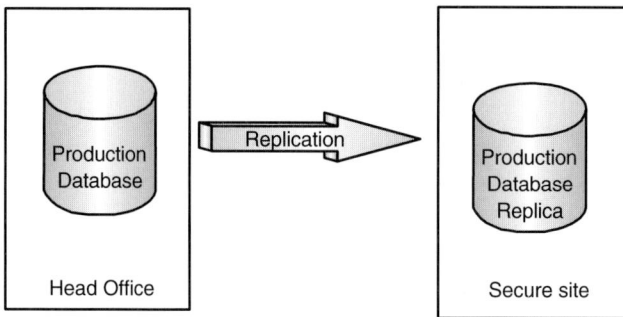

Figure 4–10 Database replication for disaster recovery.

Activity number:	DE-4
Activity name:	Design database security and audit schemes
Purpose:	To design and create the database security and audit schemes that are required to control the physical accesses to the databases
Inputs:	AN-T8 System security and control requirements DE-T3 Physical database design
Outputs:	DE-T4 Database security and audit schemes design
Activity description:	• Review the application security requirements that were identified during the analysis phase. • For each identified database security requirement, perform the following tasks: *Application users* • Identify the various categories of users who will use the client-server application.

- For each distinct category of users, determine the types of database access privileges they must be provided with to perform their business tasks, based on their job functions and responsibilities.
- Regroup each set of database access privileges into distinct user roles.
- Assign each category of users to a distinct user role.
- Construct all the required application user roles and privileges, using the CREATE ROLE, SET ROLE, and GRANT SQL commands.

Database administrator
- Determine the database privileges that should be assigned to the database administrator role, including:
  - Creation and maintenance of user roles for specific database application instances
  - Administration of the database access privileges assigned to each type of user role
  - Creation and administration of database objects, such as tables, indexes, views, etc.
  - Creation and administration of stored procedures and triggers
- Construct the database administrator role, along with its appropriate database privileges.

Application developers
- Determine the database privileges that should be assigned to the application developer role, including:
  - Creation and manipulation of specific database tables and objects
  - Creation of stored procedures
- Construct the application developer role, along with its appropriate privileges.
- Walk through the database control and security procedure deliverables.

4.5   DESIGN DATABASE SECURITY AND AUDIT SCHEMES

4.5.1   OVERVIEW

A preliminary investigation of the different classes of data that must be manipulated by the client-server or Web database system was conducted with the users earlier during the analysis phase. The end result of this study was a broad assessment of the general security measures that should be enforced to control the accesses to each distinct category of data stored in the database and who should have access to what functions.

In this current activity, specific users or groups of users will be provided with different types of access rights to a variety of database objects.

During the design phase, the specific data confidentiality requirements can be addressed further by elaborating multiple database access controls schemes. Most often than not, two major categories of data access controls can be used to satisfy the database security needs in a client-server environment, namely: discretionary or mandatory access controls.

4.5.2   DISCRETIONARY ACCESS CONTROLS

The database administrator uses the discretionary access controls to regulate all user accesses to the data that is stored in the database. Typically, granting database accesses is done by means of implementing some or all of the client-server database security features that are indicated in Table 4-16.

Table 4–16 Database Security Features

• Privileges
• Roles
• Views
• Stored Procedures
• Triggers

The following section discusses the particular merits of each database-related security feature indicated in Table 4-16.

4.5.3   PRIVILEGES

A privilege is a permission to perform a particular database operation, such as querying, updating, deleting, or inserting data in a relational database table. Without privileges, a user cannot access the information that is stored in the relational database. The database access privileges are controlled with GRANT statements. The most elementary database security rule is fairly simple: grant the users only the strict minimum set of privileges that they require to accomplish their normal day-to-day business tasks. Nothing more, nothing less.

Consequently, you need to ensure that the selected relational database system can implement this "only on a need-to-know basis" security policy, by default. With such a policy, nobody can have database access privileges unless she is specifically granted permission to use database privileges.

As shown in Figure 4-11, this approach ensures that the database system retains full control over who accesses the data stored in the database. It eliminates the possible scenario in which a user might attempt to bypass the application and its related security mechanisms by accessing the data directly, with an ad hoc database query tool, for instance.

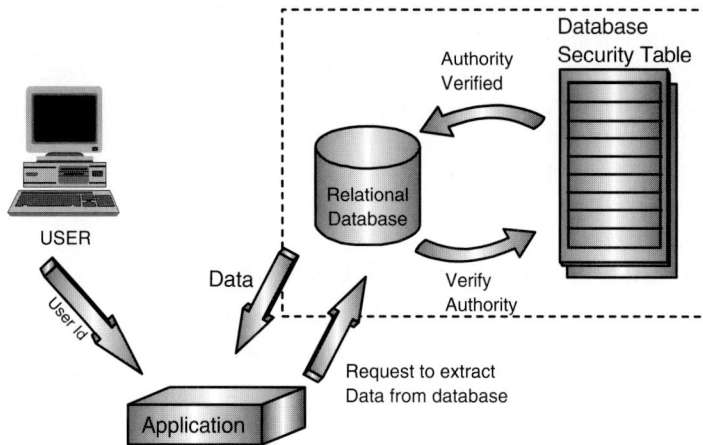

Figure 4–11 Database security.

The database administrator should review the security requirements that were defined during the analysis phase, along with any change that might have occurred since then. Then the different security rules that any particular individual or any group of users needs are defined by the database administrator. Table 4-17 lists the different access types that can be assigned to an Oracle database object.

Table 4–17 Database Object Access Rules

• Select
• Insert, update, delete
• Execute (for stored procedures)
• Index, reference, alter, grant
• All

Typically, the users are allowed only select, insert, update, and delete accesses to a database object.

4.5.4 ROLES

Privileges can be explicitly granted to specific users, such as granting John or Mary a read-only access to the table "Personnel." However, this approach might prove to be not very practical when the client-server application is used by a large number of users. In such situations, the concept of roles can be used to ease the administration of database privileges.

A role is a collection of pre-defined privileges that can be granted either to users or to other roles. Instead of explicitly granting the same privileges to all the users one after the other, the privileges for a group of users who perform a common business function can be granted to a specific role. Once a specific role has been created, each user in that group can be then granted this specific role. In the following example, a role identified as Human_Resource.Rep has the authority to execute SELECT, UPDATE, INSERT, and DELETE operations against the Eng_Dept table:

CREATE ROLE Human_Resource.Rep;
GRANT SELECT, UPDATE, INSERT,
DELETE
ON Eng_Dept TO Human_Resource.Rep;

Having this single role defined, you can grant it to several users, with the following instructions:

GRANT Human_Resource.Rep to Paul,
Mary;

With most relational database servers, a role may be assigned a password, which can provide an additional layer of security:

CREATE ROLE Human_Resource.Rep
IDENTIFIED BY "Password xyz";

The user is prompted for a password whenever the role is invoked. If the password is invalid, the user will not be able to use the set of privileges that were defined for this particular role.

A role can also be activated directly within an application to constrain the users to exercising their privileges only within the boundaries of that application. As soon as the users quit the application, their privileges are revoked immediately. By enforcing this additional precautionary database security measure, the database administrator can prevent a potentially hazardous situation in which users can execute destructive SQL statements against database tables while utilizing online ad hoc database query tools with the privileges that were granted to them via a user role.

When defining various user roles, take into consideration real-life situations that frequently occur in the workplace. For example, a user may temporarily replace the supervisor for a short period of time. Hence, this particular individual may require some additional database access capabilities for the duration of that temporary assignment.

4.5.5 DATABASE VIEWS

Database views can be utilized advantageously as another technique to exert more control on the user's ability to access the information that is stored in the database. As an example, a simple database view can be created to display only relevant columns in a database, as illustrated in the following example:

```
CREATE VIEWEmp_Supv AS
SELECT emp_name, emp_id, emp_supv
FROMemp_table;
```

With this view, the users can access only the 'emp_name, emp_id and emp_supv' fields from the 'emp_table' and nothing else.

4.5.6   STORED PROCEDURES

Another method for controlling security at the database level is to code the data access rules inside a stored procedure. A stored procedure can be created to perform a function with all the necessary database access privileges. Then the permission to execute this stored procedure is granted to certain users. This authorization is done, though, without granting the users any direct access rights to the tables and SQL operations that are used by the stored procedure.

With this technique, the users are granted EXECUTE privileges on the stored procedure itself, and the only possible way for them to access the data in the database is through the stored procedure. In other words, the data accesses are encapsulated at the level of the stored procedure. This technique should be considered only when security cannot be implemented through roles.

Stored procedures are discussed in more detail in Section 4.6.1, "Design database stored procedures."

4.5.7   DATABASE TRIGGERS

Database triggers can also be used to exert tighter access control against the database. The trigger execution follows a pattern similar to a stored procedure, with the exception that the trigger is fired automatically as soon as a delete, insert, or update operation is performed against a database table.

Contrary to a stored procedure, the user who executes the database operation has no control whatsoever over the execution of the database trigger. With this technique, enterprise-wide business rules can be enforced across all corporate applications at the level of the database trigger, based on predetermined business events.

Database triggers are discussed in more details in Section 4.6.2, "Design database triggers."

4.5.8   APPLICATION-LEVEL SECURITY

An alternative method to limit access to data is to include the access rules within the application code itself, as indicated in Figure 4-12. With this scenario, the application itself controls the data access. While this technique enforces a certain level of security when the users operate within the internal boundaries of the application, it might present serious shortcomings when the users attempt to bypass the application and access the data directly via an ad hoc query tool, for instance.

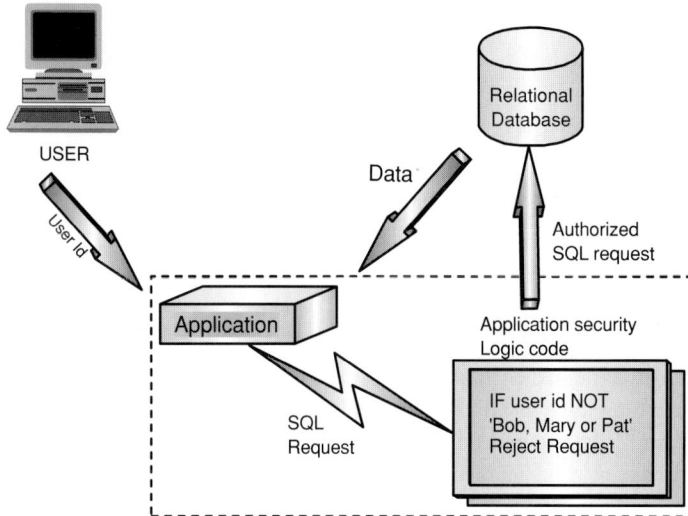

Figure 4–12 Application security.

4.5.9 MANDATORY ACCESS CONTROLS

In specific situations, the standard discretionary database access control mechanisms may simply be insufficient to secure highly sensitive information. Typically, organizations that process highly sensitive information might require more stringent levels of security to control the user accesses to the database system. Quite often, such a situation might be the case for applications that are developed by government, commercial, and intelligence agencies that use highly sensitive data.

In a robust multi-level secure database server, all the database objects, such as the tables, rows, and procedures, are labeled according to their level of sensitivity. These labels cannot be altered by the users of the database. Furthermore, the users can get to just the data that match the range of labels they are authorized to access, according to special security clearance tables. Figure 4-13 shows an example in which a government agency has labeled its database objects in accordance to the following classification: unclassified, classified, secret, and top secret.

In addition to the standard discretionary privileges that are provided by the database server, the mandatory access controls (i.e., READUP, WRITEUP, WRITE-DOWN) ensure that the users can only read, write, and modify the data that precisely match their sensitivity label. Furthermore, the users can read only in a downward fashion the data that reside at lower levels. In the example provided in Figure 4-13, user1

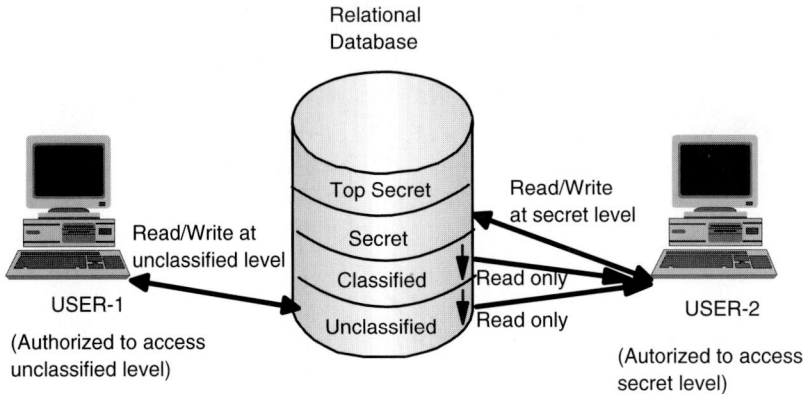

Figure 4–13 Multi-level secure database.

is connected to the database with an unclassified level. Thus user1 can read, write, and modify public data. However, user1 cannot access the data labeled as 'classified,' 'secret,' or 'top secret.' On the other hand, user2 can read, write, and modify data at the 'secret' level. However, user2 can only read down the data labeled as classified and unclassified. User2 cannot access the upper-level data tagged with the label 'top secret.'

In a typical multilevel secure database server environment that utilizes mandatory access controls, only the security administrator can manage and administer the data accesses in the database system. This arrangement is quite a departure from discretionary access controls, in which the owners of the database objects might be able to grant access to the data they control to other users.

4.5.10 DATABASE ENCRYPTION

As you have seen in the analysis phase, encryption is a special technique that is used to convert readable data into an unreadable format. Those people who know the algorithmic key that was used to originally encrypt them can decrypt the data. If the users do not have access to the proper key, then they cannot read the encrypted data.

Encryption is primarily utilized to scramble information used in digital transmissions but can also be used to secure the information contained in a database or other types of data storage facilities. Encrypting an entire database can adversely affect its overall performance because of the overhead associated with encrypting or decrypting information every time it is modified by the users. For this reason, this technique is not used frequently for an ordinary database application, unless some very stringent security requirements demand such a drastic security measure.

Nevertheless, the organization might decide to encrypt selective segments of information that are stored on the databases and that are highly sensitive. In such a situation, only a very small number of carefully chosen individuals are provided with the capability of decrypting the encrypted data.

Although most client-server database systems usually do not provide industrial-strength encrypting functionality in their software, several third-party vendors offer robust commercial encryption algorithms. In certain cases, though, specific encrypting technologies might be subject to rigorous export restrictions in the U.S.

The following Web site addresses are provided for those readers who want more information on some vendors that offer different encryption software solutions.

http://www.axent.com(Omniguard/Enterprise Access Control)
http://www.entrust.com(Entrust)
http://www.worldtalk.com(World-Secure Server)
http://www.redcreek.com(Ravlin 4)

4.5.11 DATABASE AUDITING REQUIREMENTS

For certain categories of systems, such as financial applications for instance, keeping a record of all physical database activities might be important to ensure that the users are held responsible for their actions.

If keeping database modification traces is the case for the application at hand, then the production database server must be able to provide some form of traceability for all the database operations that are performed by the users.

Most relational database server systems provide at least some basic form of audit trail capabilities. Some of the most common built-in database auditing features that can be used to design and implement an automated database audit trail subsystem are listed in Table 4-18.

Table 4–18 Database Audit Facilities

Database Audit Feature	Description
Database audit reporting facility	Some general database reporting facilities are provided to produce various database audit reports and also to support ad-hoc queries against the audit information that is centrally accumulated and stored in a system database.
DML/DDL auditing	Standard auditing facilities are provided to allow the automatic auditing of various data manipulation language (DML) and data definition language (DDL) statements, for all types of database objects and structures.
Database user connections auditing	Standard auditing facilities are provided to allow the auditing of all the attempts that are made to connect with or disconnect from the database.
Database user activity auditing	A standard auditing facility is provided to allow the auditing of all database activity by operation, by utilization of database system privileges, by objects, or by the user.

The granularity and scope of the database audit functions can be as generic as auditing all the database accesses that are made by the users across the enterprise or as confined as auditing the database activities of a particular individual.

However, you want to ensure that the implementation of the database auditing functions does not adversely affect the performance of the production databases. For this reason, the potential database overhead that can be generated by implementing database auditing functions must be assessed when designing the application database audit trails.

Database triggers can sometimes be utilized to replace or supplement the built-in database audit features. For instance, database triggers can be used to audit specific database activities against particular database operations, such as triggering automatically an audit trail process every time an employee updates the employee salary database table.

4.6 DESIGN SHARED, REUSABLE SOFTWARE COMPONENTS

Several types of software components can be reused in large software applications or across multiple applications. Some of the most common types of software components that can be shared in the context of an enterprise-wide application architecture are the database stored procedures, the database triggers, and the remote procedure subroutines. Reusable code can drastically ease application maintenance later on, simply by avoiding code duplication.

Consequently, the shared application components should always be among the first software objects to be designed, coded, and tested, so they can then be shared among all application developers, preferably at the level of the enterprise.

The next three technical activities cover the design of database stored procedures, triggers, and remote procedures.

Activity number:	DE-5A
Activity name:	Design database stored procedures
Purpose:	To design and create the database stored procedures that are required to support the application
Inputs:	AN-T3 System transactions DE-T3 Physical database design
Outputs:	DE-T5A Database stored procedures

Activity description:	• For each system transaction that requires the creation of a stored procedure:
	  – Review the detailed system transaction requirements that must be satisfied via the creation of a stored procedure
	  – For each stored procedure:

- Identify the types of parameters that need to be passed by the calling application to the stored procedure
- Identify the types of parameters that will be returned by the stored procedure to the calling application
  - Design and code the stored procedure
    - Create the database accesses using the proper SQL statements
    - Include the procedural logic code that is required to satisfy the system transaction requirements
    - Consider the specific handling of:
      - Security requirements
      - Procedural errors
      - Database access errors
      - Audit and control requirements
- Document how the stored procedure can be invoked by an application program or other procedures or triggers
- Walk through the database stored procedure deliverables

4.6.1 DESIGN DATABASE STORED PROCEDURES

A stored procedure is a collection of pre-compiled and pre-optimized SQL statements that are centrally stored on the server database rather than in each application. Any application can then execute the stored procedure, simply by invoking it. Besides the usual SQL constructs, most relational database software management systems allow the inclusion of additional control statements within the stored procedure. These additional control statements support the usual repetition and conditional programming language constructs such as LOOP, IF THEN ELSE, and CASE.

The execution of the stored procedure is triggered via a CALL statement from the client program. This CALL statement is usually invoked by an application, a trigger, or another stored procedure. Parameters are ordinarily passed along via the CALL statement and return values are sent back to the caller.

As shown in Figure 4-15, the execution of a stored procedure is far more efficient than a dynamic SQL query.

At creation time, the stored procedure is verified for correct syntax and subsequently saved in the system tables. When the stored procedure is invoked for the first time by an application, it is retrieved from the system tables, compiled, and stored into the virtual memory of the server database. From there, it is finally executed. Since the stored procedure is compiled and optimized only once and then stored permanently

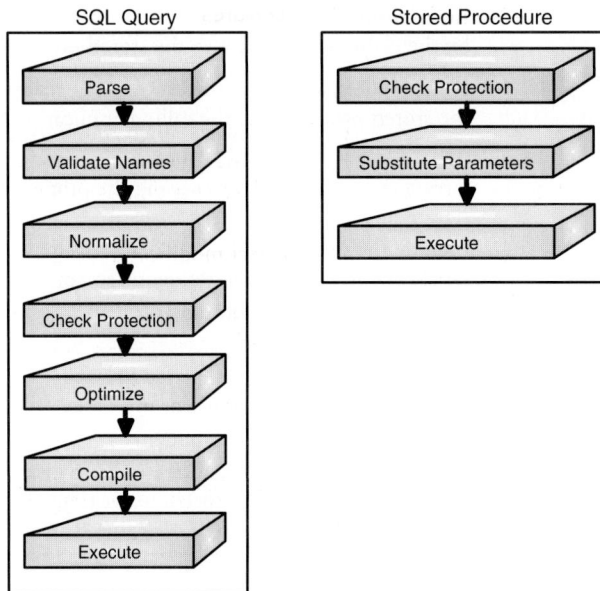

Figure 4–15 Stored procedures versus dynamic SQL queries.

on the database server, subsequent executions of the procedure that are requested by any client application will be performed immediately by the database server.

On the other hand, when a dynamic SQL query is sent from the client workstation to the database server, the server parses the command, verifies the syntax and names utilized, verifies the protection levels, optimize the search, creates an execution plan, and then compiles and executes it. This process must be repeated entirely every time a query is fired from the client workstation.

Some experts have claimed that stored procedures can sometimes be executed as much as 50 to 100% more quickly than the equivalent set of dynamic SQL statements.

The advantages and potential disadvantages of using stored procedures in a client-server system are summarized in Table 4-19.

Stored procedures can be used quite favorably in several instances during the development of a large client-server or Web database application, as indicated in Table 4-20.

Based on all the information provided on stored procedures, developers should carefully analyze the data access specifications that are documented in the data access matrices to identify the critical system transactions that are characterized with high frequency usage and/or high data access. These system transactions are likely candidates for stored procedures, which can be also reused for other business applications in the corporation.

Table 4–19 Stored Procedures

ADVANTAGES	POTENTIAL DRAWBACKS
• Usually executes more quickly than dynamic SQL • Promotes code reusability • Reduces network traffic by returning to the calling application (normally the client) only the required rows • Promotes standardization and modularity since the stored procedure is physically stored on the database server and therefore is independent of any particular application system • Can be utilized to enhance security and data integrity when used for database updates • Reduces maintenance; if a stored procedure is modified, all changes are made in one central location, and all applications using it will automatically get the new functionality	• Can limit the application independence toward the database software since stored procedures can tie you to a proprietary database language • Incorrect modifications that can be applied inadvertently to a stored procedure can affect adversely several applications or several programs within the same application • Improper use or inefficient codification of SQL calls in the stored procedures can result in system performance degradation

Table 4–20 When To Use Stored Procedures

- To reduce the overall network traffic between the client and the server caused by the frequent execution of large database transactions
- To code only once the set of SQL functions that are commonly used and shared across multiple applications or by certain programs within the same application; stored procedures can be used in the context of a reusable code enterprise program
- To standardize any set of SQL actions that are executed by more than one program within a client-server application
- To improve security, since the users can be allowed to execute a stored procedure even if they were not granted permissions to access directly the database tables or views that are referenced in it
- To centralize and enforce business rules at a single location such as the server level

Activity number:	DE-5B
Activity name:	Design database triggers
Purpose:	To design and create the database triggers that are required to support the application
Inputs:	AN-T3 System transactions DE-T3 Physical database design
Outputs:	DE-T5B Database triggers

Activity description:	• Review the business data model that was created during the analysis phase, along with its set of business rules
	• Identify the critical set of business rules that must be enforced centrally, above all applications, and activated automatically as soon as a database update, delete, or insert event is triggered by the application
	• For each business rule that must be enforced via the use of a database trigger, perform the following steps:
	  – Construct the database trigger statement, using the CREATE TRIGGER SQL command
	    – Indicate whether the trigger should be fired before or after executing the database update, delete, or insert event
	    – Indicate whether the trigger should be executed when
	      – a DELETE statement removes a row from the selected table
	      – an INSERT statement adds a row to the table
	      – an UPDATE statement modifies a value in one of the columns of the table that is subject to firing the trigger
	    – Design and code the set of logical operations that must be performed when the database trigger is executed
	• Walk through the database trigger deliverables

4.6.2 DESIGN DATABASE TRIGGERS

A trigger is a special form of stored procedure that is invoked by the database server when an attempt is made at updating the data that is stored in the relational tables.

Contrary to a stored procedure, though, triggers cannot be called directly by an application or a user. Rather, the database server automatically executes them only when data they are associated with are modified. In that respect, we can say that triggers are data-driven events.

The vast majority of relational database servers support the use of triggers. However, their implementation might differ slightly from one relational DBMS vendor to another.

Triggers are automatically fired whenever an insert, update, or delete SQL operation is performed on the table identified in the trigger, as shown in Figure 4-16.

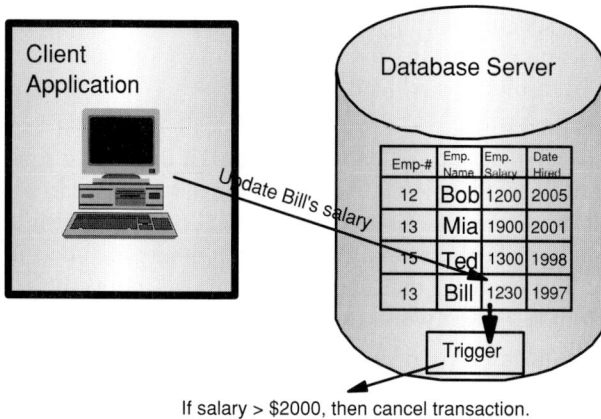

Figure 4–16 Database triggers.

Once triggers are created, they are stored on the database server and stay there until they are explicitly deleted. Most RDBMSs usually support the common types of triggers that are shown in Table 4-21.

Table 4–21 Trigger Types

TYPE OF TRIGGER	INVOCATION EVENT
INSERT	Invoked when a new row is inserted into the table associated with the trigger
DELETE	Invoked when a row is deleted in the table associated with the trigger
UPDATE	Invoked when a row in the table associated with the trigger is updated
UPDATE OF Column-List	Invoked when a row in the table associated with the trigger is updated and a column in the column list has been changed

Each type of trigger shown in Table 4-21 can be set for automatic execution either before or after the insert, update, or delete SQL request is performed.

Whenever the referential integrity features supported by a given RDBMS are not sufficient, triggers can always be used to enforce specific or additional constraints on data.

As a rule of thumb, the set of application business rules that is directly associated with the creation, update, or deletion of data can often benefit from the implementation of triggers. Similarly, potential candidates for triggers can also be found by carefully examining the business events (external, internal and temporal) that were documented in the business process model, during the analysis phase. Whenever a situation arises in which a specific action must be accomplished automatically in response to some modifications made to the database, triggers should be considered seriously as one of the best solutions at hand.

In such instances, utilizing triggers is far more efficient instead of executing an equivalent set of procedural logic at the client workstation. If the procedure is executed at the client workstation, then at least one more call to the database becomes necessary. The net result adds up to an increase in network traffic combined with a potential diminution of performance. Furthermore, the SQL statements included in a trigger often can be optimized in such a way that they will execute far more efficiently than if they were submitted from the client workstation.

A trigger can also be seen as a form of reusable code, since the logic it executes does not have to be replicated by different business applications.

Triggers can be used in numerous pre-defined situations in a client-server or Web database application, such as those indicated in Table 4-22.

Table 4–22 When To Use Database Triggers

- To logging the major activities/events performed against all database tables, independently of the different applications accessing them
- To support complex, detailed auditing measures; for example, you can monitor value changes by accumulating detailed update information in specific audit tables
- To enforce elaborate security authorizations to verify specific data changes
- To perform complex validations on data or various types of calculations such as summarization of data
- To automatically update data values in other tables based on changes performed against a specific table
- To automatically enforce referential integrity across several database servers; you can also enforce complex constraints that cannot be implemented through the regular integrity features that are supported by the database
- To automatically produce derived column values; for example, you can create values for derived columns automatically when you modify the columns on which they are constructed
- To circumvent invalid transactions
- To enforce enterprise-wide compliance to fundamental corporate business rules
- To notify users through electronic mail messages when specific database change events are triggered

Table 4-23 summarizes the common advantages and potential disadvantages of using database triggers.

Table 4–23 Database Triggers Advantages And Disadvantages

ADVANTAGES	DISADVANTAGES
• Complex business rules, integrity constraints, and procedural logic can be segregated from the applications and independently enforced at the database server level; useful in the context of an enterprise-wide application architecture • Easier to maintain • Ability to link a data-driven event to the specific data that triggers the event	• Improper testing and implementation can adversely affect several applications by generating unexpected results • Can increase consumption of system resources and cause performance deterioration if not well optimized

Since a trigger must be compiled the very first time it is fired, and every time it is modified, I recommend limiting the size of the trigger body to no more than 60 lines of code. The compilation of small triggers will minimally affect the overall performance of the system.

If the business rule that must be enforced is so complex that it requires more than 60 lines of code, I suggest encapsulating the coding instructions that must be executed by the trigger in a stored procedure. With this technique, the trigger can call the stored procedure, which is already compiled, therefore saving some execution time.

Activity number:	DE-5C
Activity name:	Design remote procedures
Purpose:	To design and create the set of remote procedures that are required to support the client-server application
Inputs:	AN-T3 System transactions DE-T3 Physical database design
Outputs:	DE-T5C Remote procedures
Activity description:	• For each system transaction that requires the creation of a remote procedure: – Review the system transaction requirements that must be satisfied via the design and construction of a remote procedure

- Determine whether special hardware, software, or
  networking facilities will be required on either the client or
  server side to support the remote procedure design process
- Design and code the remote procedure
- Design and code the business procedural logic that must be
  performed by the remote procedure
- Design and code the recovery mechanisms that might be
  required to handle potential hardware failure from either
  the computing platform where the caller of the remote
  procedure resides or the platform on which the remote
  procedure call will be executed
- Design and code the procedural security or control logic
  that must be implemented within the remote procedure
- Design and code the logic required to handle potential
  system or network errors
- Walk through the remote procedure deliverables

4.6.3   DESIGN REMOTE PROCEDURES

In a traditional mainframe environment, the communications between a main program and its subroutine modules are handled within the confines of a single computer, as shown in Figure 4-17.

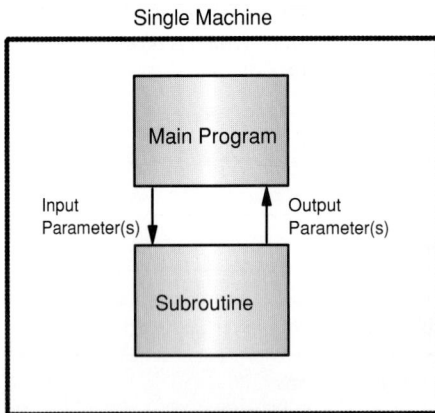

Figure 4–17 A local procedure call.

In a client-server environment, the procedural logic of a single program can be implemented partially in a client module and partially in a server module. Furthermore, you can have both routines run on a different physical platform machine, as illustrated in Figure 4-18. The subroutine that runs on a different physical computer from its calling procedure is called a remote procedure.

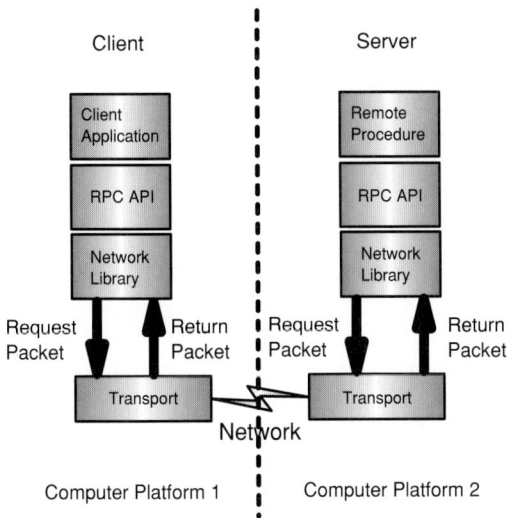

Figure 4–18 Remote procedure call.

Remote procedure calls (RPCs) provide a method of communicating in a distributed environment. Functions can be invoked and executed with processors that can run on different operating systems and computer platforms. The RPC tool provides the mechanism for the client to invoke the server module as if both modules were physically part of the same piece of code logic.

RPCs hide from the developers all the intricacies and complexities of network protocols. In fact, from a programmer's standpoint, RPCs are transparent and operate in the same manner as a traditional function call, with the distinction, though, that the function is executed on a different machine from the one calling it. Since the application interfaces with the RPC API layer and not the network, modifications at the network level do not adversely affect the application.

The rationale behind the use of RPCs is to distribute the work and data over the network to maximize resources. It also enables the design and construction of modular code, with the use of subroutines that are stored on a machine where everyone can access them. RPCs can help standardize the way programmers are creating their subroutine calls in a way that remote procedures can recognize them and execute the requests.

For the most part, the technology supporting RPCs relies heavily on direct synchronous connections between two machines. Because of this architectural particularity, RPCs' performance for industrial-strength applications can be very dependent on the robustness of the network supporting them. Furthermore, if the application attempts to invoke a remote function located on an application server that is down or very busy, then the application must wait until the call is satisfied. No other tasks on the client machine can be performed until the remote procedure call is satisfied.

The interfacing between the client and the server in a remote procedure call is generally implemented via a framework that was standardized by the Open Software Foundation (OSF) with their specification for the Distributed Computing Environment standard (DCE). Remote procedures can be advantageously used in the context of an enterprise-wide application architecture, since they represent a form of reusable code. I provide more information on DCE in Chapters 7, 9, and 11.

4.7 DESIGN DETAILED CUSTOM APPLICATION SOFTWARE COMPONENTS

At this stage, the application graphical user interface prototype that was built earlier during the analysis phase is refined and augmented with all the detailed functional specifications that are required to deliver a complete system. The initial prototype is gradually transformed into a fully functional system on its own. The application system is designed to meet not only all the detailed functional requirements but also all the stated operational requirements. This task must be achieved within the constraints imposed by the existing corporate application and technology architecture standards.

The complete set of system reports is also designed, along with any additional specialized graphical interface that might need to be grafted to the new system, such as special multimedia, fax, or e-mail application interfaces, for example.

The next series of technical activities, ranging from the completion of the detailed custom graphical user interface/program design and up to the design of the specialized pen-based interface application, cover these subjects.

Activity number:	DE-6A
Activity name:	Complete detailed graphical user interface/program design
Purpose:	To finalize the design of the application graphical user interface and its corresponding program(s)
Inputs:	AN-T3 System transactions AN-T5 System graphical user interface prototype DE-T3 Physical database design
Outputs:	DE-T6A Detailed GUI/program design
Activity description:	• Review the initial system graphical user interface prototype that was created during the analysis phase and augment it with the complete set of detailed functional features that are required by the new system. • For each system transaction that requires the creation of a graphical user interface:

- Review the set of detailed operations that must be executed inside the system transaction
- Review the system transaction database access requirements
- Identify the set of window(s) that are required to automate the basic operations that are contained in the system transaction
- For each distinct window, identify its main characteristics, including:
  - Its modality—modal (i.e., response window) or non-modal (i.e., independent window)
  - Its type
    - Main window
    - Child window
    - Response window
    - Frame window
  - Its main behavior characteristics
- Verify whether the window can inherit some or all of its components and behavior from a window ancestor class
- Design and construct each window
  - Assign to the window its general physical attributes
  - Assign a unique name and a descriptive title to the window
  - Determine its default position on the screen
  - Determine the window color background and size attributes
  - Determine whether the window needs minimizing and maximizing boxes and scroll bars
  - Determine whether the window will be resizable or not resizable
  - Determine whether the window requires a toolbar
  - Determine whether the window requires a status bar at its bottom
  - Create the basic window layout
  - Identify the various data fields that must be placed on the window and, if necessary, arrange the related data fields into logical groupings
- Place the individual data fields and control buttons in the window appropriately; uniquely identify them with descriptive labels
- Add the basic functionality that is required to support each window data field, including the necessary edit and validation rules
- Add the basic functionality that is required to support the control buttons

- Create the application windows navigational model
  - Identify how the users will navigate between the different application windows, based on the various user scenarios that were developed during the analysis phase
  - Place the individual window GUI controls that will be used to navigate between the different windows in an appropriate manner and identify each of them with descriptive names
  - Add the basic functionality that is required to support each navigation control element
- Create the window control menu
  - Determine whether the window needs a control menu
  - For each menu:
    - Determine its type
      - Window menu
      - Pop-up menu
    - Assign a unique name to the menu
    - Place the required menu items across the menu bar and organize them in a logical sequence
      - Place the drop-down and cascade menu items in a logical sequence
    - Uniquely identify each menu item with a brief but descriptive name
    - Add the basic functionality that is required to support each menu item
- Actively review the application graphical user interface with the users, gradually adding the required detailed functionality and refining its overall "look and feel"

4.7.1 COMPLETE DETAILED GRAPHICAL USER INTERFACE/PROGRAM DESIGN

In this activity, the initial graphical user interface prototype that was built earlier during the analysis phase is refined and augmented with the complete set of detailed functional features that are required for the new system.

You can consult Chapters 11 and 12 to obtain additional information on some basic graphical user interface concepts and design guidelines.

Activity number:	DE-6B
Activity name:	Design detailed system reports
Purpose:	To design and create all the business reports that are required for the application

| **Inputs:** | AN-T3 System transactions |
| | DE-T3 Physical database design |

| **Outputs:** | DE-T6B Detailed system reports design |

| **Activity description:** | • For each system transaction that requires the creation of report(s): |

- Review the detailed report data requirements
  - Determine the elementary data fields that are required to produce the report
  - Determine the data fields that may need to be derived via computational algorithms
  - Determine whether existing report layout templates can be used to develop the new report
- Design the detailed graphical report layout, covering its main features, such as:
  - Standard report header requirements, including, for instance, the display of a standard company logo and placement of the calendar date
  - Main body structure, including specific needs such as:
    - logical grouping of information
    - physical placement of data, graphs, and/or pictures
    - data sequencing and sorting
    - page and control breaks
    - totals and subtotals
    - field label descriptions
  - Standard report footer requirements, including, for instance, a page number indicator or a security classification label
  - Potential use of color to enhance the look of various report elements such as the background and field labels
  - Display and positioning of graphics and images
  - Fonts, including the use of bold, underline, and italic features
  - Paper type and size
- Walk through the application report deliverables

4.7.2   DESIGN DETAILED SYSTEM REPORTS

This section discusses the detailed steps involved in designing the system reports. If some of these reports must be printed on special forms, then it is important to ensure that the form layouts can be printed with the technology currently in place in the enterprise. If brand new technologies are introduced in the workplace, then it is important to double-check the functionality of these technologies, such as the printing of specialized forms.

Overview

In a typical client-server environment, most business reports can be processed in a batch mode, or they can be displayed directly on a window. The time and amount of resources the system takes to generate the report will determine whether the report should be processed in an online or batch mode.

Figure 4-19 shows a holistic view of a client-server infrastructure that supports a batch-processing environment. This environment also supports the automatic scheduling and production of batch reports.

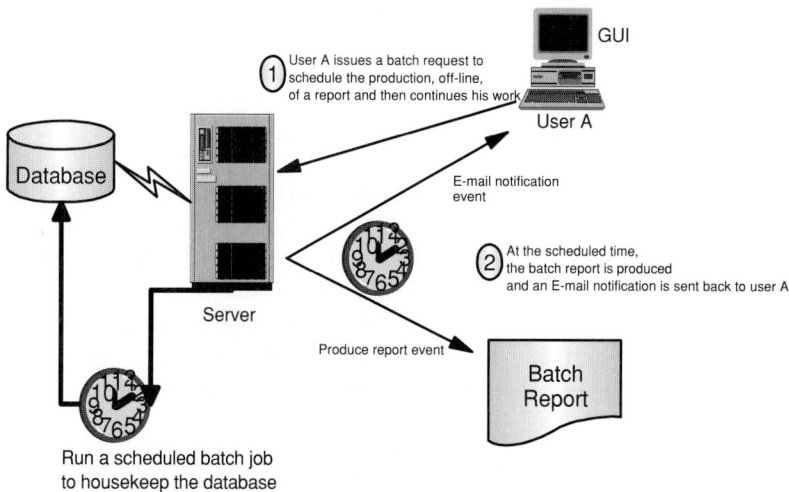

Figure 4–19 Client-server batch environment.

Client-server online reports are specifically formatted to summarize and display data directly on a window. However, the users cannot interactively modify the data that is shown on the window. These reports are simply static online versions of printed reports. The developers should always provide the users with a print option for this type of reports. With this option, the users can then print the whole report or a portion of the report, if necessary. This design strategy will help to reduce paper waste in the enterprise.

However, in a large enterprise, in many situations, complex corporate reports might need to be designed from the ground up specifically for a traditional medium such as paper.

Most RAD client-server tools provide extensive facilities to design very sophisticated layouts for reports, including the insertion of graphs, pictures or images, cross-tabulation, and so forth.

REPORT LAYOUT GUIDELINES

This section provides some basic guidelines for the design of simple report layouts. The use of standard report layout templates should be utilized to ensure adherence to the company standards and to create reports that have a uniform "look and feel" across the enterprise.

Figure 4-20 schematically shows the structure of a generic report template.

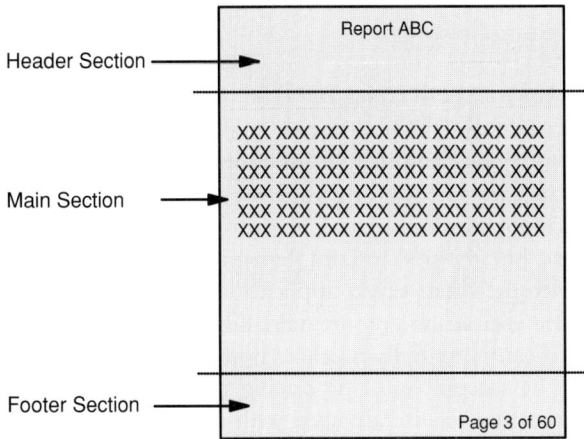

Figure 4–20 Report layout sections.

REPORT LAYOUT HEADER

The header section typically contains standard, repetitive information. Style elements usually include data such as the report name, report number, report title, report creation, date and time, and the names of the report columns headings. An official company logo can also be judiciously placed in the report header section. The header section is normally identical on all pages in the report.

MAIN BODY

The main body of the report displays the detailed data fields that must be shown on the report, in the sequence requested by the user. If graphs and images are embedded in the report, they should be placed in a non-obtrusive area to avoid cluttering the textual information.

The placement of the data on the report should facilitate its reading by the user. The information should be organized in a sequence that reduces eye fatigue. Related report data should be organized into logical groupings. Page and control breaks should be provided to improve the report's overall readability.

FOOTER

The footer section might contain various types of information such as the page number, copyright notices, and report security classifications.

SECURITY CONSIDERATIONS

If the printed report contains sensitive data, then you might want to implement additional control procedures to address various usage policies and security issues, such as report distribution to authorized recipients, report retention period, and report final disposition. An approved distribution list of users might be required and the circulation of the report tightly controlled.

USER AD HOC QUERY AND REPORTING TOOLS

Several specialized client-server and Web reporting tools are available on the market. These tools facilitate the creation of simple to fairly sophisticated reports by power users. As part of the infrastructure surrounding your production client-server environment, such user-friendly reporting tools could be provided to the users. They could then produce their own ad hoc reports, to complement the set of predetermined reports that are provided with the client-server application.

However, processing the user ad hoc report demands directly against the production database environment can potentially overload both the servers and the network. Such an environment can be acceptable for producing smaller reports occasionally or when you have only a few computer-literate users with minimal demands.

If the users require a more robust and scalable ad hoc information environment that can process a significant volume of data, then you may need to set up a more robust decision-support reporting environment completely separate from the production operational databases. Section 4.10, "Design application ad hoc report and query environment," provides additional information on this subject.

INTERNET/INTRANET REPORTING CONSIDERATIONS

Several client-server reporting tools allow the automatic conversion of the client-server reports into HTML format. The converted reports can then be deployed and viewed directly in an Internet/intranet environment, with the use of any standard Web browser.

Chapter 9 provides additional information on the concept of enterprise reporting and also on Web-based reporting tools.

CLIENT-SERVER BATCH PROCESSING

One of the most common fallacies that is associated with the client-server paradigm is that no more batch processing requirements exist in such an environment.

In a typical client-server environment, many reports can be provided interactively to the users. As you have seen previously in this section, the online reports are designed in such a way that they can be viewed directly on the user's workstation screen. The user is provided also with the option of printing them, when required. However, in several situations, reports still might need to be processed as a batch request. In a financial client-server system, for instance, what about the need for weekly, monthly, and annual aggregation of fiscal data? What about reports that can be extremely compute-intensive and demand a large amount of time to manipulate and format a colossal volume of data? What about a payroll client-server application that must create and print thousands of paychecks?

Figure 4-19 illustrates schematically a client-server environment where batch processing jobs can be triggered for asynchronous processing while the client continues performing other tasks once it has initiated the batch requests. The development environment required to support batch processing in a client-server environment will vary from one organization to another, depending on the type of technology infrastructure that is currently in place.

CLIENT OR SERVER BATCH PROCESSING

Batch processing requests that can be executed rather quickly and that do not generate intensive network traffic can be executed directly on the client workstation. If the data is not volatile, it can be cached on the client workstation to reduce unnecessary network traffic. If the batch processing requests are very data-intensive or require some lengthy processing, then you might need to execute them on the server that houses the data or on an application server, if a three-tier architecture supports the client-server environment.

BATCH PROCESSING RUN TIME ESTIMATES

Be sure to estimate the total run time of each large batch program to ensure that it will fit in the overall window allocated to the processing of the entire batch job streams. Several batch programs can be combined into a job stream if they are interdependent and can only be executed sequentially, one after the other.

Automated batch scheduler software might be required to launch the application batch jobs at regular times during the day or the night.

Other batch performance metrics that might require some further investigation include overall batch programs resource utilization, more specifically: CPU processing, I/Os, and network traffic. Can the application batch processing performance objectives that were previously established with the users be met?

REUSABLE MODULES AND STRUCTURE CHARTS

If, through earlier projects, the enterprise has assembled a library of reusable modules or templates for developing batch programs, then the designers should search this reusable library to see whether existing modules can be utilized to satisfy the processing logic of the new batch programs. If several batch programs must be written, then you might want to develop a generic batch skeleton program that will form a basis from which to construct all other batch programs, within a standard development framework.

This batch software component approach will increase the productivity of large development teams, since it will enforce a standard approach to develop batch programs. Also, all the procedural logic that was already coded and tested for the previous applications can be reused by the developers, hence reducing the likelihood of introducing additional bugs in the new programs. Figure 4-21 shows a simple batch program structure chart that can be modified or complemented to satisfy the specific needs of any enterprise.

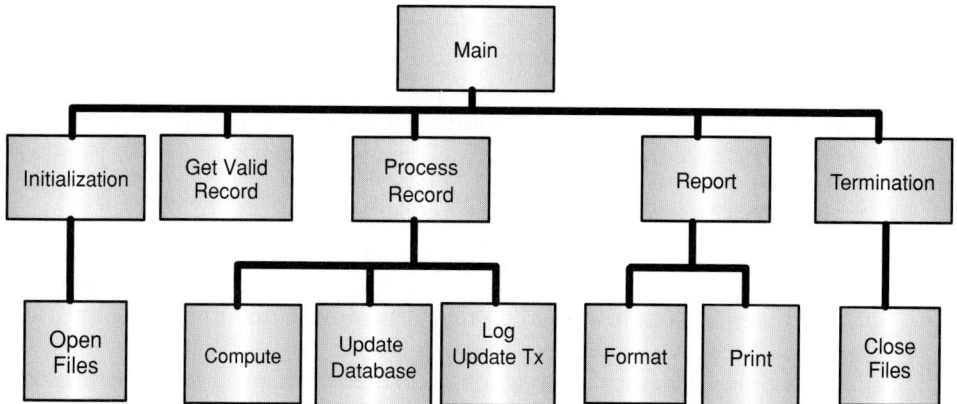

Figure 4–21 Generic structured chart.

BATCH REPORT DESIGN SPECIFICATIONS

As I previously stated, the designers should challenge the users' printed reports requirements, especially for users who were accustomed to receiving several printed reports in a legacy mainframe environment. In a client-server or Internet/intranet environment, reports that are not too voluminous can easily be viewed online, offering report printing as an additional option to cover situations in which a printed copy is still required.

For large reports that are lengthy and voluminous, batch processing might be the only viable option. Besides the usual batch reporting processing requirements, additional administrative considerations should be addressed when the production of voluminous printed outputs is a necessity in a large corporation, as indicated in Table 4-24.

Table 4–24 Batch Reports Usage Procedures

- What security measures must be put in place to identify who will have access to these reports?
- What will be the strategy to distribute the reports to all intended recipients?
- What will be the frequency for producing those reports?
- Do you need to design special security measures for the handling of printed reports that contain sensitive information, such as payroll or human resource information?
- Will special forms or stationery be used to print reports, or will the printed report forms be designed with the report facilities provided by the client-server development software?

4.7.3 DESIGN SPECIALIZED GRAPHICAL USER INTERFACES

The next set of technical activities specifically addresses some potential design challenges that relate to the integration of various multimedia, fax, email, bar code, or pen-based commercial software with the current application graphical user interface.

Activity number:	DE-6C
Activity name:	Design multimedia interface
Purpose:	To design all the multimedia interfaces required for the client-server application
Inputs:	AN-T3 System transactions DE-T3 Physical database design
Outputs:	DE-T6C Multimedia interface design

Activity description:	• For each system transaction that requires the creation of a multimedia interface:
	  – Review the detailed multimedia requirements for:
	    – audio
	    – 2-D, 3-D graphical animation
	    – video
	  – Determine whether some special hardware, software, or networking facilities and equipment will be required on either the client or server side to support the multimedia functions. Some of the items that might be required can include special sound or video compression algorithms, special software drivers, sound cards and speakers, digital video capture cards, sound digitizers, frame-grabbers, hardware audio/video compression/decompression cards, encoding/decoding software, and digital cameras and videos.
	  – Design and create the application interface for audio
	    – Create the sound effects and audio segments that must be inserted into the user interface
	    – Design the mechanism by which the sound effects and audio segments will be triggered, either automatically or via the use of GUI controls such as images, control buttons, etc.
	  – Design and create the application interface for 2-D or 3-D graphical images and animation:

- Create the 2-D or 3-D graphical animation effects that must be inserted into the user interface. If necessary, synchronize the animation with the supporting audio sequences.
- Design the mechanism by which the 2-D or 3-D graphical animation effects will be triggered, either automatically or via the use of GUI controls such as images, control buttons, etc.
  - Design and create the application interface for video:
    - Create the video segments that must be inserted into the user interface. If necessary, synchronize with the audio sequences.
    - Design the mechanism by which the video will be triggered, either automatically or via the use of GUI controls such as images, control buttons, etc.
- Integrate the sound, 2-D/3-D graphical images, animation, and video controls into the graphical user interface, along with the other textual or graphical control interface elements
- Walk through the application multimedia interface deliverables

DESIGN THE MULTIMEDIA INTERFACE

This section discusses the detailed steps involved in designing the system multimedia interface. It also provides some tips and guidelines on how to execute this process.

Overview

Certain types of client-server applications literally beg for the insertion of sophisticated multimedia data. For example, a traveling agency will want to use extensive multimedia features to display exotic images of their most popular travel destinations, along with text, pictures, videos, and exotic background music. A real-estate application will show images and videos of the properties that are for sale, with some text describing the main characteristics of the properties and their neighborhood, such as the house total square footage, special features, and so forth. Interactive audio segments might also be provided with the video. Education and training agencies will demand training applications that are computer-based, with several integrated multimedia features.

The multimedia trend that is growing in the training business is not surprising, since several studies have shown that the use of well designed multimedia applications can reduce training time as much as 50% and increase retention of what the trainees have learned by 15% to 40%.

Even the more traditional business-oriented client-server applications suddenly become more compelling with the effective use of multimedia. Humans absorb more rapidly and retain for larger periods of time the information that is provided to them via a slick user interface design that naturally excites both their visual and auditory senses. Some of the many areas where client-server multimedia application can be advantageously used are listed in Table 4-25.

Table 4–25 Examples Of Application Opportunities For Client-server Multimedia Applications

- Employee interactive training
- Internal communications
- Point-of-sale kiosks
- Multimedia catalogs
- Marketing application systems
- Entertainment industry
- Healthcare application systems

However, the developers must carefully assess the impact that rich multimedia features might have on the client-server system performance. The simultaneous delivery of full-motion, full-screen video, and high-fidelity audio to multiple client desktops over the enterprise network can quickly push to its limits a corporate client-server infrastructure that is not robust and upward scalable.

Following are some basic guidelines to consider while designing a client-server application with built-in multimedia features.

Multimedia Controls Buttons

The use of various types of multimedia controls should be integrated harmoniously with the more traditional user interface elements such as graphics, tables, GUI controls, and textual information.

The access to distinct multimedia sources that deliver the same kind of information via different channels should be provided in a consistent manner throughout the application. For instance, if specific icons are utilized to deliver a message in a video/audio format, then similar icons should be used to allow the users to access the same message in a textual format. The multimedia icons should also be designed to reflect as closely as possible the themes that are conveyed by the video and audio segments.

Multimedia Controls And A Real-life Metaphor

Controls that emulate real-life metaphors can be used advantageously when designing multimedia interfaces. For example, horizontal scroll bars can be used on the window interface to control the advance of video and audio segments. Single-arrow and double-arrow control buttons similar to those used for a VCR machine can be utilized to control the audio or video interfaces (i.e., play, pause, stop, fast forward, and fast backward). Using GUI controls that match real-life objects might help lessen the information overload a user may encounter while working with client-server multimedia applications.

Performance Considerations

The impact that the use of multimedia elements might have on various components of the enterprise client-server infrastructure, such as the server or the corporate network, for example, should be carefully assessed by the system designers. Sophisticated multimedia features such as videos, sophisticated images, sound, and 3-D animation frequently demand a large bandwidth from networks, even if the multimedia objects are compressed at a maximum level.

If the multimedia objects are stored on the server, will the network bandwidth be capable of supporting the transmission of the video file to the client workstation at a reasonable rate and, if so, will the client workstation be able to play it at an acceptable pace? Similarly, if some of the multimedia objects will reside on the client workstation, does the workstation have the proper hardware/software configuration to support it?

A large, scalable system bus combined with fast disk storage components and a high-performance network are the key characteristics of a robust multimedia server.

Use Of Images

Table 4-26 shows some of the most popular image formats that exist on the market, along with a brief description of their characteristics.

Table 4–26 Image Formats

Image format	Number of bits per pixel	Number of colors supported	Image size	Compression technique(s)	Loss of color
.GIF	8	256	65,535X65535	LZW	LOSSLESS
JPEG	24	16,555,216	65,535X65,535	JPEG	LOSSY
.BMP	24	16,555,216	65,535X65,535	RLE*	LOSSLESS
.PCX	24	16,555,216	65,535X65,535	RLE	LOSSLESS
.PNG	48	281,454,956,510,656	2,145,483,645 X 2,145,483,645	DEFLATION (LZ55 VARIATION)	LOSSLESS
TIFF	24	16,555,216	4,294,965,295	LZW,RLE, and OTHERS	LOSSLESS

Legend: *Compression is optional, RLE=Run Length Encoding, LZW=Lempel-Ziv-Welch, JPEG = Joint Photographic Experts Group

The rule of thumb with graphical images is simple: the larger the image file size, the harder storing and manipulating this image in your client-server or intranet application will be.

Quite often, compressing images or reducing the number of colors that are displayed in them can generally drastically reduce the size of certain image files. Another approach is to crop or scale down large images to get smaller images. Most of the time, these image reduction techniques can be done without much affecting the visual quality of the image. Several commercial image editing software can be used for that purpose. As a last note, images that must be printed on paper demand higher resolutions, such as 600 to 1200 dots per inch (dpi) and more, than images that will need to be displayed only on a window. On a screen, the image resolution rarely goes higher than 72 dpi.

Use Of Sound

Sound effects other than a soft human voice may be associated with some specific events and should always be used parsimoniously. Once the initial excitements have vanished, too many sound effects might seriously annoy the users rather than stimulate them.

Sound files can be compressed like images, although the compression techniques are very different. As with images, the difficulty with sound is achieving a balance between file size and quality. Table 4-27 identifies the most common sound formats that are used in client-server and Web applications.

Table 4–27 File Formats For Sound

Sound Format	Description	Compression Scheme
AIFF/AIFC	Developed by Apple for music and sound.	Lossy
WAV/WAVE	Developed by Microsoft/IBM. Primarily used with PC/Windows applications.	Lossy
AU	Developed by Sun and NeXT. Works cross-platform. Used widely for Unix platforms.	Lossy
RA/RAM	Sound format developed by RealAudio. This format is called streamed audio, since it can be played while the sound file is downloaded from the Web, for instance.	

Use Of Video

Small video clips such as a short animation or some live action can be used to carry out some very effective messages. Because of the enormous size that even a small video clip can take for storage or manipulation, some client-server or Web applications might use video frame rates that are usually lower than 30 frames per second. They might also use reduced frame sizes to play the video sequence, such as 25% of all the screen space available. As with image and audio, but more so for video files, the compression and decompression algorithms for video are extremely important. Table 4-28 describes some of the most common formats that are available for digital video.

Table 4–28 Video Formats

Video Format	Description	Compression Scheme
AVI	Developed by Microsoft for PC/Windows. Mostly used on the Windows platform.	Lossy
QuickTime	Developed by Apple. Provides wide cross-platform support capabilities.	Lossy
MPEG	Provides very good picture quality but can be slow to decompress. The decompression process is often hardware-assisted to ensure smooth playback.	Lossy

Beware Of User Software/hardware Equipment Limitations

When designing the multimedia interfaces, the designers must be prepared to support users that might have diversified workstations.

Many of these client workstations might not necessarily have the latest multimedia hardware or software equipment required to support sophisticated multimedia interfaces. In such situations, provide more traditional alternatives to the users. Due to the isochronous (time-dependent) nature of video, I strongly recommend equipping each client workstation with, at the bare minimum, a dedicated 10BaseT network connector to ensure the constant delivery of the video stream.

Universal Servers And Multimedia Applications

A universal server is a relational database management system that has been extended to manage complex data types such as those indicated in Table 4-29.

Table 4–29 Complex Data Types Supported By A Universal RDBMS

- Spatial
- Text
- Image
- Video and audio
- Time-series

A universal server should support the complex data types that are shown in the previous table with some powerful data functions and access techniques. It should also be capable of supporting open, extensible user-defined data types. The architecture of a universal RDBMS must be open to provide the flexibility necessary to adapt to evolving user needs and the emergence of new data types in the future.

The universal server technology should be tightly integrated into the enterprise client-server, intranet, or Internet architectures to improve the performance, reliability, and scalability of mission-critical multimedia business applications.

The video and audio extensions that are provided by a universal server enable the developers to store, manage, and deliver full-motion, full-screen video and high-quality audio to multiple users over the enterprise network, with a highly scalable scheme. With the use of additional software plug-ins, the developers can also stream full-motion, full-screen video and audio into a Web browser. Then they can deploy almost instantaneously rich multimedia application data directly into their corporate intranets.

Figure 4-22 shows a generic technology framework that supports a universal server for video applications. Chapter 9 provides more detailed information on Web-based push technologies.

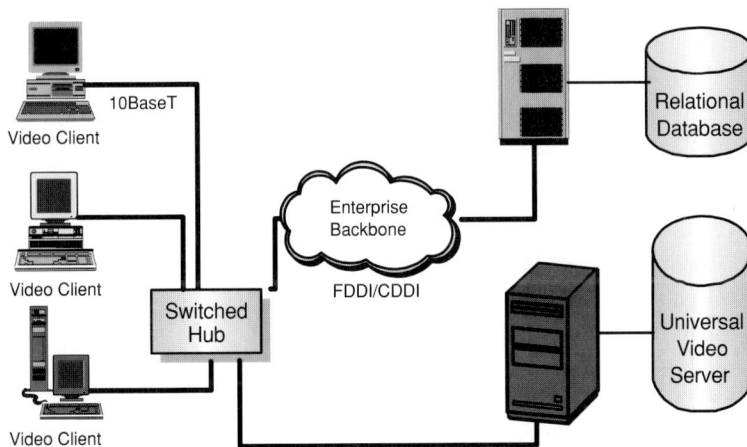

Figure 4–22 Video universal server.

When designing the multimedia interface, take into consideration the special needs of people who might be physically challenged. For example, some of the users might have difficulties discerning certain colors, such as red. Others might have hearing disabilities or impaired vision. For people with low vision, the user interface should provide zoom in and out facilities to improve their views of the application. The interface should also provide the users with the option to choose larger font sizes. Provide special screen displays that deliver output by synthesized voice or refreshable Braille to users who have low vision disabilities.

Activity number:	DE-6D
Activity name:	Design the bar code interface
Purpose:	To design all the bar code interfaces required from the application
Inputs:	AN-T3 System transactions DE-T3 Physical database design
Outputs:	DE-T6D Bar code interface design

Activity description:	• For each system transaction that requires the creation of a bar code interface:
	  – Review the detailed bar coding requirements
	  – Determine whether special hardware, software, or networking facilities will be required on either the client or server side to support the required bar coding functions
	  – Design and create the bar code interface
	  – Identify the data elements that are involved in the input/output bar coding processes
	  – Design and create the programs that are required to manipulate the bar codes, including:
	    – capturing and validating the data elements that are coded on the bar codes
	    – creating and printing bar code labels
	  – Ensure that all the data elements involved in the bar coding tasks are properly defined in the physical databases that were created to support the application
	• Walk through the bar codes interface deliverables

DESIGN THE BAR CODE INTERFACE

Bar codes are special graphic codes that contain parallel dark bars and spaces of varying width. The bars and spaces are organized in a predetermined pattern and uniquely identify different types of information. Often, bar codes are used to encode specific application data such as purchase orders, parts serial numbers, and various product identification numbers.

Bar Code Advantages

Bar code labels can be recognized very easily by a computer. When a special input device equipped with a scanner reads bar codes symbols, they are translated back into their original set of character strings.

One of the biggest advantages of bar codes is that they can be scanned with a very high level of accuracy. Good bar code readers will rarely generate data entry errors, as opposed to the manual data entry functions that are traditionally performed by a clerk using a keyboard. Furthermore, the use of bar codes can drastically reduce labor by its sheer execution speed. Scanning a bar code with a machine gun is a lot faster than using a keyboard to manually enter the data into the client-server system. In some specific instances, bar codes can be scanned even with no human intervention at all.

BAR CODE USAGE

Several manufacturing, retail, distribution, shipping, and warehousing industries advantageously use the bar code technology to streamline and automate their processes. Business operations, which must manipulate a large number of various products, can be improved significantly with the use of bar codes, as shown in Table 4-30.

Table 4–30 Bar Code Candidate Business Operations

• Point-of-sale scanning of products
• Price markdowns and verification
• In-store inventory management
• Tracking anything that you can stick a bar code label on such as: books, tools, equipment, parts, and instruments
• Receiving (identifying the different parts contained in various shipment boxes or containers)
• Shelf price audits
• Stock transfers

Typically, the bar code labels are fixed to the various products that very likely will undergo several manipulations later on, such as inventory parts, for example. Subsequently, the inventory parts are scanned with a bar code reader. During the scanning process, the bar code reader decodes the parts bar code labels and automatically relays the captured information to an application system, where it can be processed according to the application business needs.

PRINTING BAR CODES

Bar codes can be printed on labels with any of the printer devices that are listed in Table 4-31, using a font that is created specially for bar codes.

BAR CODE FONTS

In a Windows environment, several categories of bar code True Type fonts can be used to print bar codes within a client-server application. Similarly, bar code True Type fonts can also be used to insert bar codes directly into a business document with the use of commercial word processing programs such as Corel WordPerfect or Microsoft

Table 4–31 Different Categories Of Bar Code Printers

- Lasers
- Ink Jets
- Dot Matrix
- Direct Thermal Printers
- Thermal Transfer Printers

Word, for instance. Bar code True Type fonts can also be used to produce printed bar code labels.

BAR CODE SCANNING DEVICES

A bar code scanning device identifies and decodes the bar code symbols. Basically, two types of bar code input devices can be used to read bar codes: the hand-held portable scanners and those that are stationary. Table 4-32 lists different types of scanners, along with a brief description of their most basic characteristics.

Table 4–32 Bar Code Hardware Devices

Scanner Type	Characteristics
Wand Scanner	• Portable, hand-held scanner that usually looks like a large pen. Sometimes referred to as a light pen • A contact bar code reader, which means it must make contact with the bar code label; to read the bar code, the light pen is moved manually across the symbol from one side to the other
Charged Couple Device (CCD) Scanner	• A bar code reader that utilizes a CCD to capture the bar code image • These scanners can read the bar code labels without the need to be in contact with the symbol; the maximum distance from which they can read a bar code symbol is approximately 4 inches • Faster than a wand scanner • The physical length of the bar code must be taken into consideration since the optical head of the CCD scanner must cover entirely the complete bar code
Laser Scanner	• An optical bar code scanner that utilizes a low-energy laser beam as its source of light to capture the bar code symbol • Faster than a wand or CCD scanner • Can read a bar code label up to a distance of 15 inches

BAR CODE SYMBOLOGY

Several categories of bar code symbologies are on the market. Prior to implementing a bar code interface with your client-server application, select the type of bar code symbology that is appropriate for your application.

First and most important, try to verify whether an industry standard already exists for your type of business. Several industries have developed specific bar code standards, which are peculiar to their sectors of business and the type of business operations they conduct. Each specific industry segment has defined its own set of specifications for bar codes, usually covering the criteria that are listed in Table 4-33.

Table 4–33 Bar Code Specification Criteria By Industry Segment

- The specific type of data that can be encoded and decoded
- How the bar code symbols can be used within that industry
- The particular fields that contain information and their format description
- The location and size of the bar codes for a data item

Table 4-34 presents some of the most widely used bar code types that exist in industry, along with a brief description of their basic characteristics.

Table 4–34 Bar Code Standards

Bar Code Type	Industry	Characteristics
Code 39	Used widely for inventory, tracking, and distribution applications in various industry sectors such as manufacturing and warehouses. For instance, most video rental businesses use Code 39 to track their videotapes.	• Alphanumeric characters • Variable length code • Bi-directional scanning (Can be read from left to right and vice-versa) • Can be read by several popular scanners
Uniform product code (UPC)	Used for a wide variety of retail applications in industry sectors such as convenience stores, food supermarkets (extensive use), drug stores, and department stores.	• Numeric characters only • Fixed length code • 12 characters • Bi-directional scanning
Interleaved Code 2 of 5	Used widely for various shipping and warehousing applications in several industry sectors such as manufacturing, shipping, and distribution, for instance.	• Numeric characters only • Variable length code • Bi-directional scanning

Table 4–34 Bar Code Standards (cont.)

Postnet	Used to encode ZIP codes on U.S. mail.	• Supports 5-digit, 9-digit ZIP+4, 11-digit delivery point bar code
Health industry bar code (HIBC)	Used for encoding/ decoding bar codes within the health industry.	

A FINAL NOTE ON AUTOMATED IDENTIFICATION TECHNOLOGIES

Automatic product identification technologies are not limited to bar code but rather encompass a vast array of technologies. Discussing them in detail is beyond the scope of this book. Nevertheless, Table 4-35 provides a brief list of useful automated identification technologies.

Table 4–35 Different Types Of Automated Identification Technologies

- Magnetic ink character recognition (MICR)
- Optical character recognition (OCR)
- Voice pattern recognition
- Light pens
- Pen-based computer devices
- Smart cards
- Optical mark readers
- Radio frequency (RF) identification devices
- Touch screens
- Two-dimensional bar codes

Activity number:	DE-6E
Activity name:	Design e-mail interface
Purpose:	To design all the e-mail interfaces required for the application
Inputs:	AN-T3 System transactions DE-T3 Physical database design
Outputs:	DE-T6E E-mail interface design
Activity description:	• For each system transaction that requires the creation of an electronic mail interface: – Review the detailed electronic mail interface requirements

- – Determine whether special hardware, software, or networking facilities will be required on either the client or server side to support the required e-mail interface application functions
- – Design and create the application e-mail interface:
  - – Determine the data elements that are required by the interface
- – Design the user interface that is required to perform some or all the following operations:
  - – Send mail and append textual or graphical information attachments that were produced by the application
  - – Send mail when a specific event has occurred during the execution of a particular task in the application
  - – Send mail within the business application to solicit information from other people
  - – Receive mail directly within the application
- – Design and create the mechanisms by which the e-mail interface will be invoked inside the application, either automatically or via the use of specific GUI control buttons or menu items
- – Create the e-mail user interface
- • Walk through the e-mail interface deliverables

DESIGN THE E-MAIL INTERFACE

This section discusses the different steps involved in creating the system e-mail interfaces. It also provides tips and guidelines on how to perform this process.

E-mail Requirements

One of the business application requirements might involve the need to interface with an e-mail system, as schematically illustrated in Figure 4-23. This particular figure also identifies other possible application interfaces such as a link with a word processor and a spreadsheet.

In the context shown in Figure 4-23, the business application must be able to send electronic messages to individuals inside or outside the enterprise. The application must also be capable of receiving electronic messages that were sent by users outside the application, via an electronic mail software system.

E-MAIL PROTOCOLS

Some e-mail protocols can support different platforms simultaneously. For instance, the most widely used e-mail standard that exists for the Internet is the Simple Mail Transfer Protocol (SMTP).

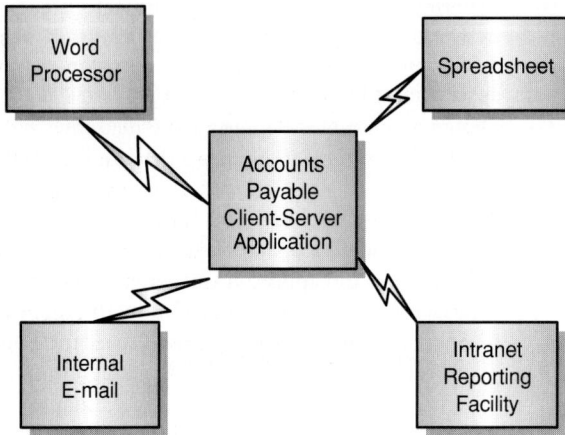

Figure 4–23 E-mail interface.

In the Windows environment, two major e-mail protocols are available: MAPI and VIM.

MAPI stands for Messaging Application Programming Interface and is supported primarily by Microsoft and its followers. VIM stands for Vendor Independent Messaging and is primarily supported by vendors such as IBM/LOTUS (i.e., cc:Mail and Lotus Notes), Apple, and Novell. Lotus has developed a VIM interface to MAPI.

With most client-server RAD tools available today, developers can build business applications that can support a direct access to a particular e-mail system and protocol. However, communicating among different e-mail systems is not always a trivial exercise. Nonetheless, the OSI standard called X.400 can be used to achieve communication between different e-mail/protocol systems via a special gateway, as shown in Figure 4-24.

The X.400 gateway will translate an e-mail message from its native format to the format of the destination e-mail system, allowing two user groups that utilize a different e-mail protocol to communicate together and exchange information.

Chapter 9 provides additional information on Web-based e-mail systems.

DESIGN THE FAX/OPTICAL CHARACTER RECOGNITION (OCR) INTERFACE

This section describes the detailed steps involved in creating the fax/optical character recognition design process. It also provides some tips and guidelines on how to perform this process.

Overview

For the vast majority of enterprises all around the world, fax-based communications have become a universal method to quickly send or receive business documents. Several areas in the world are not yet networked, despite the constant progress that is

X.400 Gateway

Local Area Network

Lotus Note Users   Microsoft Mail Users

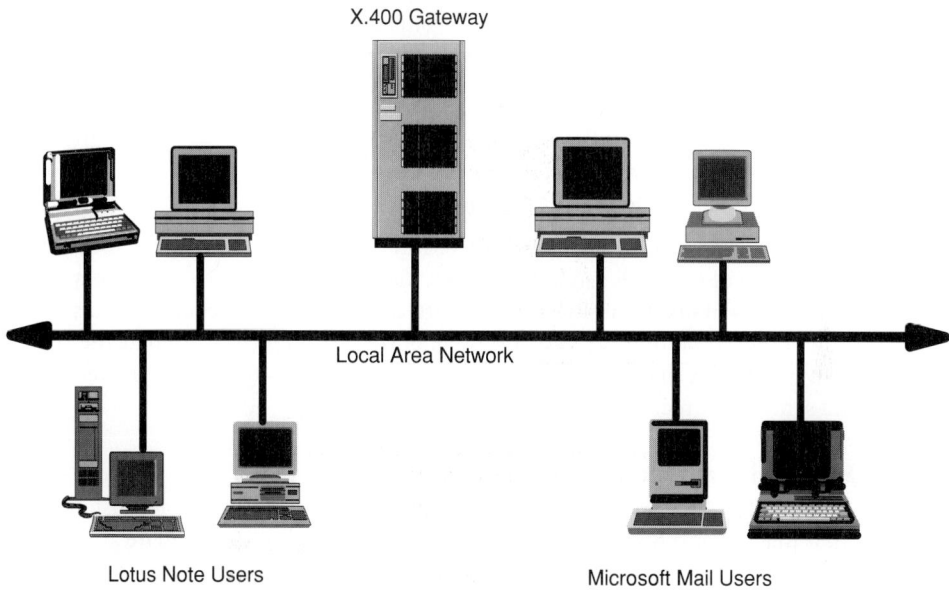

Figure 4–24 X.400 e-mail gateway.

Activity number:	DE-6F
Activity name:	Design Fax/Optical Character Recognition (OCR) interface
Purpose:	To design all the fax/optical character recognition (OCR) interfaces required from the application
Inputs:	AN-T3 System transactions DE-T3 Physical database design
Outputs:	DE-T6F Fax/optical character recognition interface design

Activity description:	• For each system transaction that requires the creation of a fax and/or an OCR interface:
	  – Review the detailed requirements for fax and/or OCR
	  – Determine whether special hardware (i.e., fax/voice modems, fax server cards, scanners), software (i.e., fax modules, optical character readers), or networking facilities will be required on either the client or server side to support the application fax and/or OCR processing needs
	  – Design the fax/OCR interface
	    – Determine the types of data and documents that need to be faxed or processed via an OCR software interface

- Design the fax templates (i.e., cover sheets, main body)
  in accordance with existing company standards
- Design the various programs required to manipulate the
  fax/OCR interface
- Create the fax/OCR interface
• Walk through the fax/OCR interface deliverables

made in the field of electronic mail and advanced telecommunication technologies.
But even the countries that are not yet fully networked still use fax machines.

Because of the widespread use of fax machines, more and more users demand that
some forms of fax capabilities be supported directly within their business applications.
The potential savings are very tangible. Several studies indicate that the time to manually send a fax via a standalone fax machine is up to ten times greater than sending
the same fax directly via a client workstation.

Fax Hardware Equipment

The users can be provided with single fax/voice modems that are installed locally on
their machines. This approach, although it can provide an adequate automated fax solution for small businesses that have single-user workstation platforms, is somewhat
limiting in terms of overall functionality for the larger organizations. For this reason,
most large organizations use sophisticated fax server software that is tightly integrated
with their networks and also tied to complementary technologies such as voice mail,
imaging systems, e-mail, and even wireless communications devices such as pagers.

Scanner devices might be required to capture various types of printed documents
or images that need to be faxed via the workstation. If the application requires color-
faxing capabilities, then a color scanner might also become a necessity for capturing
color printed documents.

FAX STANDARDS/PROTOCOLS

Several fax standards and protocols exist for fax machines. Table 4-36 identifies the
most common ones that are used in the industry.

Fax modems are defined with different class levels, as indicated in Table 4-37.

Fax Server Software

Most fax server software will support different operating system platforms and several
categories of fax cards. I include some of the criteria that must be considered while selecting specific fax server software in Table 4-38.

Table 4–36 Different Fax Machine Groups

FAX MACHINE GROUP	DESCRIPTION
GROUP 1	Group 1 fax machines were the earliest machines. They were quite slow compared to today's machines. Transmitting a one-page document took 5-6 minutes.
GROUP 2	Group 2 fax machines started to appear in the late 50s. With the introduction of new compression algorithms, these machines were able to transmit a one-page document in approximately 3 minutes.
GROUP 3	Group 3 fax machines can transmit data at speeds up to 14,400 bits per seconds, with the v.15 protocol. The T.4 protocol regulates features such as page size, resolution, and transmission time.
GROUP 4	Group 4 fax machines are constructed to specifically support the faster digital ISDN lines.

Table 4–37 Fax Modem Class Types

FAX MODEM CLASS TYPE	DESCRIPTION
CLASS 1	The class 1 fax modems are characterized with extensions to their command sets that permit them to operate as group 3 fax machines.
CLASS 2	The class 2 fax modems take care of most of the processing logic that was done by the CPU for class 1 modems.
CLASS 3	The class 3 modems can convert data streams into images.
CLASS 4	The class 4 modems include buffers that permit the CPU to process different tasks, during a short period of time, without having to respond immediately to the fax data.

Adding Fax Capabilities Within The Application

The developers must determine with the users what type of fax functionality should be supported within the business application. Several possibilities exist, including those indicated in Table 4-39.

The various fax input and output templates that are designed for the client-server business application should adhere closely to the existing enterprise standards. For ex-

Table 4–38 Fax Server Selection Criteria

- Scalability to support fax applications that must handle high-volume traffic
- Integration with different e-mail messaging systems (via fax gateways) such as:
  - Vendor Independent Messaging (VIM)
  - Mail Applications Programming Interface (MAPI)
  - Message Handling System (MHS)
- Fax security features that support various encryption/decryption mechanisms
- Automatic routing of received faxed to internal recipients
- Server-based OCR capabilities
- General fax status reporting and administration features
- Accessing a personal fax mailbox through a Web browser, from within the office or any location around the world, and allowing sending, receiving, routing, deleting, and printing of faxes

Table 4–39 Fax Application Functionality

- Sending documents that are created by the client-server application system to different recipients via faxes, either manually or automatically via event triggers
- Receiving faxes inside the application or storing received faxes
- Allowing the translation of received fax documents into editable text
- Using e-mail as a vehicle to create a document and then send it as a fax
- Using e-mail as a potential vehicle to receive faxes

ample, most organizations have defined a standard cover page form, which is always transmitted as the first page of a document that is transmitted via fax. Also, several fax software systems provide various options that allow the users to utilize a standard word processing template to create the document that will be faxed within the application.

Chapter 9 provides additional information on Web-based faxing solutions.

Activity number:	DE-6G
Activity name:	Design pen-based interface
Purpose:	To design all the pen interfaces required from the application
Inputs:	AN-T3 System transactions DE-T3 Physical database design
Outputs:	DE-T6G Pen-based interface design
Activity description:	• For each system transaction that requires the creation of a pen-based interface: – Review the detailed pen-based requirements

- Determine whether special hardware, software, or networking facilities will be required on either the client or server side to support the required pen-based processes
- Design the pen-based interface
  - Identify the data elements that are required in the pen-based operations
- Design the graphical user interface that is required to support the pen-based operations
- Design the various programs that are required to manipulate the pen-based interface, including:
  - The capturing of data elements
  - The capturing of graphical elements such as signatures and diagrams
- Ensure that all the data elements involved in the pen-based operations are existing in the physical databases that were created to support the application; ensure that the application database or other software filing facilities can also store the graphical data elements that are created with the pen-based interface
- Create the pen-based interface
- Walk through the application pen-based interface deliverables

DESIGN PEN-BASED INTERFACES

This section discusses the detailed steps involved in creating the pen-based interface design. It also presents some tips and guidelines on how to perform this process.

Overview

Several client-server RAD tools, such as PowerBuilder and Visual Basic to name a couple, provide special software libraries that contain several functions that support the development of pen-aware client-server applications. With the use of these extended software libraries, the developers construct graphical user interface (GUI) applications that can run unmodified either on a workstation or on a hand-held pen computing device.

In addition to the usual GUI objects (i.e., icons, pull-down menus, dialog boxes, etc.) that can be used to design traditional client-server systems, pen-aware applications can also support specific pen-input objects such as those indicated in Table 4-40.

Typically, a mobile user performs certain data capture tasks by writing on a pen device display screen with a stylus or using intuitive point-and-click GUI controls.

Design Guidelines

Table 4-41 contains a brief list of design guidelines that you should take into consideration while developing a graphical user interface for a pen-aware application.

Table 4–40 Pen-aware GUI Objects

- Signatures
- Sketches that are hand-drawn by the operator of the hand-held pen device
- Handwritings
- A virtual keyboard (i.e., software generated) that allows a pen device operator to enter characters one at a time on the computer screen with a stylus, as a method of inputting data. Usually, the keyboard can be either a numeric keypad or a full alphanumeric keyboard.
- Boxed edit (i.e., comb edit) controls that are used to enter textual data. Boxed edit controls are composed of regularly spaced vertical lines that allow character separation, which in turn allows the pen software to recognize easily the characters that are entered one-by-one by the operator.

Table 4–41 Pen-aware Basic GUI Design Guidelines

- The design of the user interface should remain as simple and intuitive as possible. Avoid adding extra controls that are not absolutely required to support the application.
- Considering the limited size of most pen display screens, the number of windows that can be opened at a single point in time should be minimized as much as possible.
- Since the number of colors supported is often limited to 16 levels of gray scale, carefully assess where the gray scale colors will be used to differentiate the important items that are shown on the graphical user interface limited display area.
- The mobile users that are utilizing pen devices must be able to quickly capture data with a minimum effort. Hence, try to reduce as much as possible the entry of textual data by providing GUI objects such as toolbars, control buttons, checkboxes, list boxes, radio buttons, and scroll bars.
- Icons and buttons should be instantly recognizable and big enough to be viewed clearly by the pen-device operator. This guideline is important, since the screen resolution of most pen-devices is lower than the usual desktop screen resolutions. Icons should also be big enough to be clearly identifiable with underwritten identifiers that are meaningful and easy to read.
- In applications in which handwriting must be supported as a method of data entry, leave enough room on the display screen for users to write data in delimited writing areas such as comb edit controls. This design approach will help the pen-based computer hardware and software equipment more easily recognize handwritten characters.
- In applications in which hand-drawn sketches must be supported, leave enough room on the display screen for users to draw the sketches.
- In situations in which a numeric field must be entered, provide editing and validation facilities that allow only numeric data.

Pen-aware Applications
Portable pen computers can be used in several types of applications in which mobile users must collect and communicate information anywhere in the field.

Table 4-42 enumerates a brief list of different types of business applications in which pen-aware technology can be used advantageously.

Table 4–42 Examples Of Pen-based Applications

- Utilities, including natural gas and electricity companies, that might use pen computers to collect information in the field such as metering data
- Transportation companies that, among other things, use portable pen computers to track shipments and capture client signatures when delivering the goods
- Warehouse and distribution facilities who receive, track, store, and retrieve diversified goods and materials
- Police forces that use pen computers to perform routine tasks such as roadside vehicle inspections, violation codes, or sketching a picture at the scene of an accident or at a crime scene investigation
- Retail companies that use pen-based applications for inventory control and stock management purposes

Activity number:	DE-7
Activity name:	Design system interfaces
Purpose:	To design the interfaces that are required to provide a bridge between the new system and existing applications
Inputs:	AN-T3 System transactions AN-T7 System interface requirements DE-T3 Physical database design
Outputs:	DE-T7 System interfaces design

Activity description:	• For each required system interface, perform the following tasks:
	  – Review the detailed interface requirements
	  – Determine whether special hardware, software, or networking facilities will be required on either the client or server side to support the required automated interface
	  – Design the program that will support the system interface
	    – Identify the input files/databases/data elements and also the output files/databases/data elements
	    – If required, derive from the business procedural logic that was created for that specific interface, the detailed program specifications, covering:
	      – the logic required to edit and validate the input data streams

— the processing logic required to transform the input
data streams into output data streams or to update
existing files/databases
— the logic required to handle errors or exception cases
— the requirements to sort the input data into a specific
sequence
- If the interface program is exceptionally large and highly
complex, consider developing a structure chart that
breaks the program into a set of highly functional
modules that are used to:
— read or write data
— validate or edit data
— transform data
— compute data
— format the output data
— handle errors or exception cases
— handle program initialization or termination
routines
— handle the security requirements
— handle the control logic
— handle the database access logic
- Verify whether existing program templates or reusable
software modules can be utilized for this purpose
• Walk through the system interface design deliverables

4.8   DESIGN SYSTEM INTERFACES

This section discusses the detailed steps involved in creating the system interfaces. It
also presents some tips and guidelines on how to perform this process.

4.8.1   INTRODUCTION

In large and complex environments, you frequently encounter client-server or Web
database applications that must interface with different types of systems which reside
either on the mainframe or on different client-server computing platforms.

Depending on the technology architecture that is currently in place in the enterprise, the client-server system might have to create some files that, at a certain point
in time during the day, will be uploaded to the mainframe for further processing. The
reverse might also be true. Files might be downloaded from the mainframe system for
further processing by the client-server system. Performance issues might constrain the
designers to resorting to some form of batch processing or database replication, using
a gateway middleware.

4.8.2   INTERFACE DESIGN SPECIFICATIONS

If interfaces must be constructed between the client-server application software and other systems, then be sure to review the initial interface strategy that was developed during the analysis phase. Can new information cause a change of strategy?

Table 4-43 enumerates a list of simple questions that should help to validate the interface design strategy.

Table 4–43 Application Interface Design Strategy Checklist

- Does a need exist for database middleware software that allows the client-server or Web system to access files and databases that reside on a mainframe platform? On a different client-server platform such as from a UNIX to an Intel-based computer platform?
- Did the estimated volume of data for the interface change since the last development phase? Was the potentially large volume of data peak and low variations accounted for, based on daily, weekly, monthly, or yearly processing cycles? What about the estimated volume of data growth figures per unit of time?
- Did the frequency (i.e., hourly, daily, weekly, monthly, yearly, or on-demand) at which the interface must be processed changed?
- Will some form of file reconciliation mechanism exist between the system donor and the system receiver?
- Does a need exist for some recovery/restart mechanism if the batch interface program "abends" right in the middle of the job? What about checkpoints or rerun procedures?
- Must security measures be enforced to prevent unauthorized access to or submissions of the batch interface files/programs?

Activity number:	DE-8
Activity name:	Design data conversion programs
Purpose:	To design the data conversion programs
Inputs:	AN-T3 System transactions AN-T11 Initial data conversion strategy DE-T3 Physical database design
Outputs:	DE-T8 Data conversion programs design
Activity description:	• Review the initial data conversion strategy and requirements that were outlined during the analysis phase; if required, refine the preliminary data conversion requirements in light of any additional information that might have been derived since then • Determine whether special hardware, software, or networking facilities will be required to support the activities that are outlined in the application data conversion strategy

- For each manual or automated file/database that needs to be converted, perform the following tasks:
  - Determine the most appropriate method to convert the data, based on the type of medium that is currently used to manage the legacy data
  - Identify the legacy data elements that will need to be converted into the new system and map them to the data elements of the new system
  - Derive the detailed data conversion specifications
  - Define, if required, the techniques that will be used to reconcile the converted data with the data that is contained in the old systems
  - Define the data conversion acceptance criteria that will be used to confirm that the data conversion process has been successfully completed
  - Design the data conversion program(s)
  - Refine the estimated volume of data that must be processed during the conversion effort
  - Assess the level of "readiness" of the legacy data; if necessary, define a strategy to improve the integrity of the legacy data or purge any invalid data, prior to the actual conversion process
- For the brand-new data elements that will be used in the client-server system, perform the following tasks:
  - Identify the specific data elements that are required to populate the new client-server files/database structures
  - Determine the most appropriate method to populate the new client-server files and databases with the new data
- Design and code the custom program(s) that are required to populate the client-server files/databases with the new data elements.
- Design the security and control mechanisms that might need to be enforced during the overall data conversion process
- Design the various types of reports that might be required to support and manage the overall data conversion efforts
- Define a fallback scenario in case the data conversion process fails
- Walk through the data conversion program deliverables

4.9   DESIGN DATA CONVERSION PROGRAMS

This section discusses the detailed steps involved in the design of the data conversion programs. It also presents some tips and guidelines on how to perform this process.

4.9.1 DATA CONVERSION METHODS

Several data conversion techniques can be used to capture and convert data from the old systems to the new client-server system. Depending on the type of media that is currently used to manage the legacy data, some of the data conversion options that might be available to capture and convert information appear in Table 4-44.

Table 4–44 Manual And Automated Data Conversion Processes

Manual data conversion processes	Automated data conversion processes
• Manual data entry (in-house)	• Custom data conversion programs, batch, and/or online
• Manual data entry (service bureau)	• Existing client-server file/database utilities
• Scanners to capture existing paper documents and transform them into data or images that can be manipulated with a computer	• Magnetic tape/cartridge to disk file conversion
• Bar code reading	

Quite often, a combination of many of the different data conversion techniques that are indicated in Table 4-44 are used to convert the large volumes of data that exist in huge application systems.

In certain instances, the data that needs to be loaded in the new system can be acquired from third-party vendors, such as various customer/supplier lists or competitive information addressing specific types of vertical market segments.

4.9.2 CONVERSION DATA SOURCES

Table 4-45 enumerates the various categories of manual/automated data sources that are candidates to be converted and migrated into the new client-server or Web database system.

4.9.3 MAPPING THE CONVERSION DATA ELEMENTS

Once all the data conversion source files have been identified, the old data elements for each of these files are mapped against the data elements of the target client-server system. The most common types data conversion events appear in Table 4-46.

The data selection criteria that will be used to transfer a data element, drop a data element, create a new data element, or transform the source data elements should be clearly spelled out at this stage. They will serve as a foundation for developing the automated data conversion algorithms. Of course, the conversion of manual data will re-

Table 4–45 Manual And Automated Sources Of Data

Manual Sources of Data	Automated Sources of Data
• Printed reports	• Sequential files (tapes or disks)
• Manuals	• Random files (disks)
• Filled-in business forms	• Databases
• Catalogs (i.e., price list, etc.)	• Video segments
• Printed pictures, images, and graphics	• Audio segments
• Microfiche (historical data)	• Computer graphics and images

Table 4–46 Various Types Of Data Conversion Events

- Transfer the data element as is, with no modification
- Transfer the data element, applying some additional translation/conversion procedures
- Do not transfer the data element to the new system
- Create the new target data element from scratch
- Create the new target data element by manipulating some legacy data elements

quire some human intervention. This manual conversion activity should be supported by a well documented decision-making process.

4.9.4 DESIGNING THE ONLINE CONVERSION GUI PROGRAMS

Quite often, the new data elements that need to be created for the target client-server system can be entered directly by using the new GUI windows that are developed for that application, applying the same set of data validation and editing rules that are currently associated with these fields.

4.9.5 DESIGNING THE BATCH DATA CONVERSION PROGRAMS

At this point in the project, the physical data structures of the new client-server system can be accurately compared with those of the old files and databases systems. This comparison can be performed by viewing any file/database that must be converted as being the major component of the input leg of a conversion program, while the output leg represents the data structures that are required by the new system. In the middle is the main transform process that will read the data elements that are stored in the old data structures, convert them according to predetermined transformation algorithms, and then store the results in the physical data structures of the new system. Figure 4-25 illustrates this concept with two relatively simple data structures.

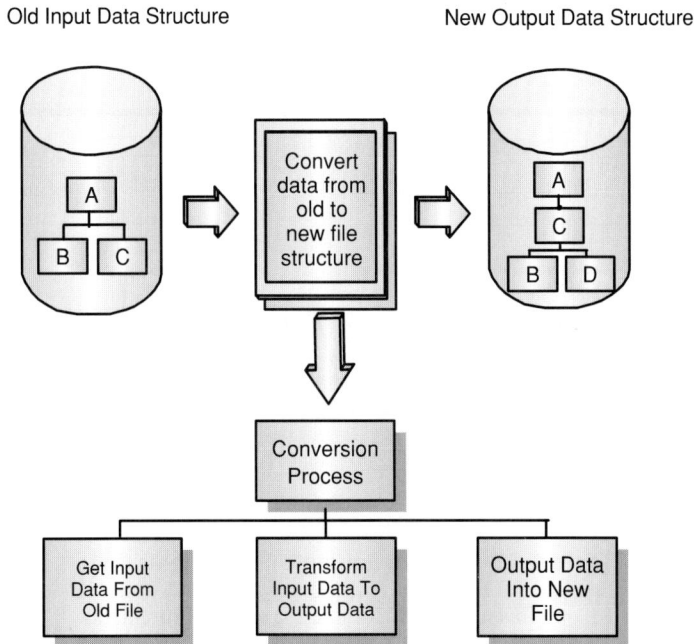

Figure 4–25 Data conversion process.

For each identified transform process, the detailed algorithmic operations that must be performed to convert the input data into the desired output data formats can be described with action diagram constructs, when complex data conversion procedures need to be developed for the new application.

Although relatively simple conversion programs such as the one shown in Figure 4-25 might not warrant the use of a structure chart, you might want to design the complex data conversion programs with the use of pre-defined structure charts and reusable batch program templates, as indicated in Figure 4-26.

The structure chart template shown in Figure 4-26 should be augmented with the set of generic modules that are required to handle the most common set of conversion tasks indicated in Table 4-47.

Depending on the level of complexity that characterizes the overall file/database conversion process, the data conversion algorithms might indeed include several of the operations that are enumerated in Table 4-48.

4.9.6 DATA CONVERSION SYSTEM DIAGRAM

In large data conversion applications, you might want to draw simple data conversion system diagrams. Such diagrams show the major components and tasks that are required to execute the conversion process, along with a visualization of the interde-

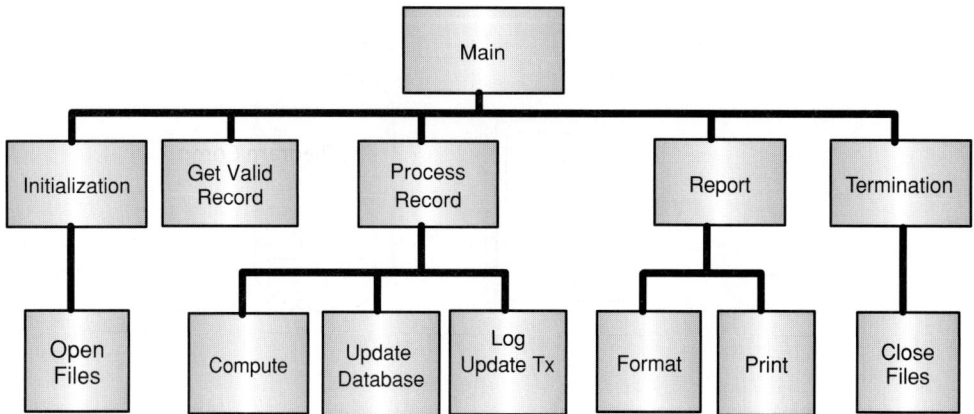

Figure 4–26 Generic structured chart.

Table 4–47 Program Reusable Components

• Error handling logic (i.e., invalid data, incomplete data, duplicate data)
• File/database error recovery logic
• Security or control logic
• File/database reconciliation or balancing logic
• Validation and editing logic
• Data formatting logic

Table 4–48 Data Conversion Operations

• Convert data from one internal computer representation format to another (i.e., from mainframe EBCDIC to non-packed, ASCII format)
• Validate the content of data elements
• Compare/manipulate various data elements that originate from different legacy files and databases sources and that are stored in multiple forms and formats
• Establish relationships or dependencies among different data elements that are currently stored in different files/databases located on different platforms
• Synchronize several files/databases at the same time
• Expand or shorten the size of legacy data elements
• Sort data elements in different sequences
• Modify the contents of data elements
• Select criteria to extract data from legacy systems

pendencies that exist between them. The various types of components that can be depicted in a data conversion system diagram appear in Table 4-49. Figure 4-27 shows an example of a generic data conversion diagram.

Table 4–49 Data Conversion System Diagram Components

- Source and target data files/databases
- Sequence and inter-relationships between the intermediate and major conversion steps
- Batch conversion programs
- Data entry GUI windows that are used to load new data in the new databases

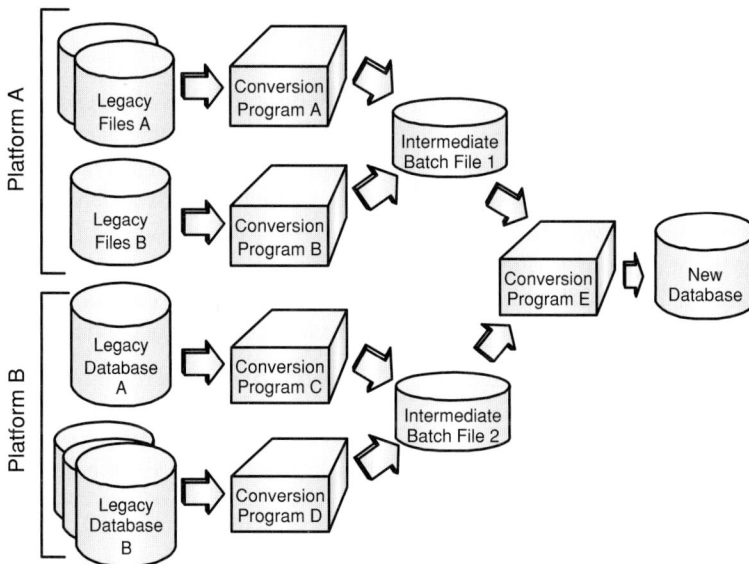

Figure 4–27 Data conversion system diagram.

In the heterogeneous world of client-server databases, the various data types that exist from one database environment to another have, for the most part, very similar internal configurations.

In a few instances, though, some subtle variations can exist in the way each distinct RDBMS internally stores certain data types. These minor discrepancies may occasionally cause some tough bugs that are hard to catch when the data is converted from one database format to another, since sometimes they are simply not reported by the DBMS software during the conversion process. These potentially dangerous conversion conditions should be taken into consideration before the execution of the actual conversion effort itself.

4.9.7   ASSESS THE CURRENT LEVEL OF READINESS OF THE LEGACY DATA

Before starting the conversion effort itself, I strongly recommend verifying the level of data integrity of the current files and databases, whether these are manual or automated, if this has not yet been done. If the existing files/databases contain too many errors, invalid values, or data inconsistencies, some extra efforts will be required to correct these errors. Ignoring these issues can only compound the problem during the implementation phase.

Many people would readily assume that, by default, the data currently stored in the manual files of the legacy systems are probably more error-prone than those in the automated files and databases of the current systems. Unfortunately, this assumption is not always the case, especially for the old automated files/databases that were created many years ago. Furthermore, this situation might even prevail in some relatively new client-server systems!

A low level of integration and poor data validation practices often characterize these old files/databases. For example, in these environments, the same data element can be duplicated in several different files. They can also be used in a slightly different manner by different legacy applications. Sometimes the same logical data element will carry a different field length from one file to another. For instance, in one file, the data field might have four characters, and in another file, the same data element might have three characters. In situations like these, the users should vigorously intervene and decide which data element in which application file is the most accurate.

Some of the strategies that might be put forward to improve the integrity of the legacy data are indicated in Table 4-50.

Table 4–50 Legacy Files/Databases Data Clean-up Strategies

• Use the existing system batch and online transactions to correct invalid data
• Develop special programs to identify anomalies with current data and subsequently correct them prior to the conversion process
• Develop a mechanism to reject any invalid data that are caught during the actual conversion process and store them in a suspense file. The data in the suspense file are corrected once the major conversion process is completed and re-submitted later on as a new input file to the application conversion subsystem.

4.9.8   DESIGNING THE DATA CONVERSION REPORTS

The layout and data content of the different types of reports that might be required to verify that the conversion programs have been executed successfully should be designed with the active participation of the users. Use existing standard report templates for this purpose.

Activity number:	DE-9
Activity name:	Design ad hoc report and query environment
Purpose:	To design and construct the interfaces between the application operational databases and the enterprise ad hoc report and query environment
Inputs:	AN-T3 System transactions AN-T9 System operational requirements AN-T10 Initial capacity plan DE-T3 Physical database design
Outputs:	DE-T9 Ad hoc report and query environment
Activity description:	• Review the end-user ad hoc reporting and querying application requirements • Verify whether the structure of the operational databases can support the ad hoc reporting and querying information needs, without affecting adversely the performance of the online transaction processing system • Determine whether separate databases should be set up to satisfy the users' needs for ad hoc information via the use of a distinct reporting and querying database environment • If required, design and create the automated interfaces between the application operational databases and the separate ad hoc reporting and querying database environment • Walk through the database operational/ad hoc data interface design deliverables

4.10 DESIGN THE AD HOC REPORT AND QUERY ENVIRONMENT

This section discusses the detailed steps that are involved in the design of the ad hoc report and query environment.

4.10.1 OVERVIEW

The developers might need to address two broad categories of reports and queries during the system development cycle, to satisfy the user needs for turning data into useful information.

The first category consists of reports and queries that are fairly static and well structured. These reports are the regular, pre-formatted type of reports for which the detailed information requirements are well defined and complete. These reports are usually created by the developers and exhibit some, if not most, of the characteristics that you see in Table 4-51.

Table 4–51 Pre-defined Reports Characteristics

- The types of data that go in the reports are well known by the users
- The reporting data requirements are fairly static as opposed to volatile
- The production of the reports is scheduled on a regular basis or on demand
- Some of the reports can be high-volume reports
- The integrity of the data shown on the reports must be very high
- The report presentation layout may range from very simple to very complex
- The report data can be extracted directly from the operational production database
- The reports are managed with an emphasis on efficient report distribution and control
- The application programs that produce the reports are fine-tuned to optimize the database accesses and not adversely affect the overall performance of the online transactions

The second category of reports and queries are those for which the users never know exactly what type of information will be required from one day to another. Very often, a sophisticated data reporting and querying environment must be set up beside the operational database environment to satisfy the user needs for ad hoc information. This special reporting and querying environment contains mostly static, historical data that is refreshed on a regular basis, such as daily, weekly, quarterly and annually.

Figure 4-28 shows an example of the type of enterprise information technology architecture that could be set up to support all types of user ad hoc reporting and unstructured query demands.

In such an environment, different types of raw data are retrieved from the back-end operational databases periodically. The extracted data is then staged in special databases such as data warehouse, data mart or online analytical processing (OLAP) servers.

Inside the data warehouse or OLAP servers, the extracted data is logically structured in a manner that addresses the shortcomings of the traditional online transaction processing (OLTP) environments, such as their inability or inefficiency to support various multidimensional views of the data or complex ad hoc queries.

At the front end of the spectrum, the users are utilizing sophisticated online analytical tools that allow them to perform complex multidimensional and time-series analysis studies. They can combine or aggregate data in various forms and shapes to address a specific business need. More specifically, the users can consolidate data into different levels of aggregation, drill down into the data warehouse database to increasingly dig up more detailed information on a particular subject, or slice and dice the information that is contained in the OLAP database from multiple viewpoints.

The design and construction of data warehouses and OLAP systems are well beyond the scope of this book. Thus, I assume here that the enterprise already has im-

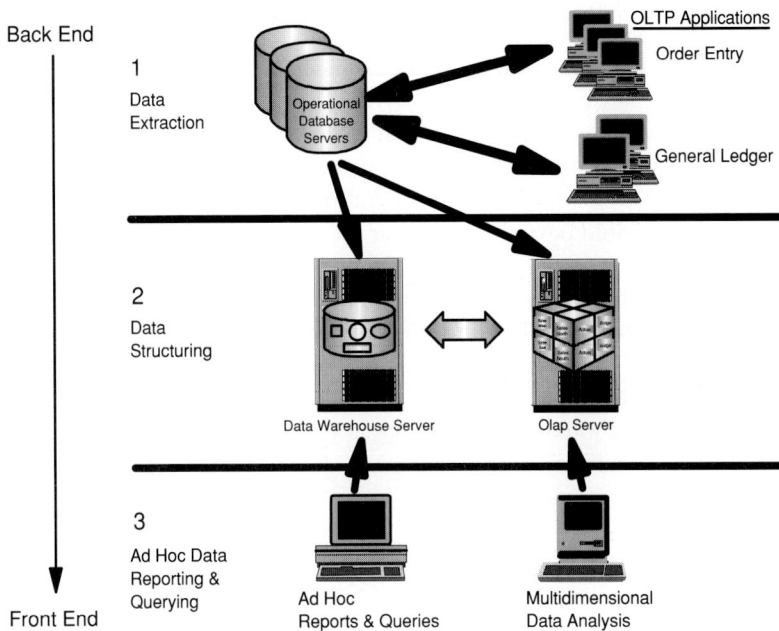

Figure 4–28 Data warehouse/OLAP environment.

plemented a specialized data warehouse, data mart or OLAP environment to satisfy the user needs that relate to ad hoc reports and queries.[3]

Chapter 9 also discusses in more detail, Web-based data warehouse and OLAP solutions.

4.10.2 INTERFACE DESIGN

As described in the activity interface design shown above, the prime objective of the current activity is to design and construct the interface that bridges the application operational databases to the enterprise ad hoc database report and query environment.

---

3. Data warehouses and data marts are designed using a special data modeling technique called dimensional modeling. Whereas entity-relationship modeling and normalization center on data performance and integrity, dimensional modeling centers primarily on business processes and the formulation of business questions. In dimensional modeling, the data is designed around a star schema, which usually contains a very large table called the fact table. The fact table is centered around smaller satellite tables, called dimension tables. The dimension tables are joined to the fact table in a star-shape pattern. Some of the logical and physical data modeling tools listed in Section 4.4.10 support dimensional modeling.

The frequency at which data will be transferred from the operational application databases to the separate ad hoc report and query environment is determined by the users, along with the identification of the specific data fields that must be migrated for this purpose.

The developers should also ensure that the users can live with the fact that the ad hoc report and query environment might contain data that are not necessarily as current as the data that are housed in the operational databases.

The interface should be designed so that the required data gets transferred automatically at periodical intervals, preferably without any human intervention. If necessary, brand-new programs can be created to migrate the data between the two environments, or you can refine and extend existing business transactions specifically for this purpose.

Database replication facilities can also be used to copy the data from the operational databases to the data warehouse databases, at predetermined time intervals.

Activity number:	DE-10
Activity name:	Create preliminary system documentation
Purpose:	To develop initial prototypes and/or templates of the required system documentation guide(s)
Inputs:	AN-T3 System transactions DE-T3 Physical database design DE-T7 System interfaces design DE-T9 Ad hoc reports and query environment design Shared software components design Application software components design
Outputs:	DE-T10 Preliminary system documentation

Activity description:	• Determine the system documentation requirements with the users and the data center personnel
	• Review existing enterprise standards and guidelines for producing system documentation
	• Determine the special hardware and software tools and facilities that might be necessary to support the process of developing all required system documentation components
	• Create initial prototypes and/or templates of the following documentation guides:
	  − User Guide
	  − Online Help Guide
	  − System Operations Guide
	  − Technical Reference Guide
	• Walk through the initial system documentation deliverables

4.11 CREATE PRELIMINARY SYSTEM DOCUMENTATION

Table 4-52 provides a list and brief description of the most common types of guides that can be produced for the new system.

Table 4–52 Brief Description Of Different Types Of System Guides

User Guide	Documents the set of procedures that the users can use to interact with the system
Online Help Guide	Provides the users with an online description of the system functions and facilities, including suggestions on how to best use the graphical user interface, description of the fields contained on each specific screen or form, how to deal with errors, generic search facilities, and so forth
System Operations Guide	Documents the set of technical procedures that are required to operate the system in the production environment, such as the backup and recovery procedures, the performance monitoring procedures, and the security procedures
Technical Reference Guide	Documents the technical components of the system for those individuals who will maintain and evolve the system, once it is transferred into its final production environment

As shown in Table 4-52, the User and Online Help Guides target the user community as their prime audience. At the opposite end, the System Operations and Technical Reference Guides primarily target the Data Center and Systems Maintenance groups as their main customers. The User and Online Help Guides are business-oriented, whereas the System Operations and Technical Reference Guides are technical.

The User Guide describes, in non-technical language, the various tasks that the users must follow to interface with the new software system while doing their regular jobs. It contains a set of operational instructions on how to best use the new system, from an end-user perspective. The User Guide can also be used to train new users long after the system has been transferred into its production environment, if it is kept up-to-date.

The Online Help Guide contains system-related documentation that the users can interactively reference while using the actual system. Some organizations might decide to create an Online Help Guide and then print it so it can also be used as a User Guide in a paper format.

The System Operations Guide describes the tasks that are required to operate the system in its production environment. Typically, the intended audience for this guide is the Operations Systems personnel who will run and support the system in the production environment.

The Technical Reference Guide describes the internal architecture of the system. It is primarily targeted at the systems professionals who will maintain the production system.

At this stage, the developers should discuss with the different user groups who will eventually utilize the system or those technical groups who will operate or support it, what their essential requirements for system documentation are.

The need or extent to which all these application documentation guides should be (or should not be) produced might vary from one project to another and even from one organization to another.

For instance, if the same people who are developing the new system will also be called upon to maintain it, then the technical reference guide might not be necessary at all. Or if it is still required, then it might contain high-level technical information instead of containing information at a very detailed level. On the other end, if the people who will support the system will not be those who developed it, then the technical reference guide will likely require a more detailed description of the most critical technical aspects of the new system and its maintenance environment.

Once the basic requirements for the system documentation have been determined, along with a brief explanation of how they will be used, the proposed format and overall content of each guide should be discussed with each involved party. Also, the type of medium that will be used to deliver the system guides should be decided at this stage. For example, will the guides be provided in soft or hard copy, or both? Will they be available in an intranet environment?

As much as possible, the format and content of the various system documentation guides should not be re-created from scratch. If enterprise documentation standards exist, the development team should use them or even recycle existing documents that were produced from previous projects as much as possible.

Quickly developing an initial prototype of the Online Help Guide is probably one of the most effective ways of demonstrating to the users the "look and feel" of this particular system documentation component. Similarly, show some representative samples of the other guides to the users or data center personnel to firm up the system documentation requirements and manage expectations.

At the bare minimum, produce a draft table of content for each type of documentation guide and review it with some representatives of the targeted audience. The table of contents should provide a list of the major chapters that will be included in the guide and the general organization of the guide.

The detailed sections and content of each guide can be developed later during the next system development phase. For very large projects, a slight variation to this approach might consist of developing a complete sample of a representative chapter for each guide and then reviewing these samples with the users or operations systems staff.

Tables 4-53 and 4-54 show an example of a table of contents for a User Guide and a System Operations Guide. These 'table of contents' may be adapted and tailored to satisfy the specific needs of any particular project.

Table 4–53 Table Of Contents For The User Guide

INTRODUCTION
- Purpose of this guide
- Intended audience
- Assumptions
- How to use this guide
- General conventions

SYSTEM OVERVIEW
- System mission
- Situation of the system within the organization
- System context diagram
- Summary description of major system functional components
  - Online transactions
  - Online reports
  - Batch reports
  - Ad hoc reports
  - Batch job descriptions

GRAPHICAL USER INTERFACE
- Introduction
- General menu/toolbar options
- Online help facility
- Detailed screen(s) or report layout(s) description
- Data fields and control descriptions
- General task flow diagram
- Detailed task(s) description
  - Why?
  - When?
  - Pre-requisites
  - How?
  - Error handling

MISCELLANEOUS
- Appendix
- Glossary of terms
- Index
- Reader's comment form

Table 4–54 Table Of Contents For The System Operations Guide

INTRODUCTION
- Purpose of this guide
- Intended audience
- Assumptions
- How to use this guide
- General conventions

SYSTEM OVERVIEW
- System technology architecture
- General description of the major system technical components
- General description of the system operating procedures
  - Hardware maintenance procedures
  - Software maintenance procedures
  - Networking maintenance procedures
- Detailed system operations procedures
- Detailed task(s) description
  - Why?
  - When?
  - Prerequisites
  - How?
  - Error handling

MISCELLANEOUS
- Appendix
- Glossary of terms
- Index
- Reader's comment form

Activity number:	DE-11
Activity name:	Finalize detailed training strategy
Purpose:	To finalize the detailed strategy required for satisfying the user/ data center staff training requirements
Inputs:	AN-T14 Initial training strategy
Outputs:	DE-T11 Detailed system training strategy

Activity description:
- Review the initial training strategy that was developed during the analysis phase
- Produce the detailed training strategy covering, for each specific targeted audience, the following items:
  - Scope and objectives of the training program
  - Training methods recommended
  - Determination of who will provide the training
  - Description of the physical facilities that are needed to deliver the training effort
  - Description of any special office equipment required to support the training effort
  - Detailed description of any special hardware/software/networking equipment that might be required to support the training effort
  - Detailed description of specific training material that needs to be developed
  - Identification of the different locations where the personnel will be trained
  - General timing, duration, sequencing, and dependencies among the major training events
- If necessary, design the specific test cases that will be used to verify the system training environment and facilities
- Walk through the detailed training strategy deliverable

4.12 FINALIZE THE DETAILED TRAINING STRATEGY

The first step in this activity involves reviewing the detailed changes that the new system will introduce into the work environment, refining the list of different categories of personnel who will be affected by these changes, and completing the description of the most essential training requirements in detail.

In addition, the detailed estimates of the total number of people who will need to be trained per major category of users should be carefully revisited with each affected business area's user representative.

Once the above-mentioned prerequisite tasks have been completed, the detailed training strategy can be finalized with the active participation of the users.

Table 4-55 summarizes some of the most essential elements that should be covered in the detailed training strategy.

Quality training is worth the expense if the enterprise wants to achieve higher productivity levels in the workplace. However, you still need to clearly highlight to management the benefits that will result by setting up an effective training program. Presenting the training costs to management is relatively easy. Presenting the training benefits in quantifiable terms is much more difficult.

Table 4–55 Detailed Training Strategy

Target audience	Who will be trained? Every user in all areas, or some selected users who in turn will train other users? How many individuals per major user category must be trained? Should the courses be tailored to suit the specific needs of each category of users (i.e., people on shop floor, clerical staff, office workers, managers, executives)? What should be the level of training: Basic? Intermediate? Advanced? Will the data center staff be trained too? What are the current skills of the different groups of users who need training?
Training methods	Which type of training method is recommended? The instructor-led approach with hands-on exercises? The self-study approach? On-the-job coaching? Audiovisuals? Formal presentations? Tutorials? Seminars? Interactive computer-based training? Pilot project? Will some mechanisms be required to evaluate the effectiveness of the training materials?
Physical facilities/ office equipment	What type of facilities is required to train the staff? Where will they be trained, in-house or at external locations? In a general-purpose classroom or in a dedicated training center? On site, in their own particular working environment? How many people can attend a single training session? What type of office equipment is required (overhead projector, 35 mm slide projector, televisions, video machines, whiteboards, flip charts)?
Training material	What type of material is required to train the staff? Are special forms needed? Will pre-assignment booklets used? What type of documents will be provided to the trainee during and/or after the course: a copy of the presentation overheads, classroom notes? Will the new User Guide and System Operations Guide documents be used during the training sessions?
Timing, duration, sequencing, and dependencies	When will the training sessions be scheduled? What will be the duration of the training sessions? What will be the sequence? Will the staff be trained at one physical location at a time? One regional site at a time? All at once? Do any training dependencies exist among the various releases of the system?
People and resources	How many trainers will be required? Will a "train-the-trainer" strategy be used?
Hardware/software/ networking equipment	Will some special hardware equipment be required to train the staff? Dedicated workstations and printers? What about the software facilities? Will the new system itself be used to train the staff?

Typically, as the project progresses through the various software development stages, the pressure to deliver the system on time and within budget often increases significantly. Consequently, downgrading the training effort might be tempting, especially if management is not convinced of the payoffs and if the initial project delivery date has already been delayed.

In an attempt to overcome these potential shortcomings, the detailed training strategy and the resulting educational cost-benefit figures should be carefully examined at this stage of the project and included in the project plans covering the subsequent development stages.

Furthermore, if the training plan is presented as a one-time effort, then the investment spent in developing a sophisticated user training environment might be hard to sell to management. On the other end, if the training program is designed to evolve with the system, then its usefulness will be greatly enhanced.

Activity number:	DE-12
Activity name:	Finalize detailed testing strategy
Purpose:	To finalize the detailed strategy required to test the new system
Inputs:	AN-T13 Initial testing strategy
Outputs:	DE-T12 Detailed testing strategy
Activity description:	• Review the initial testing requirements and strategy that were developed earlier during the analysis phase • Based on the detailed functional and technical solutions that will be used to construct the new system, complete the detailed software testing strategy and plan • Describe the detailed hardware/software/networking tools and facilities that are required during each specific testing phase; ensure that all required testing equipment and facilities can be acquired, installed, and properly configured in time to support the testing effort and its different test environments • Determine the detailed manual and/or automated test library control mechanisms that will be set up to manage the complete test environment • Determine the detailed set of procedures that will be implemented to manage the overall testing process • Determine the detailed test data storage estimates • Confirm, if required, the different sites where the testing process will be performed • Finalize the roles and responsibilities of each major group that will participate in the testing process or support it • Walk through the detailed testing strategy and plan deliverable

4.13 FINALIZE THE DETAILED TESTING STRATEGY

In this activity, the scope of the system testing effort is finalized in its entirety with the user representatives. This step is done based on the detailed information that has been captured so far on the system and its automated components.

The testing scope will likely vary from one system to another, depending on a variety of factors such as the type of system being developed, the selected computer platform(s), the system's size and complexity, and the type of software technology used.

The detailed application testing requirements should be finalized at this stage, along with the broad types of testing scenarios that will be used to verify the system. Similarly, the initial testing strategy document should be refined and augmented with more detailed and complete information.

Besides presenting a broad picture of the game plan for testing the functionality of the new system, the detailed testing strategy should also determine the management process that will be used to track defects and resolve them. If necessary, the setup of a regression test environment might also be required to help verify that unexpected side effects are not inadvertently introduced when corrected programs are re-inserted into a specific test environment. Any potential constraints such as possible system resources limitations or testing duration should be clearly described and documented in the test plan. Specific tools might be required to accurately manage and track different testing events, such as problem reported, problem being fixed, program fix in system test, program fix accepted for release.

If additional software programs must be created to support specific system interface, training, or conversion requirements, then the testing strategy should also cover the approach that will be used to test these components.

Create a table listing all the specific testing tools that will be used to create test data and execute the test cases and compare results.

Finally, the description of the detailed testing strategy leads to the creation of a detailed test plan, which describes the set of major testing activities that need to be performed during the overall testing process. The test plan should also cover the appropriate testing time frames and resources.

The next four technical activities describe the detailed steps that are required to design the various categories of test cases, which will be executed later on during the construction phase, while performing the unit, integration, system, and user acceptance testing stages.

The actual test data that will be used to run the different test cases can be created either during the design phase or during the construction phase.

Lastly, much more additional information on the client-server and Web testing process is provided in Chapter 8.

Activity number:	DE-12A
Activity name:	Design unit test cases
Purpose:	To design the unit test cases that are required to verify thoroughly the application system modules and programs
Inputs:	AN-T13 Initial testing strategy DE-T3 Physical database design DE-T7 System interfaces design DE-T8 Data conversion programs design DE-T9 Ad hoc report and query environment design Shared software components design Application software components design
Outputs:	DE-T12A Unit test cases design

Activity description:	• Review and refine the high-level strategy that was developed during the analysis phase to unit test the system modules and programs
	• For the online programs:
	  − Define the technique(s) that will be used to unit test the graphical user interface of each online program
	  − Define the criteria that will be used to determine the successful completion of the online unit test process
	  − Define the approach that will be used to track the execution of the unit tests for the online programs/modules, including the handling and resolution of uncovered defects
	  − Define the specific categories of unit test cases that will be used to verify:
	    − All the GUI window components
	    − All the functionality provided by each module or program
	    − The adherence to the enterprise-wide GUI and program naming, coding, and documentation standards
	    − The level of utilization of reusable components
	  − Develop the unit test cases that are required to verify the online programs/modules
	  − If appropriate at this stage, create the test data that are required to exercise the online test cases
	• For the batch programs:
	  − Define the technique(s) that will be used to unit test each batch program or module
	  − Define the criteria that will be used to determine the successful completion of the batch unit test process

- Define the approach that will be used to track the execution of the unit tests for the batch programs/modules, including the handling and resolution of uncovered defects
- Define the specific categories of unit test cases that will be used to verify:
  - All the functionality provided by each batch program or module
  - The adherence to the enterprise-wide program naming, coding, and documentation standards
  - The level of utilization of reusable components
- Develop the unit test cases that are required to verify the batch programs/modules
- If appropriate at this stage, create the test data that is required to exercise the batch test cases
- Walk through the unit test case deliverables

4.13.1 DESIGN THE UNIT TEST CASES

This section describes the detailed steps involved in the design of the unit test cases. It also presents some tips and guidelines on how to perform this process.

UNIT TESTING OBJECTIVES

Unit testing is the most elementary level of testing that can be performed while developing a client-server or Web database system.

The unit tests verify that all the individual programs/modules work according to their design specifications, prior to combining them into larger objects and ultimately into a complete client-server or Web database system.

An important objective of unit testing is to uncover and correct as many defects as possible in each individual program prior to integrating them together. The rationale behind unit testing is simple: locating and fixing errors in a single, isolated program is easier than when the program is integrated with the entire application system.

UNIT TESTING AND RAD

Two categories of programs can be unit tested in a client-server environment: the on-line programs, along with their graphical user interfaces, and the batch programs.

The GUI programs can be unit tested more or less independently by the programmers themselves as the required application programs/modules are developed incrementally, preferably with the use of an iterative prototyping approach. They can also be unit tested more formally once they have been expanded with their complete functionality.

The batch programs can be unit tested with a more traditional approach. They can be verified thoroughly once they have been entirely coded as a whole unit or module-by-module, in the case of large and complex batch programs.

DECIDING WHO CONDUCTS THE UNIT TESTS

Basically, unit testing can be conducted by the developers themselves or by independent testing groups specializing in client-server or Web database testing. A variant approach would be to have the unit tests performed by programmers other than those who originally developed the programs. Figure 4-29 illustrates the concept of independent testing.

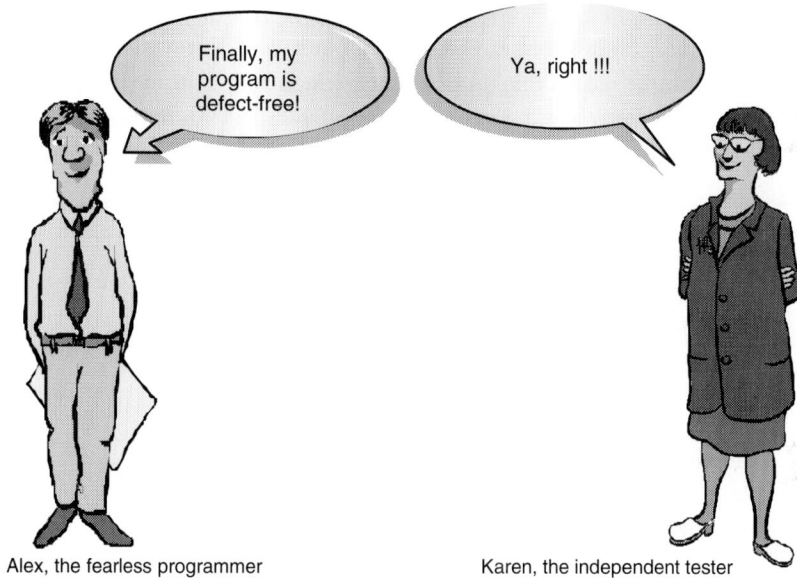

Figure 4–29 Independent testing team.

Several studies have demonstrated that the number of defects that are normally uncovered by an independent testing team is significantly greater than the number of defects that are uncovered by the authors of the programs themselves. Table 4-56 indicates some of the reasons that could explain why software testing performed by independent testing teams is usually more effective than when the developers do the testing themselves.

The level of formality that should be applied to the unit testing process, including the decision to enforce or not a rigorous tracking of the total unit testing effort, will vary from one project to another. Several factors will likely influence this important decision, such as the total number of programs that must be tested, for that application, along with an appreciation of their size and complexity. Table 4-57 provides a list of simple metrics that can be used to gauge the size and complexity of a program.

Some organizations let the developers do their own unit testing but provide them with sound unit testing standards and guidelines. Other organizations will assign to a programmer's peer the responsibility of conducting the unit tests. At the end of the

Table 4–56 Reasons Why Developers Perform Less Effective Testing Than Independent Testers

- The increasing pressure the developers might have to produce their programs as soon as possible, especially when the project is late
- The very limited amount of time allowed to the programmers for testing their programs, due to the lack of an effective testing strategy and test plan
- The lack of developers' training and experience in creating effective test cases
- The subconscious desire of the developers to prove that their programs work instead of systematically creating test cases that could potentially destroy their programs
- A poor attitude such as thinking that uncovering errors is the job of the users
- The lack of effective testing tools, techniques, and standards in the enterprise

Table 4–57 Program Size And Complexity Metrics

- Complexity of the program procedural logic
  - number of conditional statements
  - number of iterative loops
  - number of branching statements
  - number of database calls
- Complexity of the graphical user interface (GUI) window
  - number of GUI controls
  - level of interdependency among the GUI controls
  - number of data elements
- Size of the program
  - number of lines of code

spectrum, some organizations will have even the unit tests performed by completely independent testers.

GUI TEST CASES

Various test cases can be constructed to fully exercise the windows interface. The different user scenarios that were developed during the analysis phase should provide the developers with an important source of information to help them create test cases that are representative of the types of business operations that the users will likely perform while accomplishing their day-to-day tasks. Another important source of information is the set of business rules that were documented during the construction of the data model and the set of permissible values that the system data elements could take.

Additional test cases should also be engineered to ensure proper coverage of various situations in which invalid or unexpected data would be submitted inadvertently by the users.

Since unit testing is a white-box testing process, artificial test data can be used for unit testing, to ensure more complete coverage of the most common testing situations.

The unit test cases should exercise all the specific events that can be triggered while selecting the GUI objects that are shown on the windows, such as those that are enumerated in Table 4-58.

Table 4–58 GUI Test Cases

- Menu bar actions
- Toolbar actions
- Control button actions
- Field level testing (validation, formatting, masking, and editing of data entry fields)
- Field length
- Permissible values, default values, numeric ranges
- Upper and lower case
- Cross-field dependencies in a single window or across different windows
- Change of field visibility depending on the context
- Display of error messages
- Interfaces to various software facilities such as word processors, spreadsheets, e-mail, optical character readers, bar code readers
- Database accesses
- Special window navigational controls such as tab folders

First, specific test cases should be constructed to exercise the windows control buttons as independent entities within the window. Second, another series of test cases should be created to verify the interactions between the various command buttons, based on their interdependent relationships, but still within the boundary limits of a single window.

Test cases should then be developed to verify the operations and levels of navigability between different windows such as:

- How does the user navigate through the client-server system, from one major window to its subordinate windows?

- Should specific windows be easily accessible to the user at a given point in time?

- Are some windows fully dependent on other windows?

Besides the usual test cases that are triggered by various sequences of mouse clicks, additional test cases should be developed specifically to verify that all keyboard shortcuts and accelerator keys are working correctly, in each individual application window. The testers should also verify that users can tab through the GUI controls in the correct sequence. This test case is critical for keystroke-optimized data entry applications.

CONTROL-ACTION-RESPONSE (CAR) DIAGRAM

For complex windows, a Control-Action-Response (CAR) diagram can be used to depict, at a high level, how a window should respond to certain user actions. Based on the particular sequence of actions that is shown in the CAR diagram, test cases can be developed to exercise specific test conditions and verify the expected results. CAR diagrams can also be used for documentation purposes or to develop high-level program specifications. Figure 4-30 shows a CAR diagram.

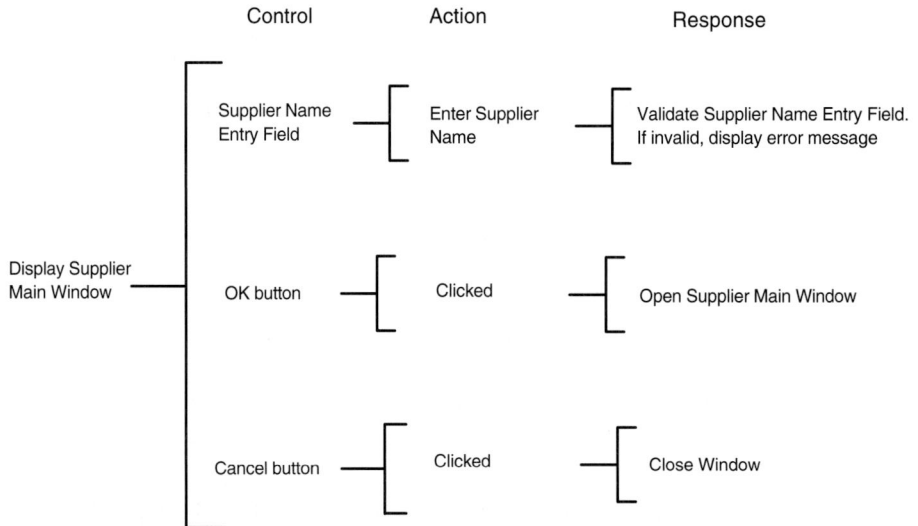

Figure 4–30 Control-Action Response (CAR) diagram.

The control buttons and data entry objects that are shown on a CAR diagram are GUI objects that can be clicked on or triggered by the users to initiate predetermined actions in a window. The control objects can be items such as:

• a data entry field such as a single line edit control item

• control buttons that activate events such as "Cancel," "Add," "Delete," "Select"

• a list box that shows a list of option items from which to select

For each single GUI control object, one or more actions can be carried out. Once an action is triggered by the user, such as clicking on a control button with a mouse, for instance, a response is activated accordingly. The response event is written in very simple English sentences. Each small sentence documents which activity needs to be performed for each action as well as what should happen next to the graphical user interface.

The detailed processing logic code that should be performed for each action is not shown on a CAR diagram. The CAR diagram depicts only what needs to be done at a high level, not how to do it. It is a logical representation of the business logic performed by a window, independent of the physical implementation of the application.

UNIT TESTING AND AUTOMATED TESTING TOOLS

For small client-server systems, effective unit testing can be performed manually by the developers, in less time than setting up an automated testing environment, training the developers on how to use the tool, capturing the GUI test scripts, and replaying them with an automated testing tool.

For this reason, the decision to use an automated testing tool to unit test a small client-server application should be carefully assessed by the development team, especially if the development is done under a tight budget constraint. A well orchestrated manual testing approach might be more appropriate unless the automated testing tool will be used for integration and system testing later on. If the automated testing tool will be used for integration and system testing, then the unit test scripts should be engineered for reusability during integration, system, and user acceptance testing.

WHITE-BOX TESTING TECHNIQUES

White-box testing, also known as structural testing, is a testing method for which the test case data is created with the intent of verifying the internal structure of a program and its procedural logic. Figure 4-31 pictorially illustrates the white-box testing concept.

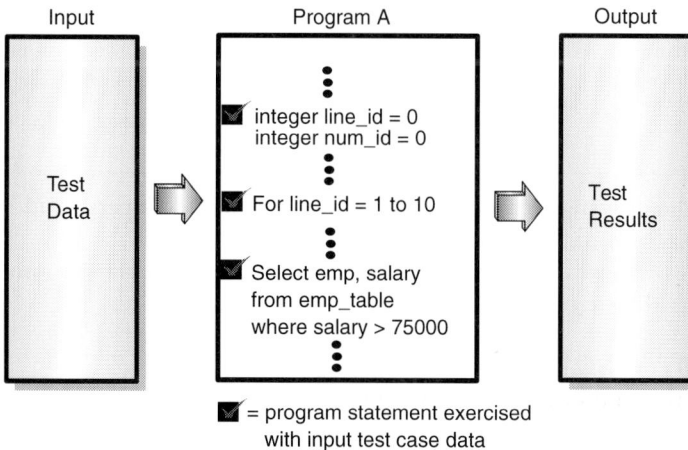

Input	Program A	Output

```
Test
Data
```

```
        •
        •
        •
☑ integer line_id = 0
  integer num_id = 0
        •
        •
        •
☑ For line_id = 1 to 10
        •
        •
        •
☑ Select emp, salary
  from emp_table
  where salary > 75000
        •
        •
        •
```

```
Test
Results
```

☑ = program statement exercised
with input test case data

Figure 4–31 White-box testing.

Similarly, Figure 4-32 shows some of the most popular white-box testing techniques, which can be applied to the testing of client-server or Web database programs or modules.

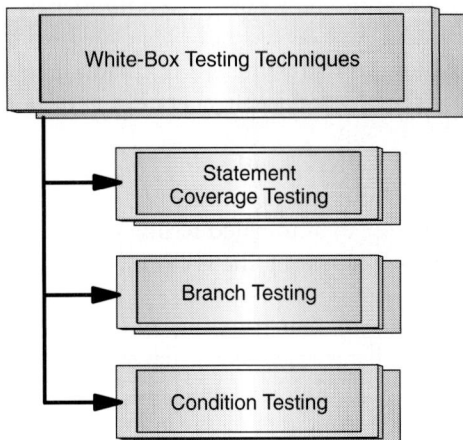

Figure 4–32 Three popular white-box testing techniques.

Table 4-59 provides a brief description of the three white-box testing techniques that Figure 4-32 displays.

Table 4–59 White-box Testing Techniques

White-Box Testing Technique	Description
Statement Testing	Each statement in a program is executed at least once during the program tests
Condition Testing	Each possible outcome on each decision point is executed at least once during the program tests
Branch Testing	Each possible branch option is executed at least once during the program tests

The white-box testing techniques can be used by the developers or independent testers to develop effective unit test cases.

As I stated earlier, white-box testing often uses artificial test data to thoroughly exercise the internal logic of a program.

BLACK-BOX TESTING TECHNIQUES
Black-box testing, also known as functional testing, is a testing method for which the test cases are created with the intent of verifying the functional requirements of the application, regardless of the internal structure of the programs. Figure 4-33 pictorially illustrates the black-box testing concept.

Similarly, Figure 4-34 shows some of the most popular black-box testing techniques that can be applied to the testing of client-server or Web database programs or modules.

Table 4-60 provides a brief description of the black-box testing techniques depicted in Figure 4-34.

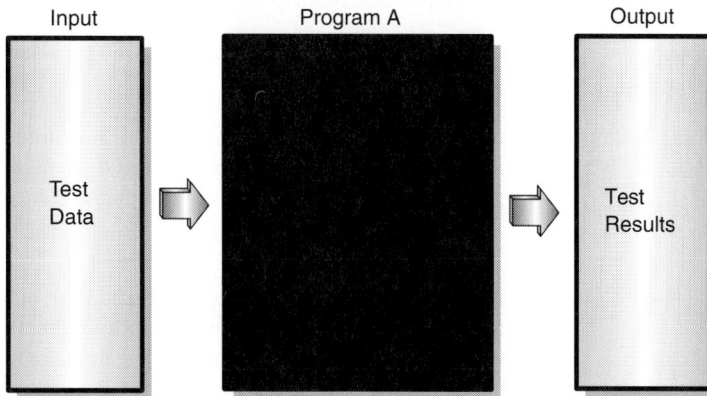

Figure 4–33 Black-box testing.

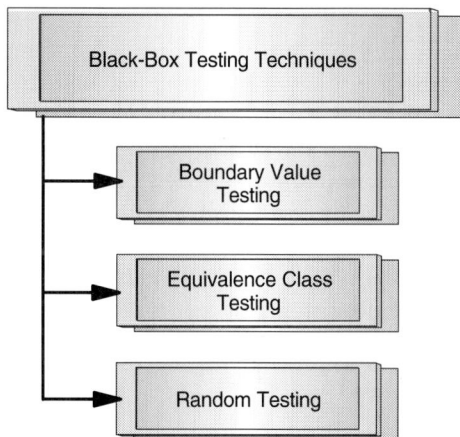

Figure 4–34 Three popular black-box testing techniques.

The developers or independent testers can use the black-box testing techniques to develop effective unit test cases. Black-box testing can use both artificial and real-life test data.

CREATING UNIT TEST DATA AND ORGANIZING THEM INTO TEST CYCLES

A test cycle is a set of test cases that are executed in a specific order. Unit test data can be organized into a series of distinct test cycles. Each test cycle verifies the procedural logic of a specific program component, such as certain fields in a data entry window, for instance.

Table 4–60 Black-box Testing Techniques

Black-Box Testing Technique	Description
Boundary Value Testing	Multiple test cases are developed to test the boundaries of input and output domain classes, file data structures, and program parameters. The conditions that are tested include value ranges that are on and outside (i.e., above and below) the established boundary limits.
Equivalence Class Testing	Multiple test cases are developed based on the functional specifications of the application. Each functional specification that is supported by the program should be tested at least once. The input test data is then segregated into two equivalence classes: the first class contains representative, valid test data, and the second class contains invalid test data.
Random Testing	The program is tested with randomly generated test data.

The unit test cycles should be engineered to complement each other. Once they are assembled together, they should test the complete set of procedural logic that is coded in the program.

Later on, the test cycles aimed at integration and system testing can be constructed by re-using selective test data from the previous unit test cycles. They can also be augmented with test data that address the specific test objectives of the integration and system testing phases.

The following example illustrates how a unit test cycle is gradually constructed to verify the logic of a simple data entry window program:

Step 1:   Create valid test data to verify the normal conditions of each single operation that is supported by the data entry window program

Step 2:   Create invalid test data to verify how each single operation that is supported by the data entry window program reacts to unusual data conditions

Step 3:   Combine valid and invalid test data together to verify each single operation that is supported by the data entry window program

Step 4:   Combine valid and invalid test data to verify the complete procedural workflow that is supported by the data entry window program

The creation of effective test cases and the data required to exercise them demands a good dose of creativity and intuition. But they are not enough. The construction of sound test cases and data also requires discipline. Table 4-61 shows, as an example, how you can construct, in a systematic manner, a representative set of test cases that can be used to thoroughly verify some data entry fields in a window.

Table 4–61 Test Case Samples

Test Cycle	Test Case	Anticipated Result
• Test the numeric data entry fields	• Input valid numbers	• Accepted
•	• Input all 9s (boundary value)	• Accepted
•	• Input all 0s (boundary value)	• Accepted
•	• Input negative numbers (invalid data)	• Rejected if negative numbers are not acceptable; proper error message displayed
•	• Input non-numeric characters (invalid data)	• Rejected and proper error message displayed
•	• Input no data at all	• Rejected if field data is mandatory
• Test the alphabetic data entry fields	• Input valid alphabetic fields	• Accepted
•	• Input numeric data	• Rejected and proper error message displayed
•	• Input field filled with spaces	• Rejected if field is mandatory
•	• Input no data at all	• Rejected if field data is mandatory
• Test the date fields	• Input valid dates	• Accepted
•	• Input invalid dates	• Rejected and proper error message displayed
•	• Input no data at all	• Rejected if field data is mandatory

Also develop additional test cases to verify all the specific business rules that apply to each data entry element shown in the window.

Activity number:	DE-12B
Activity name:	Design integration test cases
Purpose:	To design the system integration test cases that are required to verify the progressive integration of all programs into a single, comprehensive system
Inputs:	AN-T3 Initial testing strategy DE-T3 Physical database design

	DE-T7 System interfaces design DE-T8 Data conversion programs design DE-T9 Ad hoc report and query environment design Shared software components design Application software interfaces design
Outputs:	DE-T12B Integration test cases design

Activity description:	• Review and refine the high-level strategy that was developed during the analysis phase to plan and execute the system integration tests
	• For the online programs:
	  – Define the technique(s) that will be used to progressively integrate and test all the graphical user interface programs into a comprehensive subsystem
	  – Define the major categories of integration test cases that will be used to verify:
	    – the combination of all the application GUI windows into a whole
	    – the complete functionality provided by the combined online programs
	    – all the database server stored procedures and triggers
	    – all the application remote procedures
	    – the adherence to the enterprise-wide GUI and program naming, coding, and documentation standards
	    – the level of utilization of reusable components
	  – Develop the online integration test cases that are required to verify thoroughly the complete online programs subsystem
	  – Create the data that are required to exercise the online integration test cases
	  – Define the cycles and sequence into which the online application programs will be incrementally assembled together and tested as a whole, including the strategy to control the transition from one test cycle to the next
	  – Define the approach that will be used to track the execution of the online integration tests, including the handling and resolution of uncovered defects
	• For the batch programs:
	  – Define the technique(s) that will be used to test the progressive integration of the batch programs into a comprehensive subsystem
	  – Define the major categories of integration test cases that will be used to verify:

- the complete functionality provided by the combined batch programs into a subsystem
- all the database server stored procedures and triggers
- all the application system remote procedure calls
- the adherence to the enterprise-wide batch program naming, coding, and documentation standards
- the level of utilization of reusable components
- Develop the batch integration test cases that are required to verify thoroughly the batch subsystem
- If appropriate at this stage, create the data that are required to exercise the batch integration test cases
- Define the cycles and sequence into which the batch application programs will be incrementally assembled together and tested as a whole, including the strategy to control the transition from one test cycle to the next
- Define the approach that will be used to track the execution of the batch integration tests, including the handling and resolution of uncovered defects
- Walk through the system integration test case deliverables

4.13.2 DESIGN THE INTEGRATION TEST CASES

This section discusses the detailed steps involved in the design of the system integration test cases. It also presents some tips and guidelines on how to perform this process.

INTEGRATION TESTING OBJECTIVES

Integration testing is the process by which the unit tested client-server or Web database modules and/or programs are assembled together and gradually tested as a complete, cohesive system.

The integration tests verify that:

- All the modules and their interfaces work properly when they are integrated together into complete programs

- All the programs work properly when they are integrated into a complete application

- All the external interfaces that exist between the client-server system and other systems work properly

- Verification of the application look and feel standards

As shown in Figure 4-35, during integration testing, all the software components that reside on the front end, middle layer, and back end of the client-server application spectrum must be tested thoroughly as a complete, integrated system. Different types of test cases should be developed to verify all the application procedural code that resides specifically at the presentation layer, the application middleware layer, or the database server layer. Additional test cases should also be developed to verify the three layers and their interface points simultaneously.

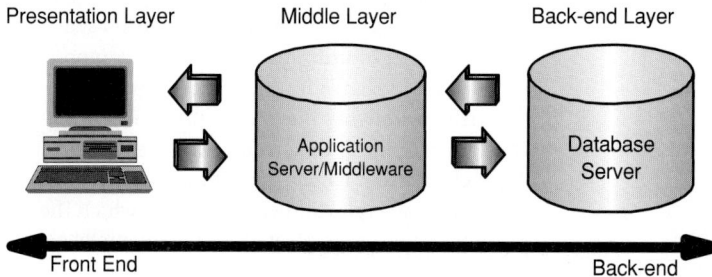

Figure 4–35 The three major layers of client-server integration testing.

THE INTEGRATION TESTING STRATEGY

During the unit testing process, the system programs were tested individually. During integration testing, the different programs are incrementally regrouped together and tested according to a predetermined, upward integration sequence. For large client-server systems, you frequently have several cycles of integration, as shown in Figure 4-36.

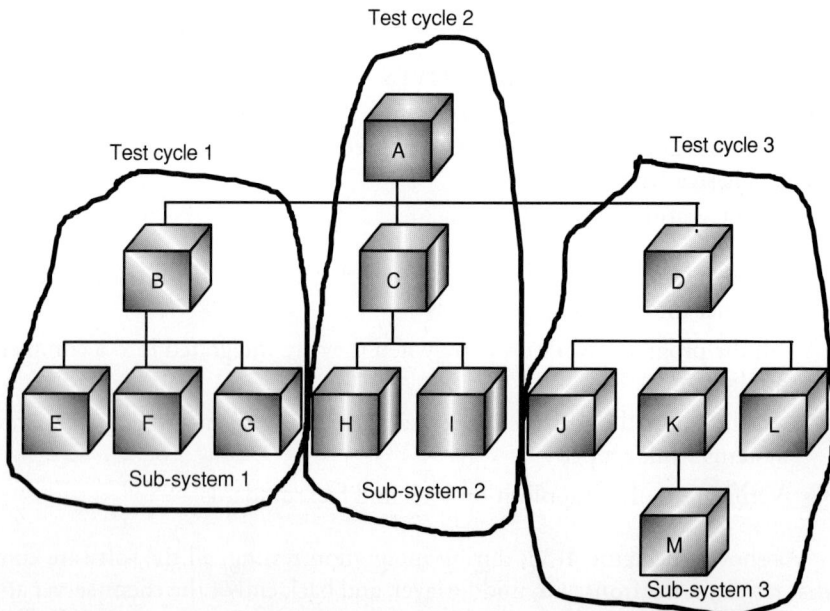

Figure 4–36 Multiple integration testing cycles.

The integration tests should be considered completed only when all the batch and online application programs are tested and successfully integrated into a complete and fully functional operational system.

The multiple integration test cycles that must be constructed to incrementally verify the different components of the client-server system are defined based on the various factors that are indicated in Table 4-62.

Table 4–62 System Integration Testing Test Cycle Factors

• The number of programs that need to be integrated together
• The dependencies that might exist between some programs
• The complexity of the application interfaces with other systems
• The amount of time allocated to integration testing
• The size and complexity of the programs to be tested
• The different platforms on which the programs operate
• The functional affinities that might exist between certain programs

You can consider several alternatives in order to determine how the different programs will be integrated incrementally together and tested accordingly. Some of the most popular integration testing strategies are listed in Table 4-63. Following is a brief description of each strategy shown in that table.

Table 4–63 System Integration Testing Strategies

• "Big Bang"
• Top-Down
• Bottom-Up
• Functional Threads

With the **Big Bang** approach, all the programs are integrated together and tested simultaneously as a complete application. This integration testing approach is more suited for small client-server applications.

With the **Top-Down** approach, the programs are tested in a top-down manner, with stubs that might be used for some lower-level modules that are not yet fully developed.

With the **Bottom-Up** approach, the most basic, lower-level modules or programs are integrated and tested together. This testing cycle continues incrementally until all the application programs have been combined and tested in an upward sequence.

With the **Functional Threads** approach, the programs that service a common function are assembled together and tested as a single functional unit. This approach works well for client-server applications that support business functions that are relatively independent from one another.

INTEGRATION TEST CASES

Several categories of test cases must be engineered to verify that the individual application programs are functioning properly as a complete system. Some of the most efficient and comprehensive unit test cases that were developed originally to test the individual programs should be merged with the new integration test cases, to complement them. This way, testing becomes a recycling process!

Likewise, some of the integration test case scenarios should exercise the distinct application features that each category of users will use, ranging from the novice, to intermediate, and finally to expert categories.

Tables 4-64, 4-65, and 4-66 enumerate some of the different types of integration test cases that should be created to verify the various software components of the client-server system, covering the client, database server layers, and application/middleware.

Activity number:	DE-12C
Activity name:	Design system test cases
Purpose:	To design the system test cases that are required to verify that the system operates successfully as per its design specifications and meets the agreed service-level performance requirements
Inputs:	AN-T3 Initial testing strategy DE-T3 Physical database design DE-T7 System interfaces design DE-T8 Data conversion programs design DE-T9 Ad hoc report and query environment design Shared software components design Application software components design
Outputs:	DE-T12C System test cases design

Activity description:	• Review and refine the high-level strategy that was developed earlier during the analysis phase to plan and execute the application system tests
	• Define the testing technique(s) that will be used to verify that the system meets all the functional and service-level performance requirements that were originally developed with the users for the application
	• Define the major categories of system test cases that will be used to verify the following system functional and operational characteristics:
	  – overall system functionality
	  – overall system performance
	  – overall system reliability and robustness
	  – system security, data integrity, and control mechanisms

- interfaces with other systems
- system file and database backup, recovery, and restart procedures
- user and systems documentation
- Develop the system test cases
- If appropriate at this stage, create the data that is required to exercise the system test cases
- Define the cycles into which the different categories of system test cases will be conducted
- Define the approach that will be used to track the execution of the system tests, including the handling and resolution of uncovered defects
- Walk through the system test case deliverables

Table 4–64 Cross-window Integration Tests

- Verify that the interfaces between the major functional windows are working properly
- Verify that the interfaces between a major functional window and all its subordinate windows are working correctly
- Verify that the integrated application windows adhere to the standards that were established for the presentation interface
  - Are the windows using colors in a consistent manner?
  - Are the windows using fonts in a consistent way?
  - Are the windows text, data, headings, and labels used in a consistent manner?

Table 4–65 Database Server Integration Cases

- Verify that all the database triggers have been exercised successfully
- Verify that all the database middleware (i.e., database gateways) facilities have been tested and proven to work correctly
- Verify that the database stored procedures are working properly and return to the client the required data correctly

4.13.3 DESIGN SYSTEM TEST CASES

This section describes the detailed steps involved in the design of the system test cases. It also provides some tips and guidelines on how to perform this process.

SYSTEM TESTING OBJECTIVES

System testing is conducted after integration testing. In system testing, the client-server application is verified against the business and service-level performance objectives

Table 4–66 Application Server And Middleware Integration Test Cases

- Verify that the procedural logic that is contained in all the client-server programs is executed as per their documented specifications and works properly when it is integrated into a complete application
- Verify that the GUI and batch programs read, create, update, or delete correctly the proper data into the application databases
- Verify that the remote procedures work correctly and interface as expected with the software components that invoke them
- Verify that the various software middleware facilities (i.e., internal or cross-platform communications, etc.) work correctly with the application software components that interface with them
- Verify that all the custom application programs interface correctly with third-party application facilities such as spreadsheets, word processors, e-mail functions, fax functions, help subsystem, and various general-purpose utility software

that were originally defined with the users. More precisely, the system testing process should ensure that the client-server or Web database system:

- operates successfully as per its design specifications
- satisfies the stated application service-level objectives
- behaves appropriately when operating under potentially stressful conditions

The scope and depth at which system testing should be performed will largely depend on the criticality, size, and complexity of the client-server or Web database system. A small and relatively simple client-server system might not need all the rigor and detailed level of testing that a large and complex mission-critical client-server system might require.

SYSTEM TEST CASES

The representative set of test cases that was developed earlier for the unit and integration testing processes should be augmented with specific test conditions to distinctly address the above-mentioned system test objectives. As I previously stated, testing is a recycling process.

Table 4- 67 lists the different types of test case scenarios that might help validate the whole system (i.e., software, hardware, documentation, and graphical user interface).

The system testers should carefully review the user acceptance testing strategy that was created in the previous development phase. The objective is to ensure that the system test cases that will be designed to verify the behavior of the total system are complete and will indeed exercise all of the system functions and facilities.

The ultimate goal is to ensure that once the system tests are completed, the system has demonstrated that it can satisfy all the system acceptance criteria that were set originally with the users. At this advanced stage in the software development life cycle pro-

Table 4–67 System Test Cases

• Volume testing	• System interface testing
• Security testing	• Configuration testing
• Stress testing	• Multi-site testing
• Backup/recovery testing	• Disaster recovery testing
• Usability testing	• Performance testing
• Documentation testing	

cess, the client-server or Web system should generate a no-surprise situation during the final user acceptance testing process.

The following section describes more explicitly each type of system test conditions that are listed in Table 4-67. Additional information and insight are provided on this subject in Chapter 8, which is dedicated to client-server and Web database application testing.

VOLUME TESTING

Volume test cases verify that the system can handle the maximum volumes of data that were specified for the client-server or Web database system. Representative test cases and their appropriate test data should be developed to verify that the system can process reasonably well the maximum volume of batch and online business transactions per unit of time.

SECURITY TESTING

Security test cases verify the system's ability to prevent or detect unauthorized access or improper use of the application system facilities and resources.

All security control mechanisms should be tested thoroughly, including system accesses via remote sites.

STRESS TESTING

Stress testing verifies the behavior of the client-server application under unusually high volumes of data over a short time frame. These tests are performed in a real or simulated mode of operation. Variable transaction workloads can be submitted simultaneously to overload the system and see how it behaves.

The objective of stress testing is to strain the client and server machines well beyond their normal capacity limits and ultimately attempt to break them.

In a mission-critical client-server environment, stress testing is often essential to determine what the true break points are whereby the client or server machines will crash while running a very large number of transactions. It can also be helpful to attempt to detect memory leaks or network inefficiencies.

BACKUP/RECOVERY/RESTART TESTING

Backup, recovery, and restart testing verifies that the application can recover from a system hardware, software, or networking failure. Test cases can be constructed to intentionally cause system crashes and then check whether the client-server application can be restored back to specific points in time, prior to the failure events.

USABILITY TESTING

Usability testing verifies the overall ease of use of the client-server application. It can highlight GUI-related features that prove to be not user-friendly and therefore can be difficult to learn or operate by the users of the application. Usability testing should be done as early as possible in the development process so that critical user interface problems can be uncovered and quickly rectified before the software system is ready to be released into production.

DOCUMENTATION TESTING

Documentation and manual procedure testing verifies the accuracy, relevancy, user-friendliness, and completeness of the user and system operations written documentation. It should equally cover the application online help facility and the manual procedures that must be carried out by the users.

SYSTEM INTERFACE TESTING

This testing verifies that the system correctly receives or sends data from or to other systems, covering all possible conditions and time periods, such as daily, weekly, monthly, yearly, or on-demand requests.

CONFIGURATION TESTING

Desktop configuration testing verifies that the client-server system operates consistently on different client desktop machine configurations. Configuration testing can also be extended to the various categories of system server machines, network, specialized hardware/software equipment, and middleware components. In a real life environment, users will likely run the new application concurrently with other software such as their word processor, spreadsheet or other custom applications. Consequently, it is important to test the new application while other applications run at the same time, to simulate an environment where several applications might compete for the same system resources.

MULTI-SITE TESTING

Multi-site testing verifies that all client-server software and supporting technology infrastructure components operate satisfactorily and in synchronization with one another, when they are distributed across multiple geographical sites.

DISASTER RECOVERY TESTING

Disaster recovery testing verifies that the client-server system can switch over to a parallel machine in case a serious hardware failure occurs and hence remain fully operational or be quickly reinstated into another production environment after the occurrence of a major disaster.

PERFORMANCE TESTING

Performance testing verifies how well the application measures up against the multiple performance service-level requirements that were defined with the users during the analysis and design phases. Performance testing is conducted under varying loads of data, but still within the limits of normal, acceptable operating conditions. In system testing, the testers should run the performance tests with the same types of machines that the users will utilize in the production environment.

Activity number:	DE-12D
Activity name:	Design user acceptance test cases
Purpose:	To design the user acceptance test cases that are required to verify that the system operates successfully as per the stated specifications and meets its service-level requirements
Inputs:	AN-T3 Initial testing strategy DE-T3 Physical database design DE-T7 System interfaces design DE-T8 Data conversion programs design DE-T9 Ad hoc report and query environment design Shared software components design Application software components design
Outputs:	DE-T12D User acceptance test cases design
Activity description:	• Review and refine the high-level strategy that was developed during the analysis phase to plan and execute the application system user acceptance tests • Define the testing technique(s) that will be used to verify the set of functional requirements, business objectives, and user acceptance criteria that were originally determined for the application system • Define the major categories of user acceptance test cases that will be used to verify the application: – overall functionality – overall usability – overall reliability and robustness – security, integrity, and control mechanisms

   – interfaces with other systems
   – system file and database backup, recovery, and restart
     procedures
   – user and systems documentation along with the system
     manual procedures
- Develop the user acceptance test cases
- If appropriate at this stage, create the data that are required to
  exercise the system test cases
- Define the cycles into which the different categories of user
  acceptance test cases will be conducted
- Define the approach that will be used to track the execution of
  the user acceptance tests, including the handling and
  resolution of uncovered defects
- Walk through the user acceptance test case deliverables

4.13.4 DESIGN USER ACCEPTANCE TEST CASES

This section discusses the detailed steps involved in the design of the user acceptance test cases. It also presents some tips and guidelines on how to perform this process.

USER ACCEPTANCE TESTING OBJECTIVES

User acceptance testing follows integration testing. It is the last major testing process that must be executed prior to transferring the system into production.

User acceptance's prime objective is to demonstrate that the client-server or Web database system meets all the business and operational objectives that were originally formulated by the users for the application. User acceptance testing should also ensure that the system manual procedures are complete, accurate, and in line with the system automated functions.

USER ACCEPTANCE TEST CASES

The user acceptance test cases are primarily developed by the users themselves, in accordance with the acceptance criteria that were formalized during the analysis phase, for the client-server system at hand. User acceptance test cases can be formulated using the user scenarios that were created during the analysis phase.[4] Additional user acceptance test scripts can also be constructed around the external business events that were identified in the business process model.

Some of the test cases that can be developed to support the acceptance testing process are listed in Table 4-68.

---

4. For more information on user scenarios, please refer back to section 3.5.6, titled "Developing user scenarios", in Chapter 3, Analysis.

Table 4–68 User Acceptance Test Cases

- Test cases that simulate a normal utilization of the system business transactions
- Test cases that validate that the batch programs operate correctly, including the submission of input data and creation of output data
- Test cases that simulate abnormal conditions or the submission of invalid data
- Test cases that validate the ease of use of the system and the level of integration that exist between the manual and automated business tasks
- Test cases that exercise the system functions from the keyboard instead of the mouse or other pointing devices
- Test cases that validate the completeness, accuracy, and clarity of the system documentation
- Test cases that exercise all the windows, reports, and forms created or used by the system
- Test cases that exercise and validate the system security and control mechanisms
- Test cases that validate the level of clarity of the system error messages and the corrective actions that are suggested to fix the problems

USER ACCEPTANCE AND OPERATIONS SUPPORT GROUPS

In some organizations, the Information System Operations department may also participate actively in the final acceptance of the system. Their goal is to verify that the system meets the set of operational standards that must be enforced at the enterprise level. For instance, the client-server system can break new ground in the enterprise and introduce some brand-new technologies, which must be integrated with the existing technical infrastructure. In such a situation, the various operations support groups within Information Systems might want to verify some or all the items that are outlined in Table 4-69 and consequently develop appropriate test cases.

Table 4–69 Operations Support Considerations

- Client workstation support procedures
- General business application support procedures (Help Desk functions)
- Network support procedures (LAN, Metropolitan Area Network/MAN, WAN)
- Authorization and security support procedures
- Miscellaneous computer operating support procedures (i.e., server startup/shutdown procedures, backup/recovery operations, reports distribution, monitoring procedures)
- Local printing support procedures

USER ACCEPTANCE TESTING STRATEGIES

You can follow several approaches to conduct acceptance testing. Some of the most popular strategies are indicated in Table 4-70.

Table 4–70 User Acceptance Testing Strategies

• Conducting the acceptance tests of the new system in parallel with the old system
• Conducting the new client-server system acceptance tests at only one physical location in a pilot mode
• Running the acceptance tests in a test environment that simulates as much as possible the production environment

Activity number:	DE-13
Activity name:	Finalize detailed data conversion strategy
Purpose:	To refine and finalize the detailed strategy required for converting existing legacy data and migrating it to the new system
Inputs:	AN-T11 Initial data conversion strategy DE-T8 Data conversion programs design
Outputs:	DE-T13 Detailed data conversion strategy
Activity description:	• Review the initial data conversion strategy deliverable that was produced earlier during the analysis phase – Finalize the detailed data conversion strategy, based on all the detailed information that has been gathered so far on the conversion process • Walk through the detailed data conversion strategy deliverable

4.14 FINALIZE THE DETAILED DATA CONVERSION STRATEGY

The broad data conversion strategy that was elaborated earlier during the analysis phase should now be revisited in light of the detailed information that has been accumulated so far on the new system.

Depending on the scope of the data conversion effort, the conversion process can become a major sub-phase of a project and should then be treated as a sub-project on its own.

Among other things, expand the initial data conversion strategy to cover all the detailed conversion steps that are required to perform the conversion process, along with their sequences and dependencies.

In addition, clearly define the following conversion subjects and finalize them with the users and any other MIS groups that might be involved in the conversion effort:

• Scope and objectives of the conversion effort

• Roles and responsibilities of each group implicated in the conversion effort

- Description and acquisition of any special software tool and hardware/networking equipment
- Estimated duration time of the entire conversion process
- Detailed description of the proposed cut-over scenario to phase out the old system components (i.e., flat files and databases)
- Detailed description of the fallback procedures, in case of unanticipated major conversion problems

In some cases, the user and system personnel might also need to receive some special training to perform the conversion process. If so, the training strategy should reflect such a need.

In some organizations, where very large volumes of data are to be processed during the conversion effort, the conversion effort is considered so crucial to the success of the project that the conversion programs are developed and tested very early during the construction phase. Then the conversion programs are used to populate the new system test files and databases with real-life production data samples. This approach also allows the development team to more accurately estimate the total processing time needed to convert all the old system data, based on the actual time converting a subset of the legacy files/databases took.

Activity number:	DE-14
Activity name:	Finalize detailed capacity plan
Purpose:	To refine and finalize the detailed capacity plan
Inputs:	AN-T10 Initial capacity plan
Outputs:	DE-T14 Detailed capacity plan
Activity description:	• Review the initial capacity plan that was developed earlier during the analysis phase • Finalize the detailed capacity plan based on the detailed information available at this stage • Walk through the detailed capacity plan

4.15 FINALIZE THE DETAILED CAPACITY PLAN

The initial capacity plan that was developed earlier during the analysis phase is converted into the detailed capacity plan. The capacity plan should be kept up-to-date as soon as new volumetric information becomes available during the subsequent development phases. However, a good practice is to review the detailed capacity plan immediately after the physical databases have been created.

Some of the most critical components that should be revised include:

- Overall disk space estimates
- Application network traffic estimates
- Network capacity estimates
- Overall CPU processing estimates
- Memory sizing estimates
- System transaction volume estimates and transaction rate per unit of time
- Physical database sizing estimates

Construction

5.1 INTRODUCTION

The prime objective of the construction phase is to code and test the detailed set of programs that are required by the application. The programs are developed as per the system design specifications and/or prototypes that have been created so far. As the individual programmers complete their programs, they themselves can unit test these immediately.

The coding and unit testing process is predominantly iterative in nature, meaning that the programs are coded, and tested, defects are corrected, and the programs are then re-tested. Once all programs work in a satisfactory manner, they are then gradually integrated into a complete system and tested as a whole. Subsequent testing activities include the system and user acceptance testing processes.

Table 5-1 describes a set of objectives for the construction phase.

Table 5–1 Construction Phase Objectives

- Develop detailed application code as per design specifications
- Thoroughly test the application system and correct defects
- Ensure that programs are properly documented and maintainable
- Conduct user acceptance testing

Table 5-2 summarizes the major technical activities that are conducted during the construction phase, along with a list of the anticipated technical deliverables.

Figure 5-1 pictorially presents, at a high level, the relationships that exist among the individual activities of the construction phase.

Table 5–2 Construction Phase

ACTIVITY	DELIVERABLE(S)
1. Determine programming standards and guidelines	1. Programming standards and guidelines
2. Create the application development and test environment	2. Application development and test environment
3. Develop application programs	3. Application programs
4. Conduct unit testing	4. Unit testing completion report
5. Conduct integration testing	5. Integration testing completion report
6. Conduct system testing	6. System testing completion report
7. Conduct user acceptance testing	7. User acceptance testing completion report
8. Create the installation strategy	8. Installation strategy
9. Create the system cut-over strategy	9. System cut-over strategy

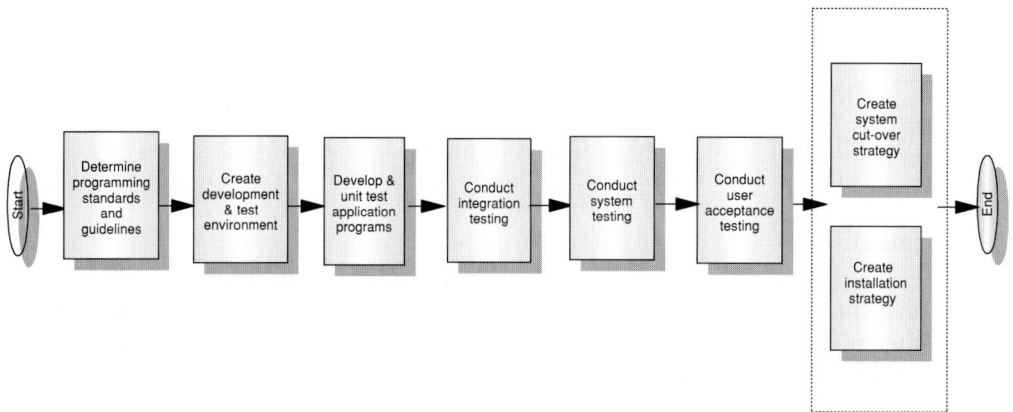

Figure 5–1 Construction phase activities.

Although the linear sequence in which the construction phase activities appear in Figure 5-1 might suggest that one specific activity must be completed prior to beginning the next one, in fact they can be performed in parallel or in different sequences.

Furthermore, several of these activities can be performed with an iterative approach, gradually refining the activity deliverables in incremental steps. On the other hand, certain types of activities might not easily lend themselves to an iterative development approach.

At the completion of each major construction phase activity, a formal walkthrough should be scheduled to review the final outcome of each activity, which is comprised of a set of specific system deliverables.

Activity number:	CO-1
Activity name:	Determine programming standards and guidelines
Purpose:	To describe the minimum set of standards and conventions that will be used to construct the application
Inputs:	Existing system development standards and guidelines
Outputs:	CO-T1 Programming standards and guidelines

Activity description:	Describe the minimum set of standards that should apply to the construction of the application software, covering the following items:
	• Standard naming conventions for application development objects
	  – Standard reusable software modules and object class naming conventions
	  – Standard database object naming conventions
	  – Standard file directory naming conventions
	  – Standard security object naming conventions
	  – Standard program documentation conventions
	  – Standard error message handling and naming conventions
	  – Standard help facility display and naming conventions
	  – Standard batch program templates
	  – Standard online program templates
	  – Software development tool "dos and don'ts"
	• Walk through the minimum set of programming standards and guidelines to which the developers should adhere

5.2 DETERMINE PROGRAMMING STANDARDS AND GUIDELINES

This section discusses a variety of programming standards, guidelines and conventions that can be used while developing the application programs.

5.2.1 OVERVIEW

The minimum but essential set of application development standards, guidelines, and conventions that will be used to construct the various application software components must be thoroughly discussed with all the development team members.

The construction standards review process is a very crucial activity to ensure building a quality system, especially when many construction teams are called upon to develop simultaneously different components of a large and complex client-server or

Web database application. Failure to clearly spell out the most critical system development conventions might result in reduced application consistency, usability, and maintainability. On the other hand, applying too rigid standards that do not add value might impede the productivity of the developers.

Section 5.2.2 discusses the different types of development standards and conventions that usually apply to the construction of a large-scale client-server or Web database application. It also includes advice and commentary on each major set of proposed standards. The major standards that I cover include:

- Application object naming conventions
- GUI controls naming conventions
- Database objects naming conventions
- General programming conventions
- Program documentation conventions
- Program error-handling conventions

5.2.2   APPLICATION OBJECT NAMING CONVENTIONS

While developing a sizable client-server or Web database application, a large number of different objects will probably be created by several developers, such as windows, menus, controls, events, and functional scripts software components. A good naming convention must be set up to uniquely identify all these software objects if the developers want to enforce software naming consistency standards within the same application or across multiple applications. Moreover, appropriate application object naming standards will increase productivity by facilitating the overall maintenance process, once the application runs in a production environment.

As a rule of thumb, the use of meaningful, prolonged names should be promoted widely in the software factory shop. The vast majority of modern client-server development tools support long names that can contain a large number of characters.

In general, the naming convention for application objects is fairly simple. The first few letters of the object identifier designate a prefix that identifies the type of object it represents. Then an underscore character '_' is typed, followed by a string of characters that uniquely describes this specific object.

Table 5-3 shows a simple naming convention that could be used to identify the most basic objects that are usually created with a typical rapid application development client-server tool.

Table 5–3 General Application Object Naming Conventions

OBJECT TYPE	NAMING CONVENTION	EXAMPLE
Application	a_	a_order_processing_rlse1
Window	w_	w_login
Menu	m_	m_customer
Function	f_	f_verify_customer_data
Structure	s_	s_customer_data
Query	q_	q_customer_order

5.2.3 GUI CONTROLS NAMING CONVENTIONS

The naming convention for GUI controls can be fairly simple. The first few letters of the GUI control identifier can designate a prefix that identifies the type of control it represents. Then an underscore character '_' is typed, followed by a string of characters that uniquely describes this specific control.

Table 5-4 shows a simple naming convention that can be used to identify the most common GUI control elements that are usually created in a client-server application. The convention that you see here is typically used for applications that are developed with the Powerbuilder client-server development tool. However, the developers can slightly modify or extend the proposed convention to satisfy their own specific needs.

Table 5–4 GUI Controls Naming Conventions

CONTROL TYPE	NAMING CONVENTION	EXAMPLE
CheckBox	cbx_	cbx_operation
DropDownListBox	ddlb_	ddlb_gender
PictureButton	pb_	pb_customer
SingleLineEdit	sle_	sle_customer_name
RadioButton	rb_	rb_customer_type
ListBox	lb_	lb_day
StaticText	st_	st_customer_info
MultiLineEdit	mle_	mle_comments
DataWindow	dw_	dw_customer_list

5.2.4   DATABASE OBJECTS NAMING CONVENTIONS

A suggested approach for the identification of database objects appears in Table 5-5.[1]
The proposed conventions can be adapted to meet the requirements of a specific relational data base management system (RDBMS).

Table 5–5 Database Objects Naming Conventions

DATABASE OBJECT	NAMING CONVENTION	EXAMPLE
Database	[Database name]_db	Customer_db
Table	[Table name]_table	Customer_table
View	[View name]_view	Customer_Order_view
Indexes	[Table name]_ndx_#	Customer_table_ndx_1
Stored procedures	[Stored procedure name]_sp	Validate_customer_sp
Update trigger	[Update trigger name]_updtrg	Change_stock_updtrg
Delete trigger	[Delete trigger name]_deltrg	Delete_employee_deltrg
Insert trigger	[Insert trigger name]_instrg	Insert_part_number_instrg

5.2.5   GENERAL PROGRAMMING CONVENTIONS

In large multi-developer environments, good programming standards should be well
documented and consistently enforced across all applications. Simple, down-to-earth
standards will greatly enhance the quality of the applications, making them easier to
debug and maintain once they are transferred into a production environment.

Describing in detail the best programming standard practices that might exist today
is well beyond the scope of this book. Nevertheless, basic programming standards that
reflect common sense should definitely encourage the use of best practices, such as
code modularization, to name one. Modularization of the code into distinct functional areas and segregation of the code that contains common application functionality
will lead to easier maintenance and open the door to more code reusability, which in
return should result in better overall software quality.

In programming environments that truly support object orientation, observance of
the best object-oriented coding practices, such as the use of generic references instead
of hard-coded references, for example, should be clearly documented and consistently
enforced across the system development organization. Taking full advantage of the basic tenets of object-oriented coding techniques, such as encapsulation, inheritance,

---

1. In this example, the object identifier type is used as a suffix. However, the object identifier type
   can also become a prefix. For instance, Customer_db would become db_customer.

and polymorphism, will lead to more code reusability. However, the dos and don'ts while using the development tools and recommended object-oriented practices must remain practical. For instance, developing application code that uses too many levels of inheritance might generate an adverse effect on the system and impede its overall performance. Using eight levels of inheritance might not be a practical technique.

5.2.6   PROGRAM DOCUMENTATION CONVENTIONS

Most rapid application development client-server tools use some form of scripting language to code the procedural logic that is required to support the business application. Lay out simple rules that indicate how to comment the code inside a program prior to coding the application, and then systematically enforce them to ensure consistency. Similarly, the rules that explain how the application code should be structured should cover at least the most basic elements that are indicated in Table 5-6.

Table 5–6 Code Structure Conventions

- Spaces should be inserted before and after operators (i.e., +, -, =, >), between statements, etc.
- Code indentation for statements such as IF...THEN...ELSE and DO...LOOP should be enforced
- Descriptive comments should be interspersed throughout the major sections of the script to explain what the code does in complex event and function scripts
- At the beginning of a functional script, the following information should be provided as a generic script header:
  - Name of the script
  - Purpose of the script
  - Author(s)
  - Creation date
  - Revision dates history with brief description of major changes
  - Description of input/output arguments

Applying the code structure conventions described in Table 5-6 will facilitate future support of the system in production.

5.2.7   PROGRAM ERROR-HANDLING CONVENTIONS

Programming housekeeping chores such as the proper handling of system errors can be standardized and processed centrally by invoking generic, reusable error-handling modules to execute functions, such as displaying error messages, displaying warning notifications, writing detailed information on the occurrence of error events in a log file, and so forth.

The adoption of a centralized error-handling approach should help ensure that the handling of application errors will be processed the same way across multiple applications. The maintenance of all error messages that are located in a central table or file can then be greatly simplified. The complete set of error messages can be accessed by a particular application from a unique central location.

Be sure to insert the proper error-handling routines at the strategic points where the application procedural code interfaces with other software components. Some of the most common types of errors that can be processed through the use of reusable error handling routines appear in Table 5-7.

Table 5–7 Common Types Of Errors In A Client-server Environment

- Network communications errors
- Database server access errors
- Application server access errors
- File server access errors
- External libraries access errors (i.e., dynamic link libraries, etc.)
- Application programming interface (API) errors
- Data entry errors
- Print server errors

5.2.8 HELP SYSTEM CONVENTIONS

These conventions include those on context sensitivity and the different types of help that will be provided at the level of the application, at the level of a specific system transaction, at the level of the fields on a screen, and so forth. Provide a generic help template so developers can apply similar documentation techniques for their help sub-systems.

Activity number:	CO-2
Activity name:	Create application development and test environments
Purpose:	To create the application development and test environments that will be used to develop and thoroughly verify the application
Inputs:	DE-T12 Detailed testing strategy
Outputs:	CO-T2 Application development and test environments
Activity description:	• Ensure that each testing site has been properly prepared to accept the new hardware/software/networking equipment and facilities that will be used to develop and test the system

- For each distinct testing environment that is required, perform the following tasks:
  - Install the required hardware equipment and facilities
  - Install the required software facilities
  - Install the required networking equipment and facilities
- Test the core functionality of each specific testing component to ensure that it works properly in a standalone manner
- Verify the interoperability of the testing components when operating with each other
- Set up the test libraries that are required to support each particular testing stage
  - Acquire the disk space required to support the testing process
  - Set up the library control procedures required to manage each test environment
  - Create the different database and file libraries that are required in each testing environment
  - Initialize the database and file libraries
  - Populate the database and file libraries with the proper test data
  - Populate the libraries that will contain all the application software programs and utilities
  - Set up the proper security mechanisms to control the access to the application development and test environments
- Create, if necessary, a test environment guide that describes how to use the various software utilities provided with each specific test environment
- Back up the application development and test environments
- Walk through the application and test environment deliverables

5.3 CREATE APPLICATION DEVELOPMENT AND TEST ENVIRONMENTS

This section discusses the detailed steps involved in the creation of the application development and test environments. It also presents some tips and guidelines on how to perform this process.

5.3.1 INTRODUCTION

Certain projects might require the installation of new hardware/software/networking equipment and facilities before you can begin to develop and test the system, especially for new client-server and Web database applications for which special hardware equipment might be needed, such as a database, application, or Web servers. On the software side, the required application development tools or middleware software components should be installed and thoroughly tested prior to handing them over to the application development or testing teams.

Often you find a large diversity of hardware, software, and networking equipment that comes from different vendors which needs to be installed and properly configured for large client-server and Web applications. Often, ensuring that each component is compatible with the others it must interface with is a challenge, especially when different computing platforms are involved. Sometimes even the installation of a new version of a software product might cause some interoperability issues that might have never been experienced with the preceding version.

For large projects, the reception and installation of different application development and testing equipment and facilities will likely involve the participation of several technical groups, such as hardware and software vendor representatives, database experts, software experts, and networking experts. The amount of time required to coordinate the delivery and proper installation of all the required material can be significant. In some instances, you might even need to dedicate one person, on a full-time basis, to manage the process of preparing the development and testing site(s), acquiring all equipment and facilities, installing them, configuring them properly, and testing them thoroughly.

Plan reasonable time allowances to cover some potentially critical situations such as missed delivery dates, unforeseen environmental problems, or defective equipment.

Create a comprehensive testing environment to support the overall testing process. However, the different testing environments that are required for this purpose do not necessarily need to be created all at once. Instead, you can construct them at different stages of the development life cycle, when they are required.

The number of testing libraries and source/object code that must be controlled by the development team of a large project can be fairly significant. For large systems, you might have to assign on a full-time basis a person whose unique responsibility is strictly to manage and keep up to date the system's various test libraries and their content. You might also need to install tools to handle version control and software configuration management.

Depending on the level of sophistication that was used to create and automate the various facilities provided by the test environment, developing a thorough test environment guide might be appropriate. Some of the sections that could be included in such a document appear in Table 5-8.

You can provide the guide to the developers either via a traditional medium such as paper, or implement it in an HTML format and then quickly migrate it to the enterprise's intranet.

Table 5–8 A Test Environment Guide

- Contents at a glance
- Introduction
  - The purpose of this guide
  - How this guide is organized
- Main Body
  - A brief description of the different test libraries and how to use them
  - A brief description of the hardware/software/networking facilities that are provided with the test environment
  - A brief description of the software utilities that can be used to create or automatically generate test data, to run the tests, to verify the results, to copy a test database, to refresh a test database, and so forth.
- Appendixes

5.3.2 LOCAL VERSUS CENTRALIZED UNIT TEST DATABASES

This section discusses the respective merits of providing each developer with either his own copy of the unit test databases or a central copy that is stored on the server machine. When stored on the server, all developers share a centralized unit test database via the network. Figure 5-2 pictorially illustrates these two options.

5.3.3 THE LOCAL UNIT TEST DATABASE APPROACH

With this scenario, each developer has a local copy of the unit test database. Such an approach might be attractive to developers who work in a decentralized environment or in a situation in which they cannot easily connect to a network, such as when they are working at home or in a remote location. Most relational database vendors provide a lighter version of their more robust, industrial-strength database engine. The lighter but often fully functional version can be easily installed on a laptop. One possible disadvantage with this approach might be that you have to re-install the database on each workstation if its structure needs some modifications, for instance in the middle of the unit testing process.

5.3.4 THE NETWORK UNIT TEST DATABASE APPROACH

With this scenario, all developers share a common unit test database, which is implemented on a database server machine. The maintenance of the database is easy since the database administrator has to make database changes only in one central location. More advanced client-server application functions, such as database stored procedures, can also be tested more easily in such an environment. The centralized unit test database environment is usually more representative of what the future database production environment could be.

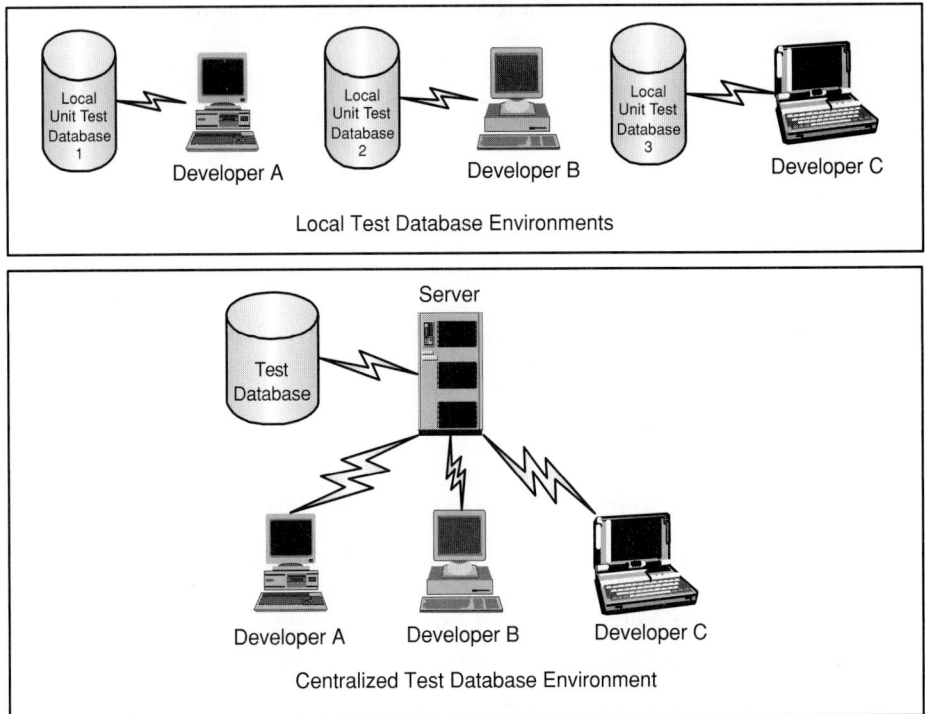

Figure 5–2 Local versus centralized unit test databases.

5.3.5   VERSION CONTROL TOOLS

When building large client-server or Web database applications, the developers must create and manage carefully a myriad of different types of files.

In general, the application development files can reside either on the developers' workstations or on the file servers or database servers. Table 5-9 lists some of the different types of application files that may be required to support a typical client-server application in a Windows environment.

Several additional types of application files must also be created to store multiple classes of various application objects, such as those enumerated in Table 5-10.

Because, for a large project, a large number of software components in different versions need to be stored in different test environments, the migration of multiple application objects from one development test library to another one is often managed with the assistance of an automated version control tool. These tools can automatically manage and control the large number of application development files that are spread on multiple servers. Similarly, these servers can reside on the same platform or across different platforms. In large projects, one project team member is usually responsible

Table 5–9 Different Application File Types

Application File Type	Description
DLL	Dynamic linked library
SQL	SQL query script
EXE	Executable module
TXT	Text file
DOC	General purpose documentation file
C	Source program in C language
RES	Resource file for C
HLP	Help file
HTM	Source file for HTML internet/intranet code
RTF	Rich text format file
LIB	Windows static library
A	UNIX static library
ICO	File for icons
BMP	File for BMP images
BAT	Batch file
AWK	UNIX script file

Table 5–10 Additional Application Objects

• Menus	• Windows
• GUI controls	• Functions
• Scripts	• Structures
• Projects	

for managing the migration of the multiple files and application objects between the different development libraries.

Following are some Web site addresses of software configuration management tool vendors:

http://www.intersolv.com	(PVCS)
http://www.pureatria.com	(ClearCase)
http://www.microsoft.com	(SourceSafe)

5.3.6   FILE DIRECTORY AND AUTHORIZATION STRUCTURES

Prior to starting the actual application coding process, create a standard directory and file authorization structure for all application development and test environments. The use of a standard directory and file authorization structure will increase the efficiency of the developers because they will use and share common application file structures that are similar from one environment to another.

In an environment where the application libraries are well organized, the time a developer might take to locate a particular application object can be greatly reduced since all the required file types have been set up in an optimal configuration. Figure 5-3 shows a sample of a generic file directory structure. You can customize it to satisfy the particular needs of a specific application development project.

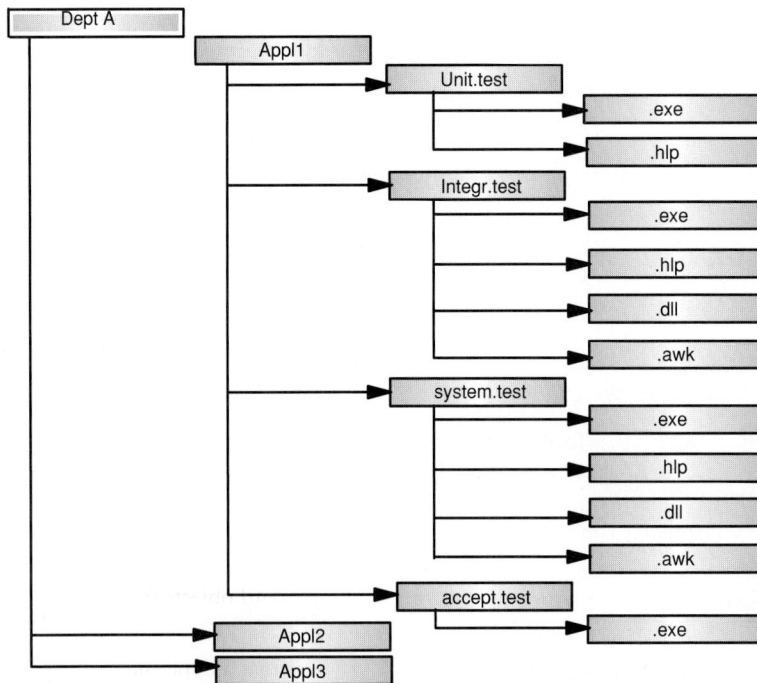

Figure 5–3 Directory structure.

5.3.7   APPLICATION DEVELOPMENT LIBRARIES AND PERFORMANCE
CONSIDERATIONS

Several client-server visual RAD tools, such as Powerbuilder, do not impose a limit on how large the particular application development libraries can be. However, the guidelines that are provided in Table 5-11 should help the developers avoid potential performance problems when they code and test a large client-server system. Although these guidelines are specifically aimed at a Power Builder development environment, the high-level principles can still apply to similar object-oriented visual development tools.

Table 5–11 Performance Considerations For Application Development Libraries

- Try to maintain the size of the application development libraries at a reasonable size, preferably smaller than 900K. This will allow an acceptable performance level as the RAD tool searches various application objects that are opened or saved frequently during the entire development process.
- Try to impose a limit on the number of libraries that contain only a few application objects. This approach will improve the response time of the RAD tool while it has to search the application development libraries to locate a specific software object.
- Try to limit the number of application objects that can be contained in a library to a manageable level.

5.3.8 LIBRARY CONSIDERATIONS FOR OBJECT INHERITANCE

For a very simple client-server application, you might be able to store all the application objects into a single library. However, a large-scale client-server application will definitely require the development of a significant number of objects. In turn, these objects will need to be stored in multiple distinct libraries. The libraries that store the application objects can be organized to advantageously exploit the object-inheritance capabilities that are supported by several categories of RAD tools.

Figure 5-4 illustrates a possible organization scheme that takes full advantage of object-inheritance.

Table 5-12 describes the application libraries shown in Figure 5-4 and their contents.

Table 5–12 Different Application Libraries

Ancestor. lib	This library contains all the ancestor objects that are utilized in the application
Common. lib	This library contains all the standard objects that are used across applications
Appl. A lib	This library contains the objects that are specific to application A
Appl. B lib	This library contains the objects that are specific to application B

Activity number:	**CO-3**
Activity name:	Develop application programs
Purpose:	To generate all the source code modules and programs required by the system, using the pertinent application development tool

Inputs:	DE-T3 Physical database design
	DE-T7 System interfaces design
	DE-T8 Data conversion programs design
	DE-T9 Ad hoc report and query environment design
	CO-T2 Application development and test environments
	Shared software components design
	Application software components design
Outputs:	CO-T3 Application programs
Activity description:	• Review the appropriate program specifications
	• Create all the online and batch source code modules and programs that are required for the system
	• Obtain a clean compilation of the source code for each module and program
	• Provide an appropriate level of documentation inside each module and program as per the enterprise's programming and documentation standards

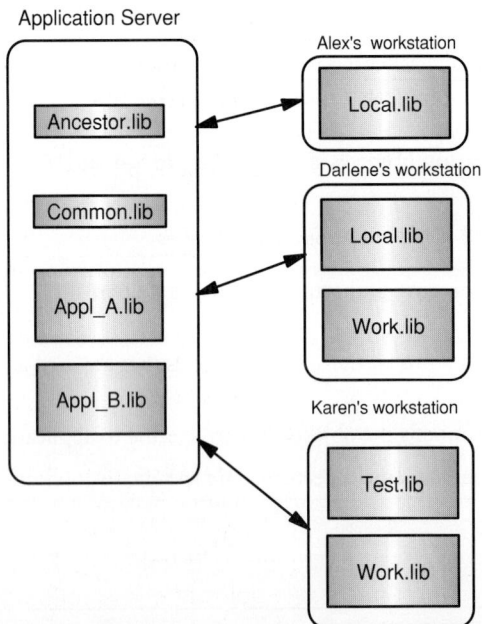

Figure 5–4 Library structure.

5.4 DEVELOP APPLICATION PROGRAMS

In this activity, you create the complete set of application modules and programs with the pertinent application development tools. The coding process is highly iterative in nature. Typically, the developers start by coding a small module or section of a program, test its functionality, fix the defects that have been detected, and once it works, add more functionality to it.

All system modules and programs should conform to the enterprise naming conventions and coding standards.

Ideally, complex procedural logic should be directly documented inside the program's source code. Also, appropriate comments should be provided to document various information such as the purpose of the module or program, the author, and any particular peculiarities.

The developers should always structure the programs and their source code in a manner that will enhance their future maintainability. Table 5-13 lists some of the most common quality guidelines that are generally prescribed to enhance the future maintainability of the software programs.

Table 5–13 Basic Guidelines To Enhance Software Program Maintainability

- Adhere to structured coding standards (modularity and simplicity: sequence, iteration, and selection constructs)
- Create single entry and single exit point constructs
- Ensure traceability of the program code back to the design specifications
- Embed small documentation blocks directly in the programs
- Use local variables instead of shared or global variables, whenever possible
- Reuse procedural logic code or graphical user interface objects via inheritance mechanisms or shared software components

For large and complex client-server and Web database systems, you might find it worthwhile to conduct informal or even formal reviews of the most critical online and batch programs to ensure they are optimized and comply to the enterprise application development standards. Table 5-14 enumerates some of the standards that the developers could verify while reviewing these critical programs.

The level of formality that should be applied to the code review process will likely vary from one organization to another depending on their corporate culture and commitment to deliver high-quality products. As a simple rule of thumb, the level of formality that should be applied while conducting technical peer reviews should be commensurate to the level of criticality and complexity of the online or batch programs.

The use of powerful RAD tools, combined with the utilization of robust debugging and automated testing tools, can definitely help the developers test their client-server systems in an effective and efficient manner. Nevertheless, simple code review

Table 5–14 Application Development Standards

- Corporate GUI design standards (consistency of windows look and feel)
- Object-oriented programming standards (i.e., inheritance, encapsulation, polymorphism)
- Program documentation standards
- Program naming standards
- Database access standards
- Error- and exception-handling standards
- Standards for coding stored procedures, remote procedures, and database triggers
- Reusability standards
- Code maintainability standards
- Cross-platform development standards
- Quality standards

techniques such as those you see in Figure 5-5 might still prove to be valuable alternatives in order to help identify potential errors or inconsistencies in mission-critical programs.

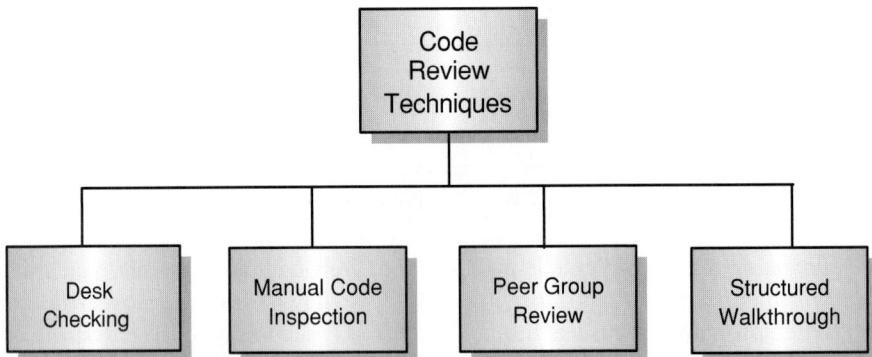

Figure 5–5 Code review techniques.

If some of the review techniques shown in Figure 5-5 are used in a disciplined, yet pragmatic manner, then they might definitely have their place in the arsenal of techniques that the developers can use to improve the overall quality of their software deliverables.

Table 5-15 lists some of the potential benefits that can be associated with code review techniques if they are implemented in a disciplined, yet flexible and pragmatic approach.

Table 5–15 Code Review Benefits

- Decreased error-debugging time
- Early detection of defects that would be much more costly to fix in later phases of the development cycle or worse, in production
- Enforced, better adherence to established standards
- Increased program readability
- Increased program maintainability
- Detection of serious design flaws and code inefficiencies
- Sharing of best object-oriented coding practices with peers

Activity number:	CO-4
Activity name:	Conduct unit testing
Purpose:	To test each application module/program to uncover potential defects in its internal logic or procedural code
Inputs:	CO-T2 Application development and test environments CO-T3 Application programs
Outputs:	CO-T4 Unit testing completion report

Activity description:	• If this step was not done during the design phase, construct a representative set of test cases and test data to exercise the internal procedural logic of each application batch or online program
	• Execute the unit tests against each specific application program
	• Analyze and compare actual test results against expected results
	• If defects are found, determine their root cause
	  – If it is a coding or program logic defect, correct the program and re-execute the required unit test(s)
	  – If the defects are major and originate from incorrect analysis or program design specifications, follow the required change control procedures to log the identified problem and develop an adequate solution to resolve it
	• When all unit test cases have been exercised successfully, document the unit test results and promote the tested programs to the application integration test libraries

5.5   CONDUCT UNIT TESTING

Unit testing is performed against each program to ensure that all modules operate according to their design specifications. The tests are executed independently of other programs, in a standalone manner.

In many cases, the same individual who developed the program creates the unit test data and performs unit testing. In some organizations, however, an independent group that did not participate in the development of the programs handles the overall unit testing process. The proponents of this approach believe that "outsiders" who have not been involved in the creation of the application code will not have "psychological" difficulties in attempting to intentionally "destroy" the programs. Experience has shown that projects that use an independent testing team will likely identify more defects than the original development team would normally do, while spending the same amount of effort on such a task. If, for whatever reasons, this approach cannot be used, an acceptable alternative could be to ask programmer X to test the programs written by programmer Y and vice versa.

Usually, the unit test data is fictitious. However, the unit test cases should not be randomly selected but should be carefully constructed to exercise all the procedural statements in the program.

Perform functional testing first with valid test data to ensure that the program works well in a normal situation and satisfies the program specifications. Then use specific test data that simulate abnormal situations to verify that the program works as expected under borderline conditions. Also, create specific test data to verify how the program handles exceptions. Lastly, perform destructive testing using extreme test cases in a definite attempt to break the program.

Even though sound unit test cases can be built to exercise full coverage of the program's entire executable source code statements, you still have no guarantee that the program will be totally defect-free. Rather, test cases only certify that the internal logic of the program works with the test cases that have been used to exercise the procedural code.

Still, though, you need to come up with a test completion measure that will indicate to the software tester that the internal logic of the program has been adequately tested and, therefore, that the unit test process for this program can be recognized as complete. Two of the most widely used unit testing completion criteria are indicated in Table 5-16.

Table 5–16 Unit Testing Completion Criteria

Statement coverage	At the bare minimum, all the program's executable source code statements have been executed at least once
Branch coverage	Each branching statement of a program is executed at least once for each alternative execution path

Perform unit testing uniquely with "live" production data with extreme caution because you have no guarantee that all the logic paths of the program will be fully exercised during the testing process. Once again, performing quality unit testing is not necessarily a question of volume of data, but rather of engineering a representative yet minimal set of test data samples that will uncover as many internal defects as possible.

Save the most representative unit test cases and data that were created to uncover program logic defects in a special project library for the duration of the project in case retests become necessary. For this purpose, an automated testing tool that can store the test results and test cases can become quite useful for large projects. Developing, updating, and maintaining test cases might become a burden, as their number rapidly increases when testing a large and complex system which contains several graphical user interface components. Maintaining the test cases and test data in a central location will make them readily available to everyone who might need them and make them easily modified or augmented to meet new testing criteria. This way, the test cases and data can be recycled for other use.

Activity number:	CO-5
Activity name:	Conduct integration testing
Purpose:	To integrate the application modules/programs with each other and progressively test them as a combined set
Inputs:	CO-T2 Application development and test environments CO-T3 Application programs
Outputs:	CO-T5 Integration testing completion report
Activity description:	• If this step is not already done, identify the set of programs that will be integrated into distinct test cycles and how they will be incrementally tested to ensure they work properly, when assembled together as a whole • Create the integration test data for each testing cycle • Execute the application integration testing cycles • Analyze the outcome of the tests and compare them against the expected results • If defects are found, determine their root cause; if required, demote the defective programs to the unit test environment and issue a system change request to resolve the problems encountered during the application integration testing process • When the integrated programs work well as a whole, promote them to the system test libraries

5.6   CONDUCT INTEGRATION TESTING

The primary purpose of the application integration testing process is to demonstrate that the unit-tested programs do work properly with each other when they are progressively assembled together to eventually operate as a cohesive, integrated system.

A critical success factor inherent in application integration testing is the establishment of a sound problem-reporting procedure. The problems that are uncovered during this testing phase must be properly documented and ideally should be logged in a central repository. Then, prioritize and assign them to programmers for resolution. Also track them while the programs are being repaired. Once the problems are fixed, retest the programs, and review again and approve the test results. The corrected programs are repromoted in the integration test environment and integration testing is then performed again.

Most of the time, a lead tester or an independent testing team does integration testing. The "politics" of testing will often start to surface during the application integration testing process. When defects are detected in the software programs, some programmers might react as if they were the victims of an organized witch-hunt, especially if the lead tester or independent testing group views the testing cycle as a destructive process. Moreover, the programmers who might be busy coding other programs might view the retesting process as additional work.

The best way to avoid such potential problems is to educate the programmers on the concept of destructiveness and how it applies to software testing. Also, the project leader or manager must acknowledge the need for programmers to repair their programs. Consequently, the testing schedule should reflect this harsh reality by including some additional time for the programmers to find the source of the reported problems, fix them, and retest their programs.

The second category of people to consider are the project managers. If too many problems are uncovered during application integration testing, the project managers might start to feel threatened by the concept of destructive testing because this probably means some schedule slippage for the project. The project manager might then be tempted to document only the identified problems and see that they get resolved with the delivery of the next release. This delay-to-later approach might work fine for minor problems but certainly will not work for major ones.

Another type of problem might arise when the application integration testing process is done at a high level, since the programmers assume by default that the users are responsible for fully demonstrating that the entire system satisfies their original requirements. At this point, you might explain to the management team the rationale behind the philosophy of destructive testing and emphasize that uncovering and resolving these defects now is far better than doing so when the system goes into production. Finally, the same set of software testing tools that were used during unit testing can also be used for the application integration testing process.

Activity number:	CO-6
Activity name:	Conduct system testing
Purpose:	To verify the full functionality and operational characteristics of the complete application, in an environment that mirrors as much as possible the production environment
Inputs:	CO-T2 Application development and test environments CO-T3 Application programs
Outputs:	CO-T6 System testing completion report
Activity description:	• Organize the system testing activities as documented in the system testing strategy • Create the system test data • Execute the system testing process • Analyze the outcome of the system tests and compare them against the expected results • If defects are found, determine their root cause; if required, demote the defective programs to the application integration test environment and issue a system change request to resolve the problems encountered during the system testing process • When the reported defects have been fixed and successfully re-tested, promote the programs to the user acceptance test libraries

5.7 CONDUCT SYSTEM TESTING

The prime objective of the system testing process is to test the complete application system to demonstrate that it truly satisfies the users' business requirements, within the constraints of the available technology. The system testing process must also demonstrate that the application can satisfy its operational requirements.

Consequently, the system testing process should encompass not only functional testing but also testing of the system main security, performance, and backup/recovery features, along with any specific operating constraints that must be satisfied by the system. Similarly, the system must also be carefully tested to verify its ability to satisfy the stated service-level objectives. Ideally, the system tests should be conducted in an environment that mirrors as much as possible the future production environment.

Depending on the different characteristics of the system at hand, different categories of tests can be executed at varying levels of granularity, as you see in Table 5-17.

The system tests should verify the extent to which the system is reliable and help detect potential faulty equipment. The tests are executed in a wide context and should cover the online, batch, and even manual components of the system.

Table 5–17 Different System Testing Scenarios

- Usability tests
- Stress and volume tests
- Security, controls, and audit tests
- Performance tests
- Cross-platform interoperability tests
- Backup/recovery tests
- System interfaces tests

Although the data processing staff performs system testing, sometimes you might find it useful to involve some key user representatives in the execution of the system test activities. User participation in the system testing process allows key user personnel who will be involved in conducting the user acceptance testing process to better prepare themselves for that assignment.

Depending on the type of defects that are uncovered during application system testing, some level of regression testing might be required to ensure that the corrected programs do not inadvertently introduce new defects into other components of the system.

Finally, the system tests should also cover the programs that will be used to perform the conversion of legacy data into the new formats required by the new system.

Activity number:	CO-7
Activity name:	Conduct user acceptance testing
Purpose:	To allow the users to verify that the system satisfies the stated business requirements and objectives
Inputs:	CO-T2 Application development and test environments CO-T3 Application programs
Outputs:	CO-T7 User acceptance testing completion report
Activity description:	• Organize the user acceptance testing activities as documented in the acceptance testing strategy; if necessary, train the user acceptance test team that will be called upon to perform the overall testing process • Create the user acceptance test cases • Execute the user acceptance testing process • Analyze the outcome of the tests and compare it against the expected results

- If defects are found, determine their root cause; if required, demote the defective programs to the system test environment and issue a system change request to resolve the problems encountered during the user acceptance testing process
- When the reported defects have been fixed and successfully re-tested, promote the programs to the set of libraries that will be transferred into the final production environment

5.8 CONDUCT USER ACCEPTANCE TESTING

The prime objective of user acceptance testing is to allow the users to test the complete system's functionality and ensure that it satisfies the business objectives and requirements that were originally documented with the users. The user acceptance testing process should also demonstrate that the system satisfies the formally documented operational and environmental constraints and service levels. The user acceptance tests are executed in an environment that should reflect a standard business mode of operations.

To a large extent, the development team already tested the functionality of the system during the application system testing process, but the users themselves must verify its functionality carefully to finally approve the new system.

Contrary to application system testing, where the developers were accountable for executing all the test cases, the users are responsible for testing the system during the user acceptance testing process. Representatives of the departments who will use the system most heavily should actively participate in the user acceptance testing process. The role of the developers is a support role. They are responsible for setting up and supporting the user acceptance test environment and for assisting the users when they perform the user acceptance tests.

The acceptance tests should cover the system in its entirety, from all the automated components up to and including all the manual procedures. A large portion of the most representative test cases and data that were used to execute the system testing process can be recycled for the user acceptance testing process. However, the users need to create their own set of test cases and data to verify the system. The user tests should allow the users to validate the acceptance criteria that were originally stated for the system, such as the original performance objectives. The users also need to verify the detailed conversion strategy and test all the conversion programs that will be used to transform the legacy data into the specific formats that are required by the new system.

Be very sure to put in place the proper test control procedures that are required to successfully manage the user acceptance testing process. These include the proper library control, change control, problem reporting, problem tracking, and problem resolution procedures.

Several organizations might insist that various data center operations groups directly participate in the user acceptance testing effort, especially for large projects. Together with the users, the system operations groups then test the system, while performing their regular, day-to-day operations support activities, to ensure that the system can fit within the established data center operations schedule. They also verify that the system can operate well in its target business production environment. In such a context, the user acceptance testing effort encompasses those people who must create input data for the system, those people who must operate and support the system, and those who might have to distribute various system outputs such as printed reports.

Activity number:	CO-8
Activity name:	Create the installation strategy
Purpose:	To create an application installation strategy for the production environment
Inputs:	AN-T15 Hardware/software/networking requirements
Outputs:	CO-T8 Installation strategy
Activity description:	• Develop a strategy to migrate the new system application components to the production environment and install all the equipment and facilities that are required by the users to use the new system • Walk through the detailed application installation strategy

5.9 CREATE THE INSTALLATION STRATEGY

The installation strategy describes the detailed sequence of tasks that is required to install the new application system components in the production environment. It also provides a detailed description of the procedures that must be followed to install, configure, and test all the hardware, software, and networking equipment and facilities that are required in the user areas, along with the sequence in which these installations must be performed.

Typically, a specialized department within the Information Systems organization performs the installation of the hardware and software equipment and facilities in the user environment.

Activity number:	CO-9
Activity name:	Create the system cut-over strategy
Purpose:	To develop the system cut-over strategy that will be used to migrate the new system to production and turn it on

Inputs:	DE-T13 Detailed data conversion strategy CO-T8 Installation strategy
Outputs:	CO-T9 System cut-over strategy
Activity description:	• Develop the detailed strategy that will be used to perform the conversion process, turn the new system on, and phase out the old system • Walk through the cut-over strategy

5.10 CREATE THE SYSTEM CUT-OVER STRATEGY

The cut-over strategy describes the detailed activities that will be used to perform the data conversion process, activate the new system in its production environment, and phase out the old system. It also documents the sequence in which all these activities need to be performed.

The cut-over strategy should cover the items that you see in Table 5-18.

Table 5–18 The System Cut-over Strategy

- How will the conversion process be handled?
- How will the new system be activated?
- How will the interfaces between the new system and existing systems be activated? In which sequence?
- How will the old system be phased out?
- How will the new system be supported during its initial shakedown period?
- Do specific cut-over issues need to be handled in a non-standard manner?

6

Implementation

6.1 INTRODUCTION

The prime objective of the implementation phase is to install the new system in its production environment and ensure that it is fully operational.

Table 6-1 describes a set of core objectives for the implementation phase.

Table 6–1 Implementation Phase Objectives

- Train the various users on how to best utilize the new system
- Train the data center personnel on how to operate the new system
- Train the application support personnel on how to maintain and evolve the new system
- Install the new system in its production environment and turn it on
- Fine-tune the new system

Table 6-2 summarizes the major technical activities that are conducted during the implementation phase, along with a list of the anticipated technical deliverables.

Figure 6-1 pictorially presents, at a high level, the relationships that exist among the individual activities of the implementation phase.

Although the linear sequence in which you see the implementation phase activities in Figure 6-1 might suggest that one specific activity must be completed prior to beginning the next one, in fact, they can be performed concurrently or in different sequences.

Furthermore, several of these activities can be performed with an iterative approach, gradually refining the activity deliverables in incremental steps. On the other hand, certain types of activities might not easily lend themselves to an iterative development approach.

Table 6–2 Implementation Phase

ACTIVITY	DELIVERABLE(S)
1. Perform data conversion and verification	1. The data conversion and verification report
2. Install hardware/software/networking equipment and facilities in the user environment	2. Hardware/software/networking equipment and facilities installation report
3. Complete the detailed system documentation guides	3. Detailed system documentation guides
4. Finalize the system training package	4. The final training package
5. Train the users and data center/ application support personnel	5. The final system training report
6. Migrate the new system into production and turn it on	6. The system migration report
7. Fine-tune the new production system	7. The system optimization report
8. Develop the system support and evolution strategy	8. The system support and evolution strategy
9. Conduct the project post-mortem	9. The project post-mortem report

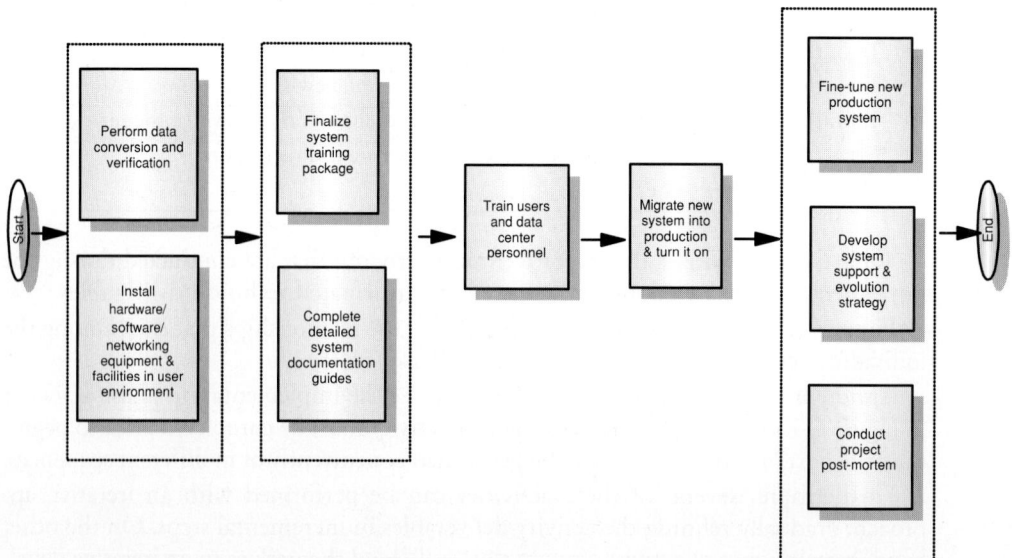

Figure 6–1 Implementation phase activities.

At the completion of each major implementation phase activity, a formal walk-through should be scheduled to review the final outcome of each activity, which is comprised of a set of specific system deliverables.

Activity number:	IM-1
Activity name:	Perform data conversion and verification
Purpose:	To convert legacy data from the old production system to the new production system
Inputs:	DE-T3 Detailed data conversion strategy
Outputs:	IM-T1 Data conversion and verification report

Activity description:	• Ensure that all the hardware, operating system software, and application software required for the conversion process have been properly installed, configured, and tested to ensure that it is fully operational
	• If necessary, verify that the source data has been carefully cleaned up prior to launching the conversion process
	• Execute the conversion programs and procedures in accordance with the sequence of events documented in the detailed data conversion strategy and detailed execution plan
	  – If required, download the source data from the mainframe system and create ASCII flat files
	  – Execute any required data translation or transformation
	  – Transfer the data into the new production system files and databases
	• Verify that the converted data contained in the new system production files and databases has been properly converted and is complete and accurate
	• If defects or discrepancies are found, determine their root cause and apply the appropriate corrective measures
	• If necessary, archive the old system files and databases for future references or audit purposes
	• Create the data conversion completion report

6.2 PERFORM DATA CONVERSION AND VERIFICATION

The prime objective of the data conversion process is to convert all required legacy data from the old production system into the new production system, using the proper data conversion programs and software utilities. Data conversion is a very crucial process. Depending on the complexity of the overall conversion process, you might need to train the users on how to adequately prepare themselves to perform the various data conversion activities in the most effective manner possible, such as preparing forms, data entry, and manual conversion procedures.

After each step of the data conversion process, the users need to verify and validate the converted data and ensure that it is complete and accurate. If they detect errors, quickly correct them. Once the data conversion process has been successfully completed, then all the data required by the new system is ready to be used in the production environment.

The data conversion process can be executed all at once or phased over an extended period of time, depending on the amount of data to be converted and its location. For some very large systems, the conversion process can turn out to be a complex, labor-intensive multi-step process, which might extend over a few days, weeks, or even several months. The data conversion process must be scheduled to terminate in time for the agreed system production target date.

If the data conversion process must be extended over a prolonged period of time, you must maintain the integrity of the legacy and new data files and databases. This data synchronization task might be required throughout the period of time that is required to successfully complete the entire conversion process.

For large systems, the data conversion process is usually performed during off-peak hours to ensure that the additional processing load created by converting the data from the old system to the new system does not adversely affect the regular data center operations or the user's ongoing business processes. During the data conversion process, the users momentarily stop entering new data into the old system to ensure that no data is missed during the conversion process.

The data conversion process often involves the migration of not only computerized data, but also manual data that was contained on printed reports, forms, or other types of paper-based media. In such instances, you might need to specifically train the data entry personnel on how to validate the input data, enter it into the new system, and correct errors when they occur.

Prior to converting data, you must ensure that the data "cleansing" procedures for cleaning up the legacy data have been successfully executed.

Finally, for certain types of systems, you might need to store the legacy data into historical files, which can be restored and accessed later on, whenever necessary. For instance, you might have to archive financial data to address future audit processes.

Activity number:	IM-2
Activity name:	Install hardware/software/networking equipment and facilities in user environment
Purpose:	To receive and install at each required user location the hardware/software/networking equipment and facilities required for providing access to the new system and supporting it

Inputs:	CO-T8 Installation strategy
Outputs:	IM-T2 Hardware/software/networking equipment and facilities installation report
Activity description:	• Verify that each user installation site was properly prepared to accept the new computer equipment and facilities • Receive and install the new hardware/software/networking equipment and facilities • Configure and verify the hardware/software/networking equipment and facilities • Test the equipment and facilities with the standard installation scripts and test cases to ensure that they work properly in both a standalone and integrated mode of operation • If necessary, verify that any special computer supplies have been received in sufficient quantities in each user area • Produce the final hardware/software/networking installation completion report

6.3 INSTALL HARDWARE/SOFTWARE/NETWORKING EQUIPMENT AND FACILITIES

In this activity, all the hardware, software, and networking equipment and facilities that are required to utilize the production system in the various user work environments are successfully installed and configured.

The installation process might cover the following items:

- Hardware equipment such as monitors, workstations, and printers and specialized hardware components such as bar code guns and scanners

- Software products such as operating system software and report writers

- Custom application development software such as programs executables

- Database middleware such as ODBC drivers or native database APIs

- Network hardware and software equipment

Be certain to allocate sufficient time to install not only the equipment and facilities in the user work environment but also to configure them properly and ensure that they inter-operate well. Any issues related to the proper configuration of the equipment and facilities or their interoperability must be resolved prior to turning on the new system once it is migrated into production.

Activity number:	IM-3
Activity name:	Complete detailed system documentation guides
Purpose:	To complete the production of the various documentation guides that are required by the users and systems personnel for the new system
Inputs:	DE-T10 Preliminary system documentation
Outputs:	IM-T3 Detailed system documentation guides

Activity description:	• Review the minimum set of documentation standards that were retained for developing the different types of system guides that will be used by the users, the data center, or application support personnel
	• Prepare the technical environment that will be used to develop the system guides and ensure that the various software tools that are required to create the required guides are properly installed and configured
	• Complete the final version of the following system documentation guides:
	  – User Guide
	  – Online Help Guide
	  – System Operations Guide
	  – Technical Reference Guide
	• Walk through the system documentation deliverables for completeness, accuracy, consistency, and ease of use

6.4 COMPLETE DETAILED SYSTEM DOCUMENTATION

This activity focuses on revising and completing all required printed and online help documentation for the new application. During the previous construction phase, the content of the various system documentation guides should have been updated in parallel with the system and user acceptance testing stages. During implementation, the final versions of the guides are completed and then can be used to teach the users how to use the new system. Table 6-3 provides a brief summary of the different types of system guides that can be produced for the application system.

The level of granularity of the various guides shown in Table 6-3 will depend on the number and complexity of the business tasks that are automated by the system. The user-oriented guides might not need to be extensive for relatively small and simple applications. Ditto for the data center personnel who will have to operate and support the system.

Table 6–3 A Brief Description Of Different Types Of System Guides

User Guide	The User Guide provides a detailed description of all the critical functions and facilities that are supported by the new application. It documents the set of procedures that are required to use the system in response to all the business events to which the system must react in a preplanned manner.
Online Help Guide	This document provides the users with an online description of the system's major characteristics. These can include information on how to best interact with the graphical user interface, descriptions of the data fields contained on each specific screen, how to deal with error messages, how to use the system's generic search facilities, and so forth.
System Operations Guide	The System Operations Guide documents the set of technical procedures that are required to operate the new system in the production environment such as the backup and recovery procedures, the performance monitoring procedures, and the security procedures.
Technical Reference Guide	The Technical Reference Guide documents the core technical components of the system for those who will be called upon to support and evolve the new system once it is transferred into its final production environment.

Depending on the target audience that is being addressed by the user-oriented guides, you might want to involve professional technical writers in the system documentation process as early as possible to develop high-quality and user-friendly guides. This approach might be necessary, as developers might be neither skilled in creating user-friendly system documentation guides nor highly motivated to do so.

A preliminary version of the Online Help facility should also be prototyped with the active participation of the users, during the analysis phase, for instance, when the developers build a functional prototype. The online help prototype allows the users to provide important feedback on the basic content and "look and feel" of the online help facility.

Several specialized software-authoring tools are available on the market to automate the development of online help systems, such as for a Windows client-server environment. Following are the Web addresses of two software-authoring tool vendors that support the Windows development environment:

http://www.blue-sky.com   RoboHELP
http://www.wextech.com   Doc-To-Help

Several HTML-based authoring tools have emerged to provide an alternative way to display online help in a Web-based environment.[1] For instance, Microsoft is using a standard called HTML Help while Netscape is using a standard called NetHelp. The HTML-based Web authoring tools for online help usually support Java applets and scripting languages such as JavaScript or VBScript. As the Web technology advances, help authors will be able to benefit from more advanced HTML-based features can and integrate them into their online help systems. The two Windows-based software-authoring tool vendors listed earlier also provide a Web-based version of their client-server authoring tools.

If a cross-platform help solution is required for the new system, then you need to verify whether the Web-based software authoring tool vendor supports the standard HTML format or has extended it with specific features that might not be fully supported by all current Web browsers. For instance, if Microsoft uses embedded ActiveX controls in HTML Help, then only browsers that support the ActiveX technology will be able to display HTML Help.

Finally, preliminary templates and sample chapters of the User Guide and User Reference Guide should be reviewed with the users as early as possible to obtain feedback on their proposed organization and content.

Activity number:	IM-4
Activity name:	Finalize system training package
Purpose:	To refine and complete all the components included in the final system-training package
Inputs:	DE-T11 Detailed system training strategy
Outputs:	IM-T4 Final training package
Activity description:	• Review and finalize the contents of the system training package in light of all the information gathered so far on the new system • Evaluate the duration of each particular type of training session and prepare the detailed training schedule, based on the number of different groups of users requiring training; complete the appropriate lists of attendees for each training session • Confirm, if required, the availability of the various training facilities (i.e., classroom sessions, computer-based training, training rooms, and equipment) • Walk through the final training package

---

1. For additional information on HTML-based help tools, refer to Chapter 11.

6.5   FINALIZE THE SYSTEM TRAINING PACKAGE

The formal training material should be prepared so that the users and operations systems personnel can be trained on how to use, operate, and support the new system in the most effective manner, prior to its implementation in the production environment.

The training material can include various items such as student handouts, slides, overhead transparencies, video segments, computer-based training modules, and case studies. It can also include the various system documentation guides that were developed to assist the users in performing their business activities with the new application. The most effective training sessions often include hands-on interaction with the new system functions. Such an approach will increase the confidence of the users in their ability to use the new system in an efficient manner.

The training material should be organized in a top-down manner, describing the system from a general level, down to a more detailed level of information. In some instances, you might need to tailor some specific components of the training package to suit the specific needs of the targeted audience. A separate training environment is the preferred approach for large systems, especially if a large number of users need to be trained over an extended period of time. Sometimes, the user acceptance test environment is used for this purpose, once the acceptance test process has been completed successfully.

For large systems, one of the best ways to verify the effectiveness and technical accuracy of the training material is to conduct small pilot sessions during which selective end user and operations systems representatives are trained with the appropriate material. This approach will allow the trainers to receive constructive feedback on how well the training objectives can be met. The trainers will also be in a better position to evaluate the overall duration of the training sessions and subsequently adjust the training schedules if necessary. Divide the training sessions into manageable segments that do not overwhelm the students with too much information at once.

Be sure to discuss and negotiate with the users what the most appropriate training schedules could be, in order to minimize the potentially disruptive impact of the training process on their daily operations. Ideally, the training process should be delivered as close as possible to the date on which the new system will be transferred into its production environment.

Activity number:	IM-5
Activity name:	Train users and data center personnel
Purpose:	To formally train the user personnel to use the new system and the operations systems staff on how to operate it
Inputs:	IM-T4 Final training package

Outputs:	IM-T5 Final system training report
Activity description:	• Finalize the detailed training schedules with all affected personnel • Train all user groups and their managers to use the new system • Train the operations systems personnel to support the system and its users • If necessary, train the systems developers who will maintain and evolve the new system • Produce the final training completion report

6.6 TRAIN THE USERS AND DATA CENTER/APPLICATION SUPPORT PERSONNEL

In this activity, the users are trained to effectively use the various manual and automated components of the new system. The data center staff also is trained to operate the new system. This formal training will allow the operations personnel to operate and support the new system in the most effective manner possible. Some representatives of the Help Desk should also be trained at the same time the users are being trained so they can develop a high-level understanding of the major functions supported by the new system.

Basically, you can use three different strategies to train the users: the direct training, "train the trainer," or computer-based approaches. In the direct training approach, the development team members directly train the users. In the "train the trainer" approach, the development team trains a given number of user instructors who, in turn, will provide training to all the end users. In the computer-based training approach, the users can be trained individually at their own convenience. However, computer-based training is not always the most effective way of teaching the users how to use the new system because this approach does not provide direct interactions between the users and the teacher such as in a classroom, instructor-led approach.

No matter which training strategy is used, ensure that the trainees fill in the course evaluation forms at the end of each training session. This task is important to allow the trainers to assess the effectiveness of the training programs and ensure that the user trainees acquire the new skills they require for performing their business activities with the assistance of the new system.

Schedule the user training sessions in a just-in-time mode as much as possible. Ideally, the users should be trained on how to use the system just before they start to use it. Otherwise, a high risk exists that they will forget much of what they have been taught during the training sessions. Also, a preferable approach is to train the users in a remote location away from the user's work area, to allow the users to concentrate on training rather than work-related issues.

Finally, the responsibility to provide ongoing training to new users often falls on a special user group, especially when the user population is fairly large. If this approach turns out to be the case in your organization, then carefully train this special group to use the system. Moreover, train them to use the training material that will be put at their disposal to train people later on, long after the system has been transferred into production.

Activity number:	IM-6
Activity name:	Migrate new system into production and turn it on
Purpose:	To migrate all required application development deliverables from the user acceptance environment into the production environment
Inputs:	CO-T9 System cut-over strategy
Outputs:	IM-T6 System migration report
Activity description:	• Transfer all required application development software deliverables from the development environment to the production environment • Verify that all the proper system components were successfully transferred into the production libraries • Distribute the sets of paper or electronic system guides to users and operation systems representatives • Turn the production system on and verify that its level of operability and functionality is adequate • Turn over the system to the users • If applicable, phase out the old system • Complete the production system migration report

6.7 MIGRATE THE NEW SYSTEM INTO PRODUCTION AND TURN IT ON

In this activity, all the application software components that are required to run the new system are finally transferred into the production environment. The production data was migrated during the data conversion process with specific software conversion programs and utilities.

The application software components are migrated into the production libraries and submitted to a production change and software configuration management control process. The new system is finally turned on.

If the new system replaces an older system, then the old system is phased out. Prior to phasing out the old system and turning off the switch, you might need to archive all the old system programs and data. The old hardware, software, and networking equipment and facilities can then be removed from the current production environment. The complete phase-out of the old system is usually done a couple of days after the new system has been in use, to ensure that everything works well. During this time, the old system can be accessed usually in a read-only mode to maintain the data integrity of the new system.

Activity number:	IM-7
Activity name:	Fine-tune new production system
Purpose:	To fix minor problems detected after the new system was transferred into its production environment, and to optimize its operations, where required
Inputs:	New system documentation
Outputs:	IM-T7 System optimization report

Activity description:	• Monitor the application system in the production environment and assess the overall levels of performance, reliability, and operability, covering the following points:
	  – System response time
	  – Execution time of batch jobs
	  – Execution time of software utility programs such as backup/recovery
	  – Security operations
	  – Reliability of client workstations and related computing equipment
	  – Inaccuracies in user and system documentation guides
	  – Network performance
	  – Inter-operability issues
	• Identify the specific areas where the original service level agreements have not been attained satisfactorily; determine the root causes of the identified problems and apply the appropriate solutions.

6.8   OPTIMIZE AND FINE-TUNE THE NEW PRODUCTION SYSTEM

Despite all the efforts spent in trying to meet the established system operational requirements while designing, developing, and testing the new software application, chances are that a large and complex system will still need to be optimized and fine-tuned shortly after it has been transferred into its production environment.

For example, the fine-tuning of the most critical online transactions might become an important issue because the performance of the entire online environment might drastically suffer if these critical transactions do not perform as planned.

Typically, the post-implementation system fine-tuning process can take up to two months for a large and complex system. At the same time, the documentation of the system should be completed, if not yet done, prior to releasing all the development team members.

Centralize the reporting of problems to ensure that all issues are known to the MIS organization in a controlled manner. Usually, the users will report the system problems through the Help Desk department.

However, the developers need to remain alert and closely monitor and respond to system problems in a very pro-active manner following the transfer of the system into its production environment. Ideally, the proper tools that will allow you to adequately monitor the overall system performance have been already installed in the production environment, and specific hooks into the new application were made to monitor and analyze the response time of the most critical transactions and quickly make corrections where appropriate.

Once the system has been fine-tuned and has reached a stable performance level, then the system is transitioned into a regular maintenance mode. The system's shake-down period is then officially terminated.

Activity number:	IM-8
Activity name:	Develop system support and evolution strategy
Purpose:	To finalize the system support strategy that is required to evolve the system over its useful lifetime
Inputs:	New system documentation
Outputs:	IM-T8 System support and evolution strategy
Activity description:	• Develop the system support and evolution strategy taking into consideration the following points: – System change requests that were officially approved during the development cycle but were purposely deferred until the system maintenance and evolution phase – Total MIS personnel required to support the new system – System releases that have been planned in the near future – Ongoing system housekeeping activities – Ongoing system training activities

6.9   DEVELOP THE SYSTEM SUPPORT AND EVOLUTION STRATEGY

In this activity, the list of future system enhancements are reviewed with the users and prioritized accordingly. Depending on the amount of work involved and available resources, the planned enhancements can be grouped into different implementation releases.

If the initial developers of the new system will not participate in its maintenance and evolution, then transfer their most critical system knowledge to those individuals who will maintain and evolve the system, over a reasonable period of time.

Activity number:	IM-9
Activity name:	Conduct project post-mortem
Purpose:	To examine the development processes used during the project and determine their effectiveness in satisfying the business needs of the organization
Inputs:	New system documentation
	Project management documentation
Outputs:	IM-T9 Project post-mortem report
Activity description:	• Gather the following information from the users and their management: – General level of user satisfaction attained with the new system – Level of usability achieved by the system and the extent to which it is used by the users – Timeliness, correctness, accuracy, and effectiveness of the information processed by the new system – Level of performance achieved by the new system versus the original requirements – Adequacy, timeliness, and effectiveness of the training provided to the user personnel – Appropriateness, completeness, and accuracy of the user documentation guides (i.e., paper and electronic formats) – Verification of the internal controls embedded in the new system – Reliability of the hardware/software/networking equipment and facilities – Effectiveness of the security and control procedures put in place to prevent system abuses

- Relevance, reliability, and effectiveness of the manual or automated system interfaces that have been implemented with other systems
- Timeliness and quality of the support services provided by the system operations and maintenance staff
- Positive and negative impacts of the new system on the users and their business environment
- Relevance and effectiveness of the technology used to implement the new system

• Gather the following information from the users and system professionals who participated in the development of the new system:
- Appropriateness and effectiveness of the technical processes, activities, standards, and guidelines prescribed by the development methodology
- Adequacy and accuracy of the development time estimates
- Reasons for deviating from the original schedules
- An assessment as to whether the scope of the project was appropriate and the extent to which it was controlled during the entire project
- Level of quality achieved while developing the technical deliverables
- Effectiveness and level of completeness of the testing process and its supportive test environments
- Relevance and effectiveness of the automated tools used to analyze, prototype, design, code, and test the system
- Relevance and effectiveness of the automated tools used for version control and software configuration management
- Relevance and effectiveness of the technology used to implement the new system, including the hardware, software, and network components and facilities
- Appropriateness and effectiveness of the project management processes, tools, activities, standards, and guidelines prescribed by the methodology for planning, estimating, controlling, and monitoring the development of the new system
- Potential suggestions to improve the performance of the development team

• Gather the following information from the system operations professionals who must operate the new system:
- Level of completeness, technical relevance, and effectiveness of the computer operations guides and procedures used to operate the new system in production
- Description of the major system production problems encountered so far, if any

- Gather the following information from the system maintenance professionals who must support and evolve the new system:
  - Type and number of requests received for system enhancements
  - Type and number of defects encountered while supporting the new system
  - The effectiveness of the knowledge transfer process from the developers to the system support team
  - Completeness and effectiveness of the technical system documentation guides
  - Level of maintainability and flexibility achieved by the system (quality of design, coding, and internal program documentation)
- Review and consolidate all the findings of the study in terms of problems and successes encountered during the development cycle and after the installation of the system in its production environment
- Provide recommendations on how to avoid in the future the problems that were experienced during the system development stages; document the recommendations on how to modify the methodology to improve the overall system development process based on lessons learned
- Walk through the project post-mortem report

6.10 CONDUCT THE PROJECT POST-MORTEM

Traditionally, the primary goal of the post-mortem review is to carefully examine the system with the users and evaluate its effectiveness in satisfying the stated business objectives. Based on the outcome of the post-mortem study, suggested changes might be proposed to enhance the newly implemented system.

However, the post-mortem study should also be extended to a variety of sources such as those people who developed the system and those who maintain and operate the system in the production environment. This enlarged scope is essential to improve not only the resulting system products but also to refine the critical software development processes that are prescribed by the methodology. Consequently, the post-mortem study should be directly integrated into the system development life cycle as an integral part of the overall process of building and maintaining the application systems.

In some organizations, the post-mortem study is conducted only after the final outcome of the project is not successful. In such organizations, the only reason to conduct the post-mortem study is to identify scapegoats who can then be blamed for all the problems encountered during the project, rather than try to concentrate efforts on identifying what could be wrong with the current development processes, project management practices, and infrastructure. The post-mortem process should never be used to conduct individual performance assessments of the developers. The post-mortem assessment is entirely process-driven. It focuses on capturing the best internal development practices and continually improving them over time.

Be sure to conduct the post-mortem study for all projects, successful or not, in an open and honest atmosphere that is conducive to gaining the cooperation of people rather than scaring them to death. You definitely should inform the affected staff and its direct management about the real objectives of the study, how it will be conducted, and the anticipated benefits. Management at all levels must be very supportive of the process and foster an atmosphere in which people can speak and learn from their mistakes without feeling threatened by possible retaliation.

The entire post-mortem assessment process should be geared toward gaining experience and learning from the challenges and problems encountered during and after the project. The Information Systems department needs to understand what works and what does not work in their particular development environment and share that information with the rest of the organization. This evaluation process is the only way an organization can learn to avoid the mistakes of the past and use the newly acquired knowledge to improve the way future projects will be conducted. At the same time, be sure to highlight those aspects of the project that turned out to be very positive. These should be used to reinforce and solidify the current system development processes and best practices.

Sometimes, post-mortem reviews are not conducted simply because the organization is very busy and does not feel it can afford the time to do so. In such circumstances, the organization has failed to recognize post-mortem evaluation reviews as an extremely valuable approach to improve the current system development and project management processes and practices, which can help to deliver high-quality software systems in a consistent and predictable manner.

Proper timing of the study is very important. The best time to schedule the study is approximately three months after the system has been delivered to its users. Before then, the users probably will not have had the opportunity to familiarize themselves with all the functions and facilities offered by the system. At the end of three months, the system should be relatively stable, and you should have already discovered and resolved most of the major problems. Furthermore, the users will have had enough time to drop the old habits they might have developed while working with the legacy system.

Ideally, the people who conduct the post-mortem study should be objective and experienced individuals who are well respected in both the user and information systems communities. In some organizations, an independent group sometimes performs the study in order to preserve objectivity.

7

Software Reusability

7.1 INTRODUCTION

The need for faster application development naturally leads to the concept of software reusability. A software factory that has successfully implemented and thereafter carefully managed a rich library of software reusable objects across the enterprise can significantly reduce the time needed to deliver new application systems. In addition to speedier development, software reusability often equates to increased system quality and lower system development costs, in a medium- to long-term horizon.

At least three major types of technologies support the concept of software reusability, procedural libraries such as dynamic link libraries, object-oriented class libraries and component-based software.

I briefly discuss these three different types of reusable technologies in this chapter. These technologies are not necessarily incompatible with each other. In fact, sometimes they can be used to complement each other. In some instances, the use of one particular reusable technology might still be the best solution to solve a particular situation.

7.2 A "COMPONENTIZED" APPROACH TO APPLICATION DEVELOPMENT

In a client-server or Web system development environment, the concept of reusability should not be limited solely to the traditional scheme of reusable chunks of modularized code. Rather, the concept should also be extended to several GUI and non-GUI software components such as those listed in Table 7-1.

Table 7–1 Reusable Software Components

- Generic application development frameworks
- Generic application object templates
- Business form templates
- Batch program templates
- Reports templates
- Stored procedure templates
- Remote procedure call (RPC) templates
- Database trigger templates
- Online transaction templates
- Graphical user interface (GUI) classes
- Generic windows classes
- Generic menu classes
- Generic GUI control classes
- JAVA applets and JavaBeans
- ActiveX controls
- JavaScript components

The whole client-server and Web development process must adopt a *componentized* approach to software design and construction. The ultimate objective of reusable software development is to reuse, adapt, or, as a last resort, design from scratch as many reusable software components as possible. However, not all software components could be designed for broad reusability in a single application or across several applications. After all, situations will always arise in which unique, context-specific business procedures must be applied to satisfy the peculiar needs of a business application.

Figure 7-1 presents a sampling of a very small set of generic software components that qualify as strong candidates for reusability. With not much extra effort, these software components can be designed to become generic reusable software modules which then can be shared across multiple applications throughout the enterprise or in different parts of the same application. For this sharing to happen, the MIS organization must extend its horizon beyond the development of standalone, monolithic applications. They must embrace a component-based development strategy.

Table 7-2 provides a brief description of the most common client-server and Web application functions that are strong candidates for reusability. These functions can be designed into reusable components that encapsulate specific system or business processes.

Figure 7-2 illustrates three basic options that are available to software developers when the decision has been made to assemble a library of generic reusable software components.

A large variety of generic application frameworks or specific pre-built reusable object libraries are available commercially. These libraries provide a large and diversified

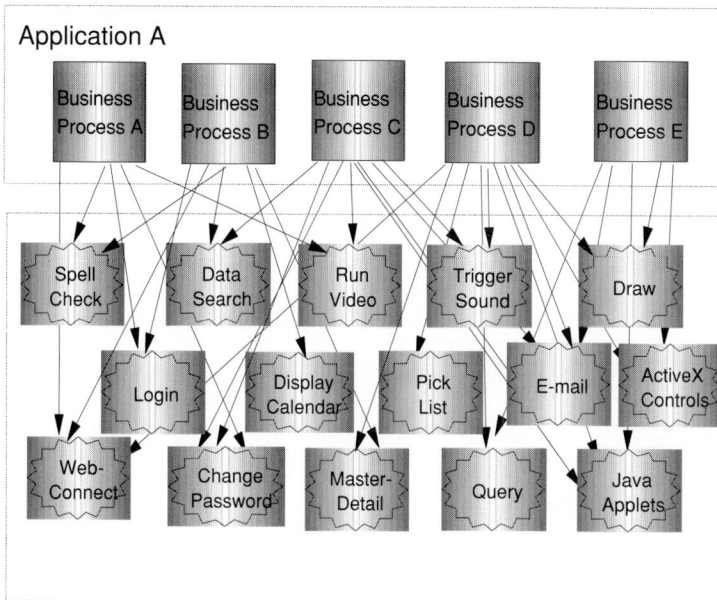

Figure 7–1 Reusable software components.

Table 7–2 Reusability Candidates

GENERIC APPLICATION FUNCTIONS	DESCRIPTION
Security functions	Common set of functions that are used to control and manage the access to data or other application objects
Error-handling functions	Common set of functions that are used to provide comprehensive warnings or error messages to the front-end programs. Depending on the severity level of the error, the program will resume processing or terminate the application
Audit and control functions	Common set of functions that are used to perform generic audit and control activities that are triggered by specific application events
Database access functions	Common set of functions that are used to perform standard database operations such as connecting to the database, navigating through the database structure to locate specific data, etc.
Data integrity functions	Common set of functions that are used to apply data integrity rules to the database structure

Table 7-2 Reusability Candidates (cont.)

Reporting functions	Common set of functions that are used to lay out various report format components such as standard report headings, footers, page breaks, summarization of totals, etc.
Editing and validation functions	Common set of functions that are used to perform various data entry validation and editing routines
Generic business functions	Common set of business functions that are used to perform generic types of calculations or algorithmic tasks that are highly repetitive in nature

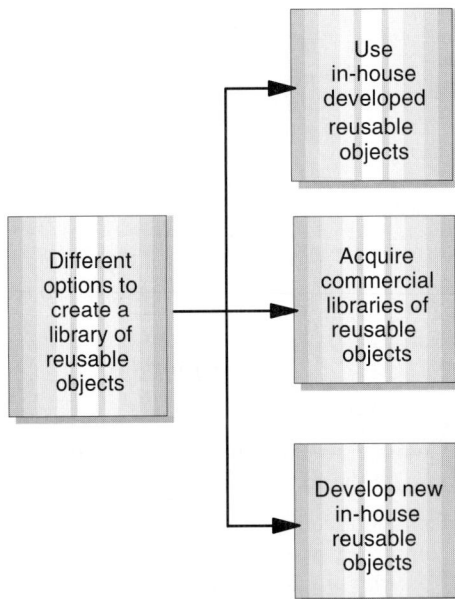

Figure 7-2 Different options for assembling a library of software reusable components.

set of software reusable components which can be directly used, with various categories of RAD client-server and Web application development tools.

7.3 THE CONCEPT OF OBJECT-ORIENTED INHERITANCE

Several client-server application development tools support important object-oriented programming principles such as those indicated in Table 7-3.

Table 7–3 Object-oriented Programming Principles

- Inheritance
- Encapsulation
- Polymorphism
- Binding

Although this book does not discuss in detail all these features, this section briefly discusses the concept of inheritance and its relevancy to the design and construction of reusable software objects classes. However, many of the concepts discussed in this chapter can be applied when performing the system development activities described in Chapter 3 (Analysis), Chapter 4 (Design), and Chapter 5 (Construction).

CLASS LIBRARY DEFINITION

A class library is defined as a collection of pre-built and pre-tested objects that can be reused in different applications or multiple areas within the same application.

Inheritance is a special object-oriented technique whereby an object acquires its behavior and properties from another object. This technique allows the development of a basic collection of application base objects (or ancestor objects). These high level ancestor objects carry a particular set of attributes and behaviors which can be reused by lower-level descendent objects.

The prime objective of object-oriented inheritance is to create an object hierarchy whereby the application base objects that are at the very top of the hierarchy are defined with generic functionality, while the specific, detailed functionality is defined in the application objects that reside at the bottom of the hierarchy.

Figure 7-3 shows a window type of reusable object hierarchy. This hierarchy supports three levels of functionality. The windows objects at the top and middle levels are defined with some very generic functional characteristics and behaviors. However, the windows at the bottom of the hierarchy are defined with specific functionality that extends, and possibly overrides, the properties and behaviors that are embedded in the top- and middle-level window objects.

True inheritance permits descendant objects to not only inherit the properties and behaviors of their ancestors but also to extend and override them, while still retaining the core set of functionality that was embedded in the ancestor objects.

This important characteristic of object inheritance is made possible because the inherited objects do not merely duplicate or copy the properties and behavior of their base object classes. Instead, they refer directly to them. For the same reasons, its descendants automatically pick up any modifications that are made to an ancestor object.

Sections 7.3.1 to 7.3.3 provide additional information on some of the most common types of visual object hierarchies that software developers can construct using the object inheritance concept in sophisticated client-server environments.

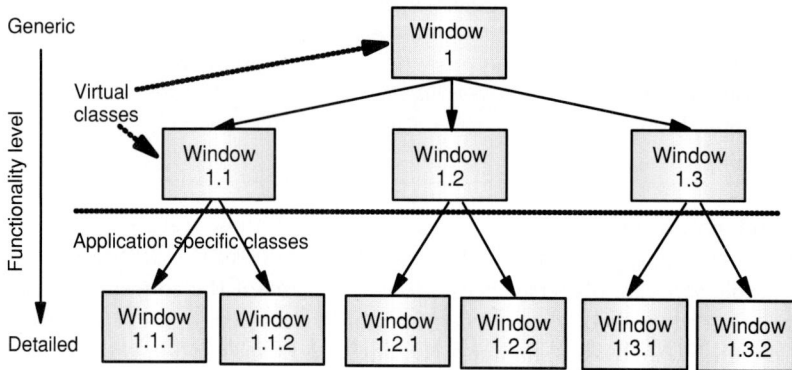

Figure 7–3 A windows type of reusable object hierarchy.

7.3.1   COMMAND BUTTONS HIERARCHY

This is a hierarchy of generic control buttons that are constructed to support the most elementary actions that are performed in an application window such as OK, CANCEL, NEW, BROWSE, CLOSE, and DELETE.

Once the ancestor hierarchy is created, all its command buttons, along with the corresponding events that are triggered when they are selected by the user with a mouse click, can be extended with additional events and behavior to address the specific needs of a given application.

At the limit, all the action-driven control buttons that are used in the application can be inherited from a single ancestor. Such an approach would force the applications to behave in a more consistent manner since the behavior of several of the objects used in them would be inherited from a unique command button ancestor.

The most obvious command buttons that are good candidates to be regrouped under a generic button class library include: About, Browse, Cancel, Close, Delete, Help, Insert, New, OK, Open, Print, Retrieve, Save, Search, and Select.

7.3.2   MENU HIERARCHY

This is a hierarchy of generic menu commands that is required to support the most frequent actions that are performed by a user in a window menu. For example, the ancestor menu base class can include standard menu commands such as File, Edit, Window, and Help.

The most basic events and corresponding behaviors that are encapsulated with each menu object could be extended or overridden to satisfy the peculiar needs of each new, distinct application.

7.3.3   WINDOWS HIERARCHY

A windows hierarchy includes a set of ancestor windows that describe the most generic types of windows that are frequently used in a typical application. Some of the reusable objects that could be included in this windows class hierarchy are pop-up windows, maintenance windows, simple query windows, pick-list windows, master-detail windows, display error windows, display warning windows, login windows, and change password windows.

Figures 7.4 through 7.7 demonstrate how the concept of inheritance can be used to define a window base class for a basic set of client-server applications.

The top-level ancestor window that you see in Figure 7-4 contains only a couple of control elements that are used to display the company's logo and name.

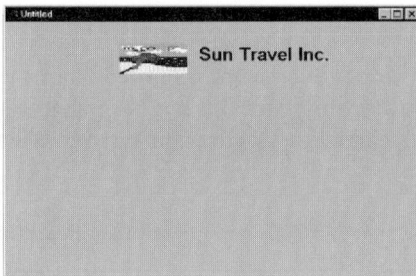

Figure 7–4   Ancestor window.

Figure 7-5 shows the next window, which is also a base class window. This base class window is inherited from the ancestor window in Figure 7-4. As you can see, this base class window is a bit more specialized and includes a few more control elements.

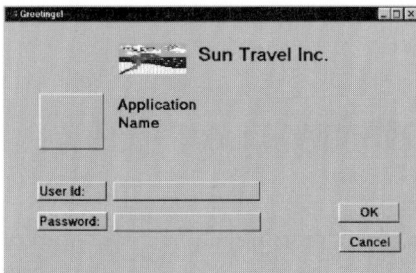

Figure 7–5   Base class window.

The window in Figure 7-6 is inherited from the base class window illustrated in Figure 7-5. As you see in the picture, though, the window's control buttons are more specialized than those that are shown in the ancestor window. The scripts that are associated with these control buttons are customized to address the specific application processing needs of a specific application, called Worldwide Agencies Application.

Figure 7–6 Worldwide agencies application window.

Finally, Figure 7-7 shows another window that is also inherited from the window shown in Figure 7-5. However, the window in Figure 7-7 has been slightly modified to satisfy the specific needs of another enterprise application system called the Accounts Receivable Application.

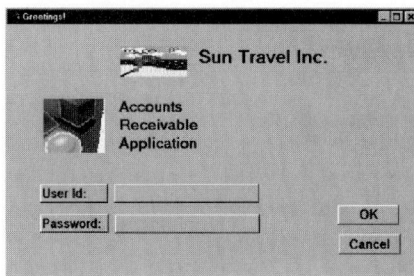

Figure 7–7 Accounts receivable application.

7.4 SOFTWARE REUSABILITY ADVANTAGES AND DISADVANTAGES

Some advantages and potential disadvantages of using reusable software components in client-server or Web development, through inheritance or other means, are summarized in Table 7-4.

Table 7–4 Reusable Software Components

ADVANTAGES	DRAWBACKS
• Reduced development cycle time because the multiple application objects are assembled with pre-existing, pre-tested components instead of being developed from scratch • Lower development costs since the use of application reusable components saves both development and testing time • Increased quality, assuming that the software reusable modules were constructed with the best design techniques and were well tested, making them less likely to have defects or omissions • Promotes overall application software standardization and modularity. For instance, the utilization of reusable GUI objects enforces a more consistent user interface either within a large application or across several applications • Reduced maintenance efforts since the reusable code is shared throughout an application, thus eliminating duplicate code and reducing the time needed to find and fix defects	• Can result in system performance degradation if the reusable object class libraries are poorly designed or introduce superfluous levels of inheritance • Incorrect modifications made to a virtual class of objects or a reusable module can affect adversely one or several applications at once • Might be difficult to agree on what could constitute the most common set of features that are needed in the descendant objects to be used by an application or across applications • Can be difficult to design reusable object class libraries that are generic, flexible, and relatively easy to modify but remain very efficient • As the reusable library grows in size and complexity, managing it or enforcing its consistent use across the various application development and maintenance groups might be difficult

7.5 SOFTWARE REUSABILITY IN THE CONTEXT OF DYNAMIC LINK LIBRARIES (DLL)

In a typical Windows environment, reusable client-server modules can be stored in dynamic link libraries (DLLs). A dynamic link library is a special library that contains compiled programs that, when they are invoked by other programs, are dynamically loaded and linked at execution time only.

When developing Windows client-server application systems, the use of dynamic link libraries presents several advantages, as indicated in Table 7-5.

Table 7–5 Dynamic Link Library Advantages

Ease of maintenance	When modifications are required, only the dynamic link library that is affected needs to be redistributed, as opposed to the entire application software
Modularity	DLLs facilitate the breakup of the application into a set of smaller, more modularized executable files, allowing the executable application module to remain smaller
Efficiency	DLLs allow a more efficient use of memory, since the modules that are stored in a dynamic link library are loaded only when needed
Reusability	Several applications can commonly reuse the procedural components that are stored in a dynamic link library

7.6 SOFTWARE REUSABILITY TECHNICAL INFRASTRUCTURE AND MANAGEMENT CHALLENGES

The reusability concept is certainly not new to veteran developers. However, software reusability has remained elusive in several large IT organizations. Many technical or managerial reasons can come to one's mind to explain this situation.

Assuredly, the IT organization must face several technical challenges while embracing the concept of software reusability. One of the major challenges is to lay down a sound technical foundation for an enterprise-wide component-based architecture, one that fosters true cross-platform interoperability and reusability across several projects.

Figure 7-8 presents a holistic view of an application development infrastructure that promotes the use of various types of reusable software components and templates.

A well architected reusable software component infrastructure advantageously supports the construction of several client-server or Web applications, throughout the enterprise. It is composed primarily of multiple class hierarchies of reusable software components that support the rapid development of different categories of business application systems. The reusable software components must deliver functionality in a manner that can be easily understood by the developers.

If a similar infrastructure does not exist yet in the enterprise, then the multiple application development groups that exist in a large organization are likely condemned to develop their own application software functionality from scratch, time after time. Such an approach can greatly reduce the MIS organization's overall productivity and hamper its ability to deliver corporate client-server and Web application systems rapidly.

On the other hand, once the initial investment that is required to create such a reusable application development architecture has been made by management, then the new application systems that need to be developed can take advantage of all the reusable functionality already built into this architecture.

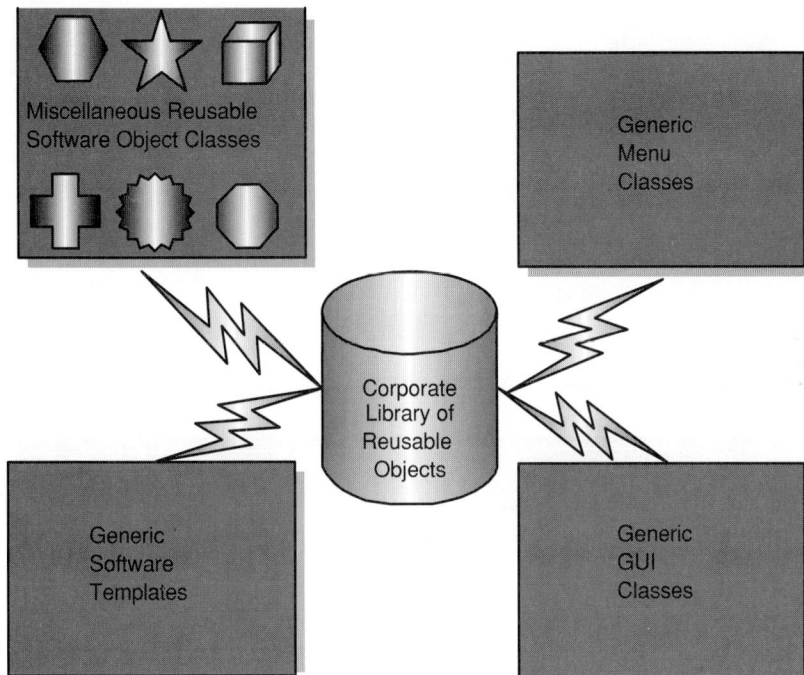

Figure 7–8 A holistic view of a corporate infrastructure for reusable software objects.

To be truly useful, all the reusable software class libraries need an indexing mechanism that makes searching the required reusable modules a relatively easy and effective process for the software developers. The functionality that is embedded in each particular reusable object must also be well described and documented, preferably with the inclusion of some meaningful examples that explain in simple terms how to use them and for which purpose. The Web technology can be advantageously used to quickly develop all the functionality required to support a reusable software environment with strong indexing capabilities. Application developers could then use powerful Web-based search engines to locate the reusable modules they need to build their applications. A universal Web interface would also be used to update and manage the libraries of reusable software components.

Figure 7-9 shows another picture in which global and application-specific sets of software reusable class libraries have been set up to support and accelerate the system development life cycle process, at the level of the enterprise.

The various reusable components might reflect either a business service such as print a check, or a business object such as a supplier. Nevertheless, the business-oriented reusable components should always be designed in a way such that they remain flexible, so they can accommodate unavoidable business changes.

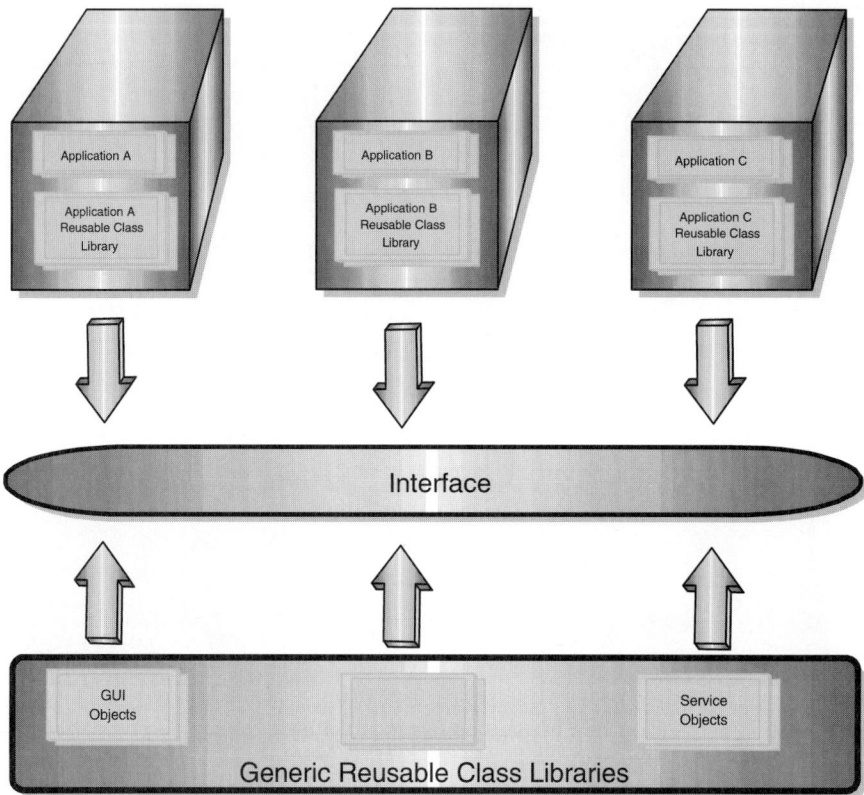

Figure 7–9 Generic reusable class libraries at the level of the enterprise.

Figure 7-10 presents a small sample of the different types of GUI objects that can be added to the visual GUI object class library that you see in Figure 7-9.

Figure 7-11 presents a small sample of additional types of visual and non-visual reusable objects that can be added to the service-related class library that is shown in Figure 7-9. The non-visual reusable objects, such as the generic database connection components, do not have a graphical interface.

To remain truly effective, the reusable component-based development strategy must find a way to minimize the number of technology platforms and related skills that the developers must assimilate to develop applications. Similarly, the software reusable class libraries and components should be implemented with a technology architecture that is based on industry-wide standards that are truly opened.

Putting aside the technical challenges of software reusability, there are several management-oriented issues that must be properly addressed by the Information Systems organization.

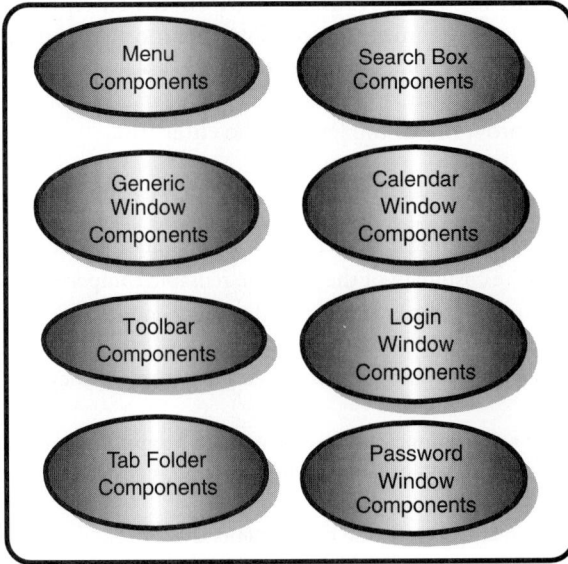

Figure 7–10 Visual objects reusable class library.

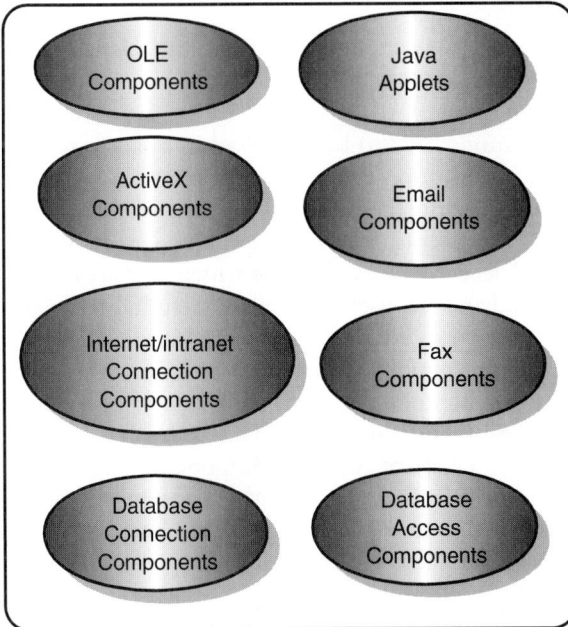

Figure 7–11 Service objects reusable class library.

In fact, the success or failure of software reusability within the enterprise can largely be influenced by the ability of the organization to resolve the most critical cultural and organizational issues surrounding the reusability paradigm. Table 7-6 lists some of the most basic questions that need to be answered by the organization prior to launching a major software reusability program, at the level of the enterprise.

Table 7–6 Software Reusability Management Challenges

- Who will be responsible for acquiring or developing the reusable components?
- Who will own or become the custodian of the software reusable components?
- Who will maintain the software component library that will contain the reusable components?
- Who will manage the component-based software environment and manage its evolution?
- Who will be responsible for managing changes that need to be applied to reusable software components? Who will pay for the development and maintenance of reusable components?
- What are the criteria to identify the software components that are good candidates for reusability? What are the recommended guidelines and standards to design and document software reusable components?
- What types of software reusability concepts, rules and guidelines should be implemented in the enterprise and where in the system development life cycle should these concepts, rules and guidelines be stated explicitly?
- What mechanisms can be implemented to enforce the software reusability concepts, rules and guidelines across the software factory shop?

All these fundamental questions need to be addressed in a satisfactory manner by the Information Technology organization to ensure that reusability truly has a chance to succeed and flourish at the enterprise level. Quality is also a strong requirement. Developers will reuse software components only if they were designed with high quality standards, have proven to be defect-free, are well documented, and are truly easy to use.

Similarly, significant cultural and mindset changes will definitely be required in the Information Technology organization, such as re-evaluating the types of metrics that are currently used to measure the application developers' productivity in terms of the traditional lines of codes or function points. New metrics, such as the number of re-usable components developed during the design and construction of an enterprise application system or the number of existing reusable components used by developers in their new application, should be introduced to provide an incentive for developers to adopt and support the reusability concept. Rewards should also be provided to those who truly endorse the reusability concept and effectively create or utilize reusable components while developing new applications.

From another cultural standpoint, in some organizations, you might have difficulty convincing management to invest additional time, resources, and money to lay down the initial infrastructure foundation required to sustain a viable component-based development process across the enterprise. If the IT organization does not acknowledge that the higher costs initially incurred to allow the development of reusable software components can be amortized only across several projects, project managers will not provide the additional resources needed to launch a viable software reusable process.

If the software organization constantly focuses its time and energy on developing and shipping software products that must satisfy overly aggressive and unrealistic target implementation dates, then its chances of succeeding in attempting to introduce the software reusability concept might be diminished dramatically. Such software development practices not only result in software applications of inferior quality but also in software applications that are rarely designed for reusability.

Figure 7-12 presents a holistic view of the type of organizational infrastructure that needs to be set up to support software reusability at the level of the enterprise.

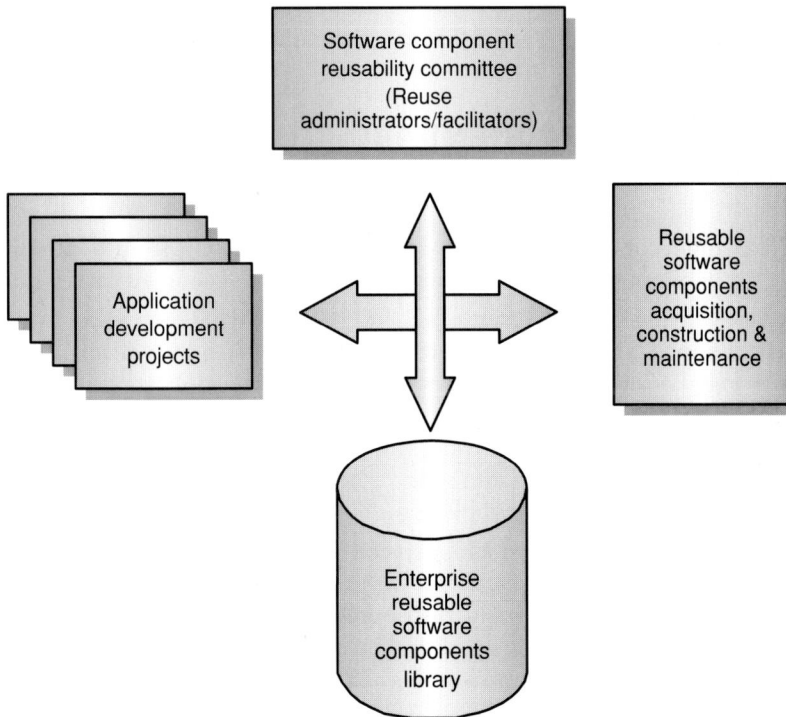

Figure 7–12 Organization infrastructure supporting the reusability paradigm.

As shown in Figure 7-12, a reusable software component committee is set up with the mission of laying down the foundation elements necessary to support an enterprise-wide component-based infrastructure effort. The committee is responsible for setting the high-level technical and management practices by which the software reusability concept will be implemented and supported at the level of the enterprise.

Software reusability must be built into the software development process. Business processes must be broken down into a set of modular functional components, with specific roles. Then the smaller functional components that are likely candidates for reusability must be clearly identified as early as possible during the software development life cycle of a business system, such as during the analysis phase. Subsequently, these functional components must be specifically designed for reusability during the design phase. Finally, they must be coded and tested for reusability as early as possible either at the end of the design phase or very early on during the construction phase.

To resume this section, enterprise business applications must be engineered proactively for reusability by partitioning business processes and data structures into highly granular components that remain loosely coupled. This partitioning-for-reusability process starts early during the development life cycle, such as during the analysis phase where opportunities for reuse are discovered. Similarly, the enterprise technology architecture must facilitate reusability by implementing a consistent set of hardware and software technology components that are standardized across the organization.

7.7 DISTRIBUTED COMPONENT ARCHITECTURES FOR WEB APPLICATIONS

The Web application development paradigm is no different from the traditional client-server development process. Using small, reusable client- or server-side components can accelerate the Web-based application development process.

First, the application is logically broken into discrete chunks of small presentation, business logic, or data-oriented components. Then, the application is constructed by assembling various application components or objects that were already developed during previous projects, or by using readily available commercial reusable components, or simply by creating, from scratch, new custom application components that embed the required chunks of application business logic.

The software developers can adopt several Web-based component models to develop Web-enabled database applications, within the framework of a distributed component architecture. Fundamentally, distributed software components are objects that can be distributed across the network and on different platforms and that can be used, shared, or reused by distinct applications as if they were local on a single computer.

Each object (or distributed component) is characterized by some specific attributes that define it in a unique manner. Each object is also characterized by specific methods that outline the behavior of the object. The objects interact with each other within an application or across applications through a messaging mechanism that invokes the object methods. Object brokers are components of middleware that are used to dynamically locate all the objects in a distributed environment and allow them to interact with each other over the network. Figure 7-13 schematically illustrates the relationships between the different components of a generic distributed object model.

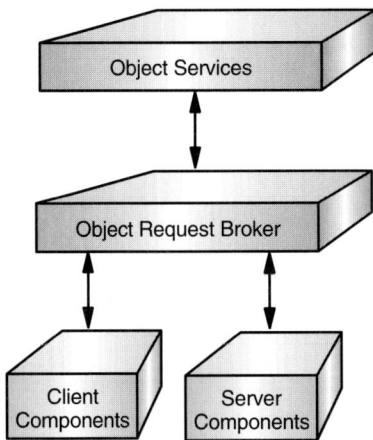

Figure 7–13 Generic distributed object model.

Figure 7-14 lists four major models that emerged in the industry to support a more robust distributed component-based architecture.

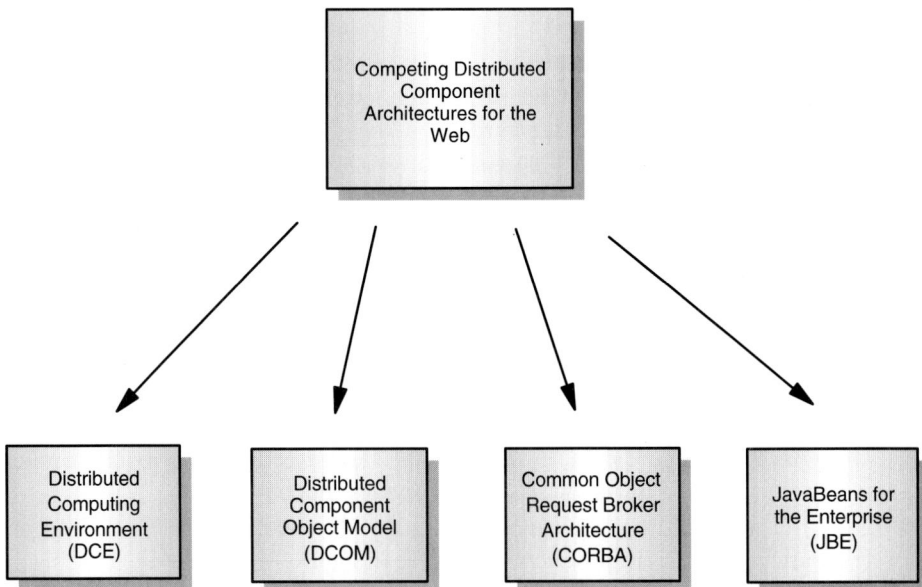

Figure 7–14 Distributed component-based models.

Simply stated, each of these powerful technologies can be seen as a form of middleware technology that supports a type of distributed component-based model, which is rooted on the object request broker paradigm. The object request broker is invoked by a specific object and passes along the object's message to another remote object.

Each of these distributed component-based models has the potential to modify significantly the approach used to construct business applications. They might deliver the ability to construct business applications with the use of plug-and-play software components that can be assembled the way a car is assembled from different components and sub-components such as wheels, engine parts, body parts, and so forth.

Following is a very brief overview of each of the dominant distributed component models shown in Figure 7-14.

7.7.1   DCOM/ACTIVEX

ActiveX can be viewed as an integration technology or inter-operability standard that permits different application software components that were created with various programming languages to interact with each other as part of an integrated interactive Web application, including Java applets. Microsoft is targeting its ActiveX/DCOM technology as an integrated environment for distributed components.

However, ActiveX-enabled Web pages work only with Web browsers that support the ActiveX technology. At the time of this writing, only the Microsoft Internet Explorer Web browser supports the ActiveX technology. However, Ncompass Labs (http://www.ncompasslabs.com) provides an ActiveX plug-in for the Netscape Web browser.

The ActiveX technology framework is built primarily on Microsoft's Component Object Model (COM) standard and its newer sibling, the Distributed Component Object Model (DCOM) standard.

The Microsoft COM standard lets objects interact with each other by utilizing links. It was originally designed to operate on desktop machines. DCOM is a Microsoft networking protocol that enables inter-connectivity between various network components, including ActiveX control objects. With the COM/DCOM technology, software application components can be partitioned into self-contained binary objects that are called ActiveX controls. ActiveX controls (a.k.a. ActiveX components) are self-contained code that can be created to run on either client or server machines. In fact, these ActiveX controls can be executed across the Internet or across corporate Intranets. Figure 7-15 provides a holistic view of the ActiveX/DCOM technology.

As seen in Figure 7-15, DCOM can be viewed as the object request broker middleware that is used in the ActiveX component model.

In reality, ActiveX is composed of a set of different Microsoft technologies that use a variety of different products, as you see in Figure 7-16.

Table 7-7 provides a high-level description of the core ActiveX components that are shown in Figure 7-16.

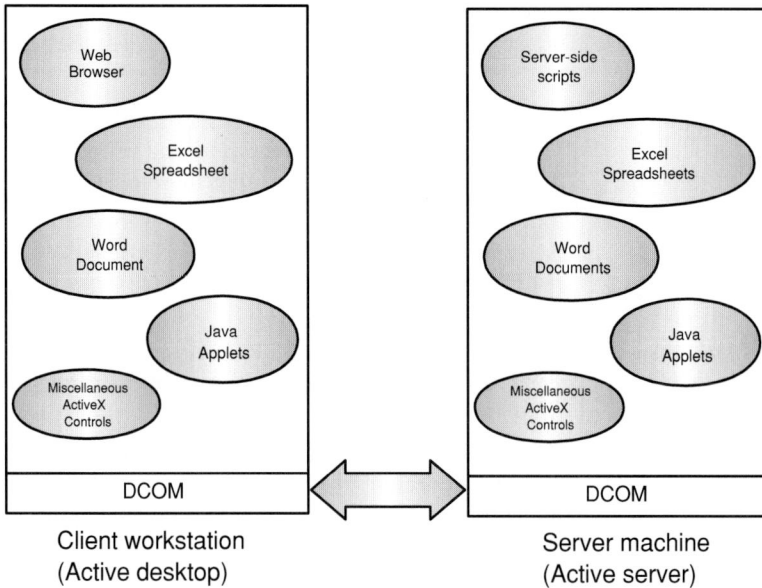

Figure 7–15 ActiveX/DCOM technology.

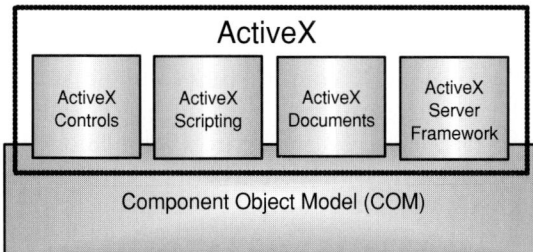

Figure 7–16 ActiveX major components.

While the ActiveX Server Framework component was conceived precisely for Web servers, the ActiveX controls, scripting, and document components were designed primarily for clients, such as Web browsers. The following section provides more details on the major elements that compose the ActiveX technology framework.

Table 7–7 ActiveX Enabling Technologies

NAME	DESCRIPTION
ActiveX Controls	ActiveX controls are interactive objects that are embedded in a Web page to extend the functionality and behavior of a Web application. Users can interact directly with an ActiveX object that was added to a Web page.
ActiveX Scripting	ActiveX scripts are used to control the behavior of a set of ActiveX controls from a client Web browser or Web server that supports the ActiveX technology.
ActiveX Documents	ActiveX documents allow a user to directly view various types of documents inside other applications, within the framework of a Web browser.
ActiveX Server Framework	The ActiveX Server Framework is comprised of several Web server-based features that extend the functionality of a Web application, such as security, database access, and state/session management.

ACTIVEX CONTROLS

ActiveX controls originate from the older Microsoft Object Linking and Embedding (OLE) technology. Although the Microsoft Component Object Model (COM) still serves as a foundation for both OLE and ActiveX technologies, they both serve two different purposes. Whereas the OLE technology was originally created specifically for use on desktop machines, ActiveX has been designed to make object linking work in an Internet or intranet context.

Among other things, ActiveX controls can be reduced in size by up to 75%, compared to the more traditional OLE controls. ActiveX controls also introduce asynchronous connections, meaning that ActiveX controls can continue processing and perform other tasks while other resources are being used, such as downloading a file. With the traditional OLE controls, the access to resources is synchronous, meaning that they have to wait and stay idle until the specific tasks they initiated were entirely completed.

The ActiveX control objects themselves can be created with a variety of programming languages and integrated development tools including Sybase/Powersoft's Powerbuilder, Microsoft's Visual Basic and C++, Borland's Delphi and C++, and a number of Java visual development tools, for instance. As a matter of fact, the Java programming language can be used by Web application developers to construct cross-platform ActiveX controls.

Microsoft has indicated its intention to offer the ActiveX technology as a true cross-platform solution, supporting not only the current Windows operating systems but also the Macintosh and UNIX computer platforms. At the time of this writing, whether Microsoft will succeed in providing developers with a true cross-platform software component solution remains to be seen.

From a security standpoint, the ActiveX controls can be downloaded on the client machine only if the appropriate ActiveX enabled Web browser security parameters have been configured to allow downloading. Since downloading objects on a client-workstation from the Internet can be a dangerous thing to do, Microsoft decided to make ActiveX controls more secure by using digital signatures. Digital signatures are utilized to authenticate the creators of the ActiveX controls. The developers of an ActiveX control must apply for a digital certificate from a certificate authority if they want to officially authenticate their controls. With such an approach, a user can, in principle, verify that a control was indeed developed by a legitimate software vendor, which presumably can be trusted, based on its established reputation.

Microsoft has implemented the ActiveX and DCOM technology frameworks in such a way as to be able to leverage existing COM and OLE technologies. Since existing OLE controls can be re-engineered relatively quickly into ActiveX controls, an extensive collection of ActiveX controls is available on the market as freeware, shareware, or commercial products. In the context of a software reusability framework, various types of ActiveX control objects can be used by Web application developers as ready-to-use building blocks for their Web applications, and these control objects are reusable across applications.

CLIENT-SIDE SCRIPTING

The ActiveX technology framework supports a scripting language interface. With this scripting interface, developers can control the use of ActiveX objects that are executed within Internet Explorer on the client machine. ActiveX scripting allows developers to automate intercommunication between several software components including ActiveX controls, ActiveX documents, and Java applets, making these various objects work harmoniously together. Two common scripting languages that can be used to control ActiveX objects are Microsoft's VBScript or Netscape's JavaScript. As you have seen in other sections of this book, scripting on the client side can be used advantageously for a variety of business application processes, such as providing interactive data validation capabilities to HTML forms.

ActiveX controls are executed on the client machine. The Microsoft Web browser, Internet Explorer, was engineered as a container application inside which ActiveX controls can be inserted. The process works as follows.

An HTML page contains an <object> tag, which indicates a URL address pointing to the location where the ActiveX control resides. When the Internet Explorer browser encounters the <object> tag, it determines whether the ActiveX control is already installed. If it is not, then the browser will download the ActiveX control from the server and install it on the client machine. Finally, the Web browser activates the ActiveX control, allowing the functionality that is embedded in it to be executed. A control needs to be downloaded only once and from there on will remain available on the client machine.

Table 7-8 shows the basic syntax that is used to embed a typical ActiveX control in an HTML Web page.

Table 7–8 An ActiveX Control Embedded In An Html Page

```
<HTML>
<HEAD>
<TITLE> A typical ActiveX control </TITLE>
</HEAD>
<BODY>
<OBJECT
    CLASSID="clsid:99B33230-4ED3-22A1-B1B4-00BB11B36FF"
    WIDTH=300
    HEIGHT=55
    VSPACE=0
    ALIGN=RIGHT>
</OBJECT>
</BODY>
</HTML>
```

Classid, width, height, vspace, and *align* are some of the typical attributes that can be used to set various characteristics of your ActiveX object. For instance, the *vspace* attribute is used to set the vertical spacing around the ActiveX object, and the *height* attribute is used to set the object's height.

SERVER-SIDE SCRIPTING

The Microsoft Web server supports Active Server Pages, which are also commonly referred to as ASP files. You can also embed VBScript or JavaScript code directly into ASP files. By doing so, scripts can then be executed on the Web server instead of the client machine. The server-side scripting approach can help reduce potential browser incompatibilities, since only standard HTML data is returned to the client machine. Additional features are also provided with the ActiveX Server Pages technology framework, such as session management, which permits tracking the state of the user's transactions.

ACTIVEX DOCUMENTS

ActiveX-enabled documents are constructed with a given application and subsequently can be dropped into another application. The ActiveX documents can be created with several OLE-compliant desktop applications such as Microsoft Word or Excel and Visio Corporation's Visio. For example, a Word document that is ActiveX-enabled can be viewed and edited directly inside the Internet Explorer Web browser or any other software application that supports ActiveX documents. The ActiveX-enabled documents are displayed live inside the native desktop applications that were used to create them, with the appropriate toolbars and menus.

ACTIVEX SERVER FRAMEWORK

ActiveX controls can retrieve data from any network facility that supports the ActiveX technology. So, data that resides on commercial relational databases can be accessed with the Open DataBase Connectivity (ODBC) standard. Similarly, the retrieved data can be viewed within all ActiveX enabled facilities, such as within Internet Explorer, Microsoft Office software, or an ActiveX control that was created by a third-party vendor. Other features that are supported by the Microsoft ActiveX Server Framework include Active Server Pages, which, among other things, allow transactions session management.

SUMMARY

Microsoft has transitioned ActiveX into an independent industry standards organization.

Whether the ActiveX technology will, in the long run, become truly platform-independent or will remain platform-specific is difficult to assess. For this reason, you might want to develop binary ActiveX controls with the Java language, at least for Web applications that must operate in a cross-platform environment, such as Windows and UNIX.

For those developers who want to create sophisticated Web applications that will run in a homogenous Windows platform, ActiveX is certainly quite a powerful technology.

For more information on ActiveX, consult the following Microsoft Web sites:

http://www.microsoft.com/activex
http://www.microsoft.com/intdev

7.7.2 CORBA

The CORBA model provides a set of standards that describe how different types of objects can interact with each other over the Internet or internal networks, utilizing a piece of middleware called Object Request Brokers (ORBs).

In other words, CORBA has formulated standards for object interoperability, facilitating the communications between distributed objects that execute on clients and servers. It embodies the methods that objects utilize to find and initiate other objects across a network, disregarding the types of platforms and programming languages that created the software objects. The ORB technology is used to develop multi-tier client-server or Web-based applications.

The Object Management Group (OMG) consortium formulated the specifications that define the CORBA model. Many important software vendors are backing up the CORBA model, as defined by OMG. Some of the most preeminent supporters of the CORBA specification include major software vendors such as IBM, Sun Microsystems, Hewlett-Packard, Netscape, and Oracle.

All these vendors formed an alliance to ensure that their distinct implementations of the CORBA model via different ORBs will be portable and compatible with each other. ORB software products are available on a large number of computing platforms, such as most UNIX, Windows, Macintosh, and a variety of Web server platforms.

An important subset of the CORBA standard was defined to address the specific needs of the Internet world. This subset of CORBA is called the Internet Interoperable ORB Protocol (IIOP). IIOP embodies a standard approach that allows various ORBs to communicate with each other in an Internet/intranet environment. In other words, IIOP is the central protocol of the CORBA distributed component model.

Although various vendors' ORB-based tools can interoperate transparently using the IIOP protocol, developers might want to use cross-platform ORB-based tools that are not locked into any specific software vendor, operating system, or computer platform. These cross-platform ORB-based tools might be more appropriate for constructing large and complex business applications which need to scale up at the enterprise level.

Thirteen major CORBA services are available, as indicated in Table 7-9. Commercially available ORB-based tools do not necessarily support the thirteen services that are shown in the table. On the other hand, not all developers might need the complete set of services that are embedded in the CORBA model.

Table 7–9 The Different Corba Distributed Object Services

SERVICE	DESCRIPTION
Concurrency Control	Allows several clients to manage access to shared resources and controls the concurrent use of resources with locks
Events	Supplies elementary features that can be defined in a flexible way including asynchronous events and dependable event delivery mechanisms
Externalization	Formulates protocols used to externalize and internalize objects
Interface	Formulates fixed point extensions to the existing Interface Definition Language (IDE) in CORBA 2.0.
Licensing	Defines a technique for object developers to control the use of their objects
Life Cycle	Provides standards and protocols that are used to construct, delete, copy, and move objects
Naming	Provides the capability to tie a name to an object pertinent to a naming context
Persistence	Provides a group of common interfaces to mechanisms that are utilized to control the persistent state of objects

Table 7–9 The Different Corba Distributed Object Services (cont.)

Query	Provides a mechanism for users and objects to invoke queries on a class of other objects or in databases
Relationship	Provides the ability to represent entities and relationships in an explicit manner
Replication	Provides the capability to automate the replication of objects across applications
Security	Provides mechanisms to enforce data integrity and confidentiality
Transaction	Provides the ability to support common transaction models that can be implemented in Transaction Processing (TP) monitors, as well as interoperability between different programming languages

Following are some Web site addresses, if you want some specific vendor information on different Object Request Broker tools:

http://www.visigenic.com	(Product: VisiBroker)
http://www.iona.com	(Product: Orbix)
http://www.sun.com/sunsoft	(Product: Joe)
http://www.hp.com	(Product: ORBplus)

The following Web site address is provided, if you want more information on the CORBA specification itself:

http://www.omg.org

7.7.3 DISTRIBUTED COMPUTING ENVIRONMENT (DCE)

The Distributed Computing Environment (DCE) model is based on a set of open standards for a distributed computing environment. It is a collection of services that help software developers build, use, and manage applications in a distributed computing environment. The Open Group oversees DCE.

DCE was one of the first attempts by some major software vendors to standardize the basic infrastructure for supporting distributed applications. Some of the software vendors that back the DCE model include Digital Equipment, Hewlett-Packard, and IBM.

At the heart of the DCE model is a set of standards for remote procedure calls (RPCs), distributed file systems, network security, and directory services. The DCE model also includes additional services for a thread package as well as a time synchronization facility.

Since the DCE model has been around for a couple of years now, it has been ported by many software vendors to more platforms than any other distributed middleware technology. DCE support has even been embedded in several leading operating systems. However, because of its complexity and weakness in object technology support,

DCE is gradually losing ground as the newer CORBA, DCOM, and JBE models gain momentum.

7.7.4   JAVABEANS FOR ENTERPRISE (JBE)

The JavaBeans for Enterprise (JBE) model, as defined by Sun Microsystems, is one of the most recent models that was proposed to implement a distributed component architecture for Web-based applications. JBE is being proposed as an alternative or a complement to the DCOM and CORBA models. Some major software vendors such as IBM, Netscape Communications, Oracle, and Borland International have endorsed JavaBeans.

The JavaBeans component model provides a standard specification for reusable, prefabricated Java components. Using the JavaBeans model, third-party software vendors can develop and sell multiple Java reusable software components. These standard reusable Java components can range from visual control widgets, such as a button or a gauge indicator, to full-fledged applications, such as a Web browser, a word processor or a business function. JavaBeans components may or may not be visible to users. Some internal JavaBeans do not have an on-screen appearance. Developers can acquire different JavaBeans software components to rapidly construct and assemble Web-based applications.

As such, the JavaBeans component model resembles the ActiveX component model. However, JavaBeans components can be built only by using the Java programming language, in contrast to the Microsoft's ActiveX technology. With the ActiveX technology, ActiveX components can be developed with several types of programming languages, since ActiveX encapsulates components written in different languages. However, the ActiveX-based applications are limited to run only on platforms on which ActiveX is supported, which currently primarily include the Microsoft Win32 environments. On the other hand, since the Java language is platform-independent, JavaBeans are equally platform independent, which can prove to be a significant advantage for cross-platform software developers. In principle, JavaBeans should be fully portable from one platform to another.

A JavaBean software component is characterized by three major features, namely, its properties, methods, and events. The properties of a JavaBean are its regular attributes, such as its color and its position, for a visible JavaBean. The methods are the set of functions that the JavaBean component can perform to modify its internal state or to communicate with other JavaBeans components. Finally, events are specific conditions that cause the launching of discrete tasks when internal or external signals occur.

JavaBeans modular components can be reused inside the same application or across applications. They can also be customized to meet the differing needs of specific applications.

The JavaBeans component model allows developers to build component-based software applications that can be integrated with other major software component-based architectures, such as CORBA and ActiveX, via the use of bi-directional bridges.

Figure 7-17 presents a holistic view of the JavaBeans for Enterprise architecture.

A brief description of its major components appears in Table 7-10.

JavaBeans For Enterprise Architecture

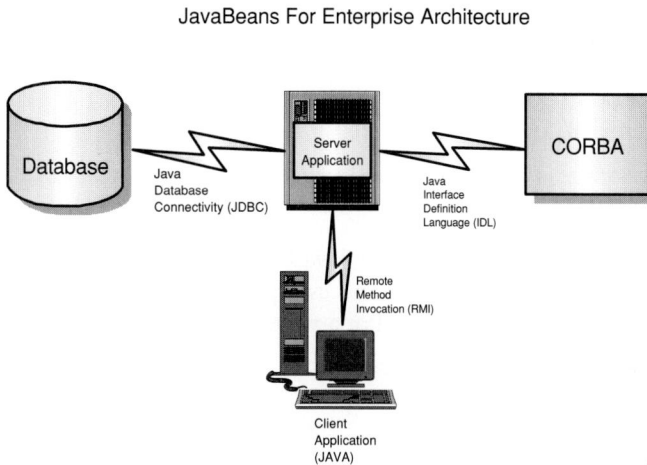

Figure 7–17 JavaBeans for Enterprise architecture.

Table 7–10 Major Components Of The Javabeans Enterprise Architecture

Component	Description
JDBC	The Java Database Connectivity (JDBC) standard API component provides relational database connectivity for Java applications. With JDBC, a Java application can send SQL statements to almost any major relational database system such as Oracle, Sybase, or Informix. The JDBC standard also supports an ODBC bridge, which allows JDBC to utilize some elements of the ODBC standard functionality to access relational databases.
IDL	The Java Interface Definition Language (IDL) API component allows Java applications to interface with the OMG CORBA standard IDL protocol.
RMI	The Remote Method Invocation (RMI) API component supports distributed computing. RMI allows JavaBeans components that run on one virtual machine to invoke methods on remote JavaBeans components as if they were local, whether these reside on another host or even across a network.

When the RMI, JDBC, IDL, and JavaBeans open standards are combined together, developers can construct large-scale Internet/intranet applications with the Java language.

Following are Web site addresses for more information on the JavaBeans specification and also on the Java language in general:

http://www.javasoft.com/beans
http://www.gamelan.com

7.7.5 CONCLUSION

The use of DCOM-, CORBA-, DCE-, or JavaBeans-based distributed component technologies might provide the plumbing necessary to allow developers to construct large-scale applications that are composed of a variety of components that might run on different platforms, providing their services through well-defined interfaces.

Fundamentally, the application can, to some extent, be developed by assembling custom and various prefabricated software objects that inter-operate with each other. This process can be done the same way a building would be assembled with prefabricated structural components. After all, the development process ultimately has only one objective, which is the rapid delivery of a quality application. However, do not view this approach as a silver bullet. A component-based development approach might still require significant programming from the developers, especially for large applications. But using components that are available commercially will help to speed up the development process over time.

Is a specific component-based architecture available that developers should adopt over others? Several factors come into play when the time comes to make the proper decision, such as those indicated in Table 7-11.

Table 7–11 Factors Influencing The Selection Of A Specific
Distributed Component-based Architecture

- The size, complexity, and level of scalability required by the applications being developed
- The types of existing or new hardware platforms that are used to implement the applications
- The types of software environments that are used to run the applications
- The level of compatibility of the different components that are assembled to create the application
- The level of stability of the application functions themselves
- The experience and programming skills of the current staff
- The number of third-party, shrink-wrapped components that are commercially available for each specific component-based computing platform
- The existence of visual and non-visual client or server-based components that can address a broad range of required functionality
- The type of component-based development tools that are commercially available to model, construct, assemble, and test component-based applications, the computing platforms they support, and their level of scalability to support large and complex applications

Choosing and implementing a particular component-based distributed model might demand significant investments in technology infrastructures to support it adequately, and, therefore, such a selection might have a long-lasting impact on the organization. Hence, pick a component-based technology infrastructure that will satisfy the specific needs of your organization.

If the software development organization is primarily Windows-centric, then DCOM/ActiveX might be the most obvious way to go. ActiveX should remain well integrated and fine-tuned with Microsoft's current and future technology architectures. If the software development organization is primarily UNIX-based or if you have a multi-platform environment, then OMG's CORBA ORBs might be a more appropriate way to go, given their cross-platform orientation and multi-vendor availability. Finally, if your software development organization is strongly committed to Java and will use it extensively in the future, then the appropriate way to go might be Sun's JavaBeans for Enterprise. Like CORBA, JavaBeans can be used equally for applications that must run on multi-platform computing environments.

Also keep in mind that the distributed component technologies described in earlier sections are not necessarily mutually exclusive. In fact, they sometimes can be used as complementary technologies. Similarly, some vendors have started to provide bridging software products that will likely support DCOM-to-CORBA with two-way communications. However, at the time of this writing, it is too early yet to tell whether these initiatives will be fully successful in the long term. Sun's JavaBeans, OMG's CORBA, and Microsoft ActiveX distributed component-based models will inevitably evolve over time and, I hope, will learn to co-exist peacefully with each other for the benefit of the developers. Interoperability standards and APIs will hopefully emerge as the distributed component-based market evolves and matures.

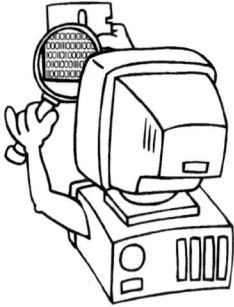

8

Client-Server and Web Testing

PART I: CLIENT-SERVER TESTING

8.1 INTRODUCTION TO CLIENT-SERVER TESTING

The development of increasingly large and complex client-server and Web database application systems poses unique challenges to developers. For example, you can see some of the various system components that must be successfully integrated to deliver a fully functional client-server application in Table 8-1.

Table 8–1 Various Components Of A Client-Server Or Web Database Application

- Sophisticated event-driven GUI-based programs
- Multi-vendor hardware equipment
- Heterogeneous client desktop and server operating systems
- Proprietary software middleware and gateways
- Multiple database servers
- Local and wide area networks operating across a wide range of protocols
- Multi-tiered distributed architecture interfaces
- Client-server rapid application development tools

Looking only at the first item in Table 8-1, the graphical user interface, you can have no doubt that GUI-based client-server applications provide the users with significant increases in flexibility and productivity through the use of powerful and user-friendly graphical user interfaces.

However, graphical elements such as intertwined windows, pull-down and pop-up menus, icons and toolbars, scroll bars, multiple-choice drop-down list boxes, and radio buttons add a myriad of variables that must be thoroughly tested prior to delivering a quality system to the user. And this testing is just the tip of the iceberg, because the GUI represents only the front end of the application, the part that is visible to the user. Behind the scenes are the database servers, the application servers, and other software facilities that need to be tested carefully.

Table 8-2 lists some of the most common GUI elements that are frequently utilized to design a simple graphical user interface.

Table 8–2 Most Common Graphical User Interface (GUI) Elements

Windows	Allow the user to view and manipulate information and initiate actions
Static text	Textual description of information
Single-line edit	Allows one line of text to be viewed or entered by the user
Multi-line edit	Allows several lines of text to be viewed or entered by the user
List box	Presents information displayed in a vertical list of entries
Picture	Displays information in a graphical format as opposed to a textual format
Drop-down list box	Does not display information choices unless the user clicks the down arrow on the right side of the box
Icons	Small graphical representations of main functions, programs and files
Checkbox	Represents yes-no information that the user can select
Radio button	The user selects mutually exclusive information by clicking on a circle button
Mouse pointer	Indicates the location of the mouse pointing device
Scroll bars	Displace the window up or down, left or right
Command button	When clicked on, executes a script in response to an event
Graph	Displays information using a graphical format
Drop-down menu	User initiates actions in a window by selecting items from a vertical list
Tool bar	Displays icon buttons corresponding to frequently selected menu items
Pop-up Menu	Allows the user to initiate action by popping up a menu within a window
Response window	Prompts the user to consider displayed information and take action on it
Tab folder	Container for tabbed pages that display other GUI controls

Not surprisingly, several studies clearly indicate that testing an application in a client-server environment is far more challenging than in a traditional mainframe, character-based development environment.

The multiple challenges that confront developers while testing client-server applications are shedding light on the necessity to implement an effective client-server testing process. Keeping this goal in mind, this chapter covers the process of systematically testing client-server and Web applications and demonstrates how this process is tightly integrated in the system development life cycle. It also complements all the detailed testing information that is provided in the design, construction, and implementation Chapters 4, 5 and 6 of this book.

As a final note, realize that testing is a highly complex and cognitive process in which creativity has a very important place so that it can be truly effective. Effective testers need workmanship and perspicacity in order to create tests that help discover all significant software defects.

8.2   TESTING DURING THE SYSTEM DEVELOPMENT LIFE CYCLE PROCESS AND BEYOND

Figure 8-1 conceptually shows how the client-server testing process maps to the system development life cycle (SDLC) process.

Clearly, Figure 8-1 highlights a very important point: the testing process in client-server and Web application development is not an after-the-fact event that typically occurs at the back end of the development effort, once all the programs have been coded by the programmers. On the contrary, the testing process is tightly interwoven with the system development life cycle process, from the early stages of application analysis straight down to system implementation and maintenance.

This approach places a high priority on software quality and ensures that testing becomes an intrinsic part of the software development process, from early beginning to end. This approach also helps to minimize the pernicious effects of the classical testing time compression syndrome, as often occurs in traditional software development life cycle, as illustrated in Figure 8-2.

Similarly, testing should not be perceived as being the sole responsibility of a particular group of people. Everyone involved in the various development stages of a software system should be held responsible for the quality of his/her work as it is being done.

The software testing process has a life of its own that parallels the system development and maintenance processes. The major generic stages that compose the software testing life cycle (STLC) are indicated in Table 8-3.

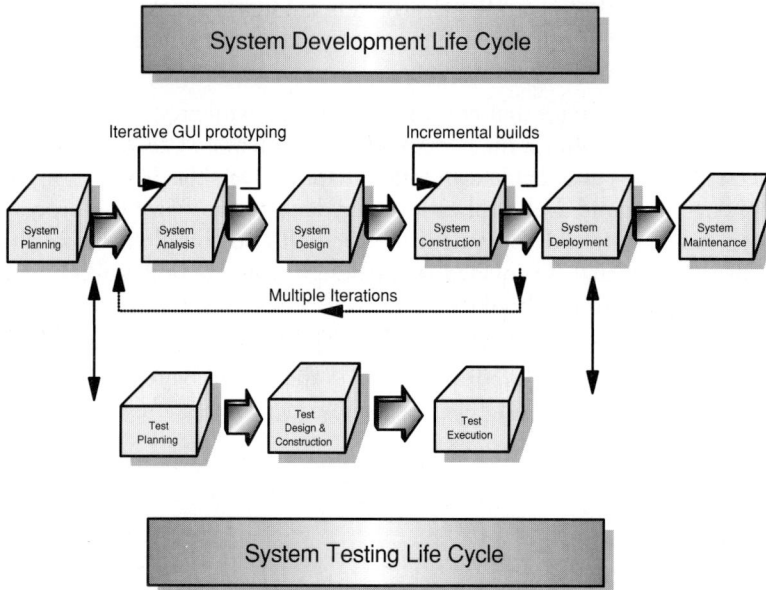

Figure 8–1 Positioning of the client-server testing process relative to the SDLC process.

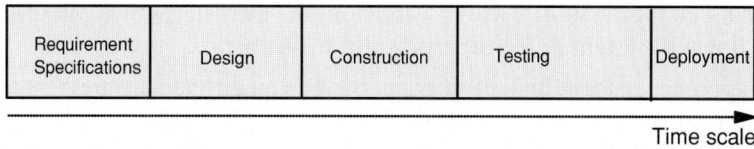

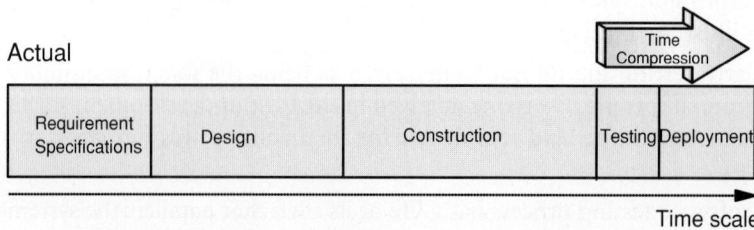

Figure 8–2 Traditional testing life cycle.

Table 8–3 Software Testing Life Cycle Generic Stages

SOFTWARE TESTING LIFE CYCLE PROCESS	DESCRIPTION
Test Planning	The test planning stage identifies the high-level application testing requirements. It also describes the overall client-server testing strategy, which covers the scope, approach, resources, and schedule of the complete testing effort.
Test Design	The test design stage identifies the client-server application features that will be tested, along with those that will not be tested. The various categorics of test procedures and test cases that will be exercised to verify the system are also defined. This stage overlaps both the SDLC design and system development stages.
Test Construction	The test construction stage allows the creation of test procedures and test data.
Test Execution	The test execution stage starts immediately after the first graphical user interface and application code modules have been developed by the programmers. (In a Rapid Application Development context, testing starts as soon as the first draft of the user interface is iteratively constructed with the users.) The test procedures and test cases are executed against the software to verify compliance to the stated system requirements.
Software Defect Tracking and Resolution	Test results are analyzed based on pass/fail test criteria and defects investigated and fixed.

8.3 THE FOUR SYSTEM DEVELOPMENT TESTING STAGES

During the system development life cycle, the testing of a large-scale client-server or Web application embodies four distinct levels of testing stages, as shown in Figure 8-3.

As discussed in several parts of this book, client-server and Web testing should occur as early and as often as possible. The powerful RAD tools that exist today, combined with effective iterative prototyping techniques, allow the initial testing of several components of the system as early as the analysis phase.

As the construction of the system gradually evolves through the various development stages, more thorough and systematic testing is required for mission-critical client-server systems. These corporate systems must work flawlessly the first time to ensure the survival of the business enterprise.

Figure 8-4 illustrates the sequence in which the major application testing stages occur against the level at which they are performed (i.e., program, system, or business levels).

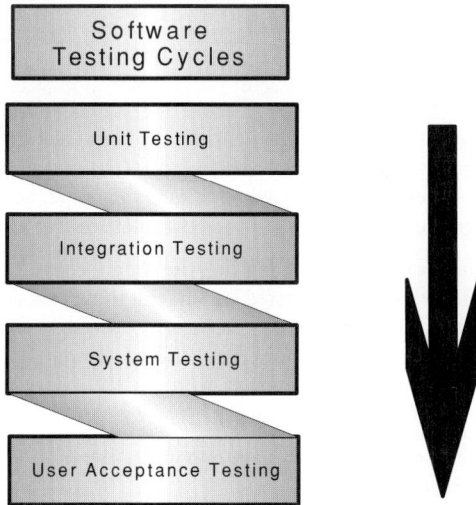

Figure 8–3 The four major software testing cycles.

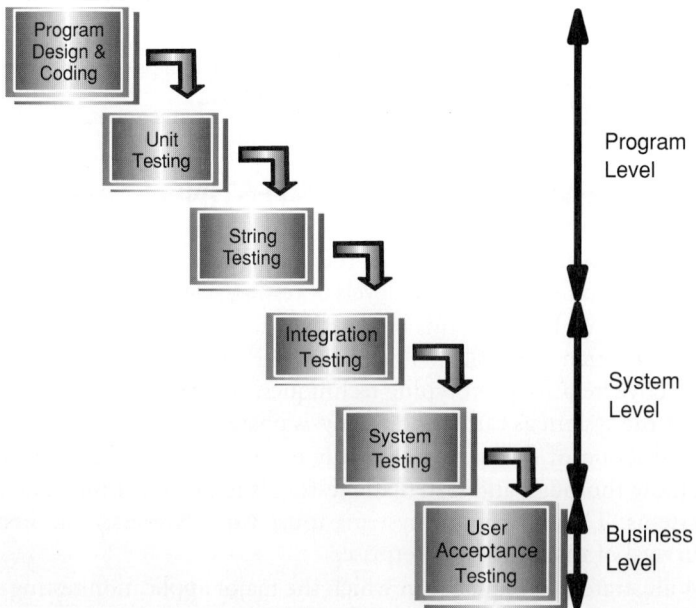

Figure 8–4 Major software testing stages.

The following sections provide a brief description of each major testing stage that you see in Figure 8-2.

8.3.1 UNIT TESTING

The goal of unit testing is to verify that the smallest logical units of application code work as per their corresponding software design specifications. Unit testing is a highly iterative process which starts as soon as the first application modules or programs are coded by the developers. This can be as early as the analysis phase, when an evolutionary prototype of the graphical user interface is built with the users. The software program specifications are used as the main source of information to derive sound unit test procedures and test cases.

During the unit testing process, all program lines of code should be executed at least once to help validate the procedural logic of the program.[1] In many organizations, the programmers themselves often test the software modules and programs. Several types of debugging tools are used to help detect, track, and resolve defects during the unit testing cycle.

In some cases, small code modules might not yet be fully assembled in a complete program. Then the use of drivers simulating the higher level structures of the program is quite frequent. Stubs might also be utilized to emulate the subroutines that are called by the application modules being tested.

Even though unit testing represents the most elementary level of testing, manage it carefully, to ease the transition to the next testing stage, integration testing. Table 8-4 indicates some of the various coding elements that are usually unit tested by the programmers.

8.3.2 INTEGRATION TESTING

The goal of integration testing is to verify that the multiple software modules or programs still work properly according to the specifications, when they are gradually combined with one another. If this verification was not already done during unit testing, the modules are systematically integrated into complete programs, which are subsequently integrated into subsystems. In turn, the subsystems are ultimately combined into a fully functional system.

---

1. Be careful, though! Coverage testing should never be used as an indication that the software is defect-free, simply because all lines of code have been exercised at least once. Additional testing techniques, combined with representative test cases, are required to help uncover the most important defects, such as the boundary-value analysis technique, for example.

Table 8–4 Unit Test Cases

- Procedural business logic
- Conditional paths
- Internal data structures
- Boundary value conditions (e.g., tables)
- Output conditions (i.e., reports, database/file updates, displays, error messages, creation of output files)
- Input conditions (i.e., data entry capturing, validation, formatting, editing)
- Graphical user interface behavior (menus, control objects inside a window)
- Error-handling procedures
- Module-to-module communication interfaces inside the program
- Control and security conditions
- Handling of invalid data values, data types, data formats, combination of data values
- Handling of valid data values
- Date processing (previous dates, current dates, aged dates)
- Passing of parameters between internal program modules
- Period-end processing (i.e., hourly, daily, weekly, monthly, yearly, on-demand)

Table 8-5 lists some of the specific software elements that are usually tested during the integration testing stage.

Table 8–5 Integration Test Cases

- Interfaces between programs
- Interfaces with specialized applications such as e-mail, fax facilities, access to the Internet/intranet
- Client-based business application logic
- Middleware-based testing
- Server-based business application logic

8.3.3   SYSTEM TESTING

System testing starts after integration testing and ends before user acceptance testing. The prime objective of system testing is to verify that the complete system successfully performs all the business functions that were documented in the system requirement deliverables.

System testing should equally demonstrate that the service-level performance and operational criteria are successfully met by the new business application.

Table 8-6 lists some of the major system components and characteristics that are typically exercised during the system tests, besides the functional tests.

Table 8–6 System Test Cases

• Volume testing	• Destructive testing
• Security testing	• Performance testing
• Stress testing	• Middleware testing
• Usability testing	• Compliance testing
• Documentation testing	• Backup/recovery testing
• System interface testing	• International customization testing
• Configuration testing	• Multi-site testing
• Data conversion testing	• Fail-over and high-availability testing
• Error message testing	
• Reliability testing	

During system testing, the multiple hardware and software components that compose the client-server architecture are jointly tested to verify their level of interoperability. This testing process encompasses the client workstations, the application and database servers, the gateways, the LAN, the WAN, and any other pieces of peripheral equipment that might be used with the client-server application, such as scanners, plotters, and bar coding devices.

The original development team or an independent testing group can perform system testing. Sometimes, the IS testing team that executes the system tests is assisted by user representatives.

In unit testing, and to some extent in integration testing, the programs that implemented specific system functions were tested more or less in isolation from each other. In system testing, the complete system functionality is tested as a whole. Consequently, an important task is creating task-oriented test cases that exercise a series of interactions between different functions of the system, as the users would normally do to perform their business tasks. For instance, a good test case to verify how well different functions of word-processing software interact together would be:

1. Open a file
2. Edit a document
   - Modify a page
   - Print the modified page
3. Save the document

The testers must develop the functional test cases to simulate representative user tasks, which inter-operate with one another. The user scenarios that were developed during analysis can be used for this purpose. For functional testing, having a member of the testing team who understands the domain of functionality provided by the new system is useful. Such a person can be extremely helpful in creating test cases that uncover defects that relate to specific business scenarios that would be overlooked by a neophyte.

For a simple example, assume that the system that might be tested is a general ledger system. In such a situation, having someone on the testing team who has a general background in finance and accounting might be useful, in creating task-oriented test cases that exercise a representative sequence of business tasks.

8.3.4   USER ACCEPTANCE TESTING

User acceptance testing validates the functionality of the entire system, including the manual procedures. It ensures that the system meets all the business requirements that the users identified for this system.

User acceptance testing covers all the elements of the system including the software, hardware, documentation, and the graphical user interface components. Wherever possible to do so, the system should be tested in an environment that closely emulates the targeted production environment.

In user acceptance testing, the system test cases are designed, constructed, and executed by the users themselves. Additionally, certain components of the system might also be tested by the IS operational groups who will be responsible for supporting the client-server application after it is transferred to the production environment.

8.4   DIFFERENT TYPES OF CLIENT-SERVER TEST CASE SCENARIOS

This section describes the different types of test conditions that you can develop to thoroughly exercise all aspects of the client-server system and ensure that it operates efficiently on the targeted software, hardware, and networking deployment platforms. Depending on the functional and technological characteristics of the application to be constructed, specific testing conditions may not be required.

8.4.1   DESKTOP CONFIGURATION TESTING

Desktop configuration testing verifies that the client-server system operates well and in a consistent manner on different types of client desktop machines. With a large variety of video graphic cards, sound boards, monitors, network interface cards, keyboards, and modems, desktop workstations can sometimes be a veritable puzzle of hardware components, often competing for the same shared resources and not always compatible with one another.

The desktop configuration test cases can be exercised either sequentially or simultaneously against multiple workstations that are configured with different categories of hardware and/or software components.

Desktop configuration tests can help to detect incompatible hardware components or software interface problems that cause the system to behave incorrectly. Desktop configuration tests are useful when multiple vendors supply different client-server components or even when a unique vendor supplies various components that operate under different releases and/or configurations.

Desktop configuration testing can also be exercised to determine the minimal or optimal configuration setups that can be used for the client desktop machines to run the application.

Figure 8-5 illustrates a desktop configuration-testing environment, which is composed of several types of client machines.

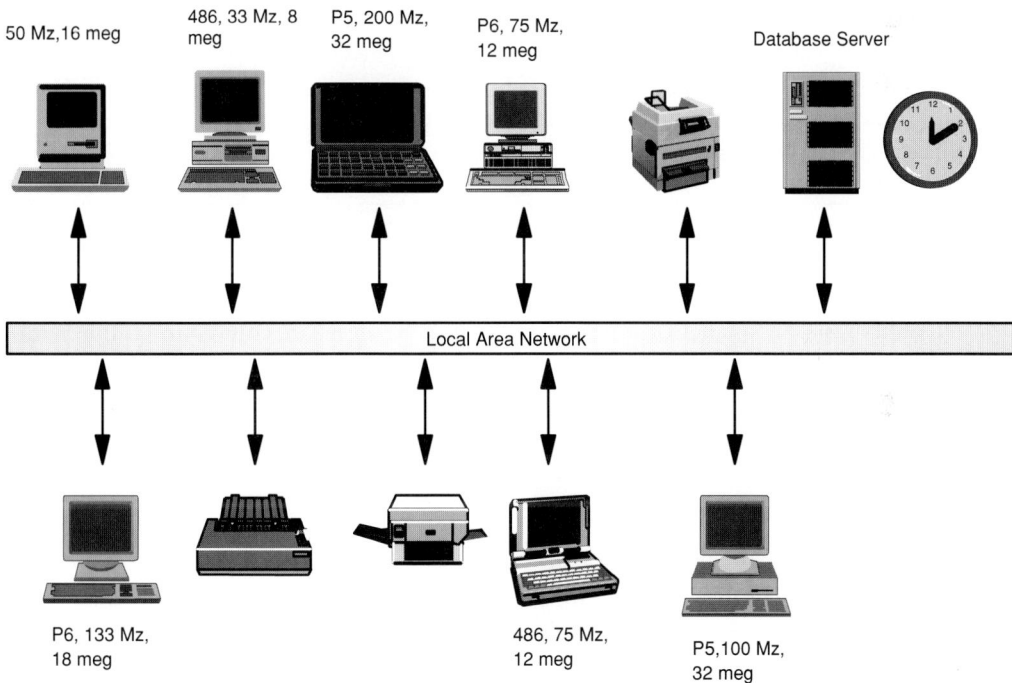

Figure 8–5 Desktop configuration testing.

8.4.2   USABILITY TESTING

Usability testing verifies that the users can easily operate the client-server application. It can highlight GUI-related features that prove to be user-unfriendly and counter-productive for the users of the application. Table 8-7 lists common system usability issues that can surface while designing client-server graphical user interfaces.

Table 8–7 System Usability Issues

- The system is difficult to learn
- The system is overly complex for no reason
- The system is difficult to use and annoys the average users
- The error messages that are displayed by the system are cryptic and meaningless to the users
- The system forces the users to memorize too much data while performing a single business task
- No online help facility is available
- The user procedure manual is incomplete or difficult to understand
- The graphical user interface is inconsistent from one screen to another
- The levels of resolution supported by the display monitors are inadequate for the kind of reports and graphics that are generated by the system
- The graphical user interface does not support the natural sequence in which the users perform their day-to-day business tasks

In some large organizations, human-factor professionals, with the active participation of a representative group of application users or targeted customers, conduct usability tests. In smaller organizations, the usability tests are conducted simply with a representative set of junior and senior users who have hands-on practices with the system interface. In all cases, usability testing should always involve users. Developers alone should never perform it.

The usability testing process truly must verify simple user interface characteristics such as the following:

- How easily the users can navigate from one screen to another
- How the various GUI control buttons, icons, and menus are organized on the windows for ease-of-use and effectiveness
- Whether the GUIs are designed in a consistent manner within the same application or across multiple corporate applications

The users perform usability testing to determine how well the business flow that is implemented by the client-server or Web application matches the natural sequence in which the users perform their business tasks. If the graphical user interface is very intuitive, then the users can concentrate their efforts on accomplishing their daily tasks rather than fighting the system interface.

Usability testing can pinpoint areas of poorly designed graphical user interfaces that, once corrected, can increase significantly user productivity and reduce user training costs. In fact, several professional studies have demonstrated that usability testing can result in $2 savings in user time for every dollar spent on testing the user interface, for relatively small home-grown applications. For large applications, the savings can increase to $100 user timesaving per dollar invested in testing the system user interface. The return on investment can grow by leaps and bounds as the number of users increases drastically. Table 8-8 illustrates this point.

Table 8–8 Usability Testing Costs Versus Savings

CLIENT-SERVER	USABILITY TESTING COSTS	USER TIME SAVINGS
Small Client-Server Application	$1	$2
Large Client-Server Application	$1	$100 and more

8.4.3 DOCUMENTATION TESTING

Documentation testing verifies the accuracy, relevancy, user-friendliness, and completeness of the user manuals and system operations documentation.

Users should exercise all the application functions while at the same time inspecting the system documentation manuals to identify potential inconsistencies, ambiguities, and errors.

Documentation testing should equally cover the application online help facility and the set of system manual procedures that the users must carry out. In a GUI system, the online help function is generally supported at two distinct levels.

The first level of help consists of a simple context-sensitive help facility that is frequently provided at the bottom of the window screen, such as the Microsoft Windows MicroHelp facility. This specific area of the window can display a simple but meaningful textual description of the functionality indicated by the menu or toolbar labels.

The second level of help, which is much more sophisticated than the first level, usually involves the creation of a complete online help subsystem. In a sophisticated client-server system, the online help facility will include pop-up windows, jumptext, and graphical hotspots.

Pop-up windows are displayed when a user clicks on a highlighted word to provide additional information about this word.

Jumptext lets the users click on a word and go directly to the help topic that is associated with this word.

Hotspots are utilized with bitmap images to highlight some areas of interest to the users. When the users move the mouse over the bitmap image, the pointer is usually transformed into a hand. This transformation indicates to the users that they can access additional information on the area or subject that has been hotspotted.

8.4.4   SECURITY TESTING

Security testing verifies that the application is immune to unauthorized attempts to access it. Security test cases are designed with the firm intent of breaking the application by bypassing its security features. Table 8-9 lists some of the functional elements that should be verified while conducting the security tests.

Table 8–9 Security Test Cases

- Sign-on and password procedures to access the application
- Security features to control access to specific application windows
- Security features to control access to the Internet
- Security features to control access to specific menu items or control objects that are displayed in the windows
- Security features to control access to the application databases or flat files
- Security features to control access to the application from remote sites
- Security procedures to control access to applications intended for mobile computing
- Potential ways of accessing the database servers via other means than the application programs themselves, such as a database query tool or utility
- Security features related to controlling the use of electronic authorization procedures and signatures
- Change password procedures

A physical dimension to security also exists. Hence, security test cases should be developed to verify the physical access controls to the different locations where the client workstations, the application servers, and the database servers are deployed throughout the enterprise and at off-site areas. The security testing process should also cover the access to and control of system documents such as sensitive reports and forms.

8.4.5   ERROR MESSAGE TESTING

Error message testing verifies the known error conditions that must be handled properly by the application. The various error messages that can be displayed by the application should be tested thoroughly to ensure that they are relevant to the type of error conditions that might arise while using that application. Also, the content of the error message should be verified for ease of understanding from a user standpoint.

In a client-server system, application errors are normally managed at four different levels, as indicated in the following:

- Field data entry level
- Window level
- Database level
- Network level

At the field data entry level, the system simply will not allow the user to enter invalid data. The invalid data field immediately gets focus, and a context-sensitive error message displays, along with an explanation of what corrective measures the user can take to attempt to fix the problem.

At the window level, prior to saving the data, the system will verify all field values to ensure that they are valid. If invalid data is encountered, an error message displays along with a general explanation of what the problem is. Control is then passed back to the user, who might have to do some extra work to locate the field in error and fix it. This approach is less effective than error checking at the field level.

At the database level, the results of an SQL call to the database are verified immediately by the program and, if the call is invalid, a meaningful error message displays back to the user, explaining what is going on in business terms that the user can easily understand.

At the network level, the error message displays back to the user with a meaningful message. Since the network layer should be completely transparent to the user, these messages are usually aimed more at the MIS staff. The IT experts use the network error messages to help fix particular network infrastructure problems, such as a network error message that is triggered by a defective remote procedure call.

Some client-server systems are also designed in such a way that error log files are created every time specific error conditions that need to be tracked occur within the application. In such a context, the content of the error log files should be thoroughly tested by the developers and carefully examined to ensure that they capture the right information.

8.4.6 DESTRUCTIVE TESTING

Destructive testing verifies how the application responds to unusual or unexpected situations. For instance, how will the application behave when only spaces are entered in an input field that normally requires any alphabetic characters other than spaces? How will the application behave when a user clicks on several control buttons that are displayed on a window in an unusual sequence?

Another aspect of destructive testing relates to hardware equipment. In order to test hardware failures and how the system reacts to them, the testers might purposely make various hardware devices look as if they would not be available (i.e., turn off the power unit) or broken, by simulating a hardware failure with specialized software facilities.

8.4.7　STRESS TESTING

Stress testing verifies the behavior of the client-server application under very high volumes of data, usually over a short period of time. These tests are performed in either a real or a simulated mode of operation. Variable workloads of transactions can be submitted simultaneously to overload the system.

The objective of stress testing is to strain the client and server machines well beyond their capacity limits and ultimately attempt to break them.

In a mission-critical client-server environment, stress testing is often essential to determine the true break points at which the client or server machines will crash while running a large number of transactions. It can also be used to detect potential memory leaks or network inefficiencies. Memory leaks occur when chunks of memory still remain allocated after a program terminates. This situation may cause a program to run out of memory after running for a significant period of time.

The rationale behind such a destructive process is to better assess and delineate the boundary limits of the system to further improve its overall reliability. Stress testing is also useful to detect faulty hardware equipment long before the system gets transferred into a production environment.

Table 8-10 lists some of the hardware/software/networking system components that are good candidates for stress testing in a typical client-server or intranet environment setup.

Stress testing generally targets system areas that put the greatest load on the client-server system and the technology infrastructure that supports it. By purposely overloading the system and the hardware equipment, the ultimate break points and potential bottlenecks areas are usually assessed within an acceptable precision range.

Once you know the critical saturation thresholds of the software, hardware, and networking facilities, the metric data that was gathered during the stress tests are used to help fix unforeseen problems and monitor the system performance behavior when the system is migrated into production.

Table 8-11 lists some of the most representative test cases that a comprehensive stress test plan should cover.

8.4.8　PERFORMANCE TESTING

Performance testing verifies how well the application measures up against the stated system service-level requirements, such as for response time transactions, under normal operating conditions, but with varying loads of data.

Table 8–10 Stress Testing Components

- Client workstation memory
- CPU capacity
- Application servers
- Client-server middleware software
- Database servers and gateways
- Fax servers
- Middleware
- Local area networks
- Metropolitan area networks
- Wide area networks
- Print servers
- Network file sharing (NFS) servers
- Client-server networks
- I/O channels
- Memory management facilities
- Printer spoolers
- Tasks or job schedulers
- Printers, monitors (graphical display capabilities)
- Special hardware devices
- Firewalls
- Web servers

Some of the issues that you can uncover when performance testing is performed over extended periods of time at or near peak load capacity appear in Table 8-12.

Performance testing is critical when Rapid Application Development (RAD) techniques are used to develop the system incrementally with the active participation of a relatively small number of users. Problems arise, however, when the client-server application suddenly needs to scale up to a full-fledged production environment and must support a very large number of users. Then some serious bottlenecks can occur at the level of the client, the server, or the network. For instance, is the application's response time acceptable when a large number of users are simultaneously running a large number of on-line transactions?

Whenever practical and feasible, execute the performance tests in a test environment that simulates as closely as possible the real-life production environment. After all, the odds are that in a real-life situation, several other applications will likely compete against one another to have access to the same servers and network resources.

Figure 8-12 schematically illustrates the need to measure a transaction response time for an N-tier client-server application.

Table 8–11 Stress Test Cases

- High transaction volumes for all mission-critical business functions, either batch or online
- Overall resource utilization
- Overall response time
- Overall turnaround time
- Overall batch processing window time
- Overall number of concurrent users
- Overall number of concurrent transactions that can be processed while updating single or multiple databases
- High volumes of data transferred between the system and its external interfaces
- Run time of critical batch programs
- Overall network throughput (LAN, MAN, WAN)
- Overall system network and backup recovery capabilities after various system failures
- Distribution of large reports across the network
- Distribution of multimedia data across the network such as audio and video clips
- Gateway connections to the mainframe environment

Table 8–12 Performance Test Cases

- Application logic errors spread over the clients, servers, or mainframe
- Various client, server, or network bottlenecks
- System throughput limitations
- Disk I/O bottlenecks
- Poor transaction response time while retrieving or updating the application databases
- Verification that the system data locking, access, and modification mechanisms work in a multi-user environment
- Memory leaks
- Verification that events that trigger other events across the application behave properly
- Storage capacity limitations
- Client or server disk space limitations
- Interfacing problems with external modules such as faxing facilities, e-mail, word processing, etc.
- Interfacing problems with other systems
- File sharing server problems
- Adherence to remote interface standards (remote procedures) problems
- Print server problems

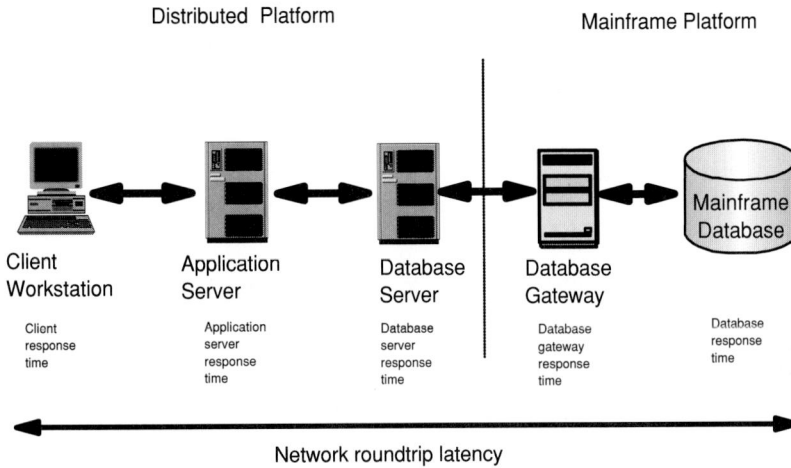

Figure 8–6 Monitoring overall transaction response time.

8.4.9 MIDDLEWARE TESTING

The purpose of middleware testing is to ensure that the client-server application interfaces correctly with all the multiple and heterogeneous layers of software components that reside somewhere between the enterprise network infrastructure layer and the business application software layer. Client-server applications often require multiple levels of connectivity software, often generically referred to as middleware. Broadly speaking, software middleware glues, in a transparent manner, various client-server (and non-client-server) components together.

Middleware software controls and manages the flow of information and activities that occur between application clients and servers components. In fact, middleware software can provide multiple functions that often are very important for large and complex client-server applications, such as:

- Access to heterogeneous relational databases
- Gateways to remote databases or flat files that reside on the mainframe
- Distribution of the business application software components across multiple heterogeneous hardware platforms

Some of the different types of middleware software include:

- Client ODBC driver modules middleware
- Native database APIs middleware
- Message-oriented middleware (MOM)
- Relational and non-relational database gateways middleware

- Remote data access (RDA) middleware to access data located in a remote location
- Remote procedure calls (RPCs), directory, and security services for distributed application middleware
- Distributed transaction processing middleware

For more detailed information on the middleware subject, consult Chapter 9.

8.4.10 MULTI-SITE TESTING

Multi-site testing verifies that all the client-server and supporting infrastructure components that are distributed across multiple geographical sites operate satisfactorily and in synchronization with one another. Table 8-13 lists some of the elements to verify while conducting multi-site tests.

Table 8–13 Multi-site Test Cases

- Network bandwidth between different sites
- Synchronization and convergence of data across geographically dispersed sites and time zones
- Integrity of data regularly replicated across several database servers
- Distribution of business functions across multiple sites
- Conformance to established security and control access procedures across multiple sites

8.4.11 COMPLIANCE TESTING

Compliance testing ensures that the client-server application conforms with the system development and software quality standards that were set for the enterprise at large.

Compliance testing should happen as early as possible in the application development cycle to validate the quality of the software deliverables that are produced during each development phase.

Table 8-14 indicates some of the types of test cases that can be exercised during compliance testing.

8.4.12 BACKUP/RECOVERY TESTING

Backup and recovery testing verifies that the application software can gracefully recover from a hardware, software, or networking failure. Test cases can be constructed to intentionally cause system crashes and then verify whether the client-server application can be restored back to specific points in time prior to the failure events. Table 8-15 lists some examples of test case scenarios.

Table 8–14 Compliance Test Cases

- Naming conventions
- Programming conventions
- Documentation conventions
- File directory structure conventions
- System specification conventions
- System requirement conventions
- Graphical user interface conventions

Table 8–15 Backup/recovery/restart Test Cases

- Backup of complete databases and flat files
- Restoration of complete databases and flat files
- Backup of selective databases and flat files
- Restoration of selective databases and flat files
- Recovery of databases and flat files back to some specific checkpoints
- Impact assessment of the recovery procedures on other components of the client-server system or other applications
- Verification of the system and database transaction logs

8.4.13 VOLUME TESTING

Volume testing verifies that the system can handle the maximum volumes of data that were specified for the client-server application during the requirement development stage.

8.4.14 INTERNATIONAL CUSTOMIZATION TESTING

Customization testing verifies local versions of the application that have been customized for an international market.

The local versions of the application are tested to ensure that they still work correctly and that the foreign words used for the translations are accurate and culturally unbiased.

8.4.15 REGRESSION TESTING

Fundamentally, two stages are used to test the client-server application. The first stage is called progressive testing, as opposed to regression testing for the second stage.

During the progressive testing stage, the developers incrementally add new functionality to the system. At this stage, the developers put the emphasis on verifying the new functions to uncover problems that might occur in the newly introduced programs.

During the regression testing stage, the application is tested to verify that the newly added programs, or changes made to existing programs, do not adversely affect other parts of the system that were already tested. Figure 8-7 illustrates the relationship between regression testing and the other stages of the testing life cycle.

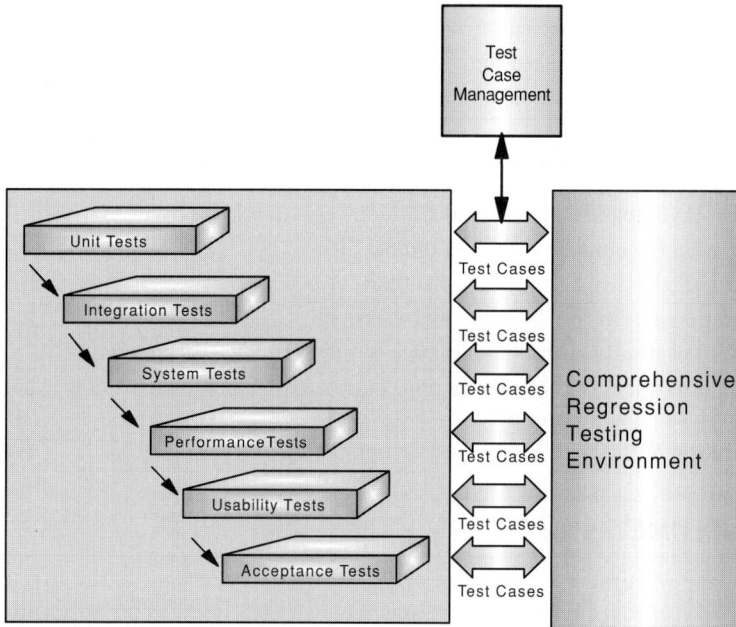

Figure 8–7 Relationship between regression testing and the other phases of the testing life cycle.

Regression testing can be performed at any stage of the testing life cycle, including unit, integration, system, and user acceptance testing. Ideally, a comprehensive regression test environment is composed of the following components:

- A detailed index of all the test cases that are currently stored in the regression testing libraries, along with a description of the expected results
- For each test case, a brief description of the system components it exercises and the relevant test case objectives
- A brief description of how, when, and where to use the test cases

Usually, test regression files are progressively built during the design and coding stages of the client-server application. Selective subsets of unit, integration, system, and user acceptance test cases are gradually assembled to ultimately create a thorough integration test environment that can be used to verify the whole system.

The regression testing process is a strong candidate for automation since most regression test cases must be repeated each time major changes are applied to the application.

8.4.16 CLIENT GRAPHICAL USER INTERFACE (GUI) TESTING

Configurable graphical user interfaces greatly increase the productivity of the users. With a mouse, users can point and click on a variety of windows, pull-down menus, control buttons, and icons on toolbars in any sequence they like. They can fill in data entry fields and so forth. The users are in full control of the application.

However, the event-driven nature of these highly sophisticated graphical user interfaces necessitates extensive testing to verify that their functionality works properly.

Figure 8-8 illustrates the different types of test cases that can be created to exercise the system graphical user interface.

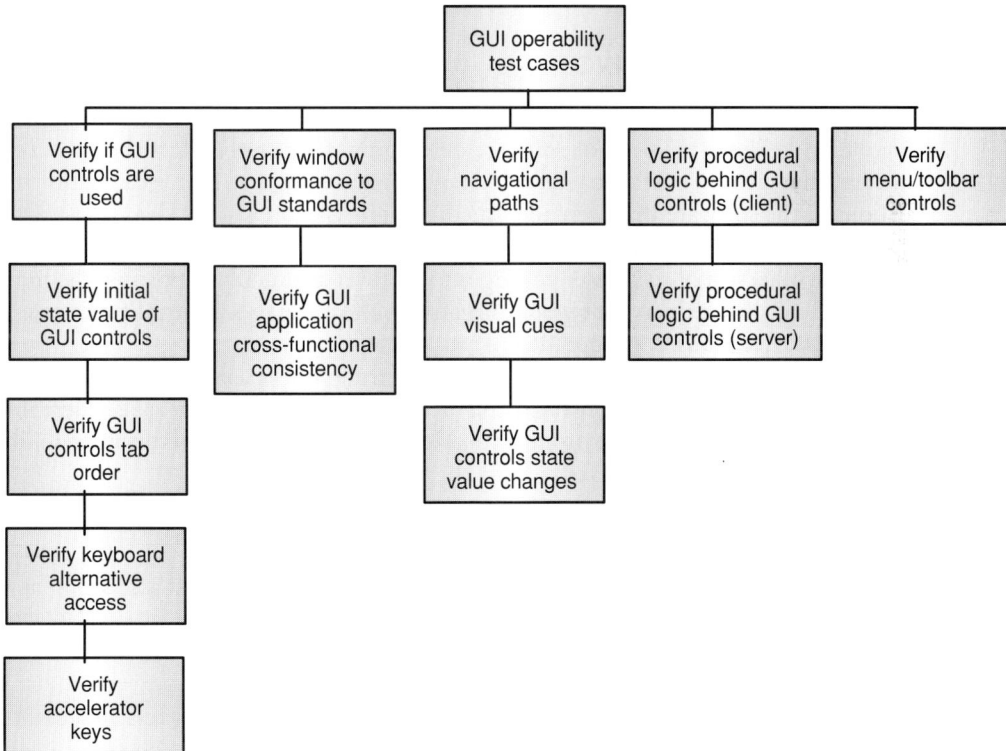

Figure 8–8 GUI test cases.

At their basic levels, the developers can manually test GUIs. However, a manual testing approach might turn out to be a labor-intensive task for a very large and complex client-server system. In such cases, automated GUI testing tools can complement the manual testing approach and facilitate the job of the developers.

Automated testing tools can automatically capture the multiple keystrokes, mouse clicks, and selection of control object operations that are usually performed by the users. All the user interactions are stored in test script files along with the expected results. The automated testing tools can then replay the various test scripts when the application code or user interface has been changed and verify whether or not the actual output results compare favorably with the previously established baselines. Refer to Section 8.6 for more information on this subject.

8.4.17 DOMAIN TESTING

Domain testing, also called boundary value testing, exercises the programs with test data that are characterized by ranges of values, invalid values, random values, out-of-boundary values, and normal values.

8.4.18 RISK-BASED TESTING

In risk-based testing, the tester will analyze the software and identify the different areas where the likelihood of a major software defect might adversely affect the user. Test data are then created based on this risk analysis assessment and exercised against the portions of the software that were identified as high-risk zones.

Testers use risk-based testing when time to test software is significantly compressed. The prime objective of risk-based testing is to uncover as quickly as possible the most important software defects that would negatively affect the most critical functions of the software, from a user standpoint.

Table 8-16 provides a typical breakdown of software zones based on user access likelihood. Testers can use such software zone breakdown lists to identify areas where important problems in a software product might have a severe impact on the user's ability to perform his/her business tasks.

Table 8–16 Identification Of Software Risk Zones By User Access Likelihood

Compulsory	This is an area of the software that the average user must access most of the time, such as when he accesses the application login screen to enter the appropriate user id and password, create a file, open a file, print a document, and so forth.
Frequent	This is an area of the software that the average user will access most of the time during a regular session with the software.
Sporadic	This is an area of the software that the average user might access once in a while during a regular session with the software.
Seldom	This is an area of the software that the average user might access very rarely during a regular session with the software.

Table 8-17 provides a breakdown of different levels of impact that a defect might have on a typical user. The impact is listed in a most damaging to a less damaging sequence order.

Table 8–17 Classification Of Defects Based On Impact On Users

Disastrous	The system crashes or freezes and becomes inoperable. The users cannot utilize the system.
Harmful	The system does not necessarily crash but may cause data to be lost or corrupted. Certain system functions may be inoperable.
Hampering	The system works relatively well, but in certain situations, the users must use a workaround solution to complete their business tasks.
Irritating	The system works well, but the execution of certain business tasks is cumbersome to the average users.

Testers can use the information provided in Tables 8.16 and 8.17 to help identify and locate the high-risk zones for software failure, the potential impact of software defects on the users, and the likelihood failure will occur. Armed with this information, they can organize a plan to test the software based on the priority assigned to each identified software high-risk area.

The areas of high risk should be tested first and much more intensely than the areas of low risk, where the discovery of a defect, even an important one, is likely to have a minor impact on the user.

8.4.19 SYSTEM INTERFACE TESTING

The system interface test cases and data verify all the functional processes that exchange data between the new system and other systems.

8.4.20 DATA INTEGRITY TESTING

The data integrity test cases verify that the data stored in the system files/databases are safeguarded from potential loss or corruption while using the system transactions. The business application software should not cause unsolicited loss or modification of data. If the software functionality degrades or fails, it should do so as gracefully as possible.

8.4.21 INSTALLATION TESTING

The installation test cases verify that all application software components can be installed on their target computing platform(s) with ease and correctly, even on the same platform but with different hardware/software configuration components. Verify the installation process and its supporting procedures to ensure that it is as foolproof as possible, especially if it will be installed by average users instead of professionals.

8.4.22 CO-EXISTENCE TESTING

Co-existence testing ensures that the application software is compatible and works in harmony with a variety of other software objects such as other systems, middleware, databases, and operating systems. It verifies that—even if the application software has been successfully installed, configured, and runs smoothly—the software does not cause any harm to other already installed software components. Co-existence testing should also verify that the new application system is backward compatible with earlier versions of it, where applicable. Co-existence testing assumes that the software functionality has been tested previously.

8.4.23 PRINTER TESTING

The printer test cases verify that all appropriate application documents and objects can be printed properly with a variety of printers provided by different manufacturers' printing devices. Are documents such as special reports and forms printed as expected on each particular printing devices? What about printer drivers? Have different printer drivers been tested for compatibility with the application and different corporate printing devices?

8.4.24 TECHNOLOGY INFRASTRUCTURE TESTING

Technology infrastructure testing verifies the many layers of inter-operable hardware, software, middleware, and networking devices and facilities that need to be implemented and work together to support the business applications. Technology infrastructure testing should include test cases for verifying interoperability, performance, and scalability. Perform technology infrastructure testing when new technologies are implemented in the enterprise.

In large organizations, a separate project can be used to quickly build a sample application or prototype to verify the overall effectiveness of the enterprise technology infrastructure, preferably ahead of the implementation of the application development infrastructure or new application system.

8.4.25 DATA CONVERSION TESTING

Data conversion testing verifies that all conversion programs have been thoroughly verified for the accuracy of each conversion process. Specific tests are also devised to verify the effectiveness of all data validation and transformation routines.

8.5 TESTING STRATEGY

The software testing strategy describes the approach that will be used to manage the overall testing process, covering the entire application development cycle. The major constituents of the software testing strategy are initially formulated during the analysis phase. Later, they are finalized with the last details during the design and construction system development stages. The outcome of this activity is the application test plan deliverable. Figure 8-9 describes the major points that you should cover in the software testing strategy.

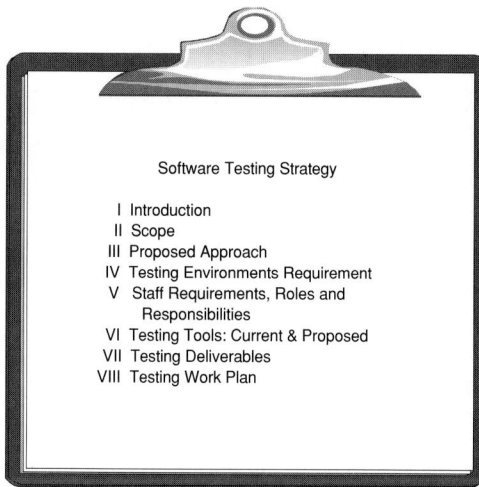

Software Testing Strategy

   I Introduction
  II Scope
 III Proposed Approach
 IV Testing Environments Requirement
  V Staff Requirements, Roles and
      Responsibilities
 VI Testing Tools: Current & Proposed
VII Testing Deliverables
VIII Testing Work Plan

Figure 8–9 Software testing strategy outline.

Section 8.5.1 provides a brief description of each item shown in Figure 8-9.

8.5.1 INTRODUCTION

This section states the prime purpose of the testing strategy and provides some high-level information about the application system that is being developed. It also describes the major objectives of the testing process in relation to the client-server or Web database application at hand. This task is primarily done based on the system functional requirements and the type of technology that will be used to develop and operate the system.

8.5.2 SCOPE

This section delineates the size and scope of the overall testing effort, covering various areas such as those indicated in Table 8-18.

Table 8–18 Testing Scope

- Conformance to existing system development quality standards
- System functions and facilities that will be tested
- System functions and facilities that will not be tested or are excluded
- System functions and facilities that will be deferred
- Critical system performance and user acceptance criteria that must be verified
- Major system operational features
- External system interfaces
- Specific components of the technology infrastructure that will or will not be tested.

A high-level diagram describing the major components of the technical architecture that will be used to develop and implement the system should be useful to pinpoint the potential areas where the risks of failure are high. Figure 8-10 shows the major components of a generic three-tier client-server technical architecture.

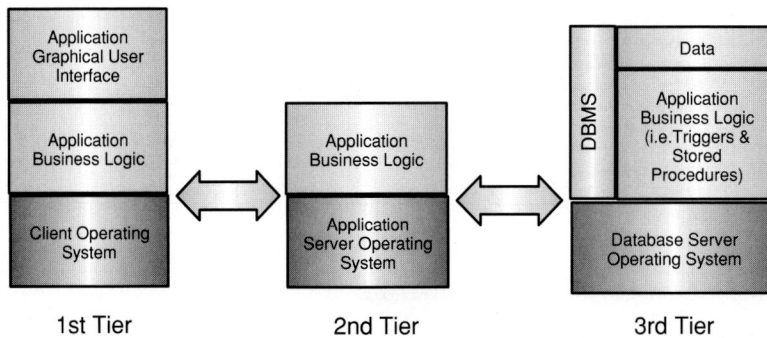

Figure 8–10 Generic, three-tier client-server technical architecture components.

The scope of the testing effort should reflect the set of requirements that have been identified by the users for the client-server system. The scope will vary project by project, but should clearly indicate the major components that are in and out of scope of the planned testing effort.

8.5.3 PROPOSED APPROACH

This section describes the strategy that you will use to manage the overall testing process. The plan of attack might cover various topics such as those indicated in Table 8-19.

The approach should also define the specific testing objectives that will apply uniquely to each particular major testing cycle: unit, integration, system, and user acceptance.

In the test game plan, carefully document the section that describes how the defect tracking and reporting process will be managed. Clearly identify the type of reports

Table 8–19 Testing Game Plan

- The set of various techniques that will used to create test data and verify the functionality and operational characteristics of the client-server or Web application
- The pass/fail criteria for each distinct testing cycle
- The procedures for reporting defects
- The procedures to control error corrections and program revisions
- The high-level start and stop mechanisms for each major testing phases (i.e., completion criteria)
- The procedures to promote or demote software components from one testing environment to another one
- How test cases and test data will be created, reused, and managed across the different testing cycles

that will be used to control and manage this process. Each report should include the name of the recipients, the frequency at which these reports will be produced, their delivery mechanisms, and so forth. Several automated testing tools now offer facilities to automate this process.

Set up a mechanism to prioritize the defects based on their impact on the users. Table 8-20 provides a simple approach to help prioritize defects.

Table 8–20 Defect Prioritization Process

Defect Impact	Priority	Description
Disastrous	1	Disastrous defects are defects that are real showstoppers. The system function or characteristic being tested cannot be used without causing a system crash or freeze.
Critical	2	Harmful defects are defects that cause some specific area of the system to not work properly as per its original specification. However, the system remains operational.
Hampering	3	The system works relatively well, but in certain situations, the users must utilize a workaround solution in order to complete their business tasks.
Minor	4	The system works well, but the execution of certain business tasks is cumbersome to the average users. Some irregularities might occur, such as misspelled labels or incorrect formatting and display of data. The graphical user interface might not satisfy the corporate GUI standards.

Also document the process used to report defects. As much as possible, the reports that will be used to document important defects should provide the information indicated in Table 8-21.

Table 8–21 Important Defect Reporting Data

- A brief description of the defect that was uncovered and what should have happened in a normal situation
- A brief description of how to reproduce the defect
- A clear indication of the severity of the defect and its potential impact on the user

8.5.4 TESTING ENVIRONMENT REQUIREMENTS

This section describes the set of client and server hardware, software, local area network, and middleware facilities and resources that will be required to support the unit, integration, system, and user acceptance testing cycles for each chosen development and deployment computer platform(s). You should identify the physical locations where testing will likely be performed in this section.

You should also describe the strategy that will be used to assign sufficient resources for the allocation of various libraries to house the current and/or previous versions of test programs and their associated test data files and databases for each respective test environment.

8.5.5 STAFF REQUIREMENTS, ROLES, AND RESPONSIBILITIES

This section identifies the various organizations that will participate in the software testing process, along with a brief description of their respective roles and responsibilities. For each group, an estimate of the number of staff resources should be provided along with a description of any specialized skill sets that the staff must possess or will need to acquire in order to perform successful testing.

8.5.6 TESTING EQUIPMENT AND TOOLS: CURRENT AND PROPOSED

This section identifies the categories of software testing tools and equipment that will be required to design and generate test data, run the different test cases, and verify the test results.

Additional categories of tools might be required to conduct system performance monitoring activities, to generate testing reports, and to manage the testing process itself. The type of information that should be provided for each type of testing tool is indicated in Table 8-22.

8.5.7 TESTING DELIVERABLES

This section describes the types of deliverables that will be produced during each major test cycle such as activity logs, incident reports, test coverage reports, test completion reports, test plans, test cases, and test data.

Table 8–22 Testing Tool Documentation

- Product name
- Testing tool purpose with a brief description of the functionality provided
- Vendor
- Release and version number
- Configuration requirements
- Computing platform supported (hardware and operating system)
- Level of compatibility with other testing tools and development environment

8.5.8 TESTING WORK PLAN

This section describes the major milestones, time estimates, and schedules that are required to plan, prepare, execute, and complete the entire testing process activities. It also describes the relationships and dependencies that exist among the major testing activities.

While preparing the work plan schedule, take into consideration unknown testing factors that might influence the time needed to perform the testing activities, as indicated in Table 8-23.

Table 8–23 Testing Soft Factors

- Number of errors that will be detected during testing
- Level of difficulty associated with the task of locating and fixing the errors
- Number of additional tests that will be required to ensure that the errors are fixed correctly and do not introduce, inadvertently, new errors
- Time needed to compare the actual test results against the results that were expected prior to executing the tests
- Level of availability of the testing tools and supporting resources that are shared with other testing teams
- Level of expertise of the software testers

If any constraints will affect the work plan, then they should be clearly spelled out, such as system resources or time limitations.

8.6 AUTOMATED CLIENT-SERVER TESTING TOOLS

So far, you have seen in this chapter that a thorough testing process which is closely integrated with the development cycle itself is essential to the successful deployment of quality client-server applications.

In today's competitive environment, software failures in a mission-critical application can easily translate into the loss of substantial amounts of revenues for an enterprise, not to mention the potential loss of lives in critical applications developed for the medical field. All in all, the testing philosophy I prescribe in this book is simple— test as early as possible during the development cycle and as frequently as possible.

Nonetheless, for medium to large client-server projects, testing might also translate directly into substantial costs. In some studies, testing client-server applications accounted for as much as 50% of the total application development effort. These costs are primarily incurred through the acquisition of testing tools, workstations, and servers that are required to perform the tests. Testing also entails investing a considerable amount of time and resources in performing the testing process and managing it, not to mention the time needed to train people in using various testing tools efficiently.

At this point, automated client-server testing tools can be used to help accelerate the testing cycles for large client-server systems while not having to compromise on its quality and effectiveness. Automated client-server testing tools can facilitate the creation, housekeeping, and execution of both client and server test cases and data, such as those indicated in Table 8-24.

Table 8–24 Automated Test Case Candidates

- Client graphical user interfaces, with multiple variations of windows, menus, objects, and icons
- Client workstation load testing
- Server load testing
- Combined client/server load testing
- Client testing with variable workstation configurations
- Middleware testing
- Local area network load testing

Figure 8-11 shows the various generic categories of client-server and Web testing tools that are available on the market.

Table 8-25 lists high-level selection criteria that can help to select client-server automated testing tools. You can supplement this list with your own selection criteria.

As a final observation on automated testing tools, software test automation is not replacing manual testing but simply can complement it in certain areas. More often than not, automated testing tools require additional time and resources on a project. Furthermore, emerging studies reveal that the number of critical defects uncovered with manual testing far outweigh the number of critical defects identified with automated testing tools. Some specific areas where automated testing tools can be really useful is in stress and load testing, regression testing, and configuration testing.

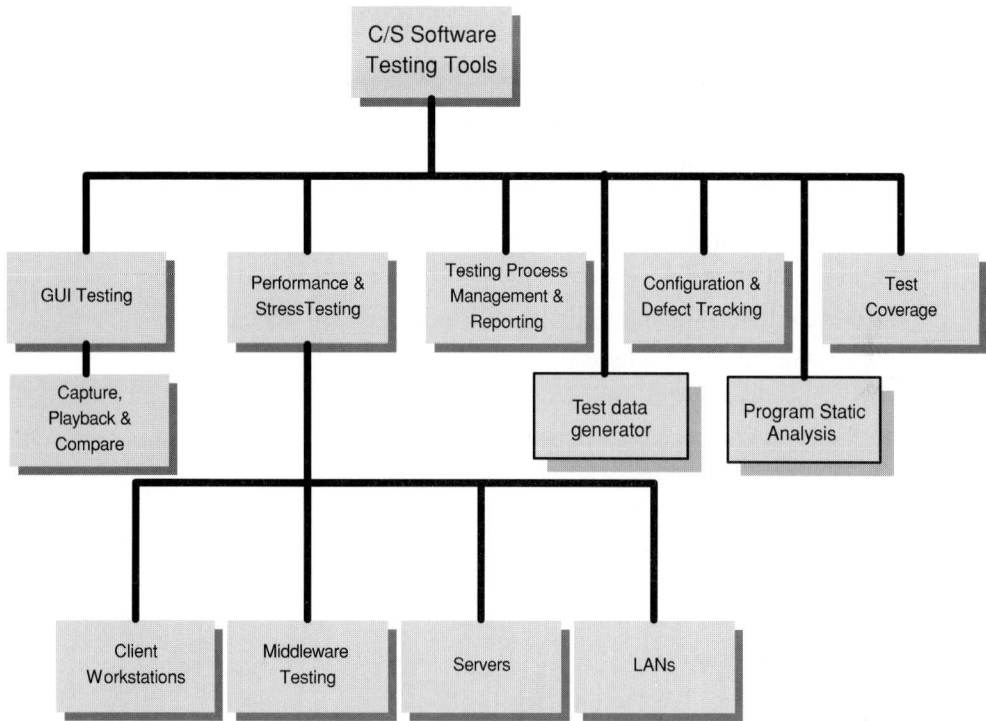

Figure 8–11 Various categories of client-server testing tools.

Table 8–25 Client-server Testing Tool Selection Criteria

	C/S Test Tool 1	・・・	C/S Test Tool 'N'
Ease of Use			
Client GUI Testing			
• Object-Level Recording			
• Object-Level Playback			
Scripting Language(s)			
• Creation			
• Execution			
• Debugging			
• Proprietary			
• Non-Proprietary			
Cross-Platform Support			

Table 8–25 Client-server Testing Tool Selection Criteria (cont.)

Support of Foreign Language(s)

Unattended Testing Features

Defect Tracking and Resolution

Coverage Analysis

Regression Testing

Client Load/Stress Testing

Server Load/Stress Testing

Middleware Load/Stress Testing

Client-Server Load/Stress Testing

Test Life Cycle Management Facilities

Test Plan Creation

Test Reporting Facilities

Test Data Creation and Maintenance

Online Data Analysis Facilities

Network Load Capacity

Support of Formal Test Methodology

Rapid Application Development (RAD)
Tools Supported

- Standard Objects Supported
- Images
- Control Buttons
- Menu Items
- Memory
- List
- Clipboard
- Alphanumeric variables
- Textual information

Error Logging

Integrated Test Repository

Documentation

Integration with Client-Server CASE
Tools

Table 8–25 Client-server Testing Tool Selection Criteria (cont.)

Customer Support
- Hotline
- Web
- Fax
- Bulletin Board
- Local Offices

On-Site Training Course(s)

Online Help Facility

Test Portability

8.7 MANAGING THE TESTING PROCESS

As you have seen throughout this chapter, the careful planning of the client-server testing process entails multiple activities that span several development phases. Figure 8-12 presents another holistic view of the testing process.

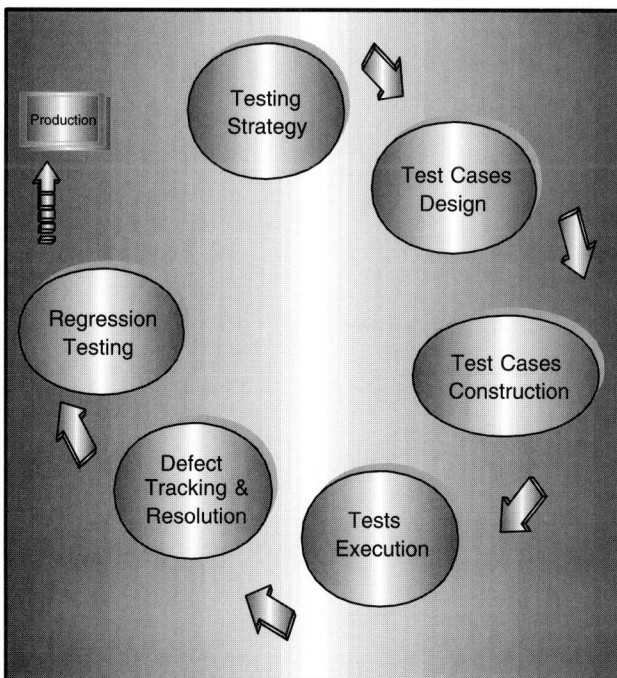

Figure 8–12 A holistic view of the testing process.

The testing process can prove to be rather complex for very large-scale client-server applications. Because of its inherent complexities, the execution of the testing effort can be chaotic and inefficient if it is not planned early and managed properly thereafter. To assist the application development team in planning and estimating the overall testing effort, Table 8-26 enumerates some of the generic testing activities and events that will likely occur during the software testing life cycle of a mission-critical client-server development project.

Table 8–26 List Of Generic Testing Activities

- Identify and document inconsistencies and failures (incident reports)
- Maintain the test activity log and the status progress report
- Develop the testing strategy
- Define and set up test environment(s)
- Maintain test environment(s)
- Decompose client-server functional specifications into testing requirements
- Specify system and performance testing requirements
- Define test procedures
- Define test cases
- Create test data and expected results
- Construct different test cycles
- Define test requirements coverage
- Schedule tests
- Run tests
- Evaluate test results
- Investigate failures
- Verify test completion criteria
- Debug and resolve failures
- Retest application modules
- Control the promotion/demotion of software objects from one testing library to another one
- Ensure that all test cases are exercised and verified
- Assess the coverage of test requirements
- Manage testing resources and assign priorities
- Track the progress of testing activities
- Perform regression testing

8.8 CHARACTERISTICS OF GOOD TEST DATA

Although several mechanical ways to generate test data exist, the creation of highly effective test data is still a process that relies heavily on the creative skills and level of expertise of the testers. The system testers must possess a killer instinct to generate test data conditions that will have a high probability of uncovering defects that can have a disastrous impact on the users.

Good test data should include not only valid data that demonstrate that the system does what it is supposed to do but also invalid data to verify how the system responds to totally unexpected test data conditions. Table 8-27 shows some of the most desirable characteristics of good test data.

Table 8–27 Characteristics Of Good Test Data

- Possess a high probability of uncovering as many defects as possible with as few test data as possible
- Can be repeated and predicted
- Have expected results that can be verified
- Can be traceable back to the original testing requirements
- Can be easily created or adapted

PART II: INTERNET/INTRANET TESTING

8.9 INTRODUCTION TO INTERNET/INTRANET TESTING

Today, several companies are implementing mission-critical Web database applications. Invariably, the vast majority of these applications all aim at developing closer communications with their customers, suppliers, partners, and employees.

However, the creation and deployment of a sophisticated Internet/intranet database application require a robust, industrial-strength application development environment similar to those available for the more traditional client-server systems. Closer to the testing arena, verifying the correctness of a large and complex Web transactional application requires separate unit, integration, system, and user acceptance test environments.

Additionally, a sound testing strategy must be created to thoroughly verify the reliability, content, functionality, performance, and scalability characteristics of the Web application.

The following sections 8.10 to 8.14 cover the process of Web application database testing. The material provided below is primarily targeted at testing large-scale and overly complex N-tiered Web database applications that interactively update corporate databases. However, the information provided can remain useful to testing smaller Web applications, even the much simpler publishing applications that display only static information on the Web.

8.10 ANATOMY OF A WEB-BROWSER-BASED GRAPHICAL USER

INTERFACE

Prior to diving into more detailed information on Web testing, I want to review, at a high level, a typical Web graphical user interface. Figure 8-13 illustrates the major components that make up a standard Web-browser-based application interface.

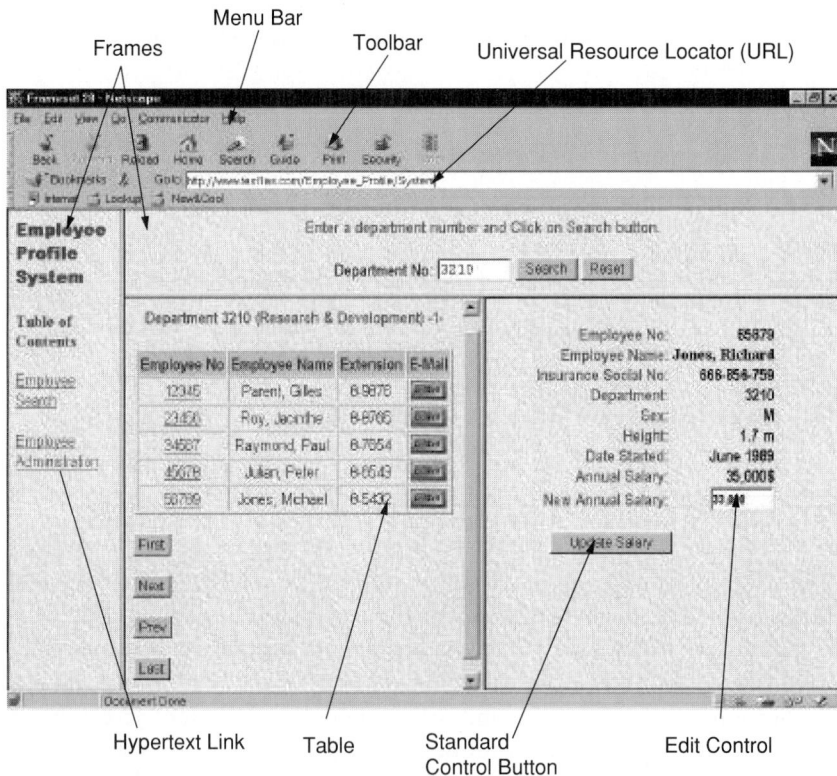

Figure 8–13 Components of a Web-browser-based application. *Source:* Copyright 1996 Netscape Communications Corp. Used with permission. All Rights Reserved. This electronic file or page may not be reprinted or copied without the express written permission of Netscape.

Following is a short description of each of the elements shown in the Web graphical user interface. The first section briefly describes the more traditional Web-based GUI elements that are also commonly used in client-server systems. The second section describes the GUI elements that are more specific to a Web system.

8.10.1 STANDARD GUI WINDOWS CONTROLS

Control buttons. Control buttons are represented under the form of a rectangle that is labeled with text to identify its function. Control buttons trigger events to initiate or conclude an operation.

Check boxes. Check boxes are used solely to set choices that are not mutually exclusive. Check boxes do not initiate or terminate an operation.

Radio buttons. Radio buttons are used to set choices which are mutually exclusive. Radio buttons do not initiate or terminate an operation.

Drop-down list boxes. List boxes are used to provide a list of mutually exclusive choices. They are illustrated by rectangles with downward-pointing arrows at the right-hand side of the rectangle.

Cursor. The cursor indicates the point of action or insertion on the window. Cursors are often utilized to indicate the state of the application. For example, an hourglass cursor will indicate to the user to wait while the system is busy performing a particular task.

Dialog boxes. Dialog boxes are special types of windows that provide information or options to the user. Dialog boxes are modal windows, since the user must dismiss them by clicking either the "**CANCEL**" or "**OK**" control buttons before further processing can take place.

Pull-down menus. Pull-down menus are used to initiate some action by selecting a specific menu item.

Icons. Icons are graphic representations of objects that are displayed in the graphical user interface.

For a more detailed discussion of the traditional GUI window controls and their usage, please refer to Chapter 12.

8.10.2 WEB-BROWSER-SPECIFIC GUI CONTROLS

Following is a brief description of the major GUI elements that are peculiar to a Web HTML document.

Text links. Text links are used to connect one hypertext document to another, or to other HTML resources, either inside the same Web application or outside the Web application. Text links are highlighted in different ways. Usually, they are identified with:

- Text identified in italics
- A color that is different from the color used for the main text
- Underlined text

Links can be identified by pointing the mouse cursor over an HTML page. The cursor will transform its shape, usually into a hand, to indicate a selectable item or hotspot.

Image links. Image links are graphical representations that are used to connect one hypertext document to another, or to other HTML resources. Image links are usually surrounded by an outline to differentiate them from regular graphical images. Image links are frequently used by Web GUI designers to highlight the specific paths a user can take to navigate through a Web document. The most common image links are represented by navigational icons or buttons to go forward, backward, up, down, or home.

Image maps. An image map is a graphic inline image that is used to execute different actions, depending on where the users click on the image with their mouse.

Tables. Tables are two-dimensional objects that are composed of rows and columns. Tables are used to display textual information or graphics on an HTML page with a grid structure. The text or graphical elements shown in a table cell can also be links.

Frames. Frames divide the display area of the browser windows into a variety of scrollable panels. Each panel behaves independently of the other panels.

Forms. A form is an HTML object that is used to enter input data via the Web-browser interface and submit it to the Web server for further processing. It can also display back data via the Web-browser interface, such as information from a corporate database. The basic elements that compose a form can include radio buttons, control buttons, check boxes, text fields, drop-down list boxes, and standard edit control fields.

Discussing the additional HTML tags that are used to structure the Web pages of a document goes well beyond the scope of this book. For more information on this subject, the reader can consult the bibliography provided at the end of this book.

8.11 ANATOMY OF A COMPLETE WEB APPLICATION

As you have seen in Section 8.10 which describes the anatomy of a Web GUI, a typical Web application can include several graphical user interface objects. However, the Web user interface represents only the tip of the iceberg. In fact, a sophisticated Web database application must be supported by a complex Internet/intranet system configuration infrastructure, as schematically illustrated in Figure 8-14.

Besides the various hardware, software, and networking software products that must work harmoniously together behind the scenes, a myriad of additional components are also required to support the functionality of the Web database application. Some of these programming elements might include JAVA applets, Microsoft ActiveX controls, Common Gateway Interface (CGI) scripts, and extensive SQL code to access the application databases. In this respect, Web database applications are no different from the more traditional client-server systems. Thus, all the major Web database application constituents must be tested thoroughly to ensure that the application is reliable, is defect-free, and meets its original design specifications.

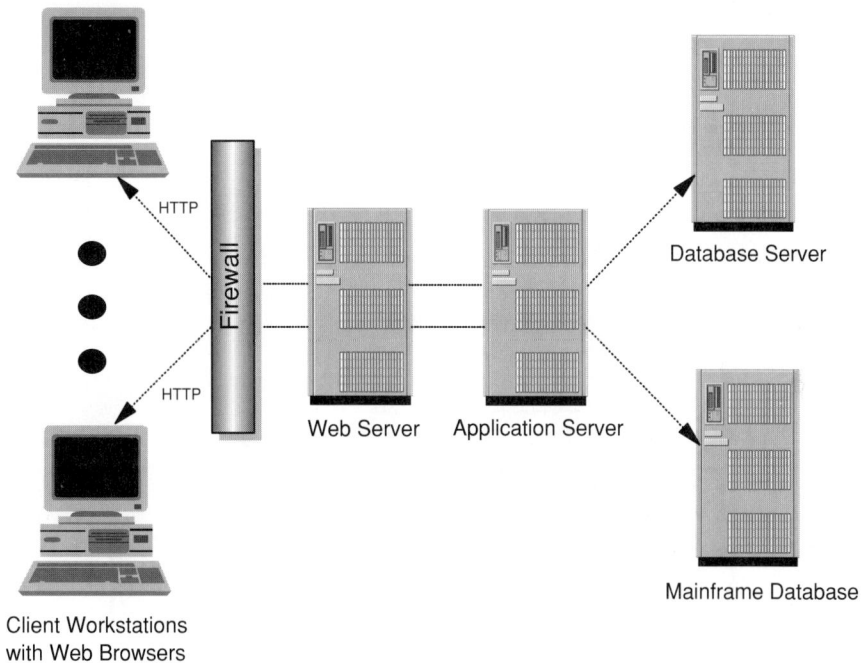

Figure 8–14 Internet infrastructure.

8.12 DIFFERENT TYPES OF WEB APPLICATION TEST CASE SCENARIOS

This section describes the different categories of test case scenarios that can be created to verify that the Web database application operates correctly, in accordance with its design specifications.

Figure 8-15 depicts a holistic view of the most common Web database application components and extensions that should be tested carefully by the developers.

8.12.1 BROWSER COMPATIBILITY TESTING

Browser compatibility testing verifies that the Web application operates correctly and consistently on different types of Web browsers and platforms. Browser compatibility testing is particularly important for the Web applications that will run on the Internet, since different browsers support different levels of HTML standards and extensions.

Cross-browser portability might be less crucial for organizations that deploy their Web applications on an intranet, since internally these organizations can standardize the use of a unique Web browser. However, it might be imperative to test carefully the

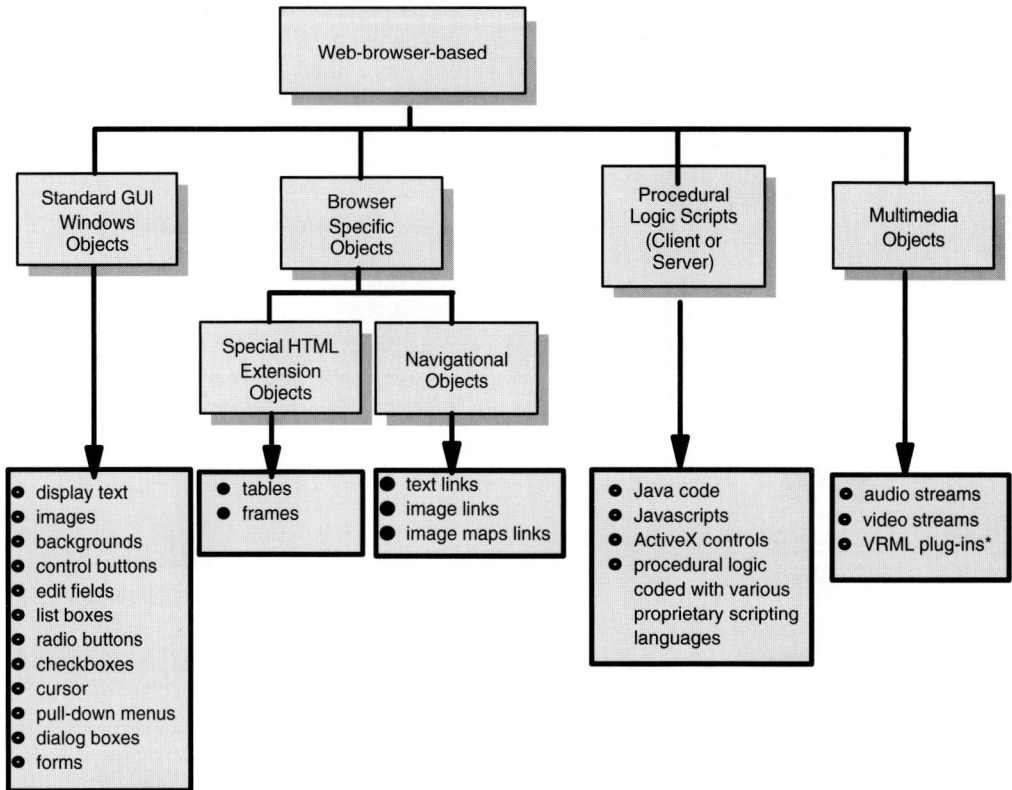

Figure 8–15 A holistic view of the most common Web database application components.

web interface's behavior when running the application with different releases of the same web browser.

8.12.2 DESKTOP CONFIGURATION TESTING

Desktop configuration testing verifies that the client side of the Web application operates consistently on different categories of client desktop machines with different configurations.

8.12.3 USABILITY TESTING

Usability testing verifies that the user interface of the Web application has been designed with a user-centric approach. The user interface of a sophisticated Web database application may contain several forms of interactive media including sounds, graphics, videos, and the more traditional HTML defined controls such as forms, radio buttons, edit fields, and so forth. Verify, with the active participation of the users, that the sequence of interactions that are supported by the Web graphical interface matches closely the users' own natural business tasks flow.

8.12.4 DOCUMENTATION TESTING

Documentation testing verifies the accuracy, relevancy, user-friendliness, and completeness of the written user guide and the context-sensitive online help facility that are provided with the Web application.

8.12.5 SECURITY TESTING

Security testing verifies that the Web application is immune from unauthorized attempts to access it. Some of the different test case scenarios that might be exercised appear in Table 8-28.

Table 8–28 Web Security Test Cases

- Attempts to bypass the Web firewall security mechanism
- Attempts to bypass the standard Web application sign-on and password procedures
- Verification of the change password procedure
- Attempts to access other hosts through the Web application
- Attempts to get access to a Web site restricted area
- Verification of potential alterations of data during network data transmissions
- Verification of potential attempts to change the static content of the Web files without proper authorization
- Verification that the data encryption algorithms used while transmitting data or passwords cannot be bypassed or broken
- Verification that Web components that are associated with special security issues and that can be downloaded from your Web site are correctly signed
- Verification that users are prompted when they attempt to download Web components but their Web browser does not allow this action; a prompting message should provide the users with the appropriate instructions that will allow them to change their Web browser settings
- If the Web application uses cookies to save data on the client machine but the users' Web browsers have been configured to refuse cookies, will the application prompt the user to cover such a situation?
- Testing digital certificates
- Testing plug-ins behavior

The content of an enterprise Web site is a direct reflection of the company. Thus, especially for Web Internet applications, regular verification of the information provided on the Web site is important. This verification is necessary to ensure that no embarrassing modifications have been made by intruders. You might also want to verify that the hyperlinks cannot be modified to send legitimate users off into "wrong" areas of the Web.

8.12.6 ERROR MESSAGE TESTING

Error message testing verifies the known error conditions that must be handled properly by the Web application. The various error messages that can be displayed by the Web application should be tested thoroughly to ensure that they are easily understandable from a user perspective.

8.12.7 CLIENT LOAD TESTING

Client load testing verifies the scalability of the Web-based application client-side while running under different volumes of data. Automated Web load testing tools can be useful to simulate hundreds or even thousands of users who would connect to the Web site and interact with the application. The client-side response time of the Web application is then measured under varying loads. The client-side of the Web application is also verified to ensure that no subtle defect surfaces unexpectedly with different browsers when the application runs under heavy loads.

8.12.8 CROSS-PLATFORM PORTABILITY

Cross-platform portability testing verifies that the Web application's functional behavior is consistent when operating on different client Web-browser platforms such as Microsoft Windows, Mac, or UNIX.

Table 8-29 shows a simple matrix structure that can be used by Web testers to help plan which type and version of browsers they will test against which type and version of computing platforms to verify the Web application's level of portability.

The Web database application can be tested on the different platforms and Web browsers using different levels of testing based on factors such as code complexity and use of HTML advanced features, as illustrated in Table 8-30.

Some of the most frequent problems that are commonly experienced when testing Web applications on different platforms are indicated in Table 8-31.

8.12.9 WEB SERVER LOAD TESTING

Web server load testing verifies the Web application performance when the Web server operates under peak loads. The Web server must be able to process efficiently thousands of requests from multiple clients which can be running with different Web browsers. The results of these performance tests are used to better predict the overall Web application response time under varying loads and also to fine-tune the hardware/software Web server configurations.

Table 8–29 Cross-platform Portability Testing

	Windows 95/98	Windows NT	UNIX HP	UNIX AIX	UNIX Solaris
Netscape Web browser (version X)					
Netscape Web browser (version Y)					
MS Internet Explorer (version A)					
MS Internet Explorer (version B)					

Table 8–30 Testing The Web Application's Portability

Advanced features testing	The most advanced features of the Web application are tested with different browsers and platforms which use sophisticated scripting languages (i.e., JavaScripts, VBScripts, Java applets, ActiveX components, and Dynamic HTML)
Common features testing	The more standard scripts and HTML features that are used in the Web application are tested on the different platforms and Web browsers
Basic features testing	The very basic scripting and HTML features of the Web application are tested on different Web browsers and platforms

Table 8–31 Common Web Cross-platform Problems

- The use of character sets that contain some signs that are not supported on each type of platform where the Web application will run
- Case sensitivity issues: the Windows and Mac platforms are not case-sensitive, whereas the UNIX platform is case-sensitive. This difference can create problems for inexperienced developers. For example, Uniform Resource Locator (URL) addresses that do not exactly match their filenames with the proper uppercase and lowercase characters will fail on a UNIX server.
- URL addresses that contain filenames with space in them. Some Web browsers do not handle spaces well in their pathname sequence.

8.12.10 NETWORK LOAD TESTING

Network load testing verifies, in an intranet environment, the throughput performance of the network when the Web applications are operating under heavy loads of data.

8.12.11 APPLICATION SERVER LOAD TESTING

Application server load testing verifies the performance of the Web application server under varying loads.

8.12.12 DATABASE SERVER LOAD TESTING

Database server load testing verifies the performance of the database server when the multiple users of the Web application fire large numbers of SQL calls against the database servers.

8.12.13 APPLET/SCRIPT TESTING

Applet testing verifies the behavior of the Web application when various components such as JAVA applets, scripts, plug-ins, or ActiveX controls are downloaded and executed on the client-side Web browser.

8.12.14 GRAPHICAL USER INTERFACE TESTING

Graphical user interface testing verifies the overall functionality of the Web application. Table 8-32 lists several categories of test cases that can be developed to exercise, as thoroughly as possible, the functionality that should be provided by the Web application via its GUI interface.

8.13 WEB AUTOMATED TESTING TOOLS

As an organization gradually develops larger-scale Web database applications, automated Web testing tools can be used in a comprehensive manner to complement the manual testing of its major functional features. Similarly, automated Web testing tools can help assess the Web application performance capabilities under varying loads of data and users.

Several automated testing tools have been either developed from the ground up or extended to satisfy the unique challenges of testing an Internet/intranet application. A good Web automated testing tool should exhibit the characteristics indicated in Table 8-33.

Table 8–32 Web-based GUI Test Cases

- HTML-defined Windows controls (e.g., behavior of edit fields, check boxes, radio buttons, list boxes, control buttons, dialog boxes)
- Do the control fields inter-operate well with each other?
- Are controls assigned proper default values?
- Pull-down menus
- Navigational objects (e.g., behavior of text links, image links, image maps)
- Does the navigational link go somewhere?
- Does the navigational link go to the intended destination?
- Did some navigational links disappear between the transition from an older version of the application to a newer release?
- Are Web pages, graphics or images missing?
- Forms (e.g., submit valid and invalid input data)
- Frames (e.g., simulate events that will lead to the alteration of the objects displayed in frames)
- HTML tables (content and properties of the objects displayed in table cells)
- HTML source code
- Dynamic HTML and associated scripting source code (state testing, etc.)

Table 8–33 Web Automated Testing Tool Characteristics

- Ability to support functional regression testing
- Ability to test the Web application GUI interface with an automatic capture and replay method based on object-oriented recording for all standard HTML objects
- Ability to simulate client load/stress testing
- Ability to test automatically the Web application navigational facilities such as text and image hyperlinks and image maps
- Ability to test automatically Web forms, tables, and frames
- Ability to test automatically third-party Web-browser downloaded components such as Java applets, Microsoft ActiveX controls and plug-ins, and JavaScripts
- Ability to automatically test cross-browser compatibility for the Web application
- Ability to simulate Web server load/stress testing
- Ability to simulate Web application server load/stress testing
- Ability to simulate Web database server load/stress testing
- Ability to simulate combined Web browser, Web server, Web application server, and Web database server load/stress testing
- Ability to verify the connections among the Web browser, Web server, Web application server, and Web database server
- Ability to verify Web-browser and Web-server security and data integrity features
- Ability to verify data encryption
- Ability to provide cross-platform testing portability
- Ability to provide extensive test management facilities to help plan, organize, track, and monitor the testing activities as they unfold
- Ability to support different Web browser software

Following is a list of Web sites of some vendors who offer various types of client-server and/or Web automated testing tools:

http://www.segue.com
http://www.mercury.com
http://www.gauge.com
http://www.platinum.com
http://www.sqa.com
http://www.pureatria.com
http://www.autotester.com
http://www.suntest.com
http://www.radview.com
http://www.rswsoftware.com

8.14 ALTERNATIVES TO IN-HOUSE TESTING

An alternative or potential extension to in-house testing is to use the services of a firm that specializes in testing client-server and/or Web application systems. Several test-outsourcing firms offer a wide variety of testing services, for client-server application systems, Web application systems, or both. Some of the most common testing services that are provided by these firms are indicated in Table 8-34.

Table 8–34 Common Testing Services

- Benchmarking the performance of hardware equipment and software under varying configurations and load conditions
- Functional testing to verify the application requirements
- Compatibility testing to verify different combinations of hardware, software, and networking equipment and facilities under different configurations
- Performance/stress testing to verify the level of scalability of an application on a single platform or on different platforms
- Security testing
- Localization testing to verify that an application was correctly translated and adapted for use in foreign countries

Following are a few Web site addresses of companies that provide a variety of testing services in client-server or Web application testing.

http://www.stlabs.com
http://www.systest.com
http://www.ntsl.com

Client-Server and Web Technology Architecture and Support Services

9.1 INTRODUCTION

In today's highly competitive global business environment, several organizations feverishly attempt to re-engineer their core business processes and restructure themselves to achieve more efficient and leaner operations.

The stakes are high. Once their mission-critical business processes have been streamlined to attain sizable productivity gains, several enterprises then look upon their Information Technology organizations to rapidly develop and implement new, scalable client-server or Web database applications that provide flexible solutions to their information needs.

When deploying large client-server or Web database systems, the Information Systems organization wants to achieve the set of critical enterprise goals that are highlighted in Table 9-1.

Table 9–1 Enterprise Application Development Critical Goals

- Increase the competitiveness of the enterprise by introducing flexible systems that can adapt easily and quickly when business requirements change
- Empower the enterprise to maximize business opportunities that can be enabled by the deployment of new technology paradigms
- Improve employees' productivity
- Reduce business processes cycle time

However, a highly scalable and adaptive technology infrastructure is essential to allow the rapid design, construction, testing, deployment, and thereafter successful support and evolution of large and complex mission-critical client-server and Web database applications. Figure 9-1 illustrates three major infrastructure ingredients that must be harmonized to successfully implement a sound client-server and Web technology architecture.

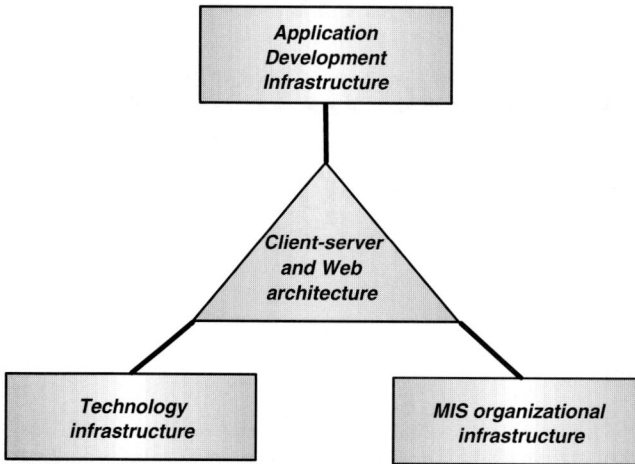

Figure 9–1 Three major infrastructure ingredients for a sound client-server/Web architecture.

Depending on where the enterprises stand in the evolutionary spectrum to distributed processing, the shift to a robust, large-scale client-server and interactive Web computing environment might force several of them to seriously overhaul their existing technology, application development, and organizational infrastructure.

In some extreme instances, as they revamp outdated business processes, enterprises might even consider rebuilding their technology infrastructure from scratch to better adapt to a new distributed platform paradigm.

You can see some of the fundamental benefits that most large corporations seek to achieve when developing and gradually implementing a robust and highly adaptive enterprise information technology infrastructure in Table 9-2.

Unfortunately, several MIS departments have learned the hard way the importance of careful planning regarding transitioning their organizations as a whole to new technology paradigms such as powerful client-server and Web technologies. The best management practices required to successfully acquire, deploy, and support new major technologies in large organizations are as important, if not more so, as selecting the technology itself. Today most organizations have access to the same business-enabling technologies as do their competitors. Unfortunately not all organizations have access

Table 9–2 Enterprise Information Technology Infrastructure Benefits

- To streamline and harmonize the various and often incompatible systems environments that typically characterize several large enterprises; this situation is primarily due to the uncontrolled propagation of incompatible and sometimes redundant hardware, software, and networking products and protocols. A standardized IT architecture helps to leverage IT employee skills, optimize training and simplify maintenance and support. The end result is reduced technology costs for the enterprise.
- To foster an application development environment that increases the speed at which application systems are developed and deployed across the enterprise
- To develop an application development framework that fosters the creation and utilization of reusable functional components and shareable software services and resources
- To minimize and control the proliferation of redundant data and automated business processes across the enterprise, therefore enabling the corporate need to quickly access and share information across and beyond the traditional enterprise boundaries
- To provide a standardized technology setting for corporate data warehouses and data marts
- To provide a standard distributed computing environment that makes possible a better integration of third-party software packages
- To provide a solid framework that clearly delineates the roles and responsibilities of the different IS groups (and possibly some specific user groups) that must be involved in implementing and thereafter supporting the enterprise information technology architecture
- To expedite and simplify changes in business processes and the software applications that enable them, therefore providing competitive advantage against rival companies

to the same quality managerial and technology players who can help them to successfully implement a sound business-enabling technology infrastructure.

In an attempt to reduce the potential risks of failures, this chapter provides a holistic view of a conceptual framework for a generic client-server and Web technology infrastructure. It also proposes some important insights into the kind of organizational infrastructure issues that must be addressed to efficiently and effectively implement and support a large-scale, enterprise-wide client-server and Web database computing environment.

To a lesser extent, it also addresses some of the most frequently overlooked people and skills issues that might surface during the various stages of developing and implementing an enterprise-wide distributed environment.

Although devising an information technology infrastructure that has very deep roots in supporting and satisfying the strategic business initiatives of the enterprise as a whole is of the utmost importance, I do not cover in this chapter this important dimension of the enterprise infrastructure planning process.

Nonetheless, keep in mind, as you move along in the next sections of this chapter, that building an information technology architecture infrastructure is not a strategy unto itself. Its sole "raison d'être" is to help achieve the strategic goals of the business enterprise and its core business processes as illustrated in Figure 9-2.[1] In other words, the IT infrastructure must be business process-driven.

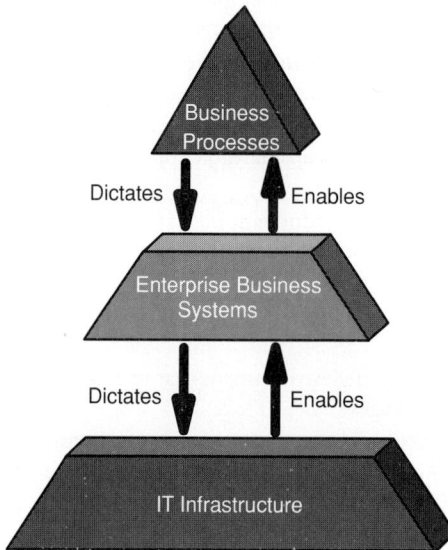

Figure 9–2 Information technology infrastructure positioning.

Finally, although I do not provide the detailed steps involved in creating an enter-prise-wide information technology infrastructure in this book, I do offer a simple def-inition for two of its major components, the enterprise information technology infrastructure and application systems plans, as described in Table 9-3 and Table 9-4.

To ensure proper buy-in, the IT infrastructure standards must be developed with the active support of key business managers. It must also be widely communicated and enforced across the enterprise to all IT personnel and all the distinct lines of the busi-ness organizations. The success and level of adherence to the standards proposed in the

---

1. Conventional wisdom recommends aligning IT with the business processes. However, the re-verse can sometimes apply whereby the enterprise must align business processes with IT. From time to time, new technology might offer such a strong opportunity for competitive advantage that the enterprise decides to adapt its processes to take full advantage of the technology. In both cases, the key word here is alignment.

Table 9–3 Enterprise-wide Information Technology Infrastructure Plan

- An enterprise information technology infrastructure plan consists of the formulation of the strategic set of policies, standards, and guiding principles that are used to plan, assemble, and support the hardware, software, networking, middleware components, facilities, and services required to successfully sustain the core enterprise business operations over a two- to five-year time span.
- The information technology infrastructure plan must emphasize the need to share and reuse prevailing technology resources as much as possible, including:
  - Common technology components, such as standard platforms, operating systems, middleware, and network operating systems
  - Common services to be provided by inter-operable technology components
  - Common, reusable, and maintainable business functions, services, and corporate data

Table 9–4 Enterprise-wide Application Systems Plan

- An entrprise application systems plan consists of a description of the mission-critical applications that are required to fulfill the strategic, tactical, and operational needs of the enterprise along with their interdependencies.
- It also consists of a description of the central scheme that will be retained to deploy and integrate or interconnect these applications over the next 2 to 5 years.
- At last, the corporate application systems plan provides a description of the set of development tools, techniques, and standards that will be used to deploy mission-critical applications across the enterprise in line with the enterprise information technology infrastructure policies, standards, and guiding principles.

IT infrastructure standards is largely proportional to the level of comprehension and support provided by power users and business line managers.

Ideally, the enterprise information technology and the application systems infrastructures must be architected for flexibility and scalability so they can both quickly adapt to evolving business needs, with the least disruption to the enterprise core lines of business. The IT infrastructure must be engineered for change and adaptability right from its initial inception.

9.2 TWO-TIER VERSUS THREE-TIER CLIENT-SERVER ARCHITECTURES

Basically, there are two types of architecture to develop client-server systems. As shown in Figure 9-3, the first category is a two-tier client-server architecture.

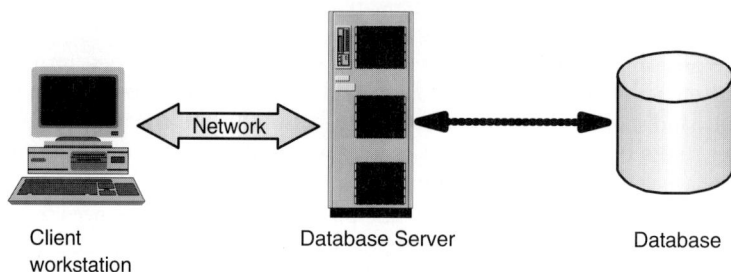

Figure 9–3 Two-tier client-server architecture.

9.2.1   TWO-TIER ARCHITECTURES

With a two-tier client-server architecture, an application is typically divided into two logical segments, or more precisely, two tiers. The first tier is the front-end client, which is comprised of the graphical user interface and the application business logic that runs on the client workstation. Typically, the second tier is the back-end database server. The primary function of the database server is to service the front-end client by providing to that client all the data that it requires to perform its automated business processes.

The partitioning of the client and database server tiers represents not only a functional division of work but also a hardware and a software division. In other words, each tier can run on a separate set of hardware and software components.

As you have just seen, the vast majority of the application business processing logic is performed at the client workstation. However, certain business rules can not only be directly embedded in the client application side but also physically bundled in the database server side. When bundled in the database server side, the business rules are usually implemented with stored procedures and database triggers.

Several client-server applications are successfully developed with a two-tier architecture with the use of powerful RAD tools. Two-tier client-server architectures work best for applications that are implemented in more or less homogeneous computing platform environments where:

- The number of users is not too high (i.e., a couple dozen to a few hundred)
- The application business logic is not necessarily simple but not overly complex either
- The volume of online transactions is relatively low

Client-server two-tier architectures tend to lose their efficiency and effectiveness when they must be scaled up to support large-scale computing environments that service several hundreds or thousands of clients. They do not scale well for large, enterprise-wide applications since most of the business logic resides in a fat client workstation which in turn creates heavy network traffic between the client and database server. Client-server three-tier architectures overcome this limitation.

9.2.2 THREE-TIER ARCHITECTURES

With three-tier client-server architecture, an application is typically divided into three logical segments, or tiers, as illustrated in Figure 9-4.

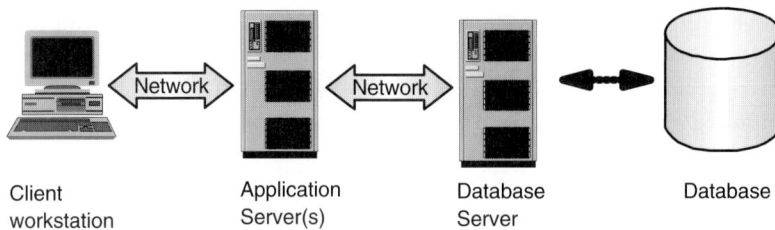

Figure 9–4 Three-tier client-server architecture.

In a three-tier client-server architecture, most of the business processing logic is taken out of the client tier and placed on a separate middle tier, the application server. This intermediate layer can also support a variety of distributed computing services. The application server can contain the entire application processing logic. More often, though, the application server shares the application logic with other servers or clients.

Because of its flexibility, the business processing logic is frequently partitioned across each of the distinct three-tier components (i.e., the client, the application server, and the database server) and possibly across different types of computing platforms in order to achieve optimal performance and response time.

Three-tier client-server architectures offer several benefits over two-tier architectures, especially for large, enterprise-wide, mission-critical applications, as you see in Table 9-5.

The potential down side of a three-tier architecture is that three-tier client-server applications are usually more complex to create than two-tier applications and thus demand more effort initially.

To conclude, Figure 9-5 illustrates the basic positioning of a three-tier client-server architecture versus a two-tier architecture, depending on the number of users and volume of transactions that the client-server application must process per second.

Table 9–5 Three-tier Client-server Architecture Benefits

- A simplified software distribution process for large enterprise systems
- An established standardized software infrastructure
- Scalability in supporting high transaction volumes with a large number of clients (i.e., thousands of customers with several transactions per second) without a major redesign of the application; you can add a new middle-tier application server or extend the processing capacity of the current ones
- Ability to support transaction processing monitors (TP monitors)
- Ability to port the client user interface code to more than one computing platform, such as Windows, UNIX, OS/2, and Macintosh, with a minimum of re-coding effort
- Application partitioning which allows the development and physical distribution of different segments of processing logic on the client, application servers, or database servers based on performance optimization considerations
- Inter-operability across heterogeneous computing platforms
- Improved maintainability since most of the application processing logic and business rules can be centrally located on the application servers; making changes to the core application business logic and rules is easier since it does not necessitate the need to upgrade every client workstation with new versions of the business application code
- A solid foundation for distributed objects
- Connecting existing business processes to an Internet/intranetenvironment

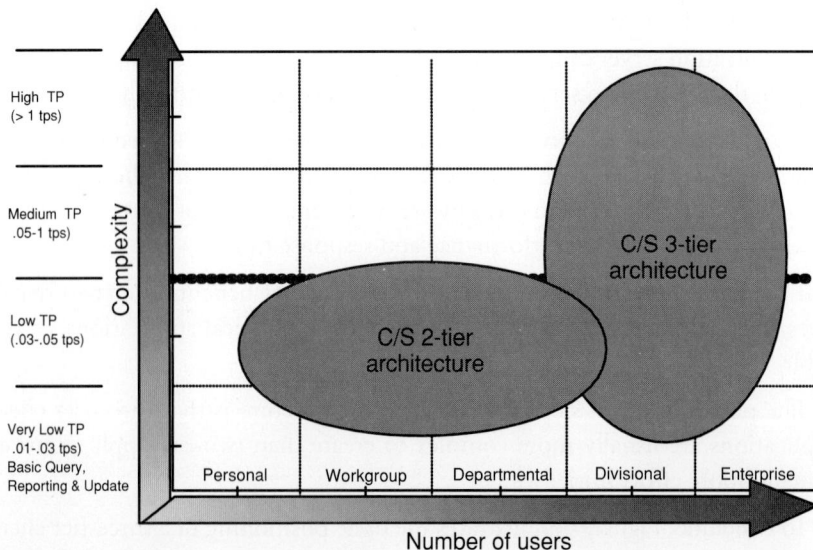

Figure 9–5 Positioning of client-server 2-tier and 3-tier architectures.

The following Web site addresses point to some vendors that offer high-end three-tier client-server application development tools:

http://www.forte.com
http://www.dynasty.com
http://www.seer.com

9.2.3   PLACEMENT OF BUSINESS PROCESSES AND DATA

In a two-tier architecture, the distribution of procedural logic can be done on either the client platform or the database servers. In a three-tier architecture, the distribution of procedural logic can be done on the client platform, the application servers, or the database servers. Table 9-6 provides a basic set of rules that can be used to help determine the optimal placement of different procedural logic or data components on the client, application or database server platforms.

However, do not see these rules as absolute. In fact, they might not necessarily apply in some specific circumstances. Distribution of business procedural logic and data on different client, application, or database computing platforms will likely be influenced by a large variety of design factors. Some of these design factors include: the desired level of application responsiveness, the overall volume of computational processing that needs to be satisfied by the application, the level of application maintainability that must be met, the volume of database accesses, and the enterprise network performance capabilities. Compromises might be necessary to obtain an appropriate equilibrium among all these factors.

Table 9–6 Some Rules Of Thumb For The
Optimal Placement Of Business Procedural Logic Or Data

- Ideally, the presentation logic should be separated from the procedural logic. The presentation logic usually resides on the client platform. In Web database applications, the Web browser handles the graphical user interface on most types of hardware client machines.
- Reusable business logic should be clearly separated from context-specific business logic. Reusable business logic should be implemented as much as possible on the server platform.
- Basic input field validations and calculations are usually executed more quickly when they are performed directly on the client platform than those that require a round trip to the server platform.
- Application components that have tight interconnections (e.g., functional components that communicate with one another very often, database tables that are joined repeatedly) should not be implemented on different machines.
- Large and complex business processes that are resource-intensive should be implemented on the server, which usually has more processing power than the client workstations.

Table 9–6 Some Rules Of Thumb For The
Optimal Placement Of Business Procedural Logic Or Data (cont.)

- Complex or resource-intensive data accesses should be implemented with stored procedures, since we have seen in Chapter 4 that stored procedures are pre-compiled objects and optimized to improve performance.
- The data traffic across the network from and to the client to the servers should be minimized as much as possible. The use of stored procedures should be encouraged to implement data-intensive processes on the database server. Also, very large transmissions of data can be improved by compressing the data prior to transmitting it across the network.
- Large business processes that consume a significant amount of resources should be broken down into smaller chunks of procedural logic segments and implemented in an asynchronous rather than a synchronous mode of operation, whenever possible to do so.
- The distribution of business procedural logic and data should be minimized, wherever possible, especially when it must be done across WANs, where reducing network traffic is important.
- If the application procedural logic will be frequently updated, then placing the application procedural logic in a central location such as on an application server might be preferable. Doing so will facilitate updating the procedural code in one unique location, as opposed to having to distribute application code changes on all the client workstation machines.

9.3 CLIENT-SERVER MIDDLEWARE

Client-server middleware tools are used primarily to tie together the different tiers that compose the client-server architectures. Table 9-7 lists three common middleware protocols that are often used with client-server technology.

I discuss middleware in more detail in Section 9.6.20, "Bringing Legacy Systems to the Web."

9.4 TAXONOMY OF CLIENT-SERVER TECHNOLOGY ARCHITECTURE

The enterprise client-server technology architecture is usually comprised of several important technological components such as those indicated in Figure 9-6.

Each particular technology component that appears in Figure 9-6 should be carefully assessed for its ability to satisfy the overall enterprise technology requirements for the development, deployment, and support of mission-critical, large-scale client-server or Web applications.

The enterprise client-server technology architecture should not describe solely the different technologies that need to be successfully interwoven to support the business

Table 9–7 Client-server Middleware Protocols

Remote Procedure Calls (RPCs)	A remote procedure call is a technique that allows a program that resides on one physical platform to call a procedure that is located on another platform. The term RPC is generic. Several industry providers have implemented different implementations of the RPC protocol.
Distributed Computing Environment (DCE)	DCE is a standard defined by the Open Systems Foundation (OSF) that supports the transmission of data and messages across platforms. DCE encompasses RPC capabilities and different services such as directory services, security services, presentation services, thread and time services, and distributed file systems.
Common Object Request Broker Architecture (CORBA)	CORBA is a standard that was defined by the Object Management Group (OMG) that can be used to deploy low-level objects across a network while supporting messaging services between those objects.

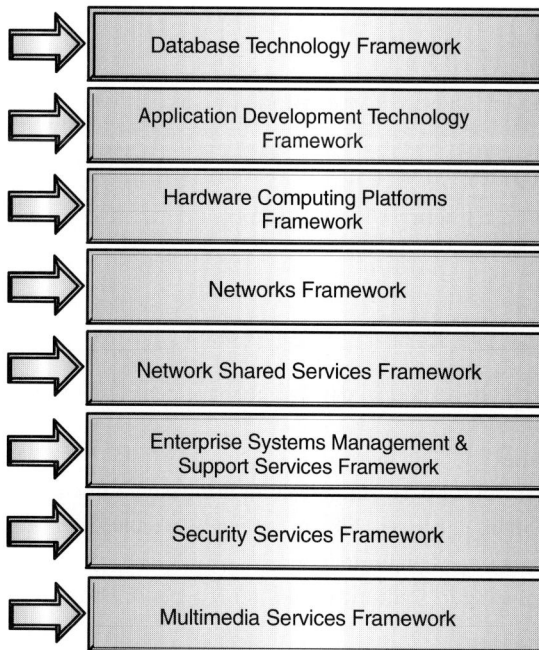

Figure 9–6 Major client-server technology architecture components.

application needs of the enterprise. It should also describe the wide range of technology services that the Information Technology organization must enable across the enterprise such as generic end-user computing and reporting, corporate file services, corporate printing services, corporate groupware services, and so forth.

Sections 9.4.1 through 9.4.8 briefly discuss each particular technology component or service shown in Figure 9-6. When they are joined together, these technology components and services are used to lay down the foundation for a sound enterprise client-server technology framework. This technology framework can be used to successfully enable and support a variety of client-server and Web applications across the enterprise.

9.4.1   THE DATABASE TECHNOLOGY FRAMEWORK

In this component, you make decisions as to which type of database technology will be used to support the global data requirements of the enterprise. The most common types of database technologies that currently exist in the industry appear in Table 9-8.

Table 9–8 Database Technology Models

- Relational (SQL) databases
- Object-oriented databases
- Universal database servers
- Mainframe databases (relational, hierarchical, network, or flat file)

Several factors which might influence the selection of a peculiar database technology are highlighted in Table 9-9.

Table 9–9 Database Selection Criteria

- The need for a highly scalable transactional database management system on a single platform or on different platforms
- The need for data warehouses and data marts
- The need for databases that can support a mobile computing environment
- The need for highly distributed databases with strong database replication features
- The need for workgroup and/or personal databases
- The need for databases that support multimedia and other types of non-relational objects
- The need for databases that can scale up from a workgroup level to an enterprise level with very large volumes of data

9.4.2　THE APPLICATION DEVELOPMENT TECHNOLOGY FRAMEWORK

In this component, essential decisions are made as to which type of client-server multi-tier model and RAD tools will be used to develop robust client-server applications. The most common client-server architecture models include:

- Two-tier client-server architecture
- Three-tier client-server architecture

As for the application development tools, the selection of a RAD tool will be largely influenced by the types of strategic programming languages the organization decides to support, such as C, C++, object-oriented Cobol, Visual Basic-like, or Java.

Also, the different categories of middleware tools that might be required to support the client-server technology architecture should be clearly identified. Several options are available such as those in Table 9-10.

Table 9–10 Different Application-related Middleware Components

- Database middleware to access mainframe relational and non-relational databases
- Database middleware to access heterogeneous relational data sources, such as:
  - Open Database Connectivity (ODBC)
  - Proprietary Application Programming Interfaces (native APIs)
  - Java Database Connectivity (JDBC)
- Remote Procedure Calls /Message Queuing
- Conversational protocols such as:
  - LU6.2
  - TCP sockets
  - NetBIOS
  - Named pipes
- Transaction processing (TP) monitors such as:
  - AT&T Tuxedo
  - Transarc Encina
  - IBM CICS

I discuss middleware in more detail in Section 9.6.20, "Bringing Legacy Systems to the Web."

9.4.3　THE HARDWARE COMPUTING PLATFORMS FRAMEWORK

In this segment, some basic decisions are made as to which type of client and server hardware computing platforms will be used to develop and deploy the enterprise business applications, covering the specific requirements of each distinct computing layer.

Figure 9-7 shows a holistic view of how the client and server computing platforms must be integrated with appropriate operating systems and network operating system protocols to ensure that all the technology architecture components can smoothly inter-operate.

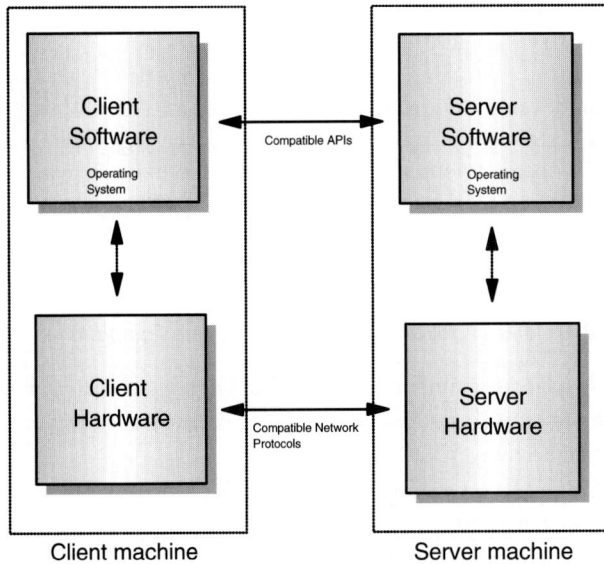

Figure 9–7 Client-server computing platforms.

The most common types of computing platforms that are used in the industry at large for physical desktop workstations and servers appear in Table 9-11.

Table 9–11 Different Client And Server Hardware Computing Platforms

- Desktop Workstations
  - PC-based
  - UNIX-based
  - Macintosh-based
  - PC Network-based computer (i.e. thin client workstation)
- Physical Servers (Workgroup and Enterprise)
  - PC LAN servers
  - RISC-based servers
  - UNIX-based servers
  - Mainframe as a host server

For each specific hardware computing platform, the set of detailed configuration elements that characterizes its major technology components should be described, as indicated in Table 9-12.

Table 9–12 Different Client And Server Hardware Configuration Elements

- Processor type
- Processing power
- Bus architecture type
- Type of internal memory and level of expandability
- Sound card type
- Video card type
- Monitor type and size
- Hard disk type and size
- Supporting peripheral types such as:
  - Scanners
  - Bar code readers
  - Bar code printers
  - Mouse, pen, micros
  - CD drives
  - Tape drives
- Network interface card (NIC) type

Finally, the type of operating systems that will run on each computing platform should also be determined at this stage. Two of the most common software operating systems that are widely used in the industry include different flavors of UNIX and Windows NT.

9.4.4 THE NETWORK FRAMEWORK

In this segment, decisions are made as to which types of physical networks are required to support the corporate client-server or web computing platforms. These decisions will be largely influenced by a variety of factors such as the different geographical locations where the enterprise runs its business and the total volume of data, voice, and video traffic that must be supported between the various operations sites.

The enterprise should implement an open, standards-based network infrastructure that will lay down the foundation required for running mission-critical client-server and web-based applications. The network infrastructure must also be designed to offer better connectivity for the mobile workforce as more and more applications are gradually shifted to a mobile environment, as opposed to the more traditional office environment.

Be sure to estimate the total volume of data that will circulate through the entire network during different time periods of the day and also determine the different service-levels that need to be supported. Also assess the volume growth estimates for network bandwidth over a five-year horizon.

In case of a network failure, determine the lengths of delays that can be indulged by the users without threatening the most critical business operations of the enterprise.

Table 9-13 provides some information as to the theoretical bandwidth supported by different types of network connections. Bandwidth is measured either in kilobytes or megabytes transmitted per second. Thus, a T3 connection line would theoretically allow an organization to transmit 45 megabits of data per second through its wide-area pipeline (a T3 connection line can provide approximately the equivalent bandwidth of twenty-eight T1 connection circuits).

Table 9–13 Network Bandwidth Capacity/Speed

Network Connectivity Type	Bandwidth/Speed
Conventional (telephone) dial-up modem	9.6, 14.4, 28.8, 56 Kbps
ISDN modem	56–128 Kbps
Direct broadcast satellite	400 Kbps–30 Mbps
Cable modem	10–40 Mbps
T1 connection	1.54 Mbps
High-Bit-Rate Digital Subscriber Line (HDSL)	1.54 Mbps
Asymmetrical Digital Subscriber Line (ADSL)	1.54–8 Mbps
Ethernet connection	10 Mbps
Token Ring connection	4–16 Mbps
T3 connection	45 Mbps
Very-high-bit-rate Digital Subscriber Line (VDSL)	51–55 Mbps
FDDI	100 Mbps
Fast Ethernet	100 Mbps
ATM (OC3)	155 Mbps
ATM (OC12)	622 Mbps

To provide you with a better appreciation of the speed at which data can be transmitted with the use of different types of network connections, Table 9-14 provides an estimation of the time needed to transmit 10 megabytes of data using different network connections.

Create different diagrams that illustrate the various components of the global enterprise network architecture, including the LANs, WANS, MANs, and the main net-

Table 9–14 Transfer Rates For 10 Megabytes Of Data

Network Connectivity Type	Estimated Transmission Time
14.4 Kbps	90 minutes
28.8 Kbps	45 minutes
56 Kbps	25 minutes
128 Kbps	12 minutes
1.54 Mbps	50 seconds
10 Mbps	9 seconds

work access points. The overall bandwidth capacity that the network must support should also be documented, for each major segment of the enterprise network topology. You can see the minimum set of elements that should be depicted in the network diagrams in Table 9-15.

Table 9–15 Network Topology Diagram Elements

- The geographical locations of the different sites that are supported by the network
- The LAN topologies including interconnections between specific user groups or different platforms such as connections to mainframe hosts
- The MAN/WAN services used and the different locations that are connected via these networking services
- The multiple network equipment and facilities that are used across the enterprise network, covering various elements such as bridges, routers, wiring hubs, protocol gateways or converters, and type of network cabling used

A backbone network is a high-capacity network that links together other networks of less capacity. A typical local backbone network would be a FDDI network that links together several local area networks (LANs) that are located in the same building. A typical wide area backbone network would utilize digital leased circuits combined with routers and multiplexers to interconnect major business units that are located in different cities, possibly across the country or around the world.

In today's age of sophisticated client-server and Web applications, enterprise backbone networks need to be capable of supporting combined data, voice, and video traffic. Some of the most common backbone networks switching technologies that are used in the industry appear in Table 9-16.

You can see the most common types of physical networks in Table 9-17.

Table 9–16 Backbone Networks Switching Technologies

- Packet switching
- Fast packet switching
- Time division multiplexing (TDM)
- Asynchronous transfer mode (ATM)
- Circuit switching
- Fiber data distribution interface (FDDI)

Table 9–17 Physical Network Types

- Local area networks (LANs)
- Metropolitan area networks (MANs)
- Wide area networks (WANs)

Following is a brief description of each physical type of networks that you see in Table 9-17.

LOCAL AREA NETWORKS (LANs)

LANs are used primarily to interconnect the various client workstations, servers, and mainframe hosts that are located within a confined geographical area, such as inside a single building or specific floors within the same building. The most common topologies that are used for LANs appear in Table 9-18.

Table 9–18 Common Lan Transmission Network Topologies

- Ethernet (IEEE 802.3 standard[a]). Ethernet is based on a bus network topology.
- Token Ring (IEEE 802.5 standard)
- Fiber data distribution interface (FDDI) (ANSI X3T9.5 standard)

a. IEEE stands for Institute of Electrical and Electronic Engineers. It is a U.S. publishing and standards organization responsible for many data processing standards.

You might also want to describe the type of cabling that will be used to interconnect the different hardware components that are hooked on the local area network, such as those highlighted in Table 9-19.

Table 9–19 Different Types Of Network Wiring Cables

- Coaxial
- Fiber optics
- Twisted pair wiring

Finally, the different technology components that are used to interconnect various physical segments of the local area network should also be documented, such as those indicated in Table 9-20.

Table 9–20 Network Connectors

- Routers
- Bridges
- Repeaters
- Gateways

A brief description of the network connectors that you see above is provided in "Define the Hardware/Software/Networking Requirements" in Chapter 3.

METROPOLITAN AREA NETWORKS (MANS)

MANs are primarily used to interconnect different sites that operate within a reasonably close vicinity of each other such as different buildings in the same city, for instance.

WIDE AREA NETWORKS (WANS)

WANs are primarily used to interconnect the enterprise sites that are widely dispersed across different states, countries, or continents.

9.4.5   THE NETWORK SHARED SERVICES FRAMEWORK

In this segment, you make decisions as to which type of network shared services will be provided within the enterprise. You can see some of the most common types of network shared services that are provided in enterprise-wide client-server architectures in Table 9-21.

Table 9–21 Network Shared Services

- Directory services
- File sharing services
- Print services
- Fax services
- Electronic mail services

The next five sections briefly discuss each network shared service that you see in Table 9-21.

DIRECTORY SERVICES

Directory services allow users or different software system components to identify different resources or destinations that are shared across the network.

Basically, two types of directory services exist, which are commonly referred to as *white pages* services or *yellow pages* services.

The white pages service indexes the names of different components that are specific constituents of the corporate network. These easy-to-remember names are automatically translated into physical network addresses, in a manner that is completely transparent to the users. The yellow pages service indexes a resource category. When the users search this resource category, then the network automatically produces a list of the servers that can provide that type of service.

You can have different implementation schemes for a variety of directory services, many of which are proprietary to the type of technology used. For instance, an enterprise electronic mail software facility might use its own proprietary directory service. A network operating system might also use its own proprietary directory service. Providing inter-operability among different proprietary directory services might be a daunting task. Nonetheless, the various corporate standards that are implemented to address the various types of directory services supported within the enterprise should at least cover the following items:

- Network resources identification, description, and location, including the various file, print, fax, multimedia, and e-mail servers

- Client-server applications identification, description, and location

- Databases identification, description, and location

- Data fields identification, description, and location

Directory services are gradually evolving toward the adoption of international open standards, which should help alleviate some of the shortcomings currently associated with having to manage different proprietary directory services that are not necessarily automatically interoperable.

FILE SHARING SERVICES

File sharing services store various types of application-related files on shared file servers that are usually supported across a corporate network. The file sharing services might include a variety of services, such as the ability to share various types of documents across the network with all users that are supported on it, the ability to provide hard disk backup facilities, and so forth.

Once the enterprise requirements for file sharing services are identified, documented, and well understood, then you select the preferred technology platform(s) that are required to satisfy these shared file services requirements. The selection of a proper file server platform can be influenced by several factors such as:

- The type of services that are provided by the file sharing service, such as the backup of client workstation hard disks, the sharing of documents with other users across the network, the support of data archiving facilities, and so forth
- The total number of users that will use the network file sharing service
- The geographic locations where the users work

The different types of file sharing server platforms might include:

- UNIX file servers (i.e., Sun's Network File System—NFS)
- Mainframe-based host file servers
- PC-based file server (i.e., Novell NetWare, Microsoft LAN Manager, Banyan Vines)

PRINT SERVICES

Print server services provide the users with facilities that allow them to route their printed documents to different types of printers that can be located in different areas of the enterprise and that are supported via the corporate network.

Table 9-22 provides a basic list of different types of printers that are commonly used in large organizations.

Table 9–22 Different Types Of Printers

- Black and white laser printers
- Color laser printers
- Thermal color printers
- Dye sublimation color printers
- Inkjet printers
- Impact/dot matrix printers

Prior to documenting the corporate standards for the print server services, estimate the total printing requirements of each specific geographical site where the enterprise operates its business. Once these requirements are well defined, then you can determine the number of print servers required, based on their print capacity and overall performance levels. The different types of standard printers supported within the enterprise can also be determined at this stage.

Some of the major components that need to be identified to support the print service functionality include:

- The type of software required for the print servers and the client workstations
- The types of printer drivers required to support various applications on specific computing platforms

- Print spoolers and gateways
- Printer description languages (i.e., PCL5/6, PostScript I and II, and so forth)

FAX SERVICES

Fax services send or receive faxes from all the workstations that are supported by the network. The fax server requirements should provide estimates for the total number of users and volume of faxes transmitted or received per unit of time, along with the identification of the different user locations involved in the process. The different hardware and software components that are required to implement the fax services are then identified including:

- Number of fax servers required
- Type of software required to support the fax services made available from the client workstations

ELECTRONIC MAIL SERVICES

Electronic mail services support store-and-forward text and file transmissions to all users that are hooked into the network. The type of computing platforms required to support e-mail servers are defined according to the following considerations:

- E-mail systems that are currently supported across the enterprise, possibly on different computing platforms, including:
  - PC-based servers
  - UNIX-based servers
  - Mainframe-based servers
  - Internet-based servers
- The number of users to be supported across the enterprise and the volume, type of e-mail messages, and frequency of message transmissions that must be sustained over a given period of time

If the e-mail services need to support heterogeneous environments, then describe in detail the different gateways that might be required to convert the e-mail messages (and their different types of attachments) from one computing platform format to another.

Although inter-connectivity is possible between e-mail systems that operate on different computing platforms, ensure which e-mail functions are supported by the gateway and which ones are not, since full functional compatibility between different e-mail systems is rarely achieved in practice.

9.4.6   THE SECURITY SERVICES FRAMEWORK

The security standards and facilities that must be supported at large by the enterprise information technology architecture should cover the following elements for all types of required computing platforms:

- Network, server, host accesses
- Database, table, data field accesses
- E-mail, fax, file server accesses
- Application transaction accesses
- Central, local, or remote accesses

If required, investigate the need for data encryption services, taking into consideration the current or targeted enterprise technology architecture major constituencies. Some of the areas to investigate might include:

- Corporate backbone networks
- Local area networks
- Corporate data sets stored on local or mobile workstations, servers, and host computers

The need for corporate anti-virus software for each type of computing platform that must be supported should also be investigated, at the level of the enterprise.

At last, if the enterprise needs to provide authentication services for all computing platforms, then document in detail the type of technology that is required to support user authentication by validating their identities. Some of the most common authentication technologies available today include:

- Passwords and user ids
- Keycards, smart cards, and secur-id cards
- Voice prints

The enterprise security architecture should be documented, covering the potential needs for various hardware and software components such as:

- Data encryption hardware devices and software
- Master-key devices and facilities
- Key-distribution servers
- Smart cards
- Workstation locking devices and software
- Authentication servers

9.4.7   THE MULTIMEDIA SERVICES FRAMEWORK

The different types of multimedia services that might be offered at the enterprise level can include video, voice, and image processing, either separately or simultaneously combined. Following is a brief description of each of these facilities.

VIDEO PROCESSING

Video processing services consist of all the different technologies that can be used to capture video segments, store them, and display them to all users who have access to the enterprise network. Some of the most common services for video processing might include:

- Real-time video conferencing
- Computer-based training (CBT)
- Business applications that contain some multimedia-oriented video segments

Some of the most common technology components that might be required to support client-server video processing include:

- Analog or digital cameras
- Data storage devices, such as jukeboxes, CD-ROMs, or videodiscs
- Video editing software
- Video encoding/decoding cards
- Video compression hardware/software protocols

VOICE PROCESSING

Voice processing services consist of all the technologies that can be used to capture voice signals and transform them into a digital format. The digitized voice documents are then stored in shared files that can be accessed or delivered to all users that have access to the enterprise network. Voice processing can also be utilized as an input device to interact with an application or an output device that the computer uses to respond verbally to a user request.

IMAGE PROCESSING

Image processing consists of all the technologies that can be used to scan various types of documents, store the resulting scanned document images in shared files, and provide various search indexes to retrieve these documents.

The scanned images are stored in corporate files that can be shared among all users that are supported on the corporate network. The users can not only retrieve and view the various types of scanned documents directly from their workstations, but they can also print them, fax them, or convert them back into text if required. Some of the most common technology components that might be required to support client-server image processing include:

- Scanners
- Data storage devices, such as jukeboxes
- Document indexing and retrieval software

Figure 9-8 illustrates the major architectural components that are required to support a generic client-server imaging framework.

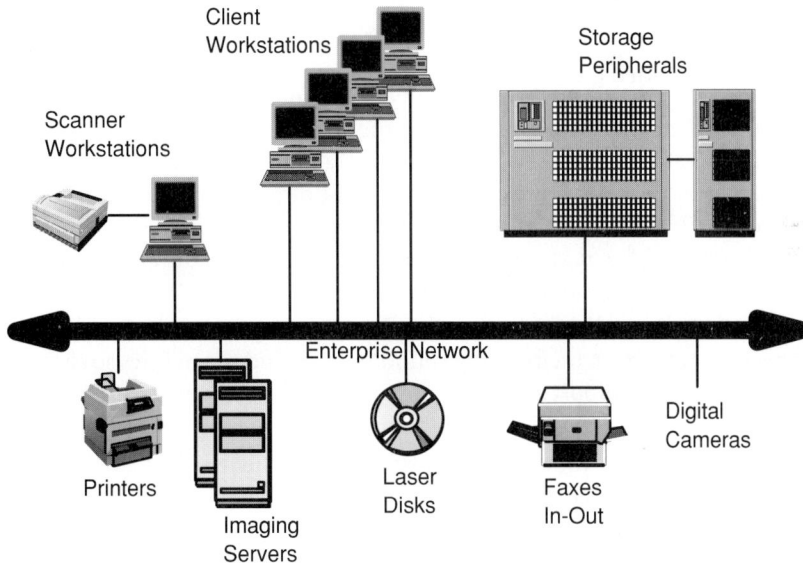

Figure 9–8 Client-server imaging framework.

9.4.8   FILE TRANSMISSION SERVICES

File transmission services provide corporate standard facilities to manually or automatically transfer files from one computing environment to another such as from a PC-based environment to a mainframe environment. File transmission services can also provide facilities that support the transmission of files from one geographical location to another.

9.5   ENTERPRISE SYSTEMS MANAGEMENT (ESM) AND SUPPORT SERVICES

The quick deployment of small and simple client-server and Web database applications will certainly bring appreciable benefits to an organization. However, the long-term success of an enterprise-wide distributed environment will be based primarily on the organization's ability to keep mission-critical distributed applications up and running in a stable operational environment and evolve them gradually through their useful corporate life cycle.

Quite often, many organizations might assume by default that the same levels of operational support and services or system availability they were accustomed to in a traditional mainframe environment will naturally be provided in a distributed system environment. This assumption is far from the harsh realities of life. In fact, a distributed environment will often be far more complicated than a traditional mainframe-computing environment.

A large-scale, distributed computing environment will likely contain more potential failure points than you can count on the fingers of your two hands. Hence, be sure to set up and adhere to a set of Information Technology standards that will minimize or at least help to better control the number of different technologies that need to be deployed in the enterprise to satisfy critical business requirements. The IT standards should be enforced across the enterprise so the introduction of marginal technology be reduced and always remain under control.

The real challenge lies not only in implementing the enterprise-wide IT distributed architecture but also in establishing sound policies and procedures so that the software development and support processes are executed in harmony with the architecture's corporate standards.

Yet the objective is to keep the mission-critical client-server and Internet/intranet systems up and running smoothly in a production environment, on a 24-hour basis, 7 days a week, 52 weeks a year, with 0% downtime. Even the most sophisticated, user-friendly, and productive Web database application is useless if its application or database servers are down and the users or customers cannot access the data they need to perform their most critical business operations.

For this reason, you need to develop and implement not only a sound information technology infrastructure but also a sound distributed system management process, as early as possible and preferably at the level of the enterprise. Then you also want to implement the system management process in an incremental fashion, based on the specific priorities and most urgent needs that are dictated by the implementation of mission-critical distributed systems across the enterprise.

Figure 9-9 shows some of the core system management categories that constitute a holistic view of a distributed system management infrastructure, for a large enterprise.

I address, at a high level, each major system management operational process that you see in Figure 9-9 and provide a rationale for its use and implementation. As each organization most likely will have different distributed computing needs and resources, the system management functions shown in Figure 9-9 do not necessarily need to be implemented all at once. For inexperienced organizations, this effort could be a daunting task. It can presumably lead to a total disaster. Devising a migration plan that remains pragmatic and incremental in nature might be far better.

An organization might only need to implement a few critical system management functions in order to satisfy its most urgent needs and then take it from there. Since I discuss the client-server technology architecture dimension in Section 9.4, I do not cover the technology environment component in this section.

Enterprise Systems Management (ESM)

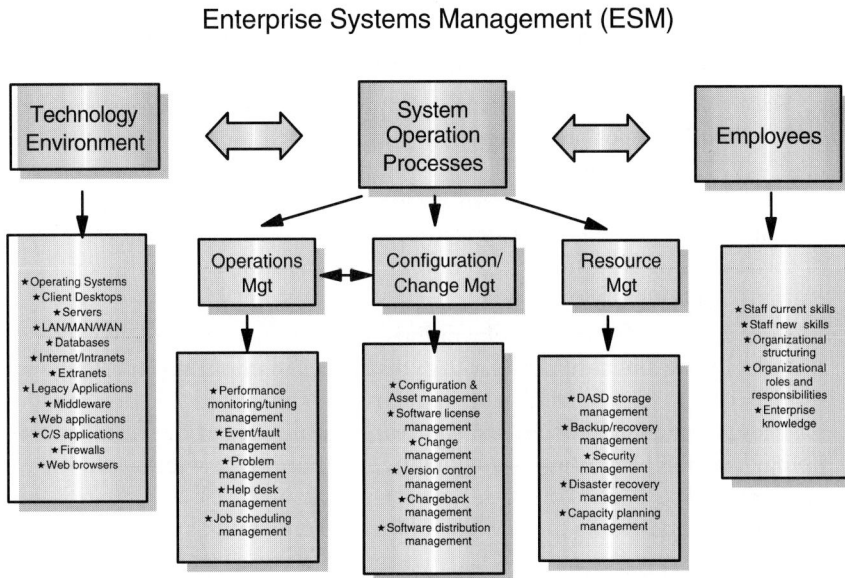

Figure 9–9 Core system management categories.

As for the third major component in Figure 9-9, the people dimension, this book cannot cover in detail this crucial aspect of an enterprise system management architecture. Nevertheless, let me point out that building a sound enterprise system management infrastructure will require the active participation of several project teams from different MIS organizational groups and will necessitate a wide variety of current and new technical skills.

Quite often, the organization unfortunately concentrates most of its efforts on the technology and process management sides of implementing an enterprise system management infrastructure, to the detriment of the people side. In reality, the people side is extremely important, since the implementation of an enterprise-wide system management architecture will likely bring with it the need for a new set of technology skills for the MIS staff. Similarly, as enterprises gradually deploy distributed technologies in various geographical areas around the country or around the world, users will also need to be trained in a variety of technology support roles that were traditionally reserved to IT staff.

Some of these skills might be the new programming skills necessary to write scripts that will generate automated processes when an alarm is triggered by an intelligent agent of the enterprise system management environment. Another required skill is the ability to carefully analyze and interpret data collected by the enterprise system management applications and pinpoint the actual source of a problem, which can reside at the level of the network, server, client, middleware, or application components.

Hence, the operations staff members might require some special training on how to effectively use the various integrated systems components that exist in the enterprise system management environment.

Finally, from an organizational standpoint, the MIS organization will have to determine what type of organizational structure is required to manage each discrete operational process shown in Figure 9-9 in the most efficient and effective manner possible. MIS also needs to determine who will be responsible to manage each process. To avoid any potential confusion, clearly outline the support roles and responsibilities of the revitalized Information Technology organization, especially for the various Operations Support departments.

Only a strong, focused IT Operations Support organization can succeed in successfully deploying and supporting a large distributed computing environment. Any communication barriers that might exist among diversified IT departments must be slashed down, as such issues can sometimes easily supercede the most complex technology issues. Quite often, implementing an enterprise-wide distributed technology architecture has a lot to do with how the people in the IT organization can deal with change. Understanding the new technologies is one thing, but like anything else in this world, if the IT organization is not managed by good coaches, then the chances of failure are high.

Sections 9.5.1 through 9.5.18 present a brief discussion of each major system management operational process shown in Figure 9-9.

9.5.1   EVENT AND FAULT MANAGEMENT

Event and fault management can be defined as the set of processes that are used to identify, diagnose, and recover from hardware, software, or networking faults. A critical issue in event and fault management is the avoidance of information overload. Different ESM components use a variety of distributed intelligent agents to trigger some specific events when thresholds are exceeded or certain physical computing devices fail.

If not careful, the MIS staff can set up the ESM agents to monitor too many components with too many events, thus creating an extraneous amount of information to analyze and support. In some instances, the level of intrusion that the ESM products generate can even cause an unacceptable level of overhead on the infrastructure. In such a case, the ESM products generate performance problems instead of helping to solve them.

Consequently, you have to decide which hardware components you want to monitor, based on the level of criticality of the services they provide, what types of events will be supported, and how the different system events will be managed and resolved when problems occur.

Furthermore, specific filtering mechanisms must be implemented to minimize the number of events and supporting information that are collected by the agents. Some

ESM tools provide a facility that allows the operations staff to customize a set of rules that can be used to help pinpoint the root cause of a problem.

Automated event management tools should provide a robust notification facility, which contains the following characteristics:

- Direct access to a central database for support-related information, such as support analyst pager number and range of support hours
- Alert of a critical event via a pager, telephone, e-mail, and so forth
- Reliability and security
- Ability to interface with different types of system management tools

9.5.2 CLIENT WORKSTATION MANAGEMENT

The Information System organization must define and properly address the management and support levels that must be provided to the various types of client workstations that are spread across the enterprise. The specific areas they might need to cover include:

- Client workstation hardware, software, and networking installation and configuration management
- Client workstation software updates and distribution
- Client workstation files backup
- Client workstation maintenance

Establishing sound policies and standards is one of the best strategies to control the proliferation of incompatible desktops across the enterprise. The enterprise must come up with a set of standard desktop configurations to simplify the technical support of desktops, saving both time and money. If the users do not want to use these corporate standards, then they should either provide their own support or contract for outsourcing support. Several companies also adopt a policy whereby the vast majority of standard business applications are supported centrally on servers, where they can be accessed via the corporate network. This approach makes supporting desktop management a lot easier, since most applications are located on a few servers instead of a large number of desktops.

An important area that requires some attention in desktop management is ensuring that all desktops are equipped with some anti-virus protection software.

9.5.3 SERVER MANAGEMENT

The management and support levels that must be provided to the different servers that are spread across the enterprise must be defined and properly addressed by the Information System organization. The specific areas that need to be covered for each type of central and remote server include:

- Server hardware, software, and networking configuration management

- Server application, system, and database software updates and distribution

- Server files backup and recovery

- Server capacity management (memory, processing capacity, disk space, CPU, swap)

- Server housekeeping maintenance

- Server performance monitoring and tuning

- Server remote system control and diagnostic capabilities

Each time a production server is down, the enterprise most likely loses productivity or revenues. Different types of reports can be produced to monitor key metric information that relates to service-level performance in a distributed environment. Such reports can be a very important communication tool for providing both customer and IS management with key metric information as to the overall IS service-level performance. As an example of such reports, Figure 9-10 illustrates a simple graphical report that can be used to show production server availability on a monthly basis.

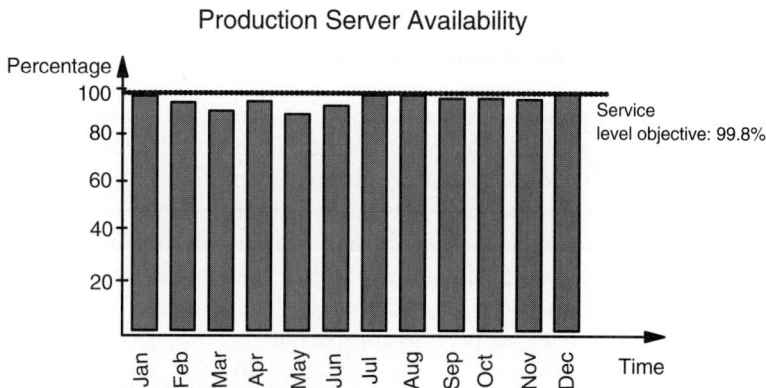

Figure 9–10 Production server availability.

9.5.4 NETWORK MANAGEMENT

The management and support levels that must be provided for the different networks that are implemented across the enterprise must be defined and properly addressed by the Information System organization. The specific areas that need to be covered for each type of network include:

- Network hardware and software configuration management

- Network capacity planning (bandwidth)

- Network housekeeping core routines maintenance

- Network performance monitoring and tuning

- Network remote system control and diagnostic capabilities

In the client-server world, the requirement for networking between the client workstations and the servers is paramount. Networks need to be architected across the enterprise with a unified approach to ensure maximum inter-operability and re-liability. Otherwise, operational incompatibilities and cost inefficiencies will surface everywhere.

Depending on the baseline network framework, network connectivity standards and also operating maintenance and monitoring procedures must be set up to ensure optimal performance from the WANs, LANs, bridges, routers, gateways, and servers that compose the enterprise network topology.

Network downtime can be disastrous for strategic business operations. It can lead to direct loss of current and potential customers. It can threaten a competitive advantage through an inability to provide quality and timely services to internal and external customers. Through sound routine housekeeping practices, network outages should be prevented, and in the event of a failure, network recovery should be as fast as possible in order to minimize the impact on the users. In the case of mission-critical systems, alternative network routes should be planned, should a drastic network outage occur due to a networking hardware malfunction.

9.5.5 PROBLEM MANAGEMENT

Problem management encompasses the set of processes that are used to quickly detect, record, track, and correct any types of malfunctions in client-server or Web database applications or their supporting hardware/software/networking equipment and facilities. Problem management issues can be largely amplified in a client-server or Internet/intranet environment due to the heterogeneous nature of the technologies used and the numerous hardware, software and middleware components that must be connected together to operate as smoothly as possible. Problems are usually reported through the help desk and should be resolved within pre-established times. The Help Desk staff monitor the progression and resolution of the reported problems to ensure that those agreed-upon service-levels are maintained.

Table 9-23 provides a non-exhaustive list of candidate problem areas that need to be closely managed with a structured problem management process.

Table 9–23 Subjects That Should Be Controlled
Under A Structured Problem Management Process

- Hardware failures
- Middleware failures
- Network failures
- Application system failures
- Environmental failures
- Database failures
- Job scheduling failures
- Transaction failures

9.5.6　PERFORMANCE MANAGEMENT

Performance management includes the set of processes that are used to predict and assess current systems performance, avoid system performance degradation, and fine-tune the response time of the most critical system transactions. The performance management function also measures the service-levels that must be satisfied by technology components based on pre-established objectives. Client-server and Internet/intranet technologies do not eliminate the need for performance monitoring and tuning. Table 9-24 shows typical service-levels that users have been accustomed to with traditional mainframe environments. Make no mistake, your customers will demand the same results in a distributed world.

Table 9–24 Service-level Agreements In A Mainframe Environment

Overall network performance	97% responses less than 3 seconds
Overall network availability	99.5 to 100%
Mean time between hardware failures	1.5 months
Mean time between software failures	1.5 months
Mean time to repair	1 hour

Collecting, monitoring, analyzing, and reacting in a timely manner to client-server and Web applications performance statistics and also to various technology component key metrics will help prevent serious performance degradation before it adversely affects the users. However, performance tuning requirements might differ for each specific category of components that compose a distributed environment. For example, different categories of real-time performance monitoring tools might be required to verify the software operating systems, networks, and database components.

A real-time performance monitoring process should allow the verification of server CPU and memory resource consumption and input-output (I/O) channel throughput as the client-server and Web applications are running. The resource consumption patterns are often investigated at the time the users experience performance problems.

However, you cannot constantly monitor the performance of all distributed hardware and software components in a real-time mode, because of the overhead that can be associated with an ongoing monitoring process. Consequently, the performance monitoring tools should also be able to capture snapshots of resource consumption for different servers, at sporadic points in time instead of continuously. Another approach consists of activating the collection of data only after a certain threshold has been exceeded, instead of constantly collecting performance information in a real-time mode.

Typically, the performance trend analysis task is performed with the assistance of a special ESM monitoring agent, which is installed on each server that needs to be analyzed. The agent works in the background and captures various server resource consumption information that is accumulated in a log file. Subsequently, systems professionals, to detect and prevent potential system performance bottlenecks before they become a problem, analyze the performance statistics with specialized analysis tools and take corrective measures.

For example, carefully select specific network parameters to regularly evaluate the performance of the corporate networks. Table 9-25 provides a brief list of some useful parameters that can be used to monitor the performance of the network.

Table 9–25 Network Performance Monitoring Parameters

• Network overall utilization	• Packet transfer rates
• Response times	• Error rates
• Downtime duration and frequencies	• Packet loss rates

For each type of network supported, set up some specific thresholds. For instance, Ethernet network usage should not surpass 40–45 percent, while occasional peaks should not be tolerated beyond 70–75 percent. For FDDI, the maximum usage should be between 70–80 percent. For WANs, the maximum use should not be greater than 80 percent. Finally, for Token Ring, the maximum usage should be around 50–55 percent, while peaks should not exceed 75–80 percent.

The most common network performance monitoring tasks should be automated by setting up the thresholds that I discussed in the previous paragraph, and alarms should be automatically triggered for unusual network events, such as significant network utilization, error rates, and lost connections.

9.5.7   SOFTWARE DISTRIBUTION MANAGEMENT

Software distribution management is the process used to remotely install and dynamically configure business application or system software components on different client workstations and server platforms, possibly across different types of networks. Figure 9-11 illustrates the software distribution concept in a distributed client-server environment.

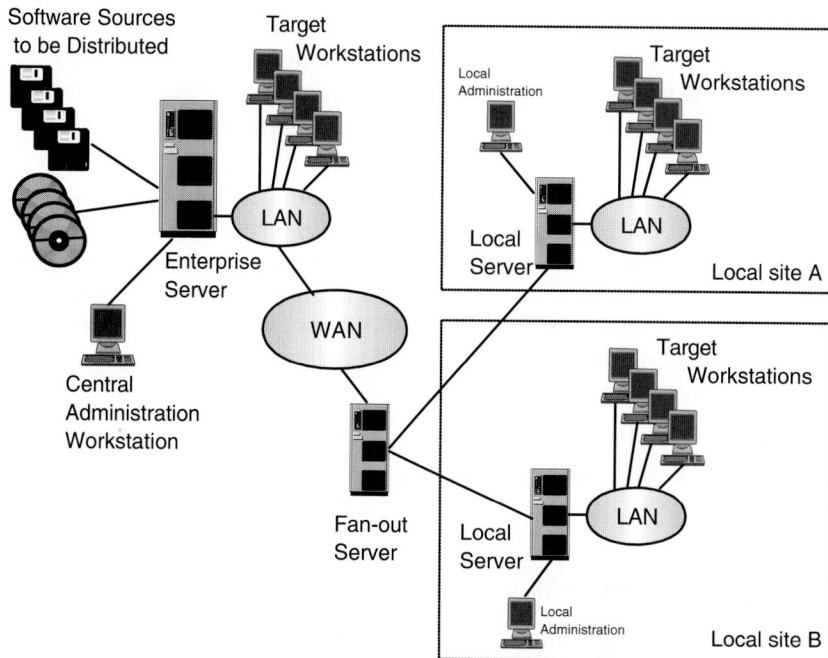

Figure 9–11 Software distribution concept.

An automated software distribution process might be less critical in environments that use a fat server strategy, such as Web database applications in intranet or Internet environments. However, software distribution can be critical in environments that invest heavily in large client-server applications with a fat client strategy, where a sizable portion of the application logic is processed on the client workstations instead of on the centralized servers.

The global costs of manually installing and administering software in a large distributed environment can surpass the initial acquisition costs of the software products themselves. Consequently, you need not only to automate the software distribution process but also to develop sound internal standards and scripts that describe how to install and configure client workstations. These standards can become essential to the enterprise's success with distributed systems. Some of the most common automated software distribution tasks that are performed by enterprise-wide software distribution tools are listed in Table 9-26.

Table 9–26 Automated Software Distribution Functions

- Creation of automated software distribution schedules, based on date, time, or other triggering parameters
- Push (server-initiated) or pull (client-initiated) software distribution, installation, configuration, and update
- Event software delivery monitoring and automated responses
- Automatic software de-installation and removal
- Centralized inventory of all software installed on the entire network
- Automated software distribution on multi-platform and multi-protocol environments
- Purchased desktop software license management, tracking, and enforcement
- Automated detection and creation of software and hardware inventories across the entire enterprise network
- Software regression capabilities that allow to return to the older software version if a problem is detected with the newer version

9.5.8   CONFIGURATION/ASSET/CHANGE MANAGEMENT

The set of processes that is used to define, track, modify, and control the entire spectrum of client-server and Web computing components and resources that are distributed across the enterprise. The control of client workstation configurations is essential to ensure smooth operations in a client-server and Web environment.

The organizations should not underestimate the importance to standardize as early as possible all elements of the distributed environment, from the client up to the servers, including the middleware that lies between these two extreme layers.

In distributed environments, several layers of software products must reside on the clients and servers to allow the applications to work smoothly in a complex and constantly evolving distributed world. Thus, you need to ensure that the right combination of different releases and versions of software components are carefully assembled together to work harmoniously and interconnect properly with each other, based on a standardized configuration scheme. Also keep an accurate inventory of the hardware equipment, its location, and modification status.

An application that has been properly running for awhile might suddenly fail to execute if the client workstation software configuration is modified to accommodate the installation of a new application. These types of problems can be amplified if the users are able to modify their workstation configuration once the initial configuration has been done. This change can create a situation in which an application that used to work properly suddenly fails to work when a new software product is installed.

Also, you might want to develop a fallback strategy should the automated installation of a new application release across hundreds or thousands of workstations suddenly fail for whatever reason. A good configuration management tool should be able to track the dependencies between software components.

Asset management in large distributed environments can be an enormous task if done manually. Several distributed system management tools offer automatic detection and identification of software and hardware inventories for most computing platforms.

Finally, change management and version control of different releases of numerous client-server and Web applications will facilitate the application development and maintenance process, especially for large and complex development and maintenance systems for which several developers can make changes to the same software component at the same time.

Table 9-27 provides a brief list of some of the major types of planned changes that need to be controlled by the ITS Operations department. If these planned changes are not carefully controlled in the new distributed production environment, then the stability of this environment can be seriously compromised. It can negatively affect the service-level agreements that were negotiated with your customers for uninterrupted services in the distributed computing environment. Similarly, contingency plans should be produced for restoring the distributed computing environment back to its previous state if the planned change does not work as expected.

Table 9–27 Examples Of Major Changes That Need To Be Controlled In A Typical Distributed Production Environment

Application systems	• Implementation of new application systems
	• Addition of new batch jobs
	• Addition of new online transactions
	• Changes to production batch jobs schedule
	• Changes to batch job dependencies
	• Application system modifications and enhancements
Operating systems/ middleware	• Implementation of new releases
	• Implementation of software patches
	• Major modifications to software configurations
Hardware	• Implementation of new hardware devices
	• Removal of hardware devices
	• Modifications of hardware configurations

Schedule in advance and plan all major changes. A change management team should approve them. Send a formal notification to all parties that might be affected by the upcoming change. The notification time interval might vary, depending on the risk associated with the change and the impact it can have on the users that work in the distributed computing environment. A sound change management process will ensure that all major changes that might affect the distributed computing environment are applied in a controlled and disciplined approach. This is a necessary process if you want to ensure that you can meet the service-level agreements you negotiated with your customers.

Similarly, also set up a specific process to handle emergency system changes. This is necessary to not delay the normal operations of the data center.

9.5.9   AUTOMATED SYSTEM OPERATIONS MANAGEMENT

Automated system operations management encompasses the set of processes that are utilized to automatically coordinate the use of distributed computing resources and operations, such as batch jobs scheduling, load balancing, event alert management, print management, and other similar routine operations system administration tasks.

A sound production job scheduling process is mandatory in a distributed computing environment, as it is in a more traditional mainframe environment. A robust automated job scheduling tool will greatly facilitate the process of scheduling and executing batch jobs in a distributed computing platform.

9.5.10 SECURITY MANAGEMENT

Security management encompasses the set of processes that are implemented to protect sensitive data and applications from unauthorized use, at the level of the enterprise. Among other things, security management encompasses the administration of user passwords (i.e., assigning, revoking, and changing them), identification codes, user access rights/profiles/privileges, handling of security incidents, and education on security matters.

Security prevention and enforcement should not be set up in a piecemeal approach, isolating one specific technology component to the detriment of other major components. For instance, distributed database security should not be implemented in a standalone mode, ignoring the need to integrate it with application and network security. In fact, an effective security action plan should be based on a strategy that emphasizes the integration of all security-related technologies so they remain closely wired with existing corporate security policies and procedures.

Internal threats should also be managed appropriately. Several security studies demonstrate that the largest security threats come from the inside, either from dishonest or disgruntled employees who seek revenge, or honest employees who are not using proper security procedures. For instance, some users could steal sensitive information simply by downloading data onto diskettes. On the other hand, the ability that the users have to load diskettes in individual client workstations that are connected to the network signifies that potentially thousands of different entry points can be used to inadvertently introduce computer viruses, whether firewalls are implemented or not.

9.5.11 HELP DESK SERVICES MANAGEMENT

The Help Desk department is composed of a group of highly trained individuals who are responsible to help users fix minor problems identified by them. The help desk staff carry out first-line problem resolution. However, if the problem is major, then the help desk mandates expert groups in the MIS department to resolve the reported problem. Effective customer support structures such as the help desk function become essential for large client-server and Web database applications.

Once a user has reported a problem, a trouble ticket is usually opened by the help desk and closed when the problem has been fixed. To some extent, though, certain types of problems can be automatically detected through the implementation of ESM intelligent event agents. The agents automatically trigger alarms and generate a trouble ticket and a problem report when a major computing device such as a server is failing.

Some help-desk support groups also use intelligent, knowledge-based databases, which contain historical information on various types of problems and how they were resolved.

9.5.12 BACKUP AND RECOVERY MANAGEMENT

Backup and recovery procedures and services must be set up for the client-server and Web environments. Two of the fundamental points that must be addressed in the file/database arena relate to who will be responsible for backing up the data that may reside on the different enterprise computer platforms and where the backups are performed. Furthermore, will only the data that resides on the enterprise servers be backed up? What about the servers that are located in remote locations? Will an incremental back-up strategy be adopted?

Some of the responsibilities that traditionally were assigned to Information Systems might now be shifted to the business areas. For example, will the data that reside on the clients workstations be backed up by the users themselves? These simple questions must be answered before the first client-server or Web database application goes into production. Using tools that can provide a centralized backup strategy is often one of the best way to manage the backup of mission-critical servers that are located in different locations.

9.5.13 SOFTWARE LICENSING MANAGEMENT

The use, distribution, and licensing of a multitude of different vendor software on hundreds of client workstations and servers can become a support nightmare if it is not properly managed right at the outset. The tracking and monitoring of software licenses can be critical to avoid buying unnecessary software and to manage the current corporate licensing schemes.

Software metering tools can be used to manage the number of users accessing a given software product, as long as the enterprise has set up standard desktop configurations.

9.5.14 HIERARCHICAL STORAGE MANAGEMENT

Hierarchical storage management is the process used to allocate data files to the most appropriate storage devices, usually based on the frequency with which the data is accessed. It evolves from the most active data files to the less active data files. The HSM systems provide a way to migrate aging files to increasingly less expensive data storage media while still providing rapid access.

9.5.15 CAPACITY PLANNING AND MANAGEMENT

Capacity planning is the process by which projections of how much computing resources will actually be consumed by all client-server and Web system software and applications across the enterprise, within specific time periods. Capacity management is the process of identifying and implementing the hardware, software, networking, and configuration changes that are required to sustain the level of computing resources that the enterprise will need over a projected period of time.

Capacity planning and management are essential to satisfying service-level commitments that meet users' expectations in a distributed world. Service-level agreements in the distributed system world are typically expressed by at least three important metrics: system response time, system overall reliability, and system availability.

Developing a capacity planning process in a large distributed system environment is not an easy task. However, the process is not much different from the ones that have been used for traditional mainframe environments, as illustrated in Table 9-28.

Table 9–28 Capacity Planning In A Distributed Environment

- First, the capacity planners establish a baseline by identifying the total resource capacity levels that are currently available within the current distributed environment. The main areas to cover include the servers, networks, and databases.
- Second, the capacity planners identify the levels of current machine and network resource utilization to determine how much capacity is being taken up by the current system and business applications.
- Third, the capacity planners collect and analyze, on a regular basis, growth projections for new applications requirements that will translate into additional computer resource consumption further down the road for trend analysis.
- Fourth, the capacity planners monitor, collect, and analyze critical system resource metrics for desktop, server, and network resource consumption, on a regular basis. This process is on-going, allowing the enterprise to keep its finger on the pulse of the distributed environment.

Depending on the projected volumes of transactions that will be processed in the future, the distributed computing environment can be scaled up either horizontally or vertically to accommodate the anticipated loads. Horizontal scaling signifies adding new server machines to the current pool of servers. Vertical scaling signifies adding additional processing capacity to existing server machines.

Even though a distributed computing environment is scalable by having the possibility to add new servers, the network certainly remains one of the most critical technology components. Several client-server and Web application systems have failed not because of a lack of functionality but because of a lack of adequate response time under heavy production peak loads. Usually, the response time problems were caused by network bandwidth problems. Capacity planning can help the enterprise avoid these types of problems.

Table 9-29 indicates some of the most common factors that will typically lead to significant increases in network traffic.

Table 9–29 Most Common Factors Leading To Enterprise Network Traffic Increases

- Increased number of users at different locations
- Significant growths in current business
- Introduction of new lines of business
- Augmentation of networked applications, such as groupware software
- Increases in client-server and Web applications
- File transfers between different sites
- Increased use of multimedia facilities (i.e., sound, graphics, videos, and 3-D animations) across the network
- Increased use of distributed database management systems and replication
- Use of automated software distribution and configuration via the network

9.5.16 DISASTER/RECOVERY MANAGEMENT

As mission-critical client-server and Web applications are implemented, the need for a sound disaster recovery process that is specifically applicable to the distributed environment increases significantly. Thus, you must identify and prioritize which distributed applications must be recovered from a major disaster and how quickly.

Typically, the protection of the mission-critical distributed applications, along with the data they manipulate, are the most essential software elements to secure. The software applications are backed up at certain time intervals, based on the frequency of changes applied to them. The backups are usually stored at an off-site storage facility.

Similarly, the corporate data is backed up at regular time intervals and sent to off-site locations. From there, the organization can work on the recovery processes and mechanisms that need to be implemented to be back in business as soon as possible, in the event of a major disaster.

Furthermore, mission-critical hardware and networking equipment should be covered in the corporate disaster recovery strategy, should a major disaster occur. In a distributed environment, an easier approach might be to develop a strategy whereby several remote production server rooms are set up throughout the corporate network to cover any emergency.

9.5.17 PREVENTIVE MAINTENANCE MANAGEMENT

Preventive maintenance is a pro-active process by which hardware equipment in the distributed computer environment, such as servers, for instance, are routinely maintained in order to prevent potential failures. Each major critical hardware component in the distributed computing environment should have a preventive maintenance handbook describing the maintenance steps that should be executed on a regular basis to prevent potential failures. Figure 9-12 shows a sample of a brief report that was produced after a preventive maintenance process was performed against a server in production.

Preventive Maintenance Report Number: _____   Date: __-__-__
Description of Hardware Equipment: _____
Performed by: _____

Description of tasks performed:

The production server Brisbane (HR100-3) was serviced today at 8:00 P.M. A complete diagnostic was performed against the server and came up error-free.

Description of major problems encountered and fixes applied:

None.

However, the following anomalies were detected and corrected immediately:

There was an FDDI card that was a bit loose and not firmly attached. The card has been firmly secured in its socket.
The power cord was very loose at one end and bent in the middle. It was replaced with a brand-new one.

Figure 9–12 Preventive Maintenance Report Form.

9.5.18 SERVICE-LEVEL AGREEMENT MANAGEMENT

The prime purpose of a service-level agreement is to outline a framework to manage the type, quality, and quantity of services that will be provided by the IS organization to its customers.

The service-level agreement process establishes with the users a formal contract describing the expected level of services that the IS organization will provide to the users, based on their business needs. This contract clearly delineates the roles and responsibilities for both IS and customer organizations. Once agreed with the users, the services delivered by the IS organization are then monitored on a regular basis. Some of the different types of services that the IS organization can provide to its customers and that they can manage with the use of service-level agreements appear in Table 9-30.

Table 9–30 Candidate Processes For Service-level Agreements

- Hardware installations, troubleshooting, and maintenance (i.e., workstations and related peripherals, etc.)
- Software installations, troubleshooting, and maintenance (i.e., desktop operating systems, application software, etc.)
- Network connectivity troubleshooting and maintenance
- Server installation, configuration, troubleshooting, and maintenance
- Customer support help desk services
- User access control and security services (i.e., creation and maintenance of user ids, passwords, etc.)
- Problem resolution (i.e., the average time under which most user problems reported to the help desk are resolved, etc.)
- Production application systems support outside regular business hours
- Production database support outside regular business hours
- Backup and recovery of data and applications (i.e., from client desktops, from servers, frequency of backups, etc.)

9.5.19 ENTERPRISE SYSTEM MANAGEMENT TOOLS

The proliferation of mission-critical client-server and Web database systems across the enterprise and even beyond its traditional boundaries has greatly increased the visibility and importance of network and distributed systems management. Several organizations start to realize that they can achieve substantial benefits by restructuring some of their core distributed network and systems management processes into a more consolidated infrastructure.

However, as you have just seen in this chapter, the formidable task of organizing distributed systems management processes into a more consolidated enterprise-driven framework goes far beyond the "tooling" dimension. It also involves managing your staff skills and different types of operations-center processes, as well as establishing an operation center environment where the roles and responsibilities associated with the distributed systems management infrastructure are clearly delineated. The network/systems management challenge in the distributed world is also vastly compounded by the fact that several large organizations have implemented over the years a wide range of heterogeneous distributed computing platforms.

Back to the tooling aspect, enterprises can embrace two fundamental approaches when the time comes to select and gradually implement enterprise-wide network/systems management tools:

- Acquire "best of breed" point solutions and integrate them together

- Acquire a highly integrated enterprise management tool solution

Unfortunately, no easy answer helps you opt for either one of these two basic approaches, since each organization will be influenced in its decision by several factors such as its current technology infrastructure and its people skills. Nevertheless, Table 9-31 summarizes some of the most common criteria to look for if your organization is contemplating acquiring an integrated enterprise systems management tool.

Table 9–31 Enterprise Systems Management Tools Selection Criteria

FEATURES	Tool 1	...	Tool N
• Asset management			
• Automatic/on-demand discovery of network protocols and devices (SNMP-compliant or non-SNMP-compliant, such as IBM's System Network Architecture or Digital's DECnet), across virtual networks and local area networks			
• Event/alarm management (e.g., low disk space situation, etc.)			
– Operations problem management/trouble-ticket administration			
– Automated event response			
– Alarm notification via pager, e-mail, etc			
– Predetermined thresholds and filters for events/alarms			
• Service-level management			
• Disaster planning and recovery management			
• User security administration			
• Virus protection			
• Graphical display of networks and devices			
• Automatic software distribution			
• Automated systems monitoring and administration of:			
– Business applications (client-server and Web-based)			
– Heterogeneous corporate databases			

Table 9–31 Enterprise Systems Management Tools Selection Criteria (cont.)

- Help desk administration
- Automated batch job scheduling
- Automated file transfer
- Configuration/version control/change management
- Capacity planning
- Performance management and resource utilization
- Backup and recovery management
- Print management
- Standard/customizable Web-based reports and charts
- Gathering of historical statistics
- Web-based console
- Support of enterprise systems such as SAP, BAAN, or PeopleSoft
- Support of Web-Based Enterprise Management (WBEM)/Common Information Model (CIM)
- Support of Java Management API (JMAPI)
- Inter-operability with third-party systems management tool vendors
- Ease of use
  - Context-sensitive help
  - User-definable interface options
  - Web-based interface
  - Remote-access device management
- Support of different client or server-based operating systems
  - Windows NT, Unix (HP-UX, Sun Solaris, IBM AIX, SGI, IRIX)

You can get more information on various enterprise systems management tools at the following vendors' Web site addresses:

http://www.tivoli.com	(TME 10 NetView)
http://www.hp.com/go/openview	(OpenView Network Node Manager)
http://www.cai.com	(Unicenter TNG)
http://www.cabletron.com	(Spectrum Enterprise Manager)

9.6   WEB TECHNOLOGY ARCHITECTURE

9.6.1   TAXONOMY OF A WEB TECHNOLOGY ARCHITECTURE

This section discusses the basic architecture of a typical Internet/intranet environment, designed for the enterprise at large. It covers, at a high level, the basic types of technology and services that are usually provided in such an environment, sometimes with a brief discussion of potential infrastructure issues. I assume that you have a certain knowledge of networking in general.

A more detailed coverage of the technology and types of services that are provided in such an environment are beyond the scope of this book. However, I provide references to several books that treat this subject in greater detail in the bibliography section at the end of this book. In addition to these references, you might simply search the Web with your favorite Web browser and commercial search engines for information on this topic, using search keywords such as Internet, intranet, or even extranet.

9.6.2   TCP/IP NETWORK

One of the fundamental blocks of technology that is essential to the setup of an enterprise Internet/intranet environment is the deployment of the Transmission Control Protocol/Internet Protocol (TCP/IP) standard on the corporate network. TCP/IP operates on Ethernet and Token Ring local area networks, on various wide area networks, and even on customary telephone lines that are connected to a modem.

If the organization is already running the TCP/IP network protocol on its LAN and WAN networks, then the network protocol is not an issue. If the organization does not yet use the TCP/IP protocol on its corporate network, then you should acquire a commercial version and implement it across the enterprise. The vast majority of UNIX systems have implemented TCP/IP as a standard feature of their operating software. Microsoft Windows 95 and beyond, along with Windows NT, have also TCP/IP built right into their operating software. TCP/IP software is also commercially available for the Macintosh and older PC platforms.

An important aspect of your TCP/IP strategy should cover mainframe connectivity, since a large amount of data in several large corporations still reside on the mainframe. In fact, most mainframe computer vendors such as IBM and DEC provide TCP/IP software that can coexist with their proprietary networking solutions, such as IBM SNA and DEC DECnet.

9.6.3   WEB SERVER HARDWARE

Web server hardware must be acquired to run the Web server software itself. The most common types of computer platforms that are usually selected to implement Web server software include:

- UNIX (i.e., HP, Sun, IBM, or Digital physical server machines)
- Windows NT (Intel, Alpha, or RISC-based machines)
- Macintosh

Table 9-32 lists some of the most common criteria that you should consider when selecting physical server machines for your enterprise Internet/intranet environment.

Table 9–32 Internet/intranet Physical Server Selection Criteria

- Overall performance capabilities
- Scalability based on planned volume of traffic and projected growth
- Security
- Reliability
- Ease of installation and configuration
- Ease of support and administration
- Level of compatibility with existing technology infrastructure
- In-house technical expertise

9.6.4   WEB SERVER SOFTWARE

The selection of the Web server software will be influenced by the Web server hardware platform that you retained to house it. Also, most of the same selection criteria that were previously outlined for choosing a physical Web server machine apply as well for selecting appropriate Web server software, as you see in Table 9-33.

Table 9–33 Web Server Software Selection Criteria

- Overall performance capabilities
- Scalability based on planned volume of traffic and projected growth
- Security
- Reliability
- Ease of installation and configuration
- Ease of support and administration
- Level of compatibility with existing technology infrastructure
- In-house technical expertise
- Content and site management features
- Web development support
- Documentation

Table 9-34 lists some of the most common Web server software that is used in the industry, along with the operating systems for which these servers are available. This list is far from being complete, because a multitude of Web server software is available on the market, whether as a commercial product that is fully supported or freeware.

Table 9–34 Web Server Software

WEB SERVER SOFTWARE	OPERATING SYSTEM SUPPORTED							
	SunOS	Solaris	HP/UX	IBM/AIX	IRIX	Windows NT	Windows 95	OS/2
Apache	√	√	√		√			
CERN	√	√	√		√			
Microsoft IIS						√		
NCSA	√	√	√		√			
Netscape	√	√	√		√	√		

9.6.5   WEB BROWSER SOFTWARE

The selection of client Web browser software will largely be influenced by the types of computing platforms and operating software that are supported within the enterprise. Large enterprises tend to have several different computing platforms. Thus, you should assess what types of operating systems are used across the enterprise and ensure that the Web browser product is available in several versions that can support all these different operating systems, if possible.

For an intranet environment, you might want to select a unique Web browser that can be used across the enterprise. Such an approach will help to drastically reduce time spent on training and supporting the users.

Most modern Web browsers are Java-capable, an important feature to look for when selecting your Web browser.

9.6.6   HTML EDITORS/WEB PAGE AUTHORING TOOLS

Web pages can be created directly with the Hypertext Markup Language (HTML) simply by using a text editor that can produce plain ASCII text. However, you might want to provide the developers and users with HTML editor tools that can facilitate and simplify the process of creating HTML documents. Basically, two major categories of HTML editors exist:

* Web page authoring tools that provide a WYSIWYG (what you see is what you get) approach to Web publishing
* HTML editor tools that generate raw HTML markups

The WYSIWYG tools are quite powerful and often provide full-fledged authoring features, complete with sophisticated menus, macros, and automated wizards that support you through the entire Web page authoring process. These tools are very user-friendly, and since they are often used like a regular word-processing application, they do not necessitate an in-depth knowledge of the HTML language to produce attractive Web pages. For this reason, WISIWYG Web page authoring tools can be used by most users without requiring a major investment in training them in HTML coding.

Power users and professional developers can use a variety of modern Web page authoring tools to develop sophisticated Web pages that make use of the latest technology, including Dynamic HTML (DHTML), streaming multimedia, Cascading Style Sheets, and even the extensible markup language (XML).[2] Most modern Web page authoring tools also allow a direct access to the underlying HTML code they generate so developers can tweak or add functionality to a page, based on specific needs.

Table 9-35 provides a list of some of the most common selection criteria that developers can use to select a Web page authoring tool, based on their specific needs.

Table 9–35 Web Page Authoring Tool Selection Criteria

HTML Facilities	• Support HTML 3.2 and above • Support Dynamic HTML • Import and translate documents from commercial word processors' native formats to HTML • Import Rich Text Format documents • Support Cascading Style Sheets (CSS) • Import and translate documents from commercial spreadsheets' native formats to HTML • Provide font definition and support
Graphics Facilities	• Support the most common graphic file formats used on the Web, such as JPEG, PNG, BMP, and GIF • Support progressive GIF and JPEG file formats • Support both client-side and server-side image maps • Provide automated file conversion facilities • Provide basic image re-touching facilities • Provide image/graphic importing facilities
Common Editing Facilities	Provide the following basic editing facilities: Tables edition Frames edition Forms edition HTML source code customization HTML code validation User-defined tags edition

2. For more information on XML, the reader might want to access the following Web site address: http://www.w3.org/XML.

Table 9–35 Web Page Authoring Tool Selection Criteria (cont.)

Ease of Use Facilities	• Provide wizards and templates • Offer multiple undo • Provide context-sensitive help • Provide adequate documentation and tutorials • Provide color-coded HTML tags • Offer a built-in spell checker

Extension Facilities	• Support the use of:
	  – ActiveX controls
	  – JavaScript
	  – Java applets
	• Support plug-ins and Web page add-ons

Site Management Facilities	• Provide global search and replace facilities • Provide hyperlink automated verification and correction • Allow on-the-fly site structure modifications • Provide simple, user-friendly Web page uploading capabilities from the development environment to the Web server
Web Page Team Authoring Facilities	• Provide version control facilities • Offer group-authoring facilities

The HTML editor tools that generate raw HTML markup are less user-friendly then the WYSIWYG Web page authoring tools. However, power users and professional developers can use them to create complex and custom-tailored Web pages. These tools will automatically generate the HTML beginning and end tags for you while you concentrate your efforts on adding content to your document. You can also configure these tools to preview the Web page results with your favorite Web browser, at the touch of a control button.

The following Web site address can help you discover various types of HTML editors, for different computing platforms:

http://www.yahoo.com/computers/world_wide_web/html_editors/

Following is a list of Web site addresses of some vendors or lists of vendors that offer specific HTML editing or Web page authoring tools:

http://www.microsoft.com/frontpage	(FrontPage)
http://www.sausage.com/dogindex.htm	
http://www.adobe.com/prodindex/sitemill/main.html	(PageMill/SiteMill)
http://www.w3.org/hypertext/www/tools/asWedit.html	
http://www.navisoft.com/index.htm	
http://www.claris.com	(Claris Home Page)

http://www.golive.com	(CyberStudio)
http://www.macromedia.com	(Dreamweaver)
http://www.netobjects.com	(NetObjects Fusion)
http://www.softquad.com	(HotMetal Pro)
http://www.symantec.com	(Visual Page)

9.6.7   ADDITIONAL VALUE-ADDED INTERNET/INTRANET SERVICES

Besides Web publishing, the Internet/intranet infrastructure can be set up to provide additional value-added TCP/IP network services such as those in Table 9-36.

Table 9–36 Most Common Value-added Internet/intranet Services

SERVICE	DESCRIPTION
File Transfer Protocol (FTP)	The file transfer protocol service transfers files between two computers. This service can be very useful to facilitate the distribution of software by providing download capabilities in your Internet/intranet environment.
Electronic Mail	This service provides access to your standard electronic mail system via a Web browser interface.
Wide Area Information Server	The wide area information server (WAIS) service can be used primarily to index large amounts of data. This indexed data can then be searchable over a TCP/IP network.

9.6.8   HTML DOCUMENT CONVERSION TOOLS

In large enterprises, a vast majority of information might already exist under the form of legacy documents that are somehow stored in various electronic formats. If you want to make this data available on the enterprise intranet, you must somehow find a way to convert these documents into an HTML format.

Several commercial tools are available on the market, which will convert various types of existing document formats into HTML formatted documents. Most of the commercial word processors (i.e., Microsoft Office, Lotus Office, or Corel Office) and desktop publishing software products provide a facility to automatically convert their documents from their original proprietary format into HTML code. These converters can also be used to directly translate spreadsheets and presentations documents into an HTML format. Figure 9-13 schematically shows the generic process that converts a file from its native format into an HTML format.

Also, several types of standalone commercial conversion tools can convert a wide range of proprietary document formats (i.e., ASCII, Rich Text Format, PostScript, etc.) into HTML code for UNIX, Macintosh, and Intel-based platforms, including older versions of various electronic document formats. If you want to find more infor-

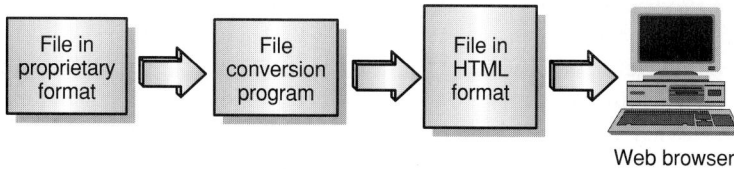

Figure 9–13 Generic file conversion process.

mation on the various types of filters that can be used to convert legacy documents into HTML code, you can access the following Web site, W3C, which is one of the best sites on the Web to locate and download a large variety of HTML converters:

http://www.w3.org/pub/WWW/Tools/Filters.html

9.6.9 WEB INTEGRATED DEVELOPMENT TOOLS

This section discusses different categories of web development tools, along with a summary description of their major characteristics.

JAVA INTEGRATED DEVELOPMENT ENVIRONMENT (IDE) TOOLS

A new breed of Rapid Application Development tools has appeared on the market to develop Web-based applications with the Java programming language. The new breed of tools is often referred to as Java Integrated Development Environments or IDEs.

The prime purpose of Java IDE tools is to assist the developers in rapidly building sophisticated Web-based applications. This is done with the use of powerful CASE tools that provide a highly visual programming interface and hide from the developers the complex infrastructure components and interfaces related to Web development.

Java Integrated Development Environment tools can be used not only to create Java applets but also to develop full-blown, standalone Java application programs that can run as standalones (i.e., they are not applets and do not need to execute in a Java-enabled Web browser). These Java applications can also access back-end corporate databases via the use of JDBC and ODBC database connection middleware, for instance.

The Java IDE tools usually provide advanced drag-and-drop visual programming interfaces that developers can use to automatically generate or manually insert Java code, build a graphical user interface, and debug the application programs with built-in graphical debuggers.

The Java RAD environments provided by these tools also include pre-built Java object and class libraries, as well as other tools to ease the programmer's burden. For instance, some of these tools include development wizards that assist the developers in building their application code. Other Java IDE tools provide a just-in-time (JIT) compiler with which the developers can compile Java bytecodes into native code for the computer machine the users are running on, avoiding the Java bytecode to be interpreted by a Java Virtual Machine.

Some of the Java RAD development tools might support different distributed object technologies such as Microsoft ActiveX, CORBA, or Sun Remote Method Invocation (RMI). Several Java IDE tool vendors are integrating the CORBA architecture with Sun Java. RMI enables a Java applet or Java application to transparently invoke an object's method across networks. To put the concept in simpler terms, a Java application that runs on one computer machine can execute a method that is embedded in a Java object that resides on another machine.

The variety of Java IDE tools that are available in industry is so broad that I cannot list all of them. However, if you want more information on these powerful tools, you might want to start your initial search at the following Web addresses:

http://www.powersoft.com	Powersoft Power J
http://www.software.ibm.com/vaj	IBM's Visual Age for Java
http://www.sun.com/developer-products/java	(Sun's JavaWorkshop)
http://.cafe.symantec.com/cafe	(Symantec's Visual Cafe Pro)
http://www.microsoft.com/visualj	(Microsoft's Visual J++)

Some of the most important technical criteria to look for when selecting a Java integrated development environment product appear in Table 9-37.

Table 9–37 Java IDE Tools Selection Criteria

FEATURES	Tool 1	...	Tool N

DEVELOPMENT FRAMEWORK

- Just-in-time (JIT) compiler
- Java Development Kit (JDK) tools supported/version level
- Graphical User Interface (GUI) design facility
- Graphical/hierarchical class browser
- ActiveX components support
- JavaBeans components support
- Database connectivity support classes
- Graphic files support (.BMP, .JPG, .GIF)

SOURCE CODE EDITOR

- Java syntax highlighting
- Scripting language type (i.e., basic-like)
- Macros support
- Support external editors
- Search/replace functions

Table 9–37 Java IDE Tools Selection Criteria (cont.)

DEBUGGING

- Integrated graphical/non-graphical debugger
- Debug Java applets in browser
- Conditional/non-conditional breakpoints
- Multiple threads debugging aid
- Remote debugging support
- Variables lookout
- Java bytecode disassembling capabilities

TEAM-BASED DEVELOPMENT FACILITIES

- Integrated source code control
- Hooks to external, third-party source code control tools

PROGRAMMERS' SUPPORT

- Context-sensitive help
- Wizard tools to help develop either Java applets or Java applications
- Online tutorials
- Online help
- Vendor support (i.e., hotline, etc.)
- Printed/online documentation

Besides these technically-oriented criteria, other additional factors might influence the selection process for picking up a Java IDE product, such as those indicated in Table 9-38.

Table 9–38 Java IDE Tools: Additional Selection Criteria

- The developers' practical knowledge of different programming languages more or less similar to Java
- The types of applications being developed
- The application development platform used by the developers
- Overall learning curve, ease of use, and level of functionality provided by the Java IDE product

WEB DATABASE APPLICATION DEVELOPMENT TOOLS

Web database application development tools are a specialized category of tools that developers can use to rapidly develop large and complex Web database applications.

Prior to moving forward on the subject though, let me point out that the Java IDE tools described earlier in "Java integrated development environment (IDE) tools" can also be used to build Web database applications. However, they are categorized as more general, broader-purpose Web development tools than the Web database application category that I cover in this section.

Although several categories of specialized tools can be used to develop Web database applications, I arbitrarily divide them into two broad categories: those tools that generate Java-based Web applications and those that generate Web database applications, which are not necessarily Java-based.

Many of the newer Web database application development tools were specifically designed from the ground up for the Web and in order to address several critical problems that are peculiar to a Web database application. I briefly discuss some of the most critical design issues that Web database application development tools must address while facilitating the development of large Web database applications in the next sections. They include:

- State management information
- Load balancing
- Concurrent database connections
- CGI connectivity

STATE INFORMATION MANAGEMENT

Typically, a Web server replies to a Web browser page request by sending an HTML page or by invoking an external application program via a server API, such as the Common Gateway Interface (CGI). Once the external application program has been executed or the Web page returned to the Web browser, the transaction process is terminated and the Web server closes the communication.

If the client Web browser sends another request for a page, the same process is repeated. The Web server simply returns another page and closes the connection once again. The Web server does not accumulate essential information about the application or the users that are utilizing it, between each user's request for a Web page. Such an approach is quite adequate for the dissemination of Web pages to a Web browser.

However, it is inadequate for Web database applications, for which you need to maintain session information or to move state information back and forth to the application users via information that is embedded in the HTML code. The approach that the Web database application development tool uses to provide session and state management is vital for its successful adoption.

LOAD BALANCING

In order to provide adequate scalability for a large-scale Web database application, the Web application server that is provided with the Web database development tool must be able to manage a significant number of concurrent transactions. Some of the most advanced tools can transparently load balance a large number of application requests among several physical server machines.

CONCURRENT DATABASE CONNECTIONS

Some Web database application development tools provide database connection caching and sharing between Web sessions while others demand a dedicated connection for each application process that is generated. The use of dedicated database connections can prove to be inefficient for huge Web database applications that are characterized by a large number of users.

CGI CONNECTIVITY

Figure 9-14 shows a typical architecture that provides Web access to a database via the Common Gateway Interface (CGI) approach.

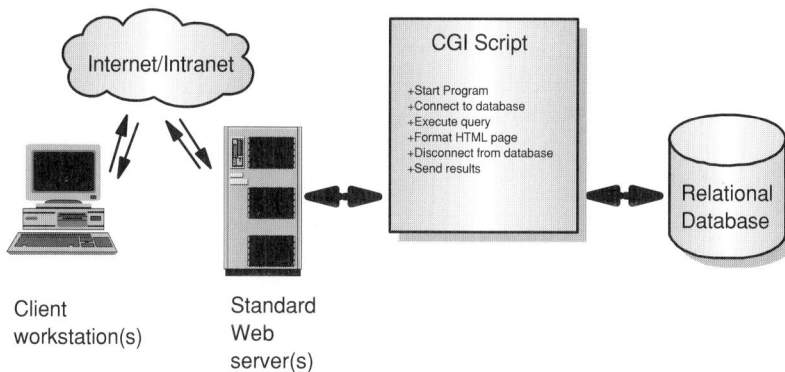

Figure 9–14 Web architecture using the common gateway interface (CGI).

Each Web browser request is serviced individually and generates substantial overhead. For each specific request, the Web server must invoke a CGI script, which connects to the relational database and executes the required database process. The data extracted from the database is subsequently formatted into some HTML code. Once the formatted Web page is returned to the client Web browser, the database connection is terminated.

This process cycle is repeated each time that a Web browser submits a request for database information. Such an approach can be quite inefficient for large Web database applications. It does not support quick response time to a large number of users' database requests and does not scale well as the demand increases on the Web application.

Most Web database application development tools offer more efficient approaches to connect a relational database management system to a Web server, using either Netscape NSAPI or Microsoft ISAPI. Both NSAPI and ISAPI are proprietary APIs that allow the Web application to work with distinct processes in a multithreaded approach.

WEB DATABASE DEVELOPMENT TOOLS SELECTION CRITERIA

Discussing in greater detail Web database application development tools is beyond the scope of this book. However, Table 9-39 lists some of the most important selection criteria that developers can use to help choose an appropriate Web database application development tool.

Table 9–39 Web Database Application Development Tools Selection Criteria

FEATURES	Tool 1	...	Tool N
GENERAL DEVELOPMENT FRAMEWORK			
• Integrated visual development interface (screen painters, etc.)			
• Plug-in or helper applications support			
• Support client- and server-side development			
• Support reusable components (i.e., JavaBeans components, ActiveX controls)			
• Generate pure Java applications on client and/or server			
• Support multi-tiered Web application deployment			
• Support development platforms (Windows/UNIX/Macintosh/OS2)			
• Integrate HTML authoring tool/third-party hooks			
• Support application server load balancing			
• Support transaction monitors			
• Support CORBA/IIOP, DCOM, RMI			
APPLICATION DEVELOPMENT PROCESS			
• Programming/scripting language supported (i.e., Java, C, Basic-like, Java Script, etc.)			
• Application-specific security features (passwords, controlled page navigation, controlled bookmark navigation, Web authentication)			
• Wizard tools to support the development process			
• Automatic generation of complex HTML reports			
• Manual/graphical query builder/SQL generator			
• Automated field creation directly from database			
• Multiple database/table joins/updates			
DEBUGGING			
• Integrated graphical/non-graphical debugger			
• Conditional/non-conditional breakpoints			
• Remote debugging support via Internet			
• Variables/points lookout			

Table 9–39 Web Database Application Development Tools Selection Criteria (cont.)

TEAM-BASED DEVELOPMENT FACILITIES

- Integrated source code versioning and control
- Hooks to external, third-party source code versioning/control tools

STATE MANAGEMENT/DATABASE CONNECTIVITY

- Provide Web application server to support persistence/state management
- Support CGI/ISAPI/NSAPI
- Support native ODBC/JDBC database drivers (Oracle/Informix/Sybase/DB2)

PROGRAMMERS' SUPPORT

- Use of wizards
- Context-sensitive help
- Online tutorials
- Online help
- Vendor support (i.e., hotline, Web-based support, classrooms, etc.)
- Printed/online documentation

Following are some Web site addresses for some detailed vendor information on different Web database application development tools:

http://www.bluestone.com	(Saphire/Web)
http://www.netdynamics.com	(Netdynamics)
http://www.next.com/webobjects	(WebObjects Pro)
http://www.haht.com	(Hahtsite)
http://webspeed.progress.com	(WebSpeed)

Most major database management system vendors have developed their own Web database application development products. For more information on this subject, consult the following database vendors' Web site addresses, searching more specifically for their Web development products.

http://www.microsoft.com
http://www.oracle.com
http://www.informix.com
http://www.sybase.com

NETSCAPE WEB APPLICATION DEVELOPMENT TOOLS

Netscape Communications provides a suite of application development tools that is aimed specifically at rapidly building and deploying Web-based applications. Netscape's Web application development suite is commonly known as Netscape One. Netscape One is in fact a network-centric Web application development environment, which is based on a variety of open, platform-independent industry standards such as:

- The HTTP protocol to support Web browsers and servers
- The Internet Inter-operable ORB Protocol (IIOP) to support CORBA services and activities across networks; IIOP is used to connect applications that run on distinct computer machines
- The Lightweight Directory Access Protocol (LDAP) for directory services
- The Simple Mail Transfer Protocol (SMTP) for electronic mail services
- The Java programming language and JavaScript scripting language
- A set of open, scalable security standards, including services such as communication encryption and certificate technologies, that are used to control accesses to Web applications

Furthermore, Netscape provides a set of Internet Foundation Classes (IFCs) to complement its Web development framework. IFCs are a set of various Java classes and components. Equivalent to Microsoft ActiveX components, IFCs provide reusable building blocks that can be assembled together to rapidly develop Web-based applications. You can find more information about the Netscape One product at the following Web site address:

http://www.netscape.com

9.6.10 WEB-BASED ENTERPRISE REPORTING/QUERY TOOLS

INTRODUCTION

This section briefly discusses the concept of enterprise reporting and the specialized sets of tools that support this concept. It also provides a brief description of the type of technology framework that is required to better support enterprise reporting at the level of the entire organization. Finally, I also provide a list of selection criteria for enterprise reporting tools, along with a brief discussion of some of the most important criteria.

Organizations could not survive long if the mission-critical information contained in a variety of operational inventory, sales, or financial reports would not be accessible to the front-line workers and supervisors on a day-to-day basis.

If you look more closely at the different reporting needs of several large organizations, at least three major types of reports are produced in the enterprise, as shown in Figure 9-15.

The first category is comprised of the production-oriented reports. The production reports contain operational data and are generally produced on a daily basis to help

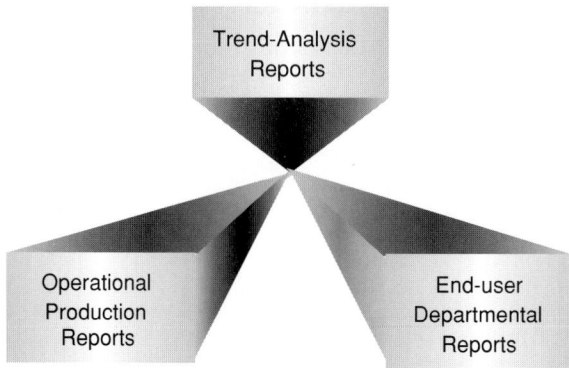

Figure 9–15 Enterprise report types.

run the business. The second category of reports includes a variety of departmental reports that are produced by the end users themselves with various user-friendly desktop-reporting tools. Finally, the third category is reports that are used for trend analysis and data mining purposes.

The production reports are usually produced by the MIS organization. These large reports are often complex and require the processing of significant volumes of data to eventually generate a variety of important business documents, such as customer credit card statements, electricity bills, or telephone bills. Usually the production-oriented reports are distributed to a large number of users or customers.

Departmental reports are relatively simple, short reports that are produced by the users themselves, without the direct support of the MIS organizations. These reports, whether created on a regular or ad hoc basis, are generated with various end-user reporting tools that do not require much programming and that primarily operate in a client-server environment.

Since the users are in control of the desktop reporting environment, they can customize their departmental reports easily with the desktop reporting tools, based on their evolving needs. Departmental desktop reports are usually developed for small user workgroups. The information can be extracted directly from the operational databases or from consolidated data warehouses.

The reports that are used for trend-analysis purposes are produced with sophisticated online analytical processing (OLAP) tools, which can slice and dice information in many different shapes and forms. The summarized information that is required to perform trend analysis is often extracted from huge, enterprise-wide data warehouses or smaller-scale data marts that focus on specific lines of business. The use of warehouses or data marts relieves the operational databases of the additional burden of processing potentially thousands of requests aimed at detecting and analyzing different types of business trends.

THREE-TIER CLIENT-SERVER REPORTING INFRASTRUCTURE

Recognizing the importance of making business reports more readily accessible to certain categories of user groups or the masses, the software reporting technology industry has evolved from a two-tier client-server architecture to a three-tier client-server architecture.

Figure 9-16 shows a traditional two-tier client-server architecture that several organizations have implemented in an attempt to satisfy various end-user reporting needs.

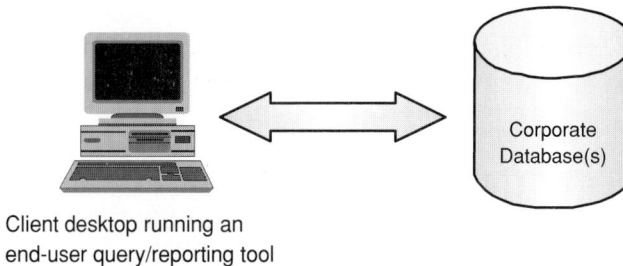

Client desktop running an
end-user query/reporting tool

Figure 9–16 Traditional two-tier client-server architecture.

The two-tier client-server reporting solution illustrated in Figure 9-16 usually consists of a fat client workstation that runs an end-user reporting tool that accesses information from a relational database server.

Although these fat-client desktop reporting tools have helped users to produce relatively simple reports or queries, they also have limitations, as indicated in Table 9-40.

Table 9–40 Two-tier Client-server Reporting Tools Limitations

• Producing reports or queries that require access to data stored in multiple, complex data structures that are scattered across the enterprise production environment is difficult.
• Performance degrades significantly as the user reports/queries necessitate the transfer of large volumes of data between the client machine and the database server, which creates an overload situation on the corporate network.
• Producing reports that require the formulation of complicated segments of business logic code is difficult.
• A strong possibility exists of overloading the database server itself with delinquent reports or queries that sequentially read the entire database for information.

In an attempt to address these limitations, the software reporting industry has introduced a three-tier client-server architecture, as illustrated in Figure 9-17.

As you see in Figure 9-17, a report server is now sitting between a thin-client desktop and the database server. The report server is used to centrally process and store business reports at the level of the entire enterprise.

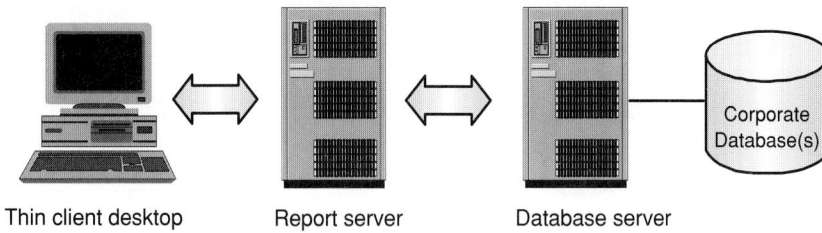

Figure 9–17 Three-tier client-server architecture.

A three-tier client-server reporting solution provides several advantages over a two-tier client-server reporting solution, as indicated in Table 9-41.

Table 9–41 Three-tier Client-server Reporting Tools Advantages

- Since the information displayed in the reports is now centrally stored in a report server, it can be distributed more rapidly to a wider audience than before.
- With this thin-client model, the desktop machines are suddenly relieved from the additional burden of producing reports, which now is done by the report server application.
- The information that is centrally stored on the report server can be more adequately managed by the MIS organization with enterprise-level backups, version control, and security mechanisms.
- This centralization scheme helps to better control the integrity of the information contained in the report server. It also helps to enforce a more consistent view of data across the enterprise by limiting the propagation of potentially dissimilar desktop-oriented versions of the same report.
- The report server architecture can scale up from a simple desktop-oriented reporting level to an enterprise-oriented reporting level, supporting potentially thousands of users.

However, with the advent of the Internet/intranet technology as the mainstream software architecture for corporate information dissemination, the three-tier client-server reporting architecture has finally evolved into an n-tier, Web-enabled client-server architecture, as illustrated in Figure 9-18.

Without a doubt, publishing various corporate reports on the Internet or in an intranet environment is one of the most efficient ways of rapidly disseminating data at large to geographically dispersed users. However, this process also brings new challenges along with it, such as deciding which reports should be accessible to which users, how the security should be handled, and whether the data should be encrypted if the reports are put on the Internet. Also, publishing a report that contains a few pages on the corporate intranet is one thing. Publishing a large and complex corporate report, which contains hundreds of pages, on the intranet is another thing. Consequently, the structure of large reports needs to be specifically adapted to the Web medium, as you see later on in this chapter.

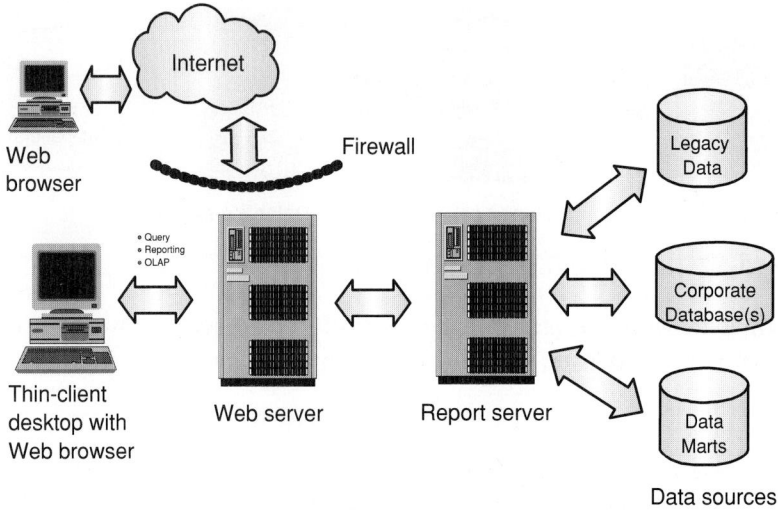

Figure 9–18 N-tier web-enabled client-server architecture.

Table 9-42 provides a list of some of the most common selection criteria that can be used for evaluating Web-enabled enterprise reporting products.

Table 9–42 Enterprise Reporting Tools Selection Criteria

FEATURES	Tool 1	...	Tool N
• 2-tier, 3-tier, or n-tier distributed architecture			
• Internet support/automated HTML report generation			
• Object-oriented, component-based reporting capability			
• Database support			
– Oracle, Sybase, Informix, SQL Server			
– Other proprietary file formats			
– Native database APIs, ODBC, JDBC			
• Report server			
– Scripting/programming language supported			
– Open API enabling integration with external applications			
• Report distribution facilities			
– E-mail attachment			

Table 9–42 Enterprise Reporting Tools Selection Criteria (cont.)

- – Automated notification of report availability/group notification
- – Automated posting on the Web (Internet or intranet)
- – Printer support
- Online viewing features
  - – Search capabilities
  - – Navigability
    - – Automated report table of contents generation with hyperlinks
    - – Hyperlinks support
      - – Inside report
      - – External to other reports
      - – Possessing drill-down capabilities
- Ability to download selective sections of report
- Web browser(s) support
- Special viewer plug-in component
- Report server administration facilities
  - – Report scheduling
  - – Report distribution
  - – Job priority management
  - – User profile/account management
  - – Security management/user authentication/encryption
  - – Printer management
- Version control management
- Scalability/performance
- Context-sensitive report help/general-purpose help facility
- Wizard tools to help users create reports
- Online tutorials
- Printed/online documentation
- Vendor support (i.e., hotline, Web site, training, etc.)

The next section briefly discusses some of the most critical selection criteria that are highlighted in the preceding table.

REPORT DISTRIBUTION

Besides creating the reports themselves, the rapid distribution of the reports is one of the important features of an enterprise report architecture. The report server should provide user-friendly facilities to e-mail reports to users with the proper attachments or to notify them of their availability and accessibility.

Another critical requirement is the ability for the users to retrieve only a few selective pages from a large report or a subsection of it, once they have reviewed the reports stored on the server in an online mode. Through the network pipeline, the report server application should be able to download from the report server only the few report pages or subsections that the user requested, instead of the whole report. This selective downloading feature is important to avoid cluttering the corporate network.

The ability to print the reports on different printing devices, such as high-speed laser printers or departmental laser printers, should also be supported across the enterprise. A flexible scheduling and distribution function must provide a variety of mechanisms to create reports on demand or in batch mode during off-peak hours, and also distribute the reports to the appropriate recipients.

INTERNET/INTRANET SUPPORT

The support of Internet/intranet environments should also be provided to allow internal or external users to access the reports via a Web browser. The reports should be structured and formatted specifically for the Web medium. A mechanism should be provided to automate the translation of client-server reports into an HTML format and place them on the intranet environment. For large reports, break them into subsections and generate a flexible table of contents that reflects this modular structure.

For example, a sales report, which displays sales information by region, should have specific entries for each region. Such a report structure allows users to view a specific sales region simply by clicking on it. Hyperlinks should also be automatically inserted into the report structure and inside the report textual data. By clicking on a hyperlink, the users can go directly to a given section of the report or simply to other related reports. Drill-down capabilities should be provided to allow users to click on a report field, button, or image to instantaneously access more detailed information, as needed.

COMPONENT-BASED FRAMEWORK

The enterprise report architecture should encourage the use of reusable software building blocks, which allow users and developers to create additional reports by assembling new and existing report object components. In fact, the report structures should be "componentized" into various objects, such as headers, footers, titles, main body, data fields, images, graphs, text, sections, sub-sections, and so forth. Professional developers can create the most complex objects. The users can then reuse these objects to develop their own reports. Figure 9-19 presents a holistic view of the component-based report architecture concept.

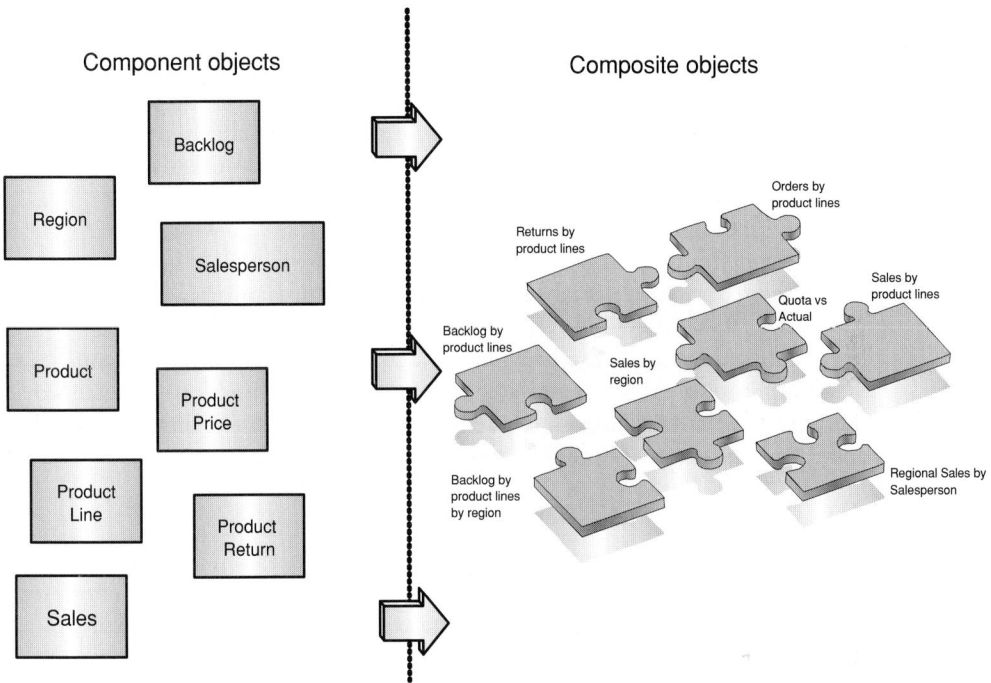

Figure 9–19 Component-based report architecture.

In a component-based report architecture, each particular report component object can be reused and shared among other objects to create more composite report objects that provide more advanced functionality without jeopardizing ease of use.

REPORT TOOLING CAPABILITIES

The enterprise report server architecture should provide the proper development and tooling environment that allows end users, power users, and professional developers to develop different types of reports. User-friendly wizards should assist the users to quickly create the reports they need. The users should be able to create reports without having the need to develop an in-depth knowledge of the enterprise database schemas. At the same time, a powerful server-based scripting or programming language should allow the professional developers to create the complex procedural logic that is required to produce the more sophisticated, production-oriented types of reports.

DISTRIBUTED ARCHITECTURE

The enterprise report architecture should support at least a three-tier architecture that allows the separation of the presentation, business procedural logic, and data into three distinct logical segments. A thin-client desktop scheme is used primarily to request and view reports, as opposed to producing them on a desktop machine, as is the case with a two-tier client-server architecture.

The distributed report architecture must be able to satisfy different reporting needs at the level of a department and at the same time be able to scale up to the level of the enterprise. At the enterprise level, the architecture should be able to produce very large reports that contain several hundreds of pages or produce thousands of small reports that are distributed to a large user population.

The report design, construction, administration, and viewing/printing services should be divided into independent but complementary functional segments that truly exploit the report server machine resources in the most optimal manner. Network traffic must be minimized and response time must be optimized.

The architecture should also provide an open API that allows external entities such as legacy applications to access and use the set of reporting functions that are provided by the report server application, hence leveraging the investments that were already made into a large number of legacy applications.

CENTRAL REPOSITORY

As the number of corporate reports and users increase over time, a central repository is mandatory to categorize, catalog, and file various types of information about reports and their recipients. Sophisticated searching features should allow the users to easily find the report information they are seeking. The meta-data repository must also offer adequate facilities to store and manage the different component objects that can be reused to create new reports.

ENTERPRISE REPORTING TOOLS VENDOR WEB SITE ADDRESSES

The following Web site addresses are provided if you want more information on vendors that offer different types of enterprise reporting tools.

http://www.actuate.com   (Actuate Software Corporation)
http://www.iqsc.com   (IQ Software Corporation)
http://www.ibi.com   (Information Builders Inc.)

9.6.11 WEB TESTING TOOLS

Chapter 8, dedicated to the particular subject of client-server and Web testing, provides detailed coverage of the Web testing process and the different types of testing tools that support it.

9.6.12 WEB-ENABLED DATA WAREHOUSE/OLAP TOOLS

This section discusses important data warehouse and OLAP concepts. It also explains how the web technology can extend the use of data warehouses and data marts way beyond the internal walls of the corporation, out to customers, partners and suppliers.

INTRODUCTION

Over the last couple of years, several organizations have built large, enterprise-based data warehouses. Most of the data warehouse implementations have been done with the traditional three-tier client-server architecture with proprietary software products.

However, as the industry makes giant progress toward mastering the Internet/intranet technologies, several organizations that have implemented large client-server data warehouses seriously contemplate the possibility of opening their warehouses to a larger internal audience with the use of the Web. Some of these organizations also want to open their warehouses to outsiders, such as customers, business partners, and suppliers.

The use of Web technology as the prime vehicle to provide easy information access to all users across the enterprise enables certain organizations to better leverage the large investments they have made in data warehouses.

Similarly, several organizations are gradually opening their data warehouses to their customers with Web technology, in an attempt to decrease their customer and client support costs. By making the information accessible via the Web, organizations can reduce and free up some of the staff who currently are supporting customers on a full-time basis by answering various requests or inquiries.

Moreover, organizations can also provide their mobile task force, such as salespeople, with immediate access to valuable competitive information that is stored in the data warehouse. Access to this competitive information from a remote location can help the salespeople to close some important sales with their customers.

WEB-ENABLED DATA WAREHOUSE CHALLENGES

The use of Web technology to support data warehouse access might present some concerns or challenges that must be overcome, such as those indicated in Table 9-43.

Table 9–43 Web-enabled Data Warehouse Challenges

- Potentially less functionality might be provided by the Web browser user interface than with proprietary client-server warehouse data access tools that offer rich online analytical processing (OLAP) capabilities
- Providing adequate security when people come through the Web interface to access corporate data
- Coping with potential bandwidth limitations via either an intranet environment or the Internet

Various approaches can be used to tighten the security of Web-based data warehouses and OLAP applications. User authentication and data encryption procedures can be used to erect safeguards against potential security threats, such as hackers or unsolicited users. The Web-enabled data warehouse or OLAP applications can also be implemented in an intranet environment, behind a firewall that controls access to these applications from inside and outside.

For companies that have extremely stringent security requirements where the above-mentioned security measures are not sufficient, they can still use dedicated communication lines and secure T1 connections that are extended to their business partners to better support the integration of Web-enabled or even traditional client-server applications.

Some of the issues associated with potential bandwidth limitations might be circumvented to some extent by using various data compression techniques to ensure that the transfer of data across the Internet/intranet environments is minimized as much as possible.

In some instances, organizations that implemented a very large data warehouse might want to integrate the Web with data marts. Data marts are comparable to enterprise-wide data warehouses but they are more restrained in scope. They usually concentrate on the needs of a specific business unit or subject area, as opposed to large data warehouses, which contain information about the entire enterprise. Table 9-44 illustrates some of the major differences between data marts and data warehouses. (The criteria shown in Table 9-44 are somewhat arbitrary and are used primarily to differentiate data marts versus data warehouses.)

Table 9–44 Data Warehouses Versus Data Marts

	Data Mart	Data Warehouse
Magnitude	Usually ranges between 1 and 60 GB	Usually ranges between 60 GB ands 2 terabytes, or more
Target	Departmental or specific subject area	Enterprise-wide (i.e., operational data collected from the entire organization)
Custodian	Departmental	MIS organization
Deployment	Averages 2 to 6 months	Averages 6 months to 2 years
Cost	Usually ranges between $10,000 and $500,000	Usually ranges between $500,000 and $10,000,000

By designing small-scale data marts for Web-enabled clients, business partners, and customers, organizations can offer to their users only the data they need, which can help to circumvent potential bandwidth limitations and even ease user searches by pointing them at specific business subject areas.

WEB-ENABLED DATA WAREHOUSE BENEFITS

Web technology offers several useful advantages over the more traditional client-server architectures, which can be used to better support data, warehouse, or decision support systems.

Table 9-45 provides a list of some of the most common benefits.

Table 9–45 Web-enabled Data Warehouse Benefits

- Users can access structured information such as word-processed documents or unstructured information such as ad hoc queries with the same user-friendly client interface, the Web browser.
- The use of a universal Web browser interface helps resolve the problem of platform compatibility. It allows users who operate with a Windows or UNIX platform to both access the data warehouse application without the need for the MIS organization to deploy and configure complex query or OLAP tools on the client workstations.
- Since several access points to connect to the Internet from almost everywhere around the world exist, organizations do not need to expand their private corporate networks to support all potential users who are located at different sites dispersed across several countries.
- The average costs for a client-based OLAP tool can easily range between $300 and $1200 per user, whereas a Web browser can cost approximately $50, when it is not free.
- Web browsers support local caching of Web page data. In the context of an OLAP client tool, the creation of repetitive analytical queries or reports can be quickly performed on the client workstation.
- The results of a query or a report can be viewed more quickly because the Web browser can start to display text and graphics before the transmission of data is entirely completed.
- Web browsers support asynchronous processing that liberates the client workstation for other tasks while a complex query is being treated

Figure 9-20 illustrates, at a high level, the basic technology architecture that is used to support generic Web-based data warehouse or OLAP products.

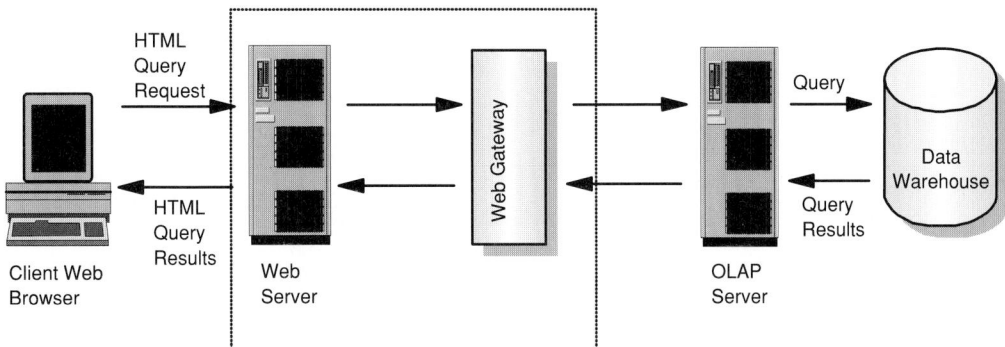

Figure 9–20 Web-based data warehouse technology architecture.

Figure 9-20 presents a summary description of how a Web-based data warehouse/ OLAP application works. First, a user creates an OLAP query via a Web browser interface. The request is passed to a Web server with some product-specific tags. The

Web server then transfers the request to a Web gateway, which formulates the original request in the application programming interface (API) supported by the OLAP server. The OLAP server retrieves the appropriate information from the data warehouse or data mart. Then the process is reversed. The OLAP server passes the returned data back to the Web gateway, which converts it into HTML code and transfers it back to the Web server. Finally, the Web server passes the query results, which are formatted as HTML pages, back to the client Web browser.

Most Web-enabled OLAP products manage all the issues related to maintaining the connection to the data source from the servers and keeping track of their clients in an interactive manner.

CONCLUSION

Most of the recent Web-based OLAP products not only bring OLAP to the desktop using Web technology, but they also offer rich functionality through their Web browser interface, such as ad hoc analysis, drill down, dynamic calculations, data pivoting, and basic data mining capabilities.

In conclusion, Web-enabled data warehouse/OLAP tools can prove to be cost-effective solutions to replace the more traditional client-server data warehousing products, especially the proprietary client-side OLAP products. What is important, though, when contemplating the acquisition of such tools is selecting products that are compatible with your current data warehouse/OLAP infrastructure.

The following Web site addresses can help if you want more information on Web-enabled warehousing solutions or Web-based decision support systems (DSS) and OLAP products in general.

http://www.strategy.com	(DSSWeb from MicroStrategy Inc.)
http://www.arborsoft.com	(Essbase from Arbor Software Corp.)
http://www.sas.com	(HTMSQL from SAS Institute Inc.)
http://www.oracle.com	(Oracle Applications Data Warehouse)
http://www.iqsc.com	(IQ/LiveWeb from IQ Software Corp.)

9.6.13 IMAGE MANIPULATION AND CONVERSION TOOLS

Various graphics and images can be used to enhance the look and feel of Web pages. Several types of image manipulation and conversion tools are on the market for this purpose. Some of them are powerful commercial graphical packages, and others are freeware or shareware, which sometimes offer almost as much core functionality as the commercial ones. Two of the most widely used image formats for publishing images on the Web are the GIF (Graphic Interchange Format) and JPEG (Joint Photographic Experts Group) formats. Most modern graphical software packages support these two popular image formats, providing various utilities to convert a large number of graphical formats into GIF or JPEG image files.

9.6.14 VIRTUAL REALITY MODELING LANGUAGE (VRML)

The virtual reality modeling language is used to display 3-D graphics in a VRML-capable Web browser and manipulate them interactively to view and move them around a virtual environment, in a near real-time mode. VRML is an open standard that can be advantageously used in various industrial types of Web applications, such as in architecture and computer-aided engineering design. The following URL provides more information on VRML in general, including VRML-capable Web browsers:

http://www.sdsc.edu.vrml
http://vag.vrml.org
http://vrml.sgi.com

9.6.15 INDEXING AND SEARCHING TOOLS

Search engine tools are commercial or proprietary software products that can be used to find several types of files that are stored on a Web server, such as plain text, sound, graphics, and video. These files can reside inside an intranet or on the Internet at large.

Most Web search tools are based on or derived from Wide Area Information Server (WAIS) technology. WAIS is a database retrieval system that searches documents that are indexed in databases across distributed networks.

Several commercial search engines are available on the market and work in a similar manner: you enter specific keywords for your query, and the search engines will find all the documents that match these keywords. You can combine multiple query fields that are associated with basic functions such as logical "AND" and "OR."

Web crawlers are indexer software tools that explore and classify the various types of documents that are stored on various Web sites, either inside an intranet or across the Internet. The inventory of Web-based documents is done using the links that are located in hypertext documents. Following the links, the indexer tools crawl through the various documents one link after another.

9.6.16 CLIENT-SIDE HELPER APPLICATIONS/PLUG-INS

Client-side helper applications are typically used to complement existing Web browser capabilities. As powerful as Web browsers can be in displaying documents and images, still a large variety of multimedia data formats out there simply cannot be handled directly by these mighty Web browsers. However, several Web browsers can call third-party software utilities that can manipulate specific media formats that the browsers cannot manipulate themselves.

These external programs are often referred to as Web browser application helpers, external viewers, or plug-ins. Quite often, shareware or commercial Web browser helper applications are used in various Internet/intranet environments to enhance the multimedia capabilities of the Web browser, such as supporting streaming audio files, video segments or animations.

Web servers and browsers use the Multi-Part Internet Mail Extensions (MIME) standard protocol to match up different types of media formats with helper applications.

The following URLs provide several references to a large number of Web browser helper applications:

> http://www.ncsa.uiuc.edu/SDG/Software/WinMosaic/viewers.htm
>   (for Windows environments)
> http://www.ncsa.uiuc.edu/SDG/Software/XMosaic/faq-software.html
>   (for UNIX environments)
> http://www.ncsa.uiuc.edu/SDG/Software/MacMosaic/helpers.html
>   (for Macintosh environments)

Also, you can get additional information on helper applications by navigating through the Web sites that are supported by companies that offer Web browsers, such as Netscape or Microsoft, for instance.

Developers can advantageously extend the functionality of Web browsers with plug-ins that, when developed with native code, can be truly optimized and offer enhanced functionality. This statement is true especially in an intranet environment that supports a single type of computing platform and a single Web browser.

However, some potential drawbacks could occur with the plug-in technology. First, the plug-ins usually must be installed on both the client and server sides. Besides the fact that downloading a plug-in might be a time-consuming process, complex installation requirements of plug-ins on client workstations might make the life of users more difficult than expected. Second, too many plug-ins can take a lot of disk space on the client workstation. Third, several plug-ins will often work well with one type of Web browser but will not be compatible with another type of Web browser. In some instances, consider extending the Web browsers' functionality with Java applets instead of plug-ins. Doing so not only will help to solve the "both-side" installation issue I just talked about, but will also provide true cross-platform applications. Fourth, if the use of plug-ins is not carefully managed in the enterprise, managing and keeping track of who has which types of plug-ins installed on their workstations and also which software versions of the plug-ins are currently running might turn out to be a time-consuming process for IS personnel. Will the same plug-ins continue to work if the intranet environment is upgraded with a new release of the standard corporate Web browser? Fifth, some add-on modules may turn out to be incompatible with in-house software.

For all those reasons, and although the use of certain plug-ins might drastically improve the productivity of the users, you still might want to set up some sound "plug-in" management policies. Do so before the use of undesired plug-ins starts to proliferate across the intranet environment and the situation suddenly gets out of control.

9.6.17 WEB-ENABLED E-MAIL TOOLS

This section discusses web-enabled electronic mail tools and facilities. It also presents open Internet e-mail standards and suggested selection criteria for choosing the Internet-based e-mail tools that are right for your enterprise.

INTRODUCTION

The Internet is gradually transforming the face of enterprise-wide e-mail systems. With the advent of open-standards-based e-mail solutions, several organizations are seriously contemplating the move from proprietary e-mail systems such as Microsoft Exchange, Novell GroupWise, Lotus Notes, and cc:Mail to IP-based e-mail.[3]

Although some will argue that the IP-based e-mail system and its supporting open standard messaging infrastructure are not yet ready to fully support large-scale, mission-critical messaging applications at the level of the enterprise, the Internet-based e-mail technology is indeed progressing very rapidly.

The Internet-based e-mail systems might not yet offer the rich feature sets of those supported by proprietary e-mail systems. Nonetheless, several small- to medium-sized organizations can implement relatively inexpensive Internet-based e-mail servers that provide not only a sound e-mail transport mechanism inside their organizations but also worldwide reach capabilities via the Internet, including remote access to electronic mail boxes for their mobile task force.

OPEN INTERNET MESSAGING STANDARDS

Table 9-46 lists some of the major Internet-based open standards that constitute the foundation of the Internet messaging services architecture. Conformance to these standards signifies, for instance, that any vendor's IMAP-compliant mail client can communicate with any other vendor's IMAP-compliant mail server. Similarly, any IMAP-compliant mail server can communicate with any other IMAP-compliant mail server, using the SMTP protocol.

Several large organizations might have experienced the dreadful challenges of sending e-mail attachments from one proprietary e-mail system to another proprietary e-mail system installed on another platform (i.e., such as from Windows to UNIX). For such organizations, as long as the mail client software is MIME-compliant, then even complex attachments can usually be transmitted in a dependable manner.

Following is a brief discussion of some of the protocols that are shown in Table 9-46.

---

3. Several large vendors of proprietary e-mail systems have embraced the open Internet e-mail standards such as SMTP, LDAP, POP3, and IMAP4, and have committed to supporting them in their own products.

Table 9–46 Open Internet Messaging Standards

POP3	The Post Office Protocol 3 (POP3) is a client-based mail protocol. Messages are downloaded from the POP3 mail server to the client workstation. Subsequently, the downloaded message is deleted from the mail server and all mail processing activities are performed locally on the client machine.
IMAP4	The Internet Message Access Protocol 4 (IMAP4) is a server-based, drop-and-store mail access protocol (i.e., the server regularly receives incoming mail and drops it into mailboxes that are located on the server; a message is stored on the server until a client moves or deletes it). IMAP4 is designed to handle either online or off-line mail messages or services. IMAP4 is an improvement over POP3 since users do not need to maintain messages. However, IMAP4 does not yet address some important mail-related issues such as e-mail directory services or centralized user management.
SMTP	The Simple Mail Transfer Protocol (SMTP) is a TCP/IP protocol, which regulates the transmission of electronic mail and its reception. It behaves as a routing vehicle between mail servers. SMTP is used by both POP and IMAP to transmit mail.
LDAP	The Lightweight Directory Access Protocol (LDAP) is a scaled-down interpretation of the X.500 directory services standard. LDAP supports specific mechanisms to name, retrieve, and search fields in a server-based directory.
X.500	The X.500 protocol is an international standard for distributed global directories that are in fact comprised of several separate servers that are accountable for managing their own content.
MIME/S-MIME	The Multipurpose Internet Mail Extensions (MIME) protocol provides a standard to add non-text files such as graphics, spreadsheets, or sound files to standard Internet mail messages. Secure-Mime (S-MIME) is a public-key encryption protocol used to transmit MIME attachments in a secure manner.
ACL	The Access Control Lists (ACL) standard is an extension of the IMAP protocol. ACL provides a security mechanism, which can be used to restrict mail access by a list of IP addresses that are defined by the mail administrator.
SSL/ X.509 Certificates	The Secure Sockets Layer (SSL) protocol is used to transmit encrypted data between a client and a server, such as a Web server. X.509 certificates are digital signatures that utilize public-key encryption to authenticate users.

X.500/LDAP PROTOCOL

The X.500 Directory Access protocol and a subset, the Lightweight Directory Access Protocol (LDAP), provide global directory services that let mail servers publish directories that mail clients can use to locate a user's e-mail address. Directory services can be viewed as the electronic counterpart of a traditional phone book, which lists e-mail users.

IMAP PROTOCOL

The IMAP protocol provides several features such as those indicated in Table 9-47.

Table 9–47 Some Imap Features

- Built-in facilities to define rules for searching, selecting, and deleting mail, based on values in the message header or the body of the message
- Selective downloading of message parts
- Server-side folder hierarchies
- Shared mail
- Mailbox synchronization

MIME PROTOCOL

The MIME protocol provides a standardized way to represent and encode a large variety of media or data types. MIME supplies a mechanism for Internet-based electronic mail software to send programs, video, graphics, sound, and other binary file types in the form of text-only mail messages.

The MIME protocol is very important, since Internet mail service is probably one of the most frequently used Internet software products beside Web browser software itself. And since Internet e-mail systems can send only messages that contain ASCII text in them, the MIME protocol goes around this limitation by extending the capabilities of Internet e-mail software. This is done by allowing binary data to be rebuilt in text form and then transmitted over the Internet in mail messages that are compliant with the original mail transport mechanisms.

Figure 9-21 shows a sample of a typical mail message header that contains a MIME attachment, which in this case is a JPEG image.

MIME-compliant e-mail user agents check incoming messages for the MIME-extended headers. Depending on the content type of the message, and some user-configurable rules that link specific content types with some specific application programs (or viewers such as a JPEG viewer, for instance), the MIME mailer sends the attachments to other application programs on the system that are qualified to work with them.

```
From: KarenF@zonax.com
To: AlexF@tampix.com
Date: Wed, 17 Aug 2002 15:21:32
Subject: MIME Example
MIME-Version: 1.0
Content-Type: image/jpeg
Content-Transfer-Encoding: base64


[...JPEG image....]
```

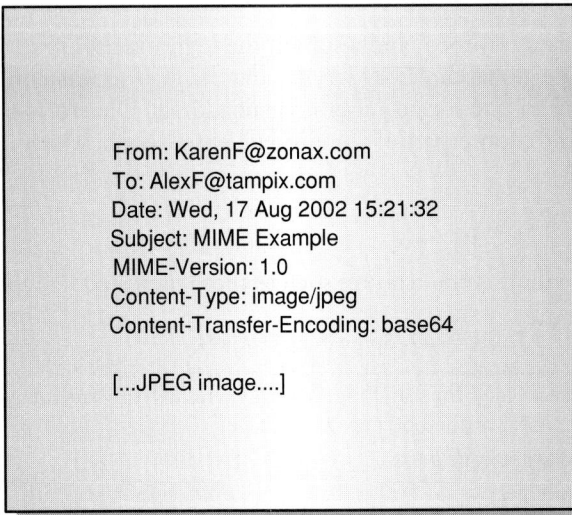

Figure 9–21 A sample e-mail message with a MIME attachment.

This process is exactly the same as that applied with a Web browser helper application. Most Web browsers that understand MIME content can send directly the data types they cannot manipulate to other application software on your system, which can handle the specific data types. Most Web browsers can be relatively easily configured to support additional MIME types that are not supported directly out of the box.

Table 9-48 shows a small subset of some of the most common MIME content and data types that are used on the Internet, along with a brief description. As shown in the table, MIME is divided into a variety of content types. Each content type is subdivided into various data types. New MIME types and subtypes continue to appear on the market as new requirements arise. They can be registered with the Internet Assigned Numbers Authority (IANU).

The following Web site address provides more information on the IMAP client and server protocol in general:

http://www.imap.org

Furthermore, you can access a comprehensive list of IMAP-compliant client and server products at the following ftp address:

ftp://ftp.cac.washington.edu/mail/imap.software

Figure 9-22 illustrates the typical path that an IP-based e-mail message follows, based on the Internet open messaging protocols. The SMTP protocol is used for sending mail, and the POP3 and IMAP4 protocols are used for receiving mail.

Table 9–48 Common Mime Types And Subtypes

TYPE	SUBTYPE	DESCRIPTION
Text	html	Hypertext Markup Language text
	plain	ASCII text with no formatting
	richtext	Text with simple formatting (i.e., word-processed formatted text)
Audio	basic	Audio data stored in 8-bit sound
	wav	Audio data stored in .WAV format
Image	gif	Color bitmapped image (8-bit) stored in .GIF format
	jpeg	Color bitmapped image (24-bit) stored in .JPEG format
Video	mpeg	Video and audio stored in MPEG format
	quicktime	Video and audio stored in Quicktime format
Application	octet-stream	Raw binary data
	postscript	A program written in PostScript
Message	rfc822	An RFC 822 mail message

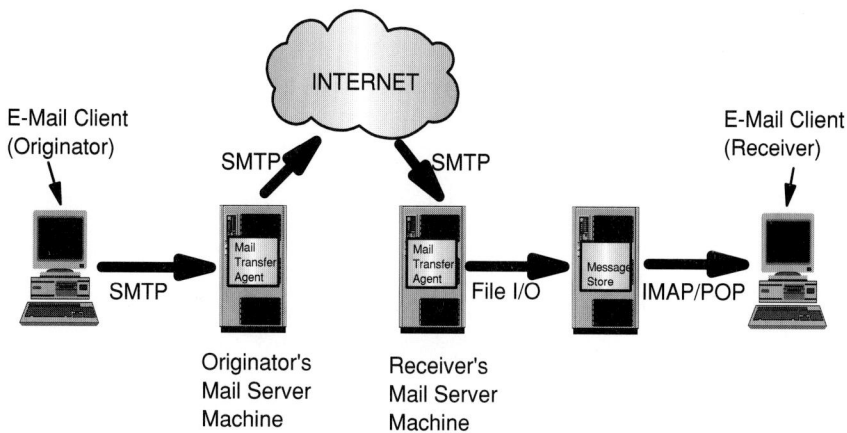

Figure 9–22 IP-based e-mail message path.

INTERNET-BASED E-MAIL TOOLS SELECTION CRITERIA

If you are interested in comparing different vendors' offerings for an IP-based e-mail system, Table 9-49 lists some of the most common selection criteria to look for when acquiring an Internet-based e-mail system. Selecting a lightweight or medium-sized IP-based e-mail system and its underlying messaging infrastructure might have a strong repercussion on other related infrastructure decisions later on. These additional infrastructure decisions relate primarily to the potential selection and acquisition of other related tools such as workflow, group collaboration, calendaring, and scheduling Web-based applications.

Table 9–49 Internet E-mail Tools Selection Criteria

FEATURES	Tool 1	...	Tool N
MESSAGING INFRASTRUCTURE			
• E-mail client or server protocols			
– POP3/IMAP4/SMTP/MIME/MAPI/VIM/S-MIME			
• Platform(s) supported			
– UNIX (HP-UX, IBM AIX, Solaris)			
– Windows (3.X, 95, NT)			
– Mac			
– OS2			
• Directory access protocol(s) supported			
– LDAP			
– X.500			
– ACAP/IMSP			
– Proprietary			
• Scripting language (VBScript, etc.)			
• Performance/scalability			
MAJOR FEATURES SUPPORTED			
• Embedded HTML/Web-browser-based administration capabilities			
• Mail scheduling			
• Multi-user/acct. support			
• Multiple MIME attachments/icon-based attachments			
• Mail client GUI customization features			
– Toolbars/notification method/signatures/pull-down menus/interface layout			
– Filter support (incoming/outgoing)			

Table 9–49 Internet E-mail Tools Selection Criteria (cont.)

- Spell checking
- Retention of mail messages/archiving
- Compression
- Backup/restore

VENDOR/TOOL SUPPORT

- Context-sensitive help/general-purpose help
- Wizard tools/online tutorials
- Vendor support (i.e., hotline, training, Web site, etc.)
- Printed/online documentation

SECURITY FEATURES

- Encryption mechanism(s)
- Authentication mechanism(s)
  - User id passwords
  - Digital signatures
- Virus protection

9.6.18 FIREWALL TOOLS

As more and more corporations connect their private networks to the Internet or other external networks, they must implement additional security mechanisms to protect their valuable data from the outside. Firewalls are a combination of hardware and software devices that sit between your internal network and the outside Internet.

The prime goal of a firewall is to limit access in and out of your network, based on your organization's security policies. Firewalls protect internal corporate networks from potential intruders, such as hackers, vandals, and even industrial spies. They can also be used to limit outgoing traffic, such as to prevent internal users from accessing the Web, for example.

To my surprising, many security attacks originate not from the outside but from the inside, by employees themselves. Hence, firewalls can also help better protect the corporation's valuable data from potential internal attacks.

Firewalls can be classified into several broad categories, based on the type of filtering mechanisms they implement. The most common categories appear in Table 9-50.

Table 9–50 Firewall Categories

- Packet filters
- Application gateways
- Circuit-level gateways
- Proxy servers
- Stateful inspection

Following is a brief description of each category of firewall filtering mechanisms.

PACKET FILTERS

A packet filtering firewall verifies each incoming IP packet as it travels through the firewall, verifying its source or destination addresses, or service type. The firewall also performs additional security checks such as ensuring that the request is coming in on a proper TCP port for the appropriate service. Some hackers have developed techniques that fool the packet filter algorithms and let them in. They are called IP spoofing. However, most packet filtering firewall vendors have beefed up their products to prevent such attacks. Despite this fact, packet filtering is rarely used by enterprises as the sole technique to protect their network from malicious attacks.

APPLICATION GATEWAYS

An application gateway is special-purpose software that confines incoming traffic to selective, specific applications, such as an e-mail system, for instance. Outgoing traffic can also be restrained if it originates from an unapproved application.

Application gateways are usually run as proxies that are implemented on the firewall, intercept IP packets, and forward them to the appropriate application. Hence, the outside users never establish a direct connection with the enterprise's internal network. Outsiders interact only with the proxy software that resides on the firewall. The proxy software will then pass the intercepted information to the approved applications it supports.

As the proxy software intercepts the incoming traffic, it can perform different inspection tasks, such as verifying the incoming traffic data, ensuring that it is a valid HTTP packet, and ensuring that the source is coming from a trusted domain. Once the verification process has been successful, the data is then forwarded to the proper application, which resides inside the walls of the corporate network.

A certain amount of work is required from the developers to ensure that the application gateway adequately supports the few applications that are allowed to receive incoming traffic from outside. When new user services or applications must be supported, the application gateway must be customized by adding new filters to accommodate these new services or applications. Depending on the level of overhead an application gateway can generate and depending on the volume of traffic that must be handled by the application gateway, performance can decrease if the traffic is very high and if the application gateway is not configured in an optimal manner.

CIRCUIT-LEVEL GATEWAYS

Circuit-level gateways operate at the session layer level instead of the application layer level like the application gateways do. A circuit-level gateway can connect an external TCP/IP port to an internal destination that is usually located inside the walls of the enterprise network, such as a network printer, for example. The circuit-level gateway uses a special access control algorithm to ensure that the user who is plugged into the external TCP/IP port is arriving from a source that is allowed to reach the printer device. If the user is authorized, then the message is transmitted without any additional verification routines, since the circuit-level gateway can't distinguish one application from another.

PROXY SERVERS

Proxy servers can be used as a form of firewalls. A proxy server, installed outside the corporate networks, provides replicated copies of Web pages for easy access by specific categories of users. The proxy server can be set up to contain public-related type of data that can be accessed by external entities without incurring the risks of having hackers infiltrate the corporate networks. The sensitive information is kept inside the walls of the corporate networks.

STATEFUL INSPECTION

Stateful inspection firewalls do not depend on packet filters or proxies. Instead, they scrutinize the protocol layers and match current sessions to previous ones to identify activities that turn out to be suspect. Stateful inspection firewalls use business rules that you create dynamically, with the assistance of the users, to support any required application. One of the most common complaints against stateful inspection is that if the table that contains the business rules or state information gets corrupted, then the corporate network suddenly becomes unprotected from the outside world.

CONCLUSION

Several firewall tools provide a combination of different filtering techniques, such as packet filtering and application gateways, for instance. Such combinations of multiple filtering techniques increase the level of protection the firewall tool can provide to the enterprise.

A firewall is useful only if it proves to be truly effective in intercepting and preventing unsolicited access attempts. Consequently, its configuration must be very carefully planned and then properly set up to prevent unsolicited access attempts and to make sure no holes are in the firewall security shield.

A good firewall tool must provide some fine granularity, which allows your organization to establish and implement the right mixture of people, controls, systems, and times required to secure your network, based on your organization's security needs. Installing and properly configuring a firewall requires a substantial investment of time and resources. Thereafter, someone must also continue to support and enhance the set of business security rules that identifies the combination of people, logical, or physical addresses and applications that are accepted or discarded through the firewall.

Some tools are available on the market to help assess your level of vulnerability to outsiders. These tools are often referred to as firewall scanners. Firewalls scanners are tools that allow you to check your corporate network to detect potential security holes either at the application level or at the operating system level. Some scanner tools are freely available, such as the famous Security Administrator Tool for Analyzing Networks (SATAN) tool, which runs on certain UNIX platforms. However, you might prefer to use a commercial version of such scanner tools. If you want more information on a specific vendor who provides a commercial firewall scanner tool, try the following Web site address:

http://www.iss.net   (Internet SafeSuite from Internet Security Systems)

Internet SafeSuite consists of a family of products aimed at testing the vulnerabilities of routers, Windows NT and UNIX servers, firewalls, and also Web sites in general.

Firewall tools can be expensive. Like any other security tools, though, the value of a firewall must be judged on the likelihood of an intrusion and the resulting damage that could occur from this unapproved access to the corporation's network.

Table 9-51 shows some of the most common features to look for when searching for a firewall that meets your specific organization's needs. You can use the table to compare different firewall products with each other or be used as a point of reference when interacting with different vendors of firewall solutions.

Table 9–51 Firewall Tools Selection Criteria

	Tool 1	...	Tool N
MISCELLANEOUS FEATURES			

- Operating system(s) supported
  - UNIX (SunOS, Solaris, HP-UX, IBM-AIX)
  - Windows (3.X and up, NT)
- National Computer Security Association (NCSA) Certified
- Network topologies supported
  - Ethernet, Fast Ethernet, Token Ring, T1, T3, ATM, FDDI
- Filtering scheme(s) supported
  - Packet filter, application gateway, circuit-level, stateful inspection
- Protocols supported
  - IP, IPX, SNA, DECNet, AppleTalk, NetBEUI
- Security mechanisms supported
  - Encryption or authentication
- Virtual Private Networks (VPNs) supported
  - Type of encryption standard(s) supported
  - Type of digital certificate standard(s) supported
- Type(s) of alert mechanism supported
  - Telephone, pager, e-mail, broadcast, SNMP, customizable alerts

Table 9–51 Firewall Tools Selection Criteria (cont.)

- Access controls supported
  - Application, address, users, time of day, user groups, address groups, application groups, user passwords, one-time passwords, IP packet signatures, reusable passwords
- Reporting features
  - Traffic statistical data, activity logs, intruder access logs
- Types of IP services supported
  - HTTP, FTP, SMTP, SSL, Telnet, CompuServe, AOL, Gopher
- Configuration management facilities
  - User-friendly graphical user interface (GUI)
  - Real-time monitoring capabilities
  - Remote monitoring capabilities
- Performance/scalability/ease of use
- Intrusion source tracing
- Vendor/tool support
  - Context-sensitive/general-purpose online help facilities
  - Wizard tools to help perform most common functions
  - Online tutorials
  - Vendor support (i.e., hotline, training, etc.)
  - Printed/online documentation

If you want more information on specific firewall vendor products, access the following Web sites:

http://www.cyberguardcorp.com	(CyberGuard Firewall)
http://www.altavista.digital.com	(AltaVista Firewall)
http://www.checkpoint.com	(Check Point Firewall-1)
http://www.milkyway.com	(Black Hole Firewall)

If you want more general information on firewalls, access the National Computer Security Association (NCSA) Web site, which contains a special segment on firewall security, at the following address:

http://www.ncsa.com

The National Computer Security Association is an international, independent association whose major objective is to promote the exchange of security information among users, vendors, and security specialists around the world. Firewall tools can be officially certified by the NCSA organization after passing a series of standardized tests.

9.6.19 JAVA APPLETS AND JDBC

As discussed in Chapter 11, Java applets are special programs that are written with the Java programming language. A Java applet resides on a Web server. When a user indirectly invokes it by requesting a Web page, the Java applet is then downloaded from the Web server onto the client desktop machine and executed within the client Web browser.

Figure 9-23 illustrates how a Java applet, which is embedded within an HTML document, can be downloaded from a Web server and executed on the client machine.

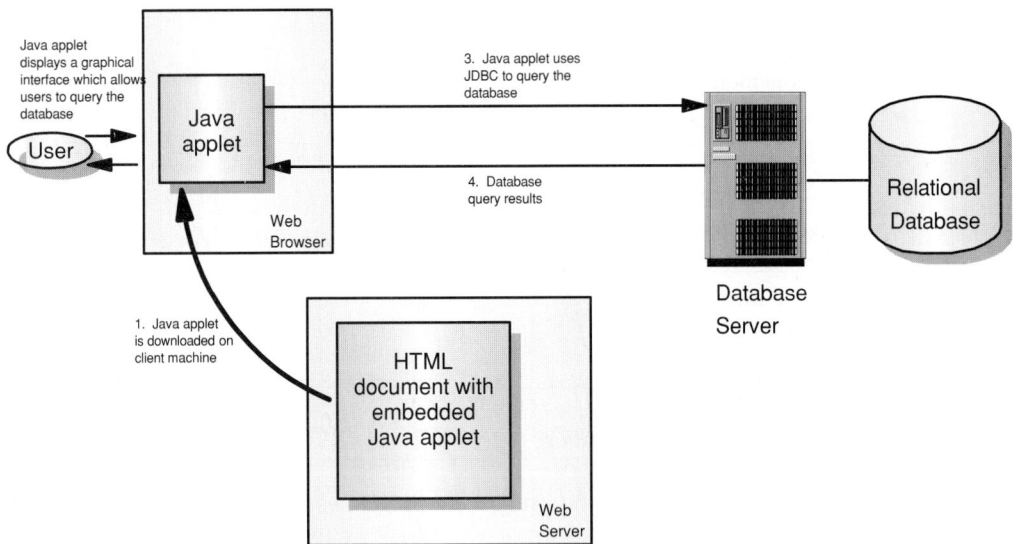

Figure 9–23 Downloading a Java applet from a Web server.

As shown in Figure 9-23, the Java applet can also use the Java Database Connectivity (JDBC) middleware standard to access a relational database located in the back end. Java applets can use JDBC to directly access a relational database and execute any type of query or modification against the data contained in the database. The vast majority of major DBMS vendors support the JDBC application programming interface (API).

Java applets can be designed with several types of graphical user interface controls, such as pull-down menus, data boxes, and other similar controls. These visual controls are supported by the Applet Window Technology (AWT) library, which consists of a series of classes that contain a collection of various user interface controls. AWT is used on all computing platforms that are Java-enabled, such as Windows and UNIX, for example. With these controls, a basic application could be constructed to provide users with a relatively simple graphical interface that would enable them to formulate dynamic database queries.

9.6.20 BRIDGING LEGACY SYSTEMS TO THE WEB

This section discusses a variety of strategies that can be used to establish connectivity between mainframe legacy systems and the Web. Different categories of middleware tools are also presented, along with a brief description of some of their major characteristics.

INTRODUCTION

Several organizations are linking their legacy applications, which might run on different computing platforms, to the Web. Some of the advantages of providing Web access to legacy applications and databases appear in Table 9-52.

Table 9–52 Web Access To Legacy Applications Advantages

- Providing a Web interface in front of a legacy application might be less expensive than rewriting it from scratch
- The Web interface is simple and user-friendly
- Exploiting new business opportunities via the combination of Web technology with mission-critical legacy applications
- Web technology allows organizations to add front-end functionality to existing applications without having to extensively modify the legacy code hidden in the back end

A large variety of Web middleware solutions attempt to connect Web technology to relational databases or legacy systems.

We can loosely define Web middleware as software bridges that help to close the gap between Web browsers and legacy systems or relational databases. In other words, Web middleware tools work behind the scenes to allow users to transparently access the information provided by legacy applications and databases via a Web browser user interface.

The market is literally flooded with a large variety of middleware tools. However, most of the major middleware tools can be loosely categorized into at least five generic classifications, as indicated in Table 9-53.

Also available is a plethora of different vendors' offerings for middleware tools that might fall in one of the five middleware categories described in Table 9-53. Discussing all these tools and middleware types in detail is well beyond the scope of this book. However, the next five sections provide a brief discussion on each middleware category and a list of some of the vendors' Web sites that offer middleware products for each category.

Table 9–53 Different Categories Of Middleware

Database Middleware	Database middleware, which is often referred to as SQL gateways, is products that are used to provide connectivity between various types of databases. Some database middleware products can connect different SQL databases from different vendors or connect SQL databases to mainframe SQL and non-SQL databases or flat files.
Message-Oriented Middleware	Message-oriented middleware (MOM) focuses on asynchronous message passing and message queuing to establish connectivity.
Object-Request Broker (ORB) Middleware	Object-request broker middleware uses an object-request broker software that allows inter-operability between objects, in a heterogeneous and distributed environment.
Remote Procedure Call (RPC) Middleware	The Remote Procedure Call middleware sends a call from one machine or process to another machine or process, for a service. The machines can be remote and run on different platforms, thus allowing applications to be distributed across a multi-tier client-server architecture.
Transaction Processing (TP) Monitor Middleware	Transaction processing monitor middleware is software used to coordinate and manage transactions processing. TP monitor middleware maintains queues that enforce message delivery.

DATABASE MIDDLEWARE TOOLS

Most major relational database management systems suppliers have developed their own database middleware products, which connect their databases to the Web. If you want more information on the different database vendors offerings for database-to-Web connectivity middleware, start your research by accessing the following Web sites and search more specifically for database gateway information:

> http://www.informix.com   (Informix Software)
> http://www.oracle.com   (Oracle Corporation)
> http://www.sybase.com   (Sybase Corporation)

The following Web site address can lead to more information on a third-party database middleware vendor that is not a specific database vendor:

> http://www.intersolv.com(Intersolv's DataDirect Sequelink)

MESSAGE-ORIENTED MIDDLEWARE TOOLS (MOM)

Several large software vendors have implemented middleware tools that focus on the message-oriented protocol. For instance, IBM is offering its MQSeries messaging middleware as a MOM solution for IBM mainframe-oriented applications and the Web. For the technically oriented readers, here is a brief explanation on how MQSeries can handle a transaction that originates from the Web:

- A Web-based application puts a message on a remote queue on the Web server. This step can be done using a Common Gateway Interface (CGI) script program.
- The queue is, at that point, attached to a local queue that resides on a host computer.
- The host application can be automatically invoked to process the message and either execute a transaction or provide some data back to the request originator that will be displayed as an HTML document.

Another vendor, Talarian, is offering another middleware tool that supports MOM, called SmartSockets.

You can get more information on these MOM tools at the following Web site addresses:

http://www.software.ibm.com	(IBM's MQSeries)
http://www.talarian.com	(Talarian's SmartSockets)

Several other vendors' offerings of MOM-based middleware tools can be found at the Message-Oriented Middleware association's Web site:

http://www.moma-inc.org

Those developers seeking to acquire a MOM-based middleware solution should verify whether it is a proprietary solution or not. Several MOM technologies originated as proprietary architectures.

OBJECT-REQUEST BROKER MIDDLEWARE TOOLS

ORB's software solutions are standardized around OMG's CORBA model. The Internet Inter-ORB Protocol (IIOP) is a CORBA-compliant protocol, which supports communications between objects and applications. IIOP applies primarily to Internet and intranet environments. Several major league software vendors are backing this protocol and many offer ORB middleware tools.

For instance, Netscape Communications has embraced the CORBA/ORB/IIOP model and implemented it in Netscape ONE Architecture. In fact, Netscape is integrating IIOP into all of its user and development tools. The Netscape Navigator 4 and beyond Web browser is an IIOP-compliant application. This means that Netscape Navigator 4 can inter-operate directly with applications that conform with the CORBA specification.

You can get more information on ORB middleware tools at the following vendors' Web site addresses:

http://www.visigenic.com   (Visigenic Software)
http://www.gemstone.com   (Gemstone's GemOrb)
http://www.iona.com   (Iona's OrbixWeb)

REMOTE PROCEDURE CALL (RPC) MIDDLEWARE TOOLS
The OSF Distributed Computing Environment (DCE) implementation of remote procedure calls is a standard that provides interoperability between DCE-compliant client and server software from different DCE vendors, across different platforms. For example, a DCE client that runs on an HP machine can communicate with a DCE server that runs on an IBM MVS machine using remote procedure calls.

OSF DCE/RPC tools are available from several vendors such as HP, IBM, and Sun. For more information on OSF DCE/RPC middleware tools, you can access the Web sites of these three major software vendors. An example of a Web middleware tool that is based on OSF's DCE protocol is WebCrusader from Gradient Technologies. You can find more information on WebCrusader at the following Web site address:

http://www.gradient.com   (Gradient Technologies WebCrusader)

TRANSACTION PROCESSING (TP) MONITOR MIDDLEWARE TOOLS
In the banking industry, every transaction must be successfully completed entirely. A classic example is a bank account credit-debit transaction. The transaction is successfully completed only if both the credit and debit operations have been successfully terminated. For this type of environment, a transaction processing (TP) monitor ensures the delivery of each transaction. TP monitors operate in a synchronous mode. This means that the computer will wait for each transaction to be fully completed before starting another one.

An example of TP monitor middleware suitable for complex networked applications is BEA's Tuxedo. BEA also provides Jolt, which provides a Web connection into Tuxedo TP Monitor and message-oriented middleware infrastructure. More information on the Tuxedo product, as well as other TP monitor middleware tools, is available at the following Web site addresses:

http://www.beasys.com   (BEA's Tuxedo)
http://www.hursley.ibm.com/cics   (IBM's Transaction Server)
http://www.kivasoft.com   (Kiva's Enterprise Server)

WEB-TO-LEGACY APPLICATION SCREEN SCRAPERS
Another approach to link a legacy application to the Web is the use of special application servers that allow developers to extract data out of the mainframe host applications and present them in an application developed precisely for a Web browser or a Java applet.

The application server middleware provides a screen scrape approach to develop host connectivity applications, with a persistent host connection.

Usually, this type of screen scrape approach works in the following manner: a special application is set up on a server to extract data from a host application using interfaces such as EHLLAPI, HLLAPI, or other similar interfaces. The application is then geared to examine 3270-like terminal screens and find the data that is embedded in them and also to navigate between different host applications to reach those terminal screens. Afterward, the application then displays the extracted data through a generated HTML document or a Java applet. All the logic performed by the application is located on the server. Only the legacy data is downloaded to the client workstation and presented in an HTML format.

Several vendors provide tools for Web-to-legacy screen scraper middleware. You will find below some Web site addresses of vendors supporting this type of middleware tool.

http://www.oc.com	(Open Connect Systems' OC://WebConnect Pro)
http://www.attachmate.com	(Attachmate's Extra! Host Publishing System)
http://www.centurasoft.com	(Centura Software's Foresite)
http://www.simware.com	(Simware's Salvo)

Most of the above-mentioned tools can support their special application server on Windows NT or different UNIX platforms. On the client side, they require either a Java-enabled Web browser or any Web browser.

CONCLUSION

The organization must understand clearly the needs that lead them to connect their legacy applications to the Web. Based on these global requirements, then you need to determine the type(s) of middleware tools you should use for the integration of legacy applications with the Internet/intranet.

Four of the most important selection criteria for middleware tools are network transparency, connectivity transparency, scalability capabilities, and overall performance based on resources used. Although point solutions might help resolve more immediate connectivity needs, you might be wise to look for proven middleware tools that are flexible enough to run with as many applications, operating systems, and platforms as possible. This advice applies especially for those developers who operate in a heterogenous platform environment.

9.6.21 INTERNET-BASED FAXING TOOLS AND TECHNOLOGY

The utilization of fax machines is still one of the most common approaches used by large, medium, and small organizations to transmit a variety of business documents worldwide. With the advent of the Web, several products and services can be used to link Internet technology to fax technology. Figure 9-24 shows the major hardware and software technology components that can be involved in supporting Internet-based faxing technologies.

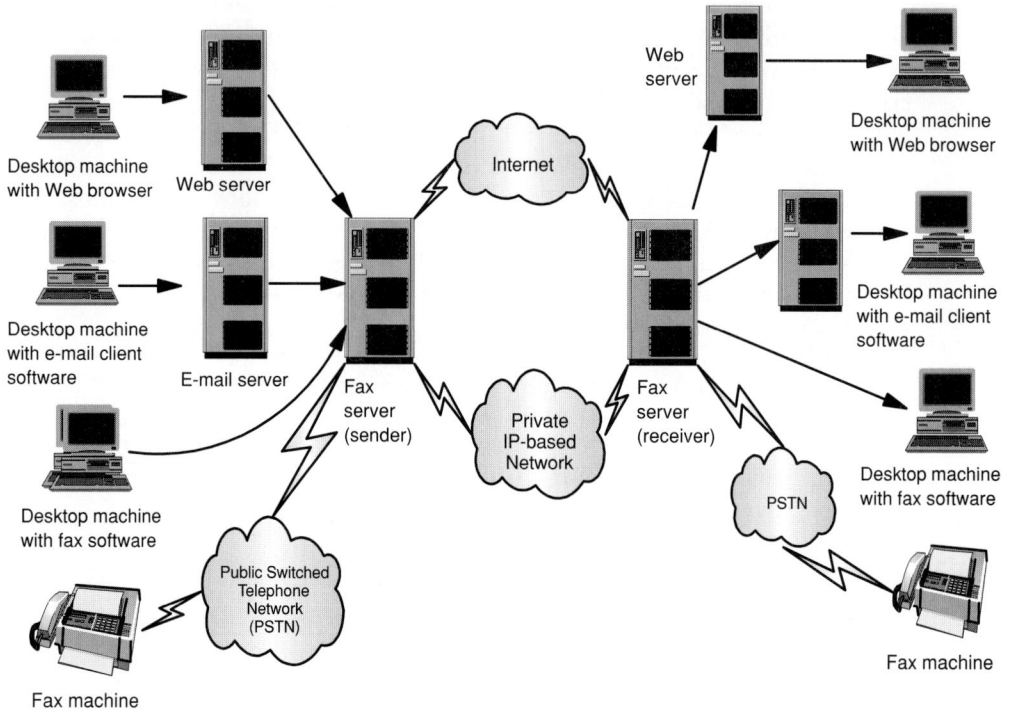

Figure 9–24 Internet-based faxing technology.

A fax can enter the system in various ways. It can be created from a desktop computer that has a Web browser interface, a client-server e-mail interface, or a fax software interface. The fax can also enter the system via a traditional fax machine device or a desktop machine that has a Web-browser-based fax application interface.

The transmission of a sending fax, from a fax machine to the fax server, is done through the Public Switched Telephone Network (PSTN). In the case of a fax-enabled client desktop machine, the sending fax document is typically transmitted by a client-based printer driver that was specifically designed for network clients and that transmits the document directly to the fax server instead of a regular printer. In the case of an e-mail-enabled client desktop, the fax document is sent to an e-mail server that, in turn, sends the fax message to the fax server. Various files such as graphics are usually attached to the e-mail message using the Multi-Purpose Internet Mail Extensions (MIME) protocol. Quite frequently, the Simple Mail Transfer Protocol (SMTP) is also used to manage the transmission between the e-mail server and the fax server. Finally, the fax document can be created by using a client desktop machine that has a Web-browser-based fax application interface. The fax document is transmitted from the Web browser client interface to a Web server. Then the Web server sends the fax document to the fax server.

Once the fax document has been captured into the system, the sending fax server machine then sends the fax document via an IP-based network to a receiving fax server that is located at the other end. The transmission of the fax can be done via either the Internet or a private IP-based network. In the last step, the fax is finally dropped by the receiving fax server into a special mailbox for a specific network client software to pick it up. If the destination device on the far end is another fax machine, then a local call is made to the destination fax machine.

At this stage, let me point out that since no industry standards yet exist to regulate this type of technology, several different protocols and operating systems are still used by Internet-faxing tools vendors. Because of this fact, the same vendor brand of fax server is likely to be mandatory on both ends of the IP-based communication lines, at least at this point in time.

Internet-based fax server vendors have come up with at least three different approaches to ensure that the fax document has been successfully and relatively quickly transmitted to its recipient(s) via an IP-based network. They are the store-and-forward, real-time, and near real-time methods.

The store-and-forward method is used primarily to send faxes, such as broadcast-based messages to thousands of recipients, for example. In such a case, real-time delivery considerations are not important with this type of fax and the sender can receive the acknowledgment of the successful transmission in a few minutes or even a few hours. The near real-time technique attempts to emulate to some extent the transmission of a fax with the traditional faxing method by displaying the progress of the fax transmission while it is in transit and up to the point when it is successfully received at the other end. Finally, the real-time method is achieved by different proprietary vendor techniques that optimize the transmission of the fax document by ensuring minimal traffic on the network, hence providing a faster response time.

SECURITY

Most Internet-based fax software products provide different mechanisms to protect the authenticity and confidentiality of the fax messages. Two of the most common security techniques that can be enforced with these tools include user authentication and message encryption.

BENEFITS

By using the Internet or a private IP-based network to transmit the fax, organizations can avoid long-distance telephone charges that are incurred with the traditional methods of sending and receiving faxes. This potential cost avoidance is achieved essentially by bypassing the public phone network services and their associated international voice rates.

Considering the fact that in the U.S. only, an estimated 35 billion dollars are spent annually on transmitting faxes, several organizations are looking at different ways of lowering their costs of doing business with faxes. The use of Internet-based faxing technologies might turn out to be one way of drastically reducing the costs associated with the transmission of faxes, for several large organizations. These savings can apply not only to international delivery faxes but also to domestic delivery faxes.

WEB SITE ADDRESSES

The following Web site addresses can help you find more detailed information on various Internet-based fax vendors and associated products.

http://www.radlinx.rad.co.il	(Radlinx Corporation)
http://www.softlinx.com	(SoftLinx Corporation)
http://www.openport.com	(Open Port Technology)
http://www.faxback.com	(FaxBack Corporation)
http://www.castelle.com	(Castelle Corporation)

9.7   WEB SITE ADMINISTRATION TOOLS

Large and mission-critical Web sites require the use of automated tools to optimize Web site performance and effectively manage their organization and content. At least four broad categories of Web site management tools can be defined, as indicated in Table 9-54.

Table 9–54 Four Major Categories Of Web Site Management Tools

- Tools that help to manage the change and configuration management process
- Tools that help to verify and maintain Web site integrity and accuracy
- Tools that gather and analyze the traffic and usage at your Web site
- Tools that help examine and manage Web site content

Section 9.7.1 briefly discusses each of these tools, at a high level.

9.7.1   WEB SITE CHANGE AND CONFIGURATION MANAGEMENT TOOLS

The system development life cycle of large and complex Web database applications is no different from the software development process that is associated with more traditional client-server applications. Usually, you assemble a large, cross-functional development team composed of distinct user and Information Systems groups to rapidly analyze, develop, test, and implement in a live production environment the Web database application.

Considering the large variety of users and system development groups that might be involved during the unit, system, and user acceptance testing of the Web database applications, distinct test environments might be required to support the complete testing process, as shown in Figure 9-25.

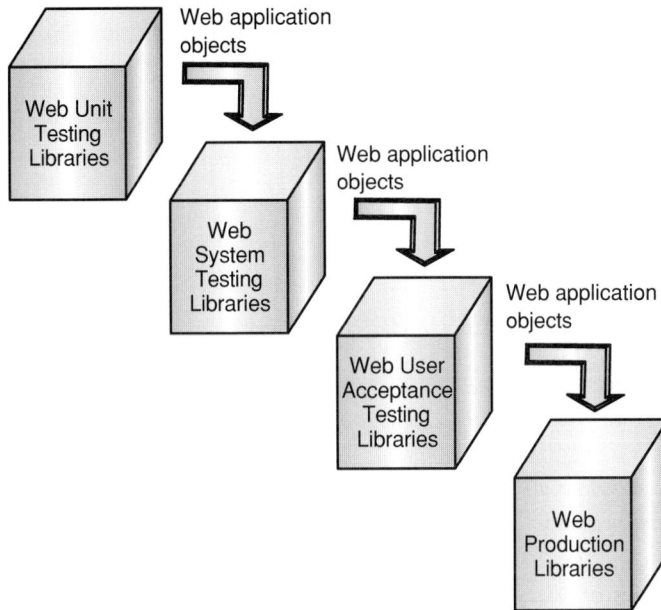

Figure 9–25 Distinct web-based test environments.

Such an approach allows each developer, quality assurance, and user group to verify different versions of the Web database application without impeding the work of others. Similarly, access to the various versions of the test libraries should also be controlled and secured in an adequate manner.

The Web development cycle is fast-paced. It frequently makes optimal use of Joint Facilitated Sessions to speed up the analysis and design processes. Rapid Application Development (RAD) tools are used to prototype and incrementally construct different functional segments of the Web database application. Once the Web application has been implemented, then multiple requests for functional changes and enhancements to the Web database application will likely require a thorough yet flexible change management and software configuration process.

In such complex Internet and intranet development environments, the use of an automated change and software configuration management (SCM) tool might quickly become essential to handle large Web development projects and possibly subprojects.

The automated SCM tool must be able to adequately manage the different releases and versions of software objects and libraries that are involved in the development of mission-critical Web database applications. The tool should be capable of protecting against possible simultaneous updates of the same software object by several developers who work on the same application in parallel. All changes to an application object should be tracked with the following basic information: who made the change, when the object was changed, and why.

Table 9-55 lists some of the most common software objects that might need to be properly managed during the development of a large Web application, as well as during its entire production life cycle.

Table 9–55 Common Web Application Software Objects

- Hypertext Markup Language files (.HTML)
- Image Files (.GIF, .JPEG, etc.)
- Java Source Code (.JAVA)
- Java Object Code (.CLASS)
- Perl Scripts (.PERL)
- C, C++ source and object code
- JavaScripts, JScripts, VBScripts
- Common Gateway Interface Scripts (.CGI)
- Legacy code
- Web helper applications and plug-ins
- Sound and video segments
- VRML segments

In addition to managing the various software objects that are used to create a Web database application, the software configuration management tool should also be able to manage the dependencies that might exist among the different Web application objects within a version. This feature will be very useful for the developers to detect missing or out-of-sync Web application objects.

The SCM tool should also provide the ability to archive different versions of the Web database applications for all test or production environments, so past versions can be rolled back if necessary.

Finally, the SCM tool should work with your Web server's security features to assign and control privileges for modifying and publishing Web pages. Only qualified developers or users should have access rights to the Web application development libraries.

An automated change request tool can also be useful to centralize the collection, prioritization, communication, and tracking of Web change requests. Such a tool can also be useful for reporting on the status of Web change requests, using a universal Web interface.

If you want more detailed information on Web software configuration and change management products, you can find more detailed information on the Web in general and particularly at the following Web sites:

http://www.mks.com
http://www.intersolv.com
http://www.starbasecorp.com
http://www.continuus.com

As a side issue to configuration management tools for Web database application, Table 9-56 lists some issues that relate to managing the static Web pages of a large Web site.

Table 9–56 Some Site Management Issues For Static Web Pages

Similar site management issues to those related to Web database applications also apply to the maintenance of a corporate Web site that contains hundreds of various static Web pages. In a corporate intranet environment, the level of control mechanisms and flexibility required to manage the testing and transfer in a production environment of static Web pages might vary considerably for different organizations, depending on a variety of factors such as:

- The level of criticality and accuracy of the static data published on the corporate intranet
- The timeliness of the data and turnaround time required to make changes to the content of the Web pages
- The level of centralization or decentralization achieved within the organization for the creation, publishing, and maintenance of the static Web pages

In an Internet environment, the testing and change management processes of static Web pages must also be carefully implemented and controlled, since the corporate Web site is a showcase for a company's products and services. It is also a direct reflection of the company's corporate image. You certainly do not want to introduce errors into your Internet Web site that might tarnish your company's corporate image and possibly deprive it from significant corporate earnings.

9.7.2 TOOLS THAT HELP TO VERIFY AND MAINTAIN WEB SITE INTEGRITY AND ACCURACY

This section discusses a variety of tools and facilities that can be used to help manage and maintain web sites.

HYPERLINK CHECKERS

Hyperlink checkers are a category of tools that are primarily used to manage the information stored on the Web server and verify how this information is linked together. These tools follow the various links that exist on a large Web site and produce various types of reports that can pinpoint any discrepancies that relate to broken hyperlinks or missing files.

These tools can usually check for dead links across the entire Web site or produce a visual map of your Web site. However, if the Web site is of any significant size, you might prefer to configure the tools to perform the link verification activities on a periodical basis while targeting specific subsections of the Web site at a time. Many of these tools allow fixing broken links on the fly as they are detected across the Web site.

9.7.3 TOOLS THAT GATHER AND ANALYZE THE TRAFFIC AND USAGE PATTERNS AT YOUR WEB SITE

Web site traffic analyzer tools track and analyze user behavior at the site. Most of these tools use a log file analyzer application that reads the log files that are created by the Web servers and report various types of statistical information on user behavior and Web server performance, such as those you see in Table 9-57.

Table 9–57 Web Site Traffic Analysis And Performance Selection Criteria

User Behavior Analysis	• Most frequent Web site paths taken by users • Number of canceled pages requests • Most frequent navigation links utilized inside or outside intranet • Identification of Web browser software utilized • Top 10 pages most and least frequently accessed • Average viewing time spent per Web site section, page • Type of modem and communication line speeds used
User Demographic Analysis	• Who accesses the Web site, from which national or international geographical locations, and how often • Top 10 pages most and least frequently accessed
Performance and Traffic Analysis	• Overall Web server reliability • Web server response time • Volume of users or visitors per unit of time • CGI events • Number and types of server errors encountered (i.e., "not found resources," internal or external dead links, etc.) • Web and FTP servers bandwidth utilization • Average time required to download Web pages and files
Web site Organization and Structure	• Actual navigation routes taken by users • Top entry and exit pages • Excessively long download time caused by oversized Web pages (too much data, too many graphics, or too many multimedia objects) • Most frequently accessed pages by directory levels • Database templates used • Pages visited and buttons clicked

The user behavior information can be useful in an intranet environment to determine which departments or types of users are utilizing the Web site the most and at which time during the day. The information can be reported in various segments such as individuals, usr groups, departments, and divisions.

In an Internet environment, the user behavior information can usually be broken down by geographic or demographic locations, such as countries and major cities, for instance.

The gathered performance-related data can be used to analyze network traffic caused by Web site usage and subsequently fine-tune the entire network or specific segments of the network, based on the Web usage findings. If the Web site is accessed by users who are located in different time zones, Web usage statistics can also help determine the best time to perform various housekeeping tasks such as Web server backups and Web page updates.

The accumulation of historical data is also essential to analyzing and plotting user behavior and Web server performance and reliability trends over extended periods of time. Several Web statistical tools gather and store critical statistical information in commercial relational databases for this specific purpose. From there, you can analyze and manipulate the collected information in different ways.

Statistical Web site tools that limit their analysis activities to only the data that were accumulated in the Web server log files might not be able to capture additional information on valuable user behavior and Web server performance data, such as:

- User Web pages that the server ignores because it is overloaded

- Users who decide to disconnect themselves from the Web server because the time needed to download information is too much or the server response time is too slow

- Network-related problems such as server re-transmissions of data that are caused by a server overloaded situation

For these reasons, you might want to select Web site analysis tools that can capture more accurate statistical data on complete transactions, such as from the moment a user requests a Web page to the moment the Web page is entirely downloaded by the Web browser. Hence, the statistical measurements apply to the number of Web pages actually received by the users instead of the number of pages that the Web server reported as transmitted. The measurements can cover various types of information such as the HTML code, the graphics, the Java applets, and other type of specialized data. These tools gather statistical data by directly analyzing the communication flow of data between Web sites and users on the network, in addition to the statistical data stored in the log files.

9.7.4 TOOLS THAT HELP EXAMINE AND MANAGE WEB SITE CONTENT

The Web site should be designed and organized for ease of maintenance right from the beginning. You can devise simple, down-to-earth strategies to save a lot of headaches when having to maintain a large Web site, such as those listed in Table 9-58.

Table 9–58 Web Site "Ease Of Maintenance" Best Practices

- Establish a naming convention for all types of Web files and objects
  - Images and graphics
  - HTML pages
  - Scripts
  - Java applets or programs
  - Multimedia objects such as sounds, videos, 3-D animations
- Use generic names for high-level Web pages such as the home pages
- Use specific, easy-to-read names for secondary Web pages
- Keep the number of Web page hierarchies at a manageable level, such as no more than three to four levels deep
- Create a Web test staging environment
- Organize intranet Web pages by internal group organizations and main subjects

Web site content analyzer tools primarily map the various files and hyperlinks that exist on the Web site. They provide a global picture on how the different links are associated to each other and how the Web site is structured.

Visual overviews of a large Web site are especially useful when the corporate intranet is organized into smaller, more manageable sub-sites. You can also produce different types of reports with these tools, covering various subjects such as what types of files and links are used in the Web site and several lists of different Web site elements displayed by size, for instance.

Following are some Web site addresses with vendor information on different types of Web log analysis tools:

http://www.accrue.com
http://www.netgen.com
http://www.interse.com

9.7.5 INTRANET DOCUMENT MANAGEMENT TOOLS

Large-scale organizations that have massive documentation requirements likely use different methods for document management. These methods can widely vary from traditional approaches, such as filing hardcopy documents, to using the most sophisticated shared network filing systems.

In most instances, the document management systems used are point solutions that are implemented by specific organizations such as engineering departments and are usually tied to some particular hardware platforms.

Enterprise-wide Web-centric document management tools can be used by large organizations to help solve these issues. They can also be used to efficiently manage the ever-growing corporate intranet sites, which can contain thousands of documents that need to be controlled and kept up-to-date. Table 9-59 highlights some of the most common types of functions that are provided by high-end Web-based document management tools.

Table 9–59 Common Web-centric Document Management Functions

Document Retrieval Capabilities	• Platform-independent access to corporate documents across the enterprise, via a Web browser
	• Flexible information searching/retrieval capabilities, including full-text searches and structured indexed searches based on various customizable attributes such as date last revised, version, author
	• Standard or customizable presentation of search results lists
	• On-the-fly document conversions from existing file formats into HTML, PDF, or other output formats, for a large variety of documents that were created on single- or multiple-platform environments
Document Management Capabilities	• Check-in contributions, via a Web browser, of HTML documents and related objects (i.e., graphics, sounds, charts, videos, 2-D and 3-D animations)
	• Check-out modifications, via a Web browser, of HTML documents and related objects
	• Document version control
	• Document revision and change history tracking
	• Collaboration by allowing more than one author to work on the same document at a time
	• Document workflow and approval
	• Usage statistical data such as who reads what, from where, when, and how often
	• Compound document management
	• Automatic archiving of aged documents
Security Capabilities	• Flexible check-in/check-out procedures
	• Ability for authorized users to post and maintain their own Web documents on the intranet without requiring the intervention of a Webmaster to manually post the HTML files

Following are some Web site addresses with vendor information on different Web-based document management tools:

http://www.documentum.com
http://www.intranetsol.com
http://www.opentext.com
http://www.netright.com

9.8   PUSH TECHNOLOGY

This section discusses important concepts that relate to the push technology. It describes different categories of push technologies and identifies potential applications where push technologies can be used effectively. Finally, it briefly covers some of the major issues that surround this powerful technology.

9.8.1   INTRODUCTION

This section provides a brief description of the push technology in general and some of the most important concepts that are associated with it.

The push technologies allow the automated delivery of content, data, or software to client desktops, servers, or a variety of different storage systems.

9.8.2   PUSH TECHNOLOGY CATEGORIES

Two fundamental categories of push technologies include automated pull and event-driven push. Figure 9-26 illustrates the automated pull concept.

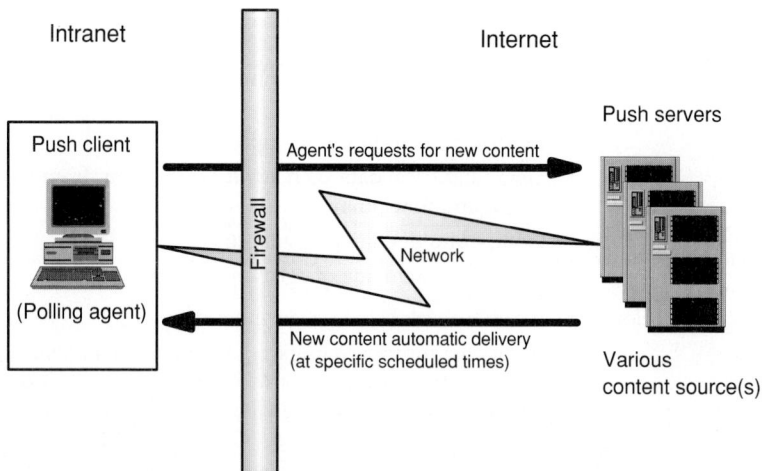

Figure 9–26 The automated pull concept.

With automated pull, the end user can request the automatic delivery of new content such as data or software updates from a variety of internal or external push servers.

The delivery of new content is performed at predetermined times or time intervals, based on the scheduling information that the pull agent has been instructed to use to periodically look for new content that is located in the identified push servers. If new content, such as software updates, for example, has been posted since the last delivery, then these software updates are transmitted to the client desktop.

The automated pull technology can be used to deliver software updates, such as during off-peak hours so as to not strain the network, as well as deliver other types of data.

Figure 9-27 illustrates the event-driven push concept.

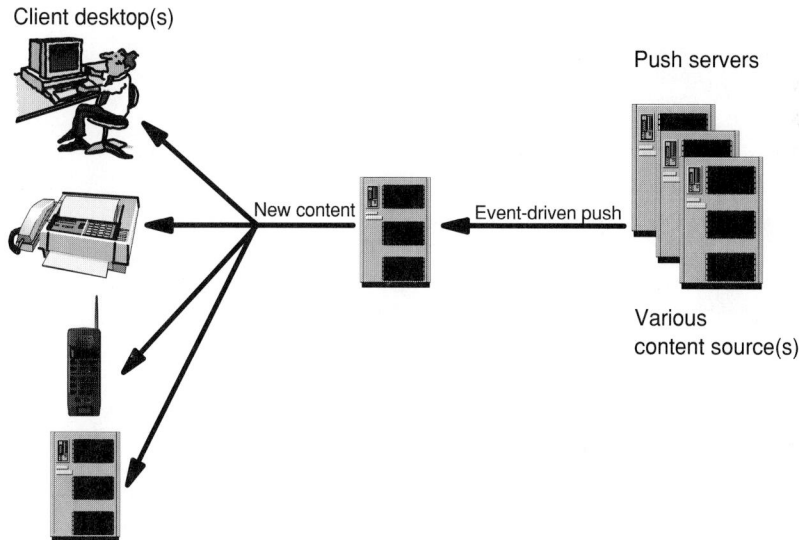

Figure 9–27 The event-driven push concept.

With event-driven push, new content is delivered to the users based on specific rules instead of a pre-defined delivery timetable. The receiver, which can be not only a client Web browser but also other devices such as a cellular phone, pager, storage device, or a fax machine, takes in new content based on the occurrence of specific events. Contrary to automated pull, the event-driven push technology usually introduces an additional middleware layer. This middleware layer is used to set up a relationship between the content and the event-driven business rules that will trigger the delivery of content to the receiver from the push server. For example, if event X occurs, then deliver some specific content from push server Y to receiver Z.

9.8.3 PUSH CONTENT DELIVERY MECHANISMS

Figure 9-28 shows three of the most common delivery mechanisms that are used to push content to an end user via a Web browser, a server, a storage device, and other similar facilities.

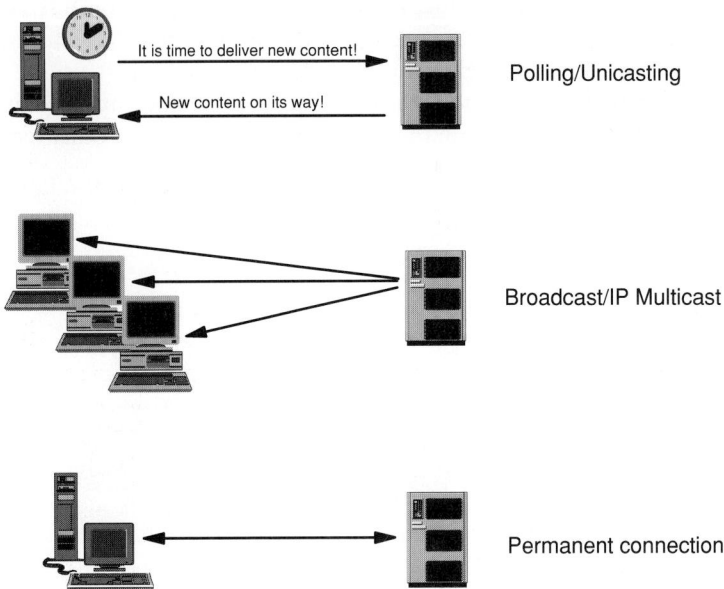

Figure 9–28 Different push mechanisms.

With polling or unicasting, content is delivered to the client workstation from the push servers at regular time intervals and automatically, such as every hour, for instance. The client polling software can also request the delivery of new content at specific times, such as at 3 p.m. every day. The delivery process is handled on a one-to-one basis. Several push technology vendors support polling/unicasting, including Netscape Netcaster, Marimba Castanet, and Microsoft Active Channels.

With broadcast and IP multicast, the delivery of content is handled on a one-to-many basis, in a real-time delivery mode. This delivery process is particularly useful to send identical content to several desktop or server receivers. However, the delivery of content with IP multicasting requires a very robust networking architecture to sustain some potentially heavy traffic.

With persistent connection, the communication is permanently hard wired between the receiving client workstation and the push server. This content delivery mode of operation is used primarily to deliver content on a continuous basis, such as trading quotes or mission-critical business transactions.

9.8.4 PUSH TECHNOLOGY APPLICATION USAGE

Push technology can be used for several types of information delivery applications, such as pushing daily news briefs to all users across the enterprise, delivering specific announcements to selective groups of users, and providing specific user groups with focused, time-critical information. Push technology can also be used to automatically deliver internal corporate reports to predetermined end users.

Most types of push applications all center around the concept of a channel that can be defined as a collection of subject-related information that is assembled together and sent to the users at regular intervals. A content channel usually contains information that focuses on a specific topic. In other words, relevant content information can be delivered with a push system to a specific category of users, depending on their particular requirements. Different delivery channels can be set up for different categories of internal user groups. A typical example of a channel is the Reuters financial news service.

Besides allowing the notification of users about various changes or new information, push technology can also be used for the distribution of software, both inside and outside corporate firewalls. For example, the Java-based push system from Marimba, called Castanet, can distribute self-installing Java-based software and related data, although Castanet can also deliver customized content channels.

9.8.5 PUSH TECHNOLOGY ISSUES

One potential drawback of the push technologies is that they can put a substantial workload on network bandwidth and cause major network traffic congestion, if they are not managed appropriately by the enterprise. For example, the newest releases of the most popular Web browsers support automated pull by default. If the enterprise does not have standards on internal content management practices or a centralized filtering mechanism such as a firewall to restrain and control the delivery of information via various push technologies, the users can easily overload the corporate network. Receiving a large amount of information that is automatically delivered to them, on a regular basis, can do the trick rather quickly. With push technology, the information is automatically pushed to the users, whether or not they look at the information that is pushed on their desktop. The content that can be delivered to the users can be not only plain text or graphics but also multimedia-rich and include audio and video data streams, which can cause an additional burden on the corporate network. Hence, the distribution of unnecessary information can quickly become an issue, if it is not properly managed at the outset.

Also, the push process needs to be managed not only from a technology standpoint but also in terms of a purely logistic standpoint. For instance, you need to identify the different types of information that should be pushed to the users, the frequency of the deliveries, where the data is coming from, and so forth.

Finally, several push technology tools are proprietary solutions, which do not necessarily support open standards. An enterprise might have difficulty supporting different proprietary push systems from several vendors until truly standard-based delivery protocols emerge in industry.

9.8.6 PUSH TECHNOLOGY TOOL VENDORS

If you want more information on different push technology tool vendors, access the following Web sites:

http://www.backweb.com	(BackWeb)
http://www.marimba.com	(Marimba's Castanet)
http://www.pointcast.com	(I-Server)
http://www.intermind.com	(Intermind Communicator)

9.9 WEB-BASED COLLABORATIVE SOFTWARE

Groupware software encompasses a wide variety of high-value business enterprise applications. You can see some of the most common types of integrated services that are usually supported by commercial groupware systems in Table 9-60.

Table 9–60 Generic Groupware Functions

Messaging	Messaging, or electronic mail, is the focal point of most groupware software systems. The e-mail function normally supports rich-text features, mail attachments, and different delivery options, and is integrated with a variety of directory services. Furthermore, gateways are frequently used to allow users to send mail to other e-mail systems.
Collaboration	Collaboration allows several users to share and collectively edit various types of documents, such as text, images, and graphics. Collaboration software also supports discussion groups.
Scheduling/ calendaring	The scheduling service provides users with functions that allow them to manage personal and group schedules and calendars, such as reserving a conference room and scheduling and confirming meeting attendance.
Personal information manager	The personal information manager service (PIM) allows users to manage a variety of personal tasks and manage their contacts folders.
Application development	The application development service provides a variety of tools to customize the groupware environment and develop custom groupware-related applications.
Administration	The administration service provides a variety of tools and facilities to monitor and manage the groupware environment configuration and mode of operation.
Workflow	The workflow service supports the automation of specific business processes in which documents or tasks are passed between different categories of people according to a pre-established delivery route, based on a set of pre-defined business rules and policies. Each participant has a specific role to play in the overall workflow process. Typical workflow processes might include insurance claims, personal loans and mortgages, and engineering change orders processing.

The leading groupware software vendors, such as Microsoft, Netscape, IBM/Lotus, and Novell, have started to migrate their proprietary systems to more open clients and Internet standards and protocols. The main advantage of the Web platform and its open standards is the support of an inter-operable, cross-platform environment. Nonetheless, at the time of this writing, all major groupware software vendors offer a combination of proprietary groupware functions and Internet standards, to some degree.

Table 9-61 provides a brief list of the major Internet standards that should be supported by Web-based groupware tools. A brief description of each Internet standard shown in the table is provided in Section 9.6.17, "Web-enabled e-mail tools."

Table 9–61 Web-based Groupware Tools Support Of Internet Standards

Generic Internet protocols/ standards supported	• Hypertext Transfer Protocol (HTTP) • Simple Mail Transfer Protocol (SMTP) • Post Office Protocol (POP) clients • Internet Message Access Protocol (IMAP) • Lightweight Directory Access Protocol (LDAP) • Network News Transfer Protocol (NNTP) • Multipurpose Internet Mail Extensions (MIME) • Secure Sockets Layer (SSL) • Java
Services supported via Web browsers	• Messaging • Collaboration • Scheduling/calendaring • Personal information manager • Application development • Administration • Workflow

The Web site addresses listed here provide some information on different Web-enabled groupware offerings supported by well established groupware software vendors.

http://www.novell.com	GroupWise
http://www.microsoft.com	Exchange Server
http://www.lotus.com	Lotus Domino
http://www.netscape.com	SuiteSpot/Communicator

Besides the seasoned groupware software vendors, a large variety of independent third-party software vendors offer different sets of groupware offerings that have been developed from the ground up with an architecture that fully embraces open Internet standards. The following Web site addresses provide more information on such Internet-based groupware tools.

http://www.altavista.software.digital.com	AltaVista Forum, AltaVista Mail
http://www.thuridion.com	CREW
http://www.webflow.com	SamePage
http://www.radnet.com	WebShare
http://www.ipswitch.com	Imail Server for Windows NT

9.10 WEB-BASED WORKFLOW TOOLS

Although some overlap might occur between workgroup and workflow tools, one of the major distinctions between them is the fact that workgroup software primarily focuses on information in general and its sharing among different individuals. Conversely, workflow applications specifically concentrate on the business process that determines cross-functional flows of information rather than on sharing information at large. Workflow automation focuses on the intelligent routing, delivery and tracking of information according to a set of pre-defined business rules and policies. Because specialized, full-fledged workflow tools are task-centric rather than people-centric, they provide much more specialized workflow-oriented functionality than the more generic workgroup tools.

Several specialized workflow tools support Internet open standards and can operate in a Web-based environment, using seamless Web browsers, which negate the need for installing additional workflow-related software components on client machines. Universal Web access also signifies that employees, customers, suppliers, and partners can participate in cross-functional workflow processes that cut across various geographic and organizational boundaries, through the use of the Internet, corporate intranets, or extranets.

Recognizing the tremendous potential of the Internet, several organizations are using Web technology to automate structured, repetitive, clerical business processes, as well as more sophisticated and ad hoc business processes, with Web-enabled workflow tools. This workflow automation process is achieved in a more cost-effective manner than with traditional client-server-based workflow solutions.

The following Web site addresses provide more information on some vendors that offer specialized, Web-enabled workgroup solutions.

http://www.actiontech.com	ActionWorks Metro
http://www.opentext.com	Open Text Livelink Intranet Suite
http://www.keyfile.com	Keyflow
http://www.ultimus1.com	Ultimus

9.11 WEB-BASED ELECTRONIC FORM TOOLS

Small to large organizations can utilize Web technology to streamline their business processes that make use of traditional paper-based forms. Following are some Web site addresses of third-party vendors that offer specialized tools to help implement Web-based electronic forms in your organization. Several of these tools can also be used to convert your existing libraries of electronic forms into Web-ready forms for your corporate intranet or even for Internet or extranet use.

http://www.caere.com	OmniForm Internet Publisher
http://www.expertelligence.com	ExperForms
http://www.adobe.com	Adobe Acrobat ESM
http://www.jetform.com	FormFlow
http://www.shana.com	Informed Designer

Besides standard form design features, most Web-based electronic form tools offer additional features such as automated data calculations, data validations, and Web connectivity to major database vendors.

Joint Facilitated Sessions

10.1 INTRODUCTION

The rapid development and delivery of quality information systems is certainly of paramount importance for any MIS organization in today's world of accelerated and constant business transformations. The Joint Facilitated Session process is a group dynamics technique that shortens the systems development process and delivers high-quality software.

The basic objective of a Joint Facilitated Session is to conduct interactive workshops with a broad group of end users at critical stages of the system development life cycle.

Each workshop, through the guidance of a facilitator, progresses through a series of structured steps to discuss and capture various bits of information that are required to develop the software system. The Joint Facilitated Session process I describe in this book builds heavily on the original Joint Application Design methodology that was developed by IBM in the early 1980s. Contrary to JAD, though, the Joint Facilitated Session process can be used for various activities other than software design during development projects.

The Joint Facilitated Session technique is an integral part of the methodology I propose in this book. It plays an important role in accelerating the system development life cycle of large systems.

For instance, a series of Joint Facilitated Sessions is conducted with the users during the analysis phase to gather their application requirements and jointly develop the system process and data models. The initial design of the system graphical user interface is also performed with users, via a series of facilitated group sessions. The Joint Facilitated Session process can also be used at the back end of the methodology, such as during the implementation phase. For example, it can be used to define the critical tasks required to transition a complex system into the production environment.

Although the Joint Facilitated Session process is centered around a structured framework, it remains a flexible method. It can be easily adapted to satisfy the specific development needs of an organization. In fact, joint facilitated sessions can be used at any point during the development process to unite developers and users together to actively participate in the development of a deliverable or to simply discuss issues and identify potential solutions.

This chapter describes detailed guidelines to plan and conduct effective Joint Facilitated Sessions.

10.2 THE JOINT FACILITATED SESSION (JFS) PROCESS LIFE CYCLE

Figure 10.1 illustrates the three major phases that comprise the Joint Facilitated Session process.

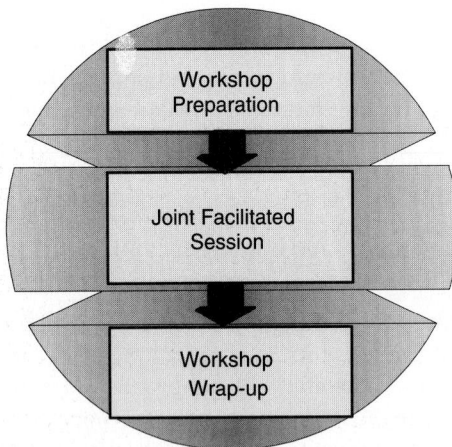

Figure 10–1 Joint facilitated session process life cycle.

Although the heart of the joint facilitated session is the actual workshop, the preparation phase is equally important. To be truly successful, the facilitated session requires careful planning activities that are performed during the preparation phase. Quite often, the preparation phase might take several days, even a week or two for complex subjects, and the workshop itself usually lasts no more than two to four days.

Once the joint facilitated session is terminated, the wrap-up phase starts. During that phase, the final outcome of the workshop, including all supporting visual aids and deliverables that were produced during the joint facilitated session, are assembled into a single document. Then the Joint Facilitated Session final document can be published throughout the organization.

Additional information on the Joint Facilitated Session process is provided in this book through chapters two and three that describe the survey and analysis system development phases.

10.3 JOINT FACILITATED SESSION BENEFITS

Table 10.1 lists some of the most common benefits that are derived from conducting Joint Facilitated Sessions.

Table 10–1 Joint Facilitated Session Benefits

- Reduces delays in the development cycle
- Increases the overall quality and business value of the software system
- Shortens the elapsed time required to capture the user requirements
- Produces more rapid system and user interface specifications
- Increases user participation and ownership
- Fosters a cross-functional team approach
- Minimizes potential business or political issues across functional organizations
- Encourages users to do some creative thinking on how to resolve issues and enhance their business processes
- Improves communication and partnership among business users

The benefits that are shown in the previous table can be realized only if the joint facilitated session process is managed with a disciplined yet flexible approach and is strongly supported by the management suite.

10.4 DETERMINING THE RELEVANCY OF USING THE JOINT FACILITATED SESSION (JFS) PROCESS

A Joint Facilitated Session is a very powerful technique to quickly capture various types of information required to build a system. Although it uses group dynamics to accomplish this objective, this is achieved by isolating several key business people in a room, away from their day-to-day work, often for several consecutive days.

Be sure to assess whether the use of the joint facilitated session technique is appropriate for the entire project or for different segments of that project. As a rule of thumb, this technique is particularly effective for projects that exhibit several of the criteria listed in Table 10.2.

On the other hand, in particular situations, the use of joint facilitated sessions can be overkill, especially when very few people, such as two or three individuals, under-

Table 10–2 Joint Facilitated Session Project Selection Criteria

- As a rule of thumb, requires a minimum of six person-months of development work
- Involves customers from different departments
- Must deal with complex business requirements
- Has a high visibility within the organization
- Has an official champion, preferably a business executive who is supportive toward the process
- Customers are committed to participate full-time during the sessions
- No single customer masters the overall big picture

stand the business processes that are under scrutiny, for instance. In such a case, less time-consuming information-gathering techniques can be substituted advantageously for joint facilitated sessions, such as simply conducting a series of more focused interviews with each particular customer.

10.5 A PROFILE OF THE JOINT FACILITATED SESSION (JFS) PARTICIPANTS

The success of the Joint Facilitated Session relies heavily on who participates in the workshop. Make sure that you have the right people for the type of session at hand. Section 10.5.1 describes the standard make-up of the workshop members, along with a short synopsis of the roles and responsibilities of each type of participant.

10.5.1 EXECUTIVE SPONSOR

The executive sponsor should be a high-level manager who comes from the ranks of the customer organization that benefits the most from the implementation of the information system. The executive sponsor must be the individual from the executive suite who has the highest authority to make decisions concerning all aspects of the project at hand. To this end, this executive has full authority to fund the project and staff it accordingly. The sponsor, who becomes the champion of the project, provides a strong management commitment to the entire joint facilitated session process.

10.5.2 SESSION FACILITATOR

The session facilitator is at the heart of the joint facilitated session activities. The role of the facilitator is to organize the workshop and then smoothly lead the team through the facilitated session process, from the beginning till the end. The facilitator must be an impartial, unbiased individual.

Ideally, the trained facilitator does not come either from the MIS department or from the user organization. The facilitator must be perceived by everyone as someone neutral who has no vested interest in the final outcome of the session results.

The facilitator must be a dynamic, well-respected individual who, besides possessing above-average communication skills, is capable of:

- Demonstrating sensitivity to corporate politics
- Demonstrating good negotiating skills
- Facilitating sessions with large groups
- Overcoming people issues with tact and diplomacy
- Releasing growing tension and keeping people at ease
- Pacing the session as per schedule
- Keeping people focused and away from tangents
- Communicating well
- Being a good listener
- Retaining a neutral position in the midst of controversy
- Enforcing the Joint Facilitated Session ground rules

Furthermore, the Joint Facilitated Session leader should be familiar, but not necessarily highly skilled, with the system development methodology and tools used in the workshop. This high level knowledge of the methodology is especially crucial when some diagramming techniques are used during the workshop to build the logical system process and data models.

The session leader should also be familiar with the basic tenets of good user interface design practices. This knowledge is paramount while conducting workshops that are aimed at designing the graphical user interface of a client-server or Web application system. If the leader does not have this knowledge, then a subject-matter expert in this area should assist the Joint Facilitated Session leader.

10.5.3 SCRIBE

The scribe assists the facilitator and records all decisions and conclusions that are made by the participants during the facilitated session. This role is critical, and must not be underestimated. This person must possess good communication skills. Ideally, the scribe should be able to follow and understand the discussions that occur during the session. During the facilitated session, the scribe always maintains a neutral attitude.

10.5.4 FULL-TIME PARTICIPANTS

Full-time participants typically involve business users and MIS staff, who are required to make decisions during the facilitated session, while the system requirements are being discussed. They are also the people who should provide all the business knowledge and expertise necessary to gradually build up all workshop deliverables.

User participants must bring their expertise on the details of the business operations that fall within the scope of the facilitated session. For a facilitated session to be truly successful, carefully select representatives who have substantial experience and a very good knowledge of the business at hand. They should also be keen to openly share their business knowledge with the other team members. They must be empowered by their respective organizations to make decisions with authority. Finally, together the team participants must represent all the business areas that will likely be affected by the system. Customer representatives may come from diverse backgrounds. They can be knowledgeable workers, clerical staff, business professionals, supervisors, and middle and even occasionally upper management.

Although a few MIS representatives might attend the session, the main focus must always remain on the user representatives. These individuals provide information on current business practices and procedures, identify problems or opportunities, and offer potential solutions.

The Information Systems representatives might assist the users by providing pertinent information on potential technology directions, issues, and existing problems with legacy systems. As a rule of thumb, a good workshop make-up ratio is approximately 75% user representatives and 25% Information Systems personnel.

10.5.5 SPECIALISTS

The specialists provide expertise on very specific subjects, on either the business or the technical side of the house. They do not attend the entire session but rather participate only when their area of expertise is required during the facilitated session. For this involvement to happen, they must make themselves available on the session days when their field of expertise is required. These experts bring in a realistic assessment of the impacts certain business or technological directions might have on the course of the future project. They can also highlight potential traps that can be costly if uncovered later in the project.

10.5.6 OBSERVERS

Observers are individuals who attend the joint facilitated session but are not allowed to participate in the discussions. Their number should be minimal, one or two individuals at the most. More often than not, an observer might be a future facilitator that needs some on-the-job exposure to the facilitation process or even a potential customer who wants to know what a joint facilitated session is. In all instances, make the observers aware that their role during the entire session must be a very silent one.

10.6 THE JOINT FACILITATED SESSION (JFS) CUSTOMIZATION PROCESS

The workshop framework must be carefully planned with the users, to ensure its effectiveness. To achieve this objective, the session facilitator meets with the project leader (and possibly some key users and system representatives) to discuss the proposed scope and objectives of the joint facilitated workshop. The core team members carefully examine potential issues and constraints that might be imposed on the conducting of the workshop. Based on the information gathered during this meeting, a strategy is then elaborated to customize the joint facilitated session process to address the specific needs of the workshop.

Another important point to discuss with the users is the number of required workshops and their respective duration. In reality, several factors might influence the number of required workshops and their respective duration, such as:

- The level of availability of the customers
- The complexity of the topics that must be addressed
- The amount of work required to adequately cover the project scope
- Project time constraints

A special Joint Facilitated Session workshop might be required to establish the scope of a large project. Such a preliminary planning workshop can last between 1 to 5 days, depending on the size and complexity of the project at hand. The outcome of this special scoping and planning workshop will be the identification of the number of subsequent workshops that are required to develop various deliverables, such as the detailed system requirements, for example.

Basically, the two basic strategies that can be pursued for scheduling the workshops are:

- Conduct all workshops sequentially, one after the other, with no interruption between them
- Conduct the workshops with some breaks interspersed between them

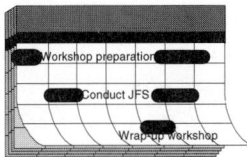
Another important question is, should the workshop last full days or half days? Full-day sessions should speed up the process. However, this approach can be strenuous for the participants. The users might lose their concentration after a couple hours of intensive participation. With half-day workshops, the participants remain more vigilant and are certainly less worried about what might be happening back at the office. Attending half-day sessions gives them the opportunity to actively participate in the sessions while still reserving some time during the day to perform their most urgent day-to-day business activities. Another advantage with half-day sessions is the extra time they provide to the facilitator, scribe, and other workshop supporting team members to prepare the material for the next morning or afternoon session. On the other hand, the full-day approach implies that all the preparatory work required for the next workshop is done once the daily session is terminated, thus during the evenings.

10.7 ROLES AND RESPONSIBILITIES OF THE JOINT FACILITATED SESSION (JFS) CORE TEAM LEADERS

The following section describes the roles and responsibilities that the executive sponsor, session facilitator, and scribe should assume before, during, and after the facilitated session workshop.

10.7.1 EXECUTIVE SPONSOR

BEFORE

- Participate, with the facilitator, project leader, and selective project team members, in the definition of the vision, purpose, scope, and objectives of the project and of the specific joint facilitated session that is currently being organized
- Explain the importance of the project and situate it within the broader view of the entire organization
- Help to select the key participants, on the business side

DURING

- Kick off the workshop by making a brief opening speech to the participants. In that speech, the sponsor:
  - Provides a strong statement of direction as to what are the major objectives of the project and those of the current facilitated session
  - Sets clear expectations for the outcome of the facilitated session
  - Instills in the team members a strong sense of commitment to actively support the facilitated session process
  - Might attend the workshop full-time, part-time, sporadically, or not at all; in any case, the sponsor should be accessible throughout the entire session to help resolve some critical management issues, such as when a serious impasse is reached during the session.

AFTER

- Follow up on the open issues that were raised during the session and that were assigned to various individuals for resolution with some specific target dates.

10.7.2 FACILITATOR

BEFORE

- Conduct interviews with the executive sponsor and with management from the customer organization to define the purpose, scope, and objectives of the facilitated session
- Help identify the business areas within the organization that should support and participate in the workshop

- Gather information on the project to prepare and organize the upcoming workshop
- Develop an agenda for the facilitated session and prepare the necessary visual aids, such as flip charts, overheads, and graphics

DURING

- Introduce the participants
- Present the agenda, explain the facilitated session process and the roles and responsibilities of each category of participants
- Explain the tools and techniques that will be used throughout the session
- Lead the joint session, smoothly guiding the participants through the agenda
- Overcome people issues
- Ensure that everyone participates actively in the discussions while maintaining a neutral attitude
- Ensure that agreements reached by the participants are properly recorded by the scribe
- Ensure that open issues are documented and assigned to someone for resolution with agreed target resolution dates
- Perform a final review of the major events and seek participants' input for the evaluation of the session
- Conclude the workshop
- Provide feedback to the project manager and project sponsor

AFTER

- Coordinate the creation, review, and distribution of the final document
- If necessary, conduct a post-session review meeting
- Provide feedback to the sponsor and project manager

10.7.3 SCRIBE

BEFORE

- Discuss his/her role with the facilitator
- Decide how the findings and agreements will be documented during the facilitated session

DURING

- At the prompting of the facilitator, document and recap decisions made during the session by the participants
- Document agreed-upon requirements or specifications
- Record action items that cover issues raised during the session and that must be resolved at a later date
- Collect and assemble all pertinent document samples provided during the session by the participants

AFTER

- Review, with the facilitator, all documentation created during the workshop
- Might help prepare the final document

10.8 THE JOINT FACILITATED SESSION (JFS) PROCESS

DETAILED ACTIVITY LIST
This section describes, in a condensed format, the detailed activities that you perform to plan the joint facilitated session, to prepare the final workshop material and facilities, to conduct the workshop, and finally to conclude it thereafter.

10.8.1 PLANNING THE JOINT FACILITATED SESSION

This section outlines the major steps involved in planning a joint facilitated session.

- Review existing documents that can prove to be pertinent to the type of information that you will cover during the facilitated session; if necessary, interview key management personnel
- Meet with the executive sponsor and the project manager to discuss the workshop mandate
  - Review the following items:
    - Project vision and background
    - Purpose and scope of the proposed Joint Facilitated Session
    - Management and business objectives for the workshop
    - Expected workshop deliverables
    - Potential issues, constraints, and assumptions that might affect the workshop

- Identification of the business areas that the outcome of the workshop can affect
  - Assist the executive sponsor and project manager in identifying and selecting the joint facilitated session participants
  - If required, conduct pre-session interviews with key users to gather information that will become the basis for the JFS
  - Identify the number of workshops required to achieve the proposed objectives, along with their respective duration
  - Discuss and finalize the schedule dates for each workshop
  - Document major findings into a JFS Management Definition Guide
  - Distribute the session invitations to the participants, including the preliminary Management Definition Guide document

10.8.2 PREPARING FOR THE JOINT FACILITATED SESSION

This section outlines the major steps involved in organizing a joint facilitated session.

- Decide with the management team whether the session will be held on-site or off-site
- Make arrangements for the session room, equipment, and supplies
- Prepare workshop visual aids, covering items such as:
  - session agenda
  - participants' familiarization with the facilitated session process
  - purpose, scope, and objectives of the facilitated session
  - issues, constraints, and assumptions
  - expected workshop deliverables
  - subject-related graphics
  - session "rules of the land"
- If required, setup a brief meeting with the team participants to review the JFS process
- If necessary, distribute to key participants a checklist of the documents they need to bring to the workshop

10.8.3 CONDUCTING THE JOINT FACILITATED SESSION CORE ACTIVITIES

This section outlines the critical activities involved in conducting a joint facilitated session.

- Prior to the session, the facilitator ensures that all conference room facilities where the workshop will be conducted are adequate, covering:
  - the physical arrangement of the tables, based on the number of participants
  - the proper positioning of all required visual aid equipment
  - the adequate provision of office supplies

- Session kickoff
  - The session facilitator introduces herself or himself, the scribe(s), and the observers
  - Welcome the participants and briefly describe the purpose of the workshop
  - Introduce the executive sponsor, who provides general opening remarks about the project, covering the following points:
    - the major business drivers behind the project and its purpose
    - the goals of the joint facilitated session
    - the expected outcomes of the workshop
    - why the current participants have been selected for this facilitated session
    - the sponsor's personal endorsement and full support of the joint facilitated process
  - Introduce the project manager, who provides a project overview covering:
    - the positioning of the current facilitated session in relation to the overall project
    - present project-specific information that is relevant to the facilitated session at hand
  - Invite the session participants to introduce themselves, covering the following items:
    - participant's name
    - the organization they represent
    - participant's current responsibilities
    - participant's current and past job experience
  - Provide an overview of the joint facilitated session process
    - Briefly explain the structure of the joint facilitated session process
    - Explain the roles and responsibilities of the session participants
  - Review with the participants the logistic aspects of the workshop, such as:
    - overall session duration
    - session daily start/stop time and breaks
    - location of restrooms and other facilities
    - the procedure for handling messages and phone calls
    - food and beverages
    - additional administrative support provided by the staff
  - Review with the team members the "rules of the land" that must be observed by everyone during the workshop
- Introduce the specific agenda of the current session, describing items such as:
  - scope
  - purpose and objectives
  - main topics to be covered during the session
  - expected results
  - constraints and assumptions
- Seek participants' feedback on potential concerns or issues to be addressed during the session, as per the proposed agenda

- Conduct the main workshop information-gathering activities
- Maintain adherence to the workshop agenda
- Maintain issue/action item lists
- Prompt the scribe to record and recap all the decisions made by the participants

10.8.4 CLOSING THE JOINT FACILITATED SESSION

This section briefly outlines the major steps involved in wrapping up and closing a joint facilitated session.

- Summarize the major accomplishments that were achieved during the session
- Review with the team participants all remaining open issues action items; ensure that each open issue action item has:
  - a target date for resolution
  - the name of the individual who is responsible to follow up on the issue
- Obtain constructive feedback from the participants on:
  - the effectiveness of the facilitated session process
  - the results achieved
- Provide positive feedback to the participants as to how well they worked as a team

10.8.5 PRODUCING THE JOINT FACILITATED SESSION FINAL DOCUMENT

This section lists the major steps involved in documenting the final outcome of a joint facilitated session.

- Gather all source documents such as the scribe notes, list of unresolved items, flip chart sheets, filled-in templates, transparencies, handwritten notes, and other pertinent information that were documented during the workshop
- Analyze, edit, format, and consolidate all session information into a final document
- Issue the final document with a covering memo, as per agreed distribution list, including all session participants and the executive sponsor
- Ensure that someone has been assigned the responsibility to monitor the timely resolution of all open issues
- If required, schedule a review of the joint facilitated session final document with session participants

10.9 THE SETUP OF THE JOINT FACILITATED SESSION (JFS) CONFERENCE ROOM

Definite advantages exist to holding the joint facilitated session off-site. For one, the participants are less likely to be interrupted or distracted by their regular day-to-day job requirements. Limited budgets might affect this decision, but whenever feasible, this option should always be considered with the project sponsor.

A good setup of the session room will definitely contribute to the success of the workshop. It will positively influence the participants and encourage them to exchange information more freely with one another. Figure 10.2 depicts a typical room layout.

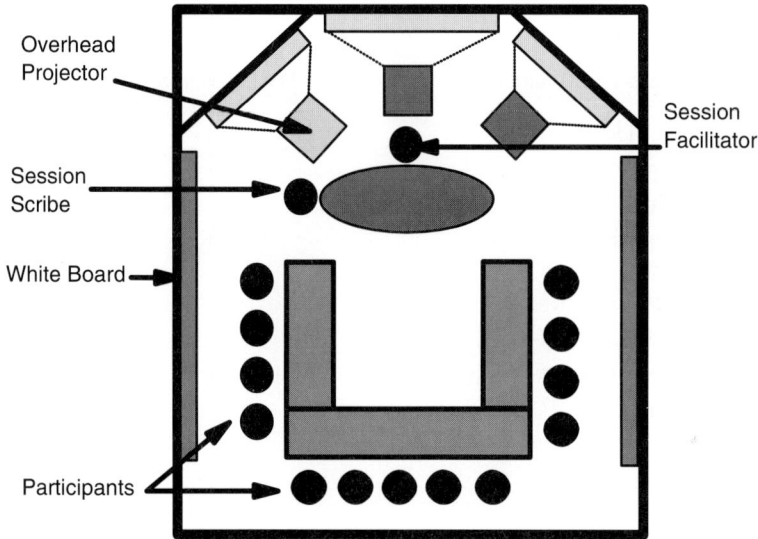

Figure 10–2 Joint facilitated session room layout.

Normally, the best seating arrangement is around a round table or in a horseshoe setup. A large table might be set up in front of the room to accommodate the facilitator and the scribe. The number of participants and room's shape and size will determine what should be the best seating arrangements. A certain amount of wall space must be reserved to stick on it various documents that must constantly be on display during the session, such as flip charts, pictures, and graphics. These visual aids must be located in such a way that they remain easily viewable by all participants, at all times.

Various pieces of equipment such as transparency or personal computer overhead projectors and flip charts must be strategically positioned so they can be easily accessible by the facilitator and scribe. However, the information that is displayed with these tools should be clearly visible for all participants. As much as possible, regular telephones, cellular telephones, and electronic beepers should be banished from the room premises. Instead, some facilities should be set up to send and receive messages for the participants in the vicinity of the room, but still outside its premise.

10.10 JOINT FACILITATED SESSION OFFICE EQUIPMENT AND SUPPLY

REQUIREMENTS

You may use several categories of support equipment during the session. The type of equipment used may vary from a few simple items to very sophisticated electronic devices. Table 10.3 provides a list of some of the most frequently used pieces of office equipment:

Table 10–3 Joint Facilitated Session Office Equipment Facilities

- Overhead and slide projectors
- Computer display projectors
- Screen projectors
- Television sets, video machines
- Digital cameras
- Video cameras
- Computer workstations or laptops
- White boards or electronic boards
- Flip chart stands
- Laser pen
- Magnetic or cork boards

The session room must also be provided with the usual, but indispensable, office supplies, such as those enumerated in Table 10.4.

Table 10–4 Joint Facilitated Session Office Supplies

- Regular pens and pencils
- Marker pens (erasable and non-erasable)
- Flip chart paper
- Transparencies
- Paper
- Standard forms
- Spare overhead projector bulbs
- Magnetic blocks
- "Mack Tak"
- Participant name tents
- Wallboard pins

As I previously indicated, keep highly visible all the major issues, action items, and decisions that are made by the participants during the entire session. A variety of visual aids is often used effectively for this purpose. The use of attractive and colorful visual aids will help retain the attention of the participants and keep them focused on the topics of the workshop. Visual aids can also be used very advantageously to pictorially depict complex session material.

10.11 USAGE OF AUTOMATED TOOLS DURING THE JOINT FACILITATED SESSIONS

During the joint facilitated session, the scribe records all the decisions made by the participants. Be sure to document as accurately as possible all the relevant information that the participants provided. These notes will be consolidated into the final output document after the joint session. Quite often, some standard, pre-defined templates are used to speed up the capturing of specific information during the workshop. For example, a template is used to quickly capture information on the various data elements that must be shown on a business report. The template already provides pre-defined field labels such as: data element name, description, length, format, and business rules.

The use of simple automated tools such as user-friendly word processing software can greatly simplify the work of the scribe. Of course, this statement is true only if the scribe possesses good enough typing skills. A one-finger typist is not a good choice in such a case.

Customized, automated templates can be developed on word processors to help quickly capture all pertinent information. As the information is entered into the computer word-processor template, a computer screen projector automatically displays it on a large surface that can be viewed by all participants.

In organizations that have successfully integrated the joint facilitated session technique with their standard system development methodology, the use of CASE tools, such as an automated data modeling tool, for instance, is frequently utilized to help capture the information that is provided by the session participants.

These organizations have gradually tailored the joint facilitated session process and its deliverables to match their existing methodology standards and guidelines.

Besides automated data modeling tools, other categories of CASE tools can be used to interactively model the information that is collected and consolidated with the session participants during the workshop.

The types of CASE tools that might be used during the session will largely depend on the type of joint facilitated session you are conducting. For instance, if you conduct a joint facilitated session aimed at creating an initial system GUI design, then a RAD client-server development tool is most likely one of the best possible choices. With such a tool, you will interactively paint your windows screens, including their proper menus and control buttons, with the direct involvement of the session participants. If you conduct a joint facilitated session for which the prime objective is to come up with a complex project milestone plan, then a PC project planning software tool will be a good choice.

Properly used, automated CASE tools can ease the creation of system information models. On the other hand, the misuse of automated tools can prove to be harmful and sometimes even fatal to the workshop. Serious problems can surface while attempting to use automated tools, as shown in Table 10.5:

Table 10–5 Potential Problems With Automated Tools

- The automated tools intimidate the session participants. The participants might not be familiar with the modeling techniques imposed by the tool and their arcane symbols and terminology.
- The tool is simply not very user-friendly, and the technician who uses it to develop the modeling information does not master it perfectly well. Instead of speeding up the information modeling session, the use of the tool slows it down.
- The facilitator tries to tailor the facilitated session process to the automated tool's own idiosyncrasies. By doing so, the facilitator destroys the group dynamic that gradually built up among the participants during the session.

Based on all the above-mentioned reasons, the decision to use automated tools in joint facilitated sessions must be carefully weighed in light of their potential pros and cons. Automated tools are not always mandatory. In fact, professional joint facilitated session leaders have conducted several joint facilitated sessions very successfully with simple visual aids such as flip charts and transparencies.

The facilitation skills of the session leader and the level of knowledge of the participants are much more critical to the success of a facilitated session than the use of automated tools and technology gadgets.

10.12 JOINT FACILITATED SESSION: THE RULES OF THE LAND

The facilitator must ensure that the workshop participants work together as a team, throughout the entire session. This teamwork can prove to be a real challenge if some ground rules are not established clearly amongst the participants, at the very beginning of the session.

Figure 10.3 enumerates some basic "rules of the land" directives that all team participants must observe during the session. The facilitator can simply review these rules and discuss them with the session participants, at the beginning of the session.

If the facilitator wants to get stronger buy-in from the participants, an alternative approach could be to list the most critical session ground rules on a flip chart. Then the participants could be solicited to suggest their own rules. Developing the ground rules progressively with the group will likely empower the participants to enforce these rules themselves as the session unfolds.

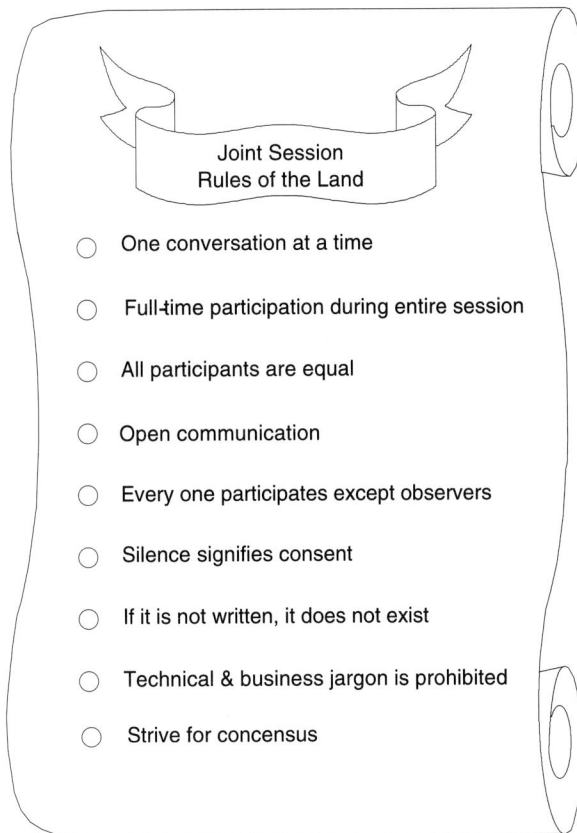

Figure 10–3 Joint facilitated session rules of the land.

10.13 ADDITIONAL SUPPORTING MATERIAL

This section provides some additional supporting material that be can used with a Joint Facilitated Session. It includes the following:

- Joint Facilitated Session open issue form (Table 10.6)

- Joint Facilitated Session list of participants form (Table 10.7)

- Joint Facilitated Session activity checklist form (Table 10.8)

This material can be tailored to better fit the custom Joint Facilitated Session requirements of your organization.

Table 10–6 Joint Facilitated Session Open Issue Form

ISSUE NUMBER	ISSUE DATE	ISSUE DESCRIPTION	ASSIGN TO	RESOLUTION DATE

Table 10–7 Joint Facilitated Session List Of Participants Form

PARTICIPANT NAME	DEPARTMENT	ROLE	PHONE NUMBER

Roles:

E: Executive Sponsor   I: MIS Representative   P: Project Manager
F: Facilitator   U: User Representative   S: Scribe
O: Observer

Table 10–8 Joint Facilitated Session Activity Checklist

Project Name: Project Manager:

Session Facilitator: Date:

ACTIVITIES

❏ Interview the project manager (JFS purpose, scope, objectives)

❏ Meet with the executive sponsor (JFS education, buy-in)

❏ Produce the JFS participation list; finalize the JFS familiarization session (advise workshop participants)

❏ Conduct the JFS familiarization workshop (provide the Pre-JFS data-gathering checklist)

❏ Finalize JFS session dates (reserve the meeting room, inform participants, secure attendance)

❏ Send a JFS cover memo (inform participants of the workshop location, date, and time, and provide directions to the location)

❏ Verify the availability of visual equipment and office supplies (e.g., participant name tags, markers, flip charts, transparencies)

❏ Prepare final workshop material

❏ Ensure that food/drinks arrangements are done

❏ Collect pre-JFS data-gathering forms

❏ Distribute the detailed agenda and JFS supporting material prior to the workshop

❏ Prepare the room for the workshop (e.g., final seating arrangements, equipment setup)

❏ Meet with the scribe

❏ Conduct the workshop

❏ Produce the JFS final document and memo

❏ Distribute the JFS final document

❏ Monitor the resolution of JFS open issues

❏ Schedule the final JFS review with participants (if necessary)

11

Web Database Application Development

11.1 INTRODUCTION

In an ever-increasing cutthroat business climate that demands the deployment of quality business applications in a drastically shortened time frame, Web database systems are becoming an essential weapon for numerous enterprises that desire to remain competitive in a global market economy.

The Internet, intranet, and extranet technology environments allow the rapid deployment of a broad range of Web database applications that can be used throughout the enterprise and also from the outside by its business partners, suppliers, and customers.

This rapid application deployment is made possible by the World Wide Web, which, through its promise of platform-independent application solutions, attempts to eliminate the traditional technological barriers that restrained the exchange of information between companies.

This chapter discusses Web technology from an application development perspective and, more particularly, the Web database application development process.

First, I provide a brief overview of the evolution and different types of applications that can be built with Web technology. Then I present some of the benefits and challenges that are associated with this technology.

Finally, I discuss different application-related topics such as security issues, application design considerations, and application programming considerations.

11.1.1 WEB APPLICATION EVOLUTION

The Web platform is increasingly used to deliver different types of business applications to the users. Table 11.1 shows the evolution of the Web application development process over time and lists three of the most common categories of business applications that can be developed in a Web environment.

Table 11–1 Three Popular Categories Of Web Applications

Generation level	1 Static document publishing applications	2 Simple dynamic Web applications	3 Complex Web database applications
Description	This type of application publishes static Web documents that may contain sophisticated graphics and multimedia objects.	This type of application contains dynamic Web pages that connect to a database for simple query purposes. Another type of application can also contain forms that allow a certain level of interactivity between the client and the Web server.	This type of interactive application manages complex Web transactional systems that can connect to several corporate databases located in the back end.
Examples	Company procedures, technical guides, plain telephone lists, description of employee benefits.	Custom or commercial Web applications that are used to directly query or occasionally update a database. Can also be used to extract database information and create reports. Telephone lists with search capabilities.	Robust, industrial-strength business applications, such as order entry and inventory systems that extensively use complex database transactions such as adds, updates, and deletes.

11.1.2 WEB APPLICATION ARCHITECTURE OVERVIEW

The basic set of Web architecture components that is required to support the three different types of Web applications I talked about in Section 11.1.1 are discussed below.

STATIC DOCUMENT PUBLISHING APPLICATIONS

Looking at Figure 11.1, the Web static document publishing application type requires a Web browser, the Internet or intranet, and a Web server. The Web server receives a request from a client Web browser for specific document(s) (under the form of HTML pages), locates them on the server, and sends them back to the client Web browser using the hypertext transfer protocol (HTTP).

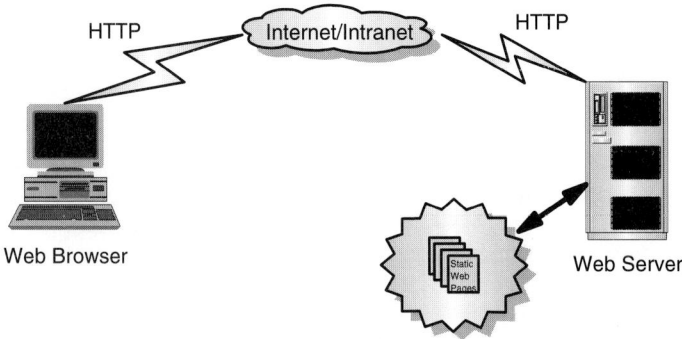

Figure 11–1 Web architecture supporting static document publishing.

SIMPLE DYNAMIC WEB APPLICATIONS

Figure 11.2 shows the Web architecture components that are required for simple dynamic Web applications.

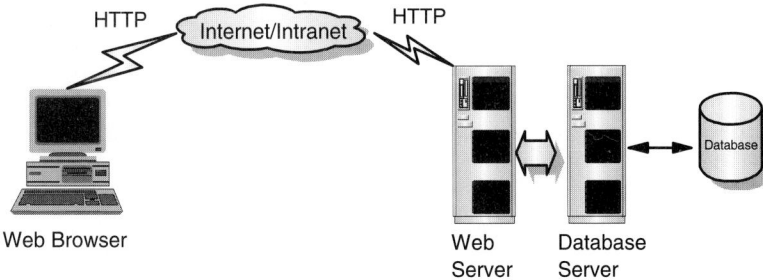

Figure 11–2 Web architecture supporting dynamic web applications.

If you compare Figure 11.2 with Figure 11.1, the only additional component that appears in Figure 11.2 is the database server. The front-end connectivity is identical to what you see in Figure 11.1. The Web client browser still connects to the Web server via the Internet/intranet HTTP protocol.

However, the Web server can connect to the database server via different protocols. The back-end database server provides the requested information back to the Web server. The Web server transforms the requested information into an HTML format and then passes back the newly generated HTML page to the client Web browser.

COMPLEX WEB DATABASE APPLICATIONS

Finally, Figure 11.3 shows the Web architecture components that are required to support the more complex Web database applications.

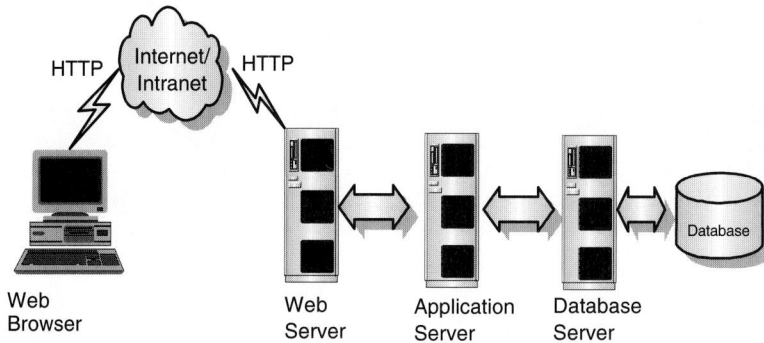

Figure 11–3 Web architecture supporting complex Web database applications.

Web database applications require an additional component that is called an application server. The application server layer provides a high-speed and scalable architecture, which is needed to support large and complex Web database applications.

The application server performs most of the application processing logic and can connect to the database server when required. In addition, the application server is also responsible for maintaining the state management and session control logic that are required for a dynamic transactional system. For example, if a user must access, in a single business transaction, multiple Web pages, then the application server handles the information flow that needs to be maintained from one Web page to another.

11.1.3 WEB TECHNOLOGY BENEFITS AND CHALLENGES

Table 11.2 highlights some of the most significant benefits that Web database applications can provide to an enterprise.

On the other hand, although providing important benefits, the Web database application and its supporting network-centric technology platform present their own challenges. Table 11.3 lists some of the major challenges that are introduced with the Web technology in general, and more specifically for large Web database applications.

11.1.4 WEB DATABASE APPLICATION SECURITY

Figure 11.4 presents a holistic view of different types of application-oriented security mechanisms that can be required to make a Web database application more secure. Each of these security options can be used to complement additional layers of Web-related security mechanisms such as firewalls and data encryption algorithms. The elements in Figure 11.4 assume that a generic four-tier Web architecture is used to im-

Table 11–2 Web Database Application Benefits

- Since the Web database application logic resides on the server rather than on the client, the cumbersome and often complex task of deploying an application to a large number of client workstations is significantly reduced in time, if not eliminated completely.
- For large applications, the reduced application deployment time and effort can be directly translated into important deployment cost reductions.
- In an Internet environment, the application is immediately accessible from anywhere in the world. In a traditional intranet environment, the application is accessible by all employees via a Web browser, regardless of the computing platform they use.
- Well-designed Web database applications can help to circumvent performance and scalability limitations that might be associated with traditional two-tier client-server applications.
- Ongoing application maintenance and enhancements can be considerably reduced, since the Web database application is centrally located on a corporate Web or application server.
- In certain environments, the Web database application can be advantageously run on "thin" client machines such as older and less powerful client workstations than the latest available machines or client network computers, thus helping to reduce the hardware acquisition and support costs.

Table 11–3 Web Technology And Database Application Challenges

Scalability	Web database applications can scale well as long as a high-performance Web architecture has been put in place. In an Internet environment, Web database applications can encounter highly variable and potentially huge transaction peak loads.
Evolving technology	The Web technology is in constant evolution. Developing large, mission-critical Web database applications might be difficult in a new technological environment where the standards still evolve relatively quickly.
Security	The security paradigm takes all its significance when corporate Web database applications are made accessible to everyone around the world via the Internet or even to internal employees via the intranet.
	Several potential security breaches associated with this technology might pose serious challenges to the developers who must secure Web applications that contain sensitive data.
State/ Persistence	The Web platform is a stateless environment where the client and the server are very loosely connected. Each particular session on a Web server is confined by the length of time needed to process a request for an HTML page. When the Web page is passed to the user who originally requested it via a Web browser, the session is closed. On the other hand, Web database applications require context-sensitive, stateful processing that keep session information maintained from one Web page to another. Stateful processing is necessary so that the users do not have to re-enter information from one request to another within the same business transaction.
Co-existence with legacy applications	The Web database application might have to co-exist with legacy applications through the creation of system interfaces. This co-existence can add complexity to the development of the application.

plement the Web database application. (i.e., client Web browser, Web server, application server, database server).

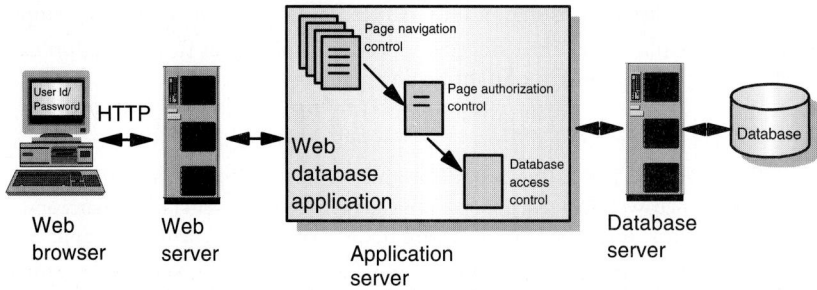

Figure 11–4 Application-driven security mechanisms.

Table 11.4 provides an overview of the different Web database application security options in Figure 11.4.

Table 11–4 Web Database Application Security Mechanisms

Security Type	Security Service Supplier	Security Mechanism Description
User authentication	Web server	The application Web server authenticates the users with special identifiers, such as a user id and a password. If the authentication process is successful, then the users are allowed to access the Web database applications.
Web page navigation flow control	Web application	The Web database application must implement a security mechanism to control how the users can navigate among the different Web pages that are provided by the application. The users should be allowed to navigate only through the legitimate access paths that were specifically set for that Web application. For instance, the Web application should not allow the users to create bookmarks that would permit them to bypass the application access control mechanisms such as the initial Web page that is used to log in into the application.

Table 11–4 Web Database Application Security Mechanisms

User authorization	Web application	Certain categories of users might have access to the entire set of Web application pages, whereas others might be restricted as to which pages of the application they can access.
Database access authorization	Database server	The user database access privileges (i.e., insert, delete, update, or read) are controlled by the internal security mechanisms that are provided by the database management system.

11.2 WEB DATABASE APPLICATION DESIGN CONSIDERATIONS

This section discusses a variety of generic topics that primarily relate to the design of a Web application, such as designing a Web application for the Internet, the layout of the Web graphical use interface, and different application-related performance issues.

11.2.1 INTERNET VERSUS INTRANET WEB DATABASE APPLICATIONS

In a corporate intranet environment, I strongly recommend selecting a specific Web browser and impose it across the enterprise as a corporate standard.

In an Internet environment, the Web database application development team has little or no control as to the type of client Web browsers that the users will utilize to interact with the application. Consequently, different users who are located all around the world might experiment some minor variations in the manner in which their Web pages will be displayed to them, depending on the type and version of Web browsers they will utilize. Nonetheless, the basic application business logic and navigational paths should not differ from one user to another, as long as the developers stick to the most common and widely accepted HTML industry standards.

Due to the diversity of Web browsers, certain Internet users might work with a text-only Web browser, and others might use a Web browser that supports only older versions of HTML. Similarly, each Web browser might offer HTML extensions that are proprietary and that simply are not supported by other Web browsers.

Based on all the above, the Web design team should decide early on during the development cycle of an Internet Web database application which type and also which level of browser display should be supported by the Web system. They can make the decision once the development team has identified with the users what the intended purpose and target audience are for the Web database application.

As a rule of thumb, the developers should consider using the lowest-level common denominator of HTML standard that can be acceptable by the users, without compromising the design integrity of the application. Such an approach might force the developers to make some tradeoffs as to the level of rendering sophistication that can be exhibited by their Web application. On the other hand, the Web application might be compatible with a larger number of Web browsers. After all, the primary intent of a commercial Internet Web application is to be accessible by the largest user audience possible.

A possible compromise between Web page originality and readability would be to allow users that possess a Web browser with limited graphical display capabilities to still access the most important information in a text-only manner without the fancy graphics, for instance. However, this approach might add to the complexity of the application and make it more difficult to maintain later on.

Finally, a diversity of Web browsers can be used to access a Web database application via the Internet. This situation will force the development team to ensure that their testing strategy takes into account the necessity of verifying the application's functionality with many different types of Web browsers and possibly different versions of the same Web browser.

11.2.2 WEB DATABASE APPLICATION DESIGN AND PERFORMANCE CONSIDERATIONS

This section discusses several topics that relate to the design and performance of web applications. It also provides different guidelines and suggestions to improve the performance and the "look and feel" of web applications.

INTRODUCTION

The occasional user might accept coping with a Web application interface that is not user-friendly or retrieves and displays information in a less than optimal timeframe. However, the frequent user of a large and mission-critical Internet/intranet Web database application will not tolerate either a poor response time or an unfriendly graphical user interface.

"Performance considerations" presents some peculiar design issues that must be taken into consideration while designing a Web database application interface.

But prior to diving deeply into any particular Web interface design considerations, peruse Table 11.5, which lists some of the most frequent user complaints that relate to the way some Web Internet/intranet sites and applications are designed. Several lessons on "things to avoid" when designing a Web page can be learned from these perfectly valid criticisms.

PERFORMANCE CONSIDERATIONS

This section discusses some important design factors that might adversely affect the performance of web applications if they are not taken into consideration early during the design process. Aesthetic and usability considerations are also covered.

Table 11–5 Web Page Design Flaws

CATEGORY	MOST COMMON USER COMPLAINTS
Organization	• No page exists to indicate the content and organization of the Web site/application
	• The structure of the Web site/application is chaotic and highly disorganized
	• No design layout consistency exists from one page to another
Response time	• The users must wait a long period of time for pages to download because they contain too many graphics, images, or multimedia elements that do not provide added value to the business process it supports
Navigation	• No assistance is provided to help guide the users in navigating through the Web site/application
	• The users must constantly scroll up and down the screen to view all the information contained in pages that are much too large
	• "Dead end" pages force the users to backtrack
	• Broken links occur between the Web site application pages
Legibility	• The Web browser window is divided into so many frames that the graphical interface confuses and disorients the users more than anything else
	• Fonts are too small to be legible at a normal distance from the screen
	• Reading the textual content of the Web pages is difficult because of poor contrast with the background
Aesthetics	• The users are annoyed by text that blinks continuously
	• Text and graphics are not well integrated with one another
	• The Web pages are visually cluttered with extraneous data

RETRIEVAL TIME

The time needed to display a Web page in a client browser can vary, depending on the type and version of the selected Web browser. Certain Web applications might also be optimized to achieve a better rendering time when operating with a specific Web browser.

Also, the decision to build an intranet database application that will be utilized by internal users who are all supported by an Ethernet network that has a data transmission capacity of 10Mbits/sec or even 100Mbits/sec might influence the design and content elements of the application Web pages. With such bandwidth capacity, you might be able to add some graphical elements that will not impede on the rapidity at which the Web transactions are executed and their results displayed back in the client Web browser.

On the other hand, if the Web application will be accessible by remote users via modems, such as field or sales representatives, then even the smallest abuse of graphics might adversely affect the time required to download the application Web pages. Thus, you need to assess the bandwidth available not only to the users located in the corporate offices but also all the different groups of external users who will become a segment of your target audience.

Besides graphics, the time needed to display unnecessarily large Web pages that contain too many data fields or too many inessential multimedia elements — such as fancy inline images, sound effects, and even video sequences — can equally adversely affect the download time of a Web page in a client browser.

Different factors other than the display of the graphical user interface can influence the overall response time of a Web database application transaction. For example, one of these factors might be the information retrieval time. Information retrieval time is the duration the application needs to access the database server in the back end and retrieve the information requested by the user.

Nonetheless, you might have to reduce to its simplest form the manner in which the retrieved information will be downloaded and displayed by the Web browser on the client workstation, especially for Web database applications that are highly transactional by nature. A more sober Web page user interface might be more effective and efficient for a Web database transactional system than a fancy and highly multimedia-oriented interface designed for a sophisticated marketing showcase Web application. The target audience is simply not the same.

READABILITY

The Web database application developers must resist the temptation to use poorly textured or colored backgrounds that make the information displayed by the client Web browser more difficult to read and interpret by the user. Like the more traditional client-server applications, the use of too many diversified fonts and font sizes will also obscure the overall readability of the information displayed by the Web graphical user interface. Images that blink on the page being displayed might be amusing when the user retrieves it for the very first time. But the same effect will quickly become less attractive and even irritating when the user accesses the same Web transaction over and over again during the course of a regular day at work. Also, the terminology should be simple and familiar to the users.

AESTHETICS

The aesthetics elements of the Web database application interface are some of the most difficult factors to evaluate without involving a certain level of subjectivity. How far the Web application interface pleases the users might be difficult to test in a quantitative manner. Nevertheless, a few aesthetics elements that are very elementary in nature can still be enforced consistently throughout the user interface.

For example, does the Web interface contain repeated patterns and cues that are consistent from one page to another? Are repetitive visual display elements repeated on different pages in a consistent manner? Do colors, if they are used, complement each other and please the eyes of a user that will utilize the application on a regular basis?

USABILITY

The usability tests that I described in previous sections of this book for the client-server applications apply also to the Web database applications. Different user case scenarios can be devised to verify the ease of use and level of effectiveness of the Web database business transactions that are supported by the interface. The users themselves should test firsthand and as early as possible the Web graphical interface and discuss with the developers any usability problems that they detect along the way.

WEB PAGE DESIGN CONSIDERATIONS

This section discusses some design considerations that primarily relate to the physical characteristics of a Web page.

PAGE SIZE

The amount of information shown on a page should not be too large, for the reasons documented in Table 11.6.

Table 11–6 Web Page Sizing Considerations

- If too much information is on a single page, the users might simply be confused or overwhelmed by the interface.
- The amount of time needed to download the page from the Web server might be too long.
- The users might have to scroll up and down the page to access all the necessary information, which might disorient them. In the worst-case scenario, scrolling up and down a page might be unacceptable for Web database application functions that contain repetitive computing tasks such as data entry transactions, for example. Instead of scrollable screens, use hypertext links where possible.

Another factor that might influence the design of Web page graphics and their size is the screen dimension and level of resolution that are supported by the user workstations. Will the users of an intranet application use a 640x480 screen resolution on a 15-inch display monitor or a 1024x760 screen resolution on a 17-inch display monitor? The designers should take this information into consideration.

For example, a page grid that is carefully and artistically designed on a 20-inch monitor can turn out to be visually outstanding on such a display device. However, you may not be able to display the same page in its entirety in a typical Web browser that operates on a standard 14- or 15-inch display monitor. For this reason, always assess the safe display zones for different screen sizes and resolutions.

PAGE TEMPLATES AND REUSABILITY

One of the best ways to ensure a consistent application look and feel is to develop a set of standard Web page templates that can be constantly reused across the enterprise, for all Web database applications. If necessary, the templates can be modified and adapted to satisfy the peculiar needs of each particular application.

A typical template for a Web page application appears in Figure 11.5.

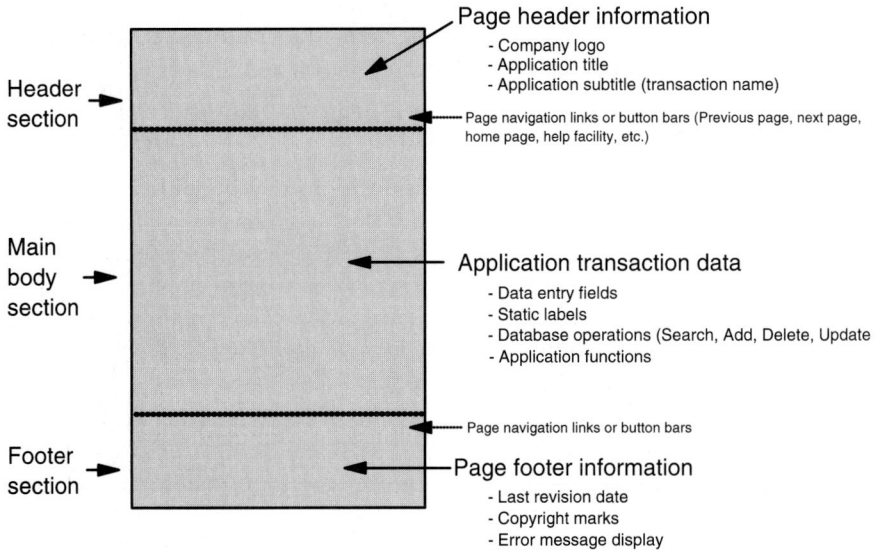

Figure 11–5 Standard Web page grid.

This template diagram illustrates one possible approach for the placement of static text, navigational page controls, functions, and data fields. The standardization of the layout of the Web pages, either in a single application or across different applications, greatly helps the users to navigate from one page to another and also quickly recognize the repetitive information and navigation cues that are consistently laid out on each page.

This technique provides the users with a secure sense of consistency and structure while interfacing with the graphical user interface. For instance, the page header and footer sections should contain information that establishes clearly the identity of your Web application. It also helps the users to quickly situate themselves visually in the Web page application structure. The users should never get confused as to where they are located in the Web database application.

For example, the header section of each application Web page should always contain a title that describes the application and a subtitle that describes the business transaction that can be performed with this Web page. If a small, recurring graphic theme such as a company logo is used to identify the Web application or the enterprise, then place it consistently at the same location across all the pages, preferably in the header section.

NAVIGATION

A button bar (or image map menu with basic navigation links) might be advantageously located in the header and the footer sections of each Web page. The button bar should contain the elementary navigation control elements that help the users to navigate through the different types of business transactions that are supported by the Web application.

Small graphic buttons or hypertext links should always be used in a consistent and predictable manner to perform the elementary page navigation tasks that you see in Table 11.7.

Table 11-7 Web Page Navigation Events

- Click a button to access a help page that contains additional information on how to use the Web business transaction
- Click a button to go back at the application top-level home page or an upper-level page
- Click a button to navigate up to the parent(s) of the current page
- Click a button to navigate down to the children of the current page
- Click a button to go back to the previous page ("Back to previous page" button)
- Click a button to go to the next page ("Forward to next page" button)
- Click a button to access a table of contents or index page
- Click a button to access utilities such as a search facility or a feedback form

Figure 11.6 illustrates a structured set of Web pages that contain related pages that are grouped into logical clusters. Convenient navigation structures are provided to the users to easily access the different logical clusters and their associated transactions in an efficient and logical manner.

The links shown in Figure 11.6 are bi-directional. The users can navigate up and down through the different levels of business transactions in a logical sequence. The users can also branch horizontally to other areas of the application, if necessary. Although not shown on the picture for clarity purposes, each page should provide a link to the home page.

Table 11.8 provides some basic guidelines on how to use various page navigation buttons.

HIERARCHICAL WEB PAGE STRUCTURES

Several types of structures can be used to link together the different Web pages of an application. However, a hierarchical page structure is often used to organize the Web pages of a corporate Web database application. A well organized Web page structure

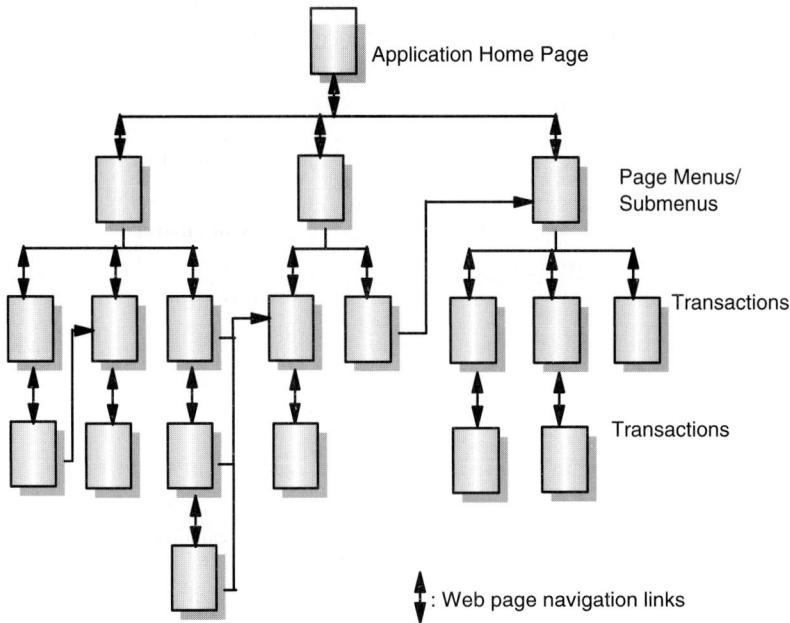

Figure 11–6 Web page navigation structures.

Table 11–8 Use Appropriate Page Navigation Buttons

- In a Web database application, use "back" and "forward" or "previous" and "next" navigation buttons in a careful and consistent manner. The use of these buttons presumes that the users know the structure of your Web application. This approach can be fine if the Web application can be accessed in a sequential, linear manner, one page at a time, using a book metaphor. However, this is rarely the case with a Web database application.

- The Web application that contains standard business transactions will likely adopt a top-down hierarchical structure to organize its pages. The most general information is usually displayed at the top levels of the hierarchy, and the more detailed information, such as the Web database transactions themselves, at the lower levels. Hence, page navigation buttons such as "back" and "forward" might signify moving either vertically up or down the hierarchy of Web pages or horizontally from left to right.

- To avoid misleading or confusing the users, properly label the page navigation buttons with a more meaningful terminology, if necessary. For example, small text that clearly indicates where the link leads the users is preferable, like "Forward to customer credit approval transaction," for instance. The link can be either textual or a graphical button with a label.

is crucial to help the users understand how the various components and subsections of your Web application have been planned and organized.

First, the different types of information requirements that must be supported by the application are grouped into clusters, based on the level of affinity that exists between the data contained in each group of information and the type of business processes that must be supported by the application. If the analysis has been done properly, the business Web application has been partitioned into a set of business transactions that are highly cohesive and modularized. Each specific logical cluster of information then can be laid out onto a Web page. Finally, all the Web pages are linked together, preferably using a generic hierarchical structure, as shown in Figure 11.7.

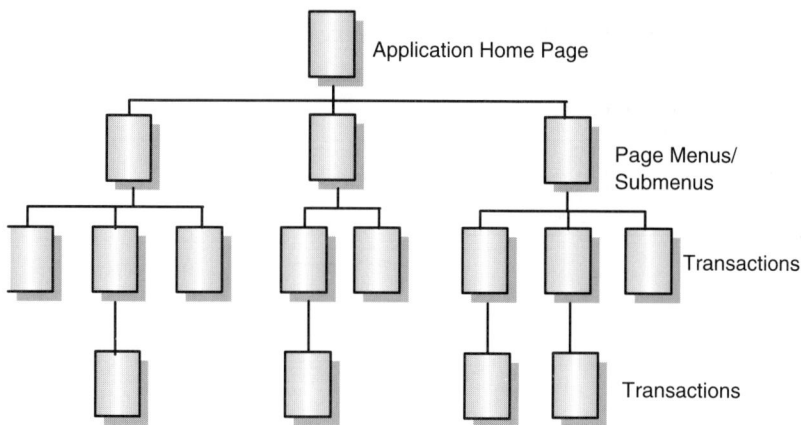

Figure 11–7 Web application hierarchical structure.

The hierarchical structure should enable the users to navigate through the different application functions in a structured fashion using a top-down approach. The application Web page structure should emulate as closely as possible the natural way in which the users would normally perform their business tasks, based on different user scenarios. The information provided by the Web application should be organized in such a way where the users are getting more and more detailed information as they navigate from the top levels down to the lower levels of the hierarchical Web page structure.

If this application is a large and rather complex one that requires a hierarchical structure with several levels of information clusters, then you might need to provide the power users with direct links to access quickly the pages/transactions that are located at the lower levels of the hierarchy. Otherwise, the users might be forced to unnecessarily follow a long path down the Web hierarchical structure to access a Web database transaction that is buried deep at the bottom of the hierarchy, several links away from the home page at the top level.

The hierarchical structure should also be designed to remain extensible. Doing so will ensure that when new business transactions are added to the current Web application structure, then the addition is done with a minimum impact on the existing sets of transactions. To keep the Web application structure flexible, use navigation links that are relative as opposed to absolute. A relative link can be more easily created and moved than an absolute link.

ADDITIONAL NAVIGATION AIDS

Several types of navigation aids other than graphical button bars, such as tables of contents and different pages of menus, can be advantageously used to help the power users rapidly access the various pages they require to perform their business tasks. These navigation aids are usually presented on a Web page under the form of hypertext textual or graphical links. Figure 11.8 shows an example of a generic Web application structure that contains an index page that points to all the pages of a Web database application.

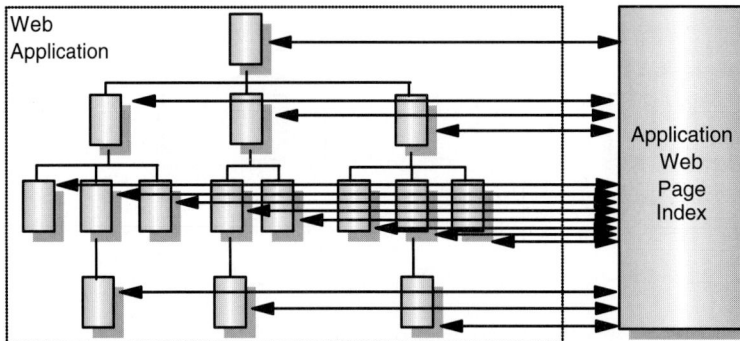

Figure 11–8 Application Web page index.

An index page can be used for relatively simple hierarchical structures. If the developers create an index page for the Web application at hand, you then should include, in the application tool bar that is located in the header section of each Web page, a hyperlink control that points to the index page. In the context of a large hierarchical structure, you might also use different local or specialized page indexes.

If textual navigation links are used to access different sections of a Web database application, then the hypertext textual links should be ordered in a logical sequence that naturally matches the way the user works. The most frequently used links should be positioned at the top of the list. The same sequence list should always be used consistently every time it is utilized in the Web application.

As a rule of thumb, the number of textual links shown in the list should not exceed 7 plus or minus 2 links. If you use more than 5 links, try to break the links into explicit groups. One advantage of using textual navigation links as opposed to graphics or small hot icons is that the users who utilize a text-only Web browser or have deactivated the graphical browsing facility of their Web browser will still be able to see the navigation links and use them.

Finally, ensure that the users never reach a dead-end page that contains no navigational options.

TYPEFACES

Certain Web browsers allow the Web designers to override the user preferences that were set in their Web browsers to view the content of a Web page with any typefaces they desire. A case in point is the Netscape Web browser, which has a tag called <Font Face>.

In many instances, you might prefer to respect the users' own preferences for typefaces. In some instances, though, you might need to override their choices of default typefaces to warrant that the Web browser displays a carefully designed Web page with its original typeface. Doing so will ensure that the original dimensions of certain display elements such as a table, for example, are not inadvertently modified by a sudden change of typeface when the client Web browser downloads the page.

FONTS

Be aware that font types are not always displayed identically on all computer platforms. For instance, a Web browser that displays a given font type in a Windows platform will appear approximately 2 to 4 points larger than the same font when it is displayed on a Macintosh platform. In some instances, this difference can seriously affect the look and feel of your Web page layout, when it is displayed on a different platform from the one originally used to design it.

FRAMES

Frames allow the display of a number of different panes in a browser window. In other words, with frames, you can display several HTML documents on a single Web page. The users can view, scroll, and update each specific frame independently of the other ones.

Frames can be quite effective to display various information elements that need to remain visible at all times in a specific pane of the Web browser display area, such as navigational buttons or textual links, for instance. The Web page is then broken into at least two frames, one which remains always visible. For example, a permanent frame placed on the left side of the browser display area can be used to list the different business transactions that are supported by a Web database application. As the users click on one of these links, the transaction data is displayed on the right side of the browser display area.

GRAPHICS

The use or abuse of graphics can seriously affect the response time of a Web database transaction system, especially for remote users that might need to access your Web application with a standard modem, via an Internet service provider.

As a rule of thumb, the more graphics you insert in your Web pages, the longer the users wait to download and display the Web pages on the client browsers. Assume a bandwidth of approximately 1 kbits/sec for an audience of Internet users who are primarily equipped with a combination of modems of different types, such as 9600, 14,400, or 28,800 bits per second.

If the Web database application will be used in the context of an intranet and the supporting ethernet network is not currently overused by other applications, then simple graphical elements might be used with moderation in the Web application to not overload the network capacity beyond its acceptable limits.

GIF FILES

The Graphic Interchange Format (GIF) is widely used to transmit various types of images across networks. The vast majority of Web browsers support the GIF file format for graphics. An effective compression algorithm is used to keep GIF files to a minimum size. The maximum number of colors supported by the GIF file format is 256. Since the compression algorithm does not cause any loss of data, the quality of the GIF pictures does not degrade when they are compressed to smaller sizes.

A typical non-interlaced GIF image will be downloaded from the Web server and displayed by the client Web browser one line of pixels at a time on the user screen, from top to bottom. In contrast, Web browsers that support the interlaced GIF file format quickly display on the user screen a full-sized interlaced GIF image, in a low-resolution mode, while it is still being downloaded from the Web server. Then the image will progressively come into focus over time. Interlaced GIF images are not downloaded more quickly than non-interlaced GIF images. However, interlaced GIF images provide the users with the advantage of quickly previewing the full area of the graphic.

The GIF89a file format allows one background color in the image to become completely transparent. Transparency is frequently used when you do not want the edges of the image to be displayed on the Web page.

JPEG FILES

The Joint Photographic Experts Group (JPEG) is another graphic file format that is widely used on the Web. In contrast to GIF images that can support only 256 colors, JPEG images can support full-color images containing more than 16,000,000 colors (24-bit true-color images). JPEG is used in Web applications when the quality of the image is paramount.

However, the more you compress a JPEG image significantly, the more the quality of the image will degrade accordingly. Like the interlaced GIF graphic file format, progressive JPEG images over standard JPEG images will be quickly displayed in their entirety at a low-level resolution as they are downloaded to then gradually come into focus over time.

> *If you decide to compress an image with JPEG, make sure you first save a copy of the uncompressed image in a safe location. Once the image has been compressed with JPEG, you cannot restore it back to its original condition. Thus, you might end up with a degraded image with no way to restore the image to its original level of resolution!*

Table 11.9 summarizes some of the benefits that can be associated with the GIF or JPEG graphics file formats.

Table 11–9 GIF Versus JPEG File Format Benefits

GIF GRAPHIC FILES	JPEG GRAPHIC FILES
• The GIF graphic file format is supported by the vast majority of Web browsers • The GIF graphic file format supports interlaced images and transparency • GIF images such as diagrams or sketches usually look sharper than equivalent JPEG images	• With the JPEG graphic file format, an image can be compressed quite significantly, even though it is a "lossy" format • JPEG can support more than 16,000,000 colors, as opposed to only 256 for GIF, which provides a larger range of colors • JPEG provides better-quality images than GIF for photographs, sophisticated artworks, or large illustrations

IMAGE MAPS

Image maps are graphics that contain "hotspots" that, once clicked over with the mouse, let the users access other areas of the Web application. As a rule of thumb, I recommend that you clearly identify the boundaries of the hotspots that are shown on image maps.

Two types of image maps exist: server-side and client-side. If the users click on a server-side image map, then the Web browser must send a request to the Web server. Subsequently, the Web server replies to this request by transmitting back the requested information. With a client-side image map, the Web browser does not need to connect to the Web server every time the users click on the image maps. The map information for the client-side image map is stored in the same HTML file that contains the image. Client-side image maps are useful when you want to minimize server traffic.

COLORED BACKGROUNDS

Most Web browsers allow you to select a specific color for the background of your Web pages. Usually, the default background color is either gray or white. For a Web database application, a neutral color such as a light gray for the background can be quite acceptable.

Several studies have demonstrated that the display of a white or soft gray background combined with the use of black text provides the best results possible for screen contrast and legibility. However, if you absolutely want to use a color background, soft colors that are not highly saturated are preferable to intense, provocative colors.

Several Web browsers allow the application developers to use different images or textures for the background of your Web pages. However, I do not recommend using these facilities, as the risk of increasing the download time of your Web pages and also decreasing the level of legibility of your textual material can be relatively high.

INTERACTIVE FORMS

Forms support interactive dialogs between the users and a Web application. They are used to input information, submit requests, and receive responses. The Web database applications use forms to create and support the set of business transactions that are required by the application. You can see the typical set of elements that can be used in a form in Table 11.10.

Table 11–10 Visual Form Elements

- Radio buttons
- Check boxes
- Pop-up menus
- Pull-down menus
- Scrolling menus
- Text fields

TABLES

Tables are similar to those used in traditional books or electronic spreadsheets. They structure information in rows and columns.

PLUG-INS APPLICATIONS

As you have seen in Chapter 9, several types of plug-in applications can be used to manipulate or display information that cannot be adequately supported by the Web browser itself. However, most plug-in applications must be configured properly if the users want to use them to display multimedia information in the Web browser's viewing window area.

If plug-in applications are used to extend the core functionality of the Web browser, make sure you clearly tell the users both how to configure them to achieve maximum efficiency and how to use them effectively.

VIDEO AND 3-D ANIMATION

Video and animation clips can sometimes advantageously complement the information that is displayed on static Web pages. They offer powerful ways to display motion pictures. Small video clips of limited duration can be very useful in the help facility to indicate to the users how to best use the application and answer the most common questions on how to use the different transactions supported by the application. However, the file sizes of even the smallest video clips can be substantial and might adversely overload the enterprise network. Also, some platform-specific requirements might need to be satisfied for the plug-in before being able to access and use the required video and animation sequences.

AUDIO AND SOUND FILES

Several audio formats are available to support the auditory requirements of the Web application. Inform the users of the plug-in applications that are necessary to use the audio clips provided by the application. Advise them how to download them, how to configure their Web browsers to invoke them, and how to use them.

WEB APPLICATION USABILITY CHECKLIST

Table 11.11 summarizes some of the most common usability elements that must be satisfied when designing any type of Web application. Although they are stated in general terms, this set of guidelines should provide a good foundation for better Web page design best practices.

Table 11–11 General Web Application Usability Checklist

Usability Characteristic	Description
Navigation	• Provide meaningful, descriptive labels on all navigation icons and images • Clearly delineate the hot regions of an image map and verify that users can differentiate static graphics from graphical links • Provide navigation aids consistently on the top and bottom of each Web page under the form of button bars or textual links • Provide a local search facility mechanism inside the application • Provide index and menu pages as additional navigation aids to the home page's table of contents • In menu pages, group transactions into logical categories • Avoid dead-end pages that have no navigation links • Provide aids to navigate downward or upward in the application hierarchical structure, which is made of different levels of Web pages • For the power or frequent users, provide optional routes to reach the most frequently used Web database transactions • Minimize the need to scroll and resize the Web pages • If the users make errors, provide alternative links so they can recover from their mistakes rapidly and easily

Table 11–11 General Web Application Usability Checklist (cont.)

Structure	• Organize the Web database application in a hierarchical structure that matches the natural steps the users follow to perform their business tasks; try to limit the structure to a maximum of three levels • Provide a panoramic view of the structure and content of the complete Web application, at the application home page level, where the users will normally enter the application • Provide meaningful page titles and subtitles to situate the users • Use consistency while designing the application pages
Accessibility	• Provide users who are equipped with text-only Web browsers with options for perusing information in a textual manner and with textual navigation links • Provide users with the option of downloading pages more quickly without having to wait unduly for large images or multimedia elements to download • Support a variety of different Web browsers if the application will be used on the Internet as opposed to an intranet
Readability	• Use font sizes that can be easily read from a comfortable distance of the screen and from different positions • Minimize the use of different types of fonts • Use backgrounds and colors on which text pages can be easily read and images easily viewed • Use terminology that is familiar to the users; avoid technical or business jargon • Provide clear, meaningful error messages
Efficiency	• Use small images with less color for faster performance • Keep the pages sizes as small as possible; use multiple pages to break up a large text; as a rule of thumb, keep the average page size below 50 KB, including both text and image files • Repeat the same images whenever possible, since once an image is downloaded, subsequently it will likely be accessed from the local memory cache instead of being downloaded again from the server • Use interlaced images, since they are usually perceived by the users to download more quickly than the non-interlaced images

WEB APPLICATION HELP FACILITIES

Several HTML-based help facilities have emerged to display online help in support of Web-based software applications. At least three major software companies have come up with their own HTML-based help standards, as indicated in Table 11.12.

Netscape and Microsoft have extended the functionality of standard HTML in order to support help-specific traditional features. Some of the help-specific features that have been implemented might include interactive tables of contents, standard naviga-

Table 11–12 HTML-based Help Authoring Facilities

Microsoft	HTML Help	http://www.microsoft.com/workshop/author/htmlhelp
Netscape	NetHelp	http://home.netscape.com/eng/help
Sun	JavaHelp	http://www.javasoft.com

tional control buttons, pop-ups, custom window sizing and placement, file compression capabilities, linking of an application with HTML files, help index, and full-text search controls. Unfortunately, the end result is two standards that currently are still proprietary in nature, even though both use the HTML standard as a common basis.

Microsoft's HTML Help uses ActiveX controls and is tightly integrated with the Internet Explorer Web browser. In fact, at the time of writing this book, Internet Explorer must be installed on the client workstation to allow HTML Help to work properly. This limitation might restrict the use of HTML Help to a Microsoft-centric development platform.

Netscape's NetHelp needs a Netscape Web browser to work properly. However, the Netscape Web browser is supported on several platforms, such as UNIX, Windows, Macintosh, and OS/2. Consequently, NetHelp can be used as a cross-platform help solution, provided that your organization is willing to use the Netscape Web browser as a cross-platform standard.

Sun has developed a standard called JavaHelp. The JavaHelp standard allows HTML-based help to be linked to Java applications, Java applets, and JavaBeans components. However, developers can also use JavaHelp for applications that are not necessarily Java-based. The JavaHelp standard will work on any computing platform that supports the Java Virtual Machine in their Web browsers and applications.

A variety of software vendors also provide software authoring tools specifically aimed at developing help-based applications. Some of these automated help authoring tools support the Microsoft- and Netscape-specific help-based standards. The use of these tools can increase the productivity of developers because they might prove to be quite user-friendly and powerful in terms of automated help-based features.

The following Web site addresses provide more information on some of these software help authoring tools.

http://www.blue-sky.com	RoboHELP
http://www.wextech.com	Doc-To-Help
http://www.ff.com	ForeHTML
http://www.hyperact.com	eAuthor/Site

Finally, Table 11.13 lists some of the most common features to look for in a Web-based help authoring tool.

Table 11–13 Web-based Help Authoring Tools Selection Criteria

Characteristics	Tool 1	Tool ...	Tool N
Provide support for standard HTML tags			
Provide support for Netscape's NetHelp standards			
Provide support for Microsoft's HTML Help standards			
Provide support for the following HTML-based help features: • Pop-up windows • Interactive table of contents • Customizable window screens • Navigational control buttons • Keyword indexes • Full-text search capabilities • GIF/JPEG image files • Image maps • Frames • Watermarks • Different font and background colors			
Provide support for HTML-based help file compression			
Provide support for a list of additional topics that relate to the current topic			
Provide support for the creation of paper-based documentation			
Provide spell-checking facilities			
Provide documentation, technical support, and training			
Provide support for converting legacy help files to the newer HTML-based help format			
Provide support for Java applets			
Provide support for JavaScript			

11.3 CLIENT-SIDE AND SERVER-SIDE PROGRAMMING

This section discusses different topics related to the different programming and scripting languages that you can use to develop Web database applications.

11.3.1 CLIENT-SIDE PROGRAMMING VERSUS SCRIPTING OPTIONS

You have several ways to extend the functionality of a Web application by executing some application code segments directly on the client workstation, as opposed to running all the application logic on the server. Well designed and tested client-side programs can sometimes provide several benefits to the developers of large and complex Web database applications, as indicated in Table 11.14.

Table 11–14 Client-side Programming Benefits

- Improve the overall application's responsiveness
- Liberate the Web server for other tasks
- Allow for more thorough programming solutions

A common approach that is frequently used to develop and execute some application code logic on a client workstation involves programming or scripting solutions such as the use of Java applets or various client-side scripting languages, as indicated in Figure 11.9.

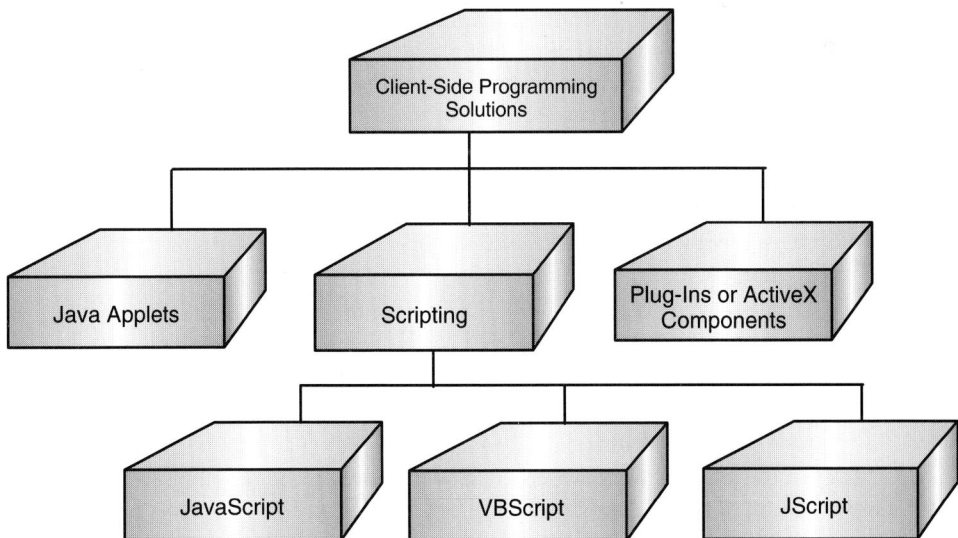

Figure 11–9 Client-side programming solutions.

You can have some potential security exposures that are inherent to the script code runtime interpreter engines that are used to execute Web scripting language programs.

As you see later in more detail, JavaScript and VBScript application routines are segments of logic code that are embedded into an HTML Web page, which will run immediately on the client workstation machine when the Web page is downloaded.

Contrary to these client-side application scripting options, Java theoretically offers a more secure environment, based on the built-in security features that were originally developed for this distributed programming language. For instance, the Java compiler checks the Java source code to ensure that unsafe operations such as attempts to access unknown memory segments with pointers are disallowed.

The next four sections briefly discuss Sun Microsystems Corp.'s Java programming language and two popular Web scripting languages that were briefly mentioned in the text above, namely Netscape JavaScript and Microsoft JScript.

Before you move ahead, note that several different Web browsers are still out there. Nonetheless, the Netscape and Microsoft Web browsers rule the market at approximately a 90% penetration level, if not more. For this reason, in the next sections, I arbitrarily limit the discussion on Web browsers' compatibility strictly to these two commercial products.

JAVA APPLETS

Java is a computer programming language that was developed by Sun Microsystems. Java can run on a variety of computing platforms, including UNIX, OS/2, Windows, and Macintosh, for instance. In fact, Java is more than a programming language; it is a software platform that can be used to execute applications on different networked computers. The Java platform resides on top of current computing platforms and executes bytecodes. Bytecodes are not specific to any particular physical computer, but are machine instructions for a virtual machine. Figure 11.10 illustrates a generic development environment that is used to code and run Java programs on different computing platforms.

First, a program is coded with the Java language. Then the program source code (.java) file is compiled to a bytecode (.class) file. At run time, the bytecode can be executed on any operating system on which the Java platform has been set up. In fact, the bytecode represents instructions that are interpreted by a Java interpreter, called the Java Virtual Machine.

With the support of a Java-enabled Web browser, the developers can create and run a special form of Java programs, which are referred to as applets, that can be downloaded from the Web server and can run as executables on the client workstations, inside a Web browser.

Being able to automatically download a Java applet from a Web server and run it on a client workstation can present an advantage for the application developers. They do not have to be concerned with providing the users with various helper applications that they need to install.

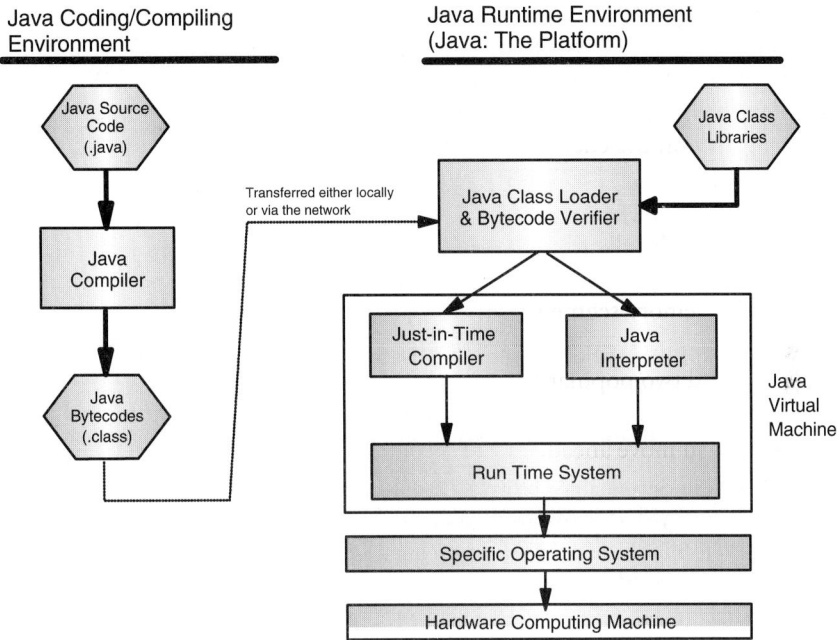

Figure 11–10 Generic Java-based computing platform.

Java applets can be used for various purposes such as displaying graphics, sounds, and animation that the users can directly interact with, in a live manner. They can also be favorably used in commercial business applications for form input validation on the client side, for instance. The application validations can then be done directly on the client workstation, saving unnecessary roundtrips to the server.

This technique can be useful for large and complex Web database applications for which response time is critical. It is quite a departure from the standard CGI approach, in which a client form submission must be sent to the server, which then triggers a CGI process to handle the data that was passed in the form. With the CGI method, if the input data is invalid, then a message must be returned back from the server to the client machine indicating that the data that was submitted is invalid. The user must then correct the data and resubmit it.

Figure 11.11 illustrates schematically how a Java-enabled browser downloads from a Web server a Web page that contains a Java applet and executes it on the client workstation.

Table 11.15 provides a description of the major steps involved in downloading a Java applet.

Table 11.16 lists some important points about Java applets.

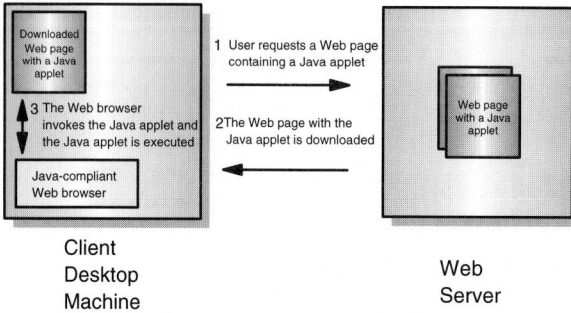

Figure 11–11 Java applet downloading process.

Table 11–15 Steps Involved In Downloading A Java Applet

STEP 1: The Java-enabled browser downloads a Web page from the Web server, following a request from a user to get an HTML document.

STEP 2: The downloaded Web page contains an HTML applet tag. This is a specific tag, which indicates to the Java-enabled Web browser that a special class of a Java program, called an applet, is associated with the Web page that was just downloaded.

STEP 3: The client Web browser downloads the Java program file, which is identified as an attribute of the HTML applet tag. The exact location where this file resides is also provided in the applet tag.

STEP 4: The client Web browser then interprets the information stored in the Java program file, which contains bytecode instructions that are directly executed on the user's machine. (Note: The original source code for the Java applet had been previously compiled by a Java compiler, which transformed the Java source code into bytecode instructions.)

STEP 5: The user then interacts with the Java applet program, based on the application functionality supported by the applet. No further downloads from the Web server are required to use the Java applet, since the bytecode contains all the instructions required to interpret the applet.

Tables 11.17 and 11.18 provide a brief description of the two major Java programming language constructs that can be used to develop distributed applications for the Web and the major components that are included in the Java Developer's Kit (JDK).

A more detailed description of the Java language and the Java Developer's Kit in general is well beyond the scope of this book. However, you can find extensive information on Java on the Web in general and particularly at the following Sun Microsystems Java site:

http://java.sun.com

Table 11–16 Additional Java Applet Considerations

- The download and execution of the Java applet on the user workstation is done in a manner that is completely transparent to the users. In other words, the download and execution processes are entirely automated and do not require any direct involvement from the user, other than downloading a Web page that contains an *applet* tag.
- The Java applet executable is platform-independent. The application developers do not need to worry about which type of computer platform the users utilize, as long as a Java interpreter, or in this case a Java-enabled browser, has been installed on their computer.
- The Java language has been built from the ground up with several security features that make it a relatively secure software environment compared to other client-side programming environments. For instance, one of the security features includes a bytecode validation routine that is embedded in the Java interpreter software. This verification routine ensures that the Java code instructions do not attempt to create pointers or access restricted memory. It also verifies that objects cannot be accessed other than according to their definition.

Table 11–17 Java Programming Language Constructs

Applets	Java programs that are associated with Web pages via the HTML *applet* tag. They are downloaded from the Web server and executed by a Java-enabled Web browser.
Applications	Java applications are usually large, standalone Java programs that are executed without the need of a Web browser. The Java application is interpreted and executed by a Java interpreter.

Table 11–18 Java Developer's Kit

Java applet viewer	The Java applet viewer is used to execute and test applets without creating an HTML Web page to reference them.
Java compiler	The Java compiler is used to generate machine-readable bytecodes from Java source code instructions.
Java debugger API	The Java debugger API is a command-line debugger, which is used to help debug Java applets or applications.
Java language runtime	The Java language runtime is the environment used to interpret Java applets or applications.

JAVASCRIPT

Netscape Communications Corporation developed JavaScript. JavaScript can be utilized as a client-side oriented application programming language that works well, especially with the Netscape Web browser. With JavaScript, developers can integrate different Web application components on an HTML page and turn them into a comprehensive Web application. Some of these components can include multiple elements such as HTML scripts and Java applets, for instance.

Among other things, JavaScript can also be used to actively verify and validate form data and improve the graphical user interface of the Web pages. This validation process is done on the client workstation, hence avoiding the need to send the input data stream across the network to execute the business logic on the server side and then send it back to the user for display if an input data field is invalid.

Intensive form validation processing that is performed on the server side might work relatively well, as long as your users are connected via an ethernet network for an intranet environment or even via an ISDN line. Otherwise, extensive server-side validation activities can sometimes have serious disadvantages, such as a poor response time.

Table 11.19 shows a generic template for a typical JavaScript program, embedded in an HTML Web page.

Table 11–19 A Generic Javascript Template

```
<HTML>
<HEAD>
<TITLE> A Sample of a JavaScript Template </TITLE>
</HEAD>
<BODY>
<SCRIPT LANGUAGE = "JavaScript">
<!-- This is a comment section that I hope will be ignored by non-compliant
JavaScript Web browsers
*** Insert the complete JavaScript code here *** -->
</SCRIPT>
</BODY>
</HTML>
```

When a JavaScript-compliant Web browser encounters the JavaScript code that is inserted in an HTML page (the script code is embedded inside the opening *<SCRIPT LANGUAGE = XXX>* tag and its closing argument *</SCRIPT>*), a built-in JavaScript interpreter then executes all the script program code. The script code can be inserted in either the <HEAD> or the <BODY> section of an HTML page.

JavaScript is tightly associated with the Netscape technology framework. Similarly, the JavaScript language and Netscape Web browser are in constant evolution. Several different versions of the Netscape Web browser might be used out there on the Internet. These different Web browser versions might not be fully backward-compatible with previous versions of the script interpreter.

In such a diversified and fast-evolving environment, a potentially quite difficult and cumbersome task is creating and maintaining Web pages that contain script code and that work flawlessly even with different releases of the same Netscape Web browser product. To achieve such a task, you might need to insert specific application logic segments to verify the appropriate version number of the Web browser. This approach can be restrictive, since the incompatibility problems can extend not only to different versions of the same Web browser product and JavaScript language, but also to different operating system platforms.

JavaScript can also be used for server-side application development tasks. JavaScript is tightly integrated with a Netscape product called LiveWire and also the Netscape family of Web servers.

In a specific Netscape technology framework, the Netscape Web servers, LiveWire, and JavaScript products are designed to provide a complete but proprietary back-end processing solution for file and database manipulations, without needing to resort to standard CGI scripts. With the assistance of another Netscape product called Live-Connect, you can link together technologies such as Java, Netscape plug-ins, and JavaScripts. You can develop scripts that modify Java applets, or you can create Java applets that invoke different script functions. You can also have plug-ins that communicate with Java applets.

Netscape Communications has developed an automated Java-based scripting tool called Visual JavaScript. As indicated by its name, Visual JavaScript provides a visual drag-and-drop programming interface. It also provides the ability to embed Java-Beans, which are Java-wrapped components, into an HTML page and a Web-based application. Furthermore, Visual JavaScript supports the OMG's Common Object Request Broker Architecture (CORBA/IIOP) communication standard.

JSCRIPT

Microsoft has created its own version of JavaScript, called JScript. JScript was intended to be a full implementation of JavaScript but with extensions that were designed to work specifically with the Microsoft Internet Explorer Web browser. JavaScript and JScript are two Web-scripting implementations that are similar in several manners but that also contain some unique features that are supported only by their specific Web browsers.

The essential differences in features can limit the use of these two scripting languages to their specific Web browser, which can potentially eliminate a significantly large number of Web visitors. This statement is especially true in the context of the Internet environment. A JavaScript-powered Web page might not work well in the Internet Explorer Web browser while a JScript-powered Web page might not work well in the Netscape Web browser.

Although you might be able to create cross-browser script code that can run in both Netscape and Microsoft Web browsers, this option might turn out to be a less-than-optimal programming solution in the long run, particularly for industrial-strength, mission-critical Web applications. This approach would mean creating and maintaining code that uses standard scripting features that are common to both languages. Unique features that are particular to one of the scripting language could be implemented in such a way that they can run in the specific Web browser that supports them but be bypassed by the other Web browser. However, the users should definitely be advised that the script utilizes a feature that is not supported by their Web browser. Another alternative would be to try to code some equivalent functionality that can work with the other Web browser and activate one of the two sets of equivalent functions, depending on the type of Web browser that is favored by the users.

Like JavaScript, JScript can also be used for server-side programming tasks, when utilized with a Microsoft-compatible Web server that supports the Active-XActiveX/ Active Server Page technology. The ActiveX technology is similar to the Netscape Live-Connect technology. It is a framework used to link various Microsoft technologies such as ActiveX controls, JScripts, and Java applets.

If you want more information on JavaScript, look on the Web in general and particularly at the following Netscape Web site:

http://home.netscape.com/eng/mozilla/3.0/handbook/javascript/index.html

If you want more information on JScript, look on the Web in general and particularly at the following Microsoft Web site:

http://www.microsoft.com/jscript/us/techinfo/jscript.doc

VBSCRIPT

VBScript is an interpreted scripting solution developed by Microsoft. Like any other interpretive language, the script code does not need to be compiled. The script code is interpreted directly, on a line-by-line basis, at the time it is executed by the client's Web browser. To be able to execute the script code, a VBScript interpreter is required. A VBScript interpreter is automatically installed with the Microsoft Internet Explorer browser product.

VBScript is a derivative of Microsoft Visual Basic programming language. VBScript can be used as a client-side programming language to verify form data, prompt the users on the same Web page with a message when a user has entered invalid input data, perform various calculations, and do other similar small application programming tasks. For example, you can use it to create interactive menus and buttons to Web pages.

VBScript was designed by Microsoft to interact with Active-XActiveX controls, meaning that ActiveX objects can be embedded in VBScript programs and their attributes can be modified by VBScript.

Table 11.20 shows a generic template for a typical VBScript program, embedded in an HTML Web page.

Table 11–20 A Generic Vbscript Template

```
<HTML>
<HEAD>
<TITLE> A Sample of a VBScript Template </TITLE>
</HEAD>
<BODY>
<SCRIPT LANGUAGE = "VBScript">
<!-- This is a comment section that I hope will be ignored by non-compliant
VBScript Web browsers
*** Insert the complete VBScript code here *** -->
</SCRIPT>
</BODY>
</HTML>
```

The begin tag *<SCRIPT>* indicates where the VBScript code starts, and the end tag *</SCRIPT>*, where it terminates. The *<SCRIPT>* tag's attribute *LANGUAGE* indicates to the Web browser that this is a VBScript program. Note that to attempt to avoid problems with non-compliant VBScript browsers, the begin tag *<SCRIPT>* is immediately followed by a comment tag.

Only Microsoft Internet Explorer fully supports VBScript. For this reason, VBScript generally turns out to be a more viable programming alternative for Microsoft-oriented development environments. Some products out there might allow the use of Active-XActiveX controls with VBScript in the Netscape Web browser, but the functionality supported by such tools might be limited.

Based on the ferocious competition that exists between the major Web technology providers, a competing browser to Microsoft's Internet Explorer is very unlikely to be able to interpret the latest enhancements to the VBScript language right the first time. The same logic also applies to the Netscape JavaScript language and Web browser. The major Web technology providers want to gain market share by differentiating their products as much as possible from the competition, and consequently they have no incentive to publicly share information on the new features that their scripting language will support in the next releases.

If you want more detailed information on VBScript and other related Microsoft products such as ActiveX, look on the Web in general and particularly at the following Microsoft Web sites:

http://www.microsoft.com/vbscript
http://www.microsoft.com/activex/controls
http://www.microsoft.com/intdev

CLIENT-SIDE WEB SCRIPTING: THE CONCLUSION

To conclude, the use of JavaScript might be more appropriate for an intranet application development environment that utilizes Netscape Web browser clients and Web server technologies. JScript and VBScript are usually more appropriate for intranet environments that use Microsoft Web browser clients and Web server technologies.

Due to the different variations that exist among the different implementations of the JavaScript languages supported by Netscape Communications and Microsoft Corporation, neither JavaScript nor VBScript nor JScript can be safely used to develop stable, mission-critical Web applications in large corporate, cross-platform environments. Java, with its support by both the UNIX and Microsoft operating system kernels, is likely to be a more viable alternative for large-scale, cross-platform development.[1]

---

1. The European Computer Manufacturers Association (ECMA) has recently proposed an industry-wide standard for JavaScript. However, it is yet too early to see whether the new emerging JavaScript standard will help resolve the current disparities that exist among the multiple vendor implementations of the JavaScript language. For more information on the forthcoming JavaScript language standard, you can access the following Web site: http://www.ecma.ch and search for the standard ECMA_262.

As a last resort, the developers themselves must decide if the inclusion of propri-etary script code in an HTML Web page will bring enough benefits that will outweigh the risks of non-compatibility with rival Web browser products or even with a future release of a given Web browser product.

11.3.2 WEB SERVER-SIDE PROGRAMMING

The right-hand side of Figure 11.12 shows some of the different programming and scripting languages that can be used to develop application logic code that runs on the server machine. The following section briefly discusses some of the most common server-side programming options.

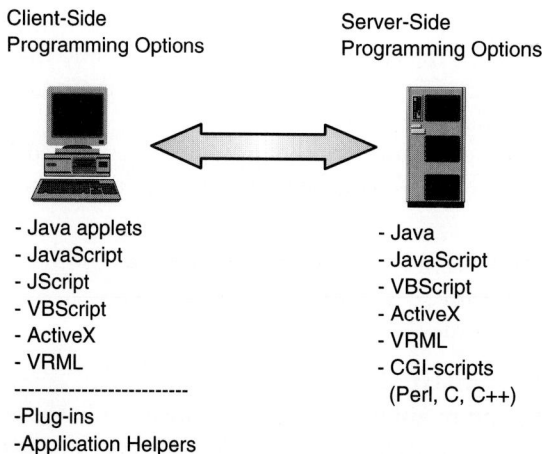

Client-Side
Programming Options

Server-Side
Programming Options

- Java applets
- JavaScript
- JScript
- VBScript
- ActiveX
- VRML

-Plug-ins
-Application Helpers

- Java
- JavaScript
- VBScript
- ActiveX
- VRML
- CGI-scripts
  (Perl, C, C++)

Figure 11–12 Different programming/scripting languages options.

COMMON GATEWAY INTERFACE (CGI) SCRIPTS

The Common Gateway Interface is a Web standard that outlines how external pro-grams are utilized on Web servers. CGI scripts, which are commonly referred to as gateway scripts, are external programs that are executed on the Web server and that act as gateways between the Web server and other applications. With CGI scripts, devel-opers can create interactive Web applications that dynamically interface with corpo-rate databases at the back end.

Figure 11.13 illustrates how a CGI script that is used to access a database is executed.

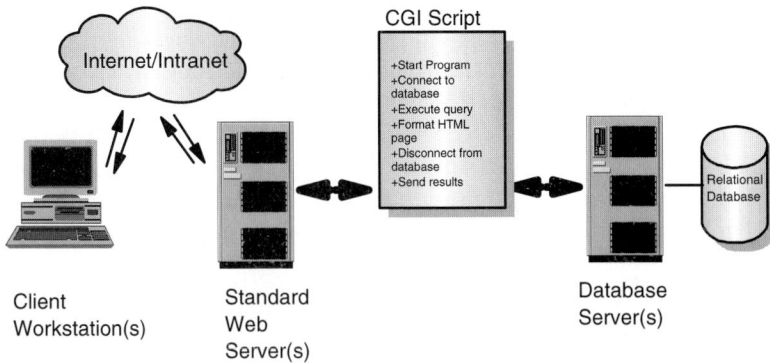

Figure 11–13 CGI scripting process.

The detailed access steps are described next.

STEP 1: The user's browser passes input data to the Web server.

STEP 2: The server passes the received input data to a CGI script.

STEP 3: The CGI script processes the input data and, if necessary, passes them to another application for further processing. When the work is completed, the resulting output is sent back to the Web server.

STEP 4: The Web server passes the output back to the user's browser, which finally displays the output back to the user.

CGI scripts can be created with a large variety of programming languages that can generate an executable file. Some of the most common programming languages that are frequently used to create gateway scripts appear in Table 11.21.

Table 11–21 Common Languages Used To Create CGI Scripts

• C	• C++
• Visual Basic	• Perl
• Bourne, C, or Korn UNIX Shell Scripting Languages	• TCL

All the different languages that appear in Table 11.21 can be used to write CGI scripts. The selection of a particular CGI scripting language over another one will vary, depending on your specific needs, current level of proficiency with some of these languages, and the type of platform that houses your Web server.

The Practical Extraction and Report Language (PERL) is especially popular for creating CGI scripts because of its advanced text manipulation characteristics and its widespread use on different computer platforms, including UNIX and PC-Intel machines. For the same reasons, C and C++ are also two other programming languages that are widely popular for creating CGI scripts.

The gateway scripts are located on the Web server. Typically, they are executed in the background to perform various tasks, such as processing the following:

- filled-out forms that the users submitted
- database queries and updates
- index searches
- documents that are interactively created on the fly

The script triggering mechanism is done automatically, without the user even being aware of it.

Scripts that reside on the Web server are commonly referred to as server-side scripts, as opposed to client-side scripts, which are embedded in HTML documents and executed by the user's browsers. Two popular client-side scripting languages are JavaScript and VBScript.

JAVA PROGRAMS EXECUTED ON THE SERVER SIDE

Java can be used to create standalone programs that are executed on the Web server side. One potential advantage of using Java on the server side, as opposed to the other CGI scripting languages, is its strong object-orientation, intrinsic security features, and its platform independence.

Key Graphical User Interface Concepts

12.1 INTRODUCTION

This chapter provides a discussion on various topics that apply to the design of client-server graphical user interfaces. Section 11.2 in Chapter 11 provides a more specific coverage for the design of Web-oriented graphical user interfaces.

12.2 ANATOMY OF A WINDOW

This section provides an overview and a brief description of the major graphical components of a window. It also suggests some basic design guidelines and advice for their creation.

Some of the GUI design guidelines that I discuss in this section might be platform-specific. For the most part, the GUI design guidelines in Table 12.1 generally apply to a Windows environment. However, you can consult the references that are provided at the end of this book if you need more information on this subject, particularly for the Windows, Macintosh, OS/2, or UNIX platforms.

Table 12–1 Window Definition

- A graphical user interface (GUI) window is an area on the display screen that contains various graphical objects (with different attributes and behaviors) that are used to exchange information between the user and the computer.
- Several windows can be shown on the screen, overlapping with one another. The user can interact with only one active window at a time, which usually appears to overlay the other windows.
- A window can display data, request data from a user, or respond to a user in reaction to some mouse or keyboard actions.

Sub-sections 12.2.1 to 12.2.8 provide brief descriptions of the major categories of visual objects that can be inserted into a typical graphical user interface window.

12.2.1 TITLE BAR

The title bar uniquely identifies a window. Table 12.2 provides some basic design guidelines for title bars.

Table 12–2 Window Title Bar Guidelines

The name of the window should always describe the type of functionality that is supported by the window.

12.2.2 MENU BAR

The menu bar contains the list of commands that the user can utilize to interact with the application. The commands that are displayed on the menu bar are used to navigate through the application, perform application functions, or set data values.

Table 12.3 provides some important menu bar guidelines.

Table 12–3 Menu Bar Guidelines

The menu bar is one of the prime tools that is put at the disposal of the user to navigate through the business application windows. Consequently, you need to organize the menu structure in the most efficient manner possible, adopting a user-centric design standpoint. • Menu items that are used repeatedly in several applications should be always named and sequenced consistently from application to application, such as: File Edit View Options Application Window Help The *Application* menu item contains the detailed submenu extensions that are specific to the application at hand. The *Options* menu item is generally a reserved area where the users are permitted to customize their GUI work environment, based on their own preferences. Sometimes, the Options menu is displayed as a submenu under the View menu. • Always provide a *Help* menu item to the users. The help menu item is generally provided at the very end of the menu bar. • Menu names should be short and descriptive of their purpose. Usually, a unique active verb or representative name is used to describe the menu item. Never use more than one or two words.

12.2.3 DROP-DOWN MENU

A drop-down menu displays the set of commands that appears when a user selects a specific menu item on the menu bar. A drop-down menu lets the users browse and select various submenu operations without the need to memorize commands. It also keeps application details out of the users' immediate sight.

Table 12.4 provides some drop-down menu guidelines.

Table 12–4 Drop-down Menu Guidelines

- Menu commands, which are frequently accessed by the users, should always have keystroke (i.e., shortcut keys) equivalents. For example, the Close menu item keystroke equivalent should be Ctrl+O.
- Each menu item should have an accelerator key, which allows the user to select a menu item directly from the keyboard, usually by pressing 'ALT+key' when the menu is displayed on the screen. The accelerator key is shown with an underline under a specific letter in the menu item name, for example, Close.
- Logically related menu commands should be regrouped together and separated from other groups of commands, under the same menu item, with straight lines.

12.2.4 CASCADING MENU

A cascading menu displays additional menu items only when a user needs to see them. It hides complexity from the user.

Table 12.5 presents basic cascading menu guidelines.

Table 12–5 Cascading Menu Guidelines

Use cascading menus sparingly, since users often find them awkward to navigate. Use them only when you must provide additional options or information to the user.

12.2.5 POP-UP MENU

A pop-up menu allows the user to initiate actions by popping up a menu within the window, instead of at the top of the window. They are context-sensitive and they are displayed at the window location where the user is working currently.

Table 12.6 presents some pop-up menu guidelines.

Table 12–6 Pop-up Menu Guidelines

- Pop-up menus are handy for experienced users who need quick access to a subset of the most frequently used operations they perform in a window or those operations that directly relate to the control element currently selected. They are also useful in windows where space is limited.
- A potential drawback with pop-up menus is that an inexperienced user has no visual clue that a pop-up menu is available.

12.2.6 STATUS AREA

A status area usually displays at the bottom of the window to show status information and various messages to the user. Status information is context-sensitive.

12.2.7 TOOLBAR

A toolbar consists of a collection of icon buttons that are usually displayed across the top of the screen. Each icon button represents a frequently used application function. Table 12.7 provides some basic guidelines on the use of toolbars.

Table 12–7 Toolbar Design Guidelines

- As a rule of thumb, the number of icon buttons displayed on a toolbar should range between five and nine buttons. Too many icons in a toolbar might cause an information overload and confuse the users rather than truly helping them out.
- Related toolbar icons should be regrouped together. Each group of icons should be delimited by spaces between them.
- Make sure that the users have the option of hiding the toolbar if they desire to do so. Users that work with smaller display screens appreciate this feature, since toolbars can occupy significant screen real estate.
- An application function that can be triggered by clicking an icon button on the toolbar should also be available via the application menu.
- The icons on the toolbar should be properly labeled. A brief description of the icon's purpose should be displayed when the user moves the mouse over them, since representing certain functions with appropriate icons that are truly intuitive is sometimes very hard.

12.2.8 SUMMARY

Table 12.8 presents a summary of the major menu-related design guidelines that I cover earlier in this section.

Table 12–8 Summary Of Menu Design Guidelines

- All frequently used menu items should always have a keyboard equivalent, allowing the power user to interact with the application without the use of a mouse
- A standard Help menu item should always be available to the users
- Menu items that, in specific contexts, are not available to users should be disabled by displaying them either like dimmed text or grayed out
- Use meaningful but short menu descriptions
- Group together menu items that share similar functionality and provide line separators between each specific group of menu items

Table 12–8 Summary Of Menu Design Guidelines (cont.)

- Create a toolbar for menu item features that users frequently utilize
- Do not go deeper than one level down when using a cascading menu
- All application-specific business functions are normally displayed via a pull-down menu

12.3 THE DIFFERENT TYPES OF WINDOWS

You can use several different types of windows to design the graphical user interface. Each type of window possesses some unique characteristics that make it the best choice for satisfying specific user needs. This section provides an overview and a brief description of the different types of windows that you can use to design the graphical user interface.

12.3.1 MAIN WINDOW

The main windows are the windows where the users perform the most important business activities that are supported by the application. Main windows are independent of all other windows. A main window is usually utilized as the prime anchor for a typical application.

12.3.2 CHILD WINDOW

A main window uses a child window to display additional information that might be required when the user performs an activity that is supported by the application. A child window is usually opened from a main window, which then can be defined as the child window's parent. A child window can exist only within the boundary of its parent window.

12.3.3 RESPONSE WINDOW

A response window notifies the users that the application has identified a peculiar condition that requires some form of action from them. The users must respond to the request before they can continue to use the application. Response windows often confirm operations that can be irreversible, such as deletes, or they simply display error or warning messages.

12.3.4 POP-UP WINDOW

A pop-up window is usually opened from another window. It is primarily a supporting window that displays additional information.

12.3.5 MULTIPLE DOCUMENT INTERFACE (MDI) WINDOW

An MDI window is a window that contains within its boundary (called a frame) multiple windows (called sheets). The sheets display different instances or views of the same document types or files. The user can navigate among the different window sheets. A typical example of a commercial MDI application is the Microsoft Word for Windows.

12.3.6 DESIGNING MODAL VERSUS MODELESS WINDOWS

A modal window is a window in which the user must somehow respond to information that is displayed in it, prior to being able to continue working on other business tasks. The *response* window type described in Section 12.3.3 is a modal window. A modeless window is a window whereby the user can initiate other tasks and access other windows without being obliged to react to the information that is currently displayed in the active window. The *main* window type described in Section 12.3.1 is a modeless window.

As a rule of thumb, system designers should carefully analyze the natural workflow of business activities and tasks that are performed by the users and the interrelationships that might exist among them. The creation of user scenarios can also serve this purpose. Wherever feasible, designers should create modeless windows that allow the users to manipulate different business transactions simultaneously and independently of one another. In other words, users should have immediate access to other windows and menus, whenever necessary.

The appropriate design of modeless windows is very important, since in a real-life environment, users might often need to perform a second or even third transaction while in the middle of processing a first transaction. For example, an order entry clerk who currently processes a customer order request might need to invoke a second window to answer a very important customer call to inquire about the status of an order. Once the second request is completed, then the user can resume the first business task and pick up the first transaction where she originally left off.

12.4 THE DIFFERENT CATEGORIES OF USERS

This section discusses the various categories of users that might be called upon to work with the client-server application. It also offers suggestions to mitigate the risks of designing a user interface that does not address well the distinct needs of different types of users.

12.4.1 TYPES OF USERS

One of the most critical success factors in designing a user-friendly graphical user interface is to develop a thorough understanding of who the users of the application are and how they accomplish their business tasks.

The user interface must be designed through the eyes of the customers. To this end, you might want to develop a brief profile of the application users or groups of users. A user profile is composed of different characteristics and facts that best describe your users.

Although space prohibits a complete explanation of all the tasks that developers can undertake to develop such profiles, the set of questions that you see in Table 12.9 should give them a good head start on this subject.

Table 12–9 Developing Application User Profiles

- How do the users work?
- How well do they know the business tasks that will be supported by the application?
- How do they perform their current tasks now?
- What are their current skill levels?
- How knowledgeable are the users about computers?
- With what computer concepts and terminology are the users familiar?
- When will they use the application?
- Where will they use the application?
- How often will the users work with the application?
- What type of training will be provided to them?
- What type of technical support will be provided to them?
- Might any specific environmental issues affect the type of input devices that will interact with the application?
- Are some users physically impaired and needing the graphical user interface to be adjusted accordingly?
- Must you take special cultural considerations into consideration while designing the interface?

If you will provide minimal training or technical support to the users, then design the graphical user interface with features that will provide more direct support to the users. Also, an occasional user might require a more intuitive GUI design than regular users, who learn the system more quickly.

For an application that will support a very large and diversified user audience, you might want to document the user profile information in the form of a simple matrix, as indicated in Table 12.10. Following is a brief description of Table 12.10 headings:

- User Category: Executive, middle management, line management, data entry operators, blue collar, white collar, secretary, professional, etc.

- Level of Expertise: Low, medium, high.

- Frequency of Use: Occasional, medium, frequent, heavy.

- Preferred GUI Characteristics: Easy to use, flexible, optimized for operational speed, and so forth.

Table 12–10 Application User Profile(S)

User Category	Level of Expertise	Frequency of Use	Preferred GUI Characteristics
Executive	Low	Occasional	Ease of use
Middle management	Medium	Medium	Flexible
...	...	...	...
Data Entry Operator	High	Heavy	Speed and accuracy

Table 12.11 provides a generic profile of three common types of users who might interact with the application graphical user interface. It also provides a brief description of their profiles and some very basic GUI design recommendations that relate to important usability issues.

If the same application must support several categories of users, then the graphical user interface should provide a combination of features that will appeal to each targeted user group. For example, the user interface can be designed to provide additional features to accommodate the power users, while at the same time also providing extensive help assistance for the novice users.

However, the extensions that are provided to the users should always remain optional. These extensions should not hinder the work of the speed users. Quite often, the speed users must perform extensive data entry functions while directly interacting live with customers. Consequently, the speed users demand a very fast application response time with an interface optimized for efficiency.

For example, if a toolbar is provided at the top of a main window, then you can provide for the users various options to show or hide the toolbar, move or resize the toolbar, or customize the toolbar.

12.5 USER-CENTRIC GUI DESIGN: SIX ESSENTIAL USABILITY CRITERIA

This section provides some basic design guidelines that are the foundation of good user-centered design practices. These GUI design guidelines are based on human behavior rather than specific technologies. They should apply to the design of any graphical user interface, no matter which type of computing platform you use to develop the visual interface.

Do not view these guidelines as a set of rigid rules. Instead, they are simple suggestions that might help the developers to truly adopt a user-centered design approach while they develop the graphical user interface. Good user interface design comes from a constant focus on the users' needs. The user interface should always be seen through the eyes of the users, never through the eyes of the developers.

Table 12–11 Generic User Profiles

USER TYPE	USER PROFILE	DESIGN GUIDELINES
Executive User	• Is a decision support user • Demands very user-friendly, intuitive GUI interfaces • Might use the application occasionally • Wants minimal training	• Provide multiple, intuitive mouse and keyboard GUI control features • Provide more windows with user feedback and assistance mechanisms, such as wizards • Provide extensive help features • Minimize mouse travel
Speed User	• Demands very fast response time • Performs repetitive data entry functions • Performs transaction-oriented processing functions • Uses the application extensively, on a regular basis • Considers accuracy vital • Wants to keep his/her hands on the keyboard, not on the mouse	• Provide extensive keyboard shortcuts and accelerators • Provide the strict minimum number of windows required for the job • Minimize data entry keystrokes to help prevent potential errors • Provide a pre-defined path for the cursor to follow when the user inputs data in a field and then presses the Tab key • Efficiency is a key factor, sometimes overriding ease of use considerations • If data must be entered into the system from paper forms, try to match the data fields' sequence to the layout displayed on the paper form, or try to adapt the paper form data layout to optimize the data entry process • Clearly indicate those data entry fields that are mandatory versus those that are optional
Power User	• Very knowledgeable and at ease with elaborate GUI applications • Often technically oriented • Exercises all available features • Demands high degree of functionality	• Provide extensive keyboard shortcuts and accelerators • Provide more levels of functionality in menus and windows • Provide interface customization features

12.5.1 GUIDELINE 1: KEEP THE GUI DESIGN AS SIMPLE AS POSSIBLE

The look and feel of the graphical user interface should always remain as straightforward and clean as possible. The graphical user interface should be considered finalized only after you have carefully streamlined it and you can take away no superfluous elements from it. If a visual element is not absolutely necessary, remove it! This minimal design approach decreases the number of information elements that must compete with each other for precious window space. It also decreases the number of options that the users can click on.

The effectiveness of the window interface can be gauged by the facility with which the users correctly identify the functionality that the application interface is trying to convey. A simple, expurgated, yet intuitive user interface always pays off quickly with less training, fewer modification requests, and happier users. Table 12.12 lists several tips that may be helpful in designing a simple graphical user interface.

Table 12–12 Tips For Designing Clean, Transparent GUIs

- Use pictures and icons that are meaningful and highly intuitive to the users
- Use metaphors that closely emulate their real-world counterparts
- Ensure that you use descriptive labels and control button names that genuinely convey their intended behavior
- Use the business language and terminology with which the users are familiar
- Hide access to business tasks that are not frequently used in the menus, instead of cluttering the window with unnecessary control buttons
- Group related tasks together to reduce overall complexity
- Avoid the extensive use of pop-up windows
- Provide windows navigational elements that are intuitive, via the effective use of menu structures, toolbars, and child windows

12.5.2 GUIDELINE 2: PUT THE USERS IN CONTROL

No matter what, users always like to be in the driver's seat. The GUI interface should adapt to the way the users usually do their work. Consequently, the user interface should not force the users to have to think unceasingly about how the application is supposed to work. Rather, the interface should become a tool that intuitively extends their ability to quickly perform their business tasks with minimal effort. In other words, the interface should be transparent to the users. It should not impede performance of the users' business work.

Try to minimize the amount of information that the users have to remember in order to perform their business tasks. As much as possible, the graphical user interface should minimize reliance on user memory. Thus, do not hesitate to use GUI features such as drop-down list boxes, pop-up lists of options, and simple list boxes that display available choices.

A well-structured interface will organize the users' tasks by presenting the GUI control objects and action buttons in a sequence that naturally maps the flow of activities they must perform to complete a business task. However, the users should still be allowed to change the order in which they perform their operations, if they desire to do so. The user interface should support different user interaction styles for applications that will be used by a broad and diversified user base.

12.5.3 GUIDELINE 3: PROVIDE USER FEEDBACK AND ASSISTANCE

Effective user awareness and assistance are essential to adequately provide the users with a good understanding of what is going on when they interact with the application. Always inform the users of what is happening at all times. For example, if the application will perform a task that will take a certain period of time, then the interface should notify the users of what is happening and indicate approximately how long it should take to complete the task.

You can provide simple yet effective user feedback mechanisms in several ways, such as those indicated in Table 12.13.

Table 12–13 User Feedback Mechanisms

Visual feedback	• Visual cues such as control buttons that get focus, control buttons that get dimmed
	• Error fields that get highlighted
	• Pointers that indicate current location
	• Progress indicators (i.e., graphical bars and gauges)
	• Cursor position
Textual feedback	• Information message boxes that indicate successful task completion
	• Error messages boxes that pop up when an error occurs and suggest possible ways to correct the error
	• Confirmation that the application has received the input data
	• Warning messages
Multimedia feedback	• Different sounds and human voice responses in view of specific user actions
	• Help facility with video demos
	• Wizard assistants

12.5.4 GUIDELINE 4: PROVIDE FORGIVENESS

Although the best cure for avoiding errors is a pro-active prevention approach, a well designed user interface should always provide a way out when the users are making mistakes. Table 12.14 provides some suggestions to help the developers design a graphical interface that allows the users to recover from errors.

Table 12–14 Application Forgiveness Characteristics

- Data entry fields should be validated as soon as the users fill them in, not once they have filled out the entire window. Also, a meaningful error message should be displayed immediately, to explain what is causing the error and provide suggestions for how the error can be corrected. The focus should be set on the field in error.
- The user interface should be designed to constantly assess the current state of the window and activate or deactivate the proper GUI commands accordingly, to prevent potential errors.
- If distinct user groups will use different application functions, consider limiting the actions that each user group can perform, by offering only the specific menu items they need to interact with the system.
- Warning messages should be displayed when a user is going to make non-reversible actions that could result in considerable loss, such as deleting a file, for instance.
- Provide some undo mechanisms that allow the users to reverse an operation, whenever doing so is feasible and practical.
- Provide clear, meaningful error messages that are easy to understand from a user perspective.
- Provide help facilities that are context-sensitive, to assist the users who need additional support in choosing the right actions.

When the users make mistakes, the error messages that the application displays should help them recover from these errors. A good error message briefly identifies what the problem is, provides an explanation of what caused the error, and offers some potential solutions, whenever feasible.

As an ideal, review the wording of error messages with users to ensure that the messages are meaningful to the users, not to the developers.

Table 12.15 provides a brief list of questions that developers can use to help formulate error messages that are truly meaningful to their users.

Table 12–15 Error Message Design Guidelines

- What type of users will read this error message?
- Is the error message formulated in simple terms that a novice user can understand?
- Does the error message help the user understand what caused the error?
- Does the error message provide guidance to the users to help them locate the error and solve the current problem?

To conclude, effective and meaningful error messages that are user-centric help to reduce the amount of technical support services that users need, once the system is transferred in production. They also indicate to your users that you truly care about them and genuinely try to help them when they make mistakes.

12.5.5 GUIDELINE 5: PROVIDE KEYBOARD SUPPORT

Power and speed users need keyboard support to accelerate the way they interact with the application. Keyboard support is also necessary in cases in which pointing devices such as mouse and pen become suddenly unusable.

12.5.6 GUIDELINE 6: PROVIDE CONSISTENCY

Windows designs should be highly consistent throughout the application and across applications and should also comply with proven corporate standards. Features that work one way in a given section of the application should work the same way throughout the entire application. A consistent user interface reduces potential user errors. It improves user effectiveness across a wide range of tasks by allowing them to leverage their knowledge once they have learned how to use specific computer-related features.

Some of the basic questions developers might ask themselves to verify that they have designed the user interface in a consistent manner appear in Table 12.16.

Table 12–16 Questions To Help Verify The GUI Consistency

- Are menu items presented in the same sequence within the same application or across different applications?
- If color is utilized, has it been utilized in an identical manner across all windows?
- Do control buttons display the same behavior within the same application or across applications?
- Is the look and feel of all windows consistent?
- Are control buttons placed consistently and do they exhibit the same visual characteristics?
- Are toolbar control buttons standardized across applications?

12.6 THE USE OF COLORS AND FONTS

This section briefly discusses the use of colors and fonts in window-based applications.

12.6.1 COLORS

The decision to use colors while designing a window must be carefully assessed in light of its advantages and disadvantages, as highlighted in Table 12.17.

Table 12.18 lists a basic set of guidelines that you should consider when using colors in a graphical user interface.

Table 12–17 Use Of Colors

ADVANTAGES	DISADVANTAGES
• Colors can be warm and engaging	• Some colors can be too provocative
• Colors can help focus attention	• Too much color can be confusing
• Colors can be used to differentiate different sections of a window or different categories of control buttons	• Approximately 10% of the population has difficulty detecting some categories of colors
	• Colors are not used in a consistent manner across the applications

Table 12–18 Guidelines For Using Colors In GUI(s)

- Use conservative, neutral colors as much as possible, such as different shades of gray, for instance.
- Use bright color sparingly and always ask yourself whether it really adds value.
- Use white, off-white, or light gray for a window background, to make sure that the graphical elements shown in a window remain clearly visible. Avoid dark backgrounds.
- If colors are used, users should be permitted to change them according to their personal preferences.

12.6.2 FONTS

The use of fonts should be carefully regulated within the application. Table 12.19 provides some basic guidelines on the use of fonts.

Table 12–19 Guidelines On The Use Of Fonts

- As a rule of thumb, use sans-serif fonts whenever possible, since they usually are easier to read on a screen than serif fonts.
- Discourage the use of different types of fonts, since they normally add noise to the user interface.
- Keep fonts as simple as possible.
- The size of the fonts should be large enough to allow the users to read text at a comfortable distance from the monitor. All titles and labels that are displayed in a window should use the same font size.

12.7 THE DIFFERENT TYPES OF WINDOW GUI CONTROLS

Following are some basic guidelines to help you decide which particular types of GUI control(s) you should select while dressing up a window. The choices available are dependent on the specific types of interactions that the users need to perform to accomplish their business tasks. These guidelines are offered as simple rules of thumb and you should therefore use them as such.

12.7.1 CONTROLS FOR MAKING CHOICES

You can use multiple types of GUI controls to allow a user to make single or multiple choices. Following is a brief description of such GUI controls, along with commentary on each of them.

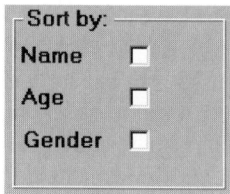

Checkbox. Checkboxes are normally used for the selection of 12 or fewer items. The number of items that may be selected and their content should be fairly static. That is, they should not change much over time. Each checkbox is independent of the others. Checkboxes can be clicked on and off. The user may select zero, one, several, or all checkboxes. Checkboxes are typically grouped in a groupbox or a rectangle to make them easier to locate and use.

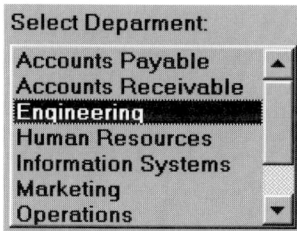

ListBox. Listboxes display a list of available choices. The list box can have scrollbars if showing all available choices at once in the listbox is impossible. The number of items that are normally displayed in a list box range from eight to twelve. One advantage of using a listbox is that users do not need to click on the listbox to display the available choices. The main disadvantage is that the listbox can take up some valuable space in the window. The listbox may allow the user to select multiple items. The items in a listbox are normally displayed in a sorted order.

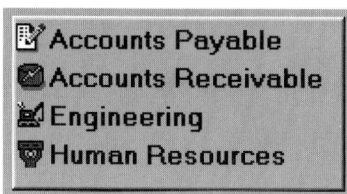

PictureListBox. PictureListBoxes are similar to listboxes with the exception that they show the available choices in combined text and images. Each image shown beside each particular available choice should add meaning to it and be intuitive to the users.

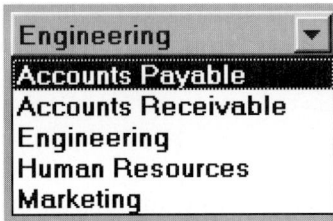

Dropdownlistbox. Dropdownlistboxes display the multiple choices that are available only once the user has clicked the down arrow that displays them. Although I do not recommend doing so, you can configure them to always display the list of items that are available for selection. The number of items that are normally displayed in a dropdownlistbox range from eight to twelve.

Dropdownlistboxes are usually used when window space is limited or for selectable items that are not used frequently. On the other hand, the use of a dropdownlistbox forces the user to do an extra keystroke and might cause a certain wait period. A particular option is always selected. The dropdownlistbox can have scrollbars if showing all available choices at once in it is impossible.

A dropdownlistbox can be either editable or non-editable. If non-editable, the user cannot type a value into the single-line edit field. Only one of the fixed set of displayed values can be selected by the user. If editable, the user can type a value in the single-line edit field. The user may type a character into the single-line edit field. Then the listbox scrolls to the first entry that begins with the typed character.

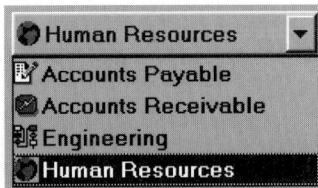

Dropdownpicturelistbox. Dropdownpicturelistboxes are almost identical to dropdownlistboxes, but they slightly differ in the way they show information. They add pictures to the textual information that is shown in the elements in the listbox.

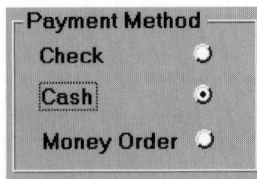

Radiobutton. Radiobuttons display mutually exclusive choices. They always exist in groups. One and only one radio button can be selected at a given time in a particular group.

Radio buttons are generally used when the number of possible choices does not exceed more than two to six different options. If more than six, users might become confused as to which choice should be selected. The data options must be static. One particular option is always initially displayed as a default value.

The order in which the radio buttons are displayed should reflect the proper sequence of natural choices. If you have no need to display them in a particular order, then sequence them in alphabetical order. The radio buttons can be placed either horizontally or vertically.

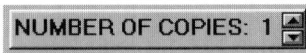

Spinbutton. Spinbuttons are special boxes that contain up and down arrows on their right-hand side, which, when the user clicks them, cycle through fixed values. Spin buttons are normally used for relatively small value ranges, such as one to fifteen.

12.7.2 CONTROLS FOR TRIGGERING ACTIONS

Following is a brief description of GUI controls that can be used to allow a user to carry out a specific action, along with commentary on each of them.

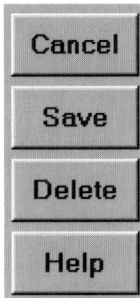

Command button. Command buttons (also referred to as push buttons) offer an intuitive way for users to carry out an action. The user simply clicks on the command button to trigger the desired action. The command buttons can be placed vertically, one above the other, in a window. They can also be placed horizontally, one beside each other, if you don't have too many.

If clicking a command button opens a window that necessitates some user interaction before any other action can take place, ellipsis points usually appear at the end of the command button text (for example, Print...).

As a rule of thumb, command buttons should always be the same size and shape. Adjacent command buttons are usually slightly set apart with a space equivalent approximately to one button's height.

Command buttons, such as *Exit* and *Cancel,* are usually placed in the lower right-hand corner of the window, since this is the area where the user naturally will focus when the time comes to exit the dialog window.

Picture button. Picture buttons are functionally identical to command buttons with the exception that they contain a picture inside them. Picture buttons frequently pictorially represent the purpose of a command button, instead of text only. Picture buttons are frequently used in toolbars. The picture in a picture button is usually centered, as well as the descriptive text shown beneath the picture. A good size for a picture button is 24 by 24 pixels.

Toolbar. A toolbar is a set of picture buttons containing specific icons that are grouped together and that provide shortcuts to frequently used actions. The user can click on a specific pictorial element of the toolbar instead of having to search through pull-down menus to locate a specific action.

A toolbar should always use icons that provide simple but effective metaphors that are easily recognizable by the users. Toolbars can be positioned vertically, horizontally, or floating in the window. They can also be hidden. The position of the toolbars should be consistent from one window to another inside an application and even across applications.

12.7.3 AESTHETIC CONTROLS

Aesthetic controls are various drawing objects that are used in a window to better organize the interface and make it look more attractive. They are used for display purposes only and do not have events associated with them. The set of drawing objects that are usually available in client-server RAD tools includes:

* straight lines
* ovals/circles
* rectangles/squares
* pictures

12.7.4 DATA DISPLAY/MANIPULATION CONTROLS

Multiple GUI controls can be used to display or manipulate data values. Following is a brief description of the most useful ones.

Static text. Static text control elements display text on a window or describe a control that does not have a textual description, such as a dropdownlistbox, for example. Users do not interact with static text controls.

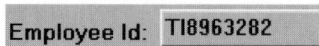

SingleLineEdit. Single line edit controls are used to enter a single line of data. They primarily support data entry operations. The textual data shown in a single-lineedit control should be left justified. Numbers should be right justified.

MultipleLineEdit. Multiple line edit controls are identical to singlelineedit controls with the exception that the user can enter more than one line of data in one. Multiple line edit controls are frequently used for free-form comments.

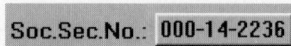

EditMask. Edit masks controls are used to allow the user to more easily enter data that have a pre-defined fixed format, such as a telephone number or a date. The edit mask consists of special characters that determine what can be entered in the box, depending on the particular type of format that needs to be emulated.

Labels. The labels associated with the data fields should be as meaningful as possible. They should not contain whole sentences but rather one or two simple descriptive words. The label descriptor usually contains a noun followed by a verb or an object followed by an action, such as "printer setup," for instance.

12.7.5 ORGANIZING CONTROLS

Organizing controls regroup related controls together to improve the window interface. Following is a description of two such controls.

GroupBox. Group box controls are used to group together several controls. Figures 12.1 and 12.2 illustrate how groupbox controls can be used.

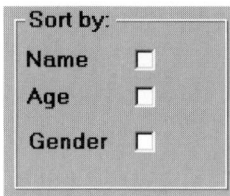

Figure 12–1 Groupbox controls.

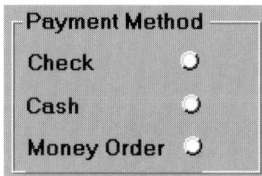

Figure 12–2 Groupbox controls.

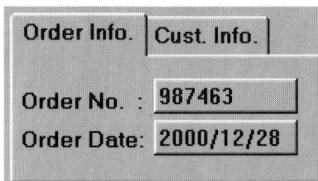

Tab control. A tab control is a container for tabbed pages that display other controls. Tab controls are usually utilized to display information that can be logically assembled together but may also be shown in discrete categories. Each major category of data appears on a different tabbed page.

In many client-server applications, the tab metaphor is frequently used to allow navigation around screens that hold more data than what can conveniently fit in a single window. To conclude, the tab metaphor, which symbolically represents traditional tabbed folders, is easily understood by the vast majority of user, even the novice users who might not be computer-literate.

Bibliography

BUSINESS REENGINEERING

Andrews, D. C., and Stalick, S. K., *Business Engineering: The Survival Guide*, New York, Yourdon Press, 1994.

Davenport, T. H., *Process Innovation: Reengineering Work Through Information Technology*, Boston, MA, Harvard Business School Press, 1993.

Hammer, M., *Beyond Reengineering: How the Process Centered Organization Is Changing Our Work and Our Lives,* New York, Harperbusiness, 1996.

Hammer, M., and Champy, J., *Reengineering the Corporation – A Manifesto for Business Revolution,* New York, HarperCollins Publishers, 1994.

CLIENT-SERVER

Berson, A., *Client-Server Architecture*, New York, McGraw-Hill, 1992.

Boar, B., *Implementing Client-Server Computing: A Strategic Perspective,* New York, McGraw-Hill, 1993.

Dewire, D. T., *Application Development for Distributed Environments,* New York, McGraw-Hill, 1994.

Dewire, D. T., *Client-Server Computing*, New York, McGraw-Hill, 1993.

Gold-Bernstein, B., and Marca, D., *Designing Enterprise Client/Server Systems*, Upper Saddle River, NJ, Prentice Hall, 1997.

Inmon, W. H., *Developing Client-Server Applications in an Architected Environment,* Wellesley, MA, QED, 1991.

631

Khanna, R., *Distributed Computing: Implementation and Management Strategies,* Englewood Cliffs, NJ, Prentice Hall, 1993.

Orfali, R., Harkey, D., Edwards, J., *The Essential Client-Server Survival Guide*, New York, John Wiley & Sons, 1997.

Renaud, P. E., *Introduction to Client-Server Systems*, New York, John Wiley & Sons, 1993.

Smith, P., *Client-Server Computing: All in One Reference for Total Systems Development,* Sams Publishing, 1992.

Vaskevitch, D., *Client-Server Strategies – A Survival Guide for Corporate Reengineers,* IDG Books Worldwide, 1995.

Watterson, K., *Client-Server Technology for Managers*, Wellesley, MA, Addison-Wesley, 1995.

DATABASE

Buretta, M., *Data Replication: Tools and Techniques for Managing Distributed Information,* New York, John Wiley & Sons, 1997.

Date, C. J., *An Introduction to Database Systems*, 6th ed., Reading, MA, Addison-Wesley, 1994.

Hogan, R., *A Practical Guide to Data Base Design,* Englewood Cliffs, NJ, Prentice Hall, 1990.

Koch, G., and Muller, R., *Oracle 7: The Complete Reference*, New York, Osborne McGraw-Hill, 1993.

Rodgers, U., *Oracle: A Database Developer's Guide*, NY, Yourdon Press, 1991.

Shasha, D. E., *Database Tuning – A Principled Approach*, Englewood Cliffs, NJ, Prentice Hall, 1992.

DATA MODELING, DATA ADMINISTRATION

Bobak, A. R., *Data Modeling and Design for Today's Architectures*, Artech House Computer Science Library, 1997.

Bruce, T. A., *Designing Quality Databases with IDEF1X Information Models*, New York, Dorset House Publishing, 1992.

Durell, W., *Data Administration: A Practical Guide to Successful Data Management,* New York, McGraw-Hill, 1985.

Flavin, M., *Fundamental Concepts of Information Modeling*, New York, Yourdon Press, 1981.

Gregory, W. W., and Reingruber, M., *The Data Modeling Handbook: A Best Practice Approach to Building Quality Data Models,* New York, John Wiley & Sons, 1994.

Loucopoulos, P., ed., *Entity-Relationship Approach–ER '94: Business Modeling and Re-Engineering,* 13th International Conference on the Entity-Relationship Approach, Springer Verlag, 1995.

DATA WAREHOUSING, DATA MINING, AND OLAP

Berson, A., and Smith, S.J., *Data Warehousing, Data Mining and OLAP,* New York, McGraw-Hill, 1997.

Burleson, D., *High Performance Oracle Data Warehousing,* Scottsdale, Arizona, Coriolis Group Books, 1997.

Inmon, W. H., and Hackathorn, R. D., *Using the Data Warehouse,* Wellesley, MA, QED Information Sciences, 1994.

Inmon, W. H., *Building a Data Warehouse,* 2nd ed., New York, John Wiley & Sons, 1996.

Inmon, W. H., *Data Architecture: The Information Paradigm,* Wellesley, MA, QED Information Sciences, 1989.

DCE, DCOM, CORBA, AND JAVABEANS

Allen, P., and Frost, S., *Component-Based Development for Enterprise Systems: Applying the Select Perspective,* Cambridge University Press, 1997.

Armstrong, T., *Designing and Using ActiveX Controls,* IDG Books Worldwide, 1997.

Chappell, D., *Understanding ActiveX and OLE,* Redmond, Washington, Microsoft Press, 1996.

Denning, A., *ActiveX Controls Inside Out,* 2nd ed., Redmond, Washington, Microsoft Press, 1997.

Downing, T. B., *RMI: Developing Distributed Java Applications with Remote Method Invocation and Object Serialization,* IDG Books Worldwide, 1998.

Englander, R., *Developing JavaBeans,* Sebastopol, CA, O'Reilly & Associates, 1997.

Lockhart, H. W., *OSF DCE: Guide to Developing Distributed Applications,* New York, McGraw-Hill, 1994.

Orfali, R., and others, *Instant CORBA,* New York, John Wiley & Sons, 1997.

Redmond, F. E. III, *DCOM: Microsoft Distributed Component Object Model,* IDG Books Worldwide, 1997.

Rogerson, D., *Inside COM,* Redmond, Washington, Microsoft Press, 1997.

Ryan, T., and Ryan, T. W., *Distributed Object Technology: Concepts and Applications,* Upper Saddle River, NJ, Prentice Hall, 1996.

ELECTRONIC MAIL

Rhoton, J., *X.400 and SMTP: The Battle of the E-Mail Protocols,* Digital Press, 1997.

ENTERPRISE INFORMATION ARCHITECTURE

Cook, M., *Building Enterprise Information Architectures: Reengineering Information Systems,* Upper Saddle River, NJ, Prentice Hall, 1996.

Hackathorn, R., *Enterprise Database Connectivity: The Key to Enterprise Applications on the Desktop,* New York, John Wiley & Sons, 1993.

Spewak, S. H., and Hill, S. C., *Enterprise Architecture Planning: Developing a Blueprint for Data, Applications and Technology,* New York, John Wiley & Sons, 1992.

GUI DESIGN

Bickford, P., Interface Design: *The Art of Developing Easy-to-Use Software*, AP Professional, 1997.

Galitz, W. O., *GUI Design Essentials,* New York, John Wiley & Sons, 1997.

Galitz, W. O., *The Essential Guide to User Interface Design: An Introduction to GUI Design Principles and Techniques,* New York, John Wiley & Sons, 1996.

Human Interface Guidelines, Apple Computer, Reading, MA, Addison-Wesley.

IBM Corp., *Object-Oriented Interface Design: IBM Common User Access Guidelines,* 1st ed., QUE Corp., 1992.

IBM Corp., *System Application Architecture: Common User Access Advanced Interface Design Guide.*

Microsoft Corp., *The GUI Guide: International Terminology for the Windows Interface,* Redmond, WA, Microsoft Press, 1993.

Nielsen, J., *Usability, Inspection Methods,* New York, John Wiley & Sons, 1994.

Nielsen, J., *Designing Websites with Authority: Secrets of an Information Architect,* New Rider Publishing, 1997.

Open Software Foundation, *OSF Motif Style Guide,* Englewood Cliffs, NJ, Prentice Hall, 1991.

Sayles, J., *GUI-Based Design and Development for Client-Server Applications: Using PowerBuilder, SQLWindows, Visual Basic, Parts Workbench,* New York, John Wiley & Sons, 1994.

The Windows Interface: An Application Design Guide, Microsoft Corporation, Microsoft Press.

JAVA

Campione, M., and Walrath, K., *The Java Tutorial: Object-Oriented Programming for the Internet,* Addison-Wesley, 1996.

Deitel, H.M., and Deitel, P.J., *Java How to Program*, Upper Saddle River, NJ, Prentice Hall, 1997.

Flanagan, D., *Java in a Nutshell*, 2nd ed., Sebastopol, CA, O'Reilly & Associates, 1997.

Morrison, M., *Java 1.1 Unleashed*, Sams.net Publishing, 1997.

Reese, G., *Database Programming with JDBC and Java*, O'Reilly & Associates, 1997.

Rice, J. C., and Salisbury, I., *Advanced Java 1.1 Programming*, New York, McGraw-Hill, 1997.

Taylor, A., *JDBC Developer's Resource: Database Programming on the Internet*, Upper Saddle River, NJ, Prentice Hall, 1997.

JOINT APPLICATION DESIGN

August, J., *Joint Application Design: The Group Session Approach to System Design*, Englewood Cliffs, NJ, Prentice Hall, 1991.

Crawford, A., *Advancing Business Concepts in JAD Workshop Setting: Business Re-Engineering and Process Redesign*, Englewood Cliffs, NJ, Yourdon Press, 1994.

Silver, D., and Wood, J., *Joint Application Design: How to Design Quality Systems in 40% Less Time*, New York, John Wiley & Sons, 1989.

MIDDLEWARE

Colonna-Romano, J., and Srite, P., *The Middleware Source Book*, Digital Press, 1995.

Korzeniowski, P., *Middleware: Achieving Open Systems for the Enterprise*, Computer Technology Research Corporation, 1997.

Simon, A. R., *Open Client/Server Computing and Middleware*, AP Professional, 1995.

NETWORKING

Jordan, L., *Communications and Networking*, Brady, 1994.

Kern, H., Johnson, R., Hawkins, M., Lyke, H., Cappel, M., *Networking the New Enterprise: The Proof not the Hype*, Upper Saddle River, NJ, Prentice Hall, 1997.

Nance, B., *Introduction to Networking*, 4th ed., QUE Corporation, 1997.

Nunemacher, G., *LAN Primer*, 3rd ed., IDG Books Worldwide, 1995.

Schnaidt, P., *Enterprise-Wide Networking: Professional Network Development Strategies for Business and Systems Administrators*, Sams Publishing, 1992.

Stang, D., *Networking Security Secrets*, New York, McGraw-Hill, 1993.

OBJECT-ORIENTED ANALYSIS, DESIGN, PROGRAMMING

Booch, G., *Object-Oriented Design with Applications*, Redwood City, CA, The Benjamin/Cummings Publishing Company, 1991.

Booch, G., *Object-Oriented Analysis and Design with Applications*, 2nd ed., Redwood City, CA, The Benjamin/Cummings Publishing Company, 1994.

Budd, T., *An Introduction to Object-Oriented Programming*, Reading, MA, Addison-Wesley, 1996.

Coad, P., and Yourdon, E., *Object-Oriented Analysis*, 2nd ed., Englewood Cliffs, NJ, Yourdon Press, 1991.

Jacobson, I., *Object-Oriented Software Engineering: A Use Case Driven Approach*, Reading, MA, Addison-Wesley, 1992.

Kroha, P., *Objects and Databases*, New York, McGraw-Hill, 1994.

Lee, G., *Object-Oriented GUI Application Development*, Englewood Cliffs, NJ, Prentice Hall, 1993.

Martin, J., and Odell, J., *Object-Oriented Methods: A Foundation*, Englewood Cliffs, NJ, Prentice Hall, 1995.

Martin, J., and Odell, J., *Object-Oriented Analysis and Design*, Englewood Cliffs, NJ, Prentice Hall, 1992.

Mellor, S. J., and Shlaer, S., *Object-Oriented Systems Analysis: Modeling the World in Data*, Englewood Cliffs, NJ, Yourdon Press, 1988.

Wirfs-Brock, R., Wilkerson, B., Wiener, L., *Designing Object-Oriented Software*, Englewood Cliffs, NJ, Prentice Hall, 1990.

Yourdon, E., *Object-Oriented Systems Design*, New York, Yourdon Press, 1994.

Yourdon, E., *Object-Oriented Systems Design: An Integrated Approach*, New York, Yourdon Press, 1994.

PROTOTYPING

Boar, B., *Application Prototyping: A Requirements Definition Strategy for the '80s*, New York, John Wiley & Sons, 1984.

Connell, J., *Object-Oriented Rapid Prototyping*, New York, Yourdon Press, 1994.

REUSE

Lim, W. C., *Managing Software Reuse*, 1st ed., Upper Saddle River, NJ, Prentice Hall, 1998.

SECURITY & FIREWALLS

Fuller, S., *Intranet Firewalls*, Ventana Communications Group Inc, 1996.

Grant, G., *Understanding Digital Signatures: Establishing Trust over the Internet and Other Networks*, New York, McGraw-Hill, 1997.

Kyas, O., *Internet Security: Risk Analysis, Strategies and Firewalls*, International Thomson Computer, 1997.

Pipkin, D. L., *Halting the Hacker: A Practical Guide to Computer Security,* Upper Saddle River, NJ, Prentice Hall, 1997.

Snyder, J., Atkins, D., Sheldon, T., Petru, T., Hare, C., *Internet Security,* 2nd ed., New Riders Publishing, 1997.

SOFTWARE DEVELOPMENT PROCESS

Barker, R., and Clegg, D., *CASE Method Fast-Track: A RAD Approach*, Reading, MA, Addison-Wesley, 1994.

Boddie, J., *Crunch Mode: Building Effective Systems on a Tight Schedule,* New York, Yourdon Press, 1987.

Fallon, H., *How to Implement Information Systems and Live to Tell about It,* New York, John Wiley & Sons, 1995.

Fournier, R., *Practical Guide to Structured System Development and Maintenance,* New York, Yourdon Press, 1991.

Humphrey, W. S., *Managing the Software Process*, Reading, MA, Addison-Wesley, 1989.

Martin, J., *Rapid Application Development*, New York, Macmillan Publishing, 1991.

TESTING

Beizer, B., *Software Testing Techniques*, New York, Van Nostrand Reinhold.

Beizer, B., *Software System Testing and Quality Assurance*, New York, Van Nostrand Reinhold.

Beizer, B., *Black-Box Testing: Techniques for Functional Testing of Software and Systems,* New York, John Wiley & Sons, 1995.

Falk, J., Kaner, C., and Nguyen, H. Q., *Testing Computer Software*, 2nd ed., New York, Von Nostrand Reinhold, 1993.

Friedman, M., and Voas, J. M., *Software Assessment: Reliability, Safety, Testability,* New York, John Wiley and Sons, 1995.

Goglia, P., *Testing Client-Server Applications*, New York, John Wiley & Sons, 1993.

Hetzel, B., *The Complete Guide to Software Testing*, 2nd ed., Wellesley, MA, QED Information Sciences, 1988.

Hopkinson, J., Tallon, H., and Wallmuller, E., *Software Quality Assurance: A Practical Approach*, Englewood Cliffs, NJ, Prentice Hall, 1993.

Marick, B., *The Craft of Software Testing*, Englewood Cliffs, NJ, Prentice Hall, 1995.

Myers, G., *The Art of Software Testing*, New York, John Wiley and Sons, 1979.

Royer, T. C., *Software Testing Management – Life on the Critical Path*, Englewood Cliffs, NJ, Prentice Hall, 1993.

WEB

Darnell, R., *Using JavaScript*, QUE Corporation, 1997.

December, J., and Ginsburg, M., *HTML 3.2 and CGI Unleashed*, Professional Reference Edition, Sams.net Publishing, 1996.

Evans, T., *Building an Intranet: A Hands-On Guide to Setting Up an Internal Web*, Sams.net Publishing, 1996.

Fisher, S., *Creating Dynamic Web Sites: A Webmaster's Guide to Interactive Multimedia*, Reading, MA, Addison-Wesley, 1997.

Hall, J. N., and Schwartz, R. L., *Effective Perl Programming: Writing Better Programs with Perl*, Reading, MA, Addison-Wesley, 1998.

Ju, P. H., *Databases on the Web: Designing and Programming for Network Access*, IDG Books Worldwide, 1997.

Ladd, E., O'Donnell, J., Ablan, J., Anthony, T., *Using HTML, Java, and CGI*, QUE Education & Training, 1996.

Tyler, D., *Microsoft FrontPage 98*, Sams.net, 1997.

Umar, A., *Application (Re) Engineering: Building Web-Based Applications and Dealing with Legacies*, Upper Saddle River, NJ, Prentice Hall, 1997.

Umar, A., *Object-Oriented Client-Server Internet Environments*, Upper Saddle River, NJ, Prentice Hall, 1997.

Williams, A., *Active Server Pages Black Book: The Professional's Guide to Developing Dynamic Interactive Web Sites*, Scottdale, AZ, Coriolis Group, 1998.

Afterword

With the Web, the world has reached the status of a global village. Readers who want to provide comments regarding this book, share their own experience on development practices or propose deliverable samples are kindly invited to forward their input to the author at the following address: rogerf@aei.ca. Your comments will help to improve this book, for the ultimate benefit of other readers like you. Thanks in advance for your feedback.

L'avènement du Web a permis au monde d'atteindre le statut de village global. Les lecteurs intéressés à commenter le contenu de ce livre, partager leur propre expérience de développement de systèmes ou proposer des exemples de biens livrables sont priés d'envoyer leurs commentaires directement à l'auteur, à l'adresse suivante: rogerf@aei.ca. Vos commentaires peuvent aider à améliorer ce livre, pour le bénéfice de tous les lecteurs. Merci à l'avance pour votre intérêt.

O Web, transformou o mundo numa aldeia global. Leitores que quierão comentar acerca deste livro ou que queirão partilhar as suas experiências e ideias acerca do desenvolvimento de práticas são encorajados a submeter as suas opiniões ao author no seguinte endereço: rogerf@aei.ca. Os vossos comentários serão utéis para melhorar este livro, para o benefício de todos. Agradeço de avanço pelo vosso interesse.

Mit dem Netz hat die Welt den Status eines globalen Dorfes erreicht. Leser, die hinsichtlich dieses Buches ihre eigene Meinung, ihre eigenen Erfahrungen auf Entwicklung und Anwendung mitteilen oder durchführbare Vorschläge machen möchten, werden gebeten, ihre Eingaben an den Author unter folgender Adresse zu richten: rogerf@aei.ca. Ihre Anregungen werden helfen, dieses Buch zu verbessern und von großem Nutzen für andere Leser, wie sie, sien. Für Ihre Teilnahme an diesem Meinungsaustausch im voraus besten Dank.

Con il Web, il mondo ha raggiunto lo stato di villaggio universale. I lettori che vogliano esprimere commenti per quanto riguarda questo libro, condividere le loro esperienze sulle pratiche di sviluppo di sistema, oppure proporre esempi di consegne techniche sono invitati ad inviarli a l'autore a l'indirizzo: rogerf@aei.ca. I vostri commenti aiuteranno a migliorare questo libro, per in fine beneficiare altri lettori come voi. Ringraziadovi in anticipo per il vostro interesso.

La llegada del Web ahora verdaderamente nos permite hablar del mundo como una aldea. Si usted es un lector interesado en comentar el contenido de este libro, en compartir sus propias experiencias en el desarrollo de sistemas, está invitado a enviar sus comentarios directamente al autor a la dirección siguiente: rogerf@aei.ca. Sus comentarios pueden ayudar a mejorar este libro para beneficiar a tantos otros lectores como usted. Gracias de antemano por su interés.

Index